Network Security 1 and 2
Companion Guide

Antoon W. Rufi

Cisco Press

800 East 96th Street

Indianapolis, Indiana 46240 USA

Network Security 1 and 2 Companion Guide

Antoon W. Rufi

Published by:
Cisco Press
800 East 96th Street
Indianapolis, IN 46240 USA

Printed in the United States of America 1 2 3 4 5 6 7 8 9 0

First Printing   October 2006

Library of Congress Cataloging-in-Publication Number: 2005932453

ISBN: 1-58713-162-5

Warning and Disclaimer

This book is designed to provide information about network security as it is explained in the Cisco Networking Academy Program Network Security courses. Every effort has been made to make this book as complete and as accurate as possible, but no warranty or fitness is implied.

The information is provided on an "as is" basis. The authors, Cisco Press, and Cisco Systems, Inc. shall have neither liability nor responsibility to any person or entity with respect to any loss or damages arising from the information contained in this book or from the use of the discs or programs that may accompany it.

The opinions expressed in this book belong to the author and are not necessarily those of Cisco Systems, Inc.

Publisher
Paul Boger

Cisco Representative
Anthony Wolfenden

Cisco Press Program Manager
Jeff Brady

Executive Editor
Mary Beth Ray

Managing Editor
Patrick Kanouse

Senior Development Editor
Christopher A. Cleveland

Senior Project Editor
San Dee Phillips

Copy Editor
Keith Cline

Technical Editors
Dale Liu
Belle Woodward

Team Coordinator
Vanessa Evans

Book and Cover Designer
Louisa Adair

Composition
Mark Shirar

Indexer
Tim Wright

Proofreader
Tonya Maddox Cupp

Trademark Acknowledgments

All terms mentioned in this book that are known to be trademarks or service marks have been appropriately capitalized. Cisco Press or Cisco Systems, Inc. cannot attest to the accuracy of this information. Use of a term in this book should not be regarded as affecting the validity of any trademark or service mark.

Feedback Information

At Cisco Press, our goal is to create in-depth technical books of the highest quality and value. Each book is crafted with care and precision, undergoing rigorous development that involves the unique expertise of members from the professional technical community.

Readers' feedback is a natural continuation of this process. If you have any comments regarding how we could improve the quality of this book, or otherwise alter it to better suit your needs, you can contact us through email at feedback@ciscopress.com. Please make sure to include the book title and ISBN in your message.

We greatly appreciate your assistance.

Corporate and Government Sales

Cisco Press offers excellent discounts on this book when ordered in quantity for bulk purchases or special sales. For more information, please contact:

U.S. Corporate and Government Sales 1-800-382-3419 corpsales@pearsontechgroup.com

For sales outside of the U.S. please contact: International Sales international@pearsoned.com

CISCO SYSTEMS

Corporate Headquarters
Cisco Systems, Inc.
170 West Tasman Drive
San Jose, CA 95134-1706
USA
www.cisco.com
Tel: 408 526-4000
    800 553-NETS (6387)
Fax: 408 526-4100

European Headquarters
Cisco Systems International BV
Haarlerbergpark
Haarlerbergweg 13-19
1101 CH Amsterdam
The Netherlands
www-europe.cisco.com
Tel: 31 0 20 357 1000
Fax: 31 0 20 357 1100

Americas Headquarters
Cisco Systems, Inc.
170 West Tasman Drive
San Jose, CA 95134-1706
USA
www.cisco.com
Tel: 408 526-7660
Fax: 408 527-0883

Asia Pacific Headquarters
Cisco Systems, Inc.
Capital Tower
168 Robinson Road
#22-01 to #29-01
Singapore 068912
www.cisco.com
Tel: +65 6317 7777
Fax: +65 6317 7799

Cisco Systems has more than 200 offices in the following countries and regions. Addresses, phone numbers, and fax numbers are listed on the
Cisco.com Web site at www.cisco.com/go/offices.

Argentina • Australia • Austria • Belgium • Brazil • Bulgaria • Canada • Chile • China PRC • Colombia • Costa Rica • Croatia • Czech Republic Denmark • Dubai, UAE • Finland • France • Germany • Greece • Hong Kong SAR • Hungary • India • Indonesia • Ireland • Israel • Italy Japan • Korea • Luxembourg • Malaysia • Mexico • The Netherlands • New Zealand • Norway • Peru • Philippines • Poland • Portugal Puerto Rico • Romania • Russia • Saudi Arabia • Scotland • Singapore • Slovakia • Slovenia • South Africa • Spain • Sweden Switzerland • Taiwan • Thailand • Turkey • Ukraine • United Kingdom • United States • Venezuela • Vietnam • Zimbabwe

Copyright © 2003 Cisco Systems, Inc. All rights reserved. CCIP, CCSP, the Cisco Arrow logo, the Cisco *Powered* Network mark, the Cisco Systems Verified logo, Cisco Unity, Follow Me Browsing, FormShare, iQ Net Readiness Scorecard, Networking Academy, and ScriptShare are trademarks of Cisco Systems, Inc.; Changing the Way We Work, Live, Play, and Learn, The Fastest Way to Increase Your Internet Quotient, and iQuick Study are service marks of Cisco Systems, Inc.; and Aironet, ASIST, BPX, Catalyst, CCDA, CCDP, CCIE, CCNA, CCNP, Cisco, the Cisco Certified Internetwork Expert logo, Cisco IOS, the Cisco IOS logo, Cisco Press, Cisco Systems, Cisco Systems Capital, the Cisco Systems logo, Empowering the Internet Generation, Enterprise/Solver, EtherChannel, EtherSwitch, Fast Step, GigaStack, Internet Quotient, IOS, IP/TV, iQ Expertise, the iQ logo, LightStream, MGX, MICA, the Networkers logo, Network Registrar, *Packet*, PIX, Post-Routing, Pre-Routing, RateMUX, Registrar, SlideCast, SMARTnet, StrataView Plus, Stratm, SwitchProbe, TeleRouter, TransPath, and VCO are registered trademarks of Cisco Systems, Inc. and/or its affiliates in the U.S. and certain other countries.

All other trademarks mentioned in this document or Web site are the property of their respective owners. The use of the word partner does not imply a partnership relationship between Cisco and any other company. (0303R)

Printed in the USA

About the Author

Antoon "Tony" W. Rufi currently attends Walden University, working on his Ph.D. in applied business management and decision sciences with a concentration in Information Systems. Tony graduated from the University of Maryland University College with a master's degree in information systems and from Southern Illinois University with a bachelor's degree in industrial technology. Tony is currently an associate dean of computer and information science CIS for all the ECPI College of Technology campuses, teaching the Cisco Academy CCNA, CCNP, Network Security, and IP Telephony curriculum. Prior to becoming an instructor for ECPI, he spent almost 30 years in the United States Air Force, working on numerous electronic and computer programs and projects. Tony lives with his wife of 33 years in Poquoson, Virginia.

About the Technical Reviewers

Dale Liu, CCAI, CCNA, CISSP, NSA IAM, NSA IEM, has been working in the computer and network fields for 20 years. His experience ranges from programming to networking to information security. He currently teaches networking, routing, and security classes, while working in the field performing security audits and infrastructure design for small to medium companies. Dale currently resides in Houston, TX.

Belle Woodward, CCNA, CCAI, CCNP, is an assistant professor in the School of Information Systems and Applied Technologies in the College of Applied Sciences and Arts at Southern Illinois University (SIU) in Carbondale, Illinois. Belle has more than 8 years' experience in the networking and network security fields. She teaches network security, advanced networking, and telecommunications. After her redesign of the networking and network security undergraduate curriculum, her students took first place at the 2006 Regional Midwestern Collegiate Cyber Defense Competition (CCDC) and fourth place at the national CCDC.

Dedication

This book is dedicated to Maxdonald and Ellen Rufi, my parents. My parents immigrated to the United States in 1960, taking a chance on the American dream. Without their sacrifices, this book would not have been possible.

Acknowledgments

I want to give special recognition to Mr. Mark Dreyfus, the president of ECPI College of Technology, and Mr. John Olson, the vice president of academic affairs. Their encouragement and support of the Cisco Academy Program at ECPI throughout the years have been instrumental in my quest to absorb as much as I can about the different Cisco platforms and to pass on this information to as many students as possible.

I also want to thank Belle Woodward for writing Chapter 7 of Course 2. She has been as good a friend as anyone could hope to have and was more than happy to lend her experience to the contents of this chapter.

Last, but not least, I want to thank my wife, Linda, who sacrificed "together" time so that I could get this project done; and my father-in-law, Dick Hamilton, who provided me with some unbiased opinions and some broad-stroke editing of the first draft even though "computers" aren't his thing.

Contents at a Glance

Contents

Course 1

Course 2

Icons Used in This Book

Communication Server · PC · PC with Software · Sun Workstation · Macintosh · Access Server · ISDN/Frame Relay Switch

Token Ring · Terminal · File Server · Web Server · Ciscoworks Workstation · ATM Switch · Modem

Printer · Laptop · IBM Mainframe · Front End Processor · Cluster Controller · Multilayer Switch

Gateway · Router · Bridge · Hub · DSU/CSU · FDDI · Catalyst Switch

Network Cloud · Line: Ethernet · Line: Serial · Line: Switched Serial

Command Syntax Conventions

The conventions used to present command syntax in this book are the same conventions used in the IOS Command Reference. The Command Reference describes these conventions as follows:

- **Bold** indicates commands and keywords that are entered literally as shown. In actual configuration examples and output (not general command syntax), boldface indicates commands that are manually input by the user (such as a **show** command).

- *Italics* indicate arguments for which you supply actual values.

- Vertical bars | separate alternative, mutually exclusive elements.

- Square brackets [ ] indicate optional elements.

- Braces { } indicate a required choice.

- Braces within brackets [{ }] indicate a required choice within an optional element.

Introduction

The *Network Security 1 and 2 Companion Guide* works with the corresponding Cisco Networking Academy Program online curriculum to provide you with a thorough introduction to network security.

The Cisco Networking Academy Program curriculum is designed to empower you to enter employment or pursue further education and training in the computer-networking field. The Network Security course is organized in two volumes.

The Network Security 1 course focuses on the overall security processes in a network with particular emphasis on hands-on skills in the following areas:

- Security policy design and management

- Security technologies, products, and solutions

- Firewall and secure router design, installation, configuration, and maintenance

- AAA implementation using routers and firewalls

- Securing the network at both Layers 2 and 3 of the OSI model

The Network Security 2 course focuses on the overall security process in a network, with particular emphasis on hands-on skills in the following areas:

- Security policy design and management

- Security technologies, products, and solutions

- Firewall and secure router design, installation, configuration, and maintenance

- Intrusion prevention system (IPS) implementation using routers and firewalls

- Virtual private network (VPN) implementation using routers and firewalls

The *Companion Guide* is designed as a portable desk reference of the course material to use anytime, anywhere. This book's features reinforce the material in the course to help you to focus on important concepts and to organize your study time for exams.

The Goal of This Book

The goal of this book is to educate you about the overall security process based on a security policy design and management. Emphasis is placed on security technologies, products, and solutions; and on firewall and secure router design, installation, configuration, and maintenance. The first section of this book covers authentication, authorization, and accounting (AAA) implementation using routers and firewalls and securing the network at both Layer 2 and 3 of the OSI model. The second section of this book covers intrusion prevention system (IPS) implementation using routers and firewalls and virtual private network (VPN) implementation using routers and firewalls. This book is designed for use in conjunction with the Cisco Networking Academy Program curriculum or as a standalone reference.

The Audience for This Book

This book is written for anyone who wants to learn about network security and overall security processes. The main target audience is students in community colleges and four-year institutions. Specifically, in an educational environment, this book could be used in the classroom as a textbook companion. This book is appropriate for readers with a CCNA certification or the equivalent knowledge. Readers should have a solid grasp of TCP/IP and fundamental networking concepts.

The secondary target audience is corporate training faculty and staff members. For corporations and academic institutions to make use of effective security measures, individuals must be trained in the design and implementation of security technologies, products, and solutions. A third target audience is general users. The book is user friendly and appeals to readers who avoid traditional technical manuals.

Book Features

Many of this book's features help facilitate a full understanding of the networking and routing covered in this book:

- **Objectives**—Each chapter starts with a list of objectives that should be mastered by the end of the chapter. The objectives provide a reference of the concepts covered in the chapter.

- **Figures, examples, tables, and scenarios**—This book contains figures, examples, and tables that help explain theories, concepts, commands, and setup sequences that reinforce concepts and help you visualize the content covered in the chapter. In addition, the specific scenarios provide real-life situations that detail the problem and the solution.

- **Chapter summaries**—At the end of each chapter is a summary of the concepts covered in the chapter. It provides a synopsis of the chapter and serves as a study aid.

- **Key terms**—Most chapters include a list of defined key terms that are covered in the chapter. These terms serve as a study aid. In addition, the key terms reinforce the concepts introduced in the chapter and help your understanding of the chapter material before you move on to new concepts. You can find the key terms highlighted with bold and italic formatting throughout the chapter where they are used in practice.

- **"Check Your Understanding" questions**—Review questions that serve as an assessment are presented at the end of each chapter. The questions reinforce the concepts introduced in the chapter and help test your understanding before you move on to other chapters.

- **Skill builders**—Throughout the book are references to lab activities found in *Cisco Networking Academy Program Network Security Lab Companion and Workbook*. These labs enable you to make a connection between theory and practice.

How This Book Is Organized

This book is divided into 18 chapters and 1 appendix:

Network Security 1:

- **Chapter 1, "Vulnerabilities, Threats, and Attacks"**—The Internet continues to grow exponentially. As personal, government, and business-critical applications become more prevalent on the Internet, there are many immediate benefits. However, these network-based applications and services can pose security risks to individuals and to the information resources of companies and government. In many cases, the rush to get connected comes at the expense of adequate network security. Information is an asset that must be protected. Without adequate protection or network security, many individuals, businesses, and governments are at risk of losing that asset. Network security is the process by which digital information assets are protected. The goals of security are to protect confidentiality, maintain integrity, and ensure availability. With this in mind, it is imperative that all networks be protected from threats and vulnerabilities for a business to achieve its fullest potential. Typically, these threats are persistent because of vulnerabilities, which can arise from misconfigured hardware or software, poor network design, inherent technology weaknesses, or end-user carelessness. This chapter provides an overview of essential network security concepts, common vulnerabilities, threats, attacks, and vulnerability analysis.

- **Chapter 2, "Security Planning and Policy"**—Security risks cannot be eliminated or prevented completely. However, effective risk management and assessment can significantly minimize the existing security risks. An acceptable level of risk depends on how much risk the business is willing to assume. A security policy is an important component in deciding how this risk is managed. A security policy is a formal statement of the rules by which people who are given access to an organization's technology and information assets must abide. A security policy can be as simple as an acceptable-use policy for network resources or it can be several hundred pages in length and detail every element of connectivity and associated policies. Routers can support a large number of network services that allow users and host processes to connect to the network. Some of these services can be restricted or disabled, improving security without affecting the operational use of the network. For security purposes, it should be a common practice for network devices to support only the traffic and protocols the network needs.

- **Chapter 3, "Security Devices"**—This chapter begins with a discussion of the network firewall. The firewall exists to enforce the enterprise security. It enables a company to do business online, while providing the necessary security between the internal network of the enterprise and an external network. In addition to access control, the firewall also provides a natural focal point for the administration of other network security measures. This chapter introduces the Cisco IOS Firewall feature set, the Cisco PIX Security Appliance and the Cisco Adaptive Security Appliance, and the Firewall Service Module. This discussion includes an overview of the various PIX Security Appliance and Adaptive Security Appliance models, their features, and their capabilities. Although security appliances are not routers, they do have certain routing capabilities. The commands used in the basic configuration of the security appliance are covered.

Security Device Manager (SDM) and Adaptive Security Device Manager (ASDM) are introduced. These device managers provide a way to configure devices quickly and easily through a graphical user interface. One aspect of understanding how TCP and UDP work with the security appliance is examining both translations and connections. It is important to learn how these items are used when traffic is going from the inside network to the outside network, or from the outside network to the inside network. In examining translations and connections, Network Address Translation (NAT) is discussed.

Port Address Translation (PAT) and configuring multiple interfaces on the PIX Security Appliance are also discussed. PAT is a translation method, like NAT, that enables network administrators to hide the inside network addressing scheme from outside hosts and allows for the conservation of IP addresses. However, unlike NAT, which leases IP addresses to inside hosts on a one-to-one basis, PAT can go a step further and allow numerous inside hosts to use a single IP address. This process is called overloading.

So that you understand how to configure multiple interfaces, this module discusses how the PIX Security Appliance supports additional perimeter interfaces.

- **Chapter 4, "Trust and Identity Technology"**—This chapter presents an overview of the authentication, authorization, and accounting (AAA) architecture and shows the importance of identity services in network security. AAA security is one of the primary components of the overall network security policy of an organization. AAA is essential to providing secure remote access to the network and remote management of network devices. After a brief discussion of AAA, several authentication methods are discussed.

  Cisco Identity Based Networking Services (IBNS) and Network Admission Control (NAC) are also introduced in this chapter. IBNS is an integrated solution combining several Cisco products that offer authentication, access control, and user policies to secure network connectivity and resources. NAC is an industry initiative, sponsored by Cisco Systems, that uses the network infrastructure to enforce security policy compliance on all devices seeking to access network computing resources, thereby limiting damage from viruses and worms.

- **Chapter 5, "Cisco Secure Access Control Server"**—Cisco Secure Access Control Server (ACS) network security software helps you authenticate users by controlling access to an AAA client. The AAA client can be any one of many network devices that can be configured to defer authentication and authorization of network users to a AAA server. Cisco Secure ACS operates as a set of Windows services that control the authentication, authorization, and accounting of users accessing networks. This chapter describes features, functions, and architectures of Cisco Secure ACS and how to configure TACACS+ and RADIUS on Cisco routers and switches to work with Cisco Secure ACS. Upon completing this chapter, you will be able to install, configure, operate, and troubleshoot Cisco Secure ACS for Windows Server. You will also be able to describe the function, features, and architecture of the three components of Cisco Secure ACS for Windows Server. In addition, you will be able to configure TACACS+ and RADIUS with the Cisco Secure ACS for Windows Server.

- **Chapter 6, "Configure Trust and Identity at Layer 3"**—Authentication proxy provides dynamic, per-user authentication and authorization, authenticating users against industry standard TACACS+ and RADIUS authentication protocols. Authenticating and authorizing connections by users provides more robust protection against network attacks. In this chapter, you learn how to configure a Cisco router to authenticate using authentication proxy. This chapter then examines how to configure, monitor, and troubleshoot AAA configurations on the PIX Security Appliance.

- **Chapter 7, "Configure Trust and Identity at Layer 2"**—Cisco Identity Based Networking Services (IBNS) is an integrated solution combining several Cisco products that offer authentication, access control, and user policies to secure network connectivity and resources. The Cisco IBNS solution enables greater security while simultaneously offering cost-effective management of changes throughout the organization. In this chapter, you are introduced to Cisco IBNS. This chapter also discusses 802.1x and Extensible Authentication Protocol (EAP) as they relate to IBNS. You also learn to configure a Cisco Secure ACS server to authenticate using EAP-MD5 and RADIUS. This chapter also discusses the use IEEE 802.1x port-based authentication to prevent unauthorized devices from gaining access to the network. As LANs extend to hotels, airports, and corporate lobbies, insecure environments can be created. The IEEE 802.1x standard defines a client/server-based access control and authentication protocol that restricts unauthorized clients from connecting to a LAN through publicly accessible ports. The authentication server authenticates each client connected to a switch port before making available any services offered by the switch or the LAN. You will also learn the steps necessary to configure 802.1x port-based authentication on a Cisco Catalyst switch.

- **Chapter 8, "Configure Filtering on a Router"**—This chapter discusses, in greater detail, how routers are used to secure a network through the use the Context-Based Access Control (CBAC) component of the Cisco IOS Firewall feature set. Access control lists (ACLs) are used to filter and secure network traffic. ACLs filter network traffic by controlling whether routed or switched packets are forwarded or blocked at the interface. Each packet is examined to determine how that packet should be handled based on the criteria specified within the ACL. One particular type of ACL implementation, CBAC, is discussed in great detail. CBAC provides a greater level of security among the ACLs by inspecting traffic at Layers 3 and higher. Information gathered by CBAC is used to create temporary openings in the firewall access lists. In this chapter, you learn the steps required to create and establish CBAC.

  In addition to applied ACLs, CBAC has several other uses. Packets entering the firewall are only inspected by CBAC if they first pass the inbound ACL at the interface. If a packet is denied by the ACL, the packet is simply dropped and not inspected by CBAC.

- **Chapter 9, "Configure Filtering on a PIX Security Appliance"**—This chapter discusses access control lists (ACLs) and how they are handled by the PIX Security Appliance. The first part of this module focuses on configuring ACLs and knowing how and when to use ACLs in different network environments. This section also discusses applet filtering and URL filtering. You learn when to use this technology and why it is necessary. This chapter also introduces you to the concept of object grouping, which puts ACLs into object groups and nested object groups. To simplify the task of creating and applying ACLs, administrators can group network objects (such as hosts) and services (such as FTP and HTTP). By grouping ACLs, you can drastically reduce the number of access lists. Modular policy provides greater granularity and more flexibility when configuring network policies. The Modular Policy Framework (MPF) provides a consistent and flexible way to configure PIX Security Appliance features. One case where MPF could be used is to create a timeout configuration specific to a particular TCP application, as opposed to one that applies to all TCP applications. This chapter concludes with a discussion of advanced protocol handling and inspection, and how you can tune it to fit the PIX Security Appliance operation. This chapter moves on to discuss the advanced protocols used for multimedia support, including real-time streaming protocols. The protocols required to support IP telephony are also covered.

- **Chapter 10, "Configure Filtering on a Switch"**—Like routers, both Layer 2 and Layer 3 switches have their own sets of network security requirements. Unlike routers, however, not much public information is available that discusses the network security risks in switches and what can be done to mitigate those risks. This module covers Layer 2 attacks and how to use Cisco IOS features to mitigate such threats to the network. This chapter introduces several types of Layer 2 attacks and explains strategies to mitigate these attacks. Upon completing this module, you will be able to mitigate network Layer 2 attacks, including content-addressable memory (CAM) table overflow, VLAN hopping, Spanning Tree Protocol (STP) manipulation, MAC address spoofing, and DHCP starvation.

Network Security 2:

- **Chapter 1, "Intrusion Detection and Prevention Technology"**—This chapter introduces the basic concepts of intrusion prevention and detection. The basic types of inspection engines used in an intrusion detection system (IDS) and an intrusion prevention system (IPS) are discussed. The chapter concludes with an introduction to the IDS and IPS devices that are part of the Cisco Self-Defending Network solution.

- **Chapter 2, "Configure Network Intrusion Detection and Prevention"**—This chapter looks at the Cisco IOS Intrusion Prevention System (IPS). Configuration of attack guards, intrusion prevention, and shunning on PIX Security Appliance are discussed.

- **Chapter 3, "Encryption and VPN Technology"**—This chapter primarily covers the virtual private network (VPN) protocols available in Cisco VPN-capable devices. A VPN provides the same network connectivity for remote users over a public infrastructure as they would have over a private network. However, before allowing a user to access a network, certain measures must be taken to ensure authenticity, data integrity, and encryption. In this chapter, you learn about each of these measures and are introduced to the two basic VPN types: site-to-site and remote-access VPNs. There is a thorough discussion of the protocols and devices used to ensure authenticity, data integrity, and confidentiality with a VPN connection.

- **Chapter 4, "Configure Site-to-Site VPN Using Pre-Shared Keys"**—This chapter covers the site-to-site virtual private network (VPN) configuration for Cisco IOS routers and PIX Security Appliances. A VPN provides the same network connectivity for remote users over a public infrastructure as they would have over a private network. However, before allowing a user to access a network, certain measures must be taken to ensure authenticity, data integrity, and encryption. This chapter discusses how to identify and configure the protocols used to ensure authenticity, data integrity, and confidentiality with a site-to-site VPN using pre-shared keys.

- **Chapter 5, "Configure Site-to-Site VPN Using Digital Certificates"**—This chapter guides you through the process of configuring a Cisco router to support certificate authorities (CAs). Included are topics on managing nonvolatile rapid-access memory (NVRAM), router date and time settings, and commands to configure RSA keys and CAs. The goal of this chapter is to prepare you to configure the Cisco IOS router and the PIX Security Appliance for a site-to-site VPN using digital certificates for authentication.

- **Chapter 6, "Configure Remote Access VPN"**—This chapter provides an introduction to the two components of Cisco Easy VPN: the Cisco Easy VPN Server and Cisco Easy VPN Remote. Both components work together to provide safe, reliable, and secure remote-access VPNs for users. The chapter discusses how Easy VPN works and how users and administrators can use it to ease the creation of secure VPNs. The configuration of routers and PIX Security Appliances as Easy VPN Servers is also explored. Configuring Easy VPN Remote with the Cisco VPN Client, Cisco routers, and the PIX 501 and 506/506E models is also covered. The chapter also provides an explanation of how to configure WebVPN on an Adaptive Security Appliance.

- **Chapter 7, "Secure Network Architecture and Management"**—This chapter begins with a discussion on best practices for Layer 2 security. You are introduced to multiple physical network scenarios and given vulnerabilities and mitigation techniques for each. The Security Device Manager (SDM) Security Audit Feature is discussed next. SDM contains a unique Security Audit Wizard that provides a comprehensive router security audit. SDM uses Cisco Technical Assistance Center (TAC)- and International Computer Security Association (ICSA)-recommended security configurations as the basis for comparisons and default settings. The enterprise management of VPNs is also explored. Management is one of the greatest challenges in the implementation of large-scale site-to-site and remote-access VPNs. The primary role of the Management Center for VPN Routers (Router MC) is to manage site-to-site VPNs. The key topics necessary to understand VPNs are explored. A firm understanding of how Router MC operates will help you better manage large-scale VPNs. Finally, you learn about the Simple Network Management Protocol (SNMP).

- **Chapter 8, "PIX Security Appliance Contexts, Failover, and Management"**—This chapter provides an overview and explanation of security contexts. A single PIX Security Appliance can be partitioned into multiple virtual firewalls, known as security contexts. Each context is an independent firewall, with its own security policy, interfaces, and administrators. Multiple contexts are similar to having multiple stand-alone firewalls. This module continues with a discussion of configuring and managing of security contexts.

Appendix:

- **Appendix A, "Check Your Understanding Answer Key"**—This appendix provides the answers to the quizzes that appear at the end of each chapter.

The **Glossary** includes key terms used throughout this book.

CHAPTER 1

Vulnerabilities, Threats, and Attacks

Upon completion of this chapter, you should be able to answer the following questions:

- What are the basics concepts of network security?
- What are some common network security vulnerabilities and threats?
- What are security attacks?
- What is the process of vulnerability analysis?

Key Terms

This chapter uses the following key terms. You can find the definitions in the glossary at the end of the book.

Unstructured threats   page 20

Structured threats   page 20

External threats   page 20

Internal threats   page 21

Hacker   page 21

Cracker   page 21

Phreaker   page 21

Spammer   page 21

Phisher   page 21

White hat   page 21

Black hat   page 21

Dictionary cracking   page 28

Brute-force computation   page 28

Trust exploitation   page 28

Port redirection   page 29

Man-in-the-middle attack   page 30

Social engineering   page 30

Phishing   page 30

The Internet continues to grow exponentially. Personal, government, and business applications continue to multiply on the Internet, with immediate benefits to end users. However, these network-based applications and services can pose security risks to individuals and to the information resources of companies and governments. Information is an asset that must be protected. Without adequate network security, many individuals, businesses, and governments risk losing that asset.

Network security is the process by which digital information assets are protected.

The goals of network security are as follows:

- Protect confidentiality
- Maintain integrity
- Ensure availability

With this in mind, it is imperative that all networks be protected from threats and vulnerabilities for a business to achieve its fullest potential.

Typically, these threats are persistent because of vulnerabilities, which can arise from the following:

Note

It is highly recommended that you study the commands covered in the chapters using the labs and the Command Reference (Cisco Security Appliance Command Reference Guide, Version 7.0, at http://www.cisco.com/application/pdf/en/us/guest/products/ps5317/c2001/cc migration_09186a008018e5 f2.pdf; and Cisco IOS Security Command Reference, Release 12.3, at http://www.cisco.com/application/pdf/en/us/guest/products/ps5317/c2001/ccmigration_09186a008018 e5f2.pdf).

Not all required commands are covered in sufficient detail in the text alone. Successful completion of this course requires a thorough knowledge of command syntax and application.

- Misconfigured hardware or software
- Poor network design
- Inherent technology weaknesses
- End-user carelessness
- Intentional end-user acts (that is, disgruntled employees)

This chapter provides an overview of essential network security concepts, common vulnerabilities, threats, attacks, and vulnerability analysis.

Introduction to Network Security

This chapter consists of an overview of what network security is all about. The sections that follow cover the following aspects of network security:

- The need for network security
- Identifying potential risks to network security
- Open versus closed security models
- Trends driving network security
- Information security organizations

The Need for Network Security

Security has one purpose: to protect assets. For most of history, this meant building strong walls to stop the enemy and establishing small, well-guarded doors to provide secure access for friends. This strategy worked well for the centralized, fortress-like world of mainframe computers and closed networks, as seen in Figure 1-1.

Figure 1-1   Closed Network

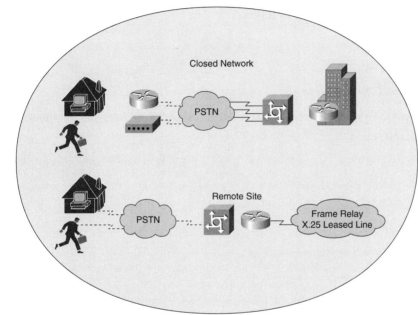

The closed network typically consists of a network designed and implemented in a corporate environment and provides connectivity only to known parties and sites without connecting to public networks. Networks were designed this way in the past and thought to be reasonably secure because of no outside connectivity.

With the advent of personal computers, LANs, and the wide-open world of the Internet, the networks of today are more open, as shown in Figure 1-2.

As e-business and Internet applications continue to grow, the key to network security lies in defining the balance between a closed and open network and differentiating the good guys from the bad guys.

With the increased number of LANs and personal computers, the Internet began to create untold numbers of security risks. Firewall devices, which are software or hardware that enforce an access control policy between two or more networks, were introduced. This technology gave businesses a balance between security and simple outbound access to the Internet, which was mostly used for e-mail and web surfing.

Figure 1-2   Open Network: The Network Today

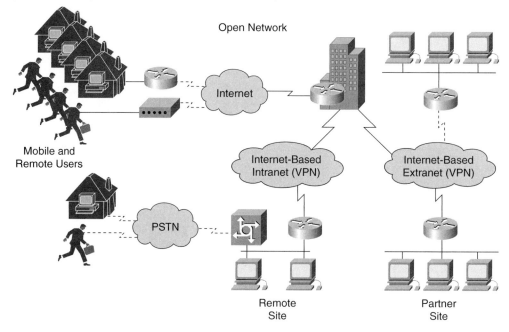

This balance was short-lived as the use of extranets began to grow, which connected internal and external business processes. Businesses were soon realizing tremendous cost savings by connecting supply-chain management and enterprise resource planning systems to their business partners, and by connecting sales-force automation systems to mobile employees, and by providing electronic commerce connections to business customers and consumers. The firewall began to include intrusion detection, authentication, authorization, and vulnerability-assessment systems. Today, successful companies have again struck a balance by keeping the enemies out with increasingly complex ways of letting friends in.

Most people expect security measures to ensure the following:

- Users can perform only authorized tasks.

- Users can obtain only authorized information.

- Users cannot cause damage to the data, applications, or operating environment of a system.

The word *security* means protection against malicious attack by outsiders (and by insiders). Statistically, there are more attacks from inside sources. Security also involves controlling the effects of errors and equipment failures. Anything that can protect against an attack will probably prevent random misfortunes, too.

Throughout this book, many definitions, acronyms, and logical device symbols dealing with security are introduced (see Figure 1-3). Refer to the glossary for further explanation when encountering unknown terms and acronyms. For a complete listing of all the graphic symbols in this book, see the Introduction.

Figure 1-3   Several Graphic Symbols Used in This Book

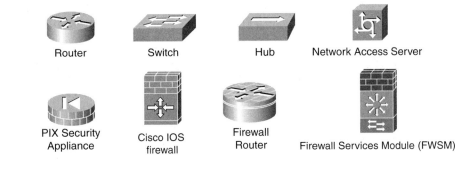

Lab 1.1.1 Student Lab Orientation

In this lab, you review the lab bundle equipment and gain an understanding of the security pod technology and the pod naming and addressing scheme. You then load a Cisco IOS Firewall image and the default lab configurations. After that, you cable the standard lab topology and, finally, test connectivity.

Identifying Potential Risks to Network Security

A risk analysis should identify the risks to the network, network resources, and data. The intent of a risk analysis is to identify the components of the network, evaluate the importance of each component, and then apply an appropriate level of security. This analysis helps to maintain a workable balance between security and required network access. The key is to identify what needs to be secured and at what cost. More money and assets would be allocated ensuring the security of a high-priced automobile versus an old junker, for example.

Asset Identification

Before the network can be secured, you must identify the individual components that make up the network. You need to create an asset inventory that includes all the network devices and endpoints, such as hosts and servers.

Vulnerability Assessment

After you have identified the network components, you can assess their vulnerabilities. These vulnerabilities could be weaknesses in the technology, configuration, or security policy. Any vulnerability you discover must be addressed to mitigate any threat that could take advantage of the vulnerability. Vulnerabilities can be fixed by various methods, including applying software patches, reconfiguring devices, or deploying countermeasures, such as firewalls and antivirus software. Many websites list the vulnerabilities of network components, and the manufacturers of operating systems and components that list vulnerabilities of their products sponsor many websites.

Threat Identification

A threat is an event that can take advantage of vulnerability and cause a negative impact on the network. Potential threats to the network need to be identified, and the related vulnerabilities need to be addressed to minimize the risk of the threat.

Open Versus Closed Security Models

With all security designs, some trade-off occurs between user productivity and security measures. The goal of any security design is to provide maximum security with minimum impact on user access and productivity. Some security measures, such as network data encryption, do not restrict access and productivity. On the other hand, cumbersome or unnecessarily redundant verification and authorization systems can frustrate users and prevent access to critical network resources. Remember that the network is a tool designed to enhance production. If the security measures that are put in place become too cumbersome, they will actually detract rather then enhance productivity.

Networks used as productivity tools should be designed so that business needs dictate the security policy. A security policy should not determine how a business operates. Because organizations are constantly subject to change, security policies must be systematically updated to reflect new business directions, technological changes, and resource allocations.

Security policies vary greatly in design. Three general types of security models are open, restrictive, and closed. Some important points are as follows (see Figure 1-4):

- Security model can be open or closed as a starting point.

- Choose the best end-to-end mix of security products and technology to implement the model.

- Application-level security can include Secure Sockets Layer (SSL) technology.

Figure 1-4   Network Security Policies

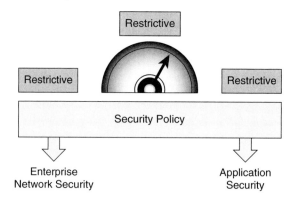

Like security models, many devices can be classified as open, restrictive, or closed. For example, routers and switches are typically open devices, allowing high functionality and services by default. On the other hand, a firewall is typically a closed system that does not allow any services until they are switched on. Server operating systems can fall into any of the three categories, depending on the vendor. It is important to understand these principles when deploying these devices.

Open Access

An open security model is the easiest to implement, as shown in Figures 1-5 and 1-6. Few security measures are implemented in this design. Administrators configure existing hardware and software basic security capabilities. Firewalls, virtual private networks (VPNs), intrusion detection systems (IDSs), and other measures that incur additional costs are typically not implemented. Simple passwords and server security become the foundation of this model. If encryption is used, it is implemented by individual users or on servers.

Figure 1-5   Open Security Policy

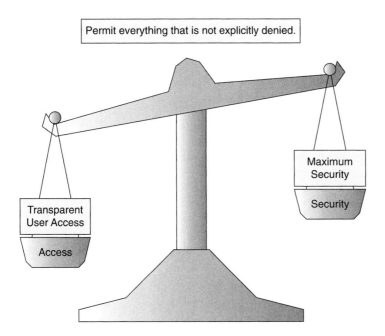

Figure 1-6   Open Security Policy Topology

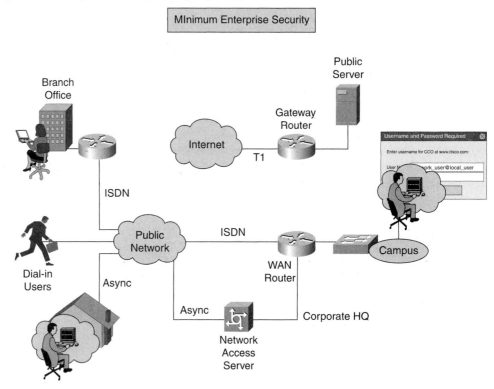

This model assumes that the protected assets are minimal, users are trusted, and threats are minimal. However, this does not exclude the need for data backup systems in most open security policy scenarios. LANs that are not connected to the Internet or public WANs are more likely to implement this type of model.

This type of network design gives users free access to all areas. When security breaches occur, they are likely to result in great damage and loss. Network administrators are usually not held responsible for network breaches or abuse.

Restrictive Access

A restrictive security model is more difficult to implement, as shown in Figures 1-7 and 1-8. Many security measures are implemented in this design. Administrators configure existing hardware and software for security capabilities in addition to deploying more costly hardware and software solutions such as firewalls, VPNs, IDSs, and identity servers. Firewalls and identity servers become the foundation of this model.

Figure 1-7   Restrictive Security Policy

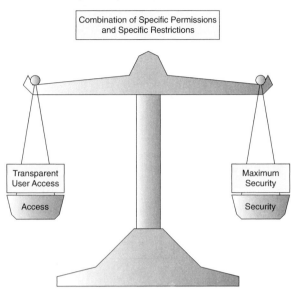

This model assumes that the protected assets are substantial, some users are not trustworthy, and that threats are likely. LANs that are connected to the Internet or public WANs are more likely to implement this type of model. Ease of use for users diminishes as security tightens.

Figure 1-8   Restrictive Security Policy Topology

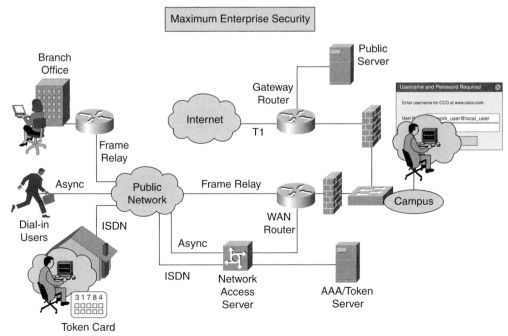

Closed Access

A closed security model is most difficult to implement. All available security measures are implemented in this design. Administrators configure existing hardware and software for maximum-security capabilities in addition to deploying more costly hardware and software solutions such as firewalls, VPNs, IDSs, and identity servers, as shown in Figures 1-9 and 1-10.

Figure 1-9   Closed Security Policy

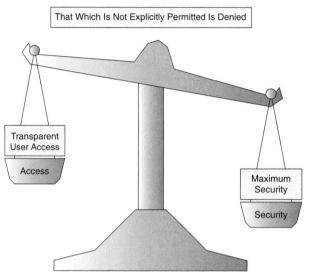

The closed security model assumes that the protected assets are premium, all users are not trustworthy, and that threats are frequent. User access is difficult and cumbersome. Network administrators require greater skills and more time to administer the network. Furthermore, companies require a higher number of and better trained network administrators to maintain this tight security.

In many corporations and organizations, these administrators are likely to be unpopular while implementing and maintaining security. Network security departments must clarify that they only implement the policy, which is designed, written, and approved by the corporation. Politics behind the closed security model can be monumental. In the event of a security breach or network outage, network administrators might be held more accountable for problems.

Trends Driving Network Security

As in any fast-growing industry, changes are to be expected. The types of potential threats to network security are always evolving. If the security of the network is compromised, there could be serious consequences, such as loss of privacy, theft of information, and even legal liability. Figure 1-11 illustrates several threats and their potential consequences.

Figure 1-10   Closed Security Policy Topology

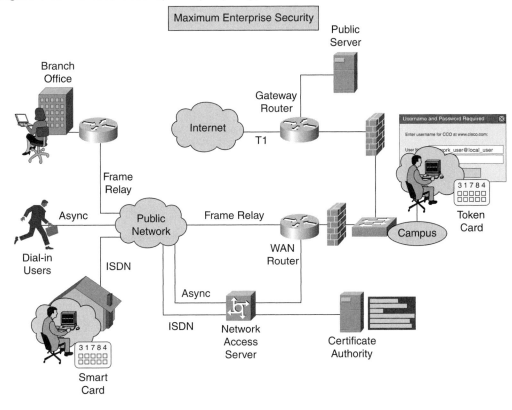

Figure 1-11   Threats and Potential Consequences

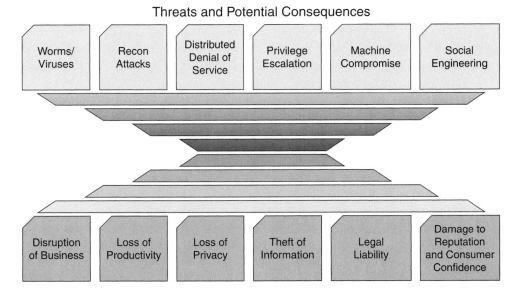

Legal Issues and Privacy Concerns

For many businesses today, one of the biggest reasons to create and follow a security policy is compliance with the law. Any business is potentially liable should a hacker or a virus take down the operation. Similarly, if a business is running a publicly held e-business and a catastrophic attack seriously impairs the business, a lawsuit is possible.

Legal liability in such cases is likely to depend on what prevention technologies and practices are available and on whether these technologies and practices are reasonably cost-effective to implement. As a result, showing due diligence will mean everything from implementing technologies such as firewalls, intrusion-detection tools, content filters, traffic analyzers, and VPNs to having best practices for continuous risk assessment and vulnerability testing. Of course, litigation is not the only legal consideration that e-businesses face today. Lawmakers concern over the lack of Internet security, particularly where it hampers rights to privacy, is growing.

Due diligence is the part of the legal equation in which the technology person researches the vulnerabilities, threats, and risks. This process determines the countermeasures that are available and gives that information to the executives, who then make the decisions based on the four mitigation strategies available:

- Transfer the risk (insurance)

- Reduce the risk (apply a mitigation)

- Accept the risk (understanding that the risk might occur and if it does the company will shoulder the loss)

- Reject the risk (it has not happened to us before, so we don't believe it will happen to use in the future)

This process is called due care on the management side: What would a prudent person do in that situation?

In 1998, the European Union passed the comprehensive Data Privacy Directives that provide consumers with strong control over their personal data. Many countries outside the United States have adopted the equivalent of these privacy principles. In the United States, more than 1000 privacy-related bills were introduced in state legislatures in 1999 and 2000, and numerous bills are currently pending.

In the United States, education, financial services, government, and health care are currently scrambling to meet federally mandated guidelines for network security and privacy. In financial services, there is the Gramm-Leach-Blilely (GLB) Act, which was passed in 1999. The GLB Act erased long-standing antitrust laws that prohibited banks, insurance companies, and securities firms from merging and sharing information with one another. The idea was that smaller firms would then be able to pursue acquisitions and alliances that would help drive competition against many of the larger financial institutions. Included in that law were several consumer privacy protections. Namely, companies must tell their customers what sorts of data they plan to share and with whom and then give customers a chance to opt out of that data sharing. The law required banks to send those notices to customers by July 1, 2001.

The U.S. government is contending with the Government Information Security Reform Act (passed in October 2002), which directs federal agencies to increase security plans for their computer systems. Representatives from the General Accounting Office (GAO) and other organizations recently told Congress that, despite this legislation, federal agencies are still falling short of dealing with key security issues.

On the health-care side, the Health Insurance Portability and Accountability Act of 1996 (HIPAA) requires the U.S. Department of Health and Human Services to develop a set of national standards for health-care transactions and provide assurance that the electronic transfer of confidential patient information will be as safe as or safer than paper-based patient records. Compliance with HIPAA is estimated to cost the health-care industry $4 billion annually.

The Family Educational Rights and Privacy Act (FERPA) is a federal law designed to protect the privacy of a student's education records. The law applies to all schools that receive funds under an applicable program of the U.S. Department of Education. When an individual requests student information from a university, the university must respond in accordance with FERPA guidelines. The Department of Education's FERPA guidelines act as the foundation.

Finally, many education institutions in the United States must comply with the Children Internet Protection Act (CIPA) if they want to receive any form of U.S. federal funding.

Wireless Access

The increasing use of wireless LAN connections and the rapid rise of Internet access from cell phones in Europe and Asia are requiring entirely whole new approaches to security. Radio frequency (RF) connections do not respect firewalls the way wired connections do. Moreover, the slow processors, small screens, and nonexistent keyboards on cell phones and personal digital assistants (PDAs) challenge many of the standard approaches to access, authentication, and authorization.

The Need for Speed

The number of broadband connections to the Internet from homes is exceeding projections. Many businesses are finding that multiple T1 or E1 connections to the Internet no longer suffice. Current software-based security approaches have problems scaling to OC-1 and higher ratings.

IT Staffing Shortages

The IT staffing shortage is especially evident in the security field. To solve this problem, many enterprises are increasingly outsourcing day-to-day security management tasks. The application service provider (ASP) business model will become increasingly common in the security world. Therefore, security solutions will need to be more manageable in this outsourced model. Clearly, there is a demand for skilled network security professionals.

ISO/IEC 17799

ISO/IEC 17799, *Information technology—Code of practice for information security management*, is an information security standard that is published by the International Organization for Standardization (ISO) and the International Electrotechnical Commission (IEC). ISO/IEC 17799 is intended to be a common basis and practical guideline for developing organizational security standards and effective security management practices.

ISO/IEC 17799 was originally published in 2000 and was revised and republished in 2005. ISO/IEC 17799 is based on the British Standard (BS7799). The 2005 revision of ISO/IEC 17799 is made up of the following 11 sections:

- Security policy

- Organization of information security

- Asset management

- Human resources security

- Physical and environmental security

- Communications and operations management

- Access control

- Information systems acquisition, development, and maintenance

- Information security incident management

- Business continuity management

- Compliance

Information Security Organizations

Many organizations provide useful information for security professionals. These organizations provide information on detecting and responding to both established and emerging information security threats. Information about operating system weaknesses, best practices for security, and security training and certification information is also available. Independent security evaluations have arisen to provide organizations with an unbiased and objective review of security products. For example, Common Criteria, Federal Information Processing Standards Publication 140 (FIPS 140), and International Computer Security Association (ICSA) are some of the independent certifications and evaluations.

CERT/CC

The CERT Coordination Center (CERT/CC) is a reporting center for Internet security issues. The CERT/CC plays a major role in coordinating responses to Internet security threats. The CERT/CC is located at the Software Engineering Institute (SEI) operated by Carnegie Mellon University.

US-CERT

The United States Computer Emergency Readiness Team (US-CERT) is a partnership between the Department of Homeland Security and the public and private sectors. US-CERT was established in 2003 to protect the nation's Internet infrastructure by coordinating defense against and responses to Internet security threats.

US-CERT is responsible for the following:

- Analyzing and reducing cyber threats and vulnerabilities
- Disseminating cyber threat warning information
- Coordinating incident-response activities

SANS Institute

The SysAdmin, Audit, Network, Security (SANS) Institute was established in 1989 as a cooperative research and education organization. The SANS Institute develops and maintains research documents about various aspects of information security. These documents are available at no cost. SANS also operates the Internet Storm Center, an early warning system for Internet security issues.

ISC^2

The International Information Systems Security Certification Consortium, Inc. (ISC^2) is a non-profit organization that maintains a collection of industry best practices for information security. The ISC^2 has created five certifications that align to these best practices, the Systems Security Certified Practitioner (SSCP), and the Certified Information Systems Security Professional (CISSP). There are two Focus certifications that one can take after the CISSP, and then there is the new Certification and Accreditation Professional (CAP) certification.

Common Criteria

The Common Criteria is an international standard for evaluating IT security. It was developed by a consortium of 14 countries to replace a number of existing country-specific security assessments and was intended to establish a single high-quality standard for international use. Although there are seven security levels defined for the Common Criteria evaluation process, Evaluation Assurance Level 4 (EAL4) is the highest universal evaluation level implemented under the Common Criteria today. Table 1-1 describes each EAL.

Table 1-1   Evaluation Assurance Levels

EAL Level	Description
EAL1	Minimal level of independently assured security
EAL2	Low to moderate level of independently assured security
EAL3	Moderate level of independently assured security
EAL4	Moderate to high level of independently assured security
EAL5-7	Specific requirements, yet to be implemented. Needed only in the most restrictive government environments

FIPS

The Federal Information Processing Standard (FIPS) 140 is a U.S. and Canadian government standard that specifies security requirements for cryptographic modules. FIPS 140 has four levels of assurance: Level 1 is the lowest, and Level 4 is the most stringent. Each level builds upon the one below it, so a Level 2 certification means that a product meets the requirements for both Level 1 and Level 2. Table 1-2 describes each FIPS security level.

Table 1-2   FIPS Security Levels

Level	Description
Level 1	Lowest level of security requirements specified for a cryptographic module
Level 2	Level 1 plus tamper-evident coatings or seals, locks on removable covers or doors
Level 3	Level 2 plus detecting and responding to attempts at physical access, use, or modification of the cryptographic module
Level 4	Highest level of security useful for operation in physically unprotected environments

ICSA

ICSA Labs tests firewalls against a standard set of functional and assurance criteria elements. ICSA Labs is presently testing firewalls against the Modular Firewall Product Certification Criteria Version 4.0. ICSA also test VPN devices for IP Security (IPsec) interoperability. IPsec interoperability testing validates a product or set of products that use cryptography to provide effective security services. ICSA certification exists to provide a set of measurable, public-domain standards for commercial security products.

Introduction to Vulnerabilities, Threats, and Attacks

When discussing network security, the three common terms used are as follows:

- **Vulnerability**—A weakness that is inherent in every network and device. This includes routers, switches, desktops, servers, and even security devices themselves.

- **Threats**—The people eager, willing, and qualified to take advantage of each security weakness, and they continually search for new exploits and weaknesses.

- **Attacks**—The threats use a variety of tools, scripts, and programs to launch attacks against networks and network devices. Typically, the network devices under attack are the endpoints, such as servers and desktops.

The sections that follow discuss vulnerabilities, threats, and attacks in further detail.

Vulnerabilities

Vulnerabilities in network security can be summed up as the "soft spots" that are present in every network. The vulnerabilities are present in the network and individual devices that make up the network.

Networks are typically plagued by one or all of three primary vulnerabilities or weaknesses:

- Technology weaknesses
- Configuration weaknesses
- Security policy weaknesses

The sections that follow examine each of these weaknesses in more detail.

Technological Weaknesses

Computer and network technologies have intrinsic security weaknesses. These include TCP/IP protocol weaknesses, operating system weaknesses, and network equipment weaknesses. Table 1-3 describes these three weaknesses.

Table 1-3   Network Security Weaknesses

Weakness	Description
TCP/IP protocol weaknesses	HTTP, FTP, and ICMP are inherently insecure. Simple Network Management Protocol (SNMP), Simple Mail Transfer Protocol (SMTP), and SYN floods are related to the inherently insecure structure upon which TCP was designed.
Operating system weaknesses	The UNIX, Linux, Macintosh, Windows NT, 9x, 2K, XP, and OS/2 operating systems all have security problems that must be addressed. These are documented in the CERT archives at http://www.cert.org.
Network equipment weaknesses	Various types of network equipment, such as routers, fire-walls, and switches, have security weaknesses that must be recognized and protected against. These weaknesses include the following: Password protection Lack of authentication Routing protocols Firewall holes

Configuration Weaknesses

Network administrators or network engineers need to learn what the configuration weaknesses are and correctly configure their computing and network devices to compensate. Table 1-4 lists some common configuration weaknesses.

Table 1-4   Configuration Weaknesses

Weakness	How the Weakness Is Exploited
Unsecured user accounts	User account information might be transmitted insecurely across the network, exposing usernames and passwords to snoopers.
System accounts with easily guessed passwords	This common problem is the result of poorly selected and easily guessed user passwords.
Misconfigured Internet services	A common problem is to turn on JavaScript in web browsers, enabling attacks by way of hostile JavaScript when accessing untrusted sites. IIS, Apache, FTP, and Terminal Services also pose problems.
Unsecured default settings within products	Many products have default settings that enable security holes.

Table 1-4   Configuration Weaknesses   *continued*

Weakness	How the Weakness Is Exploited
Misconfigured network equipment	Misconfigurations of the equipment itself can cause significant security problems. For example, misconfigured access lists, routing protocols, or SNMP community strings can open up large security holes. Misconfigured or lack of encryption and remote-access controls can also cause significant security issues, as can the practice of leaving ports open on a switch (which could allow the introduction of noncompany computing equipment).

Security Policy Weaknesses

Security policy weaknesses can create unforeseen security threats. The network can pose security risks to the network if users do not follow the security policy. Table 1-5 lists some common security policy weaknesses and how those weaknesses are exploited.

Table 1-5   Security Policy Weaknesses

Weakness	How the Weakness Is Exploited
Lack of written security policy	An unwritten policy cannot be consistently applied or enforced.
Politics	Political battles and turf wars can make it difficult to implement a consistent security policy.
Lack of continuity.	Poorly chosen, easily cracked, or default passwords can allow unauthorized access to the network.
Logical access controls. not applied	Inadequate monitoring and auditing allow attacks and unauthorized use to continue, wasting company resources. This could result in legal action or termination against IT technicians, IT management, or even company leadership that allows these unsafe conditions to persist. Lack of careful and controlled auditing can also make it hard to enforce policy and to stand up to legal challenges for "wrongful termination" and suits against the organization.
Software and hardware installation and changes do not follow policy.	Unauthorized changes to the network topology or installation of unapproved applications create security holes.
Disaster recovery plan nonexistent.	The lack of a disaster recovery plan allows chaos, panic, and is confusion to occur when someone attacks the enterprise.

Threats

There are four primary classes of threats to network security, as Figure 1-12 depicts. The list that follows describes each class of threat in more detail.

Figure 1-12   Variety of Threats

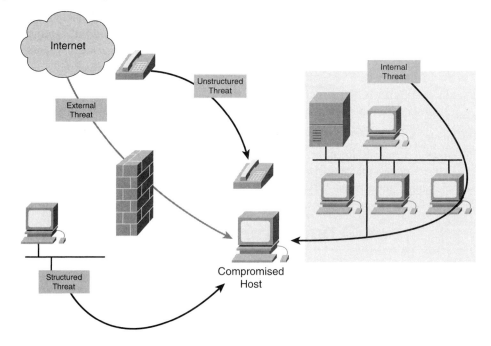

- ***Unstructured threats***—Unstructured threats consist of mostly inexperienced individuals using easily available hacking tools such as shell scripts and password crackers. Even unstructured threats that are only executed with the intent of testing and challenging a hacker's skills can still do serious damage to a company. For example, if an external company website is hacked, the integrity of the company is damaged. Even if the external website is separate from the internal information that sits behind a protective firewall, the public does not know that. All the public knows is that the site is not a safe environment to conduct business.

- ***Structured threats***— Structured threats come from hackers who are more highly motivated and technically competent. These people know system vulnerabilities and can understand and develop exploit code and scripts. They understand, develop, and use sophisticated hacking techniques to penetrate unsuspecting businesses. These groups are often involved with the major fraud and theft cases reported to law enforcement agencies.

- ***External threats***—External threats can arise from individuals or organizations working outside of a company. They do not have authorized access to the computer systems or network. They work their way into a network mainly from the Internet or dialup access servers.

- *Internal threats*—Internal threats occur when someone has authorized access to the network with either an account on a server or physical access to the network. According to the FBI, internal access and misuse account for 60 percent to 80 percent of reported incidents.

As the types of threats, attacks, and exploits have evolved, various terms have been coined to describe different groups of individuals. Some of the most common terms are as follows:

- *Hacker*—Hacker is a general term that has historically been used to describe a computer programming expert. More recently, this term is commonly used in a negative way to describe an individual who attempts to gain unauthorized access to network resources with malicious intent.

- *Cracker*—Cracker is the term that is generally regarded as the more accurate word that is used to describe an individual who attempts to gain unauthorized access to network resources with malicious intent.

- *Phreaker*—A phreaker is an individual who manipulates the phone network to cause it to perform a function that is normally not allowed. A common goal of phreaking is breaking into the phone network, usually through a payphone, to make free long-distance calls.

- *Spammer*—A spammer is an individual who sends large numbers of unsolicited e-mail messages. Spammers often use viruses to take control of home computers to use these computers to send out their bulk messages.

- *Phisher*—A phisher uses e-mail or other means in an attempt to trick others into providing sensitive information, such as credit card numbers or passwords. The phisher masquerades as a trusted party that would have a legitimate need for the sensitive information.

- *White hat*—White hat is a term used to describe individuals who use their abilities to find vulnerabilities in systems or networks and then report these vulnerabilities to the owners of the system so that they can be fixed.

- *Black hat*—Black hat is another term for individuals who use their knowledge of computer systems to break into systems or networks that they are not authorized to use.

Attacks

Four primary classes of attacks exist:

- Reconnaissance
- Access
- Denial of service
- Worms, viruses, and Trojan horses

The sections that follow cover each attack class in more detail.

Reconnaissance

Reconnaissance is the unauthorized discovery and mapping of systems, services, or vulnerabilities (see Figure 1-13). It is also known as information gathering and, in most cases, it precedes an actual access or denial-of-service (DoS) attack. Reconnaissance is somewhat analogous to a thief casing a neighborhood for vulnerable homes to break into, such as an unoccupied residence, easy-to-open doors, or open windows.

Figure 1-13   Reconnaissance

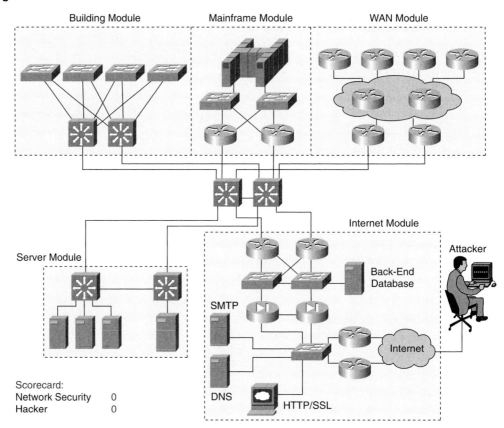

Access

System access is the ability for an unauthorized intruder to gain access to a device for which the intruder does not have an account or a password. Entering or accessing systems to which one does not have authority to access usually involves running a hack, script, or tool that exploits a known vulnerability of the system or application being attacked.

Denial of Service (DoS)

Denial of service implies that an attacker disables or corrupts networks, systems, or services with the intent to deny services to intended users. DoS attacks involve either crashing the system or slowing it down to the point that it is unusable. But DoS can also be as simple as deleting or corrupting information. In most cases, performing the attack simply involves running a hack or script. The attacker does not need prior access to the target because a way to access it is all that is usually required. For these reasons, DoS attacks are the most feared.

Worms, Viruses, and Trojan Horses

Malicious software is inserted onto a host to damage a system; corrupt a system; replicate itself; or deny services or access to networks, systems or services. They can also allow sensitive information to be copied or echoed to other systems.

Trojan horses can be used to ask the user to enter sensitive information in a commonly trusted screen. For example, an attacker might log in to a Windows box and run a program that looks like the true Windows logon screen, prompting a user to type his username and password. The program would then send the information to the attacker and then give the Windows error for bad password. The user would then log out, and the correct Windows logon screen would appear; the user is none the wiser that his password has just been stolen.

Even worse, the nature of all these threats is changing—from the relatively simple viruses of the 1980s to the more complex and damaging viruses, DoS attacks, and hacking tools in recent years. Today, these hacking tools are powerful and widespread, with the new dangers of self-spreading blended worms such as Slammer and Blaster and network DoS attacks. Also, the old days of attacks that take days or weeks to spread are over. Threats now spread worldwide in a matter of minutes. The Slammer worm of January 2003 spread around the world in less than 10 minutes.

The next generations of attacks are expected to spread in just seconds. These worms and viruses could do more than just wreak havoc by overloading network resources with the amount of traffic they generate, they could also be used to deploy damaging payloads that steal vital information or erase hard drives. Also, there is a strong concern that the threats of tomorrow will be directed at the very infrastructure of the Internet.

Attack Examples

Several types of attacks are used today, and this section looks at a representative sample in more detail.

Reconnaissance Attacks

Reconnaissance attacks can consist of the following:

- Packet sniffers

- Port scans

- Ping sweeps

- Internet information queries

A malicious intruder typically ping sweeps the target network to determine which IP addresses are alive. After this, the intruder uses a port scanner, as shown in Figure 1-14, to determine what network services or ports are active on the live IP addresses. From this information, the intruder queries the ports to determine the application type and version, and the type and version of operating system running on the target host. Based on this information, the intruder can determine whether a possible vulnerability exists that can be exploited.

Figure 1-14   Nmap

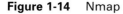

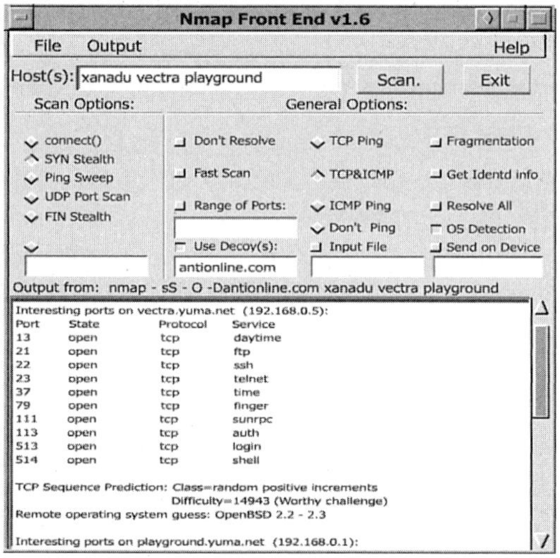

Using, for example, the Nslookup and Whois software utilities (see Figure 1-15), an attacker can easily determine the IP address space assigned to a given corporation or entity. The **ping** command tells the attacker what IP addresses are alive.

Network snooping and packet sniffing are common terms for *eavesdropping*. Eavesdropping is listening in to a conversation, spying, prying, or snooping. The information gathered by eavesdropping can be used to pose other attacks to the network.

Figure 1-15   ARIN Whois

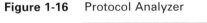

An example of data susceptible to eavesdropping is SNMP Version 1 community strings, which are sent in clear text. An intruder could eavesdrop on SNMP queries and gather valuable data on network equipment configuration. Another example is the capture of usernames and passwords as they cross a network.

Types of Eavesdropping

A common method for eavesdropping on communications is to capture TCP/IP or other protocol packets and decode the contents using a protocol analyzer or similar utility, as shown in Figure 1-16.

Figure 1-16   Protocol Analyzer

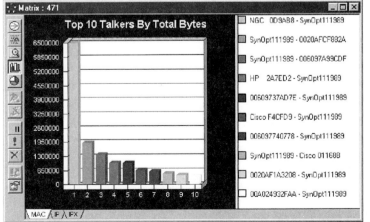

Two common uses of eavesdropping are as follows:

- **Information gathering**—Network intruders can identify usernames, passwords, or information carried in the packet such as credit card numbers or sensitive personal information.

- **Information theft**—Network eavesdropping can lead to information theft. The theft can occur as data is transmitted over the internal or external network. The network intruder can also steal data from networked computers by gaining unauthorized access. Examples include breaking into or eavesdropping on financial institutions and obtaining credit card numbers. Another example is using a computer to crack a password file.

Tools Used to Perform Eavesdropping

The following tools are used for eavesdropping:

- Network or protocol analyzers

- Packet capturing utilities on networked computers

Methods to Counteract Eavesdropping

Three of the most effective methods for counteracting eavesdropping are as follows:

- Implementing and enforcing a policy directive that forbids the use of protocols with known susceptibilities to eavesdropping

- Using encryption that meets the data security needs of the organization without imposing an excessive burden on the system resources or the users

- Using switched networks

Encrypted Data for Protection Against Reconnaissance Attacks

Encryption provides protection for data susceptible to eavesdropping attacks, password crackers, or manipulation. Some benefits of data encryption are as follows:

- Almost every company has transactions, which, if viewed by an eavesdropper, could have negative consequences. Encryption ensures that when sensitive data passes over a medium susceptible to eavesdropping, it cannot be altered or observed.

- Decryption is necessary when the data reaches the router or other termination device on the far-receiving LAN where the destination host resides.

- By encrypting after the UDP or TCP headers, so that only the IP payload data is encrypted, Cisco IOS network-layer encryption allows all intermediate routers and switches to forward the traffic as they would any other IP packets. Payload-only encryption allows flow switching and all access list features to work with the encrypted traffic just as they would with plain text traffic, thereby preserving desired quality of service (QoS) for all data.

Most encryption algorithms can be broken and the information can be revealed if the attacker has enough time, desire, and resources. A realistic goal of encryption is to make obtaining the information too work-intensive to be worth it to the attacker.

Access Attacks

Access attacks exploit known vulnerabilities in authentication services, FTP services, and web services to gain entry to web accounts, confidential databases, and other sensitive information. Access attacks can consist of the following:

- Password attacks

- Trust exploitation

- Port redirection

- Man-in-the-middle attacks

- Social engineering

- Phishing

Password Attacks

Password attacks can be implemented using several methods, including brute-force attacks, Trojan horse programs, IP spoofing, and packet sniffers. Although packet sniffers and IP spoofing can yield user accounts and passwords, password attacks usually refer to repeated attempts to identify a user account, password, or both (see Figure 1-17 for an illustration of an attempt to attack using the administrator's profile). These repeated attempts are called brute-force attacks.

Figure 1-17   Password Attack Example

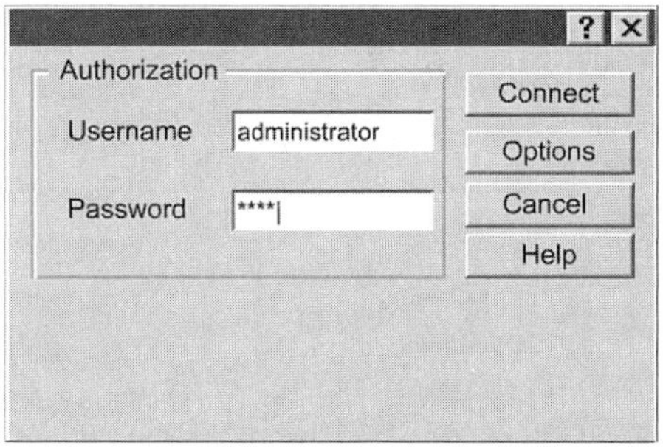

Often a brute-force attack is performed using a program that runs across the network and attempts to log in to a shared resource, such as a server. When an attacker gains access to a resource, he has the same access rights as the user whose account has been compromised. If this account has sufficient privileges, the attacker can create a back door for future access, without concern for any status and password changes to the compromised user account. In fact, not only would the attacker have the same rights as the exploited, he could attempt privilege escalation.

The following are the two methods for computing passwords:

- **Dictionary cracking**—All of the words in a dictionary file are computed and compared against the possible users' password. This method is extremely fast and finds simple passwords.

- **Brute-force computation**—This method uses a particular character set, such as A to Z, or A to Z plus 0 to 9, and computes the hash for every possible password made up of those characters. It always computes the password if that password is made up of the character set you have selected to test. The downside is that time is required for completion of this type of attack.

Trust Exploitation

Although it is more of a technique than a hack itself, ***trust exploitation***, as shown in Figure 1-18 refers to an attack in which an individual takes advantage of a trust relationship within a network. The classic example is a perimeter network connection from a corporation. These network segments often house Domain Name System (DNS), SMTP, and HTTP servers. Because all these servers reside on the same segment, the compromise of one system can lead to the compromise of other systems because these systems usually trust other systems attached to the same network.

Figure 1-18   Trust Exploitation

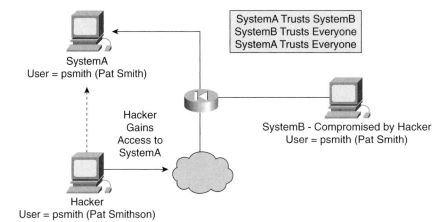

Another example is a system on the outside of a firewall that has a trust relationship with a system on the inside of a firewall. When the outside system is compromised, it can take advantage of that trust relationship to attack the inside network. Another form of an access attack involves privilege escalation. Privilege escalation occurs when a user obtains privileges or rights to objects that were not assigned to the user by an administrator. Objects can be files, commands, or other components on a network device. The intent is to gain access to information or execute unauthorized procedures. This information is used to gain administrative privileges to a system or device. They use these privileges to install sniffers, create backdoor accounts, or delete log files.

Trust exploitation-based attacks can be mitigated through tight constraints on trust levels within a network. Systems on the outside of a firewall should never be absolutely trusted by systems on the inside of a firewall. Such trust should be limited to specific protocols and should be authenticated by something other than an IP address where possible.

Port Redirection

Port redirection attacks, as shown in Figure 1-19, are a type of trust exploitation attack that uses a compromised host to pass traffic through a firewall that would otherwise be dropped. Consider a firewall with three interfaces and a host on each interface. The host on the outside can reach the host on the public services segment, but not the host on the inside. This publicly accessible segment is commonly referred to as a demilitarized zone (DMZ). The host on the public services segment can reach the host on both the outside and the inside. If hackers were able to compromise the public services segment host, they could install software to redirect traffic from the outside host directly to the inside host. Although neither communication violates the rules implemented in the firewall, the outside host has now achieved connectivity to the inside host through the port redirection process on the public services host. An example of an application that can provide this type of access is Netcat.

Figure 1-19   Protocol Analyzer

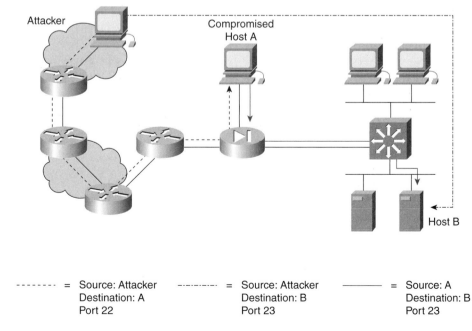

```
-------- = Source: Attacker      ---------- = Source: Attacker      ———— = Source: A
          Destination: A                     Destination: B                Destination: B
          Port 22                            Port 23                       Port 23
```

Port redirection can be mitigated primarily through the use of proper trust models, which are network specific (as mentioned earlier). Assuming a system under attack, a host-based IDS can help detect a hacker and prevent installation of such utilities on a host.

Man-in-the-Middle Attacks

A *man-in-the-middle attack* requires that the hacker have access to network packets that come across a network. An example could be someone who is working for an Internet service provider (ISP) and has access to all network packets transferred between the ISP network and any other network.

Such attacks are often implemented using network packet sniffers and routing and transport protocols. The possible uses of such attacks are theft of information, hijacking of an ongoing session to gain access to private network resources, traffic analysis to derive information about a network and its users, denial of service, corruption of transmitted data, and introduction of new information into network sessions.

Man-in-the-middle attack mitigation is achieved by encrypting traffic in an IPsec tunnel, which would allow the hacker to see only cipher text.

Social Engineering

The easiest hack (*social engineering*) involves no computer skill at all. If an intruder can trick a member of an organization into giving over valuable information, such as locations of files, and servers, and passwords, the process of hacking is made immeasurably easier.

Perhaps the simplest, but a still-effective attack is tricking a user into thinking one is an administrator and requesting a password for various purposes. Users of Internet systems frequently receive messages that request password or credit card information to "set up their account" or "reactivate settings." Users of these systems must be warned early and frequently not to divulge sensitive information, passwords or otherwise, to people claiming to be administrators. In reality, administrators of computer systems rarely, if ever, need to know the user's password to perform administrative tasks. However, even social engineering might not be necessary—in an Infosecurity survey, 90 percent of office workers gave away their password in exchange for a cheap pen.

Phishing

Phishing is a type of social-engineering attack that involves using e-mail or other types of messages in an attempt to trick others into providing sensitive information, such as credit card numbers or passwords. The phisher masquerades as a trusted party that has a seemingly legitimate need for the sensitive information. Frequent phishing scams involve sending out spam e-mails that appear to be from common online banking or auction sites. These e-mails contain hyperlinks that appear to be legitimate but actually cause users to visit a phony site set up by the phisher to capture their information. The site appears to belong to the party that was faked in the e-mail, and when users enter their information it is recorded for the phisher to use.

Denial-of-Service (DoS) Attacks

Certainly the most publicized form of attack, DoS attacks are also among the most difficult to completely eliminate. Even within the hacker community, DoS attacks are regarded as trivial and considered bad form because they require so little effort to execute. Still, because of their ease of implementation and potentially significant damage, DoS attacks deserve special attention from security administrators. If you are interested in learning more about DoS attacks, researching the methods employed by some of the better-known attacks can be useful. DoS attacks take many forms. Ultimately, they prevent authorized people from using a service by using up system resources, as shown in Figure 1-20.

Figure 1-20   Denial of Service

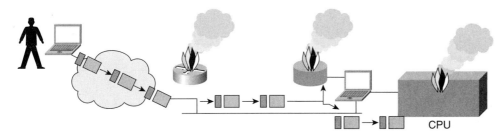

The following are some examples of common DoS threats:

- **Ping of death**—This attack modifies the IP portion of the header, indicating that there is more data in the packet than there actually is, causing the receiving system to crash, as shown in Figure 1-21.

Figure 1-21   Ping of Death

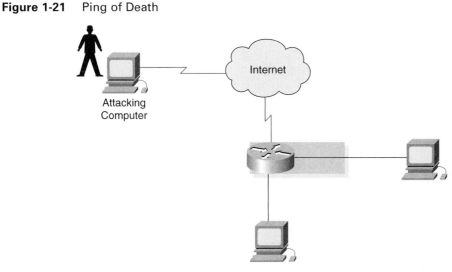

■ **SYN flood attack**— This attack randomly opens up many TCP ports, tying up the network equipment or computer with so many bogus requests that sessions are thereby denied to others. This attack is accomplished with protocol analyzers or other programs.

The SYN flood attack sends TCP connections requests faster than a machine can process them. The SYN flood attack follows these steps:

— An attacker creates a random source address for each packet.

— The SYN flag set in each packet is a request to open a new connection to the server from the spoofed IP address.

— A victim responds to spoofed IP address, and then waits for confirmation that never arrives (waits about three minutes).

— The victim's connection table fills up waiting for replies.

— After the table fills up, all new connections are ignored.

— Legitimate users are ignored, too, and cannot access the server.

— When the attacker stops flooding the server, it usually goes back to normal state (SYN floods rarely crash servers).

Newer operating systems manage resources better, making it more difficult to overflow tables, but still are vulnerable.

The SYN flood can be used as part of other attacks, such as disabling one side of a connection in TCP hijacking, or by preventing authentication or logging between servers.

■ **Packet fragmentation and reassembly**—This attack exploits a buffer–overrun bug in hosts or internetworking equipment.

■ **E-mail bombs**—Programs can send bulk e-mails to individuals, lists, or domains, monopolizing e-mail services.

■ **CPU hogging**—These attacks constitute programs such as Trojan horses or viruses that tie up CPU cycles, memory, or other resources.

■ **Malicious applets**—These attacks are Java, JavaScript, or ActiveX programs that act as Trojan horses or viruses to cause destruction or tie up computer resources.

■ **Misconfiguring routers**—Misconfiguring routers to reroute traffic disables web traffic.

■ **The chargen attack**—This attack establishes a connection between UDP services, producing a high character output. The host chargen service is connected to the echo service on the same or different systems, causing congestion on the network with echoed chargen traffic.

■ **Out-of-band attacks such as WinNuke**— These attacks send out-of-band data to port 139 on Windows 95 or Windows NT machines. The attacker needs the victim's IP address to launch this attack, as shown in Figure 1-22.

Figure 1-22   WinNuke

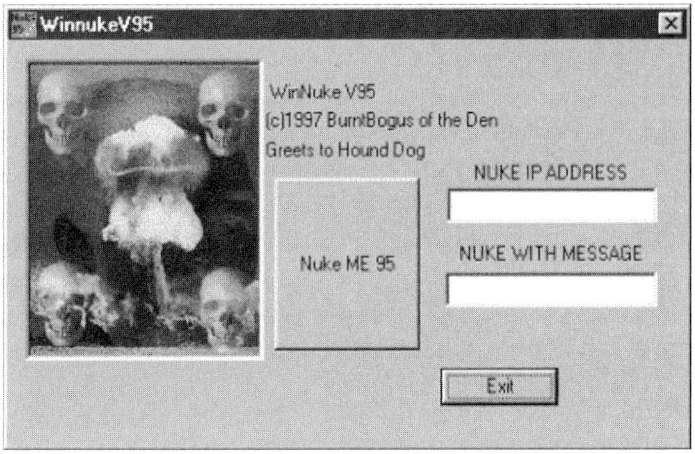

- **DoS**—DoS can occur accidentally because of misconfigurations or misuse by legitimate users or system administrators.

- **Land.c**—This program sends a TCP SYN packet that specifies the target host address as both source and destination. The program also uses the same port (such as 113 or 139) on the target host as both source and destination, causing the target system to stop functioning.

- **Teardrop.c**—In this attack, the fragmentation process of the IP is implemented in such a way that reassembly problems can cause machines to crash.

- **Targa.c**—This attack is a multiplatform DoS attack that integrates bonk, jolt, land, nestea, netear, syndrop, teardrop, and WinNuke all into one exploit.

Masquerade/IP Spoofing Attacks

With a masquerade attack, the network intruder can manipulate TCP/IP packets by IP spoofing, falsifying the source IP address, thereby appearing to be another user. The intruder assumes the identity of a valid user and gains that user's access privileges by IP spoofing. IP spoofing occurs when intruders create IP data packets with falsified source addresses.

During an IP spoofing attack, an attacker outside the network pretends to be a trusted computer. The attacker may either use an IP address that is within the range of IP addresses for the network or use an authorized external IP address that is trusted and provides access to specified resources on the network.

Normally, an IP spoofing attack is limited to the injection of data or commands into an existing stream of data passed between a client and server application or a peer-to-peer network connection. The attacker simply does not worry about receiving any response from the applications.

To enable bidirectional communication, the attacker must change all routing tables to point to the spoofed IP address. Another approach the attacker could take is to simply not worry about receiving any response from the applications.

If attackers manage to change the routing tables, they can receive all the network packets that are addressed to the spoofed address, and reply just as any trusted user can. Like packet sniffers, IP spoofing is not restricted to people who are external to the network.

Some tools used to perform IP spoofing attacks are as follows:

- Protocol analyzers, also called password sniffers
- Sequence number modification
- Scanning tools that probe TCP ports for specific services, network or system architecture, and the operating system

After obtaining information through scanning tools, the intruder looks for vulnerabilities associated with those entities.

Distributed Denial-of-Service Attacks

Distributed denial-of-service attacks (DDoS) attacks are designed to saturate network links with spurious data. This data can overwhelm an Internet link, causing legitimate traffic to be dropped. DDoS uses attack methods similar to standard DoS attacks but operates on a much larger scale. Typically hundreds or thousands of attack points attempt to overwhelm a target, as shown in Figure 1-23.

Figure 1-23   DDos Attack

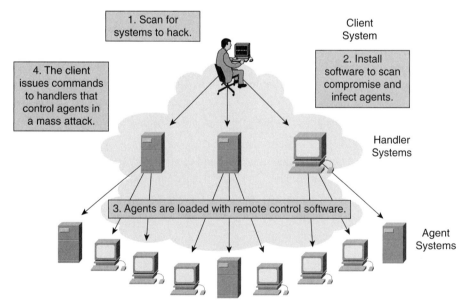

Examples of DDoS attacks include the following:

- Smurf
- Tribe Flood Network (TFN)
- Stacheldraht

The sections that follow describe each of these DDoS attacks in more detail.

Smurf Attacks

The Smurf attack starts with a perpetrator sending a large number of spoofed ICMP echo, or ping, requests to broadcast addresses, hoping that these packets will be magnified and sent to the spoofed addresses, as shown in Figure 1-24. If the routing device delivering traffic to those broadcast addresses performs the Layer 3 broadcast-to-Layer 2 broadcast function, most hosts on that IP network will each reply to the ICMP echo request with an ICMP echo reply, multiplying the traffic by the number of hosts responding. On a multi-access broadcast network, there could potentially be hundreds of machines replying to each echo packet.

Figure 1-24   Smurf Attack

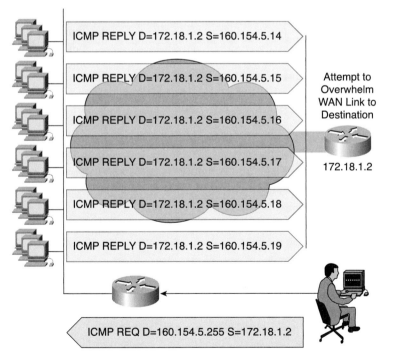

Assume the network has 100 hosts and that the attacker has a T1 link. The attacker sends a 768-kbps stream of ICMP echo, or ping packets, with a spoofed source address of the victim, to the broadcast address of the "bounce site." These ping packets hit the bounce site broadcast network of 100 hosts, and each takes the packet and responds to it, creating 100 outbound ping replies. A total of 76.8 Mbps of bandwidth is used outbound from the bounce site after the traffic is multiplied. This is then sent to the victim, or the spoofed source of the originating packets.

Turning off directed broadcast capability in the network infrastructure prevents the network from being used as a bounce site.

Tribe Flood Network (TFN)

Tribe Flood Network (TFN) and Tribe Flood Network 2000 (TFN2K) are distributed tools used to launch coordinated DoS attacks from many sources against one or more targets. A TFN attack can generate packets with spoofed source IP addresses. An intruder instructing a master to send attack instructions to a list of TFN servers or daemons carries out a DoS attack using a TFN network. The daemons then generate the specified type of DoS attack against one or more target IP addresses. Source IP addresses and source ports can be randomized, and packet sizes can be altered. Use of the TFN master requires an intruder-supplied list of IP addresses for the daemons.

Stacheldraht Attack

Stacheldraht, German for "barbed wire," combines features of several DoS attacks, including TFN. It also adds features such as encryption of communication between the attacker and Stacheldraht masters and automated update of the agents. There is an initial mass-intrusion phase, in which automated tools are used to remotely root-compromise large numbers of systems to be used in the attack. This is followed by a DoS attack phase, in which these compromised systems are used to attack one or more sites. Figure 1-25 illustrates a Stacheldraht attack.

Lab 1.3.4 Vulnerabilities and Exploits

In this lab, you examine the use of common network mapping tools, hacking programs, and scripts on a LAN and across a WAN. Where vulnerabilities are discovered, propose a fix or solution to the problem.

Malicious Code

The primary vulnerabilities for end-user workstations are worm, virus, and Trojan horse attacks. A worm executes arbitrary code and installs copies of itself in the infected computer's memory, which infects other hosts. A virus is malicious software that is attached to another program to execute a particular unwanted function on a user's workstation. A Trojan horse differs only in that the entire application was written to look like something else, when in fact it is an attack tool. Examples of attack types include the following:

- **Trojan horse**—An application written to look like something else that in fact is an attack tool

- **Worm**—An application that executes arbitrary code and installs copies of itself in the memory of the infected computer, which then infects other hosts

- **Virus**—Malicious software that is attached to another program to execute a particular unwanted function on the user workstation

Figure 1-25   Stacheldraht Attack

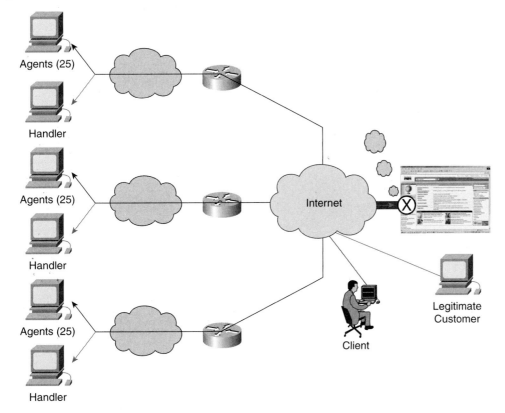

Worms

The anatomy of a worm attack is as follows:

1. **The enabling vulnerability**—A worm installs itself using an exploit vector on a vulnerable system.

2. **Propagation mechanism**—After gaining access to devices, a worm replicates and selects new targets.

3. **Payload**—After the device is infected with a worm, the attacker has access to the host—often as a privileged user. Attackers could use a local exploit to escalate their privilege level to administrator.

Typically, worms are self-contained programs that attack a system and try to exploit a specific vulnerability in the target. Upon successful exploitation of the vulnerability, the worm copies its program from the attacking host to the newly exploited system to begin the cycle again. A virus normally requires a vector to carry the virus code from one system to another. The vector can be a word processing document, an e-mail message, or an executable program. The key element that distinguishes a computer worm from a computer virus is that human interaction is required to facilitate the spread of a virus.

Worm attack mitigation, as shown in Figure 1-26, requires diligence on the part of system and network administration staff. Coordination between system administration, network engineering, and security operations personnel is critical in responding effectively to a worm incident. The following are the recommended steps for worm attack mitigation:

Step 1. Containment

Step 2. Inoculation

Step 3. Quarantine

Step 4. Treatment

Figure 1-26   Worm Attack Mitigation

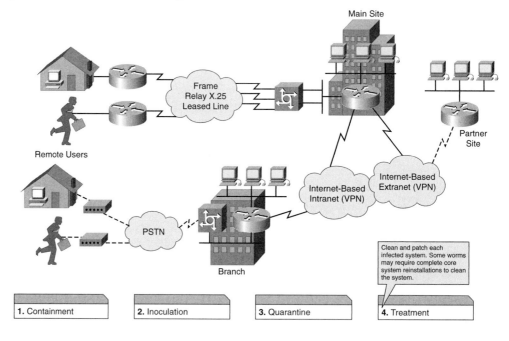

Viruses and Trojan Horses

Viruses are malicious software that is attached to another program to execute a particular unwanted function on a user's workstation. An example of a virus is a program that is attached to command.com (the primary interpreter for Windows systems) that deletes certain files and infects any other versions of command.com that it can find.

A Trojan horse differs only in that the entire application was written to look like something else, when in fact it is an attack tool. An example of a Trojan horse is a software application that runs a simple game on the user's workstation. While the user is occupied with the game, the Trojan horse mails a copy of itself to every user in the user's address book. The other users receive the game and then play it, thus spreading the Trojan horse.

These kinds of applications can be contained through the effective use of antivirus software at the user level and potentially at the network level, as depicted by Figure 1-27. Antivirus software can detect most viruses and many Trojan horse applications and prevent them from spreading in the network. Keeping current with the latest developments in these sorts of attacks can also lead to a more effective posture against these attacks. As new virus or Trojan applications are released, enterprises need to keep current with the latest antivirus software and application versions.

Figure 1-27 Virus and Trojan Horse Attack Mitigation

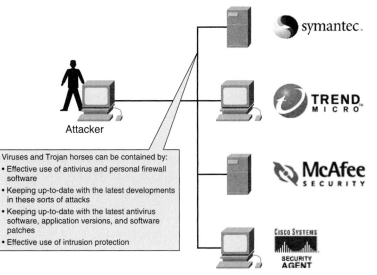

Vulnerability Analysis

Before adding new security solutions to an existing network, you need to identify the current state of the network and organizational practices to verify their current compliance with the requirements. This analysis also provides you with the opportunity to identify possible improvements and the potential need to redesign a part of the system or to rebuild a part of the system from scratch to satisfy the requirements. This analysis can be broken down into the following steps:

1. Policy identification

2. Network analysis

3. Host analysis

The remainder of this chapter looks at each of these steps in more depth and at some analysis tools.

Policy Identification

If a security policy exists, the designer should analyze it to identify the security requirements, which will influence the design of the perimeter solution. Initially, the designer should examine two basic areas of the policy:

- The policy should identify the assets that require protection. This helps the designer provide the correct level of protection for sensitive computing resources and to identify the flow of sensitive data in the network.

- The policy should identify possible attackers. This gives the designer insight into the level of trust assigned to internal and external users, ideally identified by more-specific categories such as business partners, customers of an organization, and outsourcing IT partners.

The designer should also be able to evaluate whether the policy was developed using correct risk-assessment procedures. For example, did the policy development include all relevant risks for the organization and not overlook important threats? The designer should also reevaluate the policy mitigation procedures to determine whether they satisfactorily mitigate expected threats. This ensures that the policy, which the designer will work with, is current and complete.

Organizations that need a high level of security assurance will require defense-in-depth mechanisms to be deployed to avoid single points of failure. The designer also needs to work with the organization to determine how much investment in security measures is acceptable for the resources that require protection.

The result of policy analysis will be as follows:

- The evaluation of policy correctness and completeness

- Identification of possible policy improvements, which need to be made before the security implementation stage

Network Analysis

Many industry best practices, tools, guides, and training are available to help secure network devices. These include tools from Cisco, such as AutoSecure and Cisco Output Interpreter, and from numerous web resources. Third-party resources include the U.S. National Security Agency (NSA) Cisco Router Security Recommendation Guides and the Center for Internet Security (CIS) Router Audit Tool (RAT) for auditing Cisco router and PIX Security Appliance configuration files.

Cisco AutoSecure

The Cisco AutoSecure feature is enabled from a Cisco IOS Security command-line interface (CLI) command, as shown in Table 1-6. AutoSecure enables rapid implementation of security policies and procedures to ensure secure networking services. It enables a "one-touch" device lockdown process, simplifying the security configuration of a router and hardening the router configuration. This feature simplifies the security process, thus lowering barriers to the deployment of critical security functionality.

Table 1-6   AutoSecure

Command	Description
auto secure [management | forwarding] [no-interact]	Secures the management and forwarding planes of the router. Applying the **management** keyword dictates that only the management plane will be secured. Applying the **forwarding** keyword dictates that only the forwarding plane will be secured. The **no-interact** option dictates that the user will not be prompted for any interactive configurations.
show auto secure config	Displays all configurations commands that have been added as part of the AutoSecure configuration.

Cisco Output Interpreter

The Cisco Output Interpreter (see Figure 1-28) is a troubleshooting tool that report potential problems by analyzing supported **show** command output. The Output Interpreter is available at the Cisco website to users with a valid Cisco.com.

Figure 1-28   Output Interpreter

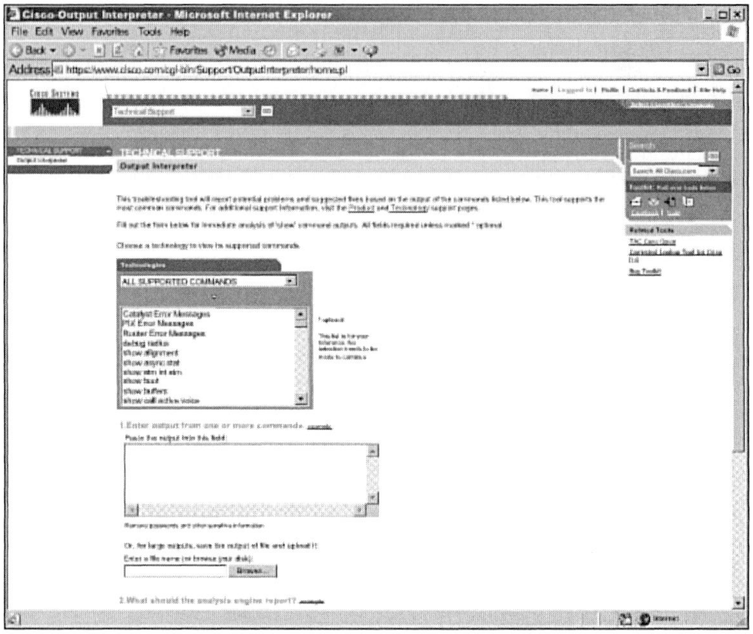

Output Interpreter supports the following functionality:

- Displays **show** command output from a router, switch, or PIX Security Appliance. A list of supported **show** commands is available at the Output Interpreter site.

- Displays error messages generated by a router, switch, or PIX Security Appliance. The error or log messages can be copied and pasted from a router, switch, or PIX Security Appliance into the Output Interpreter.

- Decodes and analyzes a router or switch **stack trace** for any possible bugs. Copy and paste the **show version** command output followed by traceback or stack trace and alignment data.

- Can convert the **apply**, **conduit**, and **outbound** statements of a PIX Security Appliance configuration to equivalent **access-list** statements. Copy and paste **show tech-support** or **write terminal** command output of the PIX Security Appliance.

- Decodes and analyzes the Configuration Register. Copy and paste the **show version** or **show tech-support** command output into the Output Interpreter.

Figure 1-29 shows an example of the output of the Output Interpreter.

Figure 1-29   Output Interpreter Results

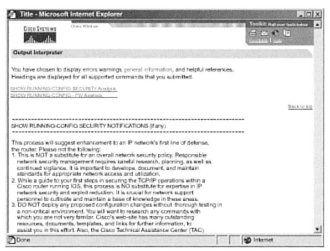

National Security Agency (NSA) Cisco Router Security Configuration Guides

The Router Security Configuration Guide (RSCG) contains principles and guidance for secure configuration of IP routers, with detailed instructions for Cisco Systems routers (http://www.nsa.gov/snac/routers/cisco_scg-1.1b.pdf). The RSCG was used extensively in the development of the Cisco Router Security course. This guide was developed in response to numerous questions and requests for assistance received by the NSA System and Network Attack Center (SNAC). The topics covered in the guide were selected on the basis of customer interest, community consensus, and the SNAC's background in securing networks. The RSCG is a large, detailed, yet readable and accessible document. It is supplemented with an Executive Summary Card, a quick checklist for securing your Cisco router.

Routers direct and control much of the data flowing across computer networks. The RSCG provides technical guidance intended to help network administrators and security officers improve the security of their networks. Using the information presented here, you can configure your routers to control access, resist attacks, shield other network components, and even protect the integrity and confidentiality of network traffic.

The goal for this guide is a simple one: improve the security provided by routers on U.S. government operational networks.

The RSCG document is only a guide to recommended security settings for IP routers, particularly routers running Cisco IOS Software Release 11 and 12. It is not meant to replace well-designed policy or sound judgment. The guide does not address site-specific configuration issues. Care must be taken when implementing the security steps specified in this guide. Ensure that all security steps and procedures chosen from this guide are thoroughly tested and reviewed prior to implementing them on an operational network.

Cisco IOS XR Software

Cisco IOS XR Software, a new member of the Cisco IOS family, is a unique self-healing and self-defending operating system designed for always-on operation while scaling system capacity up to 92 Tbps. Cisco IOS XR powers the Cisco Carrier Routing System, enabling the foundation for network and service convergence today while providing investment protection for decades to come.

Cisco Router Audit Tool (RAT)

The CIS RAT is based on the CIS Benchmark for Cisco IOS routers, a consensus-based best practice guideline for hardening Cisco routers. Version 2.2 of the RAT tool can be used to score both Cisco IOS routers and PIX Security Appliances. The RAT is available for the Windows or UNIX operating systems. Example 1-1 shows a sample RAT output display. The RAT downloads configurations of devices to be audited (optionally) and then checks them against the settings defined in the benchmark.

Example 1-1   Cisco RAT Sample Output

```
C:\CIS\RAT\bin>rat Austin1.text
Auditing Austin1.text...
Parsing: /C:\CIS\RAT/etc/configs/cisco-ios/common.conf/
Parsing: /C:\CIS\RAT/etc/configs/cisco-ios/cis-level-1.conf/
Parsing: /C:\CIS\RAT/etc/configs/cisco-ios/cis-level-2.conf/
Checking: Austin1.txt
done checking Austin1.txt.
Parsing: /C:\CIS\RAT/etc/configs/cisco-ios/common.conf/
Parsing: /C:\CIS\RAT/etc/configs/cisco-ios/cis-level-1.conf/
Parsing: /C:\CIS\RAT/etc/configs/cisco-ios/cis-level-2.conf/
ncat_report: writing Austin1.txt.ncat_fix.txt.
ncat_report: writing Austin1.txt.ncat_report.txt.
ncat_report: writing Austin1.html.
ncat_report: writing rules.html  (cisco-ios-benchmark.html).
ncat_report: writing all.ncat_fix.txt.
ncat_report: writing all.ncat_report.txt.
ncat_report: writing all.html.

C:\CIS\RAT\bin>
```

For each configuration examined, the RAT produces a report listing the following:

- A list of each rule checked with a pass/fail score
- A raw overall score

- A weighted overall score (1–10)

- A list of commands that will correct problems identified

The RAT produces a composite report listing all rules (settings) checked on all devices (and an overall score) and recommendations for improving the security of the router, as shown in Figure 1-30.

Figure 1-30   CIS RAT Report

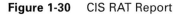

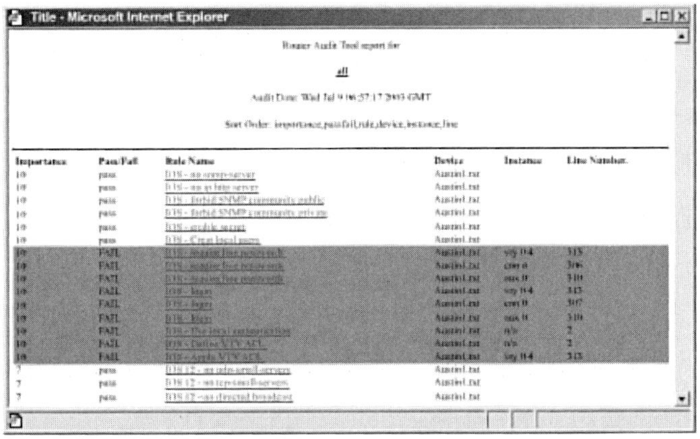

Host Analysis

The hosts that are on the network need to be considered when designing a network security solution. Determining the role in the network of each host will help to decide the steps that will be taken to secure it. The network could have many user workstations, and multiple servers that need to be accessed from both inside and outside of the network.

The types of applications and services that are running on the hosts need to be identified, and any network services and ports that are not necessary should be disabled or blocked. All operating systems should be patched as needed. Antivirus software should be installed and kept current. Some servers may be assigned static routable IP addresses to be accessible from the Internet. These hosts in particular should be monitored for signs of malicious activity.

Many tools are available to test host security. Most tools have been developed on a UNIX or Linux platform, and some of them have now been ported to other operating systems. Two of the most common tools are as follows:

- **Network Mapper (Nmap)**—Nmap is a popular free tool used for security scanning and auditing. It can rapidly perform a port scan of a single host or a range of hosts. Nmap was originally written to be run on UNIX systems, and it is now available for use on Microsoft Windows platforms, as shown in Figure 1-31.

- **Nessus**—Nessus is a vulnerability scanner that is available for UNIX and Microsoft Windows platforms. New vulnerability testing capabilities can be added to Nessus through the installation of modular plug-ins. Nessus includes a built-in port scanner, or it can be used along with Nmap. When the Nessus scan is finished, a report is created. This report displays the results of the scan and provides steps to mitigate vulnerabilities.

Figure 1-31   NMAP for Windows

Analysis Tools

Many tools are available to help to determine vulnerabilities in endpoint devices, such as network hosts and servers. You can obtain these tools from either the company that creates the operating system or a third party. In many cases, these tools are free. The sections that follow describe some of the most commonly used analysis tools.

Knoppix STD

Knoppix Security Tools Distribution (STD) is a Linux LiveCD distribution that contains many valuable security tools. The LiveCD is a bootable CD-ROM that contains the Linux operating system, along with software applications, that can be run from memory without installation on the hard drive. After the LiveCD is ejected from the CD-ROM drive, the system can be reboot-ed to return to the original operating system. Knoppix STD contains many useful features, such as the following:

- Encryption tools
- Forensics tools
- Firewall tools
- Intrusion detection tools
- Network utilities
- Password tools
- Packet sniffers
- Vulnerability assessment tools
- Wireless tools

Many additional versions of LiveCD are available. If one distribution does not support a partic-ular system or piece of hardware, it might be necessary to try another distribution. Most LiveCD releases are available as free downloads that the end user can burn to a CD.

Microsoft Baseline Security Analyzer

You can use the Microsoft Baseline Security Analyzer (MBSA) to scan hosts running Windows 2000, Windows XP, and Windows Server 2003 operating systems to determine poten-tial security risks. MBSA scans for common system misconfigurations and missing security updates. MBSA includes both a graphical interface and a CLI that can perform local or remote scans. After a system scan, the MBSA provides a report outlining potential vulnerabilities and the steps required to correct them. This tool is available as a free download from Microsoft.

Summary

This module introduced the needs, trends, and goals of network security. The exponential growth of networking has led to increased security risks. Many of these risks are due to hack-ing, device vulnerabilities, and improper uses of network resources. Awareness of the various weaknesses and vulnerabilities is critical to the success of modern networks. Security profes-sionals who can deploy secure networks are in high demand.

The four primary threats to network security include unstructured threats, structured threats, exter-nal threats, and internal threats. To defend against threats, an understanding of the common meth-ods of attack must be established, including reconnaissance, access, DoS, and malicious code.

Responses to security issues range from ignoring the problem to excessive spending on security devices and solutions. Neither approach will succeed without a good, sound policy, and highly skilled security professionals.

Check Your Understanding

Complete all the review questions listed here to test your understanding of the topics and concepts in this chapter. Answers are listed in Appendix A, "Check Your Understanding Answer Key."

1. Which of the following is not a primary network security goal?

   a. Assure the availability of corporate data

   b. Maintain integrity of corporate data

   c. Protect against denial-of-service attacks

   d. Protect the confidentiality of corporate data

2. What is the method of mapping a network called?

   a. Eavesdropping

   b. Reconnaissance

   c. Sniffing

   d. Discovery

3. Which security model would describe a CISCO PIX Appliance with a basic configuration without access control lists or conduits?

   a. Open access

   b. Hybrid access

   c. Closed access

   d. Restrictive access

4. What is a low-technology method of acquiring information for future network attacks?

   a. Man-in-the-middle

   b. Social engineering

   c. Back doors

   d. Masquerade

   e. Graffiti

5. Which will introduce an inconspicuous back door into a host?

   a. Trojan horse

   b. TCP session hijacker

   c. LophtCrack

   d. Packet sniffer

6. Which of the following would not be considered an attack?

   a. Trust exploitation

   b. Man-in-the-middle

   c. Access control

   d. Port redirection

7. What is data manipulation an attack on?

   a. Confidentiality

   b. Integrity

   c. Authentication

   d. Access

8. What would not be considered part of the security policy?

   a. Remote access

   b. Access control

   c. Employee comfort

   d. Password length

9. Which of the following is not likely to cause a denial-of-service attack?

   a. SYN flood

   b. Power outage

   c. Buffer overflow

   d. Access violation

10. A protocol analyzer can be used to do which of the following?

   a. Determine the contents of a packet

   b. Analyze the inside of a switch

   c. Determine the layers of the OSI model

   d. Rearrange the sequence numbers

CHAPTER 2

Security Planning and Policy

Upon completion of this chapter, you should be able to answer the following questions:

- What are network security and Cisco?

- What are endpoint protection and management strategies?

- What are some common network protection and management techniques?

- What is the process of security architecture?

- What are the basics of router security?

Key Terms

This chapter uses the following key terms. You can find the definitions in the glossary at the end of the book.

Stateful inspection and packet filtering   page 53

Identity Based Networking Services (IBNS) page 80

Secure Shell (SSH) page 87

Network Time Protocol (NTP)   page 104

Simple Network Management Protocol (SNMP) page 105

Domain Name System (DNS)   page 106

Security risks cannot be eliminated or prevented completely. Effective risk management and assessment can significantly minimize the existing security risks, however. An acceptable level of risk depends on how much risk the business is willing to assume. A security policy is an important component in deciding how this risk is managed. A security policy is a formal statement of the rules by which people who are given access to an organization's technology and information assets must abide. A security policy can be as simple as an acceptable-use policy for network resources or it can be several hundred pages in length and detail every element of connectivity and associated policies.

Routers can support a large number of network services that enable users and host processes to connect to the network. Some of these services can be restricted or disabled, improving security without affecting the operational use of the network. For security purposes, it should be a common practice for network devices to support only the traffic and protocols the network needs.

In addition to a general overview of security issues, this chapter provides hands-on labs for essential skills such as configuring router privileges and accounts, disabling and controlling TCP/IP services, configuring routing protocol authentication, and Secure Shell (SSH).

Discussing Network Security and Cisco

Most security incidents occur because system administrators do not implement available countermeasures, and hackers or disgruntled employees exploit the oversight. Therefore, the issue is not just one of confirming that a technical vulnerability exists and finding a countermeasure that works, it is also critical to verify that the countermeasure is in place and working properly.

The Security Wheel

This is where the Security Wheel (see Figure 2-1), a continuous process, is an effective approach. The Security Wheel promotes retesting and reapplying updated security measures on a continuous basis.

To begin the Security Wheel process, first develop a security policy that enables the application of security measures. A security policy needs to accomplish the following tasks:

- Identify the security objectives of the organization.

- Document the resources to be protected.

- Identify the network infrastructure with current maps and inventories.

- Identify the critical resources that need to be protected, such as research and development, finance, and human resources. This is called a risk analysis.

After the security policy is developed, make it the hub upon which the four steps of the Security Wheel are based. The steps are secure, monitor, test, and improve.

Figure 2-1   Security Wheel

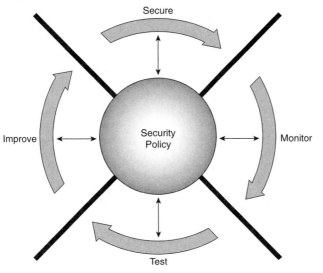

Secure

Securing the system involves implementing security devices such as firewalls, identification systems, and virtual private networks (VPNs) with the intent to prevent unauthorized access to network systems. Secure the network by applying the security policy and implementing the following security solutions, as shown in Figure 2-2:

- **Threat defense**:

    — *Stateful inspection and packet filtering*—Filter network traffic to allow only valid traffic and services.

    — **Intrusion prevention systems**—Inline intrusion detection systems (IDSs), which are better termed intrusion prevention systems (IPSs), can be deployed at the network and host level to actively stop malicious traffic.

    — **Vulnerability patching**—Apply fixes or measures to stop the exploitation of known vulnerabilities. This includes turning off services that are not needed on every system. The fewer services that are enabled, the harder it is for hackers to gain access.

- **Secure connectivity through VPNs**—Hide traffic content to prevent unwanted disclosure to unauthorized or malicious individuals.

- **Trust and identity**:

    — **Authentication**—Give access to authorized users only. One example of this is using one-time passwords.

    — **Policy enforcement**—Ensure users and end devices are in compliance with the corporate policy.

Figure 2-2   Secure the Network

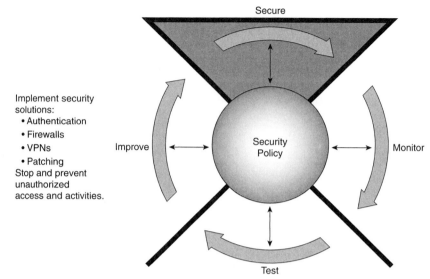

Implement security
solutions:
   • Authentication
   • Firewalls
   • VPNs
   • Patching
Stop and prevent
unauthorized
access and activities.

Monitor

Monitor the network for violations and attacks against the corporate security policy. Violations can occur within the secured perimeter of the network from a disgruntled employee or from a hacker outside the network. Monitoring the network with a real-time IDS can ensure that the security devices in the secure step of the Security Wheel have been configured properly. Monitoring security involves both active and passive methods of detecting security violations, as shown in Figure 2-3.

Figure 2-3   Secure the Network

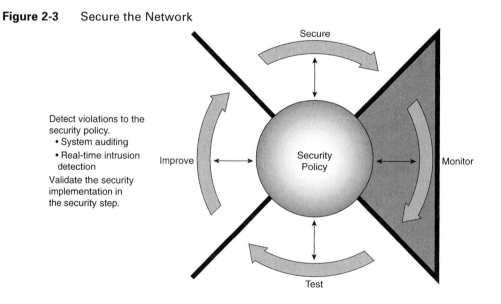

Detect violations to the
security policy.
   • System auditing
   • Real-time intrusion
     detection
Validate the security
implementation in
the security step.

The most commonly used active method is to audit host-level log files. Most operating systems include auditing functionality. System administrators for every host on the network must turn these on and take the time to check and interpret the log file entries.

Detect violations to the security policy through the following:

- System auditing

- Real-time intrusion detection

Passive methods include using IDS devices to automatically detect intrusion. This method requires only a small number of network security administrators for monitoring. These systems can detect security violations in real time and can be configured to automatically respond before an intruder does any damage.

An added benefit of network monitoring is the verification that the security devices implemented in Step 1 of the Security Wheel have been configured and are working properly.

Test

The testing phase of the Security Wheel involves analyzing the effectiveness of the security safeguards in place, using various tools to identify the security posture of the network with respect to the security procedures that form the hub of the Security Wheel. In the testing phase of the Security Wheel, the security of the network is proactively tested, as shown in Figure 2-4. Specifically, the functionality of the security solutions implemented in Step 1 and the system auditing and intrusion detection methods implemented in Step 2 must be ensured. Proper certification and accreditation of your network is a critical part of network security. Vulnerability-assessment tools such as Security Administrator's Tool for Analyzing Networks (SATAN), Nessus, or Nmap are useful for periodically testing the network security measures at the network and host level.

Figure 2-4   Test Security

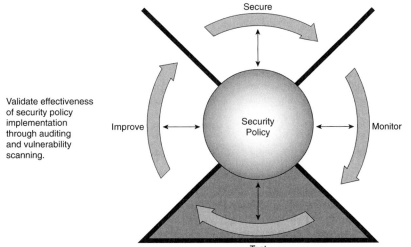

Improve

Improve corporate security by collecting and analyzing the information from the monitoring and testing phases to make security improvements. The improvement phase of the Security Wheel involves analyzing the data collected during the monitoring and testing phases and developing and implementing improvement mechanisms that feed into the security policy and the securing phase in Step 1, as shown in Figure 2-5. To keep a network as secure as possible, the cycle of the Security Wheel must be continually repeated, because new network vulnerabilities and risks are created every day.

Figure 2-5   Improve Security

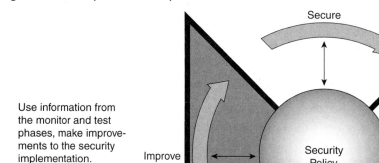

With the information collected from the monitoring and testing phases, IDSs can be used to implement improvements to the security. The security policy should be adjusted as new security vulnerabilities and risks are discovered.

All four steps should be repeated on a continuous basis and should be incorporated into updated versions of the corporate security policy.

Network Security Policy

Security policies are worth the time and effort needed to develop them. A security policy benefits a company in the following ways:

- It provides a process to audit existing network security.
- It provides a general security framework for implementing network security.

- It defines which behavior is and is not allowed.

- It often helps determine which tools and procedures are needed for the organization.

- It helps communicate consensus among a group of key decision makers and defines the responsibilities of users and administrators.

- It defines a process for handling network security incidents.

- It enables global security implementation and enforcement.

- It creates a basis for legal action if necessary

Computer security is now an enterprise-wide issue and computing sites are expected to conform to the network security policy.

Developing a Security Policy

A security policy can be as simple as a brief acceptable-use policy for network resources or can be several hundred pages long and detail every element of connectivity and associated policies. Although somewhat narrow in scope, RFC 2196 suitably defines a security policy as follows:

A security policy is a formal statement of the rules by which people who are given access to an organization's technology and information assets must abide.

It is important to understand that network security is an evolutionary process. No single product can make an organization secure. True network security comes from a combination of products and services, combined with a comprehensive security policy and a commitment to adhere to that policy from the top of the organization down. In fact, a properly implemented security policy without dedicated security hardware can be more effective at mitigating the threat to enterprise resources than a comprehensive security product implementation without an associated policy.

For a security policy to be appropriate and effective, it needs to have the acceptance and support of all levels of employees within the organization, including the following:

- Site security administrator

- Information technology technical staff, such as staff from the computing center

- Administrators of large user groups within the organization, such as business divisions or a computer science department within a university

- Security incident response team

- Representatives of the user groups affected by the security policy

- Responsible management

- Legal counsel, if needed

It is extremely important that management fully support the security policy process. Otherwise, there is little chance that the process will have the intended impact.

An effective security policy works to ensure that the network assets of the organization are protected from sabotage and from inappropriate access, both intentional and accidental. All network security features should be configured in compliance with the organization's security policy. If a security policy is not present, or if the policy is out of date, the policy should be created or updated before deciding how to configure security on any devices.

Table 2-1 illustrates the traits that any security policy should include.

Table 2-1   Important Features of a Security Policy

Procedure	Description
Statement of authority and scope	This section specifies who sponsors the security policy and what areas the policy covers.
Acceptable-use policy	This section specifies what the company will and will not allow regarding its information infrastructure.
Identification and authentication policy	This section specifies what technologies, equipment, or combination of the two the company will use to ensure that only authorized individuals have access to its data.
Internet access policy	This section specifies what the company considers ethical and proper use of its Internet access capabilities.
Campus-access policy	This section specifies how on-campus users will use the company data infrastructure.
Remote-access policy	This section specifies how remote users will access the company's data infrastructure.
Incident-handling procedure	This section specifies how the company will create an incident response team and the procedures it will use during and after incident occurs.

Developing Security Procedures

Security procedures implement security policies. Procedures define configuration, login, audit, and maintenance processes. Security procedures should be written for end users, network administrators, and security administrators. Security procedures should specify how to handle incidents. These procedures should indicate what to do and who to contact if an intrusion is detected. Security procedures can be communicated to users and administrators in instructor-led and self-paced training classes.

Lab 2.1.2 Designing a Security Plan

In this lab, you analyze, offer recommendations, and help improve the security infrastructure of a fictitious business. You analyze business application requirements, analyze security risks, identify network assets, and analyze security requirements and trade-offs.

Endpoint Protection and Management

Protecting network hosts, such as workstation PCs and servers, is critical. These hosts need to be secured (hardened) because they are added to the network and updated with security patches as they become available. The management of this process is discussed in this section.

Host- and Server-Based Security Components and Technologies

You can take additional steps to secure these hosts. Antivirus, firewall, and intrusion detection are valuable tools that can be used to secure network hosts. Because many business resources may be contained on a single file server, it is especially important for servers to be accessible and available.

Device Hardening

When a new operating system is installed on a computer, the security settings are all set to the default values. In most cases, this level of security is inadequate. You should take some simple steps that that apply to most operating systems:

- Default usernames and passwords should be changed immediately.

- Access to the system resources should be restricted to only the individuals who are authorized to use those resources.

- Any unnecessary services and applications should be turned off and uninstalled when possible.

Personal Firewalls

Personal computers connected to the Internet through a dialup connection, digital subscriber line (DSL), or cable modems are as vulnerable as corporate networks, as shown in Figure 2-6. Personal firewalls reside on the user's PC and attempt to prevent these attacks. Personal firewalls are not designed for LAN implementations such as appliance-based or server-based firewalls, and they may prevent network access if installed with other networking clients, services, protocols, or adapters. Some personal firewall software vendors are McAfee, Norton, Symantec, Zone Labs. In addition, a personal firewall is built in to the new Microsoft operating systems.

Figure 2-6   Personal Firewall

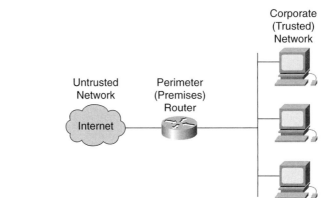

Antivirus Software

Install host antivirus software to protect against known viruses. Antivirus software can detect most viruses and many Trojan horse applications and the new addware products and prevent them from spreading in the network.

Operating System Patches

The most effective way to mitigate any worm and its variants is to patch all vulnerable systems. This is difficult with uncontrolled user systems in the local network, and even more trouble-some if these systems are remotely connected to the network via a VPN or remote-access server (RAS). Administering numerous systems involves the creation of a standard software image that is deployed on new or upgraded systems. These images might not contain the latest patch-es, and the process of continually remaking the image to integrate the latest patch may quickly become time-consuming. Pushing patches out to all systems requires that those systems be con-nected in some way to the network, which might not be possible. One solution to management of critical security patches is to create a central patch server that all systems must communicate with after a set period of time. Any patches that are not applied to a host that is available on the patch server would be automatically downloaded and installed without user intervention. However, determining which devices are exploitable can be simplified by the use of security auditing tools that look for vulnerabilities.

Intrusion Detection and Prevention

Intrusion detection is the ability to detect attacks against a network and send logs to a management console and provides the a detection defense mechanism, which identifies malicious attacks on networks including network devices and hosts. Three types of network attacks that can be detected are as follows:

- Reconnaissance
- Access
- Denial of service

On the other hand, intrusion protection is the ability to prevent attacks against the network and should provide the following active defense mechanisms:

- **Detection**—Identifies malicious attacks on network and host resources
- **Prevention**—Stops the detected attack from executing
- **Reaction**—Immunizes the system from future attacks from a malicious source

Either technology can be implemented as a network level, host level, or both for maximum protection.

Host-Based Intrusion Detection Systems

Host-based intrusion is typically implemented as inline or passive technology depending on the vendor. The passive technology, which was the first generation technology, is called host-based intrusion detection (HIDS), which basically sends logs after the attack has occurred and the damage is done. The inline technology, called host-based intrusion prevention (HIPS), actually stops the attack and prevents damage and propagation of worms and viruses.

Active detection can be set to shut down the network connection or to stop the impacted services automatically. This has the benefit of being able to quickly analyze an event and take corrective action. Cisco provides HIPS using the Cisco Security Agent software.

Current host-based intrusion prevention software requires agent software to be installed on each host, either server or desktop, to monitor activity performed on and against the host. The agent software performs the intrusion detection analysis and prevention. The agent software also sends logs and alerts to a centralized management/policy server.

The advantage of HIPS is that it can monitor operating system processes and protect critical system resources, including files that might exist only on that specific host. Therefore, it can notify network managers when some external process tries to modify a system file in a way that might include a hidden backdoor program.

Figure 2-7 illustrates a typical HIPS deployment. Agents are installed on publicly accessible servers and corporate mail and application servers. The agents report events to a central console server (CiscoWorks VPN/Security Management Solution [VMS]) located inside the corporate firewall or can e-mail an administrator.

Figure 2-7   Host-Based Intrusion Detection

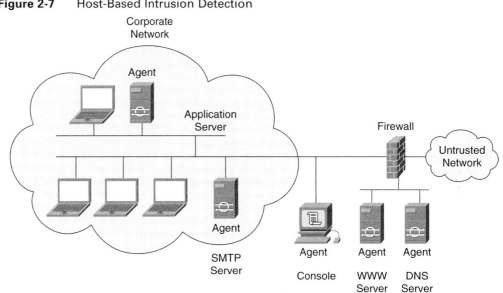

PC Management

It is extremely important to have a plan in place to manage the computers that serve as your network endpoints. Securing them (hardening) is just one aspect of this task. The sections that follow examine some other considerations.

Desktop Inventory and Maintenance

You should keep a detailed inventory of all hosts on the network, such as workstations, servers, and laptops. This inventory should include the serial number of the computer, the type of hardware and software that is installed, and the name of the individual who is responsible for the computer. It is particularly important to provide employees with adequate training to educate them about keeping laptop computers secure. Laptop computers are the most stolen piece of equipment; and in most cases, you can prevent these thefts by simply securing the laptop at the workspace with a lockdown cable. It is extremely important that at work, home, and on the road you safeguard your hardware and the sensitive information it contains.

When software, hardware components, and storage devices are replaced, you should update the inventory to reflect the change. A procedure for the disposal of hardware that is no longer being used needs to be in place. Properly dispose of any storage media to make sure that the data is not recovered by unauthorized individuals. There have been many cases of confidential data being recovered by individuals who have acquired used hard drives. Letting this data fall into the wrong hands could have serious consequences, including legal action being taken against the organization that did not take appropriate steps to make sure that the information remained private.

Update Antivirus Definitions

As new virus or Trojan horse applications are released, enterprises need to keep current with the latest antivirus software and application versions. Antivirus software can only stop viruses and Trojan horses if there is a known signature to identify the malicious object.

For virus scanning to be successful, complete the following at regular intervals (a common recommendation for acceptable minimum intervals for updates are daily for workstations and hourly for servers):

- Routine host local file scanning
- Routine virus list and signature updating
- Routine monitoring of alerts generated by the host scanners

Update HIDS and HIPS Signatures

The effectiveness of an HIDS or HIPS depends on the update status of its signature database. A brand new exploit can slip past an HIDS or HIPS that does not have the signature of that exploit yet. Another issue is that signatures can be too broad, which can generate many false positive alerts. HIDS and HIPS signatures need to be updated on a regular basis. Alerts and logs should be monitored so that ongoing tuning of HIDS and HIPS implementations can be performed.

Network Protection and Management

As important as endpoint protection and management is, network protection and management is equally important. The sections that follow examine the concepts by looking at network-based security and technologies and network security management.

Network-Based Security Components and Technologies

Several components designed to provide security for our networks, and we will examine both appliance-based and server-based firewalls and network-based IDSs. A couple of technologies that we explore in this section are VPNs and trust identity.

Appliance-Based Firewalls

A firewall is a system or group of systems that enforces an access control policy between two or more networks, as shown in Figure 2-8. Many dedicated hardware appliance-based firewalls are available to secure a network. Appliance-based firewalls typically are custom-designed platforms without hard drives. This allows them to boot faster, inspect traffic at higher data rates, and be less prone to failure. Cisco solutions include an integrated Cisco IOS Firewall (software bases and installed on the router) and a dedicated Private Internet Exchange (PIX) Security Appliance (a separate device). The Cisco IOS Firewall feature set can be installed and configured on perimeter Cisco routers. It adds features such as stateful, application-based filtering; dynamic per-user authentication and authorization; defense against network attacks; Java blocking; and real-time alerts. The PIX Security Appliance is a dedicated hardware/software security solution/appliance that provides packet-filtering and proxy server technologies. Other appliance-based firewall vendors include Juniper, Nokia, Symantec, Watchguard, and Nortel Networks. For home networks, Linksys, DLink, Netgear, and SonicWALL provide lower-cost models with basic firewall capabilities.

Figure 2-8   Host-Based Intrusion Detection

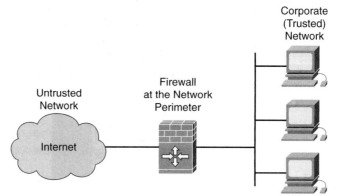

Server-Based Firewalls

A server-based security solution runs on a network operating system such as UNIX, Windows NT, or Win2K, or Novell. Figure 2-9 illustrates a sample of a server-based firewall interface, which is generally an all-in-one solution that combines a firewall, access control, and VPN features into one package. Examples of a server-based security solution include Microsoft ISA Server, Linux, Novell BorderManager, and Check Point Firewall-1.

Remember that appliance-based firewalls are specialized computers, too, but they run only a single embedded firewall application or operating system, whereas server-based firewalls run on top of a general purpose operating systems. Server-based firewalls can be less secure than dedicated firewall because of security weaknesses of the general purpose operating system. Server-based firewalls typically do not perform as well in high-bandwidth networks compared to dedicated firewalls. Furthermore, they are prone to higher failure rates because they use mechanical hard drives.

Figure 2-9   Software-Based Firewall

Network-Based Intrusion Detection Systems

Just like host-based intrusion technology, a network-based intrusion detection system (NIDS) can be based on active or passive detection. Figure 2-10 illustrates a typical network deployment of intrusion technology. Sensors are deployed at network entry points that protect critical network segments. The network segments have both internal and external corporate resources. Sensors capture and analyze the traffic as it traverses the network. Sensors are typically tuned for intrusion detection analysis. The underlying operating system is stripped of unnecessary network services, and essential services are secured. The sensors report to a central director server located inside the corporate firewall.

Unfortunately, research and experience have shown that attackers can effectively elude almost any NIDS. Attackers can hide an attack in two fundamentals ways:

■ They can change the way the attack is delivered (for example, by splitting the attack into many network packets).

■ They can alter the attack payload so that it no longer matches the NIDS signature (for example, by using a different encoding for URLs).

Unlike analysts of security protocols, who use formal threat models to evaluate the resistance of a protocol against attacks, NIDS analysts carry out their evaluation using ad-hoc methods and tools.

Figure 2-10   Network-Based Intrusion Detection

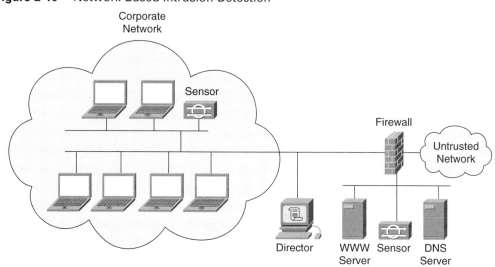

Virtual Private Networks

The broadest definition of a VPN, as shown in Figures 2-11 through 2-16, is any network built upon a public network and partitioned for use by individual users. As a result, public Frame Relay, X.25, and ATM networks are considered VPNs. These types of VPNs are generically referred to as Layer 2 VPNs. The emerging form of VPNs consists of networks constructed across shared IP backbones, referred to as IP VPNs, which focus on Layer 3.

A VPN can be defined as an encrypted connection between private networks over a public network such as the Internet, as shown in Figure 2-11.

Figure 2-11   VPN Definition

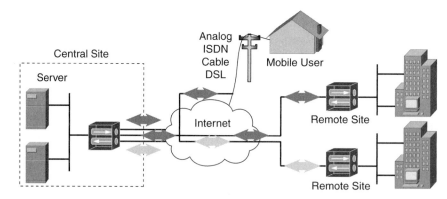

Virtual Private Network (VPN)—An Encrypted Connection Between
Private Networks over a Public Network such as the Internet

A remote-access VPN is an extension/evolution of dialup technologies, as shown in Figure 2-12.

Figure 2-12   VPN Definition

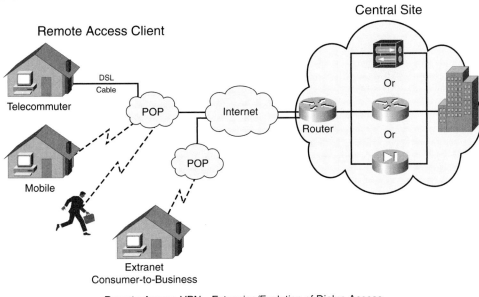

Remote Access VPN—Extension/Evolution of Dialup Access

A site-to-site VPN is an extension of the classic WAN, as shown in Figure 2-13.

Figure 2-13   VPN Definition

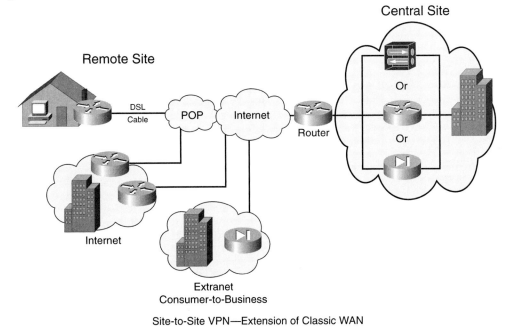

Site-to-Site VPN—Extension of Classic WAN

Figure 2-14 shows the different types of clients in a VPN environment.

Figure 2-14   VPN Clients

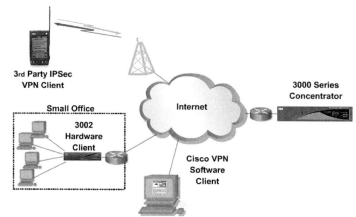

Figure 2-15 shows an example of a site-to-site VPN using different series of Cisco routers depending on need.

Figure 2-15   Site-to-Site VPNs: Cisco Routers

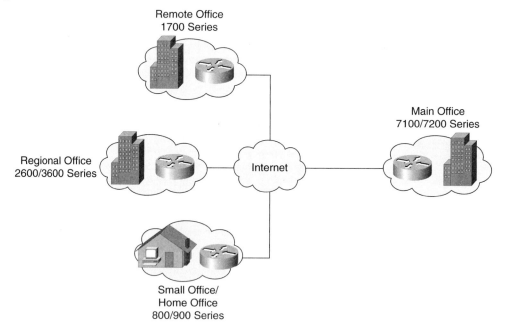

Figure 2-16 shows an example of a VPN using firewalls.

Figure 2-16   Firewall-Based VPN Solutions

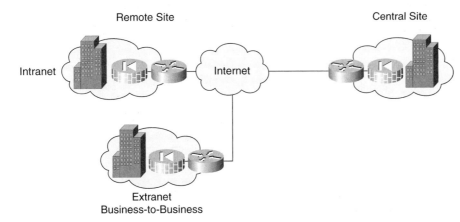

IP VPNs are not simply encrypted tunnels. IP VPNs encompass an entire spectrum of technologies and supporting products, including firewalls, encryption, authentication, intrusion detection, tunneling, quality of service (QoS), and network management. There are fundamentally three different corporate or business uses of VPNs:

- Remote-access VPNs

- Site-to-site extranet and intranet VPNs

- Campus VPNs

Trust and Identity

Identity refers to the accurate and positive identification of network users, hosts, applications, services, and resources. Standard technologies that enable identification include authentication protocols such as RADIUS and TACACS+, Kerberos, and one-time password (OTP) tools. New technologies such as digital certificates, smart cards, and directory services are beginning to play increasingly important roles in identity solutions.

Throughout this course, authentication, authorization, and access control (AAA) are incorporated into the concept of identity. Although these concepts are distinct, they all pertain to each individual user of the network, be it a person or device. Each person or device is a distinct entity that has separate abilities within the network and is allowed access to resources based on who he, she, or it is.

Network Security Management

The goal of security management is to control access to network resources according to local guidelines. This prevents the network from being sabotaged and prohibits users without appropriate authorization from accessing sensitive information. A security management subsystem, for example, can monitor users logging on to a network resource and can refuse access to those who enter inappropriate access codes.

Security management subsystems work by partitioning network resources into authorized and unauthorized areas. For some users, access to any network resource is inappropriate, mostly because such users are usually company outsiders. For internal network users working inside the company, access to information originating from a particular department is inappropriate.

Security management subsystems perform several functions. They identify sensitive network resources—including systems, files, and other entities—and determine mappings between sensitive network resources and user sets. They also monitor access points to sensitive network resources and log inappropriate access.

A typical scenario includes a management station that monitors and manages devices such as routers, firewalls, VPN devices, and IDS sensors, as shown in Figure 2-17. CiscoWorks VMS software is an example (see Figure 2-18). CiscoWorks VMS consists of a set of web-based applications for configuring, monitoring, and troubleshooting enterprise VPNs, firewalls, NIDSs, and HIDSs. CiscoWorks VMS is a scalable solution that addresses the needs of small- and large-scale VPN and security deployments.

Figure 2-17   Management Station

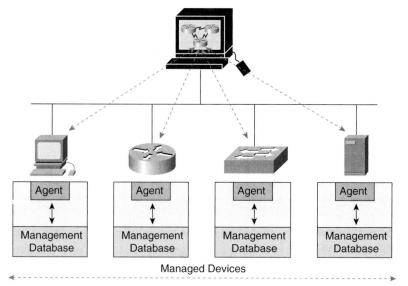

Figure 2-18   CiscoWorks VMS

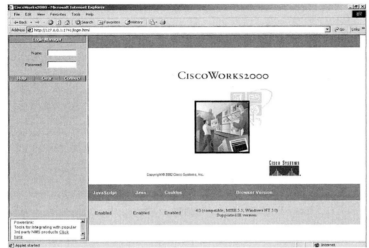

The following are the VMS features and uses:

- Security Monitor (see Figure 2-19)

- One central management station for configuring, monitoring, and troubleshooting the following:

  — VPN routers (see Figure 2-20)

  — Firewall (see Figure 2-21)

  — NIDS

  — HIPS

Figure 2-19   Monitoring Center for Security

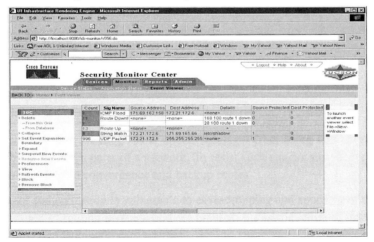

Figure 2-20   Monitoring Center for VPN Routers

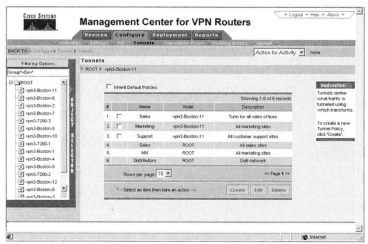

Figure 2-21   Monitoring Center for PIX Security Appliances

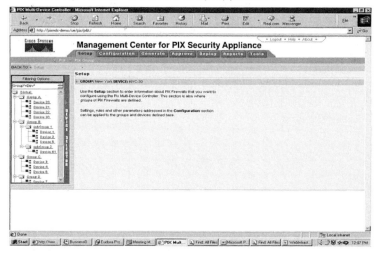

In addition to VMS, Cisco provides free graphical user interface (GUI) device managers to configure and monitor single firewalls, IDS sensors, or routers, as shown in Figures 2-22 and 2-23.

Figure 2-22   PIX Device Manager (PDM)

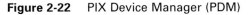

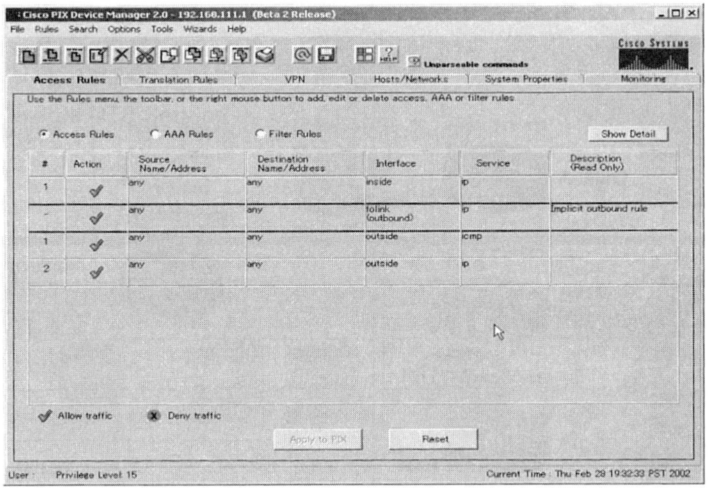

Figure 2-23   IDS Device Manager (IDM)

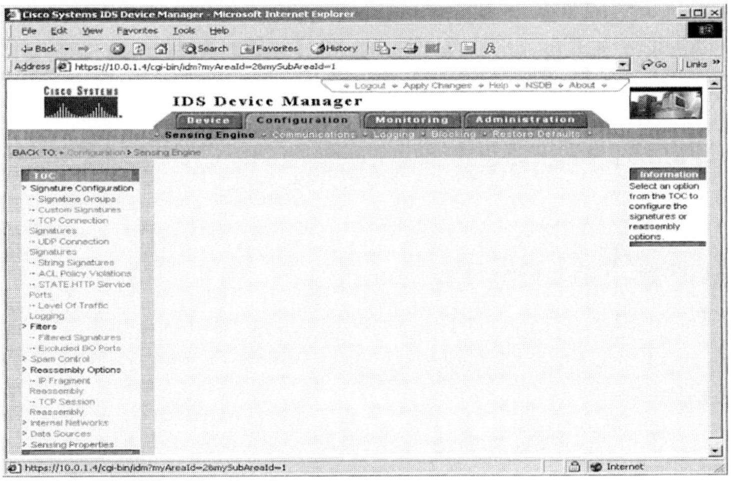

Security auditing is necessary to verify and monitor the corporate security policy. A security audit verifies the correct implementation of the security policy in the corporate network infrastructure. Subsequent logging and monitoring of events can help detect any unusual behavior and possible intrusions.

The hard part is determining what behavior is unusual. It is important to establish a baseline of normal behavior. When normal activity patterns are easily recognized, unusual activity is more readily identified.

To test the effectiveness of the security infrastructure, security auditing should occur frequently and at regular intervals. Auditing should include new system installation checks, methods to discover possible malicious insider activity, possible presence of a specific class of problems, such as denial-of-service (DoS) attacks, and overall compliance with the site security policy.

An audit log, generated by the various operating systems running in the infrastructure, can be used to determine the extent of the damage from a successful attack. Audit trails are most often put to use after the attack, during damage assessment to reconstruct what happened during the assault.

It is important to avoid logging every event. The amount of data to sift through would become insurmountable. If too much data is logged, and an intrusion does occur, that intrusion will definitely also be logged, along with hundreds of other insignificant events. The intrusion will most likely remain undetected because it was hidden under a mountain of data being generated by the system.

If the network or system is designed and implemented well, consider logging the types of activities that would most likely indicate a first-stage attack. Only the unusual events need to be logged. This information can give network administrators a warning that something is amiss, and that warning will not be buried in too much inconsequential detail.

Understanding how a system normally functions, knowing what behavior is expected and unexpected, and being familiar with how devices are usually used can help the organization detect security problems. Noticing unusual events can help catch intruders before they damage the system. Security auditing tools can help companies detect, log, and track those unusual events.

Security Architecture

This section of the chapter explores SAFE (a security blueprint for networks); the Cisco Self-Defending Network; Cisco integrated security; and the plan, design, implement, operate, and optimize (PDIOO) model.

Security Architecture (SAFE)

SAFE is a security blueprint for networks, which is based on Cisco Architecture for Voice, Video, and Integrated Data (AVVID). SAFE enables businesses to securely and successfully take advantage of e-business economies and compete in the Internet economy. SAFE provides a secure migration path for companies to implement and converge voice, video, and data networks. SAFE layers are incorporated throughout the Cisco AVVID infrastructure:

- **Infrastructure layer**—Intelligent, scalable security services in Cisco platforms, such as routers, switches, firewalls, IDSs, and other devices

- **Appliances layer**—Incorporation of key security functionality in mobile handheld devices and remote PC clients

- **Service control layer**—Critical security protocols and APIs that enable security solutions to work together cohesively

- **Applications layer**—Host- and application-based security elements that ensure the integrity of critical e-business applications

To facilitate rapidly deployable, consistent security throughout the network, SAFE consists of modules that address the distinct requirements of each network area, as shown in Figure 2-24. By adopting a SAFE blueprint, security managers do not need to redesign the entire security architecture each time a new service is added to the network. With modular templates, it is easier and more cost-effective to secure each new service as it is needed and to integrate it with the overall security architecture.

Figure 2-24   Basic SAFE Modular Blueprint

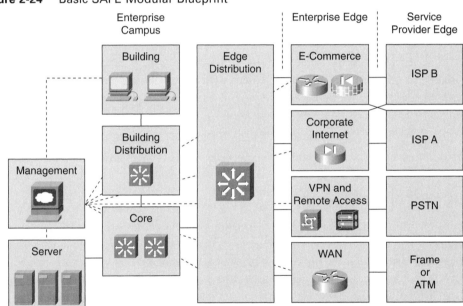

One of the unique characteristics of the SAFE blueprint is that it is the first industry blueprint that recommends exactly which security solutions should be included in each section of the network and why they should be deployed. Each module in the SAFE blueprint is designed specifically to provide maximum performance for e-business, while at the same time enabling businesses to maintain security and integrity.

The SAFE white papers provide overviews of the extended SAFE blueprint, followed by detailed descriptions of the specific modules that comprise the actual network designs.

- SAFE: A Security Blueprint for Enterprise Networks

- SAFE: Extending the Security Blueprint to Small, Midsize, and Remote-User Networks

- SAFE: VPN IPSec Virtual Private Networks in Depth

- SAFE: Wireless LAN Security in Depth—version 2
- SAFE: IP Telephony Security in Depth
- SAFE: IDS Deployment, Tuning, and Logging in Depth
- SAFE: Worm Mitigation

The Cisco Self-Defending Network

In today's environment, in which Internet worms spread across the world in a matter of minutes or seconds, security systems must react instantly. A security system that is fully integrated into all aspects of the network can recognize potential suspicious activity, identify threats, react appropriately, isolate infections, and respond to attacks in a coordinated way.

The Cisco Self-Defending Network strategy allows organizations to use their existing investments in routing, switching, wireless, and security platforms to create a system that will help to identify, prevent, and adapt to both known and unknown security threats.

The strategy consists of three systems, or pillars, each with a specific purpose:

- Secure connectivity safely transports applications across different network environments.
- Threat defense protects against both known and unknown threats.
- Trust and identity solutions supply the contextual identity required for entitlement and trust.

Secure Connectivity

Ensuring the privacy and integrity of all information is vital to businesses. As companies use the flexibility and cost-effectiveness of the Internet to extend their networks to branch offices, telecommuters, customers, and partners, security is paramount. Not only must organizations protect external communications, they must also help ensure that the information transported across an internal wired and wireless infrastructure remains confidential. Similarly, companies must secure voice and video as they use their existing network infrastructure to provide new business-enhancing services, as shown in Figure 2-25.

The following solutions are included in Cisco secure connectivity (see Figure 2-26):

- Site-to-site VPNs
- Remote-access VPNs
- Voice security
- Wireless security
- Solution management and monitoring

Figure 2-25   Security Connectivity Enhances the Business

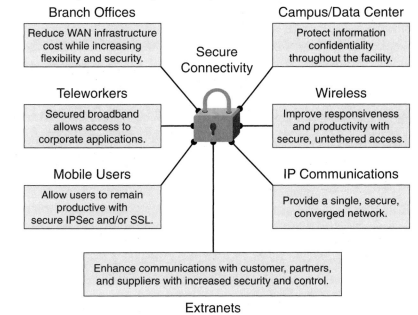

Figure 2-26   Security Connectivity Technologies

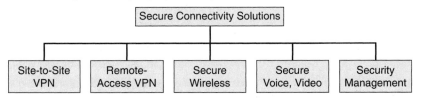

Threat Defense

The Cisco threat-defense system brings together security solutions and intelligent networking technologies to identify and mitigate both known and unknown threats from inside and outside an organization. This systems-based approach protects the network through flexible, customizable deployment of security and network services.

The elements that comprise a threat-defense system include the following features and products, as shown in Figure 2-27:

- Endpoint security
- Integrated firewalls
- Network intrusion prevention
- Content security

- Intelligent networking and security services

- Management and monitoring

Figure 2-27   Cisco Threat-Defense System

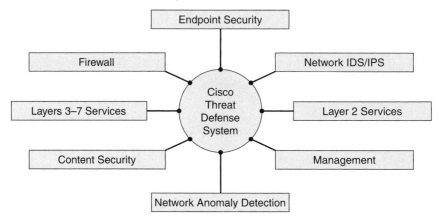

Trust and Identity Solutions

Businesses need to effectively and securely manage who and what can access the network, and when, where, and how that access can occur. Cisco trust and identity management solutions can turn virtually every network device into an integral part of an overall security strategy.

Deploying a complete trust and identity management solution lets enterprises secure network access and admission at any point in the network, and it isolates and controls infected or unpatched devices that attempt to access the network. Businesses can streamline the security management of remote network devices while taking full advantage of existing security and network investments.

With the trust and identity management solutions, the following essential security functions are provided, as shown in Figure 2-28:

- **Enforcement**—Authenticates entities and determines access privileges based on policy

- **Provisioning**—Authorizes and controls network access, and pushes access policy enforcement to network devices using VLANs and access control lists (ACLs)

- **Monitoring**—Accounting, auditing, and forensic tools allow administrators to track the who, what, when, where, and how of network activity

The Cisco trust and identity management technology is composed of three solution categories:

- **Identity management**—Guarantees the identity and integrity of every entity on the network and applies appropriate access policy. Identity management also secures the centralized management of remote devices and provides AAA functionality across all network devices.

- **Identity Based Networking Services (IBNS)**—Expands network security by using 802.1x to automatically identify users requesting network access and route them to a VLAN domain with an appropriate degree of access privilege based on policy. IBNS also prevents unauthorized network access from rogue wireless access points.

- **Network Admission Control (NAC)**—Allows network access only to trusted endpoint devices that can verify their compliance to network security policies, such as having a current antivirus image, operating system version, or patch update. NAC can permit, deny, or restrict network access to any device and quarantine and remediate noncompliant devices.

Figure 2-28   Identity Management Elements

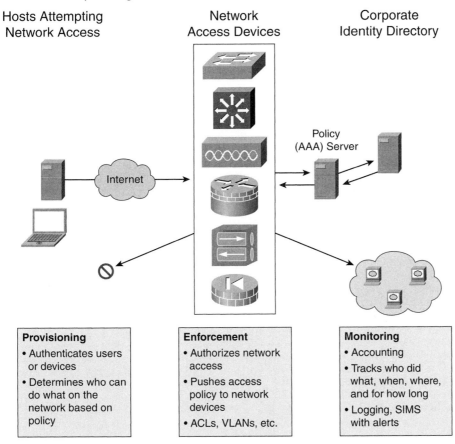

Cisco Integrated Security

Integrated security describes the security functionality that is provided on a networking device (for example on a router, switch, or wireless access point). As traffic passes through a networking device, it must be scanned and analyzed, and then allowed to continue, partitioned, or rejected. This requires that the integrated security device possess intelligence, performance, and scalability. Two Cisco functionalities that provide these services are IBNS and Cisco perimeter security.

Identity Based Networking Services

Identity Based Networking Services (IBNS) is an integrated solution combining several Cisco products that offer authentication, access control, and user policies to secure network connectivity and resources, as shown in Figure 2-29. IBNS enables greater security and allows management of changes throughout the organization.

IBNS and 802.1x are supported on all Cisco Catalyst switches, including Catalyst 6500, 4500, 3550, and 2950 switches; Cisco Access Control Server (ACS); and Cisco Aironet access points.

Figure 2-29   Identity Based Network Services

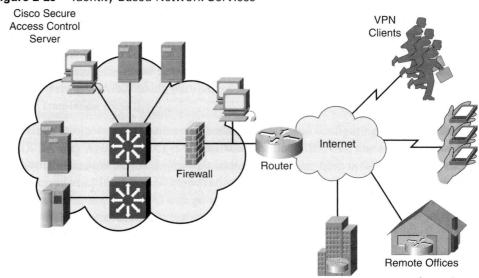

Cisco Perimeter Security

A solid perimeter security solution enables communications across it as defined by the security policy, yet protects network resources from breaches or attacks. It controls multiple network entry and exit points. It also increases user assurance by implementing multiple layers of security.

Perhaps the most familiar type of perimeter is a firewall (see Figure 2-30). PIX security appliances provide security services, including stateful inspection firewalling, standards-based IPsec VPN, intrusion protection, and many other features. Cisco IOS Firewall functionality provides advanced access control, logging, and address translation.

Figure 2-30   Firewall at Network Perimeter

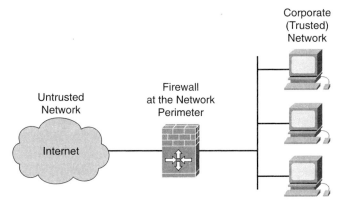

Plan, Design, Implement, Operate, Optimize (PDIOO)

As network expectations have changed, so have design principles. Enterprises no longer rely on a single vendor, technology, or protocol. The design strategy has changed dramatically to include security and scalability as primary criteria. Security has a large impact on network design.

There is greater redundancy in network designs. Organizations are focusing on increased levels of redundancy, and disaster-recovery planning is becoming a necessity. Redundancy takes many forms, including separate power sources, multiple WAN carriers, alternative cable routes, and redundant hardware. Network connectivity and services are critical components of enterprise operations. The cost of downtime is increasing at a phenomenal rate.

Designing a network is not a trivial factor. Assessing the design criteria enables designers to understand the network and what it was meant to do. Network designs must easily adapt to implement the next generation of technology. Many network designers are planning for IP telephony. These network design plans are not just for new networks but are improvements on existing ones. Properly planning networks based on sound architecture makes necessary network redesigns easier at a later stage.

Design is just one component of a network life cycle. Planning, design, implementation, operation, and optimization (PDIOO), as shown in Figure 2-31, are the stages of the network life cycle. Each stage builds on its predecessor to create a sound network that maintains its effectiveness despite changing business needs. The PDIOO methodology can be applied to all technologies. During the PDIOO process, the designer should define key deliverables and associated actions with a direct correlation to the added value and benefit for the network. For example, understanding business goals, usage characteristics, and network requirements helps to avoid unnecessary upgrades and network redesigns, thereby reducing the time it takes to introduce new services in the network.

Figure 2-31   Plan, Design, Implement, Operate, Optimize (PDIOO)

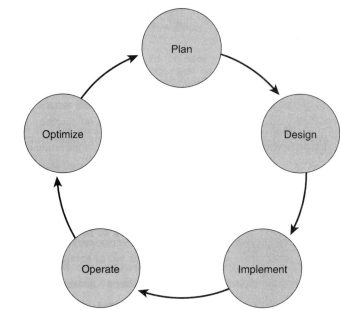

Planning Phase

During the planning stage, the logic of future designs can be tested for flaws. Planning helps avoid a logical mistake being replicated in network design that might be used as a template across a number of additional locations. The planning stage focuses on technical and financial criteria and takes into account all the requirements and constraints that were discussed in the previous section. During this phase, it is important to identify all the stakeholders to make this process a success. The stakeholders are people or organizations who have a vested interest in the environment, performance, and outcome of the project.

Design Phase

After completing the planning stage, the designer should have enough information to develop a network design. If a network is already in place, this phase can be used to review and validate the network design as it is currently implemented. At this stage, products, protocols, and features are chosen based on criteria defined in the planning stage. Network diagrams are developed to illustrate what changes will occur in the network to achieve the desired results. The more detailed the network diagram and plan, the easier it will be to anticipate the challenges during implementation.

Implementation Phase

The implementation stage provides detailed, customized deliverables to help avoid risks and meet expectations. A sound implementation plan ensures smooth deployment even when issues arise. Communicating the implementation plan to all stakeholders provides an opportunity to assess the viability of the plan. It is better to find mistakes on the drawing board than during implementation.

Good processes, such as change control, can effectively handle issues that occur during deployment. Change control provides flexibility because it is impossible to plan for every contingency, especially if the implementation has a long duration.

Note

Change control is a procedure by which authorized amendments are made to the organization's business process. It involves analyzing the problem and appending the results to a formal proposal. This proposal should be reviewed by management before being authorized.

Operation Phase

The operation phase, also known as the operational-support phase, is designed to protect the network investment and help the staff prevent problems, maximize system utility, and accelerate problem resolution.

Optimization Phase

The last step in the PDIOO process is the optimization of the network. A sound design still requires optimization and tweaking to reach its full potential. The optimization of the network can be as simple as hardening servers against security threats or adding QoS to the network for latency-sensitive traffic.

Basic Router Security

Secure configurations are necessary to protect access to routers and switches. Anyone who can log in to a router or switch can display information that should not be made available to the general public. It is important to realize that any router or switch, by default, is an open system.

Control Access to Network Devices

A user who can log in might be able to use the device as a relay for further network attacks. Anyone who can obtain privileged access to the router or switch can reconfigure it. To prevent inappropriate access, administrators need to control logins.

Although most access is disabled by default, there are exceptions. They are sessions from directly connected, asynchronous terminals, such as the console terminal, and sessions from integrated modem lines.

Console Ports

The console port of a Cisco IOS device has special privileges. In particular, if a **Break** or **Ctrl-Break** signal is sent to the console port during the first few seconds after a reboot, the password-recovery procedure can easily be used to take control of the system. Attackers who can interrupt power or induce a system crash and who have access to the console port via a hardwired terminal, a modem, a terminal server, or some other network device can take control of the system, even if they do not have physical access to it or the ability to log in to it normally (see Figure 2-32).

Figure 2-32   Connecting to Router Console Port

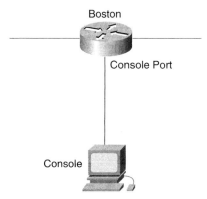

It follows that any modem or network device that gives access to the console port must be secured to the same degree as the router. At a bare minimum, any console modem should require the dialup user to supply a password for access, and the modem password should be carefully managed.

General Access

There are more ways of connecting to routers than users may realize. Cisco IOS Software, depending on the configuration and software version, can support connections through Telnet, rlogin, SSH, non-IP-based network protocols such as local-area transport (LAT), Maintenance Operation Protocol (MOP), X.29, and V.120. Connections can also be supported by way of local asynchronous connections or modem dial-ins. Additional protocols for access are always being added. Telnet access occurs not only on the standard TCP port 23, but on a variety of higher-numbered ports, too.

To configure the console port with the user-level password, follow these steps:

Step 1.   Enter console line configuration mode:

```
router(config)#line console  line-number
```

Step 2.   Enable password checking at login:

```
router(config-line)#login
```

Step 3. Set the user-level password to *password*:

```
router(config-line)#password  password
```

Step 4. Create the user-level password ConUser:

```
router(config)#  line console 0
router(config-line)#  login
router(config-line)#  password ConUser
```

The password is unencrypted.

The best way to protect a system is to make certain that appropriate controls are applied on all lines, including vty lines and tty lines. Administrators should usually make sure that logins on all lines are controlled using some sort of authentication mechanism, even on machines that are supposed to be inaccessible from untrusted networks. This is especially important for vty lines and for lines connected to modems or other remote-access devices.

Logins may be completely prevented on any line by configuring the router with the **login** and **no password** commands. This is the default configuration for vtys, but not for ttys. There are many ways to configure passwords and other forms of user authentication for tty and vty lines.

One peculiarity in using the Initial Configuration Dialog option is that the Cisco router will prompt for a vty password (unencrypted) and apply it and the **login** command to vty 0 4 as of Cisco IOS Software Release 12.3.15. The console port does not configure any password or logon, thus allowing the console port to be accessed in user EXEC mode with no password at all.

tty and AUX Local asynchronous terminals are less common than they once were, but they still exist in some installations. Even if the terminals are physically secured, the router should be configured to require users on local asynchronous terminals to log in before using the system. Most tty ports in modern routers are either connected to external modems or are implemented by integrated modems. Securing these ports is even more important than securing local terminal ports.

Step 1. Enter auxiliary line configuration mode:

```
router(config)#line aux  line-number
```

Step 2. Enable password checking at login for AUX connections:

```
router(config-line)#login
```

Step 3. Set the user-level password to *password*:

```
router(config-line)#password  password
```

Step 4. Create the user-level password ConUser:

```
router(config)#  line console 0
router(config-line)#  login
router(config-line)#  password ConUser
```

To disable the reverse Telnet feature, apply the configuration command **transport input none** to any asynchronous or modem line that should not be receiving connections from network users. If at all possible, do not use the same modems for both dialing in and dialing out and do not allow reverse Telnet connections to the lines used for dialing in.

Controlling vty Lines

Any vty should be configured to accept connections only with the protocols actually needed. This is done with the transport input command. For example, a vty that was expected to receive only Telnet sessions would be configured with **transport input telnet**, whereas a vty permitting both Telnet and SSH sessions would have **transport input telnet ssh**. If the software supports an encrypted access protocol such as SSH, it might be wise to enable only that protocol and to disable Telnet. It is also a good idea to use the **ip access-class** command to restrict the IP addresses from which the vty will accept connections.

A Cisco IOS device has a limited number of vty lines, usually five. When all the vtys are in use, no more additional remote connections can be established. This creates the opportunity for a DoS attack. If an attacker can open remote sessions to all the vtys on the system, the legitimate administrator might not be able to log in. The attacker does not have to log in to do this. The sessions can simply be left at the login prompt.

One way of reducing this exposure is to configure a more restrictive **ip access-class** command on the last vty line in the system. The last vty might be restricted to accept connections only from a single, specific administrative workstation, whereas the other vtys might accept connections from any address in a corporate network. To configure a vty user-level password, follow these steps:

Step 1. Enter vty line configuration mode and specify the range of vty lines to configure:

```
router(config)#line vty   start=line-number end=line-number
```

Step 2. Enable password checking at login for vty (Telnet) sessions:

```
router(config-line)#login
```

Step 3. Set the user-level password to *password*:

```
router(config-line)#password   password
```

Step 4. Create the user-level password ConUser:

```
router(config)#   line console 0
router(config-line)#   login
router(config-line)#   password ConUser\
```

Another useful tactic is to configure vty timeouts using the **exec-timeout** command, as follows:

```
router(config)#exec-timeout   minutes [seconds]
```

This prevents an idle session from consuming the vty line indefinitely. The default value is 10 minutes. Entering this command terminates an unattended console connection and provides an extra safety factor when an administrator walks away from an active console session.

For example, to terminate an unattended console/auxiliary connection after 3 minutes and 30 seconds, you enter the following:

```
router(config)#   line console 0
router(config-line)#   exec-timeout 3 30
router(config)#   line aux 0
```

```
router(config-line)#  exec-timeout 3 30
```

Similarly, enabling TCP keepalives on incoming connections, using the **service tcp-keepalives-in** command, can help guard against both malicious attacks and orphaned sessions caused by remote system crashes.

The configuration syntax for the **service tcp-keepalives** command is this:

```
router(config)#  service tcp-keepalives-in
router(config)#  service tcp-keepalives-out
```

Disabling all non-IP-based remote access protocols, and using SSH, Secure Sockets Layer (SSL), or IP Security (IPsec) encryption for all remote connections to the router can provide complete vty protection.

Remote Configuration Using SSH

Having remote access to network devices is critical for effectively managing a network. Traditionally, Cisco IOS Software supports Telnet, which allows users to connect to a remote router using TCP port 23. However, this method provides no security because all Telnet traffic goes over the network in clear text. *Secure Shell (SSH)* replaces Telnet to provide remote router administration with connections that support strong privacy and session integrity. This connection provides functionality that is similar to that of an outbound Telnet connection except that the connection is encrypted. With authentication and encryption, SSH allows for secure communications over an insecure network. Figure 2-33 illustrates the components that make up SSH.

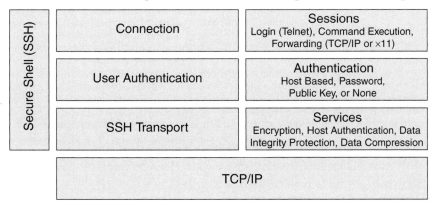

Figure 2-33 SSH Protocol Components

Currently, two versions of SSH are available: SSH Version 1 (SSHv1) and SSH Version 2 (SSHv2). SSH was introduced into Cisco IOS platforms/images in the following sequence:

- SSHv1 server was introduced in some Cisco IOS platforms/images starting in Release 12.1.(1)T.

- SSHv1 client was introduced in some Cisco IOS platforms/images starting in Release

12.1.(3).T.

- SSHv1 terminal-line access, also known as reverse-Telnet, was introduced in some Cisco IOS platforms/images starting in Release 12.2.(2).T.

- SSHv2 was introduced with Release 12.3(4)T.

The SSH terminal-line access feature enables users to configure their router with secure access and perform the following tasks:

- Connect to a router that has multiple terminal lines connected to consoles or serial ports of other routers, switches, or devices

- Simplify connectivity to a router from anywhere by securely connecting to the terminal server on a specific line

- Allow modems attached to routers to be used for dial-out securely

- Require authentication to each of the lines through a locally defined username and password, TACACS+, or RADIUS

Cisco routers can act as the SSH client and server. By default, both of these functions are enabled on the router when SSH is enabled. These two functions are detailed in the following sections.

SSH Client

The SSHv1 Integrated Client feature is an application running over the SSH protocol to provide device authentication and encryption. The SSH client enables a Cisco router or other SSH client to make a secure, encrypted connection to another Cisco router or to any other device running the SSHv1 server.

The SSH client in Cisco IOS Software works with publicly and commercially available SSH servers. The SSH client supports the ciphers of Data Encryption Standard (DES), Triple DES (3DES), and password authentication. User authentication is performed like that in the Telnet session to the router. The user authentication mechanisms supported for SSH are RADIUS, TACACS+, and the use of locally stored usernames and passwords.

SSH Server

When the SSH server function is enabled on a Cisco router or other device, an SSH client can make a secure, encrypted connection to that router or device. The SSH server in Cisco IOS Software will work with publicly and commercially available SSH clients and other Cisco routers that have SSH enabled.

When SSH is enabled on a Cisco router, it acts as both a client and a server by default. The Secure Copy Protocol (SCP) feature that is provided with SSH also allows for the secure transfer of configuration and image files.

Lab 2.5.2a Configure SSH

In this lab, you configure a router as an SSHv1 server, you install and configure a SSH client on the student PC, and you use **show** and **debug** commands to troubleshoot SSH. You also strengthen SSH by configuring SSHv2.

 Lab 2.5.2b Controlling TCP/IP Services

In this lab, you begin the process of implementing a secure perimeter router, learn to explicitly deny common TCP/IP services, and verify that TCP/IP services have been disabled.

Router Passwords

Passwords are the most critical tools in controlling access to a router. There are two password-protection schemes in Cisco IOS Software:

- Type 7 uses the Cisco-defined encryption algorithm, which is not as strong as Type 5 encryption.

- Type 5 uses a Message Digest 5 (MD5) hash, which is much stronger. Cisco recommends that Type 5 encryption be used rather than Type 7 where possible. Type 7 encryption is used by the **enable password, username**, and **line password** commands.

To protect the privileged EXEC level as much as possible, do not use the **enable password** command. Use the **enable secret** command. Even if the **enable secret** is set, do not set the **enable** password because it will not be used and may give away a system password, as demonstrated in Example 2-1.

Example 2-1   Configuring Router Passwords

```
router#  config t
Enter configuration commands, one per line. End with CNTL/Z
router(config)#  enable secret 2-mAny-rOUtEs
router(config)#  no enable password
router(config)#  end
router#
```

No user account should be created above privilege level 1 because it is not possible to use Type 5 encryption on the default EXEC login or the **username** command. User accounts should be created for auditing purposes. The **username** command should be used to create individual user accounts at the EXEC level, and then the higher privilege levels should be protected with the **enable secret** password. Users with a need to work at higher levels would be given the higher privilege level password.

If the **login** command is used to protect a line, the **password** command is the only way to set a password on a line. If the **login local** command is used to protect a line, however, the specified username and password pair is used. For access and logging reasons, use the **login local** command.

The privileged EXEC secret password should not match any other user password. Do not set any user or line password to the same value as any **enable secret** password.

The **service password-encryption** command will keep passersby from reading passwords that are displayed on the screen. Be aware that there are some secret values that **service password-encryption** does not protect. Never set any of these secret values to the same string as any other password.

Example 2-2 demonstrates encryption used for all passwords in the router configuration file.

Example 2-2   Service Password Encryption
```
router(config)#  service password-encryption
router#  show running-config
!
line con 0
password 7 0956F57A109A
!
line vty 0 4
password 7 034A18F366A0
!
line aux 0
password 7 7A4F5192306A
```

This configuration uses a weak encryption algorithm that can easily be cracked.

Good password practices include the following:

- Avoid dictionary words, names, phone numbers, and dates.

- Include at least one lowercase letter, uppercase letter, digit, and special character.

- Make all passwords at least eight characters long.

- Avoid more than four digits or same-case letters in a row.

Cisco IOS Software Release 12.3(1) and later allow administrators to set the minimum character length for all router passwords using the **security passwords** global configuration command, as shown in the figure. This command provides enhanced security access to the router by allowing you to specify a minimum password length, eliminating common passwords that are prevalent on most networks, such as lab and cisco. This command affects user passwords, enable passwords and secrets, and line passwords created after the command was executed (existing router passwords remain unaffected).

The syntax for the **security passwords** command is as follows:

```
security passwords min-length length
```

where the **min-length** keyword sets the minimum length of all Cisco IOS passwords and the *length* argument specifies the value (minimum of 10 characters is highly recommended). For example:

```
Boston(config)# security passwords min-length 10
```

By default, Cisco IOS routers allow a break sequence during power up, forcing the router into ROMMON mode. When the router is in ROMMON mode, anyone can choose to enter a new enable secret password using the well-known Cisco password-recovery procedure. This procedure, if performed correctly, leaves the router configuration intact. This scenario presents a potential security breach in that anyone who gains physical access to the router console port can enter ROMMON, reset the enable secret password, and discover the router configuration.

This potential security breach can be mitigated using the **no service password-recovery** global configuration command, as follows:

```
no service password-recovery
```

By default, Cisco routers are factory configured with **service password-recovery** set. Applying the **no** keyword prevents the console from accessing ROMMON. For example:

```
Boston(config)# no service password-recovery
WARNING:
Executing this command will disable password
recovery mechanism. Do not execute this command
without another plan for password recovery.

Are you sure you want to continue? [yes/no]: yes
Boston(config)#
```

> **Note**
>
> The **no service password-recovery** command is a hidden Cisco IOS command and is not visible in the **?** output.

If a router is configured with **no service password-recovery**, all access to the ROMMON is disabled. If the router's Flash memory does not contain a valid Cisco IOS image, you cannot use the ROMMON XMODEM command to load a new Flash image. To repair the router, you must obtain a new Cisco IOS image on a Flash SIMM or on a PCMCIA card (for example the 1600s and the 3600s). See Cisco.com for more information regarding backup Flash images.

Router Privileges and Accounts

Cisco IOS Software provides for 16 different privilege levels ranging from 0 to 15. Cisco IOS Software comes with two predefined user levels. User EXEC mode runs at privilege level 1, and the privileged EXEC mode runs at level 15. Every Cisco IOS command is pre-assigned to either level 1 or level 15. By default, Cisco provides user EXEC level 1 with a few commands that might, in terms of security, belong at a higher privilege level.

To set multiple privilege levels, enter the following:

```
router(config)#privilege mode {level level command | reset command}
```

Example 2-3 shows how to move level 1 user EXEC commands to level 15 privileged EXEC mode. This provides a more secure user EXEC mode. The last line is required to move the **show ip** command back down to level 1. For example, a site might want to set up more than the two levels of administrative access on their routers.

```
Example 2-3     Moving Commands to Privilege Mode
router(config)#  privilege exec level 15 connect
router(config)#  privilege exec level 15 telnet
router(config)#  privilege exec level 15 rlogin
router(config)#  privilege exec level 15 show ip access-lists
router(config)#  privilege exec level 15 show access-lists
router(config)#  privilege exec level 15 show logging
router(config)#  privilege exec level 1 show ip
```

Keep in mind several considerations when customizing privilege levels:

- Do not use the **username** command to set up accounts above level 1. Instead, use the **enable secret** command to set a level password.

- Be careful about moving too much access down from level 15; this could cause unexpected security holes in the system.

- Be careful about moving any part of the **configure** command down from level 15. When users have write access, they can leverage this to acquire greater access.

First, give each administrator a login account for the router. When an administrator logs in with a username and changes the configuration, the generated log message will include the name of the login account that was used. The login accounts created with the **username** command should be assigned privilege level 1. In addition, do not create any user accounts without passwords. When an administrator no longer needs access to the router, delete the account. Example 2-4 shows how to create local user accounts for users named rsmith and bjones and how to remove the local user named brian. In general, only allow accounts that are required on the router and minimize the number of users with access to configuration mode on the router.

Example 2-4   Creating Local User Accounts

```
router#  config t
Enter configuration commands, one per line. End with CNTL/Z.
router(config)#  username rsmith password 3d-zircOnia
 router(config)#  username rsmith privilege 1
router(config)#  username bjones password 2B-or-3B
router(config)#  username bjones privilege 1
router(config)#  no username brian
router(config)#  end
router#
```

Cisco IOS Network Services

Cisco routers support a large number of network services at Layers 2, 3, 4, and 7. Some of these services are application layer protocols that allow users and host processes to connect to the router. Others are automatic processes and settings intended to support legacy or specialized configurations, which are detrimental to security. Some of these services can be restricted or disabled to improve security without degrading the operational use of the router. General security practice for routers should be to support only traffic and protocols a network needs. Most of the services listed in this section are not needed.

Turning off a network service on the router itself does not prevent it from supporting a network where that protocol is used. For example, a router may support a network where the BOOTP protocol is employed, but some other host is acting as the BOOTP server. BOOTP is a UDP that can be used by Cisco routers to access copies of Cisco IOS Software on another Cisco router running the BOOTP service. In this case, the BOOTP server on the router should be disabled.

In many cases, Cisco IOS Software supports turning a service off entirely, or restricting access to particular network segments or sets of hosts. If a particular portion of a network needs a service but the rest does not, the restriction features should be employed to limit the scope of the service.

Turning off an automatic network feature usually prevents a certain kind of network traffic from being processed by the router or prevents it from traversing the router. For example, IP source routing is a little-used feature of IP that can be used in network attacks. Unless it is required for the network to operate, you should disable IP source routing.

Table 2-2 lists some of the services offered on Cisco IOS Software that can generally be turned off or disabled to avoid giving extra opportunity to hackers. This list has been kept short by including only those services and features that are security relevant and might need to be disabled. Services that are not running cannot be attacked.

Table 2-2   Securing Available Cisco IOS Services

Feature	Description	Default	Recommendation
Cisco Discovery Protocol (CDP)	Proprietary Layer 2 protocol between Cisco devices.	Enabled	CDP is almost never needed; disable it.
TCP small servers	Standard TCP network services; echo, chargen, and so on.	Disabled on Cisco IOSSoftware Release 11.3and later. Enabled on Cisco IOS Software Release 11.2	This is a legacy feature; disable it explicitly.
UDP small servers	Standard UDP network services; echo, discard, and so on.	Disabled on Cisco IOS Software Release 11.3 and later. Enabled on Cisco IOS Software Release 11.2	This is a legacy feature; disable it explicitly.
Finger	UNIX user lookup service, allows remote listing of users.	Enabled	Unauthorized persons do not need to know this; disable it.
HTTP server	Some Cisco IOS devices offer web-based configuration.	Varies by device	If not in use, explicitly disable; otherwise, restrict access.
BOOTP server	Service to allow other routers to boot from this one.	Enabled	This is rarely needed and might open a security hole; disable it.
Configuration auto-loading	Router will attempt to load its configuration via TFTP.	Disabled	This is rarely used; disable it if it is not in use.
IP source routing	IP feature that allows packets to specify their own routes.	Enabled	This rarely used feature can prove helpful in attacks; disable it.
Proxy ARP	Router will act as a proxy for Layer 2 address resolution.	Enabled	Disable this service unless the router is serving as a LAN bridge.

Table 2-2   Securing Available Cisco IOS Services   *continued*

Feature	Description	Default	Recommendation
IP directed broadcast	Packets can identify a target LAN for broadcasts.	Enabled on Cisco IOS Software Release 11.3 and earlier	Directed broadcast can be used for attacks; disable it.
Classless routing behavior	Router will forward packets with no concrete route.	Enabled	Certain attacks can benefit from this; disable it unless your network requires it.
IP unreachable notifications	Router will explicitly notify senders of incorrect IP addresses.	Enabled	Can aid network mapping; disabled on interfaces to untrusted networks
IP mask reply	Router will send an IP address mask of interface in response to an ICMP* mask request.	Disabled	Can aid IP address masking; explicitly disable on interfaces to trusted networks.
IP redirects	Router will send an ICMP redirect message in response to certain routed IP packets.	Enabled	Can aid in network mapping; disable on interfaces to untrusted networks.
NTP service	Router can act as a time server for other devices and hosts.	Enabled (if NTP is configured)	If not in use, explicitly disable; otherwise, restrict access.
Simple Network Management Protocol	Routers can support SNMP remote query and configuration.	Enabled	If not in use, explicitly disable; otherwise restrict access
Domain Name Service	Routers can perform DNS name resolution.	Enabled (broadcast)	Set the DNS server address explicitly, or disable DNS.

* ICMP = Internet Control Message Protocol

To find the services to restrict or disable, start by running the **show proc** command on the router. Next, turn off clearly unneeded facilities and services. Some services that should almost always be turned off, and the corresponding commands to disable them are as follows:

- Small services such as echo, discard, and chargen: **no service tcp-small-servers** or **no service udp-small-servers**, as demonstrated in the following

```
Austin2(config)#  no service tcp-small-servers
Austin2(config)#  no service udp-small-servers
```

- BOOTP: **no ip bootp server** (see Figure 2-34)

- Finger: **no service finger** (see Figure 2-35)

- HTTP: **no ip http server** (see Figure 2-36)

- SNMP: **no snmp-server**

Figure 2-34   Disable Boot Servers

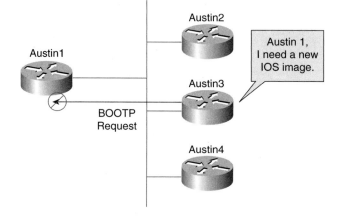

Figure 2-35 shows a sample network for which you would disable the Finger service for the Austin4 router by entering the following:

```
Austin4(config)#  no ip finger
Austin4(config)#  no service finger
Austin4(config)#  exit
Austin4#  connect 16.1.1.5 finger
Trying 16.1.1.5, 79...
% Connection refused by remote host
```

Figure 2-35   Disable Finger Service

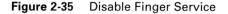

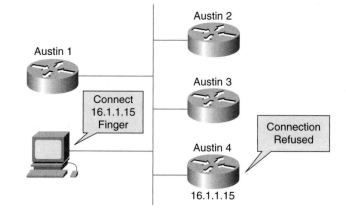

Figure 2-36 shows a sample network for which you would disable the HTTP service for the
Austin4 router by entering:

```
Austin(config)#  no ip http server
```

Figure 2-36   Disable HTTP Service

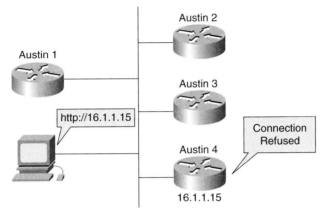

It is also important to shut down services that allow certain packets to pass through the router,
send special packets, or are used for remote router configuration. The corresponding commands
to disable them are as follows:

- CDP: **no cdp run** (see Figure 2-37)

- Remote configuration: **no service config** (see Figure 2-38)

- Source routing: **no ip source-route**

- Classless routing: **no ip classless**

Figure 2-37 shows a sample network for which you would globally disable the CDP service for
the Austin4 router by entering the following:

```
Austin4(config)#  no cdp run
```

Figure 2-37   Disable CDP Server

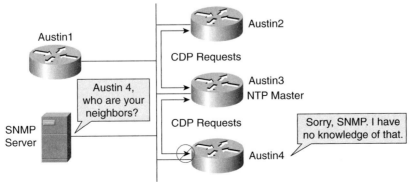

Figure 2-38 shows a sample network for which you would globally disable auto-loading services for the Austin4 router by entering the following:

```
Austin4(config)#  no boot network
Austin4(config)#tftp://AustinTFTP/TFTP/Austin4.config
Austin4(config)#  no service config
```

Figure 2-38   Disable Configuration Auto-Loading Service

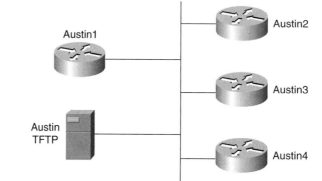

You can make the interfaces on the router more secure by using certain commands in the configure interface mode. These commands should be applied to every interface:

- Unused interfaces: **shutdown**

- No Smurf attacks: **no ip directed-broadcast**

- Ad-hoc routing: **no ip proxy-arp**

The configuration listing in Example 2-5 shows the configuration commands for disabling typically unneeded services.

Example 2-5   Disabling Unneeded Services on a Router to Reduce Vulnerability to Hacker Attacks

```
! ——- IP and network services Section no cdp run
no ip source-route no ip classless
no service tcp-small-serv no service udp-small-serv no ip finger
no service finger no ip bootp server no ip http server no ip name-server
! ——- Boot control section no boot network
no service config
! ——- SNMP Section (for totally disabling SNMP)
! set up totally restrictive access list no access-list 70
access-list 70 deny any
! make SNMP read-only and subject to access list snmp-server community
  aqiytj1726540942 ro 11
! disable SNMP trap and system-shutdown features no snmp-server enable traps
no snmp-server system-shutdown no snmp-server trap-auth
! turn off SNMP altogether no snmp-server
```

Example 2-5 Disabling Unneeded Services on a Router to Reduce Vulnerability to Hacker Attacks *continued*

```
! ——- Per-interface services section interface eth 0/0
description Outside interface to 14.1.0.0/16 net no ip proxy-arp
no ip directed-broadcast no ip unreachable
no ip redirect ntp disable exit
interface eth 0/1
description Inside interface to 14.2.9.0/24 net no ip proxy-arp
no ip directed-broadcast no ip unreachable
no ip redirect ntp disable exit
interface eth 0/2 no ip proxy-arp shutdown
no cdp enable exit
interface eth 0/3 no ip proxy-arp shutdown
no cdp enable exit
```

Routing, Proxy ARP, and ICMP

The routing process and the process of proxy ARP and ICMP can be disadvantages to your network security. The sections that follow explore these processes to see what can be done to overcome these disadvantages.

IP Source Routing

Source routing is a feature of IP whereby individual packets can specify routes. This feature is used in several kinds of attacks. Cisco routers normally accept and process source routes. Unless a network depends on source routing, you should disable it on all network routers in the network. To disable IP source routing, you enter the following:

```
router(config)#  no ip source-route
```

Proxy ARP

Network hosts use the Address Resolution Protocol (ARP) to translate network addresses into MAC addresses. Normally, ARP transactions are confined to a particular LAN segment. A Cisco router can act as an intermediary for ARP, responding to ARP queries on selected interfaces and thus enabling transparent access between multiple LAN segments. This service is called proxy ARP. Proxy ARP should be used only between two LAN segments at the same trust level, and only when absolutely necessary to support legacy network architectures.

Cisco routers perform proxy ARP by default on all IP interfaces. Disable it on each interface where it is not needed, even on interfaces that are currently idle, using the interface configuration command **no ip proxy-arp**. To disable proxy ARP on an Ethernet interface, as depicted in Figure 2-39, you enter the following:

```
Austin1(config)#  interface e0/0
Austin1(config-if)#  no ip proxy-arp
```

Figure 2-39   Disable Proxy ARP

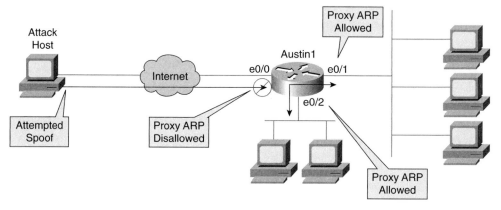

IP Directed Broadcast

Directed broadcasts permit a host on one LAN segment to initiate a physical broadcast on a different LAN segment. This technique was used in some old DoS attacks, and the default Cisco IOS Software configuration is to reject directed broadcasts. To explicitly disable directed broadcasts on each interface depicted in Figure 2-40, you would use the **no ip directed-broadcast** interface configuration command, as follows:

```
Austin2(config)#  interface e0/1
Austin2(config-if)#  no ip directed-broadcast
```

Figure 2-40   Disable IP Directed Broadcast

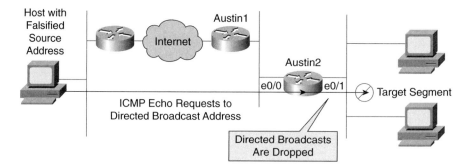

IP Classless Routing

By default, a Cisco router makes an attempt to route almost any IP packet. If a packet arrives addressed to a subnet of a network with no default network route, Cisco IOS Software uses IP classless routing to forward the packet along the best-available route. This feature is often not needed. On routers where IP classless routing is not needed, you can globally disable it as follows (see Figure 2-41):

```
Austin2(config)#  no ip classless
```

Figure 2-41   Disable IP Classless Routing Service

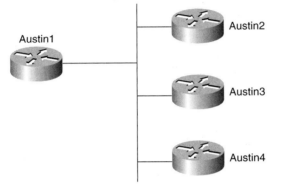

IP Unreachables, Redirects, Mask Replies

ICMP supports IP traffic by relaying information about paths, routes, and network conditions. Cisco routers automatically send ICMP messages under a wide variety of conditions. Attackers for network mapping and diagnosis commonly use three ICMP messages:

- Host Unreachable

- Redirect

- Mask Reply

To prevent attackers from exploiting the ICMP Host Unreachable message, you can enter the following:

```
Austin2(config)#  interface e0/0
Austin2(config-if)#  no ip unreachable
```

To prevent attackers from exploiting the ICMP Redirect message, you can enter the following (see Figure 2-42):

```
Austin2(config)#  interface e0/0
Austin2(config-if)#  no ip redirect
```

Figure 2-42   Disable IP Redirects

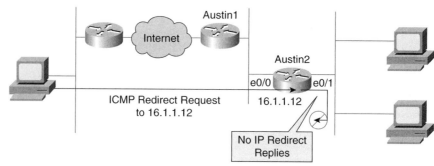

To prevent attackers from exploiting the ICMP Mask Reply message, you can enter the following (see Figure 2-43):

```
Austin2(config)#  interface e0/0
Austin2(config-if)#  no ip mask-reply
```

Figure 2-43   Disable IP Mask Replies

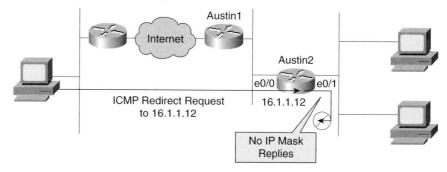

Automatic generation of these messages should be disabled on all interfaces, especially interfaces that are connected to untrusted networks.

Routing Protocol Authentication and Update Filtering

An unprotected router or routing domain is an easy target for any network-savvy adversary. For example, an attacker who sends false routing update packets to an unprotected router can easily corrupt its routing table. This enables the attacker to reroute network traffic as desired. The key to preventing this type of an attack is to protect the routing tables from unauthorized and malicious changes.

Two basic approaches enable you to protect routing table integrity:

- **Use only static routes**—This might work in small networks but is unsuitable for large networks. A static route is shown in Example 2-6.

- **Authenticate route table updates**—By using routing protocols with authentication, network administrators can deter attacks based on unauthorized routing changes. Authenticated router updates ensure that the update messages come from legitimate sources. Bogus messages are automatically discarded. You configure routing protocol authentication as demonstrated in Example 2-7.

Example 2-6   Configuring Static Routes

```
Router# config t
Enter configuration commands, one per line. End with CNTL/Z.
Router(config)# ip route 14.2.6.0 255.255.255.0 14.1.1.20 120
Router(config)# end
Router(config)#
```

Example 2-7   Configuring Routing Protocol Authentication

```
North# config t
Enter configuration commands, one per line. End with CNTL/Z.
North(config)# router ospf 1
North(config-router)# network 14.1.0.0 0.0.255.255 area 0
North(config-router)# area 0 authentication message-digest
North(config-router)# exit
North(config)# int eth0/1
North(config-if)# ip ospf message-digest-key 1 md5 r0utes-4-all
North(config-if)# end
North#
East# config t
Enter configuration commands, one per line. End with CNTL/Z.
East(config)# router ospf 1
East(config-router)# area 0 authentication message-digest
East(config-router)# network 14.1.0.0 0.0.255.255 area 0
East(config-router)# network 14.2.6.0 0.0.0.255 area 0
East(config-router)# exit
East(config)# int eth0
East(config-if)# ip ospf message-digest-key 1 md5 r0utes-4-all
East(config-if)# end
East#
```

Another attack involves preventing router update messages from being sent or received, which will result in bringing down parts of a network. To resist such attacks and recover from them quickly, routers need rapid convergence and backup routes.

Routing protocol authentication is vulnerable to eavesdropping and spoofing of routing updates. MD5 authentication of routing protocol updates prevents the introduction of unauthorized or false routing messages from unknown sources.

Cisco IOS Software supports the use of MD5 authentication of routing protocol updates for the following protocols:

- Open Shortest Path First (OSPF)

- Routing Information Protocol Version 2 (RIPv2)

- Enhanced Interior Gateway Routing Protocol (EIGRP)

- Border Gateway Protocol (BGP)

The **key-string** command defines the MD5 key that is used to create the message digest, or hash, that is exchanged with the opposite router. It is possible to specify the time period during which the key can be received and sent with the **accept-lifetime** and **send-lifetime** commands.

Static routes are manually configured on the router as the sole path to a given destination. In one sense, static routes are secure. They are not vulnerable to spoofing attacks because they do not deal with router update packets. However, exclusively using static routes will make network administration extremely difficult. Also, configuring a large network to use only static routes can make the availability of large segments of the network subject to single points of failure. Static routes cannot handle events such as router failures. However, a dynamic routing protocol, such as OSPF, can correctly reroute traffic in the case of a router failure.

Passive Interfaces

The **passive-interface** command is used to prevent other routers on the network from learning about routes dynamically. It can also be used to keep any unnecessary parties from learning about the existence of certain routes or routing protocols used. It is typically used when the wildcard specification on the network router configuration command configures more interfaces than desirable.

Lab 2.5.7 Configure Routing Authentication and Filtering

In this lab, you learn to configure routing protocol authentication and route filters to control route updates from peer routers.

NTP, SNMP, Router Name, DNS

The final four services we want to look at in this chapter are NTP, SNMP, router name, and DNS. These services all affect network security.

NTP Service

Cisco routers and other hosts use the *Network Time Protocol (NTP)* to keep their time-of-day clocks accurate and in synchrony. If possible, configure all routers as part of an NTP hierarchy.

If an NTP hierarchy is not available on the network, disable NTP as follows (see Figure 2-44).

```
Austin4(config)# interface e0/0
Austin4(config-if)# ntp disable
```

Figure 2-44   Disable NTP Service

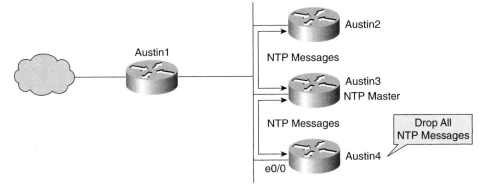

Disabling NTP on an interface will not prevent NTP messages from traversing the router. To reject all NTP messages at a particular interface, use an access list.

SNMP Services

The *Simple Network Management Protocol (SNMP)* is the standard Internet protocol for automated remote monitoring and administration. There are several different versions of SNMP with different security properties. If a network has an SNMP infrastructure in place for administration, all routers on that network should be configured to securely participate in it. In the absence of a deployed SNMP scheme, all SNMP facilities on all routers should be disabled using the following steps:

Step 1.   Erase existing community strings, and set a hard-to-guess, read-only community string.

Step 2.   Apply a simple IP access list to SNMP denying all traffic.

Step 3.   Disable SNMP system shutdown and trap features.

Disable SNMP

Figure 2-45 shows a network where disabling SNMP is a viable option for reducing security threats. Example 2-8 demonstrates the necessary configuration for disabling SNMP.

Figure 2-45 Disable SNMP

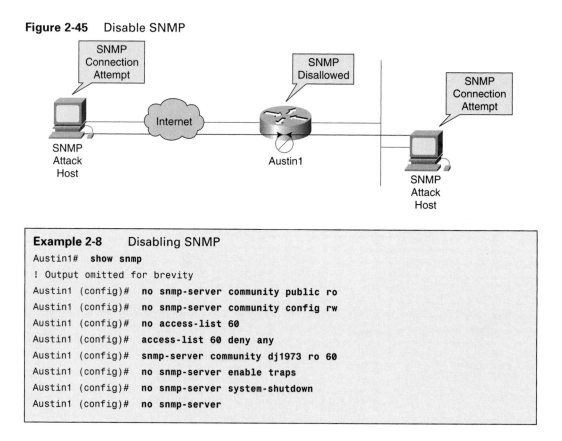

```
Example 2-8      Disabling SNMP
Austin1#  show snmp
! Output omitted for brevity
Austin1 (config)#  no snmp-server community public ro
Austin1 (config)#  no snmp-server community config rw
Austin1 (config)#  no access-list 60
Austin1 (config)#  access-list 60 deny any
Austin1 (config)#  snmp-server community dj1973 ro 60
Austin1 (config)#  no snmp-server enable traps
Austin1 (config)#  no snmp-server system-shutdown
Austin1 (config)#  no snmp-server
```

Example 2-8 starts with listing the current configuration to find the SNMP community strings. The configuration listing is often quite long, but there is no other mechanism in Cisco IOS Software for viewing the configured SNMP community strings. The command **no snmp-server** shuts down all SNMP processing on the router. When SNMP processing is shut down, SNMP configuration will not appear in any listing of the running configuration, but it might still be there.

Router Name and DNS Name Resolution

Cisco IOS supports looking up host names with the ***Domain Name System (DNS)***. DNS provides the mapping between names, such as central.mydomain.com, to IP addresses, such as 14.2.9.250. Unfortunately, the basic DNS protocol offers no authentication or integrity assurance. By default, name queries are sent to the broadcast address 255.255.255.255. If one or more name servers are available on the network, and it is desirable to use names in Cisco IOS commands, explicitly set the name server addresses using the global configuration command **ip name-server** *addresses*. Otherwise, turn off DNS name resolution with the command **no ip domain-lookup**. It is also a good idea to give the router a name, using the command

hostname. The name given to the router will appear in the prompt.

Figure 2-46 shows a network where restricting DNS service is a viable option for reducing security risks, which you can configure as follows:

```
Austin4(config)#  ip name-server 16.1.1.20
Austin3(config)#  no ip domain-lookup
```

Figure 2-46   Restricting DNS Service

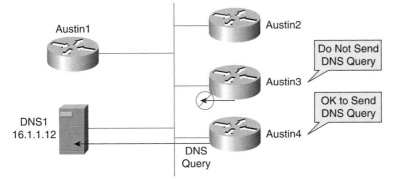

Summary

This chapter introduced the Security Wheel, a continuous process built around a security policy, which is the most critical part of network security. The Security Wheel consists of four steps: secure, monitor, test, and improve. This policy is the plan for successful network security. As the saying goes, "Fail to plan, plan to fail."

This chapter also covered techniques to control access to routers and the network by managing access at the console ports and terminal lines. It also covered setting up passwords, accounts, and privilege levels. For security purposes, you should configure network devices to support only the traffic and protocols the network needs. Furthermore, administrators should use SSH when managing routers and other key network devices to protect passwords and sensitive data.

Check Your Understanding

Complete all the review questions listed here to test your understanding of the topics and concepts in this chapter. Answers are listed in Appendix A, "Check Your Understanding Answer Key."

1. Which two steps are contained in the Security Wheel?

   a. Secure

   b. Prevent

   c. Analyze

   d. Manage

   e. Back up

2. What command would turn off Cisco Discovery Protocol at the interface?

   a. **no cdp enable**

   b. **no cdp run**

   c. **no cdp int**

   d. **cdp disable**

3. When auditors came to the network operations center, one of the documents that the network administrator showed them contained detailed information on proper login processes. In which category does this document belong?

   a. Security policy

   b. Security procedure

   c. Security monitoring

   d. Security assessment

4. What service would not normally be turned off at the router?

   a. Telnet

   b. SNMP

   c. Finger

   d. HTTP

5. A network administrator has installed a new network server and applied all patches and upgrades. What two simple steps can the administrator take to help harden the operating system? (Choose two.)

   a. Perform UDP and TCP port scan on the server

   b. Install redundant services in case on fails

   c. Change default usernames and passwords

d. Turn off unnecessary services and applications

e. Configure stateful packet inspection on network connections.

6. Cisco assigns two different default user privilege levels. What are they?

a. Level 0 user EXEC, level 1 privileged EXEC

b. Level 1 user EXEC, level 1 privileged EXEC

c. Level 1 user EXEC, level 15 privileged EXEC

d. Level 5 user EXEC, level 15 privileged EXEC

7. How many different privilege levels are there in the Cisco IOS Software?

a. 2

b. 8

c. 15

d. 25

e. 16

8. Which of the four components of a network security policy does the administrator conducting port scans of the company network fall under?

a. Secure

b. Improve

c. Monitor

d. Test

9. Which hashing algorithm, along with a passphrase, does Cisco IOS Software support for authenticating routing protocol updates?

a. SHA

b. MD5

c. AES

d. TYPE 7

10. Which benefit does SSH have over Telnet when remotely managing a router?

a. Encryption

b. TCP usage

c. Authorization

d. Connection using six VTY lines

e. UDP usage

Upon completion of this chapter, you should be able to answer the following questions:

- What are some of the device options?

- What are some uses of the Security Device Manger?

- What is the Cisco Security Appliance family?

- What is the Pix Security Appliance?

- How do I use the PIX Security Appliance translations and connections?

- How do I manage a Pix Security Appliance with Adaptive Security Device Manager?

- What are the PIX Security Appliance routing capabilities?

- How does the Firewall Services Module operate?

This chapter begins with a discussion of the network firewall. The firewall exists to enforce the enterprise security—enabling a company to do business online, while providing the necessary security between the internal network of the enterprise and an external network. In addition to access control, the firewall provides a natural focal point for the administration of other network security measures.

This chapter introduces the Cisco IOS Firewall feature set, the Cisco PIX Security Appliance and the Cisco Adaptive Security Appliance, and the Firewall Service Module. This coverage includes an overview of the various PIX Security Appliance and Adaptive Security Appliance models, their features, and their capabilities. Although Security Appliances are not routers, they do have certain routing capabilities. The commands used in the basic configuration of the Security Appliance are covered, too.

This chapter also introduces Security Device Manager (SDM) and Adaptive Security Device Manager (ASDM), which provide a way to configure devices quickly and easily through a graphical user interface.

One aspect of understanding how TCP and UDP work with the Security Appliance is examining both translations and connections. It is important to learn how these items are used when traffic is going from the inside network to the outside network, or from the outside network to the inside network. In examining translations and connections, the chapter covers Network Address Translation (NAT).

The chapter also covers Port Address Translation (PAT) and configuring multiple interfaces on the PIX Security Appliance. PAT is a translation method, like NAT, that enables network administrators to hide the inside network addressing scheme from outside hosts and allows for the conservation of IP addresses. However, unlike NAT, which leases IP addresses to inside hosts on a one-to-one basis, PAT can go a step further and allow numerous inside hosts to use a single IP address, a process called *overloading*.

Device Options

The most well-known security device is the firewall. By conventional definition, a firewall is a partition made of fireproof material designed to prevent the spread of fire from one part of a building to another. A firewall can also be used to isolate one compartment from another. A firewall is only effective if there are no holes in it to allow the fire to spread. When applying the term *firewall* to a computer network, a firewall is a system or group of systems that enforces an access control policy between two or more networks and again, the more holes you have in your computer firewall, the less effective it becomes. Figure 3-1 depicts a sample firewall topology.

Figure 3-1   Sample Firewall Topology

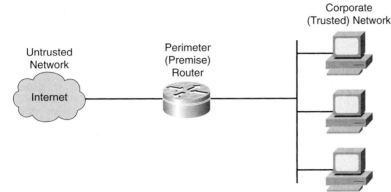

All firewalls fall within three classes:

- **Appliance-based firewalls**—Appliance-based firewalls are hardware platforms designed specifically as dedicated firewalls. The appliance might serve other functions, but they are secondary to the firewall feature set.

- **Server-based firewalls**—A server-based firewall consists of a firewall application that runs on a network operating system (NOS) such as UNIX, NT or Windows 2000, or Novell. The underlying operating system is still present, so vulnerabilities and resource use of the operating system must be considered when implementing a this type of firewall.

- **Integrated firewalls**—An integrated firewall is implemented by adding firewall functionality to an existing device.

Cisco provides a full lineup of firewall solutions. This book will help you design, install, and configure firewalls using Cisco IOS Firewall routers and PIX Security Appliances.

Although the PIX Security Appliance and Cisco IOS Firewall are the focus of this chapter, you should understand that other Cisco firewall options and other vendor firewalls are available. A basic understanding of the PIX Security Appliance and Cisco IOS Firewall should enable you to easily transition to other manufacturer firewalls if needed. Because it is beyond the scope of this book to go into detail on these products, it is recommended that you familiarize yourself with each of them.

Cisco IOS Firewall Feature Set

The Cisco IOS Firewall is a security-specific option for Cisco IOS Software that integrates robust firewall functionality, authentication proxy, and intrusion prevention for every network perimeter, and enriches existing Cisco IOS security capabilities. The Cisco IOS Firewall adds greater depth and flexibility to existing Cisco IOS security solutions by delivering state-of-the-art security features such as stateful, application-based filtering, dynamic per-user authentication and authorization, defense against network attacks, Java blocking, and real-time alerts.

When combined with Cisco IOS Internet Protocol Security (IPsec) software and other Cisco IOS Software-based technologies, such as Layer 2 Tunneling Protocol (L2TP) tunneling and quality of service (QoS), the Cisco IOS Firewall provides a complete, integrated virtual private network (VPN) solution.

The Cisco IOS Firewall feature set combines existing Cisco IOS firewall technology and the Context-Based Access Control (CBAC) feature. When the Cisco IOS Firewall is configured on a Cisco router, the router is turned into an effective, robust firewall.

The Cisco IOS Firewall features are designed to prevent unauthorized external individuals from gaining access to the internal network and to block attacks on the network, while at the same time allowing authorized users to access network resources.

You can use the Cisco IOS Firewall features to configure a Cisco IOS router as one of the following:

- An Internet firewall or part of an Internet firewall
- A firewall between groups in the internal network
- A firewall providing secure connections to or from branch offices
- A firewall between a company's network and that company's partners' networks

The Cisco IOS Firewall features provide the following benefits:

- Protection of internal networks from intrusion
- Monitoring of traffic through network perimeters
- Enabling of network commerce via the World Wide Web

Creating a Customized Firewall

To create a firewall customized to fit an organization's security policy, first determine which Cisco IOS Firewall features are appropriate, and then configure those features. At a minimum, you must configure basic traffic filtering to provide a basic firewall. You can configure a router to function as a firewall by using the following Cisco IOS Firewall features:

- Standard access lists and static extended access lists
- Dynamic, or lock-and-key, access lists
- Reflexive access lists
- TCP intercept
- CBAC
- Cisco IOS Firewall Intrusion Prevention System
- Authentication proxy
- Port-to-application mapping

- Security server support

- Network address translation

- IPsec network security

- Neighbor router authentication

- Event logging

- User authentication and authorization

PIX Security Appliance

The Cisco PIX Security Appliance 500 series scales to meet a range of requirements and network sizes. It currently consists of the following five models, as shown in Figure 3-2:

- The PIX 501 Security Appliance has an integrated 10/100BASE-T port (100BASE-T option available in Release 6.3) and an integrated four-port 10/100 switch.

- The PIX 506E Security Appliance has dual integrated 10/100BASE-T ports (100BASE-T option available in Release 6.3 for 506E only).

- The PIX 515E Security Appliance supports single-port or four-port 10/100 Ethernet cards.

- The PIX 525 Security Appliance supports single-port or four-port 10/100 Fast Ethernet and Gigabit Ethernet.

- The PIX 535 Security Appliance supports Fast Ethernet and Gigabit Ethernet. The PIX 515E, 525, and 535 Security Appliance models come with an integrated virtual private network (VPN) Accelerator (VAC) card.

Figure 3-2   PIX Security Appliance Family

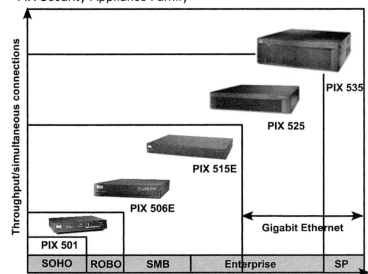

A network administrator will choose a model depending on the network requirements. Larger models offer more features, but they are more expensive. Table 3-1 outlines the targeted markets and features supported by each model in the PIX Security Appliance family.

Note

At the introduction of PIX Operating System Version 7.0, the PIX 501, PIX 506, and PIX 506E models do not support the new software.

Table 3-1   PIX Security Product Line Overview

Model	501	506E	515E	525	535
Market	SOHO	ROBO	SMB	Enterprise	Enterprise and service provider
Licensed users	10 or 50 or unlimited	Unlimited	Unlimited	Unlimited	Unlimited
Maximum VPN peers	10	25	2000	2000	2000
Size (RU)	<1	1	1	2	3
Processor	133 (MHz)	300 (MHz)	433 (MHz)	600 (MHz)	1 GHz
RAM	16 MB	32 MB	64 MB or 128 MB	256 MB	512 MB or 1 GB
Maximum interfaces	1 + 4 port switch	2	6	10	14
Failover support	No	No	Yes	Yes	Yes
Clear text (Mbps)	60	100	190	330	1650
3DES/AES (Mbps)	3/4.5	16/30	140/140	155/170	440/535
Maximum connections	75,000	25,000	130,000	280,000	500,000

Adaptive Security Appliance

The Cisco Adaptive Security Appliance 5500 Security Appliance series scales to meet a range of requirements and network sizes, as depicted in Figure 3-3. The ASA 5500 Security Appliance family currently consists of the following three models:

Figure 3-3   ASA Security Appliance Family

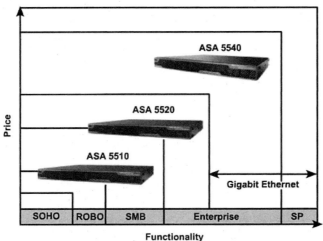

- The ASA 5510 Security Appliance, which has integrated 10/100BASE-T ports

- The ASA 5520 Security Appliance, which supports a single management 10/100 Fast Ethernet port and four Gigabit Ethernet ports

- The ASA 5540 Security Appliance, which supports a single management 10/100 Fast Ethernet port and four Gigabit Ethernet ports

The ASA Security Appliance models also support WebVPN and an optional IPS-Security Services Module (SSM).

Table 3-2 outlines the targeted markets and features supported by each model in the ASA Security Appliance family.

Note

The available features and commands used to configure the PIX Security Appliance and the Adaptive Security Appliance are the same. The only exception is the VPN over Secure Sockets Layer (SSL), or WebVPN, feature set. This feature is only available for the Adaptive Security Appliance, and not the PIX Security Appliance, for Software Version 7.0.

Table 3-2   ASA Security Product Line Overview

Model	5510	5520	5540
Key functionality characteristics	All-in-one enterprise remote office and SMB security/VPN gateway	All-in-one enterprise and SMB headend security/VPN gateway	All-in-one enterprise and SMB headend security/VPN gateway
Interface support	Up to five 10/100 Fast Ethernet Up to 10 VLANs	Five 10/100/1000 Gigabit Ethernet Up to 25 VLANs Up to 10 Contexts	Five 10/100/1000 Gigabit Ethernet Up to 100 VLANs Up to 50 Contexts
Failover support	Active/standby	Active/standby Active/active	Active/standby Active/active
VPN support	Site-to-site Remote access WebVPN	Site-to-site Remote access WebVPN	Site-to-site (5000 peers) Remote access WebVPN
AIP-SSM Option	AIP-SSM-10	AIP-SSM-10	AIP-SSM-20
Clear-text throughput (Mbps)	100	200	400
Maximum concurrent connections	64,000	130,000	280,000

Finesse Operating System

Finesse is the Cisco proprietary real-time operating system that runs directly on the hardware of the PIX Security Appliance and the Adaptive Security Appliance. It is a non-UNIX, non-Windows NT, and Cisco IOS-like operating system.

Use of Finesse eliminates the risks associated with general-purpose operating systems. It enables the PIX Security Appliance to deliver outstanding performance with up to 1,000,000 simultaneous connections depending on the model. This number is significantly greater than any software-based firewall. The Finesse operating system displays the following advantages:

- Software reusability
- Source-code portability
- Increased product quality
- Decreased testing

- Shorter time to market

- Increased return on investment for users of Cisco products

The Adaptive Security Algorithm

The heart of the Security Appliances is the Adaptive Security Algorithm (ASA). ASA maintains the secure perimeters between the networks controlled by the Security Appliance. The stateful, connection-oriented ASA design creates session flows based on source and destinations addresses. The ASA randomizes TCP sequence numbers, port numbers, and additional TCP flags before completion of the connection. This function is always in operation, monitoring return packets to ensure they are valid, and allows one-way, inside-to-outside connections without an explicit configuration for each internal system and application. The randomizing of the TCP sequence numbers is to minimize the risk of a TCP sequence number attack. Because of the ASA algorithm, the Security Appliance is less complex and more robust than a packet-filtering-designed firewall.

Stateful packet filtering is a secure method of analyzing data packets that places extensive information about a data packet into a table. Each time a TCP connection is established for inbound or outbound connections through the Security Appliance, the information about the connection is logged in a stateful session flow table. For a session to be established, information about the connection must match information stored in the table. With this methodology, the stateful filters work on the connections and not the packets, making it a more stringent security method with its sessions immune to hijacking.

Like a fingerprint, stateful packet filtering does the following:

- Obtains the session identifying parameters, IP addresses and ports for each TCP connection

- Logs the data in a stateful session flow table and creates a session object

- Compares the inbound and outbound packets against session flows in the connection table

- Allows data packets to flow through the PIX Security Appliance only if an appropriate connection exists to validate their passage

- Temporarily sets up a connection object until the connection is terminated

Firewall Services Module

The Firewall Services Module (FWSM) is a multigigabit, integrated firewall module for the Cisco Catalyst 6500 series switch and the Cisco 7600 series Internet router. It is fabric enabled and capable of interacting with the bus and the switch fabric. Based on PIX Security Appliance technology, FWSM provides stateful firewall functionality in these switches and routers.

The following are the key features of FWSM:

- High-performance, 5-Gbps throughput, full-duplex firewall functionality
- Based on Cisco PIX Security Appliance technology
- 5-Gbps throughput per module
- Support for 1000 VLANs
- 1 million concurrent connections
- LAN failover: Active or standby, and inter chassis or intra chassis
- Dynamic routing with Open Shortest Path First (OSPF) and passive Routing Information Protocol (RIP)
- Supports up to four modules per chassis

Table 3-3 shows the major differences between the PIX Firewall and FWSM.

Table 3-3   PIX Firewall and FWSM Comparison

	FWSM	PIX Firewall
Interfaces supported	1000 VLANs	100 VLANs
IPS functionality	Not Present	Present
VPN functionality	Not Present	Present
Performance	5 Gbps	1.7 Gbps

Using Security Device Manager

The Cisco Security Device Manager (SDM) is an intuitive, web-based device management tool for Cisco IOS Software-based routers. Cisco SDM simplifies router and security configuration through smart wizards, which help to quickly and easily deploy, configure, and monitor a router without requiring knowledge of the command-line interface. SDM is supported on Cisco 830 series, 1700 series, 1800 series, 2600XM series, 2800 series, 3600 series, 3700 series, and 3800 series routers, and select 7200 series and 7301 routers. Figure 3-4 shows a sample screen shot of the SDM.

Figure 3-4   Security Device Manager (SDM)

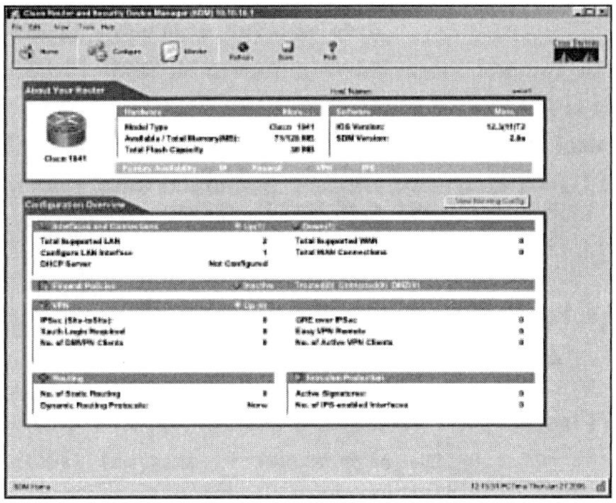

SDM allows users to easily configure routing, switching, security, and QoS services on routers while helping enable proactive management through performance monitoring. Whether deploying a new router or installing SDM on an existing router, users can now remotely configure and monitor these routers without using the Cisco IOS CLI. The SDM GUI aids non-expert users of Cisco IOS Software in their day-to-day operations, provides easy-to-use smart wizards, automates router security management, and assists users through comprehensive online help and tutorials.

SDM smart wizards guide users step by step through router and security configuration workflow by systematically configuring LAN and WAN interfaces, firewall, intrusion prevention system (IPS), and IPsec VPNs. SDM smart wizards can intelligently detect incorrect configurations and propose fixes, such as allowing DHCP traffic through a firewall if the WAN interface is DHCP addressed. Online help embedded within SDM contains appropriate background information, in addition to step-by-step procedures to help users enter correct data in the SDM. Networking and security terms and definitions that users might encounter are included in an online glossary.

For network professionals familiar with Cisco IOS Software and its security features, the SDM offers advanced configuration tools to quickly configure and fine-tune router security features, allowing network professionals to review the commands generated by the SDM before delivering the configuration changes to the router.

SDM helps administrators configure and monitor routers from remote locations using Secure Sockets Layer (SSL) and Secure Shell Version 2 (SSHv2) protocol connections. This technology helps enable a secure connection over the Internet between a web browser and the router. When deployed at a branch office, an SDM-enabled router can be configured and monitored from corporate headquarters, reducing the need for experienced network administrators at the branch office.

SDM Software

SDM comes preinstalled on several Cisco router models manufactured in June 2003 or later that were purchased with the VPN bundle.

SDM is also available as a separate option on all supported routers with Cisco IOS Software security features manufactured in June 2003 or later.

If a router does not have SDM installed, you can download SDM from Cisco.com and install it on the router. The router must contain enough Flash memory to support both the existing Flash file structure and the SDM files. The router also needs 5.2 MB RAM, or 2 MB for Express files and an additional 2 MB for wireless management applications.

Using the SDM Startup Wizard

Use the following process to access SDM for the first time. This procedure assumes that an out-of-box router with SDM installed is being used, or that a default SDM configuration was loaded into Flash:

Step 1. Connect a PC to the lowest-number LAN Ethernet port of the router using a crossover cable.

Step 2. Assign a static IP address to the PC. It is recommended to use 10.10.10.2 with a 255.255.255.0 subnet mask.

Step 3. Launch a supported web browser.

Step 4. Use the URL https://10.10.10.1. A login prompt will appear.

Step 5. Log in using the default user account:

```
Username: sdm
Password: sdm
```

The SDM Startup Wizard opens (see Figure 3-5), requiring a basic network configuration to be entered. To access SDM after the initial Startup Wizard is completed, use either **http:** or **https:**, followed by the router IP address.

When you enter **https:**, it specifies that the SSL protocol be used for a secure connection. If SSL is not available, use **http:** to access the router.

After you have configured the WAN interface, SDM is accessible through a LAN or WAN interface.

Figure 3-5   SDM Startup Wizard

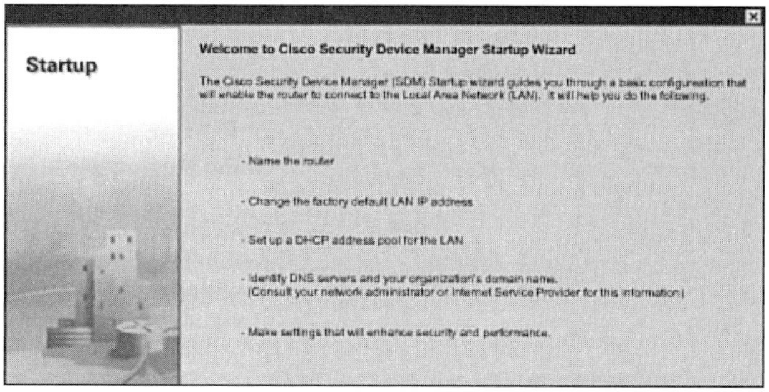

Note

The Startup Wizard information needs to be entered only once and will only appear when a default configuration is detected.

To troubleshoot SDM access problems, use the following tips:

- First determine whether there is a web browser problem by checking the following:

  - ❏ Are Java and JavaScript enabled on the browser? Enable them.

  - ❏ Are pop-up windows being blocked? Disable pop-up blockers on the PC; SDM requires pop-up windows.

  - ❏ Are there any unsupported Java plug-ins installed and running? Disable them using the Windows Control Panel.

- Is the router preventing access? Remember that certain configuration settings are required for SDM to work. Check the following:

  - ❏ Is one of the default configurations being used, or is an existing router configuration being used? Sometimes new configurations disable SDM access.

  - ❏ Is HTTP server enabled on the router? If it is not, enable it and check that other SDM prerequisite parameters are configured, too. Refer to the "Downloading and Installing Cisco SDM" document for the required settings. This document can be found at the web link below.

  - ❏ Did SDM access work before, but not now? Ensure that the PC is not being blocked by a new access control list (ACL). Remember that SDM requires HTTP, SSH, and Telnet access to the router, which could have been inadvertently disabled in a security lockdown.

- Is SDM installed?

  - ❏ The quickest way to determine this is to access it using the appropriate HTTP or HTTPS method https://<router IP address>/flash/sdm.shtml.

❑ Use the show flash command to view the Flash file system and make sure that the required SDM files are present.

Lab 3.2.3   Configure Basic Security Using Security Device Manager (SDM)

In this lab, you copy the SDM files to router Flash memory, configure the router to support SDM, configure a basic firewall, reset a router interface, configure PAT, create a banner, and configure secure management access.

SDM User Interface

The home page supplies basic information about the hardware, software, and configuration of the router, as depicted in Figure 3-6.

Figure 3-6   SDM Main Window Layout and Navigation

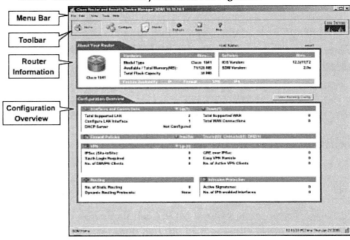

This page contains the following sections:

■ About Your Router—This section shows basic information about the router hardware and software, and contains the following fields:

— Hardware:

Model Type—Shows the router model number

Availability/Total Memory—Available RAM/Total RAM

— **Software:**

IOS Version—The version of Cisco IOS Software currently running on the router.

SDM Version—The version of Cisco Router and SDM software currently running on the router.

Total Flash Capacity—Flash plus Webflash (if applicable).

Feature Availability—The features available in the Cisco IOS image the router is using are designated by a check. The features SDM checks for are IP, firewall, VPN, and IPS.

The More link displays a pop-up window providing additional hardware and software details.

- **Configuration Overview**—This section of the home page summarizes the configuration settings that have been made. To view the running configuration, click **View Running Config**. The Configuration Overview section also contains information about the following parameters:

  — Interfaces and connections

  — Firewall policies

  — VPN

  — Routing

  — Intrusion prevention

SDM Wizards

SDM contains the following wizard options:

- **LAN wizard**—Used to configure the LAN interfaces and DHCP.

- **WAN wizard**—Used to configure PPP, Frame Relay, and High-Level Data Link Control (HDLC) WAN interfaces. Check http://www.cisco.com/go/sdm for the latest information regarding wizards and the interfaces they support.

- **Firewall wizards**—Contains two options:

  — A simple inside/outside firewall wizard.

  — A more complex inside/outside/DMZ with multiple-interfaces wizard

- **VPN wizard**—Contains three options:

  — A secure site-to-site VPN wizard

  — An Easy VPN wizard

  — A generic routing encapsulation (GRE) tunnel with IPsec wizard

- **Security Audit wizard**—Contains two options:

  — The router security audit wizard

  — An easy one-step router security lockdown wizard

Note

At the end of each wizard procedure, all changes are automatically delivered to the router using SDM-generated CLI commands. A preview of the commands to be sent is an available option. The default is to not preview the commands.

■ **Reset wizard**—Resets the router configuration back to the SDM factory default configuration settings.

Using SDM to Configure a WAN

You can use SDM to configure a WAN connection on the router. To start the WAN Wizard, click **the Interface and Connection Wizard Mode** button. The Interfaces and Connections window opens, enabling you to create new WAN connections and to view existing WAN connections.

Select a WAN Connection Type button from the list, as shown in Figure 3-7. The types shown in this list are based on the physical interfaces that are installed on the router and available for configuration. A use case scenario diagram for the selected interface type appears to the right of the list.

Figure 3-7   WAN Wizard; Create a New WAN Connection

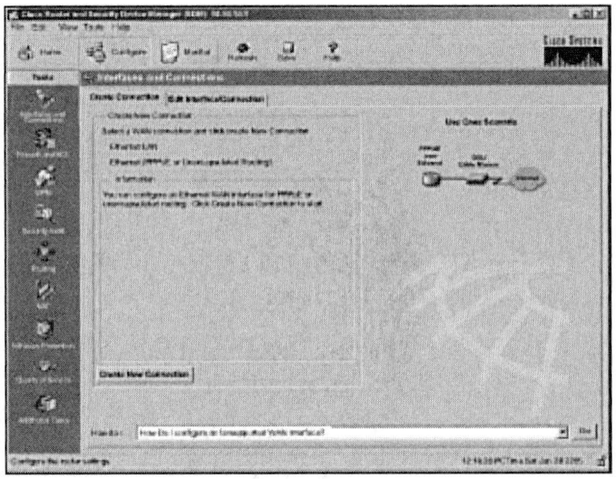

Note

If the router has interfaces that are not supported by SDM, such as an ISDN interface, or a supported interface that has an unsupported configuration that was created using the CLI, the interface will not appear in this window. If another type of connection needs to be configured, the configuration can be done by using the CLI.

Using the Factory Reset Wizard

You can reset the router to factory defaults using the SDM Reset to Factory Default Wizard, as shown in Figure 3-8.

Access the wizard by selecting **Reset to Factory Default** from the Wizard Mode category bar. The Reset to Factory Default window opens.

Figure 3-8   Reset to Factory Default Wizard

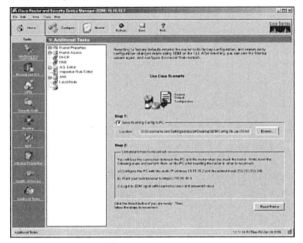

This wizard contains two steps:

Step 1.   **Save Running Config to PC**—This function copies the running configuration of the router to the SDM host PC. SDM verifies that this step is completed before allowing the user to continue with the reset procedure.

Click **Save Running Config to PC**. SDM prompts the user to select a directory on the local PC where it will store the configuration file.

Step 2.   **Reset Router**—This function performs the actual reset procedure.

Click **Reset Router**. The connection to SDM will be lost. Wait a couple of minutes while the router resets and then reloads with the default settings.

Now SDM can reconnect using the lowest-numbered LAN interface of the router.

Note

Before proceeding with Step 2, understand how to reconnect to the router following the reset procedure. The wizard window explains the process for reconnecting to the router. Make sure to read and understand this procedure before continuing with Step 2.

Monitor Mode

Monitor view lets the user view information about the router, the router interfaces, the firewall, and any active VPN connections. Any messages in the router event log are also available for viewing.

The monitor function includes the following elements:

- **Overview**—Displays the router status, including a list of the error log entries, as shown in Figure 3-9

- **Interface Status**—Used to select the interface to monitor and the conditions to view (see Figure 3-10)

- **Firewall Status**—Displays a log showing the number of entry attempts that were denied by the firewall (see Figure 3-11)

- **VPN Status**—Displays statistics about active VPN connections on the router, as shown in Figure 3-12

- **QoS Status**—Displays statistics on QoS configured on the router

- **Logging**—Displays an event log categorized by severity level, as shown in Figure 3-13

Figure 3-9   Monitor Mode

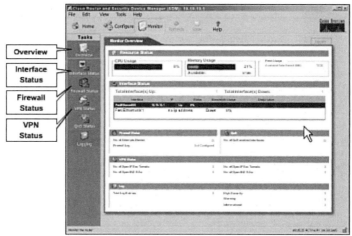

Figure 3-10   Monitor Interface Status

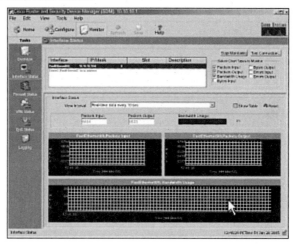

Figure 3-11   Monitor Firewall Status

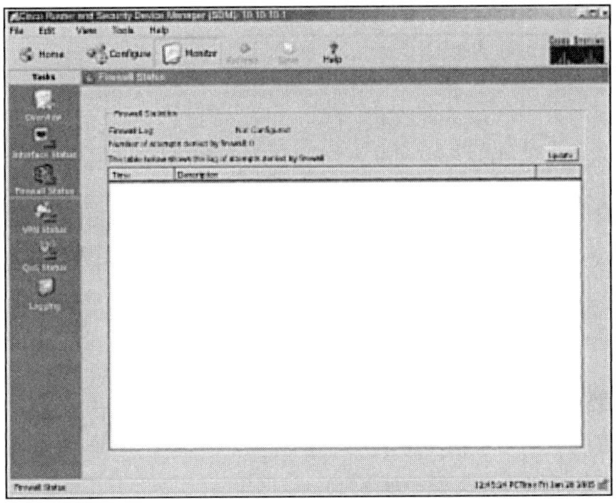

Figure 3-12   Monitor VPN Status

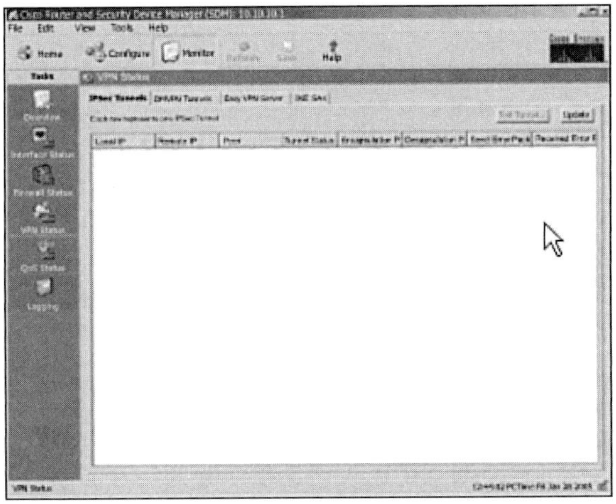

Figure 3-13   Monitor Logging

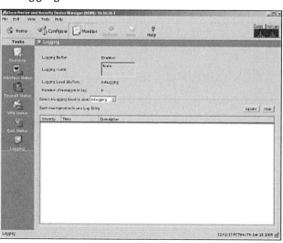

Introduction to the Cisco Security Appliance Family

The PIX Security Appliance 500 series feature set includes stateful inspection firewalling, advanced application and protocol inspection, site-to-site and remote access virtual private networking (VPN), intrusion detection and prevention, and robust multimedia and voice security. The features that are available vary by model.

PIX 501 Security Appliance

The PIX 501 Security Appliance delivers enterprise-class security for small offices and teleworkers. The PIX 501 is ideal for securing high-speed, always-on, broadband environments.

The PIX 501 Security Appliance provides a convenient way for multiple computers to share a single broadband connection. In addition to the RJ-45 9600 baud console port and the integrated 10/100BASE-T port for the outside interface, it features an integrated auto-sensing, auto-medium-dependent interface cross-over (MDIX) four-port 10/100 switch for the inside interface. Auto-MDIX support eliminates the need to use cross-over cables with devices connected to the switch.

The PIX 501 Security Appliance can also secure all network communications from remote offices to corporate networks across the Internet using its standards-based Internet Key Exchange (IKE)/IPsec VPN capabilities. The PIX 501 can act as a DHCP to automatically assign network addresses to the computers when they are powered on.

With PIX 501 Security Appliance Software Release 6.3, several product-licensing options are available. Each user license supports a maximum number of concurrent source IP addresses from the internal network to traverse through the PIX 501. 10-user, 50-user, or unlimited-user licenses are available.

For VPN encryption, there are two options, Data Encryption Standard (DES), which supports 56-bit DES encryption, or Triple-DES (3DES), which supports both 168-bit 3DES and up to 256-bit Advanced Encryption Standard (AES) encryption.

PIX 506E Security Appliance

The Cisco PIX 506E Security Appliance delivers enterprise-class security for remote office, branch office, and small-to-medium business (SMB) networks. The PIX 506E supports two 10/100 Fast Ethernet interfaces and two 802.1q-based virtual interfaces.

The PIX 506E Security Appliance license is provided in a single, unlimited-user license. There are two VPN encryption options: DES, which supports 56-bit DES encryption; or 3DES, which supports both 168-bit 3DES and up to 256-bit AES encryption.

PIX 515E Security Appliance

The Cisco PIX 515E Security Appliance delivers enterprise-class security for SMB and enterprise networks. The chassis is one-rack unit (1RU) in size. The PIX 515E supports up to six 10/100 Ethernet ports. With the restricted license, it supports 3 interfaces and 10 VLANs. With the unrestricted license (UR), it supports 6 interfaces, 25 VLANs, and 5 security contexts.

This model also features integrated hardware-based IPsec acceleration, delivering VPN performance of up to 130 Mbps while freeing system resources for other security functions. IPsec acceleration is provided by an integrated PIX Firewall VPN Accelerator Plus card (VAC+), or the PIX Security Appliance VAC. There is more information on the VAC and VAC+ cards later in this lesson.

The PIX 515E Security Appliance comes with 16 MB of Flash memory and uses TFTP for image download and upgrade.

PIX 525 Security Appliance

The PIX 525 Security Appliance delivers enterprise-class security for medium-to-large enterprise networks. The modular two-rack unit (2RU) design incorporates two 10/100 Fast Ethernet interfaces and supports a combination of additional 10/100 Fast Ethernet interfaces or Gigabit Ethernet interfaces. With the restricted license, it supports up to 6 interfaces and 25 VLANS. With the UR license, it supports up to 10 interfaces, 100 VLANs, and 50 security contexts.

The PIX 525 Security Appliance also offers multiple power-supply options. Either AC or a 48 DC power supply is available. Either option can be paired with a second power supply for redundancy and high availability.

PIX 535 Security Appliance

The PIX 535 Security Appliance delivers enterprise-class security for large enterprise and service provider networks. The modular three-rack unit (3RU) design supports a combination of up to 10/100 Fast Ethernet interfaces or Gigabit Ethernet interfaces, integrated VPN Accelerator card, and redundant power supplies. With the restricted license, it supports up to 8 interfaces and 50 VLANs. With the UR license, it supports up to 14 interfaces, 200 VLANs, and 100 security contexts.

Note

If, after configuring a PIX Security Appliance for Gigabit Ethernet cards, the cards are replaced with 10/100 Ethernet cards, the order of the cards in the configuration changes from what was originally configured. For example, if a Gigabit Ethernet card is configured as ethernet0 and assigned to the inside interface, this card might no longer appear as ethernet0 if it is replaced with a 10/100 Ethernet card

The PIX 535 Security Appliance has a throughput of 1.7 Gbps, with the ability to handle up to 500,000 concurrent connections and 5000 IPsec tunnels. The PIX 535 comes with 16 MB of Flash memory.

Adaptive Security Appliance Models

The Adaptive Security Appliance 5500 series provides a multilayered defense for enterprise networks through rich, integrated security services, including stateful inspection firewall services, advanced application and protocol inspection, site-to-site and remote-access VPN, WebVPN, intrusion prevention, and robust multimedia and voice security. The traffic throughput, number of interfaces, and number of concurrent connections vary by model.

ASA 5510 Adaptive Security Appliance

The ASA 5510 Adaptive Security Appliance delivers enterprise-class security for SMBs and enterprise networks. The modular one-rack unit (1RU) design incorporates up to five 10/100 Fast Ethernet interfaces and supports an optional Security Services Module (SSM) slot which provides inline IPS.

The ASA 5510 Adaptive Security Appliance has a throughput of 100 Mbps, with the ability to handle up to 64,000 concurrent connections. It supports active/standby failover. The ASA 5510 can deliver 150-Mbps IPS throughput when an AIP SSM model 10 is added to the appliance.

ASA 5520 Adaptive Security Appliance

The ASA 5520 Adaptive Security Appliance delivers enterprise-class security for small medium businesses and enterprise networks. The modular one-rack unit (1RU) design incorporates four 10/100/1000 Gigabit Ethernet interfaces and supports an SSM slot that provides inline IPS.

The ASA 5520 Adaptive Security Appliance has a throughput of 200 Mbps, with the ability to handle up to 130,000 concurrent connections. It supports active/standby and active/active failover. The ASA 5520 can deliver 375 Mbps IPS throughput when an AIP SSM model 20 is added to the appliance.

ASA 5540 Adaptive Security Appliance

The ASA 5540 Adaptive Security Appliance delivers enterprise-class security for enterprise networks. Its modular one-rack unit (1RU) design incorporates four 10/100/1000 Gigabit Ethernet interfaces one 10/100 Fast Ethernet management interface, and an optional SSM slot that provides inline IPS.

The ASA 5540 Adaptive Security Appliance has a throughput of 400 Mbps, with the ability to handle up to 280,000 concurrent connections. The ASA 5540 can deliver 450-Mbps IPS throughput when an AIP SSM model 20 is added to the appliance.

Front-Panel LEDs

Figure 3-14 shows the ASA 5500 family front panel with the labeled LEDs:

- **Power**—When the ASA 55X0 has power, the light shines.

- **Status**—When the power-up diagnostics are running or the system is booting, the light flashes. When the system passes power-up diagnostics, the green light shines. When power-up diagnostics fail, the amber light shines.

- **Active**—When there is network activity, the light flashes.

- **VPN**—When data is passing through the interface, the light shines.

- **Flash**—When the Compact Flash is accessed, the light shines.

Figure 3-14   ASA55X0 Front Panel

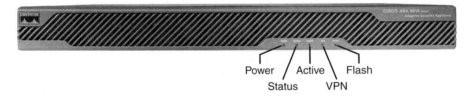

Back Panel

The ASA 5500 family back plane can be logically divided into two sections. These two sections are the fixed interfaces and the SSM slots, as shown in Figure 3-15. The fixed interfaces on an ASA 5510 provide up to five 10/100BASE-T Ethernet ports. The ASA 5520 and 5540 provide four 10/100/1000 and one 10/100BASE-T Ethernet ports. The SSM slot provides the ability to add other high-performance services to the ASA 55X0 family, such as the IPS-SSM.

Figure 3-15   ASA 55X0 Back Panel

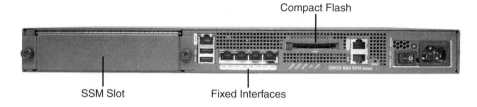

Connectors

The following lists the ASA 5520 and 5540 back-plane connectors as shown in Figure 3-16:

- Power supply—Supports either an AC or DC power supply module

- Console port—Used to connect a computer to the ASA 5520 and 5540 for console operations.

- User Compact Flash

- 10/100 out-of-band management port

- USB 2.0 ports

- Four 10/100/1000BASE-T Ethernet ports

- AUX ports

Figure 3-16   ASA55X0 Connectors

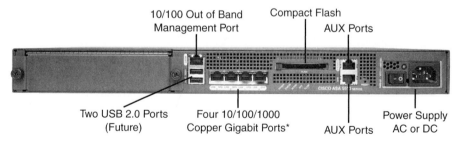

*ASA 5510 Supports 10/100 Fast Ethernet Ports

PIX Security Appliance Licensing

Current PIX Security Appliance licensing is based on a feature-based license key system. The PIX license determines the level of service it provides, its functions in a network, and the maximum number of interfaces and memory it can support.

For the PIX Security Appliance family, the following licensing is available:

■ **PIX 501 Security Appliance**—Provided with a 10-user, 50-user, or unlimited-user licenses in PIX Security Appliance Software Release 6.3. Each license allows up to a specified number of concurrent source IP addresses from the internal network to traverse the PIX. For instance, the 50-user license allows up to 50 concurrent source IP addresses from the internal network to traverse the PIX. If a PIX 501 Security Appliance requires more concurrent users, an upgrade license can be purchased.

■ **PIX 506E Security Appliance**—Provided in a single, unlimited-user license.

■ **PIX 515E Security Appliance, 525, and 535 models**—Available with the following basic license types:

— **Unrestricted (UR)**—PIX platforms in a UR license mode allow installation and use of the maximum number of interfaces and RAM supported by the platform. The UR license supports failover.

— **Restricted (R)**—PIX platforms in a restricted license mode limit the number of interfaces supported and the amount of RAM available within the system. An R licensed PIX does not support contexts or failover configurations.

— **Failover (FO) Active/Standby**—Places the PIX in a failover mode for use alongside another PIX with an unrestricted license. Only one unit can be actively processing user traffic while the other unit acts as a hot standby.

— **Failover (FO) Active/Active**—Places the PIX in a failover mode for use alongside another PIX with an unrestricted license, or two UR licenses. Both units can actively process firewall traffic while at the same time serving as a backup for their peer unit. Active/active failover is supported using security contexts.

Cisco supplies an activation key with each license. The activation key is based on the type of license and the serial number of the PIX. To enable the license features, enter the activation key into the PIX configuration. Starting with PIX Security Appliance Software Release 7.0, a PIX supports two kinds of license activation keys:

■ Existing 4-tuple license activation key for PIX Security Appliance Version 6.3

■ A new 5-tuple license activation key for PIX and ASA Security Appliance Version 7.0 only

Note

An activation key is tied to a specific PIX Security Appliance, such as PIX-serial number 12345678.

Unlike the PIX Version 6.3 which always requires a valid license key to run, PIX and ASA Version 7.0 can run without a license key, but it runs in a default settings. When upgrading from PIX Version 6.3 to PIX and ASA Version 7.0, the existing license key for PIX Version 6.3 is preserved and is saved in a central location on the Flash file system. When you downgrade from PIX and ASA Version 7.0 to PIX Version 6.2 or 6.3, the existing license key for the original PIX Version 6.2 or 6.3 that was saved during the upgrade procedure is retrieved and saved to the PIX Version 6.2 or 6.3 image.

PIX VPN Encryption License

In addition to upgrading the PIX Security Appliance license, administrators might want to add data encryption services or increase the level of data encryption that the PIX can provide. An online form at the PIX Security Appliance Software page on Cisco.com can be completed to obtain a free 56-bit DES key. There is a separate form to install or upgrade to 168-bit 3DES encryption. For failover configurations, the UR and FO Security Appliances each require their own unique corresponding DES or 3DES license for failover functionality.

A DES license provides 56-bit DES. A 3DES license provides 158-bit 3DES and an AES license provides up to 256-bit AES.

Adding cryptographic services and upgrading a PIX Security Appliance license both require obtaining and installing an activation key. You can find current information on obtaining activation keys at Cisco.com.

Security Contexts

A single UR-licensed PIX 515E, 525, or 535 Security Appliance, and a single ASA Security Appliance, can be partitioned into multiple virtual firewalls, known as *security contexts*. Each context is an independent firewall, with its own security policy, interfaces, and administrators. The number of contexts available in a PIX Security Appliance or Adaptive Security Appliance is dependent upon the model and context license. As the network grows, or requirements change, you can purchase an upgrade context license to increase the number of available contexts.

PIX Security Appliance Context Licensing

By default, two contexts are included in the UR PIX 515E, 525, or 535 Security Appliance license. A PIX 515E supports up to 5 contexts, a PIX 525 supports up to 50 contexts, and a PIX 535 supports up to 100 contexts.

Table 3-4 compares the restricted and unrestricted licenses of the PIX 515E, 525, and 535 Security Appliance models.

Table 3-4   PIX 515E, 525, and 535 License Comparison

	Features	Maximum Number of Physical Interfaces	Maximum Number of VLANs	Maximum Number of Contexts	Maximum Memory	Failover
PIX 515E	Restricted	3	10	N/A	64	No
	Unrestricted	6	25	License up to 5	128	Yes
PIX 525	Restricted	6	25	N/A	128	No
	Unrestricted	10	100	License up to 50	256	Yes
PIX 535	Restricted	8	50	N/A	512	No
	Unrestricted	14	200	License up to 100	1024	Yes

ASA Security Appliance Licensing

ASA Security Appliance licensing is also based on a feature-based license key system. The ASA Security Appliance license determines the number of contexts, type of VPN encryption, and number of VPN peers an ASA Security Appliance can support.

By default, the ASA 5520 and 5540 support two contexts. An ASA 5520 Security Appliance supports up to 10 contexts, and an ASA 5540 Security Appliance supports up to 20 contexts.

Table 3-5 compares the ASA Security Appliance license offerings. Across the top of the chart are the ASA Security Appliance features. Down the left side are the ASA5510, ASA5520, and ASA5540 licenses. Each ASA Security Appliance column compares the listed features available with each license.

Table 3-5   ASA 5510, 5520, and 5540 Comparison

Model	Licenses	Interfaces	Security Context	VLANs	IPsec VPN Peers	Failover A/S	A/S	GTP/ GPRS
ASA5510	Base	3 x 10/100	N/A	0	25	Yes	N/A	N/A
	Security +	5 x 10/100	N/A	10	100	Yes	N/A	N/A
ASA5520	Base	4 x 10/100/1000 1 x 10/100	Default of 2 Up to 10	25	300	Yes	Yes	License
	VPN +	4 x 10/100/1000 1 x 10/100	Default of 2 Up to 10	25	750	Yes	Yes	License
ASA5540	Base	4 x 10/100/1000 1 x 10/100	Default of 2 Up to 50	100	500	Yes	Yes	License
	VPN +	4 x 10/100/1000 1 x 10/100	Default of 2 Up to 50	100	2000	Yes	Yes	License
	VPN Premium	4 x 10/100/1000 1 x 10/100	Default of 2 Up to 50	100	5000	Yes	Yes	License

Expanding the Features of the PIX 515E

The two expansion slots support Fast Ethernet expansion option cards and Hardware VPN Accelerator cards. The features of both cards are as follows:

- Single-port and four-port Fast Ethernet expansion option cards are available. With the restricted license, the PIX 515E supports one additional expansion network port. With the restricted license, the PIX 515E supports up to four additional expansion network ports.

- Hardware VPN acceleration is available through the addition of a VAC or VAC+ card. Offloading encryption functions to the VAC and VAC+ cards improves IPsec encryption processing. The VAC card provides 56-bit DES and 168-bit 3DES encryption. The VAC card has a 32-bit, 33-MHz PCI interface. The VAC+ card, in addition to supporting DES and 3DES, provides 128-, 192-, and 256-bit AES encryption. The VAC+ card has a 64-bit, 66-MHz PCI interface.

Expanding the Features of the PIX 525

The PIX 525 Security Appliance supports additional network interfaces through three PCI expansion slots. It supports expansion cards including single-port Fast Ethernet cards, four-port Fast Ethernet cards, single-port Gigabit Ethernet cards, and VAC and VAC+ cards.

A maximum of six interfaces are supported with a Restricted license, and a maximum of 10 interfaces are possible with the Unrestricted license. Currently, a VAC+ card is included with every PIX 525 by default.

When connecting the network cables to the expansion interface ports, use the following guidelines. The first expansion port number, at the top left, is interface 2. Starting from that port and going from left to right and top to bottom, the next port is interface 3, the next is interface 4, and so on.

Expanding the Features of the PIX 535

Gigabit Ethernet (1GE), single- (1FE) and four-port (4FE) Fast Ethernet, and VPN Accelerator cards (VAC and VAC+) are available for the PIX 535. For most card types, there is a 33-MHz and a 66-MHz version. For example, the 1GE card has a 33-MHz PCI interface. The 1GE-66 card has a 66-MHz PCI interface. There are nine interface slots and three buses in the PIX 535.

The slots and buses are configured as follows:

- **Slots 0 and 1**—64-bit/66-MHz bus 0

- **Slots 2 and 3**—64-bit/66-MHz bus 1

- **Slots 4 to 8**—32-bit/33-MHz bus 2

For optimum performance and throughput for the interface circuit boards, use the following guidelines:

- A total of 8 interfaces are configurable on the PIX 535 with the Restricted license, and a total of 14 are configurable with the Unrestricted license.

- For best performance, the 1GE-66, 4FE-66, and VAC+ (66 MHz) circuit boards should be installed in a 64-bit/66-MHz card slot.

- The 1GE, 1FE, 4FE, and VAC (33 MHz) circuit boards should be installed in the 32-bit/33-MHz card slots.

- The 1FE circuit board (33 MHz) can be installed in any bus or slot (32 bit/33 MHz or 64 bit/66 MHz). Up to nine 1FE circuit boards or up to two 4FE circuit boards can be installed. The 1FE circuit boards should be installed in the 32-bit/33-MHz card slots first.

- Do not mix the 1FE circuit boards with the 1GE-66 circuit boards on the same 64-bit/66-MHz bus (bus 0 or bus 1). The overall speed of the bus is reduced by the lower-speed circuit board.

- If stateful failover is enabled for 1GE-66 traffic, the failover link must be PIX-1GE-66. The amount of stateful failover information is proportional to the amount of traffic flowing through the PIX Firewall and, if it is not configured properly, loss of state information or 256-byte block depletion can occur.

- The discontinued 4FE card can be installed only in a 32-bit/33-MHz card slot and must never be installed in a 64-bit/66-MHz card slot. Installation of this circuit board in a 64-bit/66-MHz card slot can cause the system to hang at boot time.

Note

The 1GE circuit board is not recommended for use in the PIX 535 because it can severely degrade performance. It is capable of only half the throughput of the 1GE-66 circuit board. If this circuit board is detected in the PIX 535, a warning about degraded performance will issue.

Expanding the Features of the Adaptive Security Appliance Family

Additional security services for the Cisco ASA 5500 Adaptive Security Appliance family are provided on the Security Services Module (SSM) plug-in hardware modules. SSMs are high-performance modules based on a Pentium 4 class processor designed to provide additional security services. Diskless (Flash-based) design provides improved reliability and a Gigabet Ethernet port for out-of-band management. The current offering is an AIP-SSM card.

The AIP-SSM card is available in two versions: the AIP-SSM-10 and the AIP-SSM-20. The AIP-SSM module can function in inline or promiscuous mode. In the inline mode, packets are sent to the AIP-SSM module, inspected, and then returned to the Adaptive Security Appliance. Operating in inline mode puts the AIP-SSM module directly into the traffic flow. In promiscuous mode, AIP-SSM module is not directly in the packet flow. The AIP-SSM performs analysis on a copy of the traffic instead of on the actual forwarded packets.

The SSM has the following LEDs:

- **Power**—When the SSM has power, the light shines.

- **Status**—When the power-up diagnostics are running or the system is booting, the light flashes. When the system passes power-up diagnostics, the green light shines. When power-up diagnostics fail, the amber light shines.

- **Speed**—With 10 Mbps of traffic, the LED is off. With 100 Mbps traffic, the LED is green. With 1000Mbps of traffic, the LED is amber.

- **Link/Act**—When there is network activity, the light flashes.

Getting Started with the PIX Security Appliance

The PIX Security Appliance contains a command set based on the Cisco IOS, and provides four administrative access modes:

- **Unprivileged mode**—This mode is available when the PIX is first accessed. The > prompt displays. This mode provides a restricted, limited view of PIX settings.

- **Privileged mode**—This mode displays the # prompt and enables users to change the current settings. Any unprivileged command also works in privileged mode.

- **Configuration mode**—This mode displays the (config)# prompt and enables users to change system configurations. All privileged, unprivileged, and configuration commands work in this mode.

- **Monitor mode**—This is a special mode that enables users to update the image over the network or to perform password recovery. While in the monitor mode, users can enter commands specifying the location of the TFTP server and the PIX software image or password-recovery binary file to download.

Within each access mode, most commands can be abbreviated down to the fewest unique characters for a command. For example, you can enter **sh run** to view the configuration instead of entering the full command **show running-config**. You can enter the abbreviation **en** rather than **enable** to start privileged mode, and **con t** rather than **configuration terminal** to start configuration mode.

Configuring the PIX Security Appliance

Upon first accessing a Security Appliance, the administrator is presented with the pixfirewall> prompt when using a PIX Security Appliance, or ciscoasa> for an Adaptive Security Appliance. This is the prompt for the unprivileged mode. This mode enables users to view restricted settings. In a previously configured PIX, pixfirewall> may be replaced with a network specific hostname prompt such as Paris>, London>, and so on.

To get started with the PIX, the first command used is the **enable** [*priv_level*] command. This command provides entrance to the privileged access modes. The *priv_level* argument specifies the privilege level, with a value of 0 to 15. After the **enable** command is entered, the PIX prompts the user for a privileged mode password. By default, a password is not required, so **Enter** can be pressed at the password prompt, or a password can be created. In privileged mode, the prompt changes to #.

To set the privileged mode password, enter the following command:

```
enable password pw [level priv_level] [encrypted]
```

The password is case sensitive and can be up to 16 characters long. You can use any character except the question mark, space, and colon. The password should be written down and stored in a manner consistent with the security policy. After this password is created, it cannot be viewed again because it is stored as an MD5 hash. The **show enable** password command lists the encrypted form of the password. After passwords are encrypted, they cannot be reversed back to plain text.

Accessing Configuration Mode

Use the **configure terminal** command to move from privileged mode to configuration mode. As soon as the command is entered, the prompt changes to (config)#. Configuration mode enables a user to change system configurations. Use the **exit** or **quit** command to exit and return to the previous mode.

Example 3-1 demonstrates accessing and exiting configuration mode

Note

You can create configurations on a text editor and then cut and paste them into the configuration. The configuration can be pasted in one line at a time, or the entire configuration can be pasted at once. Always check the configuration after pasting large blocks of text to ensure that everything has been copied.

Note

An empty password is also changed into an encrypted string.

```
Example 3-1    Moving to and Exiting from Configuration Mode
pixfirewall>enable
password:
pixfirewall#configure terminal
pixfirewall(config)#exit
pixfirewall#exit
pixfirewall>
```

The help Command

Help information is available from the PIX Security Appliance command line using the **help** [*command* | **?**] command. Entering **help?** displays all commands that are available in the current privilege level and mode, as demonstrated in Example 3-2.

You can display the help, usage, description, and syntax for an individual command by entering the **help** command followed by the command name. as follows:

```
pixfirewall>help enable
```

Example 3-2 shows the usage and description for the **enable** command by using the **help** command.

If a command string is unknown, you can enter **?** after the command. The command syntax is listed as the output.

```
Example 3-2     Using the help Command
pixfirewall>help ?

enable    Turn on privileged commands
exit      Exit the current command mode
login     Log in as a particular user
logout    Exit from current command mode, and to unprivileged mode
quit      Exit the current command mode


pixfirewall>help enable
USAGE:

 Enable [<priv_level>]

DESCRIPTION:

enable    Turn on privileged commands
```

Security Levels

The security level, as shown in Figure 3-17, designates whether an interface is trusted, and more protected, or untrusted, and less protected, relative to another interface.

Figure 3-17   ASA Security Level Example

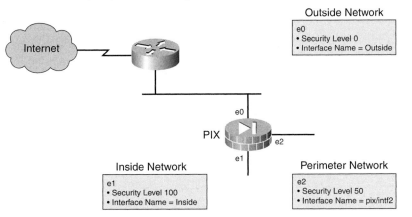

An interface is considered more trusted in relation to another interface if its security level is higher than the security level of the other interface, and is considered less trusted in relation to another interface if its security level is lower than the security level of the other interface.

The primary rule for security levels is that an interface with a higher security level can access an interface with a lower security level. Conversely, an interface with a lower security level cannot access an interface with a higher security level without an ACL. Security levels range from 0 to 100. The specific rules for these security levels are as follows:

- **Security level 0**—This is the lowest security level. It is the default setting for the outside interface of the PIX Security Appliance and cannot be changed. Because 0 is the least trusted interface security level, the least trusted network should be set behind this interface. This limits access to other interfaces unless given permission. Security level 0 is usually assigned to the interface connected to the Internet.

- **Security levels 1 through 99**—These are the security levels that can be assigned to the perimeter interface connected to the PIX Security Appliance. Security levels are assigned based on the type of access each device is desired to have.

- **Security level 100**—This is the highest security level. It is the default setting for the inside interface of the PIX Security Appliance, and it cannot be changed. Because 100 is the most trusted interface security level, the corporate network should be set up behind it. This is so it will deny any access coming from all the lower security levels except to those that are given permission. This will also allow every device behind this interface to have access outside the corporate network.

The following are examples of different interface connections between the PIX Security Appliance and other perimeter devices:

- **Higher security level interface to a lower security level interface**—For traffic originating from the inside interface of the PIX with a security level of 100 to the outside interface of the PIX with a security level of 0, all IP-based traffic is allowed unless it is restricted by ACLs, authentication, or authorization.

- **Lower security level interface to a higher security level interface**—For traffic originating from the outside interface of the PIX with a security level of 0 to the inside interface of the PIX with a security level of 100,all packets are dropped unless specifically allowed by an **access-list** command. The traffic can be restricted further if authentication and authorization is used.

- **Same secure interface to a same secure interface**—No traffic flows between two Interfaces with the same security level.

Note

The PIX Security Appliance can support up to 14 interfaces depending on the model and license.

Basic PIX Security Appliance Configuration Commands

The following are some of the primary commands necessary to configure the PIX Security Appliance:

- **hostname**—Assigns a hostname to the PIX

- **interface**—Configures the type and capability of each perimeter interface

- **nameif**—Assigns a name to each perimeter interface

- **ip address**—Assigns an IP address to each interface

- **security level**—Assigns the security level for the perimeter interface

- **speed**—Assigns the connection speed

- **duplex**—Assigns the duplex communications

hostname Command

The PIX Security Appliance default hostname label is pixfirewall. In a network of multiple PIX Security Appliances, it might be advantageous to assign a unique hostname label to each one. To accomplish this, use the following command:

```
pixfirewall(config)#hostname newname
```

The **hostname** command changes the hostname label on the prompts. The hostname can be up to 16 alphanumeric characters, and upper- and lowercase. For example, to change default hostname label of pixfirewall to fw1, you enter the following:

```
pixfirewall(config)#hostname fw1
fw1(config)#
```

The default name for the Adaptive Security Appliance is ciscoasa.

interface Command

To identify a perimeter interface and its slot location on the PIX Security Appliance, use the following command:

```
pixfirewall(config)#interface hardware_id
```

The PIX Security Appliance interfaces are numbered from 0 to *x*, *x* being the highest number interface on the PIX. The Adaptive Security Appliance interfaces are numbered 0/0, 0/1, 0/2, and so on. For each PIX in your network, enter the appropriate interface type, slot and port number. If the device is a PIX, for the Ethernet 0 interface, you enter **interface ethernet0**. If the device is an Adaptive Security Appliance, for the Gigabit Ethernet 0/0 interface, you enter **interface GigabitEthernet0/0**. After entering the interface command, the CLI prompt changes to the interface configuration subcommand level, as demonstrated here:

```
pix1(config)#interface ethernet0
pix1(config-if)#
```

In the interface configuration subcommands, you can configure the hardware speed and duplex, interface name, security level, IP address, and many other settings. For an interface to pass traffic, the **nameif**, **ip address**, **security level**, and **no shutdown** interface configuration subcommands are necessary. For physical interfaces, the default state is shut down, so you must enter the **no shutdown** command to enable the interface. The default security level for the interface can be used, or the security level can be changed so that interfaces can communicate with each other.

The syntax for the **interface** command is as follows:

```
interface {physical_interface [.subinterface] | mapped_name}
```

where:

- *physical_interface*—Specifies the type, slot, and port number as *type{slot/}port*. A space between the *type* and *slot/port* is optional. Depending on your Security Appliance model, the types can be **ethernet**, **gigabitethernet**, or **management**. If your model does not include slots, enter the type followed by the port number. If your model does include slots, enter the *type* followed by *slot/port*. See the hardware documentation that came with your model to identify the interface type, slot, and port number.

- *subinterface*—(Optional) Designates a logical subinterface with an integer between 1 and 4294967293.

- *mapped_name*—Specifies the mapped name, if assigned using the **allocate-interface** command, in multiple-context mode.

nameif Command

To assign a name to each perimeter interface on the PIX Security Appliance, use the following command:

```
pixfirewall(config-if)#nameif hardware_id if_name
```

where:

- *hardware_id*—Assigns the hardware name for the network interface that specifies the slot location of the interface on the Security Appliance motherboard. For more information on Security Appliance hardware configuration, refer to the *Cisco Security Appliance Hardware Installation Guide*.

A logical choice for an Ethernet interface is ethernet*n*. These names can also be abbreviated with any leading characters in the name, for example, ether1 or e2.

- *if_name*—Describes the perimeter interface. This name is assigned by you, and must be used in all future configuration references to the perimeter interface.

For the PIX in Figure 3-18, the first two interfaces have the default names **inside** and **outside**, while interface ethernet2 was assigned a name of dmz with the following command sequence:

```
pixfirewall(config)#interface ethernet2
pixfirewall(config-if)#nameif dmz
```

Figure 3-18   Assigning a Name to PIX Perimeter Interfaces

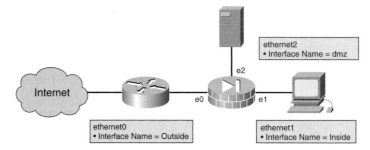

ip address Command

You can configure each interface on the PIX Security Appliance with an IP address by using the following command:

```
pixfirewall(config-if)#ip address ip_address [mask] [standby ip_address]
```

where:

- *ip_address*—Specifies the IP address of the interface.

- *mask*—(Optional) Specifies the subnet mask of the IP address. If you do not set the mask, the Security Appliance uses the default mask for the IP address class.

- *standby ip_address*—Specifies the IP address for the standby unit for failover.

The **clear ip** command resets all interface IP addresses to no IP address. For the PIX in Figure 3-19, the DMZ interface (e0) is configured with an IP address of 192.168.1.2 and a mask of 255.255.255.0 using the following command sequence:

```
pixfirewall(config)#interface ethernet0
pixfirewall(config-if)#nameif outside
pixfirewall(config-if)#ip address 192.168.1.2 255.255.255.0
```

Figure 3-19   Configuring an IP Address for a PIX Interface

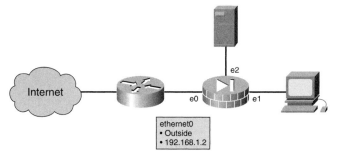

ip address dhcp Command

Instead of manually configuring an IP address on the PIX Security Appliance interface, you can use DHCP client feature to have the PIX dynamically retrieve an IP address from a DHCP server. With the PIX configured as a DHCP client, a DHCP server can configure the PIX interface with an IP address, subnet mask, and optionally a default route. Use the following command to enable this feature:

```
pixfirewall(config-if)#ip address if_name dhcp [setroute] [retry retry_cnt]
```

For the PIX in Figure 3-20, the e0 interface is configured to receive an IP address on the outside interface via DHCP using the following command sequence:

```
pixfirewall(config)#interface ethernet0
pixfirewall(config-if)#nameif outside
pixfirewall(config-if)#ip address dhcp
```

Figure 3-20   Using DHCP for a PIX Interface

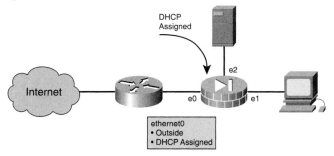

Reenter the **ip address dhcp** subcommand to release and renew a DHCP lease from the PIX Security Appliance. To delete the DHCP leased IP address, use the **no** form of this command. The **debug dhcpc event | packet | error** command provides debugging tools for the DHCP client feature.

security level Command

To specify the PIX Security Appliance security level, use the following command:

```
pixfirewall(config-if)#security-level [level]
```

Remember that the inside and outside interfaces are assigned security levels by default. The inside interface has a default security level of 100, and the outside interface has a default security level of 0. As other interfaces are named, the system assigns a default security level of 0 to each interface. For these newly named interfaces, the administrator should change the security level to a unique number between 1 and 99.

Normally, interfaces on the same security level cannot communicate. If it is necessary that interfaces with the same security level are able to communicate, use the same-security-traffic command. Two interfaces could be assigned to the same level to allow them to communicate without using NAT, if more than 100 communicating interfaces are needed, or if protection features are to be applied equally for traffic between two interfaces.

If the security level of an interface is changed, you can use the **clear xlate** command to clear all existing connections before they are timed out. Clearing the translation table disconnects all current connections.

speed Command

Although the hardware speed is set to automatic speed sensing by default, recommended practice dictates that you should specify the speed of the network interfaces. Doing so enables the PIX Security Appliance to operate in network environments that might include devices that do not handle auto-sensing correctly.

To set the speed of a Fast Ethernet or Gigabit Ethernet interface, use the **speed** command in interface configuration subcommand mode:

```
pixfirewall(config-if)#speed {auto | 10 | 100 | 1000 | nonegotiate}
```

where:

- **auto**—Automatically detects the speed.

- **10**—Sets the speed to 10BASE-T.

- **100**—Sets the speed to 100BASE-T.

- **1000**—Sets the speed to 1000BASE-T.

- **nonegotiate**—Sets the speed to 1000 Mbps for Shortest Path First (SFP) media types. SFP does not allow any other setting.

To restore the speed setting to the default, use the **no** form of this command.

duplex Command

To set the duplex of a Fast Ethernet or copper Gigabit Ethernet interface, use the following command in interface configuration mode:

```
pixfirewall(config-if)#duplex {auto | full | half}
```

where:

- **auto**—Automatically detects the duplex mode
- **full**—Sets the duplex mode to full duplex
- **half**—Sets the duplex mode to full duplex

To restore the duplex setting to the default, use the **no** form of this command.

Additional PIX Security Appliance Configuration Commands

The following are some additional configuration commands for the PIX Security Appliance:

- **nat-control**—Enables or disables the NAT configuration requirement
- **nat**—Shields IP addresses on the inside network from the outside network
- **global**—Creates a pool of one or more IP addresses for use in NAT and PAT
- **route**—Defines a static or default route for an interface

Network Address Translation (NAT)

Network Address Translation (NAT) enables internal IP addresses that are behind the PIX Security Appliance to remain unknown to external networks. NAT accomplishes this by translating the internal IP addresses, which are not globally unique, into globally accepted IP addresses before packets are forwarded to the external network. NAT is implemented in the PIX with the **nat** and **global** commands.

When an outbound IP packet that is sent from a device on the inside network reaches a PIX Security Appliance with NAT configured, the source address is extracted and compared to an internal table of existing translations. If the address of the device is not already in the table, it is then translated. A new entry is created for that device, and it is assigned an IP address from a pool of global IP addresses. This global pool is configured with the **global** command. After this translation occurs, the table is updated and the translated IP packet is forwarded. After a user-configurable timeout period, or the default of three hours, during which there have been no translated packets for that particular IP address, the entry is removed from the table, and the global address is freed for use by another inside device.

In Figure 3-21, host 10.0.0.11 starts an outbound connection. The PIX Security Appliance translates the source address to 192.168.0.20. Packets from host 10.0.0.11 are seen on the outside as having a source address of 192.168.0.20. Return packets from the outside server at IP address 192.168.10.11 are addressed to the globally assigned address, 192.168.0.20.

Figure 3-21   Network Address Translation

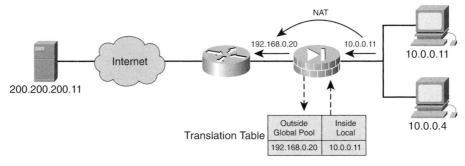

nat-control Command

To enable NAT incrementally, enter the following command:

```
pixfirewall(config)#nat-control
```

With NAT disabled, only IP addresses that need to be protected require a NAT rule. With **nat-control** enabled, all packets traversing the PIX Security Appliance require a NAT rule. There are two NAT policies: an inside NAT policy and an outside NAT policy. They are used to perform address translation on each packet that traverses the PIX. If **nat-control** is configured, the PIX enforces address hiding. Specifically, each inside address must have an inside NAT rule configured before communication is permitted through the PIX.

In addition, if outside NAT is enabled on an interface, each outside address must have an outside NAT rule configured before communication is permitted through the PIX Security Appliance. If **nat-control** is not configured, only hosts that undergo NAT need a NAT rule configured. If no NAT policy matches the traversing packet, address rewrite is not performed, and PIX Security Appliance processing continues. By default, **nat-control** is not enabled.

nat Command

The first step in enabling NAT on a PIX Security Appliance is to enter the following command:

```
pixfirewall(config)#nat [(if_name)] nat_id address [netmask] [dns] [[tcp] tcp_max_conns
[emb_limit] [norandomseq]]] [udp udp_max_conns]
```

where:

- *if_name*—Specifies the name of the interface attached to the network to be translated.

- *nat_id*—A number greater than zero (0) that specifies the global address pool you want to use for dynamic address translation.

- *address*—Specifies the IP address to be translated. You can use 0.0.0.0 to allow all hosts to start outbound connections. The 0.0.0.0 address can be abbreviated as 0.

- *netmask*—Specifies the network mask for the address. You can use the 0.0.0.0 mask to allow all outbound connections to translate with IP addresses from the global pool.

- **dns**—Specifies to use the created translation to rewrite the DNS address recorded.

- *max_conns*—Specifies the maximum number of simultaneous connections the local_ip hosts are to allow. (Idle connections are closed after the idle timeout specified by the **time-out conn** command.)

- *emb_limit*—Specifies the maximum number of embryonic connection per host. (An embryonic connection is a connection request that has not finished the necessary handshake between source and destination.) Set a small value for slower systems, and a higher value for faster systems. The default is 0, which allows unlimited embryonic connections.

- **tcp**—(Optional) Specifies that the maximum TCP connections and embryonic limit are set for the TCP protocol.

- *tcp_max_conns*—(Optional) Specifies the maximum number of simultaneous TCP connections that the **local_ip** hosts allow. Idle connections are closed after the time that is specified by the entry.

- **udp**—(Optional) Specifies a maximum number of UDP connection parameters that can be configured.

- *udp_max_conns*—(Optional) Sets the maximum number of simultaneous UDP connections that the **local_ip** hosts are each allowed to use. Idle connections are closed.

The **nat** command can specify translation for a single host or a range of hosts. The **nat** command has two major components:

- *nat_id*

- IP address or range of IP addresses

A *nat_id* is a number from 1 to 2147483647 that specifies the hosts for dynamic address translation. The dynamic addresses are chosen **from** a global address pool created with the global command. The nat command *nat_id* number must match the *nat_id* number in the global command if you want to use that specific global pool of IP addresses for the dynamic address translation.

For example, the **nat (inside) 1 10.0.0.0 255.255.255.0** command means that all outbound connections from a host within the specified network, 10.0.0.0, can pass through the PIX Security Appliance with address translation. The **nat (inside) 1 10.0.0.11 255.255.255.255** command means that only outbound connections originating from the inside host 10.0.0.11 are translated as the packet passes through the PIX. Administrators can use 0.0.0.0 to allow all hosts to be translated. The 0.0.0.0 can be abbreviated as 0. As shown in Figure 3-22, all inside hosts making outbound connections with the **nat (inside) 1 0.0.0.0 0.0.0.0** command are translated. The *nat_id* identifies the global address pool the PIX will use for the dynamic address translation.

Figure 3-22   Enabling NAT on the PIX

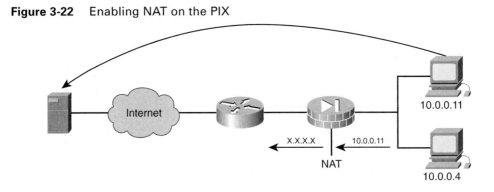

global Command

For a local address to be translated using NAT, you must define a global pool of addresses. In a PIX Security Appliance configuration, you might have more than one global pool configured. Each outbound network address translation is associated with a *nat_id*. Each global pool has a corresponding *nat_id*. The PIX uses the *nat_id* of the outbound IP packet to identify which global pool of addresses to select a translation IP address from. The *nat_id* of the outbound packet must match the *nat_id* of the global pool. The PIX assigns addresses from the designated global pool starting from the low end to the high end of the range specified in the global command. The pool of global IP addresses is configured with the following command:

```
pixfirewall(config)#global [(if_name)] nat_id {global_ip[-global_ip] [netmask
global_mask]} | interface
```

where:

- *if_name*—Describes the external network interface name where you will use the global addresses.

- *nat_id*—Identifies the global pool and matches it with its respective **nat** command.

- *global_ip*—Specifies a single IP address or the beginning IP address for a range of global IP addresses.

- *-global_ip*—Specifies the end of a range of global IP addresses.

- *global_mask*—Specifies the network mask for the *global_ip* address. If subnetting is in effect, use the subnet mask (for example, 255.255.255.128). If you specify an address range that overlaps subnets with the **netmask** command, this command will not use the broadcast or network address in the pool of global addresses. For example, if you use 255.255.255.128 and an address range of 192.150.50.20–192.150.50.140, the 192.150.50.127 broadcast address and the 192.150.50.128 network address will not be included in the pool of global addresses.

- *interface*—Specifies Port Address Translation (PAT) using the IP address at the interface.

If the **nat** command is used, the companion command, **global**, must be configured to define the pool of translated IP addresses. Use the **no global** command to delete a global entry.

In Figure 3-23, host 10.0.0.11 starts an outbound connection. The *nat_id* of the outbound packet is 1. In this instance, a global IP address pool of 192.168.0.20-254 is also identified with a *nat_id* of 1. The PIX assigns an IP address of 192.168.0.20. It is the lowest available IP address of the range specified in the **global** command. Packets from host 10.0.0.11 are seen on the outside as having a source address of 192.168.0.20.

The commands to make this possible are as follows:

```
pixfirewall(config)#nat (inside) 10.0.0.0 0.0.0.0
pixfirewall(config)#global (outside) 1 192.168.0.20-192.168.0.254
```

Figure 3-23   Translating a Local Address Using NAT via a Global Pool of Addresses

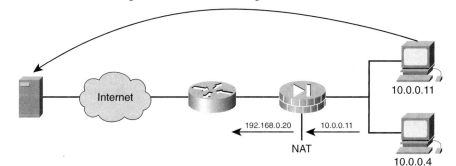

Note

The PIX Security Appliance uses the global addresses to assign a virtual IP address to an internal NAT address. After adding, changing, or removing a **global** statement, use the **clear xlate** command to make the IP addresses available in the translation table.

route Command

To enter a static route for an interface, use the following command:

```
pixfirewall(config)#route if_name ip_address netmask gateway_ip [metric]
```

where:

- *if_name*—Describes the internal or external network interface name.

- *ip_address*—Describes the internal or external IP address. Use 0.0.0.0 to specify a default route. The 0.0.0.0 IP address can be abbreviated as 0.

- *netmask*—Specifies a network mask to apply to ip_address. Use 0.0.0.0 to specify a default route. The 0.0.0.0 IP address can be abbreviated as 0.

- *gateway_ip*—Specifies the IP address of the gateway router (the next-hop address for this route).

- *metric*—Specifies the number of hops to gateway_ip. If you are not sure, enter 1. Your WAN administrator can supply this information, or you can use the **traceroute** command to obtain the number of hops. The default is 1 if a metric is not specified.

To enter a default route, set *ip_address* and *netmask* to 0.0.0.0, or the shortened form of 0. In Figure 3-24, a **route** command with the IP address of 0.0.0.0 identifies the command as the default route. The PIX transmits all destination packets not listed in its routing table out the outside interface to the router at IP address 192.168.0.1.

The commands that make this possible are as follows:

```
pixfirewall(config)#route outside 0.0.0.0 0.0.0.0 192.168.0.1.1
pixfirewall(config)#route inside 10.0.1.0 255.255.255.0 10.0.0.102 1
```

Figure 3-24   Defining a Static Route for an Interface

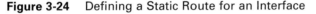
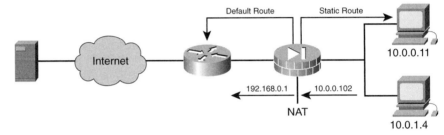

Static routes can be created to access specific networks beyond the locally connected networks. For example, in Figure 3-24, the PIX Security Appliance sends all packets destined to the 10.0.1.0 255.255.255.0 network out the inside interface to the router at IP address 10.0.0.102. This static route was created by using the command **route inside 10.0.1.0 255.255.255.0 10.0.0.102 1**. The router knows how to route the packet to the destination network of 10.0.1.0.

All routes entered using the **route** command are stored in the configuration when it is saved. The IP address of one of the interfaces of the PIX can be used as the gateway address. If this is done, the PIX broadcasts an Address Resolution Protocol (ARP) request for the MAC address of the destination IP address in the packet instead of broadcasting a request for the MAC address of the gateway IP address.

name Command

To configure a list of name-to-IP address mappings on the PIX Security Appliance, use the following command:

```
pixfirewall(config)#name ip_address name
```

where:

- *ip_address*—Specifies the IP address of the host being named

- *name*—Specifies the name being assigned to the IP address

Allowable characters for the *name* are a to z, A to Z, 0 to 9, a dash (-), and an underscore (_). The name cannot start with a number. If the name is more than 16 characters long, the command fails. The **names** command must be used to enable the use of the **name** command. The **clear names** command clears the list of names from the PIX Security Appliance configuration. The **no** names command disables the use of the text names, but does not remove them from the configuration. The **show names** command lists the **name** command statements in the configuration.

Configuring a list of name-to-IP address mappings allows the use of names in the configuration instead of IP addresses. In Figure 3-25, the IP addresses of the server and PC are mapped to the names, bastionhost and insidehost, with the following commands:

```
pixfirewall(config)#names
pixfirewall(config)#name 172.16.0.2 bastionhost
pixfirewall(config)#name 10.0.0.11 insidehost
```

Now, the names bastionhost and insidehost can be used in place of an IP address in any PIX command reference, such as in the command **ping insidehost**.

Figure 3-25   Name-to-IP Address Mappings

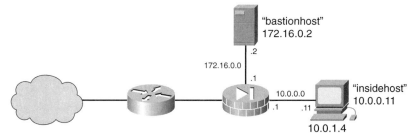

Examining the PIX Security Appliance Status

The **show** command enables the administrator to view command information. Several **show** commands display system information. You can use either **show** or **?** to view the names of the **show** commands and their descriptions. In general, **show run** plus a command displays a static screen. This typically shows the way that a parameter is configured. The **show** command plus a command displays a dynamically changing statistics screen. For example, **show run interface** displays how the interfaces are configured, a static screen. **show interface** displays a dynamic screen with numerous counters, as shown in Example 3-3.

Example 3-3   show run interface Command

```
pixfirewall (config)# show run interface
!
interface Ethernet0
  speed 100
  duplex full
  namif outside
  security-level 0
  ip address 192.168.2.2 255.255.255.0
!
interface Ethernet 1
  speed 100
  duplex full
nameif inside
security-level 100
ip address 10.0.2.1 255.255.255.0

pixfirewall(config)# show run interface
interface GigabitEthernet0/0 "outside", is up line protocol is up
  Detected: Speed 100 Mbps, Full-duplex
  Requested: Auto
  MAC address 000b.fcf8.c538, MTU1500
  IP address 192.168.1.2, subnet mask 255.255.255.0
  0 packets input,  0 bytes, 0 no buffer
  Received 0 broadcasts, 0 runts, 0 giants
  0 input errors, 0 CRC, 0 frame, 0 overun, 0 ignored, 0 abort
  0 packets output, 0 bytes, 0 undrruns
  Input queue (carr/max blocks): hardware (0/0)
  Software (0/0)
    Received 0 VLAN untagged packets, 0 bytes
    Transmitted 0 VLAN untagged packets, 0 bytes
    Dropped 0 VLAN untagged packets
```

Commonly Used **show** Commands

The **show memory** command displays a summary of the maximum physical memory, current used memory, and current free memory available to the PIX Security Appliance operating system.

The **show cpu usage** command displays CPU use.

Use the **show version** command to display the PIX Security Appliance software version, operating time since the last reboot, processor type, Flash memory type, interface boards, serial number, BIOS identification, and activation key value, as demonstrated in Example 3-4.

The **show ip address** command enables you to view the IP addresses that are assigned to the network interfaces.

Example 3-4   show version Command Output

```
pix1# show version
Cisco PIX Firewall Version 7.0
Compiled on Fri May 21 07:12:35 EDT 2004 by morlee
pix1 up 17 hours 59 mins
Hardware: PIX-515, 64 MB RAM, CPU Pentium 200 MHz
Flash i28F640J5 @ 0x300, 8 MB…
```

The **show interface** command enables you to view network interface information. This is one of the first commands you should use when trying to establish connectivity.

Use the **show nameif** command to view the named interfaces. For the PIX in Figure 3-26, the first two interfaces have the default names inside and outside. The inside interface has a default security level of 100, and the outside interface has a default security level of 0. Ethernet2 is assigned a name of dmz with a security level of 50. Example 3-5 shows this information was obtained with the **show nameif** command.

Figure 3-26   Displaying Named PIX Interface Information

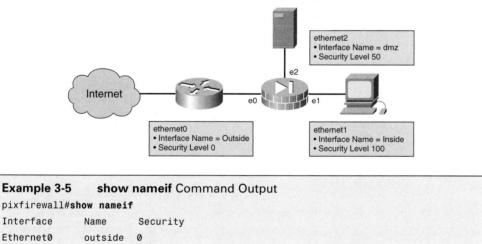

Example 3-5   show nameif Command Output

```
pixfirewall#show nameif
Interface    Name       Security
Ethernet0    outside    0
Ethernet1    inside     100
Ethernet2    dmz        50
```

Use the **show run nat** command to display a single host or range of hosts to be translated. As the following output reveals, all hosts on the 10.0.0.0 network will be translated when traversing the PIX Security Appliance (the *nat-id* is 1):

```
pix1#show run nat
nat (inside) 1 10.0.0.0 255.255.255.0 0
```

Figure 3-27 illustrates this process.

Figure 3-27   Displaying Hosts Translated with NAT

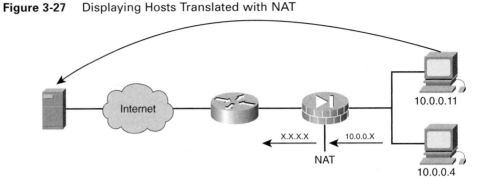

Use the **show run global** command to display the global pools of addresses configured in the PIX Security Appliance. As the following output reveals, there is currently one pool configured. The pool is configured on the outside interface. The pool has an IP address range of 192.168.0.20 to 192.168.0.254 and the *nat_id* is 1.

```
pix1#show run global
global (outside) 1 192.168.0.20-192.168.0.254
netmask 255.255.255.0
```

Figure 3-28 illustrates this process.

Figure 3-28   Displaying Global Pools of Addresses

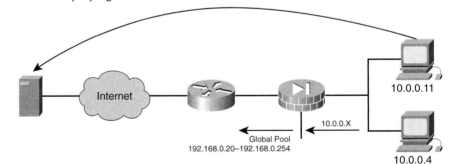

Use the **show xlate** command to display the contents of the translation slot. As the following output reveals, the number of currently used translations is 1 with a maximum count of 1. The current translation is a local IP address of 10.0.0.11 to a global IP address of 192.168.0.20:

```
pix1#show xlate
1 in use, 1 most used
Global 192.168.0.20 Local 10.0.0.11
```

Figure 3-29 illustrates this process.

Figure 3-29   Displaying Translation Slot Contents

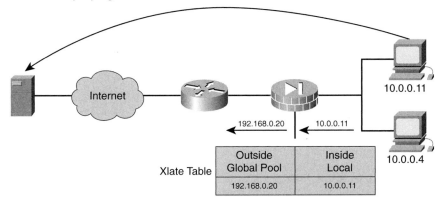

ping Command

To determine whether the PIX Security Appliance has connectivity, or whether a host is visible to the PIX on the network, use the following command:

`ping [if_name] host`

where:

- *if_name*—Specifies the network interface name. The address of the specified interface is used as the source address of the ping.

- *host*—Specifies the name or IP address of the host being pinged.

By default, the **ping** command makes three attempts to reach an IP address.

If it is necessary to allow internal hosts to be able to ping external hosts, an ACL for echo reply is necessary. If pings through the PIX Security Appliance between hosts or routers are not successful, use the **debug icmp trace** command to monitor the success of the ping.

After the PIX Security Appliance is configured and operational, a ping sent to the inside interface of the PIX from the outside network or from the outside interfaces of the PIX will not be successful. If the inside networks can be pinged from the inside interface and the outside networks can be pinged from the outside interface, the PIX is functioning normally and the routes are correct.

Lab 3.4.6a   Configure the PIX Security Appliance Using Setup Mode and the ASDM Startup Wizard

In this lab exercise, you verify that the PIX Security Appliance and a student PC are properly cabled and installed. You erase the current configuration and configure basic settings using the Interactive Setup mode. You also configure basic settings using the ASDM Startup Wizard secure management access.

Lab 3.4.6b   Configure the PIX Security Appliance Using the CLI

In this lab exercise, you execute general maintenance commands. You also configure the PIX Security Appliance inside and outside interfaces and test and verify basic PIX Security Appliance operation.

Time Setting and NTP Support

To set the PIX Security Appliance clock and enable the time, month, day, and year, enter the following command:

`clock set hh:mm:ss {month day | day month} year`

A battery on the motherboard allows the clock setting to be retained in memory when the power is off. The PIX generates syslog messages for system events and can log these messages to a syslog server. You can use the **logging timestamp** command to add a time stamp value to these messages. The **logging timestamp** command requires that the **clock set** command be used to ensure that the **correct** time appears on the syslog messages.

You can view the time with the **show clock** command, which displays the time, time zone, day, and full date. You can remove the **clock set** command with the **clear configure clock** command.

Setting Daylight Savings Time and Time Zones

Although the PIX Security Appliance clock does not adjust itself for daylight savings time changes, you can configure it to display daylight savings time by using the following command:

`clock summer-time zone recurring [week weekday month hh:mm week weekday month hh:mm] [offset]`

The **summer-time** keyword causes the PIX Security Appliance to automatically switch to summer time for display purposes only. The **recurring** keyword indicates that summer time should start and end on the days specified by the values that follow it. If no values are specified, the summer time rules default to United States rules.

For example, to specify that summer time starts on the first Sunday in April at 2 a.m. and ends on the last Sunday in October at 2 a.m., you enter the following:

`pixfirewall(config)#clock summer-time PDT recurring 1 Sunday April 2:00 last Sunday October 2:00`

To set the time zone, use the **clock timezone** *zone hours* [*minutes*] command. The **clock timezone** command sets the time zone for display purposes only. Internally, the time is kept in coordinated universal time (UTC). The **no** form of the command enables you to set the time zone to UTC. The **clear clock** command removes summer time settings and sets the time zone to UTC.

NTP

To synchronize the PIX Security Appliance with a specified network time server, use the following command:

```
pixfirewall(config)#ntp server ip_address [key number] source if_name [prefer]
```

where:

- *ip_address*—Specifies the IP address of the network time server with which to synchronize
- **key**—Specifies the authentication key
- **number**—Specifies the authentication key number (1 to 4294967295)
- **source**—Specifies the network time source
- *if_name*—Specifies the interface to use to send packets to the network time server
- **prefer**—Designates the network time server specified as the preferred server with which to synchronize time

You can configure the PIX to require authentication before synchronizing with the NTP server as demonstrated here:

```
pixfirewall(config)#ntp authentication-key 1234 md5 cisco123
pixfirewall(config)#ntp trusted-key 1234
pixfirewall(config)#ntp server 10.0.0.12 key 1234 source inside prefer
pixfirewall(config)#ntp authenticate
```

Use the **show run ntp** command to display the current NTP configuration. Use the **show ntp status** command to display the NTP clock information. The **clear configure ntp** command removes the NTP configuration, including disabling authentication and removing all authentication keys and NTP server designations.

Syslog Configuration

The PIX Security Appliance generates syslog messages for system events, such as alerts and resource depletion. Syslog messages can be used to create log files, or displayed on the console of a designated syslog host. The PIX can send syslog messages to any syslog server. In the event that all syslog servers or hosts are offline, the PIX stores up to 512 messages in its memory. Subsequent messages that arrive overwrite the buffer starting from the first line.

Logging Options

Some of the logging options available on the PIX Security Appliance are as follows:

- **Console**—Specifies that the specified log messages appear on the console as each message occurs

- **Buffered**—Sends the specified log messages to an internal buffer that can be viewed with the **show logging** command.

- **Monitor**—Specifies that the log messages appear on Telnet sessions to the PIX console

- **Host**—Specifies a log server that will receive the messages that are sent from the PIX

- **SNMP**—Enables sending log messages as Simple Network Management Protocol (SNMP) trap notifications

Messages at the specified level, and any higher severity level messages, are logged as shown in Figure 3-30.

Figure 3-30 Logging Levels

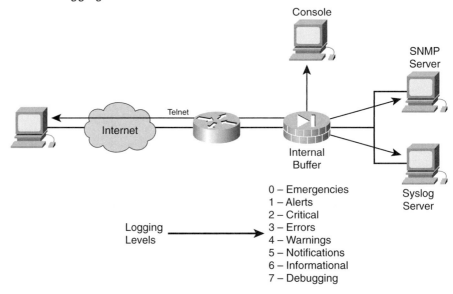

For example, if the log level is 3, the syslog displays 0, 1, 2, and 3 messages. Possible number and string level values are as follows:

- **0—emergencies**—System unusable messages

- **1—alerts**—Take immediate action

- **2—critical**—Critical condition

- **3—errors**—Error message

- **4—warnings**—Warning message

- **5—notifications**—Normal but significant condition

- **6—informational**—Information message

- **7—debugging**—Debug messages and log FTP commands and WWW URLs

Configuring Message Output

To configure the PIX Security Appliance to send the logging messages to syslog server 10.0.0.12, shown in Figure 3-31, you enter the following:

```
pixfirewall(config)#logging host inside 10.0.1.11
! Designates the Syslog host server
pixfirewall(config)#logging trap warnings
! Sets the logging level
pixfirewall(config)#logging timestamp
! Enables logging timestamp on syslog messages
pixfirewall(config)#logging device-id pix6
! Specifies a logging device ID
pixfirewall(config)#logging on
```

The messages sent will consist of warning messages and higher severity. Each message is time stamped and identified with a device-id of pix6. In the end, logging is turned on.

Figure 3-31   Configure Message Output to a Syslog Server

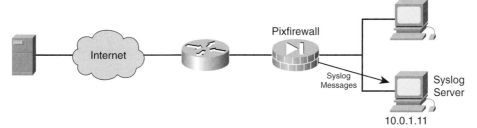

To configure the PIX Security Appliance to send warning messages, and higher severity messages, to the PIX Security Appliance logging buffer rather than a syslog server, you enter the following:

```
pixfirewall(config)#logging buffered warnings
pixfirewall(config)#logging on
```

show logging Command

Use the **show logging** command to see the logging configuration and any internally buffered messages. Use the **clear logging** buffer command to clear the buffer to make viewing the most current messages easier. As the output from **show logging** demonstrated in Example 3-6 shows, logging is enabled. The PIX Security Appliance will send warning messages, and higher severity messages, to a syslog server and the PIX internal buffer. On syslog messages, fw1 device-id and a time stamp will be appended.

Example 3-6   Display Logging Configuration an Internally Buffered Messages

```
pixfirewall(config)#show logging
Syslog logging: enabled
  Facility: 20
  Timestamp logging: enabled
  Standby logging: disabled
  Ambiguous interface parameters: 97
  Console logging: disabled
  Monitor logging: disabled
  Buffer logging: level warnings, 0 messages logged
  Trap logging: level warnings, facility 20, 0 messages logged
    Logging to inside 10.0.1.11
  History logging: disabled
  Device ID: fw1
  Mail logging: disabled
  PDM logging: disabled
```

Security Appliance Translations and Connections

Translations use NAT or PAT technologies to change the IP address of traffic as it goes across the PIX Security Appliance. For traffic going from the inside network to the outside network, this provides an additional layer of security and helps the administrator conserve IP address space. For traffic going from outside networks to inside networks, translations help simplify the router configuration on the internal, or perimeter, networks by controlling the addresses that appear on these networks.

Connections are used to create pathways through the PIX Security Appliance from lower-security networks to higher-security networks. These pathways allow traffic that would otherwise be denied by default. These pathways must be defined so that only specified traffic is allowed through.

The sections that follow examine translations and connections in detail.

Note

In the context of this chapter, the term *outbound* means connections from a more trusted side of the PIX Security Appliance to a less-trusted side of the PIX Security Appliance. The term *inbound* means connections from a less-trusted side of the PIX to a more-trusted side of the PIX.

Transport Protocols

It is important to understand the transport protocols Transmission Control Protocol (TCP) and User Datagram Protocol (UDP) to understand how the PIX Security Appliance operates.

A network session is carried out over two transport layer protocols:

■ TCP, which is easy to inspect

■ UDP, which is difficult to inspect properly

TCP

TCP is a connection-oriented protocol. When a session from a more-secure host inside the PIX Security Appliance is started, the PIX Security Appliance creates an entry in the session state filter.

The PIX Security Appliance can extract network sessions from the network flow and actively verify their validity in real time. This stateful filter maintains the state of each network connection and checks subsequent protocol units against its expectations. When a TCP session is initiated through the PIX, the PIX records the network flow and looks for an acknowledgment from the device with which the host is trying to initiate communications. The PIX then allows traffic to flow between the hosts involved in the connection based on the three-way handshake. The step-by-step process is detailed in the demonstration activity.

UDP

UDP is connectionless. The PIX Security Appliance must take other measures to ensure its security. Applications using UDP are difficult to secure properly because there is no handshaking or sequencing. It is difficult to determine the current state of a UDP transaction. It is also difficult to maintain the state of a session, because it has no clear beginning, flow state, or end. However, the PIX creates a UDP connection slot when a UDP packet is sent from a more-secure to a less-secure interface, as shown in Figure 3-32. All subsequent returned UDP packets matching the connection slot are forwarded to the inside network.

Figure 3-32   UDP

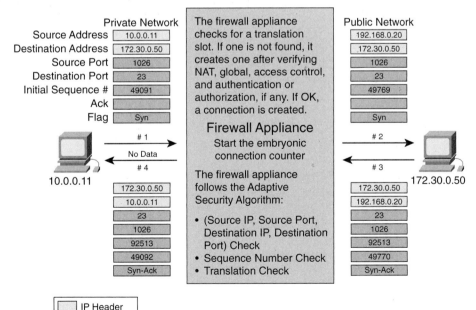

When the UDP connection slot is idle for more than the configured idle time, it is deleted from the connection table. The following are some UDP characteristics:

- UDP is an unreliable but efficient transport protocol.

- UDP has no handshaking or sequencing.

- UDP has no delivery guarantees.

- UDP has no connection setup and termination.

- UDP has no congestion management or avoidance.

NAT

NAT is critical to mitigating global Internet address depletion and was in fact created because of the rapid expansion of the Internet. Often, private networks are assigned numbers from network blocks defined in RFC 1918. Because these addresses are intended for local use only, NAT is required to connect to the Internet. In addition, NAT increases security by hiding the internal network topology.

In Figure 3-33, the private network is using private IP addressing, 10.0.0.0/24. Before a packet can be sent to the Internet, it must be translated into a public, routable address. In this example, the PIX Security Appliance translates IP address 10.0.0.11 into routable IP address 192.68.6.1.

Figure 3-33   Addressing Scenarios

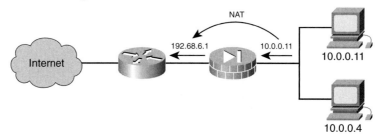

Access Through the Security Appliance

When configuring multiple interfaces, remember that the security level designates whether an interface is inside or outside relative to another interface, as shown in Figure 3-34. An interface is considered *inside* in relation to another interface if its security level is higher than the security level of the other interface, and is considered *outside* in relation to another interface if its security level is lower than the security level of the other interface.

The primary rule for security levels is that an interface with a higher security level can access an interface with a lower security level. As covered earlier in the chapter, the **nat** and **global** commands work together to enable the network to use any IP addressing scheme and to remain hidden from the external network.

An interface with a lower security level cannot access an interface with a higher security level unless it is specifically allowed by **static** and **access-list** command pairs.

Figure 3-34   Access Through the PIX Security Appliance

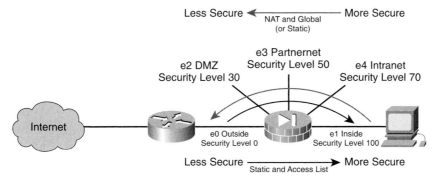

Inside Address Translation

The PIX Security Appliance supports the following two main types of address translations, as shown in Figure 3-35:

- **Dynamic translation**—Translates host addresses on more-secure interfaces to a range or pool of IP addresses on a less-secure interface. This enables internal users to share registered IP addresses and hides internal addresses from view on the public Internet.

- **Static translation**—Provides a permanent, one-to-one mapping between an IP address on a more-secure interface and an IP address on a less-secure interface. This allows an inside host to access a less-secure host, a server on the Internet, for instance, without exposing the actual IP address. Examples of static translation are static NAT and identity NAT.

Figure 3-35   Inside Address Translation

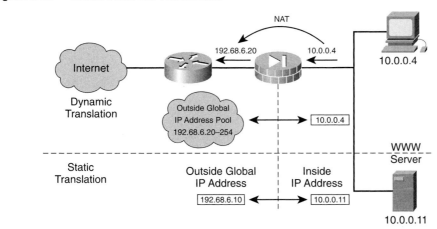

Dynamic Inside NAT

Dynamic inside translations are used for local hosts and their outbound connections. With dynamic translations, the hosts that are eligible for translation must be defined with the **nat** command, and the address pool must be defined with the **global** command. The pool for address allocation is chosen on the outgoing interface based on the *nat_id* selected with the **nat** command.

In the Figure 3-36 all hosts on the inside network are eligible for translation. The global pool of addresses assigned by the **global** command is 192.68.0.20 through 192.68.0.254, enabling up to 235 individual IP addresses:

```
nat (inside) 1 0.0.0.0 0.0.0.0
global (outside) 1 192.68.0.20 - 192.68.0.254
netmask 255.255.255.0
```

Figure 3-36   Dynamic Inside NAT

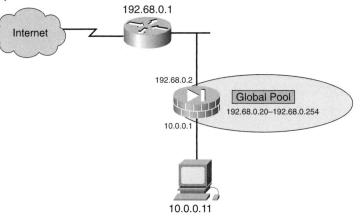

Two Interfaces with NAT

Example 3-7 demonstrates a configuration for the network in Figure 3-37 where all hosts on the inside networks can start outbound connections and a separate global pool is used for each internal network.

Example 3-7   Configuring Two Interfaces with NAT

```
pixfirewall(config)#nat (inside) 1 10.0.0.0 255.255.255.0
pixfirewall(config)#nat (inside) 2 10.2.0.0 255.255.255.0
pixfirewall(config)#global (outside) 1 192.68.0.1-192.68.0.14 netmask 255.255.255.240
pixfirewall(config)#global (outside) 2 192.68.0.17-192.68.0.30 netmask 255.255.255.240
```

Figure 3-37   Two Interfaces with NAT

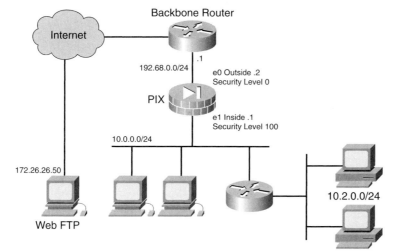

The first **nat** command statement permits all hosts on the 10.0.0.0 network to start outbound connections using the IP addresses from a global pool. The second **nat** command statement permits all hosts on the 10.2.0.0 network to do the same. The *nat_id* (1) in the first **nat** command statement tells the PIX Security Appliance to translate the 10.0.0.0 addresses to those in the global pool containing the same *nat_id*. Likewise, the *nat_id* (2) in the second **nat** command statement tells the PIX to translate addresses for hosts on network 10.2.0.0 to the addresses in the global pool containing *nat_id* 2.

Three Interfaces with NAT

Example 3-8 demonstrates a configuration for the network in Figure 3-38 where all inside users can start outbound connections to both the demilitarized zone (DMZ) and the Internet.

Figure 3-38   Three Interfaces with NAT

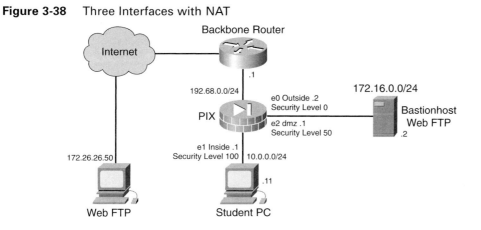

Example 3-8   Configuring Three Interfaces with NAT

```
pixfirewall(config)#nat (inside) 1 10.0.0.0 255.255.255.0
pixfirewall(config)#nat (dmz) 1 172.16.0.0 255.255.255.0
pixfirewall(config)#global (outside) 1 192.68.0.20-192.68.0.254 netmask 255.255.255.0
pixfirewall(config)#global (dmz) 1 172.16.0.20-172.16.0.254 netmask 255.255.255.0
```

The first nat command statement enables hosts on the inside interface, which has a security level of 100, to start connections to hosts on interfaces with lower security levels. In this case, that includes hosts on the outside interface and hosts on the DMZ. The second **nat** command statement enables hosts on the DMZ, which has a security level of 50, to start connections to hosts on interfaces with lower security levels. In this case, that includes only the outside interface.

Because both global pools and the **nat (inside)** command statement use a *nat_id* of 1, addresses for hosts on the 10.0.0.0 network can be translated to those in either global pool. Therefore, when users on the inside interface access hosts on the DMZ, their source addresses are translated to addresses in the 172.16.0.20 through 172.16.0.254 range from the **global (dmz)** command statement. When they access hosts on the outside, their source addresses are translated to addresses in the 192.68.0.20 through 192.68.0.254 range from the **global (outside)** command statement.

When users on the DMZ access hosts on the outside, their source addresses are always translated to addresses in the 192.68.0.20 through 2.68.0.254 range from the **global (outside)** command statement.

PAT

Typically, an enterprise network receives only a small number of routable addresses from its Internet service provider (ISP), whereas the number of hosts is much larger. To resolve this situation, you can use Port Address Translation (PAT).

With PAT, multiple connections originating from different hosts on the inside networks can be multiplexed by a single global IP address. The multiplexing identifier is the source port number. In Figure 3-39, the IP addresses of the two hosts on the inside network are translated to a PAT IP address of 192.68.0.20 source ports 2000 and 2001.

A PAT address can be a virtual address that differs from the outside address of the PIX Security Appliance. PAT should not be used when running multimedia applications through the PIX. Multimedia applications need access to specific ports and can conflict with port mappings provided by PAT.

In the example in Figure 3-40, the XYZ Company has only three registered IP addresses. One address is taken by the perimeter router, one by the PIX Security Appliance, and one by the global address.

Figure 3-39   Port Address Translation (PAT)

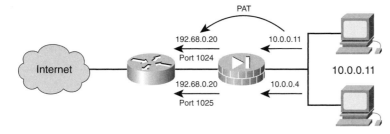

Figure 3-40   PAT Example

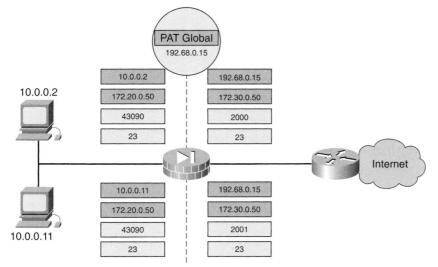

The example configuration is as follows:

```
ip address inside 10.0.0.1 255.255.255.0
ip address outside 192.68.0.2 255.255.255.0
route outside 0.0.0.0 0.0.0.0 192.68.0.1
```

IP addresses are assigned to the internal and external interfaces. A single registered IP address is put into the global pool and is shared by all outgoing access for network 10.0.0.0:

```
nat (inside) 1 10.0.0.0 255.255.0.0
global (outside) 1 192.68.0.9 netmask 255.255.255.255
```

PAT Using the Outside Interface Address

You can use the IP address of the outside interface as the PAT address by using the **interface** option of the **global** command. This is important when using the PIX Security Appliance DHCP client feature. It allows the DHCP-retrieved address to be used for PAT.

In Figure 3-41, source addresses for hosts on network 10.0.0.0 are translated to 192.68.0.2 for outgoing access, and the source port is changed to a unique number greater than 1023 as a result of the following commands:

```
pixfirewall(config)#ip address (inside) 10.0.0.1 255.255.255.0
pixfirewall(config)#ip address (outside) 192.68.0.2 255.255.255.0
pixfirewall(config)#route (outside) 0.0.0.0 0.0.0.0 192.68.0.1
pixfirewall(config)#global (outside) 1 interface
pixfirewall(config)#nat (inside) 1 10.0.0.1 255.255.255.0
```

Note

When PAT is enabled on an interface, there should be no loss of TCP, UDP, and Internet Control Message Protocol (ICMP) services. These services allow termination at outside interface of the PIX Security Appliance.

Figure 3-41   PAT Using the Outside Interface Address

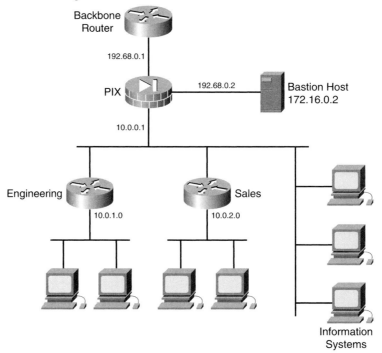

Mapping Subnets to PAT Addresses

You can specify multiple PATs to track use among different subnets. See Figure 3-41 again. Network 10.0.1.0 and network 10.0.2.0 are mapped to different PAT addresses. This is done by using a separate **nat** and **global** command pair for each network:

```
pixfirewall(config)#ip address (inside) 10.0.0.1 255.255.255.0
pixfirewall(config)#ip address (outside) 192.68.0.2 255.255.255.0
pixfirewall(config)#route (outside) 0.0.0.0 0.0.0.0 192.68.0.1
pixfirewall(config)#global (outside) 1 192.68.0.8 netmask 255.255.255.0
pixfirewall(config)#global (outside) 2 192.68.0.9 netmask 255.255.255.0
pixfirewall(config)#nat (inside) 1 10.0.1.0 255.255.255.0
pixfirewall(config)#nat (inside) 2 10.0.2.0 255.255.255.0
```

Outbound sessions from hosts on internal network 10.0.1.0 will appear to originate from address 192.68.0.8, and outbound sessions from hosts on internal network 10.0.2.0 will appear to originate from address 192.68.0.9.

Backing Up PAT Addresses by Using Multiple PATs

You can back up PAT addresses by configuring multiple global command statements with the same nat_id.

Refer to the network in Figure 3-41 again. Address 192.68.0.9 will be used for all outbound connections from network 10.0.1.0 when the port pool from 192.68.0.8 is at maximum capacity. This functionality results because of the following commands:

```
pixfirewall(config)#ip address (inside) 10.0.0.1 255.255.255.0
pixfirewall(config)#ip address (outside) 192.68.0.2 255.255.255.0
pixfirewall(config)#route (outside) 0.0.0.0 0.0.0.0 192.68.0.1
pixfirewall(config)#global (outside) 1 192.68.0.8 netmask 255.255.255.0
pixfirewall(config)#global (outside) 2 192.68.0.9 netmask 255.255.255.0
pixfirewall(config)#nat (inside) 1 10.0.1.0 255.255.255.0
```

Augmenting a Global Pool with PAT

You can also augment a pool of global addresses with PAT. When all IP addresses from the global pool are in use, the PIX Security Appliance begins PAT using the single IP address shown in the second **global** command.

See the network in Figure 3-41 again. Hosts on the 10.0.0.0 internal network are assigned addresses from the global pool 192.68.0.20 through 192.68.0.254 as they initiate outbound connections. When the addresses from the global pool are exhausted, packets from all hosts on network 10.0.0.0 appear to originate from 192.68.0.15. This functionality results because of the following commands:

```
pixfirewall(config)#ip address (inside) 10.0.0.1 255.255.255.0
pixfirewall(config)#ip address (outside) 192.68.0.2 255.255.255.0
pixfirewall(config)#route (outside) 0.0.0.0 0.0.0.0 192.68.0.1
pixfirewall(config)#global (outside) 1 192.68.0.20-192.68.0.254 netmask 255.255.255.0
pixfirewall(config)#global (outside) 2 192.68.0.15 netmask 255.255.255.0
pixfirewall(config)#nat (inside) 1 10.0.0.0 255.255.255.0
```

The static Command

Use static translations when it is necessary for an inside host to always appear with a fixed address on the PIX Security Appliance global network. Static translations are used to map an inside host address to an outside global address:

- Use the **static** command for outbound connections to ensure that packets leaving an inside host are always mapped to a specific global IP address, such as an inside DNS or mail server.

- Use the **static** command for outbound connections that must be mapped to the same global IP address.

The following information can help to determine when to use static translations in the PIX Security Appliance:

- Do not create static translations with overlapping IP addresses. Each IP address should be unique.

- **static** commands take precedence over **nat** and **global** command pairs.

- If a global IP address will be used for PAT, do not use the same global IP address for a static translation

The **static** command creates a permanent mapping, called a *static translation slot*, or *xlate*, between a local IP address and a global IP address. For outbound connections, use the **static** command to specify a global address to which the actual IP address of a local host will be translated.

Statics take precedence over **nat** and **global** command pairs. Use the **show static** command to view **static** statements in the configuration.

Net Static

Net static permanently maps a subnet from itself, to itself, on a lower-security interface. It is recommended when address translation is undesirable.

Outside NAT

NAT and PAT can be applied to traffic from an outside interface to an inside interface. This functionality is called *outside NAT*. Outside NAT/PAT is similar to inside NAT/PAT, only the address translation is applied to the source address of hosts residing on the outer (less-secure) interfaces of the PIX Security Appliance. To configure dynamic outside NAT, specify the addresses to be translated on the less-secure interface and specify the global address or addresses on the more-secure interface. To configure static outside NAT, use the **static** command to specify the one-to-one mapping.

After outside NAT is configured, when a packet arrives at the outer interface of the PIX Security Appliance, the PIX attempts to locate an existing address translation entry in the connections database. If no xlate exists, it searches the NAT policy from the running configuration. If a NAT policy is located, an xlate is created and inserted into the database. The PIX then rewrites the source address to the mapped or global address and transmits the packet on the inside interface. After the xlate is established, the addresses of any subsequent packets can be quickly translated by consulting the entries in the connections database.

outside static Command

An outside static is used to translate the source address of a packet. The **static** command for outside NAT is as follows:

```
static (outside, inside) 10.0.0.0 192.68.100.0 netmask 255.255.255.0
```

PAT with Overlapping Address Space

Figure 3-42 illustrates an example of using PAT with overlapping address space.

Figure 3-42   Overlapping Address Example

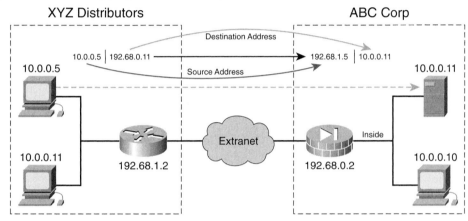

XYZ Distributors is a reseller of ABC Corporation's widgets. To place an order, XYZ Distributors order-entry host accesses a host on the ABC Corporation network. The issue is both companies use the 10.0.0.0/24 addressing space on their inside networks. To communicate, both companies must solve the overlapping address space issue. One or both companies can change their addressing space, or they can perform address translation. ABC Corporation's administrator configured a static translation and an outside static. As a packet travels through the PIX Security Appliance, the packets destination address is translated from a 192.68.11 address to an inside address of 10.0.0.11. The host source address of XYZ Distributors, 10.0.0.5, is translated to 192.68.1.5. When the ABC Corporation's server responds to the packet, it addresses the packet to 192.68.1.5, the translated address of the XYZ Distributors host. The commands needed to accomplish this are as follows:

```
pixfirewall(config)#static (extranet,inside) 192.68.1.0 10.0.0.0 netmask 255.255.255.0
pixfirewall(config)#static (inside, extranet) 192.68.0.0 10.0.0.0 netmask 255.255.255.0
```

Static PAT: Port Redirection

The PIX Security Appliance provides static PAT capability, which allows outside users to connect to a particular IP address and port and have the PIX redirect traffic to the appropriate inside server and port number. This capability can be used to send multiple inbound TCP or

UDP services to different internal hosts through a single global address. The shared address can be a unique address or a shared outbound PAT address, or it can be a shared with the external interface. If the keyword **tcp** or **udp** is specified in the **static** command, a static UDP or TCP port redirection is configured. If the keyword **interface** is specified, the outside interface address is presumed to be the global IP address. For example, if it necessary to provide a single address for global users to access FTP, HTTP, and SMTP, but these are all actually different servers on the local network, static statements can be specified as follows:

- *global_ip_A*/FTP to *local_ip_A*

- *global_ip_A*/HTTP to *local_ip_B*

- *global_ip_A*/SMTP to *local_ip_C*

This feature can also be used to translate a well-known port to a lesser-known port or vice versa. For example, if the inside web servers use port 8080, outside users can be allowed to connect to port 80, and the PIX Security Appliance will translate the connection to the correct port. Similarly, web users can be directed to connect to lesser-known port 6785, and then the PIX can be configured to translate the connections to port 80 on the local network.

static PAT Command

In Figure 3-43, an external user directs a FTP request to the PIX Security Appliance address 192.68.0.9. The redirects the request to DMZ FTP server at IP address 172.16.0.9. To enable the external user to access the FTP server, an access list would also have to be present in the configuration. Note that when port 21 is used on the PAT address, it cannot be redirected to a different inside host, a second FTP server. To access a second FTP server, the administrator would have outside clients use a different port number (for instance, port 2121). The administrator could configure the PIX Security Appliance to redirect port 2121 to the inside FTP server. The command needed to accomplish this is as follows:

```
pixfirewall(config)#static (inside,outside) tcp 192.68.0.9 ftp 172.16.0.9 ftp netmask
255.255.255.255
```

The basic syntax of this command is as follows:

```
static [(prenat_interface,postnat_interface)] {tcp | udp} {global_ip | interface}
global_port {local_ip local_port} [netmask mask]
```

The nat 0 Command

Another feature that you can use to control outbound connections is to control which internal IP addresses are visible on the outside. The **nat 0** command lets administrators disable address translation so that inside IP addresses are visible on the outside without address translation, as illustrated in Figure 3-44.

Figure 3-43   Static PAT

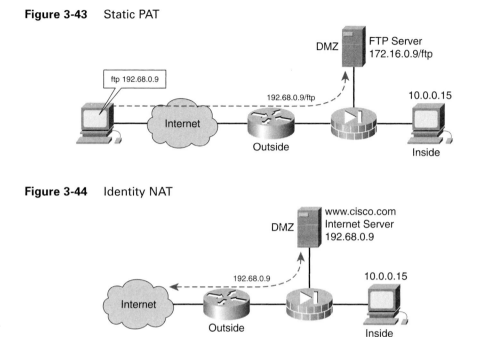

Figure 3-44   Identity NAT

You can use this feature when there are InterNIC-registered IP addresses on the inside network that need to be accessible on the outside network. Use of the **nat 0** command depends on your security policy.

If the policy allows internal clients to have their IP addresses exposed to the Internet, the **nat 0** command is used to provide that service.

For the network in Figure 3-44, the address 192.68.0.9 is not translated. When the following command is entered

```
pixfirewall(config)#nat (dmz) 0 192.68.0.9 255.255.255.255
```

the PIX Security Appliance displays the following message:

```
nat 0 192.68.0.9 will be non-translated
```

Note that NAT 0 enables the Internet server address to be visible on the outside interface. The administrator also needs to add a static address in combination with an access list to allow users on the outside to connect with the Internet server.

Connections and Translations

Translations (IP address to IP address) occur at the IP layer, and connections (TCP or UDP sessions) occur at the transport layer, TCP specifically. Connections are subsets of translations. Many connections can be open under one translation, as illustrated in Figure 3-45.

Figure 3-45   Connections Versus Translations

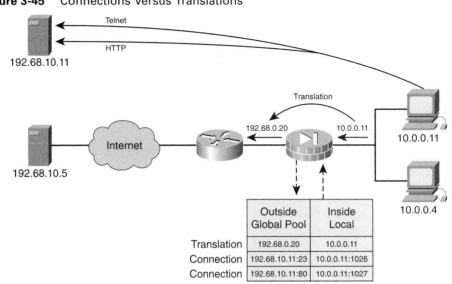

The sections that follow cover some of the **show** commands that you can use to uncover information about connections and translations.

show conn Command

To display information about the active TCP connections, enter the following command:

```
pixfirewall#show conn [count] | [detail] | [protocol tcp | udp | protocol][{foreign | local}
ip [-ip2]] [netmask mask]] [{lport | fport} port [-port2]]
```

where:

- **count**—Displays only the number of used connections. The precision of the displayed count might vary depending on traffic volume and the type of traffic passing through the Security Appliance.

- **detail**—If specified, displays translation type and interface information.

- {**foreign** | **local**} *ip* [-*ip2*]] [**netmask** *mask*]—Displays active connections by foreign IP address or by local IP address. Qualify foreign or local active connections by network mask.

- [**protocol tcp** | **udp** | *protocol*]—Displays active connections by protocol type. *protocol* is a protocol specified by number.

For the network in Figure 3-46, the output in Example 3-9 reveals that there are two connections between host 10.0.0.11 and web server 192.68.10.11. Connections are addressed to TCP port 80 on the web server. The replies are addressed host 10.0.0.11 ports 2824 and 2823.

Example 3-9   show conn Command Output

```
pixfirewall#show conn
2 in use, 2 most used
pixfirewall#show conn
2 in use, 9 most used
TCP out 192.68.10.11:80 in 10.0.0.11:2824
   idle 0:00:03 bytes 2320 flags UIO
TCP out 192.68.10.11:80 in 10.0.0.11:2823
   idle 0:00:03 bytes 3236 flags UIO
```

Figure 3-46   Displaying All Active Connections

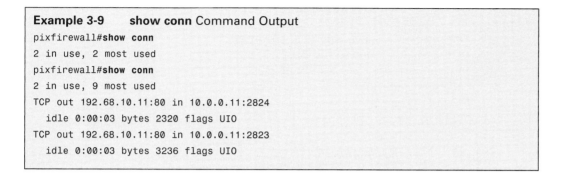

show conn detail Command

When you use **detail** option of the **show conn** command, the system displays information about the translation type, interface information, IP address/port number, and connection flags. In Example 3-10, the two connections display a flag value of UIO. According the flag definition, the connections are up. The connections are passing inbound and outbound data.

Example 3-10   show conn detail Command Output

```
pixfirewall#show conn detail
2 in use, 9 most used
TCP out 192.68.10.11:80 in 10.0.0.11:2824 idle 0:00:03 bytes 2320 flags UIO
TCP out 192.68.10.11:80 in 10.0.0.11:2823 idle 0:00:03 bytes 3236 flags UIO
pixfirewall#show conn detail
2 in use, 9 most used
Flags: A - awaiting inside ACK to SYN
       a - awaiting outside ACK to SYN
       B - initial SYN from outside, C - CTIQBE media,
       D - DNS, d - dump, E - outside back connection,
       F - outside FIN, f - inside FIN, G - group,
       g - MGCP, H - H.323, h - H.225.0,
       I - inbound data, i- incomplete, J - GTP,
```

```
Example 3-10    show conn detail Command Output    continued
        j - GTP data, k - Skinny media, M - SMTP data,
        m - SIP media, O - outbound data,
        P - inside back conn, q - SQL*Net data,
        R - outside acknowledged FIN, R - UDP RPC,
        r - inside acknowledged FIN,
        S - awaiting inside SYN,
        s - awaiting outside SYN,
        T - SIP, t - SIP transient, U - up
TCP outside:192.68.10.11/80 inside:10.0.0.11/2824 flags UIO
TCP outside:192.68.10.11/80 inside:10.0.0.11/2823 flags UIO
```

show local-host Command

To display the network states of local hosts, enter the **show local-host** [*ip_address*] command. A local-host entry is created for any host that forwards traffic to, or through, the PIX Security Appliance. This command shows the translation and connection slots for the local hosts. In the output in Example 3-11, the inside host 10.0.0.11 establishes a web connection with server 192.68.10.11.

```
Example 3-11    show local-host Command Output
pixfirewall#show local-host
Interface dmz: 0 active, 0 maximum active, 0 denied
Interface inside: 1 active, 5 maximum active, 0 denied
local host: <10.0.0.11>
  TCP flow count/limit = 2/unlimited
  TCP embryonic count to (from) host = 0 (0)
  TCP intercept watermark = unlimited
  UDP flow count/limit = 0/unlimited

  Conn:
  TCP out 192.68.10.11 :80 in 10.0.0.11 :2824 idle 0:00:05 bytes 466 flags UIO
  TCP out 192.68.10.11 :80 in 10.0.0.11 :2823 idle 0:00:05 bytes 1402 flags UIO

Interface outside: 1 active, 1 maximum active, 0 denied
local host: <192.68.10.11>
  TCP flow count/limit = 2/unlimited
  TCP embryonic count to (from) host = 0 (0)
  TCP intercept watermark = unlimited
  UDP flow count/limit = 0/unlimited

  Conn:
  TCP out 192.68.10.11 :80 in insidehost:2824 idle 0:00:05 bytes 466 flags UIO
  TCP out 192.68.10.11 :80 in insidehost:2823 idle 0:00:05 bytes 1402 flags UIO
```

This command also displays the connection limit values. In Example 3-11, the TCP flow count has no limit. If a connection limit is not set, the value displays as 0 or unlimited, and the limit is not applied. In the event of a SYN attack, with TCP intercept configured, the show local-host command output includes the number of intercepted connections in the usage count.

To clear the network state of all local hosts, or a specific IP address, enter the **clear local-host** command or the **clear local-host** [*ip_address*] command. Doing so stops all connections and xlates that are associated with the local hosts, or the specific IP address specified in the command.

show xlate Command

To display or clear the contents of the translation, or xlate slots, enter the following commands:

```
pixfirewall#show xlate [global_ip [local_ip]]
pixfirewall#clear [global_ip [local_ip]]
```

Translation slots can remain indefinitely after key changes have been made. Always use **clear xlate** or **reload** after adding, changing, or removing **access-list**, **global**, **nat**, **route**, or static commands in the configuration. For the network in Figure 3-47, host 10.0.0.11 is translated to a global address of 192.68.0.20 by the PIX Security Appliance, as you can see in the following output:

```
pixfirewall#show xlate
1 in use, 2 most used
Global 192.68.0.20 Local 10.0.0.11
```

Figure 3-47   Displaying Translation Contents

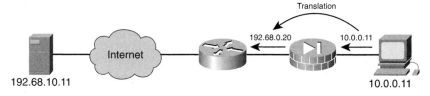

show xlate detail Command

To display information about the translation, interface information, IP address, and the type of translation, use the **show xlate detail** command.

In Example 3-12, the translation displays a flag value of i. According the flag definition, the i translation is a dynamic translation.

Example 3-12   show xlate detail Command Output

```
pixfirewall#show xlate detail
1 in use, 3 most used
Flags: D – DNS, d – dump, I – identity, i – dynamic, n – no random, r – portmap, s –
   static
NAT from inside 10.0.0.11 to outside 192.68.0.20 flags i
```

show timeout Command

The **show timeout** command displays the idle time for connection and translation slots. If the slot has not been used for the idle time specified, the resource is returned to the free pool. TCP connection slots are freed approximately 60 seconds after a normal connection close sequence.

Example 3-13 shows sample output from the **show timeout** command.

Example 3-13   show timeout Command Output

```
pixfirewall#show timeout
timeout xlate 3:00:00
timeout conn 1:00:00 half-closed 0:10:00 udp 0:02:00
```

Configuring Multiple Interfaces

The PIX Security Appliance supports up to eight additional physical interfaces for platform extensibility and security-policy enforcement on publicly accessible services. Multiple extranets or partner networks are easily connected and configured with standard firewall appliance commands. The multiple physical interfaces enable the PIX to protect publicly accessible web, mail, and Domain Name System (DNS) servers on the DMZ, as illustrated in Figure 3-48.

Figure 3-48   Additional Interface Support

Configuring Three Interfaces

The configuration in Example 3-14 shows the addition of a third interface for the network in Figure 3-49.

Figure 3-49   PIX with Three Interfaces

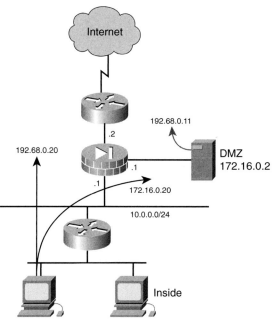

Example 3-14   Configuring a Third Interface

```
pixfirewall(config)#nameif ethernet0 outside sec0
pixfirewall(config)#nameif ethernet1 inside sec100
pixfirewall(config)#nameif ethernet2 dmz sec50

pixfirewall(config)#ip address outside 192.68.0.2 255.255.255.0
pixfirewall(config)#ip address inside 10.0.0.1 255.255.255.0
pixfirewall(config)#ip address dmz 172.16.0.1 255.255.255.0

pixfirewall(config)#global (outside) 1 192.68.0.20-192.68.0.254 netmask 255.255.255.0
pixfirewall(config)#global (dmz) 1 172.16.0.20-172.16.0.254 netmask 255.255.255.0

pixfirewall(config)#static (dmz,outside) 192.68.0.11 172.16.0.2
```

After you configure the third interface in Example 3-14, hosts on the inside network can access
the outside network. The original 10.0.0.0/24 address is assigned an address from the global
pool of 192.68.0.20-254. When an inside host accesses the DMZ, the original address is
assigned an address from the global pool of 172.16.0.20-254. Last, the DMZ server is always
translated to an outside address of 192.68.0.11.

When the PIX Security Appliance is equipped with three or more interfaces, use the following guidelines to configure it while using NAT:

- The outside interface cannot be renamed or given a different security level.

- An interface is always outside with respect to another interface that has a higher security level. Packets cannot flow between interfaces that have the same security level.

- Use a single default route statement to the outside interface only. Set the default route with the **route** command.

- Use the **nat** command to let users on the respective interfaces start outbound connections.

- Associate the *nat_id* with the *nat_id* in the **global** command statement. The valid identification numbers can be any positive number up to two billion.

- After a **global** statement is added, changed, or removed, save the configuration and enter the **clear xlate** command so that the IP addresses will be updated in the translation table.

- To permit access to servers on protected networks from a less-secure interface, use the **static** and **access-list** commands.

Configuring Four Interfaces

In Figure 3-50, the PIX Security Appliance has four interfaces. Users on the inside have access to the DMZ and the outside. The server 172.16.0.2 is visible on the outside as 192.68.0.11 and on the partnernet as 172.18 0.11. The configuration in Example 3-15 makes this possible.

Figure 3-50   Configuring Four Interfaces

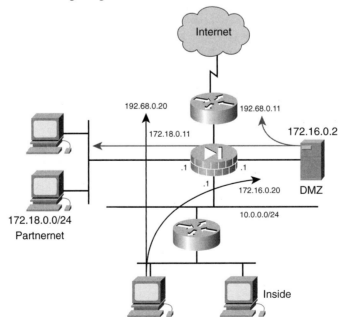

```
Example 3-15    Configuring a Fourth Interface
pixfirewall(config)#nameif ethernet0 outside sec0
pixfirewall(config)#nameif ethernet1 inside sec100
pixfirewall(config)#nameif ethernet2 dmz sec50
pixfirewall(config)#nameif ethernet3 partnernet sec40

pixfirewall(config)#ip address outside 192.68.0.2 255.255.255.0
pixfirewall(config)#ip address inside 10.0.0.1 255.255.255.0
pixfirewall(config)#ip address dmz 172.16.0.1 255.255.255.0
pixfirewall(config)#ip address partnernet 172.18.0.1 255.255.255.0

pixfirewall(config)#nat (inside) 1 10.0.0.0 255.255.255.0

pixfirewall(config)#global (outside) 1 192.68.0.20-192.68.0.254 netmask 255.255.255.0
pixfirewall(config)#global (dmz) 1 172.16.0.20-172.16.0.254 netmask 255.255.255.0

pixfirewall(config)#static (dmz,outside) 192.68.0.11 172.16.0.2
pixfirewall(config)#static (dmz,partnernet) 172.18.0.11 172.16.0.2
```

Configuring four interfaces requires more attention to detail, but the interfaces are still configured with standard PIX commands. To enable users on a higher-security level interface to access hosts on a lower-security interface, use the **nat** and **global** commands (for example, when users on the inside interface have access to the web server on the DMZ interface).

To let users on a lower-security level interface, such as users on the partnernet interface, access hosts on a higher-security interface (DMZ), use the **static** and **access-list** commands. As the third and fourth lines of Example 3-15 show, the partnernet has a security level of 40, and the DMZ has a security level of 50. The DMZ will use **nat** and **global** commands to speak with the partnernet and will use **static** commands and **access-list** commands to receive traffic originating from the partnernet.

Manage a PIX Security Appliance with Adaptive Security Device Manager

Adaptive Security Device Manager (ASDM) is a browser-based configuration tool designed to help the administrator set up, configure, and monitor a PIX or Adaptive Security Appliance graphically, without requiring an extensive knowledge of the PIX Security Appliance CLI, as shown in Figure 3-51.

Figure 3-51   ASDM Configuration Tool

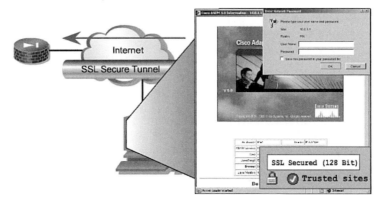

ASDM monitors and configures a single PIX Security Appliance. The administrator can use ASDM to create a new configuration and monitor and maintain current PIX Security Appliances. The administrator can point the browser to more than one PIX and administer several devices from a single workstation.

ASDM is secure, versatile, and easy to use. It can be used to manage PIX 500 series and ASA 5500 series Security Appliances and runs on a variety of platforms.

ASDM enables the administrator to securely configure and monitor a PIX Security Appliance remotely. Its ability to work with the Secure Sockets Layer (SSL) protocol ensures that communication with the PIX Security Appliance is secure, and because it is implemented in Java, it can provide robust, real-time monitoring. A single PIX can support up to 16 concurrent ASDM sessions, enabling up to 16 workstations to each have 1 browser session open with the same PIX.

ASDM works with PIX and ASA Security Appliance Software Versions 7.0 and later and comes preloaded into Flash memory on new Security Appliances running Software Versions 7.0. The administrator can download ASDM from Cisco and then copy it to the PIX via TFTP. To use ASDM, the Security Appliance must be running, at minimum, PIX or ASA Software Version 7.0. ASDM runs on Windows, Sun Solaris, and Linux platforms and requires no complex software installations.

ASDM Operating Requirements

A PIX Security Appliance must meet the following requirements to run ASDM:

- The administrator must have an activation key that enables DES or the more-secure 3DES, which ASDM requires for support of the SSL protocol. If the PIX Security Appliance is not enabled for DES, the administrator must obtain a new PIX Security Appliance activation key.

- Support for Java plug-in 1.4.2 or 1.5.0.

- Meets all requirements listed in the release notes for the PIX software version that is installed.

- Hardware model, PIX software version, and Device Manager (DM) version are compatible. Table 3-6 lists compatibility information.

Table 3-6   ASDM Compatibility Table

DM Version	Security Appliance SW Version	Security Appliance Model
PDM 1.0	6.0 or 6.1	506, 515, 520, 525, 535
PDM 1.1	6.0 or 6.1	506, 515, 520, 525, 535
PDM 2.0	6.2	501,506/506E,515/515E,520, 525, 535
PDM 2.1	6.2	501,506/506E,515/515E,520, 525, 535
PDM 3.0	6.3	501,506/506E,515/515E,520, 525, 535
ASDM 5.0	7.0	515/515E, 520, 525, 535, 5510, 5520, 5540

Workstation Requirements

To access ASDM from a browser, the workstation must meet the following requirements:

- JavaScript and Java must be enabled. If these are not enabled, ASDM prompts the administrator to enable them. When you are using a browser, Java Plug-in Version 1.4.2 or 1.5.0 is supported. To check which is running, launch ASDM. In the main ASDM menu, click **Help > About Cisco ASDM 5.0 for PIX**. When the About Cisco ASDM 5.0 for PIX window opens, it displays the browser specifications in a table, including the Java version. If an older version of Java is present, you must obtain a newer version.

- Browser support for SSL must be enabled. The supported versions of Internet Explorer and Netscape Navigator support SSL without requiring additional configuration.

- Pop-up blockers might prevent ASDM from starting. If ASDM does not start, try disabling pop-up blocking.

ASDM can operate in browsers running on Windows, Sun Solaris, or Linux operating systems. Table 3-7 lists the requirements for each operating system.

Table 3-7   ASDM Compatibility Table

Windows	Sun Solaris	Linux
Windows 2000 (Service Pack 3) or Windows XP Operating systems*.	Sun Solaris 2.8 or 2.9 running CDE window manger.	Red Hat Linux 9.0 or Red Hat Linux WS, Version 3 running the GNOME or KDE
The supported browsers are Internet Explorer 6.0 with Java Plug-in 1.4.2 or 1.5.0.	Monzilla 1.7.3 with Java Plug-in 1.4.2 or 1.5.0	Monzilla 1.7.3 with Java Plug-in 1.4.2 or 1.5.0
Any Pentium or Pentium-compatible processor running at 45MHz or higher.	SPARC microprocessor	—
At least 256 MB of RAM	At least 256 MB of RAM.	At least 256 MB of RAM
An 1024 x 768 pixel display with at least 256 colors.	An 1024 x 768 pixel display with at least 256 colors	A 1024 x 768 pixel display with at least 256 colors

*ASDM does not support use on Windows 3.1, 95, 98, Me, or NT4

General Guidelines

The following are a few general guidelines for workstations running ASDM:

- The administrator can run several ASDM sessions on a single workstation. The maximum number of ASDM sessions the administrator can run varies depending on the resources of the workstation, such as memory, CPU speed, and browser type.

- The time required to download the ASDM applet can be greatly affected by the speed of the link between the workstation and the PIX Security Appliance. A minimum 56-Kbps link speed is required, and 384 Kbps or higher is recommended. After the ASDM applet is loaded on the workstation, the link speed impact on ASDM operation is negligible.

If the resources of the workstation are running low, the administrator should close and reopen the browser before launching ASDM.

Prepare for ASDM

The PIX Security Appliance must be configured with the following information before the administrator can use ASDM. The administrator can either preconfigure a new PIX through the interactive prompts, which appear after the PIX boots, or the administrator can enter the commands shown below each information item.

- **Enable Password**—Enter an alphanumeric password to protect the privileged mode of the PIX Security Appliance. This password must be used to log in to ASDM. The command syntax for enabling a password is as follows:

```
enable password password [encrypted]
```

- **Time**—Set the PIX Security Appliance clock to universal coordinated time (UTC). Enter the UTC time in 24-hour time as *hour:minutes:seconds*. The command syntax for setting the clock is as follows:

```
clock set hh:mm:ss day month year
```

- **Inside IP address**—Specify the IP address of the inside interface of the PIX Security Appliance. The command syntax for setting an inside IP address is as follows:

```
ip address ip_address [netmask]
```

- **Hostname**—Specify up to 16 characters as a name for the PIX Security Appliance. The command syntax for setting a hostname is as follows:

```
hostname newname
```

- **Domain name**—Specify the domain name for the PIX Security Appliance. The command syntax for enabling the domain name is as follows:

```
domain-name name
```

- **IP address of the host running ASDM**—Specify the IP address of the workstation that will access ASDM from its browser. The command syntax for granting permission for a host to connect to the PIX Security Appliance with SSL is as follows:

```
http ip_address [netmask] [if_name]
```

- **HTTP server**—Enable the HTTP server on the PIX Security Appliance with the **http server enable** command.

ASDM does not support certain commands in a configuration. If these commands are present in the configuration, they are ignored when encountered by the ASDM. They display in the list of unparsed commands viewable under **Options > View Unparsed Commands**. ASDM does not change or remove these commands from the configuration.

Setup Dialog

A defaulted PIX Security Appliance starts in an interactive setup dialog to enable the administrator to perform the initial configuration required to use ASDM. The administrator can also access the setup dialog by entering setup at the configuration mode prompt.

The dialog asks for several responses, including the inside IP address, network mask, hostname, domain name, and ASDM host. The hostname and domain name are used to generate the default certificate for the SSL connection.

Example 3-16 demonstrates how to respond to the **setup** command prompts. Pressing the **Enter** key instead of entering a value at the prompt accepts the default value within the brackets. The administrator must fill in any fields that show no default values, and change default values as necessary.

After the configuration is written to Flash memory, the PIX Security Appliance is ready to start

---

Example 3-16   Responding to Setup Command Prompts in the ASDM

```
Pre-configure Firewall now through interactive prompts [yes]? <Enter>
Security Appliance Mode [routed]:
Enable Password [<use current password>]: cisco123
Allow password recovery? [yes] ?
Clock (UTC)
  Year [2006]: <Enter>
  Month [Jul]: <Enter>
  Time [10:21:49]: <Enter>
Inside IP address: 10.0.1.1
Inside network mask: 255.255.255.0
Host name: pix1
Domain name: ciscopix.com
IP address of host running PIX Device Manager: 10.0.1.11
Use this configuration and write to Flash? Y
```

Note

The clock must be set for ASDM to generate a valid certification. Set the PIX Security Appliance clock to UCT.

ASDM.

 Lab 3.6.3   Configuring the PIX Security Appliance with ASDM

In this lab exercise, you configure basic settings using ASDM, configure outbound access with NAT, and test connectivity through the PIX Security Appliance. You also configure banners and Telnet and SSH for remote access.

Using ASDM to Configure the PIX Security Appliance

You have two options for running ASDM. When first accessing ASDM via a browser, the administrator is presented with the screen in Figure 3-52.

The administrator can choose to download the ASDM application to a PC and run it locally, or run ASDM as a Java applet in a browser. With the local ASDM application option, the administrator can invoke ASDM from a desktop shortcut, no browser is required. Local installation support is only provided for Windows platforms. The other option is to run ASDM as a Java applet in a browser.

If the Java applet choice is selected, a Java applet is loaded to the PC from the PIX Security Appliance.

Figure 3-52   Running ASDM

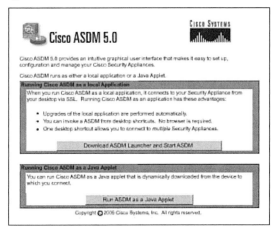

ASDM Home Window

The ASDM Home window enables the administrator to view important information about the PIX Security Appliance, such as the status of the interfaces, the version running, licensing information, and performance, as shown in Figure 3-53. Many of the details available on the ASDM Home window are available elsewhere in ASDM, but the Home window provides a useful and quick way to see how the Security Appliance is running. All information on the Home window is updated every 10 seconds, except for the device information. The administrator can access the Home window any time by clicking the Home button on the main toolbar.

Figure 3-53   ASDM Home Window

The following sections are included in the ASDM Home window:

■ **Menu bar**—Provides quick access to files, tools, options, wizards, and help.

- **Main toolbar**—Provides quick access to the Home window, configuration windows, ASDM monitoring, search, and context-sensitive help. The administrator can also save the running configuration to Flash memory by clicking the **Save** button, or reload the running configuration from Flash by clicking the **Refresh** button.

- **Device Information group box**—Displays PIX Security Appliance information in two tabs: General and License. The General tab displays PIX Security Appliance hardware and software information. The License tab displays the level of support for licensed features on a PIX Security Appliance.

- **VPN Status group box**—Displays the status of VPN tunnels, if they are configured.

- **System Resources Status group box**—Displays CPU and memory usage.

- **Interface Status group box**—Displays the interface, IP address and mask, and link status.

- **Traffic Status group box**—Displays the number of TCP and UDP connections that occur each second. Their sum displays as the total number of connections. The Interface Traffic Usage area displays the traffic going through the named interface in kilobits per second.

- **Last 10 ASDM Syslog Messages group box**—Displays the last 10 system messages generated by the PIX Security Appliance.

ASDM Configuration Window

The ASDM Configuration window includes nine icons, which enable the administrator to configure various aspects of the product as shown in Figure 3-54. ASDM Configuration enables the administrator to configure interfaces, a security policy, routing, NAT, VPN, device administration features, IPS, and miscellaneous properties. The administrator can also configure building blocks, including host and network identification and application inspection maps, to simplify configuration tasks. Some features might not be available for a particular PIX Security Appliance depending on the firewall mode and context.

Figure 3-54   ASDM Configuration Window

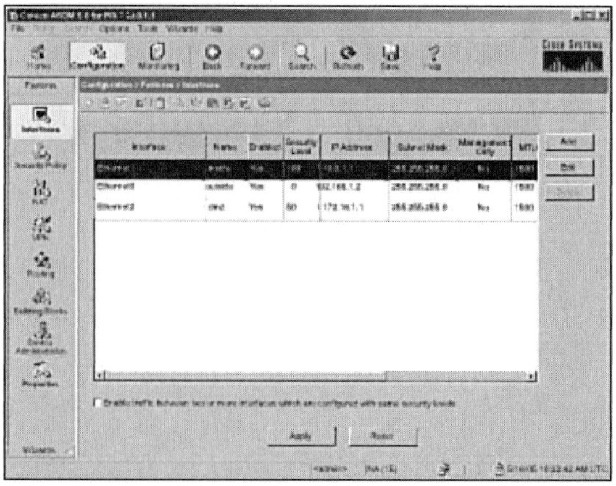

The list of available configuration feature icons is as follows:

- **Interface**—The Interfaces window displays configured interfaces and subinterfaces. The administrator can add or delete subinterfaces and enable communication between interfaces on the same security level.

- **Security Policy**—The administrator can add and delete access rules, authentication, authorization, and accounting (AAA) rules, filter rules, and service policy rules.

- **NAT**—The administrator can add, delete, and modify translation and translation exemption rules.

- **VPN**—The administrator can create and modify site-to-site and remote-access VPNs.

- **Routing**—The administrator can configure static routes, passive RIP, OSPF, IGMP, and PIM.

- **Building Blocks**—The administrator can configure IP address-to-hostname conversion, inspection maps, and time ranges.

- **Device Administration**—The administrator can set basic administration parameters for the PIX Security Appliance. You can also configure and administer certificates.

- **Properties**—The administrator can customize the PIX Security Appliance by configuring failover, logging, the static ARP table, and many other features.

Further exploration of the ASDM is conducted through the lab activities included in this course.

PIX Security Appliance Routing Capabilities

Virtual LANs

With PIX Security Appliance Software Version 6.3 and later, the administrator can assign VLANs to physical interfaces on the PIX or configure multiple logical interfaces on a single physical interface and assign each logical interface to a specific VLAN. VLANs connect devices on one or more physical LAN segments through software so that they can act as though they are attached to the same physical LAN, as depicted in Figure 3-55. The PIX supports only 802.1q VLANs.

Figure 3-55   VLANs and the PIX

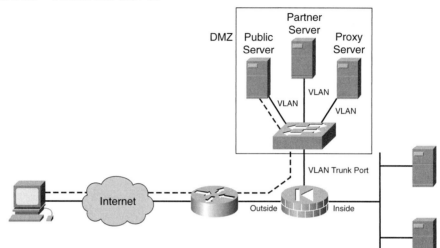

The PIX Security Appliance does not currently support executable commands for LAN trunks, the physical and logical connection between two switches, because the PIX does not negotiate or participate in any bridging protocols. The PIX only displays the VLANs on the LAN trunk. The state of the LAN trunk is considered the same as the state of the physical interface by the PIX Security Appliance. If the link is up on the physical Ethernet, the PIX considers the trunk as up as soon as a VLAN has been assigned or configured for it. In addition, the VLAN is active as soon as a VLAN ID is assigned or configured on the physical Ethernet interface of the PIX.

Physical interfaces are one per PIX Security Appliance interface, in place at boot time and not removable. Logical interfaces can be many to one for each interface, are created at runtime, and can be removed through software reconfiguration. A minimum of two physical interfaces is required for all PIX platforms to support VLANs.

Configuring Logical Interfaces

The general syntax for creating an interface is as follows:

```
pixfirewall (config)#interface {physical_interface[.subinterface] | mapped_name}
```

where:

- *physical_interface*—Designates the physical interface type, slot, and port number as *type\slot/port*. A space between the *type* and *slot/port* is optional.

Depending on your Security Appliance model, the types include **ethernet**, **gigabitethernet**, and **management**.

If your model does not include slots, enter the *type* followed by the *port_number*. If your model includes slots, enter the *type* followed by *slot/port*.

See the hardware documentation that came with your model to identify the interface type, slot, and port number.

- *subinterface*—(Optional) Designates a logical subinterface with an integer between 1 and 4294967293.

- *mapped_name*—In multiple mode, enter the mapped name if it was assigned using the **allocate-interface** command.

To create a logical subinterface, use the *.subinterface* argument of the **interface** command in global configuration mode, as demonstrated here for the network in Figure 3-56:

```
pixfirewall (config)#interface ethernet3.1
pixfirewall (config-subif)#vlan 10
```

Figure 3-56   Create Logical and Physical Interfaces

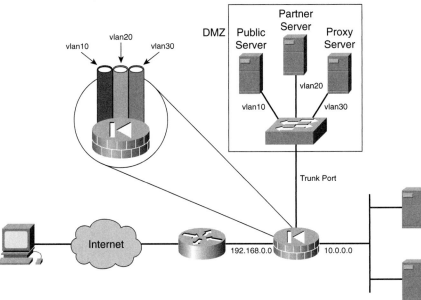

To remove a subinterface, use the **no** form of this command. A physical interface cannot be removed. You can configure a subinterface configuration mode, name, VLAN, IP address, and many other settings.

Use the **vlan** *vlan_id* command in subinterface configuration mode to assign a VLAN ID to a subinterface. The *vlan_id* is an integer between 1 and 4094. Subinterfaces require a VLAN ID to pass traffic.

If subinterfaces are enabled, the main interface is typically not configured to pass traffic, because the main interface passes untagged packets. The main interface must be configured with the **no shutdown** command to let subinterfaces be enabled. Therefore, traffic cannot be prevented from being passed through the main interface with the **shutdown** command. Instead, ensure that the main interface does not pass traffic; you do this by leaving out the **nameif** command. If the main interface is required to pass untagged packets, you can configure the **nameif** command as usual.

With the **nameif** command, the administrator defines a name for each VLAN. The interface name is used in all configuration commands on the PIX Security Appliance instead of the interface type and ID, such as fastethernet0/1, and is therefore required before traffic can pass through the interface.

To set the security level of a subinterface, use the **security-level** *number* command in subinterface configuration mode. The number can be any integer between 0 and 100.

In the example in Figure 3-57, to name vlan10 as dmz1, with a security level of 10, you enter the following:

```
pixfirewall (config)#interface ethernet3.1
pixfirewall (config-subif)#vlan 10
pixfirewall (config-subif)#nameif dmz1
pixfirewall (config-subif)#security-level 10
```

Figure 3-57   Assign VLAN Names and Security Levels

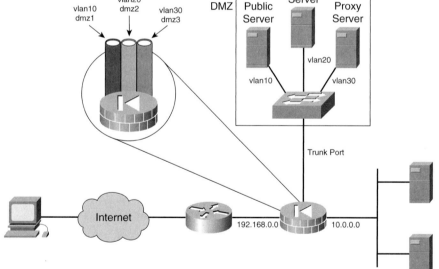

Use the **ip address** command to assign IP addresses to the VLANs. In the example in Figure 3-58, to assign dmz1 with the IP address 172.16.10.1, you enter the following:

```
pixfirewall (config)#interface ethernet3.1
pixfirewall (config-subif)#vlan 10
pixfirewall (config-subif)#nameif dmz1
```

```
pixfirewall (config-subif)#security-level 10
pixfirewall (config-subif)#ip address 172.16.10.1
```

Figure 3-58   Assign VLAN IP Addresses

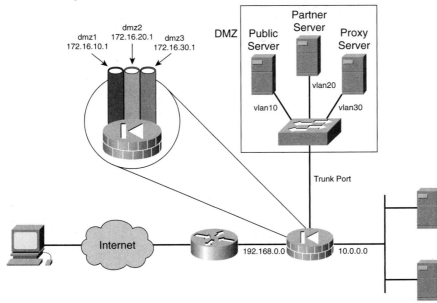

Example 3-17 details the configuration necessary to create multiple VLANs on a single physical interface for the network shown previously in Figure 3-57. In the example, VLANs 10, 20, and 30 have been created on the appropriate subinterfaces of interface Ethernet3.

Example 3-17   Configuring Multiple VLANs on a Single Physical Interface

```
Interface Ethernet3
  speed auto
  duplex auto
  no nameif
  no security-level
  no ip address
Interface Ethernet3.1
  vlan 10
  nameif dmz1
  security-level 10
  ip address 172.16.10.1
Interface Ethernet3.2
  vlan 20
  nameif dmz2
  security-level 20
  ip address 172.16.20.1
```

Example 3-17   Configuring Multiple VLANs on a Single Physical Interface   *continues*

```
Interface Ethernet3.3
  vlan 30
  nameif dmz3
  security-level 30
  ip address 172.16.30.1
```

VLAN Support

VLANs are not supported on the PIX Security Appliance 501 and 506/506E models. The number of logical interfaces that can be configured on the other PIX models varies by platform and license type. Table 3-8 and Table 3-9 define the maximum supported interfaces of the PIX Security Appliance family.

Table 3-8   Maximum Interfaces Supported in Release 7.0: PIX

	Restricted License		Unrestricted License	
	Physical Interfaces	Virtual Interfaces	Physical Interfaces	Virtual Interfaces
PIX 501	N/A	N/A	2	N/A
PIX 506E	N/A	N/A	2	2
PIX 515E	3	10	6	25
PIX 525	6	25	10	100
PIX 535	8	50	14	200

Table 3-9   Maximum Interfaces Supported in Release 7.0: ASA

	Physical Interfaces	Virtual Interfaces
ASA 5510	5	10
ASA 5520	5	25
ASA 5530	5	100

Static and RIP Routing

Although the PIX Security Appliance is not a router, it does have certain routing capabilities.

To create static routes for accessing networks outside a router on any interface, use the following command:

```
pixfirewall (config)#route interface_name ip_address netmask gateway_ip [metric]
```

In the example in Figure 3-59, the PIX sends all packets destined to the 10.1.1.0 network to the router at 10.0.0.3. All traffic for which the PIX Security Appliance has no route is sent to 192.68.0.1, the gateway in the default route. To enter a default route, set the *ip_address* and *netmask* arguments to 0.0.0.0, or the shortened form of 0. Only one default route can be used:

```
pixfirewall (config)#route outside 0.0.0.0 0.0.0.0 192.68.0.1 1
pixfirewall (config)#route inside 10.0.1.0 255.255.255.0 10.0.0.102 1
```

Figure 3-59 Static Routes

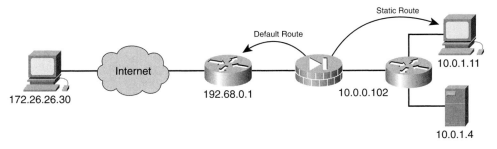

All routes entered using the **route** command are stored in the configuration when it is saved. You can display them by using the **show run route** command, and most routes can be cleared by using the **clear configure route** command. The only routes not removed with the **clear configure route** command are those that show the keyword CONNECT when the **show route** command is issued. These are routes that the PIX Security Appliance automatically creates in its routing table when an IP address is issued for a PIX interface. A route created in this manner is a route to the network directly connected to that interface. Figure 3-59 shows examples of these automatically created routes.

Although the *gateway* argument in the route command usually specifies the IP address of the gateway router, the next hop address for this route, one of the PIX Security Appliance interfaces can also be used. When a route command statement uses the IP address of one of the PIX interfaces as the gateway IP address, the PIX broadcasts an ARP request for the MAC address corresponding to the destination IP address in the packet instead of broadcasting the ARP request for the MAC address corresponding to the gateway IP address.

The following steps show how the PIX Security Appliance handles routing in this situation:

1. The PIX receives a packet from the inside interface destined to IP address *X*.

2. Because a default route is set to itself, the PIX sends out an ARP for address *X*.

3. Any Cisco router on the outside interface LAN that has a route to address *X* replies back to the PIX with its own MAC address as the next hop. Cisco IOS Software has proxy ARP enabled by default.

4. The PIX sends the packet to router.

5. The PIX adds the entry to its ARP cache for IP address *X* with the MAC address being that of the router.

Learning Dynamic Routes with RIP

Another way to build the PIX Security Appliance routing table is by enabling RIP with the **rip** command, the syntax for which is as follows:

```
pixfirewall (config)#rip if_name default | passive [version [1 | 2]][authentication [text |
md5 key key_id]]
```

where

- *if_name*—Specifies the internal or external network interface name.

- **default**—Broadcasts a default route on the interface.

- **passive**—Enables passive RIP on the interface. The Security Appliance listens for RIP routing broadcasts and uses that information to populate its routing tables.

- **version**—Specifies the version of RIP. Use Version 2 for RIP update encryption. Use Version 1 to provide backward compatibility with the older version.

- **authentication**—Enables RIP Version 2 authentication.

- **text**—Sends RIP updates in clear text.

- *key*—Specifies the key to encrypt RIP updates. This value must be the same on the routers and any other device that provides RIP Version 2 updates. The key is a text string of up to 16 characters in length.

- *key_id*—Specifies the key identification value. The *key_id* in use on the routers and any other device that provides EIP Version 2 updates.

You can configure the PIX to learn routes dynamically from RIP Version 1 or RIP Version 2 broadcasts. Although the PIX uses the dynamically learned routes itself to forward traffic to the appropriate destinations, it does not propagate learned routes to other devices. The PIX cannot pass RIP updates between interfaces. It can, however, advertise one of its interfaces as a default route.

Figure 3-60 shows the PIX Security Appliance learning routes from a router on its outside interface and broadcasting a default route on its inside interface (10.0.0.1 in this case). MD5 authentication is used on the outside interface to enable the PIX to accept the encrypted RIP updates; for example, it could learn the route to network 172.26.26.0 from Router A. Both the PIX and Router A are configured with the encryption key MKEY and its *key_id* value of 2:

```
pixfirewall (config)#rip outside passive version 2 authentication md5 MYKEY 2
pixfirewall (config)#rip inside default
```

Figure 3-60   Dynamic RIP Routes

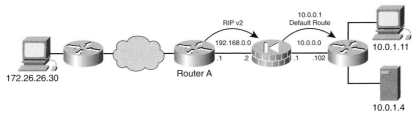

Use the **rip** command to configure the PIX Security Appliance to learn routes dynamically from RIP Version 1 or RIP Version 2 broadcasts. When RIP Version 2 is configured in passive mode, the PIX accepts RIP Version 2 multicast updates with an IP destination of 224.0.0.9. For the RIP Version 2 default mode, the PIX transmits default route updates using an IP destination of 224.0.0.9. Configuring RIP Version 2 registers the multicast address 224.0.0.9 on the interface specified in the command so that the PIX can accept multicast RIP Version 2 updates. When the RIP Version 2 commands for an interface are removed, the multicast address is unregistered from the interface card.

If RIP Version 2 is specified, RIP updates can be encrypted using MD5 encryption. The *key* and *key_id* values must be the same as on any device in the network that makes RIP Version 2 updates.

IP routing table updates are enabled by default. Use the **no rip** command to disable the PIX Security Appliance IP routing table updates. The **clear rip** command removes all the **rip** commands from the configuration.

Note

Static routes override dynamic routes.

OSPF

PIX Security Appliance Software Version 6.3 introduces support for dynamic routing using the Open Shortest Path First (OSPF) routing protocol, as illustrated in Figure 3-61.

Figure 3-61   PIX in an OSPF Environment

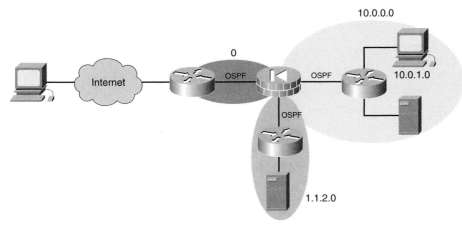

OSPF is widely deployed in large internetworks because of its efficient use of network bandwidth and its rapid convergence after changes in topology. Some of the PIX OSPF-supported features are as follows:

- Support for intra-area, interarea, and type 1 and 2 external routes

- Support for virtual links

- Authentication for OSPF packets

- Configuring the PIX Security Appliance as a designated router (DR), Area Border Router (ABR) and limited Autonomous System Boundary Router (ASBR)

- Support for stub and not-so-stubby areas (NSSAs)

- ABR type 3 link-state advertisement (LSA) filtering

- Route redistribution

Note

OSPF routing is not supported on the PIX Security Appliance 501. OSPF and RIP cannot be enabled simultaneously on the PIX Security Appliance.

To configure OSPF on the PIX Security Appliance requires the administrator to do the following:

- Enable OSPF.

- Define the PIX Security Appliance interfaces on which OSPF runs.

- Define OSPF areas.

Enable OSPF

To enable OSPF routing, use the **router ospf** *pid* command. The *pid* argument is an internally used identification parameter for an OSPF routing process. You assign it locally on the firewall, and its value can be from 1 to 65535. A unique value must be assigned for each OSPF routing process.

The PIX Security Appliance can be configured for one or two processes, or OSPF routing domains:

- One process is for public areas.

- One process is for the private areas.

If the PIX is functioning as an ABR and it is configured for one process, the PIX will pass type 3 LSA between defined OSPF areas. For the network illustrated in Figure 3-62, the PIX is configured for one OSPF process, OSPF 1, with the following command:

```
pixfirewall (config)#router ospf 1
```

Figure 3-62   Configuring the PIX for One OSPF Process

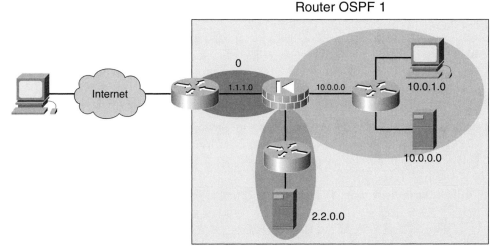

Define Network Interfaces

To define the interfaces on which OSPF runs and the area ID for those interfaces, use the following command:

```
pixfirewall (config)#network addr mask area area_id
```

where:

- *addr*—Specifies the IP address.

- **area** *area_id*—Specifies the area that is to be associated with the OSPF address range. The *area_id* can be specified in either IP address format or in decimal format. When specified in decimal format, the valid range is from 0 to 4294967295.

- *mask*—Specifies the network mask.

Example 3-18 shows how the three PIX Security Appliance interfaces for the network, shown previously in Figure 3-62, are configured for OSPF. The outside interface, network 1.1.1.0, is configured as area 0. The DMZ interface, network 2.2.1.0, is configured as network 2.2.0.0. The inside interface, network 10.0.0.0, is configured as area 10.0.0.0. LSA type 3 advertisements pass between the three interfaces.

Example 3-18   Defining OSPF Networks

```
pixfirewall(config)#router ospf 1
pixfirewall(config)#network 1.1.1.0 255.255.255.0 area 0
pixfirewall(config)#network 2.2.1.0 255.255.255.0 area 2.2.0.0
pixfirewall(config)#network 10.0.0.0 255.255.255.0 area 10.0.0.0
```

OSPF Processes

Defining a PIX Security Appliance with two OSPF processes enables the PIX to pass LSA type 3 advertisements between areas but not between processes. In Figure 3-63, for example, there are two defined process areas. OSPF process ID 1 encompasses OSPF area 0. OSPF process ID 2 encompasses areas 10.0.0.0 and 192.168.1.0. With two OSPF processes defined, LSA type 3 advertisements can pass between areas within a process (for example, 192.168.1.0 and 10.0.0.0). LSA type 3 advertisements cannot pass between areas defined by different processes. For example, 10.0.0.0 LSA type 3 advertisements cannot pass to area 0.

Figure 3-63   Two Processes

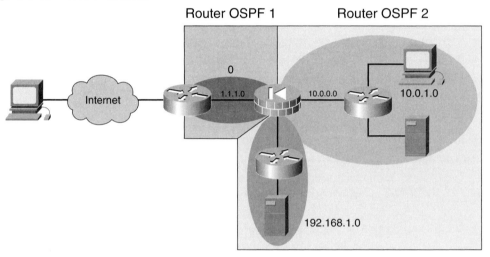

It might be advantageous to use two OSPF processes for the following scenario:

- NAT is used.

- OSPF is operating on the public and private interfaces.

- LSA type 3 advertisement filtering is required.

A maximum of two processes can be defined for each PIX Security Appliance.

OSPF Areas

To configure two areas, define the router OSPF process ID (PID) first. Next define the network and areas belonging to the OSPF PID. For the network shown previously in Figure 3-63, there are two OSPF PIDs: OSPF 1 and OSPF 2.

As demonstrated in Example 3-19, OSPF 1 is defined first. Network 1.1.1.0/24 is associated with area 0. OSPF 2 is configured next. Within OSPF 2, there are two networks: 10.0.0.0 and 192.168.1.0. Network 10.0.0.0/24 is associated with OSPF area 10.0.0.0. Network

192.168.1.0/24 is associated with area 192.168.1.0. LSA type 3 advertisements can pass between areas of OSPF 2. LSA type 3 advertisements cannot pass between OSPF 1 and 2.

Example 3-19   Defining OSPF: Two Processes

```
pixfirewall(config)#router ospf 1 //public AS
pixfirewall(config-router)#network 1.1.1.0 255.255.255.0 area 0
pixfirewall(config)#router ospf 2 //private AS
pixfirewall(config-router)#network 10.0.0.0 255.255.255.0 area 10.0.0.0
pixfirewall(config-router)#network 192.168.1.0 255.255.255.0 area 192.168.1.0
```

Multicast Routing

IP multicasting is a bandwidth-conserving technology that reduces traffic by simultaneously delivering a single stream of information to multiple recipients (see Figure 3-64). Applications that take advantage of multicast include videoconferencing, corporate communications, distance learning, and distribution of software, stock quotes, and news.

Figure 3-64   IP Multicasting

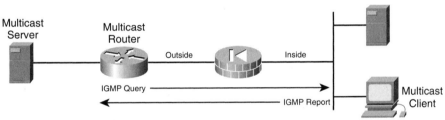

IP multicasting is actually the transmission of an IP datagram to a host group. A host group is a set of hosts identified by a single IP destination address. For this to work, hosts that wish to receive multicasts must join a multicast host group, and routers that forward multicast datagrams must know which hosts belong to which group. Routers discover this information by sending Internet Group Management Protocol (IGMP) query messages through their attached local networks. Host members of a multicast group respond to the query by sending IGMP reports noting the multicast groups to which they belong. If a host is removed from a multicast group, it sends a leave message to the multicast router.

In Software Versions 6.2 and later, the PIX Security Appliance supports Stub Multicast Routing (SMR), which enables it to pass multicast traffic. This feature is necessary when hosts that need to receive multicast transmissions are separated from the multicast router by a PIX. With SMR, the PIX acts as an IGMP proxy agent. It forwards IGMP messages from hosts to the upstream multicast router, which takes responsibility for forwarding multicast datagrams from one multicast group to all other networks that have members in the group. When SMR is used, it is not necessary to construct generic routing encapsulation (GRE) tunnels to allow multicast traffic to bypass the PIX.

Note

The GRE protocol is used for tunneling data across an IP network.

Outside Multicast Server: Configuring the Outside Interface

When hosts that need to receive a multicast transmission are separated from the multicast router by a PIX Security Appliance, configure the PIX to forward IGMP reports from the downstream hosts and to forward multicast transmissions from the upstream router (see Figure 3-65). By default, IGMP processing is enabled on an interface.

Figure 3-65   Outside Multicast Server: Configuring the Outside Interface

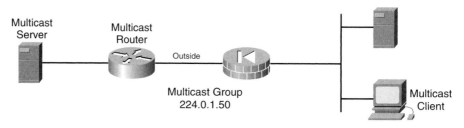

Complete the following steps to allow hosts to receive multicast transmissions through the PIX:

Step 1.   Use the **interface** command to enter the interface subcommand mode. From this prompt, you can enter the **igmp** commands for further multicast support.

Step 2.   (Optional) Use the **permit** option of the **access-list** command to configure an ACL that allows traffic to the desired Class D destination addresses. The **deny** option can also be used to deny access to transmissions from specific multicast groups. Within the ACL, the *destination-addr* argument is the Class D address of the multicast group to which multicast transmissions are to be permitted or denied. If ACLs are used for this purpose, the **igmp access-group** *acl-id* command must also be used to apply the ACL to the currently selected interface.

For the network in Figure 3-65, you configure the following:

```
pixfirewall (config)#interface ethernet0
pixfirewall (config-if)#igmp access-group 110
pixfirewall (config)#access-list 110 permit udp any host 224.0.1.50
```

Outside Multicast Server: Configuring the Inside Interface

When hosts that need to receive a multicast transmission are separated from the multicast router by a PIX Security Appliance, configure the PIX to forward IGMP reports from the downstream hosts and to forward multicast transmissions from the upstream router (see Figure 3-66).

Figure 3-66   Outside Multicast Server: Configuring the Inside Interface

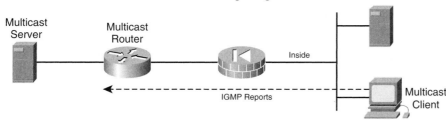

Complete the following steps to allow hosts to receive multicast transmissions through the PIX:

Step 1.   Use the **interface** command to enter the interface subcommand mode. From this prompt, you can enter the **igmp** commands for further multicast support.

Step 2.   Use the **igmp forward interface** *interface-name* command to enable IGMP forwarding on the PIX. The **igmp forward** command enables forwarding of all IGMP host report and leave messages received by the PIX to the specified interface. The interface specified is the PIX interface connected to the multicast router. In the example in Figure 3-66, this is the outside interface.

Step 3.   (Optional) Use the **igmp join-group** *group-address* command to configure the PIX to join a multicast group. This command configures the interface to be a statically connected member of the specified group. It allows the PIX to act for a client that might not be able to respond via IGMP but that still requires reception. The **igmp join-group** command is applied to the downstream interface toward the receiving hosts.

For the network in Figure 3-66, you configure the following:

```
pixfirewall (config)#interface ethernet1
pixfirewall (config-if)#igmp forward interface outside
pixfirewall (config-if)#igmp join-group 224.0.1.50
```

A multicast group is defined by a Class D IP address. Although Internet IP multicasting uses the entire range of 224.0.0.0 to 239.255.255.255, any group address that is assigned must be within the range 224.0.0.2 to 239.255.255.255. Because the address 224.0.0.0 is the base address for Internet IP multicasting, it cannot be assigned to any group. The address 224.0.0.1 is assigned to the permanent group of all IP hosts, including gateways. This is used to address all multicast hosts on the directly connected network. There is no multicast address for all hosts on the Internet.

Outside Multicast Server: Inside Receiving Hosts

To permit multicast on the dmz and inside interfaces for the network in Figure 3-67, and enable the PIX Security Appliance to forward IGMP reports from inside hosts to the multicast router on its dmz interface, you enter the following:

```
pixfirewall (config)#access-list 120 permit udp any host 224.0.1.50
pixfirewall (config)#interface ethernet2
pixfirewall (config-if)# igmp access-group 120
pixfirewall (config)#interface ethernet1
pixfirewall (config-if)#igmp forward interface dmz
```

In this example, host 10.0.0.11 joins multicast group 224.0.1.50. The PIX Security Appliance enables host 10.0.0.11 to receive multicasts from the multicast server.

Figure 3-67   Outside Multicast Server: Inside Receiving Host Example

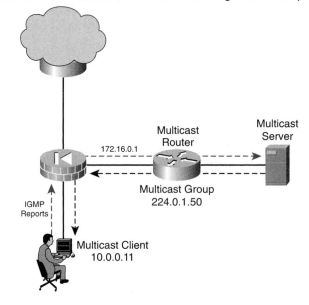

The transactions involved in this scenario are as follows:

1. Host 10.0.0.11 sends an IGMP report:

   - Source 10.0.0.11

   - Destination 224.0.1.50

   - IGMP group 224.0.1.50

2. The PIX Security Appliance accepts the packet, and IGMP places the inside interface on the output list for the group.

3. The PIX Security Appliance forwards the IGMP packet to the multicast router:

   - Source 172.16.0.1

- Destination 224.0.1.50

- IGMP group 224.0.1.50

4. The router places the input interface on the output list for the group.

5. Packets from the multicast server arrive at the router, which forwards them to the necessary interfaces.

6. The PIX Security Appliance accepts the packets and forwards them to the interfaces for the group.

Configuring Other IGMP Options

Administrators can also set other IGMP options. The administrator can choose an IGMP version and configure the IGMP timers with the **igmp query-interval** *seconds* and **igmp query-max-response-time** *seconds* commands. To specify the version of IGMP, use the **igmp** *version* command. This configures which version of IGMP is used on the subnet represented by the specified interface. The default is Version 2.

For information on the differences in Versions 1 and 2, see RFC 2236.

Use the **igmp query-interval** *seconds* command to configure the frequency at which IGMP query messages are sent by the interface. The default is 60 seconds. Use the **no** version of this command to set the query interval back to the default.

The **igmp query-max-response-time** *seconds* command specifies the maximum query response time and is only available with IGMP Version 2. The default is 10 seconds. The permitted range of values is from 1 to 65535. Use the **no** version of this command to set the query response time back to the default.

Firewall Services Module Operation

The Cisco Firewall Services Module (FWSM) is an integrated module for the Cisco Catalyst 6500 series switch and the Cisco 7600 series Internet router. The Cisco Catalyst 6500 provides intelligent services such as firewall capability, intrusion detection, and virtual private networking, along with multilayer LAN, WAN, and MAN switching capabilities. The Cisco 7600 series Internet router offers optical WAN and metropolitan-area network (MAN) networking with line-rate IP services at the network edge.

The Cisco FWSM is a high-performance firewall solution, providing 5 Gbps of throughput per module and scaling to 20 GB of bandwidth with multiple modules in one chassis. The FWSM is completely VLAN aware, offers dynamic routing, and is fully integrated within the Cisco Catalyst 6500 series switches. The FWSM is based on Cisco PIX Security Appliance technology and therefore offers the same security and reliability as the Cisco ASA and PIX Security Appliances.

The FWSM has the following benefits for the Catalyst 6500 switch (based on FWSM Version 2.2):

- Brings switching and firewalls into a single chassis

- Based on PIX Firewall technology

- Supports transparent or routed firewall mode

- Up to 100 security contexts:

    — Up to 256 VLANs per context

    — Up to 1000 VLANs for all contexts

- 5.5 GBPS throughput

- 1 million concurrent connections

- 1000,000 connections per second

- Multiple blades supported in 1 chassis (4 maximum)

- Dynamic routing via RIPv1, RIPv2, and OSPF

- High availability via intra- or inter-chassis stateful failover

The FWSM can run in one of the following modes:

- **Routed**—The FWSM is considered to be a router hop in the network. It performs NAT between connected networks, and can use OSPF or passive RIP, in single-context mode.

- **Transparent**—The FWSM acts like a "bump in the wire," and is not a router hop. The FWSM connects the same network on its inside and outside ports, but each port must be on a different VLAN.

Although a FWSM can be installed in the Catalyst 6500 series switches and the Cisco 7600 series routers, the FWSM runs its own operating system. The FWSM operating system is based on the PIX operating system. Although the FWSM operating system is similar to the PIX operating system, there are differences. Table 3-10 compares FWSM and PIX features.

Table 3-10   FWSM and PIX Feature Comparison

	FWSM	PIX Security Appliance
Performance	5.5 Gbps	1.7 Gbps
VLANs	1000	100
Interfaces	Internal VLANs	External interfaces
IDS signatures	No	Yes
VPN functionality	No	Yes
Traffic	Explicitly denied	Allowed higher to lower security level

Some of the differences are as follows:

- The FWSM has higher performance.

- The FWSM supports more VLANs.

- The FWSM does not include any external physical interfaces. Instead, it uses internal VLANs.

- Termination of VPN connections for traffic flowing through the FWSM is not supported on a FWSM. The Cisco Catalyst 6500 provides intelligent services such as intrusion detection, and virtual private networking via Intrusion Detection System (IDSM) and VPN Services Module (VPNSM) service modules.

- By default, all traffic is explicitly denied on an FWSM.

FWSM Requirements

The FWSM occupies one slot in a Cisco Catalyst 6500 switch. Up to four FWSM modules can be installed in the same switch chassis. The FWSM has the following requirements for the Catalyst 6500 switch:

- Supervisor 1A and Multilayer Switch Feature Card 2 (MSFC2)

- Supervisor 2 with MSFC2

- Supervisor 720

- Cisco IOS Software Release 12.1(13)E or later when using the Supervisor 2 option

- Cisco IOS Software Release 12.2(14)SX1 or later when using the Supervisor 720

- CatOS minimum Software Release 7.5(1) or later when using the Supervisor 2

- CatOS minimum Software Release 8.2(1) or later when using the Supervisor 720

A Cisco Catalyst 6500 switch includes a switching supervisor and an MSFC. The MSFC can be used as a router. Although the MSFC is necessary as part of the system, it does not have to be used in conjunction with a FWSM. One or more VLAN interfaces can be assigned to the MSFC, if the switch software version supports this feature.

Getting Started with the FWSM

With a PIX Security Appliance, it can be taken out of the box, hooked up to LAN cables, powered-on, and then it is ready to be configured. Remember, however, than an FWSM is not a standalone device. It is a security module within a Catalyst chassis. Before you can configure a security policy in an FWSM, you must complete the following tasks:

1. Initialize the FWSM.

2. Configure the switch VLANs.

3. Associate VLANs with the FWSM.

The switch CLI is accessible through a Telnet connection to the switch or through the switch console interface.

Verify FWSM Installation

Before you can use the FWSM, you must verify that the card is installed and recognized by the switch. Enter the **show module** [*mod-num* | **all**] command to verify that the system acknowledges the new module and has brought it online. Example 3-20 demonstrates the results of a **show module** command.

Example 3-20　　Verify FWSM Installation

```
Router#show module

Mod  Slot  Ports  Module-Type                   Model              Sub  Status
--- ---  ---    ---------------               -------------      ---  ---

1    1     2     100BaseX Supervisor           WS-X6K-S2U-MSFC2   yes  ok
15   1     1     Multilayer Switch Feature     WS-F6K-MSFC2       no   ok
2    2     48    10/100BaseTX Ethernet         WS-X6348-RJ-45     yes  ok
4    4     6     Firewall Module               WS-SVC-FWM-1       no   ok
```

Configure the Switch VLANs

The FWSM does not include any external physical interfaces. Instead, it uses VLAN interfaces. Hosts are connected to ports, and VLANs are assigned to these physical switch ports. To prevent mismatched VLANs, the administrator should first configure a VLAN on the MSFC, and then configure the VLANs on the FWSM. VLAN IDs must be the same for the switch and the FWSM. A VLAN can be linked with a specific FWSM by using the **firewall** command. After the MSFC VLAN is configured, specific VLANs can be associated with a FWSM.

The **firewall vlan-group** *firewall_group vlan_range* command creates a group of firewall VLANs named by the **vlan-group** keyword where *firewall_group* indicates the name of the firewall VLAN group and *vlan_range* is a numeric range of VLAN numbers to be included in the group.

After a group of VLANs have been assigned to a group, the **firewall module** *module_number* **vlan-group** *firewall_group* command associates a VLAN group with a specific FWSM.

Figure 3-68 shows a switch with VLANs 100, 200, and 300. To place these VLANs into Firewall VLAN-group 1 and associate the FWSM in slot 4 with VLAN-group 1, VLANs 100, 200, and 300, you enter the following commands:

```
switch(config)#firewall vlan-group 1 100,200,300
switch(config)#firewall module 4 vlan-group 1
```

Figure 3-68   Firewall VLAN Group

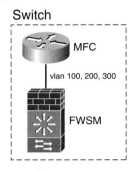

Verify the MSFC Configuration

To verify that the MSFC is properly configured for interaction with the FWSM and determine which VLANs are assigned to each firewall VLAN group, use the **show firewall vlan-group** command. To verify that the VLAN groups are assigned to the associated slot where the FWSM resides, enter the **show firewall module** command. Example 3-21 demonstrates sample output of these commands for the VLAN group illustrated previously in Figure 3-68.

Example 3-21   Verify the MSFC Configuration

```
switch#show firewall vlan-group
Group   vlans
— —.  — —.
1       100,200,300

switch#show firewall vlan-group
Module   Vlan-groups
4         1
```

Configure the FWSM Interfaces

The FWSM is now installed. The MSFC VLANs are configured. The FWSM VLANs are associated with a specific FSWM. The next step is to configure the security policy on the FWSM. You can access the FWSM by establishing a console session using the **session slot** *mod* {**processor** *processor-id*} command. The *processor-id* value should always be 1. Use the default password **cisco** for the FWSM when prompted. A prompt for an enable mode password then displays. By default, there is no password, and you can press the **Enter** key to access the enable mode. It is recommended that you change the enable password to a valid value and use this for future access to this mode.

When on the FWSM, you use the standard Security Appliance commands to configure interface names, add security levels, and specify IP addresses.

For the switch in Figure 3-69, Example 3-22 shows the use of the **nameif** command and associates VLAN 100 as the outside interface and sets the interface with a security level of 0. It also defines VLAN 200 as the inside interface. It specifies VLAN 300 as the dmz interface. In all cases, the **ip address** command is used to add an IP address to each interface.

Figure 3-69   FWSM Interfaces

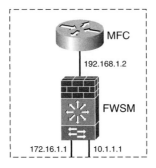

Example 3-22   Configuring the FWSM Interfaces

```
switch(config)#session slot 4 processor 1
.............
fwsm(config)#hostname FWSM1
FWSM1(config)#nameif 100 outside 0
FWSM1(config)#ip address outside 192.168.1.2 255.255.255.0
FWSM1(config)#nameif 200 inside 100
FWSM1(config)#ip address inside 10.0.0.1 255.255.255.0
FWSM1(config)#nameif 300 dmz 100
FWSM1(config)#ip address dmz 172.16.1.1 255.255.255.0
```

Configure A Default Route

You might also need to add a default route. For the switch depicted previously in Figure 3-69, to create a default route pointing to the VLAN 100 interface of the MSFC, you enter the following:

```
FWSM1(config)#route outside 0.0.0.0 0.0.0.0 192.168.1.1
```

Creating static routes might also become necessary. Multiple-context mode does not support dynamic routing, so static routes must be used to reach any networks to which the FWSM is not directly connected, such as when a router is between the destination network and the FWSM.

Static routes might be appropriate in single-context mode under the following conditions:

- The network uses a routing protocol other than RIP or OSPF.

- The network is small and static routes can be easily managed.

- The traffic or CPU overhead associated with routing protocols is to be avoided.

Configure the FWSM Access Lists

The administrator needs to create ACLs to allow outbound and inbound traffic because the FWSM, unlike the Security Appliances, denies all inbound and outbound connections that are not explicitly permitted by ACLs, as shown in Figure 3-70. To configure explicit access rules, use the **access-list** command; and to attach the ACLs to the appropriate interface, allowing traffic to pass through that interface, use the **access-group** command. Traffic that has been permitted into an interface can exit through any other interface. Return traffic matching the session information is permitted without an explicit ACL.

Figure 3-70   Permitting Traffic Through the FWSM

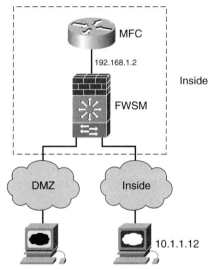

To configure an access list to permit traffic through the inside interface depicted in Figure 3-70, you enter the following:

```
FWSM1(config)#access-list 200 permit ip 10.1.1.0 255.255.255.0 any
FWSM1(config)#access-group 200 in interface inside
```

Using PDM with the FWSM

You can use PIX Device Manager (PDM) Version 4.0 to configure and monitor FWSM Version 2.2. Be sure to initialize the FWSM before attempting to install PDM. To prepare the FWSM to use PDM, follow these steps:

Step 1.   Use the **copy tftp flash** command to copy the PDM image into FWSM Flash: **copy tftp://10.1.1.1/pdm-*XXX*.bin flash:pdm** (where *XXX* = PDM image version number).

Step 2.   Enable the HTTP server on the FWSM with the **http server enable** command. Without it, PDM will not start.

Step 3.   Identify the specific hosts/networks that can access the FWSM using HTTP. To permit hosts from network 10.1.1.0 (on the inside interface) enter this: **http access http 1.1.1.0 255.255.255.0 inside**

Step 4.   Launch the browser and enter the following address: **https://10.1.1.1 (FWSM inside interface)**

Resetting and Rebooting the FWSM

If the module cannot be reached through the CLI or an external Telnet session, enter the **hw-mod module** *module_number* **reset** command to reset and reboot the module. The reset process requires several minutes.

To reset the module, installed in slot 4, from the CLI, you enter the following:

```
Router(config)#hw-mod module 4 reset

Proceed with reload of module? [confirm] y

% reset issued for module 4
```

When the FWSM initially boots, by default it runs a partial memory test. To perform a full memory test, use **the hw-mod module** *module_number* **mem-test-full** command.

A full memory test takes more time to complete than a partial memory test depending on the memory size. For 512 MB, the boot time takes about three minutes. For 1 GB, the boot time takes about six minutes.

Summary

This chapter introduced the Cisco IOS Firewall feature set, the Cisco PIX Security Appliance, and the Adaptive Security Appliance. Particular emphasis was placed on the various models, their capabilities, and how they are used in a network. Also, the basic capabilities and configuration of the PIX were discussed. This discussion included routing capabilities and user interfaces. Device configuration using SDM and ASDM was also discussed.

Translations use NAT or PAT technologies to change the IP address of traffic as it goes across the PIX Security Appliance. For traffic going from the inside network to the outside network, this provides an additional layer of security and helps the administrator conserve IP address space. For traffic going from outside networks to inside networks, translations help simplify the router configuration on the internal, or perimeter, networks by controlling the addresses that appear on these networks.

Connections are used to create pathways through the PIX Security Appliance from lower-security networks to higher-security networks. These pathways allow traffic that would otherwise be denied by default. These pathways must be defined so that only specified traffic is allowed through. The PIX uses the static and **access-list** commands to do this.

Check Your Understanding

Complete all the review questions listed here to test your understanding of the topics and concepts in this chapter. Answers are listed in Appendix A, "Check Your Understanding Answer Key."

1. Which of the following firewalls is not one of the firewall classes discussed in this chapter?

   a. Appliance-based firewalls

   b. Software-based firewalls

   c. Server-based firewalls

   d. Integrated firewalls

2. The Cisco IOS Firewall does not feature which of the following benefits?

   a. Protection of internal networks from intrusion

   b. Monitoring of traffic through network perimeters

   c. Filtering of viruses

   d. Enabling of network commerce via the World Wide Web

3. Finesse is the Cisco proprietary real-time operating system that runs directly on the hardware of the PIX Security Appliance and the Adaptive Security Appliance. It is a non-UNIX, non-Windows NT, and Cisco IOS-like operating system.

   a. True

   b. False

4. With PIX 501 Security Appliance Software Release 6.3 you have several options for product licensing. Which one of the following options is not one?

   a. 10-user license

   b. 20-user license

   c. 50-user license

   d. Unlimited-user license

5. The PIX Security Appliance contains a command set based on the Cisco IOS Software and provides which four administrative access modes?

   a. Unprivileged mode, privileged mode, configuration mode, monitor mode

   b. User mode, privileged mode, configuration mode, monitor mode

   c. Unprivileged mode, privileged mode, superuser mode, monitor mode

   d. Unprivileged mode, privileged mode, configuration mode, EXEC mode

6. A PIX Security Appliance will not allow you to cut and paste configurations.

   a. True

   b. False

7. The first step in enabling NAT on a PIX Security Appliance is entering which command?

   a. **nat**

   b. **nat enable**

   c. **nat inside**

   d. **nat enable inside**

8. The **name** command is used to configure a list of name-to-IP address mappings on the PIX Security Appliance. This allows the use of names in the configuration instead of IP addresses. This name cannot be more than how many characters in length?

   a. 5

   b. 10

   c. 12

   d. 16

9. On a PIX Security Device, the **show interface** command enables you to view network interface information.

   a. True

   b. False

10. The PIX Security Appliance supports up to how many additional interfaces?

    a. 5

    b. 8

    c. 10

    d. 16

CHAPTER 4

Trust and Identity Technology

Upon completion of this chapter, you should be able to answer the following questions:

- What is AAA?

- What are some of the authentication technologies in use today?

- How does Identity Based Network Services (IBNS) work?

- What is network admission control (NAC)?

Key Terms

This chapter uses the following key terms. You can find the definitions in the glossary at the end of the book.

Authentication, authorization, and accounting (AAA) architecture   page 220

Cisco Identity Based Networking Services (IBNS) page 220

Network Admission Control (NAC)   page 220

Terminal Access Controller Access Control System Plus (TACACS+)   page 221

Remote Authentication Dial-In User Service (RADIUS)   page 222

This chapter presents an overview of the ***authentication, authorization, and accounting (AAA) architecture*** and shows its importance to identity services in network security. AAA security is one of the primary components of the overall network security policy of an organization. AAA is essential to providing secure remote access to the network and remote management of network devices. After a brief discussion of AAA, several authentication methods are discussed.

This chapter also introduces ***Cisco Identity Based Networking Services (IBNS)*** and ***Network Admission Control (NAC)***. IBNS is an integrated solution combining several Cisco products that offer authentication, access control, and user policies to secure network connectivity and resources. NAC is an industry initiative, sponsored by Cisco Systems, that uses the network infrastructure to enforce security policy compliance on all devices seeking to access network computing resources, thereby limiting damage from viruses and worms.

AAA

Identity management is key to network security and can be accomplished using various technologies and devices. Cisco uses the term authentication, authorization, and accounting (AAA) when discussing identity management of network access using routers, switches, firewalls, and access points. Depending on the size of the network and available resources, you can implement AAA on a device and locally manage it from a central server running RADIUS or TACACS+ protocols.

The discussion in this section centers on Terminal TACACS+, RADIUS, and a comparison of TACACS+ and RADIUS.

TACACS

There are three versions of TACACS:

- TACACS
- XTACACS
- TACACS+

TACACS is an industry standard protocol specification, RFC 1492, that forwards username and password information to a centralized server. The centralized server can be either a TACACS database or a database such as the UNIX password file with TACACS protocol support. For example, the UNIX server with TACACS passes requests to the UNIX database and sends the accept or reject message back to the access server.

XTACACS

XTACACS defines the extensions that Cisco added to the TACACS protocol to support new and advanced features. XTACACS is multiprotocol and can authorize connections with Serial

Line Internet Protocol (SLIP), enable, PPP IP or Internet Packet Exchange (IPX), AppleTalk Remote Access (ARA), EXEC, and Telnet. XTACACS supports multiple TACACS servers and syslog for sending accounting information to a UNIX host; connects where the user is authenticated into the access server shell; and can Telnet or initiate SLIP, PPP, or ARA after initial authentication. XTACACS is essentially obsolete concerning Cisco AAA features and products.

TACACS+

Terminal Access Controller Access Control System Plus (TACACS+) is the enhanced and continually improved version of TACACS that allows a TACACS+ server to provide the services of AAA independently. Each service can be tied into its own database or can be used with the other services available on the server or on the network. TACACS+ forwards username and password information to a centralized security server.

TACACS+ was introduced in Cisco IOS Software Release 10.3. This protocol is a completely new version of the TACACS protocol referenced by RFC 1492 and developed by Cisco. It is not compatible with XTACACS. TACACS+ has been submitted to the Internet Engineering Task Force (IETF) as a draft proposal.

Cisco seriously evaluated RADIUS as a security protocol before it developed TACACS+. Many features were included in the TACACS+ protocol to meet the needs of the growing security market. The protocol was designed to scale as networks grow and to adapt to new security technology as the market matures.

Figure 4-1 documents the features available with TACACS+ and where it fits into the network.

Figure 4-1   TACACS+ Features

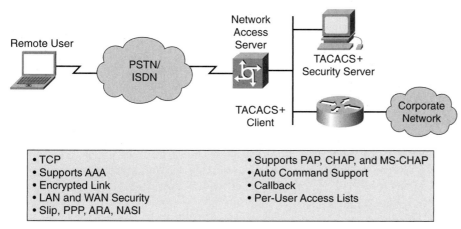

RADIUS

Remote Authentication Dial-In User Service (RADIUS) is an alternative to TACACS+ and is important to network administrators. RADIUS is an access server AAA protocol developed by Livingston Enterprises, Inc (now part of Lucent Technologies). RADIUS is a system of distributed security that secures remote access to networks and protects network services against unauthorized access. RADIUS is composed of three components:

- Protocol with a frame format that uses UDP/IP

- Server

- Client

The server runs on a central computer, typically at the customer's site; the clients reside in the dialup access servers and can be distributed throughout the network. Cisco incorporated the RADIUS client into Cisco IOS Software, starting with Cisco IOS Software Release 11.1.

Three major versions of RADIUS are available today:

- **IETF with approximately 63 attributes**—Developed and proposed to IETF by Livingston Enterprises. The RADIUS protocol is specified in RFC 2138, and RADIUS accounting in RFC 2139.

- **Cisco implementation supporting approximately 58 attributes**—Starting in Cisco IOS Software Release 11.2, an increasing number of attributes and functionality are included in each release of Cisco IOS Software and Cisco Secure Access Control Server (ACS).

- **Lucent supporting more than 254 attributes**—Lucent is constantly changing and adding vendor-specific attributes such as token caching and password changing. An application programming interface (API) enables rapid development of new extensions, making competing vendors work hard to keep up. Although Livingston Enterprises developed RADIUS originally, it was championed by Ascend.

Client/Server Model

A network access server (NAS) operates as a client of RADIUS, as shown in Figure 4-2. The client is responsible for passing user information to designated RADIUS servers and then acting on the response that is returned. RADIUS servers are responsible for receiving user connection requests, authenticating the user, and then returning all configuration information necessary for the client to deliver service to the user. The RADIUS servers can act as proxy clients to other kinds of authentication servers.

The RADIUS server can either use a local user database or can be integrated to use a Windows database or Lightweight Directory Access Protocol (LDAP) directory to validate the username and password.

You can find more information on the RADIUS protocol in RFC 2865 and RFC 2868.

Figure 4-2   Network Topology Using a RADIUS Server

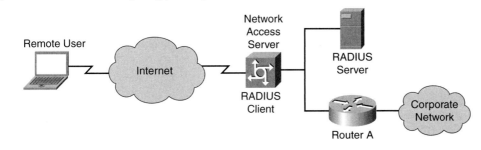

Network Security

Transactions between the client and RADIUS server are authenticated using a shared secret, which is never sent over the network. In addition, any user passwords are sent encrypted between the client and RADIUS server, to eliminate the possibility that someone snooping on an unsecured network could determine a user password.

Flexible Authentication Mechanisms

The RADIUS server supports a variety of methods to authenticate a user. When it is provided with the username and original password given by the user, it can support PPP, Password Authentication Protocol (PAP), Challenge Handshake Authentication Protocol (CHAP), or MS-CHAP, UNIX login, and other authentication mechanisms.

Comparing TACACS+ and RADIUS

Although TACACS+ and RADIUS share much of the same functionality, several important differences exist between them. To make the most appropriate choice in implementing one or both of them in a network, a network administrator should understand these differences. The list that follows and Table 4-1 outline these differences:

- **Functionality**—TACACS+ separates AAA functions according to the AAA architecture, allowing modularity of the security server implementation. RADIUS combines authentication and authorization, and separates accounting, thus allowing less flexibility in implementation.

- **Transport protocol**—TACACS+ uses TCP. RADIUS uses UDP because it simplifies client and server implementation, but it also makes the RADIUS protocol less robust and requires the server to implement reliability measures such as packet retransmission and timeouts because UDP is a connectionless protocol.

- **Challenge/response**—TACACS+ supports bidirectional challenge and response as used in CHAP between two NASs. RADIUS supports unidirectional challenge and response from the RADIUS security server to the RADIUS client.

- **Protocol support**—TACACS+ provides more complete dialup and WAN protocol support than RADIUS, which is limited to PPP.

- **Data integrity**—RADIUS encrypts only the password attribute in the Access-Request packet; however, TACACS+ encrypts the entire packet body of every packet, which makes TACACS+ more secure than RADIUS.

- **Customization**—The flexibility provided in the TACACS+ protocol allows many things to be customized on a per-user basis for customizable username and password prompts. RADIUS lacks flexibility, and therefore many features that are possible with TACACS+ are not possible with RADIUS, such as message catalogs.

- **Authorization process**—With TACACS+, the server accepts or rejects the authentication request based on the contents of the user profile. The client, or NAS, never knows the contents of the user profile. With RADIUS, all reply attributes in the user profile are sent to the NAS. The NAS accepts or rejects the authentication request based on the attributes received.

- **Accounting**—RADIUS accounting can contain more information than TACAC+ accounting records, which is the primary strength of RADIUS over TACACS+. TACACS+ accounting includes a limited number of information fields.

Table 4-1   Comparing TACACS+ and Radius

	TACACS+	RADIUS
Functionality	Separates AAA	Combines authentication and authorization
Transport protocol	TCP	UDP
CHAP	Bidirectional	Unidirectional
Protocol support	Multiprotocol support	No ARA No NetBEUI
Confidentiality	Entire packet encrypted	Password encrypted
Accounting	Limited	Extensive

TACACS+ is generally considered superior because of the following reasons:

- TACACS+ encrypts the entire TACACS+ packet, whereas RADIUS only encrypts the shared secret password portion.

- TACACS+ separates authentication and authorization, making possible distributed security services.

- RADIUS has limited name space for attributes.

Authentication Technologies

Several methods are used to authenticate who you are, in reference to network security. This section looks at static passwords, one-time passwords, token cards, digital certificates, and biometrics.

Static Passwords

Some system administrators and users decide not to use a username and password. This is obviously the least-secure option. A network intruder has to discover only the access method to gain access to the networked system.

A static username/password authentication method remains the same until changed by the system administrator or user. This method is susceptible to playback attacks, eavesdropping, theft, and password-cracking programs. Furthermore, because the password remains the same, when an attacker has access to the password, and subsequently to the network, the attacker continues to have access until the administrator or user chooses to change it.

With the aging username/password authentication method, the user is forced to change the password after a set time, usually 30 to 60 days. Although this method mitigates some risk, it is still susceptible to playback attacks, eavesdropping, theft, and password cracking until the password is changed.

Authentication of usernames and passwords is commonly used with secure Internet applications. For example, some Cisco.com applications require a user to be registered and possess a username and password assigned by CCO. When the user accesses a secure Cisco.com application using a web browser, the application causes the web browser to display a window requesting a username and password. The username and password can be validated using an AAA security server.

Figure 4-3 illustrates an example of dialup authentication using usernames and password authentication. On the client end, the Windows 2000 LAN connection prompts the user for a username and password, which is sent over communication lines using TCP/IP and PPP to a remote NAS or a security server for authentication.

Figure 4-3   Windows User's Dialup Networking Login Screen

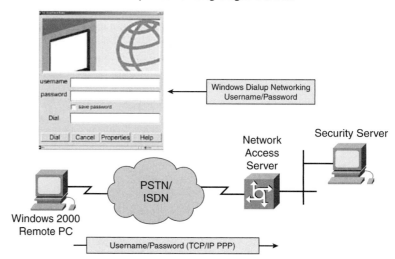

One-Time Passwords

Some remote logins send passwords over networks as clear text. An eavesdropper could capture these passwords and use them to gain unauthorized access to systems. One way to create passwords that can be safely sent over remote connections is to use a one-way hashing algorithm to create a one-time password scheme. This is what S/Key does.

S/Key uses either MD4 or MD5, one-way hashing algorithms developed by Ron Rivest, to create a one-time password system. In this system, passwords are sent in clear text over the network. However, after a password has been used, it is no longer useful to the eavesdropper. The biggest advantage of S/Key is that it protects against eavesdroppers without modification of client software and imposes only marginal inconvenience to the users.

The S/Key system involves three main components:

- **The client**—The client is responsible for providing the login shell to the user. It does not contain any persistent storage for password information

- **The host**—The host is responsible for processing the user login request. It stores the current one-time password and the login sequence number in a file. The host is also responsible for providing the client with a seed value.

- **A password calculator**—The password calculator is a one-way hashing function, which is defined as a function that loses information each time it is applied. The network protocol between the client and the host is completely independent of the hashing function.

Token Cards

Another one-time password authentication method that adds a new layer of security uses a token card or smart card and a token server. Each token card, about the size of a credit card, is programmed to a specific user, and each user has a unique PIN that can generate a password keyed strictly to the corresponding card. Token cards and servers generally work as follows:

1. The user generates a one-time password with the token card using a security algorithm.

2. The user enters the one-time password into the authentication screen generated by the remote client, the Windows Dial-Up Networking screen in Figure 4-4.

3. The remote client sends the one-time password to the token server via the network and a NAS.

4. The token server uses the same algorithm to verify the password is correct and authenticates the remote user.

Figure 4-4   Using Token Cards in the Automation Process

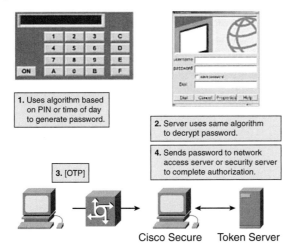

1. Uses algorithm based on PIN or time of day to generate password.

2. Server uses same algorithm to decrypt password.

4. Sends password to network access server or security server to complete authorization.

3. [OTP]

Cisco Secure   Token Server

Token Card and Server Methods

Two token card and server methods exist:

- **Time based**—In this system, the token card contains a cryptographic key and generates a password or token using a PIN entered by the user. The password is entered into the remote client, which sends it to the token server. The password is loosely synchronized in time to the token server. The server compares the token received to a token generated internally. If they match, the user is authenticated and allowed access.

- **Challenge-response**—In this system, the token card stores a cryptographic key. The token server generates a random string of digits and sends it to the remote client that is trying to access the network. The remote user enters the random string, and the token card computes a cryptographic function using the stored key. The result is sent back to the token server, which has also computed the function. If the results match, the user is authenticated.

Token cards are now implemented in software for installation on the remote client. SofToken, which generates single-use passwords without the associated cost of a hardware token, is one example of a software token card.

Digital Certificates

Printed documents are signed and notarized with a seal and a signature. Electronic documents are signed using a digital signature. A digital signature, or certificate, is an encrypted hash that is appended to a document. It can be used to confirm the identity of the sender and the integrity of the document.

Digital signatures are based on a combination of public key encryption and secure one-way hash function algorithms. A digital certificate contains information to identify a user or device, such as the name, serial number, company, department or IP address (see Figure 4-5). It also contains a copy of the entity's public key (see Figure 4-6). A certificate authority (CA) signs the certificate. The CA is a third party that is explicitly trusted by the receiver to validate identities and to create digital certificates, as shown in Figure 4-7. Digital certificates contain the following information:

- Serial number
- Validity dates
- Issuer's name
- Subject's name
- Subject's public key information
- CA signature

Figure 4-5   A Digital Certificate

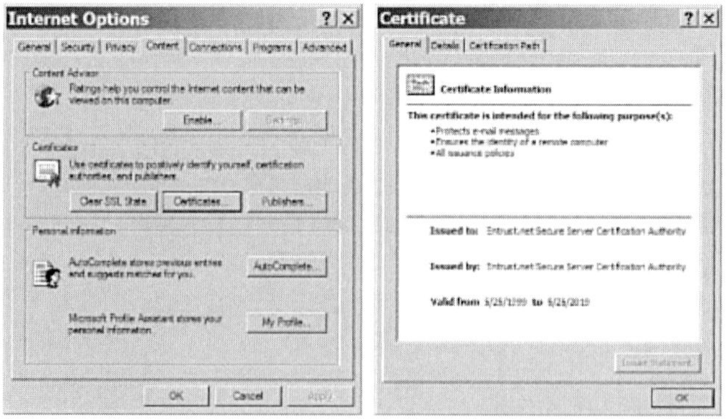

Figure 4-6   Public Key in Digital Certificate

Figure 4-7   Certificate-Based Authentication

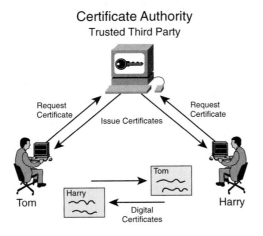

To validate the CA's signature, the receiver must first know the CA's public key. Normally, this is handled out of band or through an operation done at installation. For instance, most web browsers are configured with the public keys of several CAs by default.

Figure 4-8 and the list that follows summarize the digital signature process.

Figure 4-8   Digital Signatures

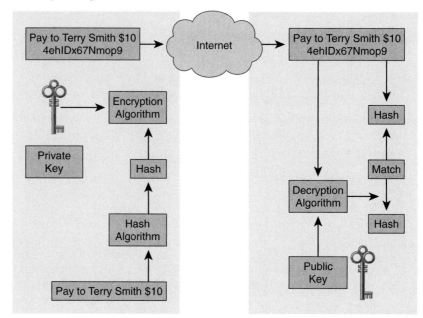

1. At the transmitting end, the private key generated by the sender is used to encrypt the hash. The encrypted hash, which is a digital signature, is attached to the message and forwarded to the remote end.

2. At the receiving end, the hash is produced by running the original message through a hash algorithm.

3. The hash that was appended to the original message is decrypted using the public key from the sender.

4. If the hashes match, the message is signed by a private key that was generated by the sender. Only a specific private key could have produced the digital signature.

Digital signatures are much more scalable than pre-shared keys. Without digital signatures, keys must be manually shared between each pair of devices. Without certificates, every new device added to the network requires a configuration change on every other device it securely communicates with. By using digital certificates, however, each device is enrolled with a CA. When two devices want to communicate, they exchange certificates and digitally sign data to authenticate each other. When a new device is added to the network, one simply enrolls that device with a CA, and none of the other devices need modification. When the new device attempts a connection, certificates are automatically exchanged and the device can be authenticated.

The two common digital signature algorithms are Rivest, Shamir, Adelman (RSA) and Directory System Agent (DSA). RSA is used commercially and is the most common. DSA is used mostly by U.S. government agencies.

Biometrics

Biometrics is the science of measuring a unique physical characteristic about an individual as an identification mechanism. A number of widely used biometric technologies and techniques exist. These techniques can be deployed to help secure the network. The most common biometric technologies are fingerprint scanning and voice recognition. Other technologies, such as face recognition and signature recognition, can also be used in biometric identification.

Biometric access methods for computer systems are gaining popularity because of increased focus on security. Numerous commercial products are already available, and the future will inevitably see all portable devices, access doors, and so on being biometrically protected. The integration of biometrics in the security policy will provide a solid foundation for developing a secure environment.

Fingerprint Scanning

Fingerprint scanning is probably the most widely used biometric technology. The fingertips of each individual have unique characteristics. These characteristics vary from the geometry to the pattern and size of the ridges. Fingerprint scanners can read the fingerprint and convert it into a digital representation. Fingerprint scanners can be small enough to fit on a laptop, keyboard, or mouse. The digital copy made by the scanner is checked against an authorized copy that is stored in a secure system so that it can be used as a comparison for authentication.

Although this technology might seem sophisticated, it has a few drawbacks. For instance, the system can be cheated because it cannot determine whether a fingerprint was made by a live user or was copied. When deciding to deploy biometrics in the network, consider commercially available computer keyboards with integrated fingerprint scanners. These are excellent and relatively cheap options.

Voice Recognition

Voice recognition, sometimes referred to as *speech analysis*, is based on vocal characteristics. Just as with fingerprints, each individual voice has unique characteristics. A few instruments and techniques are available. The most common implementation is a microphone in combination with a speech-analysis application. The purpose of all voice recognition systems is to depict the speech signal in some way and to capture and store its characteristics on a computer system. Again, these characteristics are checked against an authorized copy stored on the central computer system.

Face Recognition

Just as with other recognition techniques, face recognition uses certain parameters and characteristics to reveal an individual's identity. The U.S. Department of Defense is involved in the development of a facial-recognition technology program called FERET. Iris and retina recognition can also be categorized in this segment of biometric technology.

Signature Recognition

Signature identification systems analyze individual signatures based on factors such as speed, acceleration, velocity, pen pressure, and stroke length.

Newer biometric measurements include techniques for DNA comparisons, which will be refined in the years to come.

Identity Based Networking Services (IBNS)

Cisco Identity Based Networking Services (IBNS) is an integrated solution combining several Cisco products that offer authentication, access control, and user policies to secure network connectivity and resources (see Figure 4-9). The Cisco IBNS solution enables greater security while simultaneously offering cost-effective management of changes throughout the organization.

By offering a secure IBNS framework for enterprises to manage user mobility and reduce the overhead costs associated with granting and managing access to network resources, Cisco provides enterprises with the capability to increase user productivity and reduce operating costs.

Figure 4-9   Identity Based Networking Services

Cisco VPN Concentrators, Cisco IOS Routers, PIX Security Appliances

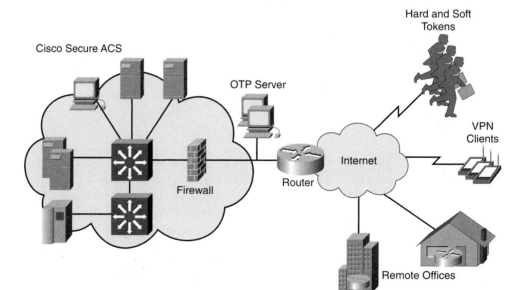

The Cisco IBNS solution provides the following benefits:

- **Intelligent adaptability for offering greater flexibility and mobility to stratified users**—Creating user or group profiles with policies that define trust relationships between users and network resources allows organizations to easily authenticate, authorize, and account for all users of wired or wireless networks.

- **A combination of authentication, access control, and user policies to secure network connectivity and resources**—Because policies are associated with users and not physical ports, users obtain more mobility and freedom, and IT administration is simplified. Greater scalability and ease of management is achieved through policy enforcement and dynamic provisioning.

- **User productivity gains and reduced operating costs**—Providing security and greater flexibility for wired or wireless network access provides enterprises with the capability to have cross-functional or new project teams form more quickly, enables secure access for trusted partners and vendors, and facilitates secure conference-room connectivity. Enabling flexibility with secure network access through centralized policy-based administration decreases the time, complexity, and effort associated with port security techniques at the MAC level.

IBNS is a solution for increasing the security of physical and logical access to an enterprise network that is built on the IEEE 802.1x standard. IBNS and 802.1x are supported on all Cisco Catalyst switches, including Catalyst 6500, 4500, 3550, and 2950 switches, Cisco ACS Server, and Cisco Aironet access points.

Cisco IBNS allows the network administrator to implement true identity-based network access control and policy enforcement at the user and port levels. It provides user and device identification using secure and reliable strong authentication technologies. This solution associates identified entities with policies. The policies are created and administered by management and provide increased granularity of control.

Cisco IBNS is a standards-based implementation of port security that is centrally managed by a RADIUS server (Cisco Secure ACS). Additionally, Cisco IBNS offers greater flexibility and mobility to users by combining access control and user profiles to secure network connectivity, services, and applications. This allows enterprises to increase user productivity and reduce operating costs.

The Cisco IBNS solution will adapt to meet the changing requirements of the standards and of customers. This phase is an early one in a multiphase implementation.

Cisco Catalyst switches support Microsoft Windows XP, Linux, and HP UNIX, with additional 802.1x client support anticipated in the future. Cisco Aironet products support all current versions of Microsoft Windows, Windows CE, Mac OS, Linux, and MS-DOS.

The Cisco IBNS solution is based on standard RADIUS and 802.1x implementations. It interoperates with all IETF authentication servers that comply with these two standards. Cisco has particularly enhanced its Secure ACS to provide a tight integration across all Cisco switches.

The Cisco IBNS solution is a standards-based (802.1x) implementation of port security centrally managed by Cisco Secure ACS. The following section looks at the 802.1x protocol. The 802.1x protocol applies to both wired and wireless networks, and IBNS can be implemented in both types of networks.

802.1x

802.1x is a standardized framework defined by the IEEE, designed to provide port-based network access. 802.1x authenticates network clients using information unique to the client and with credentials known only to the client. This service is called *port-level authentication* because, for security reasons, it is offered to a single endpoint for a given physical port. The 802.1x framework defines three roles in the authentication process (see Figure 4-10).

- The endpoint that is seeking network access is known as the *supplicant*. The supplicant may be an end user device or a standalone device, such as an IP phone.

- The device to which the supplicant directly connects and through which the supplicant obtains network access permission is known as the *authenticator*.

- The authenticator acts as a gateway to the *authentication server*, which is responsible for actually authenticating the supplicant.

Figure 4-10   802.1x Components

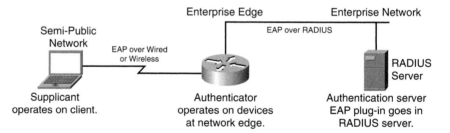

The authentication process, which consists of exchanges of Extensible Authentication Protocol (EAP) messages, occurs between the supplicant and the authentication server, as shown in Figure 4-11. The authenticator acts as a transparent relay for this exchange and as a point of enforcement for any policy configuration instructions the authentication server may send back as a result of the authentication process.

The IEEE 802.1x specification defines a new link-layer protocol, 802.1x, which is used for communications between the supplicant and the authenticator. Communications between the supplicant and authentication server also leverage the RADIUS protocol carried over standard UDP.

Figure 4-11   802.1x

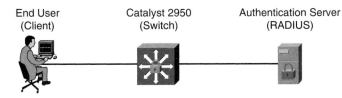

End User   Catalyst 2950   Authentication Server
(Client)   (Switch)   (RADIUS)

Table 4-2 lists some 802.1x benefits.

Table 4-2   802.1x Benefits

Feature	Benefit
802.1x authenticator support	Enables interaction between the supplicant component on workstations and application of appropriate policy.
MAC address authentication	Adds support for devices such as IP phones that do not presently include 802.1x supplicant support.
Default authorization policy	Permits access for unauthenticated devices to basic network service.
Multiple DHCP pools	Authenticated users can be assigned IP addresses from a different IP range than unauthenticated users, allowing network traffic policy application by address range.

IEEE 802.1x is a well-defined standard with industry-wide acceptance. Supplicant, authenticator, and authentication server implementations are available from many vendors, including Cisco.

Wired and Wireless Implementations

The Cisco IBNS solution uses the 802.1x port-based authentication in both a wired or wireless network. The 802.1x port-based authentication is supported in two configurations:

- Point to point
- Wireless LAN

In a point-to-point configuration, only one client can be connected to the 802.1x-enabled switch port. The switch detects the client when the port link state changes to the up state. If a client leaves or is replaced with another client, the switch changes the port link state to down, and the port returns to the unauthorized state.

Figure 4-12 shows 802.1x-port-based authentication in a wireless LAN. The 802.1x port is configured as a multiple-host port that becomes authorized as soon as one client is authenticated. When the port is authorized, all other hosts indirectly attached to the port are granted access to the network. If the port becomes unauthorized, the switch denies access to the network to all the attached clients. The port could become unauthorized if re-authentication fails or an EAP over LAN (EAPOL) logoff message is received. In this topology, the wireless access point is responsible for authenticating the clients attached to it, and the wireless access point acts as a client to the switch.

Figure 4-12   802.1x Wireless LAN Example

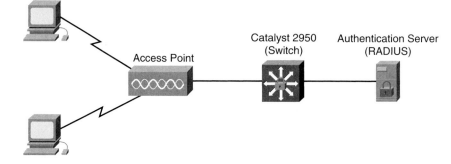

Network Admission Control (NAC)

The significant damage caused by recent worms and viruses demonstrates the inadequacy of existing safeguards. Network Admission Control (NAC), an industry initiative sponsored by Cisco Systems, uses the network infrastructure to enforce security policy compliance on all devices seeking to access network computing resources, thereby limiting damage from viruses and worms.

Using NAC, organizations can provide network access to endpoint devices such as PCs, personal digital assistants (PDAs), and servers that are verified to be fully compliant with established security policy. NAC can also identify noncompliant devices and deny them access, place them in a quarantined area, or give them restricted access to network resources. By combining information about endpoint security status with network admission enforcement, NAC enables organizations to dramatically improve the security of their computing infrastructures.

NAC is part of the Cisco Self-Defending Network. Its goal is to create greater intelligence in the network to automatically identify, prevent, and adapt to security threats.

NAC Components

As Figure 4-13 illustrates, NAC has the following components:

- **Endpoint security software, such as antivirus software, and the Cisco Trust Agent**—The Cisco Trust Agent (CTA) collects security state information from multiple security software clients, such as antivirus clients, and communicates this information to the connected Cisco network where access control decisions are enforced. Application and operating system status, such as antivirus and operating system patch levels or credentials, can be used to determine the appropriate network admission decision. Cisco and NAC cosponsors integrate the CTA with their security software clients.

- **Network access devices**—Network devices that enforce admission control policy include routers, switches, wireless access points, and security appliances. These devices demand host credentials and relay this information to policy servers where network admission control decisions are made. Based on customer-defined policy, the network enforces the appropriate admission control decision-permit, deny, quarantine, or restrict.

- **Policy server**—The policy server is responsible for evaluating the endpoint security information relayed from network devices and for determining the appropriate access policy to apply. Cisco Secure ACS, using RADIUS, is the foundation of the policy server system. It works in concert with NAC cosponsor application servers that provide deeper credential validation capabilities, such as antivirus policy servers. It also works in conjunction with audit servers, which aid in assessing systems that do not respond to NAC credential inquiries.

- **Management system**—Cisco management solutions provision the appropriate NAC elements and provide monitoring and reporting operational tools. CiscoWorks VPN/Security Management Solution (VMS) and CiscoWorks Security Information Management Solution (SIMS) form the basis for this capability. NAC cosponsors provide management solutions for their endpoint security software.

Figure 4-13   Four Components of NAC

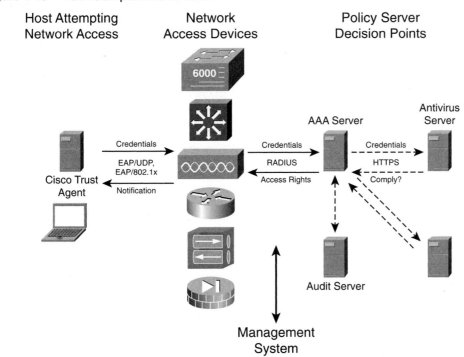

NAC Phases

The first release of NAC addresses the two most pressing compliance tests required: antivirus software and operating system information. This includes antivirus vendor software version; engine level; and signature file levels; and operating system type, patch, and hot fix. The second release of NAC addresses additional security, management, and workplace application checks.

NAC Phase 1

Phase 1 of NAC, released in June 2004, supports Cisco routers communicating with the CTA to gather endpoint security credentials and enforce admission control policy. The CTA software allows NAC to use existing Cisco network devices, Cisco Security Agent software, and cosponsor security software, including antivirus software (see Figure 4-14). Router access control lists (ACLs) restrict the communications between noncompliant hosts and other systems in the network (for example, only allowing communications to an antivirus server to download a new pattern file). NAC currently support endpoints running Microsoft Windows NT, XP, and 2000 operating systems.

Figure 4-14   Cisco Trust Agent Architecture

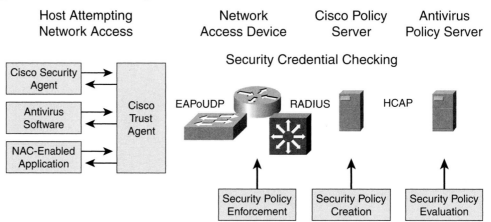

NAC is likely to first be used in monitoring mode, where host compliance is assessed without any attempt to restrict network access. During this time, noncompliant systems may be updated as needed to reach desired compliance levels.

NAC Phase 2

In Phase 2 of NAC, released in October 2005, Cisco switches can assign noncompliant hosts to quarantine VLAN segments on which only remediation servers reside. NAC 2 also supports IPsec remote-access platforms, such as the VPN 3000 concentrators, and expand support for additional endpoint operating systems. NAC 2 also expands support beyond the initial NAC cosponsors to support an even broader range of access policy assessment and enforcement through the implementation of a broad API.

Future NAC releases will support additional access devices, such as firewalls and wireless access points, and continue to expand the platforms which it will support.

NAC Operation

NAC implementation combines a number of existing protocols and Cisco products with some new products and features, including the following:

- CTA and plug-ins

- Cisco IOS network access device (NAD)

- Extensible Authentication Protocol (EAP)

- Cisco Secure ACS/RADIUS

- Posture validation/remediation server

CTA communicates with other software on the client computer over a published API and answers posture queries from the NAD. CTA also implements the communication necessary to implement NAC using EAP over UDP (EOU). The resident software includes a posture plug-in (PP) that interfaces with the CTA. The PP is an agent included with third-party software that reports on the policy and state of this software.

In the current implementation of NAC, the NAD is a Layer 3 Cisco IOS Software device that queries client machines seeking network access using EOU. Figure 4-15 and the detailed list that follows illustrate the way that the different components of the NAC solution interact.

Figure 4-15   NAC Operation

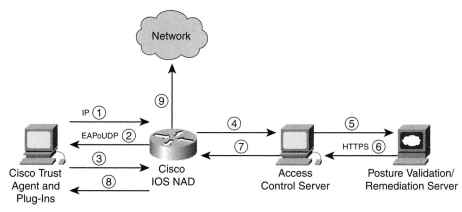

NAC component interaction occurs as follows:

1. Client sends a packet through a NAC-enabled router.

2. NAD begins posture validation using EOU. By combining information about endpoint security status with network admission enforcement, NAC enables organizations to dramatically improve the security of their computing infrastructures.

3. Client sends posture credentials using EOU to the NAD.

4. NAD sends posture to Cisco ACS using RADIUS. These posture credentials contain attributes that hold information about the current state of the client software.

5. Cisco Secure ACS requests posture validation using the Host Credential Authorization Protocol (HCAP) inside an HTTPS tunnel.

6. Posture validation/remediation server sends validation response of pass, fail, quarantine, and so on.

7. To permit or deny network access, Cisco Secure ACS sends an accept with ACLs/URL redirect.

8. NAD forwards posture response to client.

9. Client is granted or denied access, redirected, or contained.

NAC Vendor Participation

The NAC Program is a program in which Cisco shares technology features with program participants. Participants design and sell their client and server applications and services that incorporate features that are compatible with the NAC infrastructure.

Participants in the NAC Program can integrate the Cisco interfaces into their applications and test the applications according to NAC specifications at a Cisco-approved independent test facility. After entering into a NAC Program agreement and after successfully testing their applications, participants can market their devices, applications, and services as NAC enabled.

All shipping NAC-enabled products and solutions, whether from Cisco or other NAC participants, must go through a testing and validation process at an independent third-party testing facility. They are required to interact the same way with the CTA and the Cisco Secure ACS.

Cisco is currently working with the antivirus vendors Network Associates, Symantec, and Trend Micro through the NAC program, which focuses on limiting damage from emerging security threats such as viruses and worms. IBM has announced plans to integrate the Tivoli management suite into NAC. Cisco is broadening NAC vendor participation through an integration program and expects to open elements of NAC to additional industry organizations as it develops.

Cisco is licensing its CTA technology to NAC cosponsors. Antivirus products that include support for CTA include Network Associates' McAfee VirusScan Enterprise 8.0i and McAfee VirusScan Enterprise 7.x, upcoming versions of Symantec Client Security and Symantec AntiVirus Corporate Edition, and the Trend Micro OfficeScan Corporate Edition 6.5.

Table 4-3 contains examples of NAC-enabled applications. Additional products and participants will be available in the future.

Table 4-3   NAC-Enabled Applications

NAC-Enabled Applications	Vendor
eTrust AntiVirus, eTrust PestPatrol	Computer Associates International, Inc.
IBM-NAC enabled applications: Tivoli	IBM
CyberGatekeeper Server 3.1 and CyberGatekeeper Policy Manager 3.1	InfoExpress
VirusScan 7.x and 8.0i	McAfee, Inc.
Symantec AntiVirus 9.0 and Symantec Client Security 2.0	Symantec
Trend Micro OfficeScan Corporate Edition 6.5	Trend Micro, Inc.

Summary

This chapter introduced the concept of AAA security and discussed several important related topics. You should now understand why AAA security is one of the primary components of the overall network security policy of an organization. AAA is essential to providing secure remote access to the network and remote management of network devices.

The chapter also covered TACACS+ and RADIUS and how both can be used in a network to provide authentication and authorization.

Finally, the chapter introduced IBNS and NAC and how these technologies can be used to secure admission to the network

Check Your Understanding

Complete all the review questions listed here to test your understanding of the topics and concepts in this chapter. Answers are listed in Appendix A, "Check Your Understanding Answer Key."

1. TACACS+ uses which transport layer protocol?

    a. IP

    b. TCP

    c. UDP

    d. ICMP

    e. DLC

2. Which two are examples of remote-server security protocols used by AAA? (Choose two.)

    a. Telnet

    b. TACACS+

    c. RADIUS

    d. Security database on NAS

3. How are transactions between a client and a RADIUS server authenticated?

    a. One-time passwords (OTPs)

    b. Shared secret

    c. Public keys

    d. Asymmetric key

4. Why is TACACS+ generally considered to be superior to RADIUS?

    a. TACACS+ is more widely supported than RADIUS.

    b. TACACS+ uses TCP as its transport protocol.

    c. TACACS+ has a more limited name space for attributes, which eases setup.

    d. TACACS+ supports client/server operations.

5. Compared with TACACS+, which two characteristics are considered weaknesses of the RADIUS protocol? (Choose two.)

    a. Poor accounting

    b. Does not encrypt passwords

    c. Does not support CHAP

    d. Uses UDP as transport

    e. Unidirectional challenge and response

6. When using RADIUS as an authentication method, what is the network access server (NAS) acting as?

   a. Peer

   b. Server

   c. Client

   d. Agent

7. After administrators gain access to the network, what AAA function allows them to access network resources?

   a. Authentication

   b. Authorization

   c. Accounting

   d. Access control

8. Which of the following is not a feature of TACAC+?

   a. Extensive accounting

   b. Encrypts entire packet

   c. Multiprotocol support

   d. Uses TCP

CHAPTER 5

Cisco Secure Access Control Server

Upon completion of this chapter, you should be able to answer the following questions:

- What is Cisco Secure Access Control Server for Windows?

- How do I configure RADIUS and TACACS+ with Cisco Secure ACS?

Key Terms

This chapter uses the following key terms. You can find the definitions in the glossary at the end of the book.

One-time passwords (OTPs)   page 248

Database Replication   page 250

Remote Database Management System (RDBMS) page 250

Cisco Secure Access Control Server (ACS) network security software helps you authenticate users by controlling access to an authentication, authorization, and accounting (AAA) client. The AAA client can be any one of many network devices that can be configured to defer authentication and authorization of network users to an AAA server. Cisco Secure ACS operates as a set of Windows services that control the AAA of users accessing networks. This chapter describes features, functions, and architectures of Cisco Secure ACS and how to configure TACACS+ and RADIUS on Cisco routers and switches to work with Cisco Secure ACS.

Cisco Secure ACS for Windows is a network security software application that helps you control access to the campus network, dial-in access, and the Internet.

Upon completing this chapter, you will be able to install, configure, operate, and troubleshoot Cisco Secure ACS for Windows Server.

You will be able to describe the function, features, and architecture of the three components of Cisco Secure ACS for Windows Server. You will also be able to configure TACACS+ and RADIUS with the Cisco Secure ACS for Windows Server.

Cisco Secure Access Control Server Product Overview

Cisco Secure ACS for Windows Server is a network security software application that helps to control access to the campus, dial-in access, and Internet access, as shown in Figure 5-1. Cisco Secure ACS for Windows Server operates as Windows 2000 services and controls AAA of users accessing the network.

Figure 5-1   Cisco Secure ACS Products

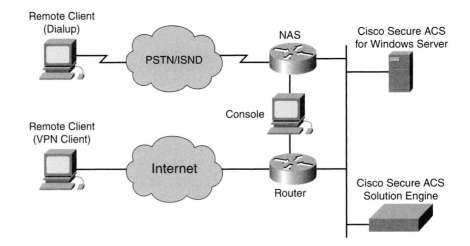

Cisco Secure ACS for Windows Server provides AAA services to network devices that function as AAA clients, such as routers, network access servers, PIX Security Appliances, and VPN 3000 concentrators. An AAA client is any device that provides AAA client functionality and uses one of the AAA protocols supported by Cisco Secure ACS. Cisco Secure ACS allows authentication against Windows 2000 user databases, ACS user databases, token servers, or other external databases. It also supports third-party devices that can be configured with TACACS+ or RADIUS protocols. Cisco Secure ACS treats all such devices as AAA clients. Cisco Secure ACS uses the TACACS+ and RADIUS protocols to provide AAA services that ensure a secure environment.

Cisco Secure ACS helps centralize access control and accounting, in addition to router and switch access management. With Cisco Secure ACS, network administrators can quickly administer accounts and globally change levels of service offerings for entire groups of users. Although the use of an external user database is optional, support for many popular user repository implementations enables companies to use the working knowledge gained from and the investment already made in building the corporate user repositories.

Cisco Secure ACS for Windows Server Version 3.3 is an easy-to-use AAA server that is simple to install and administer. It runs on the Microsoft Windows 2000 Server operating system. The Cisco Secure ACS for Windows Server administration interface is viewed using supported web browsers, making it easy to administer.

Cisco Secure ACS for Windows Server authenticates usernames and passwords against the Windows 2000 user database, the Cisco Secure ACS for Windows Server database, a token server database, or NetWare Directory Services (NDS).

You can use different levels of security with Cisco Secure ACS for different requirements. The basic user-to-network security level is Password Authentication Protocol (PAP). Although it does not represent the highest form of encrypted security, PAP does offer convenience and simplicity for the client. PAP allows authentication against the Windows 2000 database. With this configuration, users need to log in only once. Challenge Handshake Authentication Protocol (CHAP) allows a higher level of security for encrypting passwords when communicating from a client to the network access server (NAS). You can use CHAP (and MS-CHAP) with the Cisco Secure ACS user database, as illustrated in Figure 5-2.

Figure 5-2   Cisco Secure ACS General Features

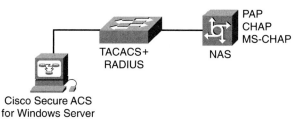

PAP
CHAP
MS-CHAP

TACACS+
RADIUS

NAS

Cisco Secure ACS
for Windows Server

The Cisco Secure ACS extends access security by combining authentication, user or administrator access, and policy control from a centralized platform, allowing greater flexibility and mobility, increased security, and user productivity. The Cisco Secure ACS reduces the administrative and management burden involved in scaling user and network administrative access. By using a central database for all user accounts, the Cisco Secure ACS centralizes the control of all user privileges and distributes them to hundreds or thousands of access points throughout the network. As an accounting service, the Cisco Secure ACS reduces IT operating costs by providing detailed reporting and monitoring capabilities of network users' behavior and by keeping a record of every access connection and device configuration change across the entire network. The Cisco Secure ACS supports a wide array of access connection types, including wired and wireless LAN, dialup, broadband, content, storage, Voice over IP, firewalls, and virtual private networks (VPNs).

Authentication and User Databases

Authentication determines user identity and verifies the information. Traditional authentication uses a name and a fixed password. More modern and secure methods use technologies such as CHAP and *one-time passwords (OTPs)*. Cisco Secure ACS supports a wide variety of these authentication methods.

A fundamental implicit relationship exists between authentication and authorization. The more authorization privileges granted to a user, the stronger the authentication should be. Cisco Secure ACS supports this fundamental relationship by providing various methods of authentication.

Network administrators who offer increased levels of security services, and corporations that want to lessen the chance of intruder access resulting from password capturing, can use an OTP. Cisco Secure ACS supports several types of OTP solutions, including PAP for PPP remote-node login. Token cards are considered one of the strongest OTP authentication mechanisms.

Cisco Secure ACS supports a variety of user databases. In addition to the Cisco Secure user database, Cisco Secure ACS supports several external user databases, including the following:

- Windows NT/2000 user database
- Generic Lightweight Directory Access Protocol (LDAP)
- Novell NDS
- Open Database Connectivity (ODBC)-compliant relational databases
- CRYPTOCard token server
- SafeWord token server
- AXENT token server
- RSA SecureID token server
- ActivCard token server
- Vasco token server

The Cisco Secure ACS User Database

The Cisco Secure ACS user database is crucial for the authorization process. Regardless of whether a user is authenticated by the internal user database or by an external user database, Cisco Secure ACS authorizes network services for users based upon group membership and specific user settings found in the Cisco Secure ACS user database. Therefore, all users authenticated by Cisco Secure ACS, even those authenticated by an external user database, have an account in the Cisco Secure ACS user database.

Figure 5-3   Cisco Secure ACS User Database

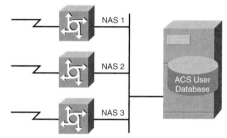

Note

External user databases can only be used to authenticate users and to determine which group Cisco Secure ACS assigns a user to. The Cisco Secure ACS user database, internal to Cisco Secure ACS for Windows Server, provides all authorization services. With few exceptions, Cisco Secure ACS cannot retrieve authorization data from external user databases.

The Cisco Secure ACS user database draws information from several data sources, including a memory-mapped, hash-indexed file, VarsDB.MDB, and the Windows Registry. VarsDB.MDB is a Microsoft Jet database formatted file that yields fast lookup times. This structure enables the Cisco Secure ACS user database to authenticate users quickly.

Unless Cisco Secure ACS is configured to authenticate users with an external user database, Cisco Secure ACS uses usernames and passwords in the Cisco Secure ACS user database during authentication.

You can create user accounts in the Cisco Secure ACS for Windows 2000 Servers in five ways. Of these, RDBMS Synchronization and CSUtil.exe support importing user accounts from external sources.

- **Cisco Secure ACS HTML interface**—The HTML interface enables you to create user accounts manually, one user at a time. Regardless of how a user account was created, a user account can be edited by using the HTML interface.

- **Unknown User Policy**—The Unknown User Policy enables Cisco Secure ACS to add users automatically when a user without an account in the Cisco Secure user database is found in an external user database. The creation of a user account in the Cisco Secure user database occurs only when the user attempts to access the network and is successfully authenticated by an external user database.

- **RDBMS Synchronization**—RDBMS Synchronization enables an administrator to create large numbers of user accounts and to configure many settings for these accounts. This feature is recommended whenever it is necessary to import users by bulk.

- **CSUtil.exe**—The CSUtil.exe command-line utility provides a simple means of creating basic user accounts. When compared to RDBMS synchronization, the functionality is limited. However, it is simple to prepare for importing basic user accounts and assigning users to groups.

- **Database Replication**—Database Replication creates user accounts on a secondary Cisco Secure ACS by overwriting all existing user accounts on a secondary Cisco Secure ACS with the user accounts from the primary Cisco Secure ACS. Any user accounts unique to a secondary Cisco Secure ACS are lost in the replication.

Keeping Databases Current

Database Replication and *Remote Database Management System (RDBMS)* Synchronization are provided with Cisco Secure ACS for Windows Server, as shown in Figure 5-4. These utilities automate the process of keeping the Cisco Secure ACS database and network configuration current. Cisco Secure ACS for Windows Server supports the import of data from ODBC-compliant databases, such as Microsoft Access and Oracle Corporation databases. Another utility, CSUtil, provides database backup and restore functionality.

Figure 5-4   Cisco Secure ACS Database Features

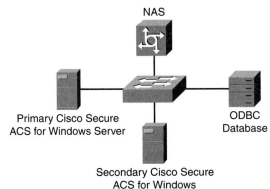

Database Replication

Database Replication enables the administrator to do the following:

- Select the parts of the primary Cisco Secure ACS configuration to be replicated

- Control the timing of the replication process, including creating schedules

- Export selected configuration items from the primary Cisco Secure ACS

- Securely transport selected configuration data from the primary Cisco Secure ACS to one or more secondary Cisco Secure ACSs

- Update the secondary Cisco Secure ACSs to create matching configurations

The primary Cisco Secure ACS sends replicated Cisco Secure database components to other Cisco Secure ACSs. The secondary Cisco Secure ACS receives replicated Cisco Secure database components from a primary Cisco Secure ACS. In the HTML interface, these are identified as replication partners. A Cisco Secure ACS can be both a primary Cisco Secure ACS and a secondary Cisco Secure ACS, provided that it is not configured to be a secondary Cisco Secure ACS to a Cisco Secure ACS for which it performs as a primary Cisco Secure ACS.

RDBMS Synchronization

The RDBMS Synchronization feature enables that administrator to update the Cisco Secure user database with information from an ODBC-compliant data source (see Figure 5-5). The ODBC-compliant data source can be the RDBMS database of a third-party application. It can also be an intermediate file or database that a third-party system updates. Regardless of where the file or database resides, Cisco Secure ACS reads the file or database via the ODBC connection. RDBMS Synchronization supports addition, modification, and deletion for all data items it can access.

Figure 5-5   RDBMS Synchronization

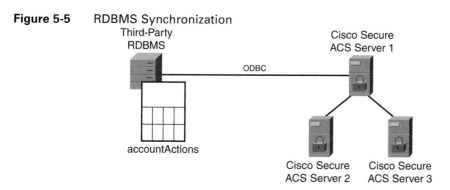

You can configure synchronization to occur on a regular schedule or manually on demand.

Synchronization performed by a single Cisco Secure ACS can update the internal databases of other Cisco Secure ACSs, so configuration of RDBMS Synchronization only needs to occur on one Cisco Secure ACS. Cisco Secure ACSs listen on TCP port 2000 for synchronization data. RDBMS Synchronization communication is encrypted using a 128-bit encrypted, proprietary algorithm.

RDBMS Synchronization Components

The RDBMS Synchronization feature comprises two components:

- **CSDBSync**—A dedicated Windows service that performs automated user and group account management services for Cisco Secure ACS

- **accountActions Table**—The data object that holds information used by CSDBSync to update the Cisco Secure user database

Note

Bidirectional replication, wherein a Cisco Secure ACS both sends database components to and receives database components from the same remote Cisco Secure ACS, is not supported. Replication fails if a Cisco Secure ACS is configured to replicate to and from the same Cisco Secure ACS.

All Cisco Secure ACSs involved in replication must run the same release of the Cisco Secure ACS software. It is strongly recommend that Cisco Secure ACSs involved in replication use the same patch level, too.

OBDC Import Definitions

Cisco Secure ACS supports the import of data from ODBC-compliant databases, such as Microsoft Access or Oracle. Importing is done using a single table to import information into one or more ACS servers.

The CSAccupdate service processes the table and updates local/remote ACS installations according to its configuration.

Cisco Secure ACS for Windows Architecture

When Cisco Secure ACS is installed, the installation adds several modular Windows 2000 services operating together on one server, as shown in Figure 5-6. The services provide the core of Cisco Secure ACS functionality and provide ACS to multiple Cisco authenticating devices. The Cisco Secure ACS services on the computer running Cisco Secure ACS include the following:

- **CSAdmin**—Provides the HTML interface for administration of Cisco Secure ACS

- **CSAuth**—Provides authentication services

- **CSDBSync**—Provides synchronization of the Cisco Secure user database with an external RDBMS application

- **CSLog**—Provides logging services, both for accounting and system activity

- **CSMon**—Provides monitoring, recording, and notification of Cisco Secure ACS performance, and includes automatic response to some scenarios

- **CSTacacs**—Provides communication between TACACS+ AAA clients and the CSAuth service

- **CSRadius**—Provides communication between RADIUS AAA clients and the CSAuth service

Figure 5-6   Cisco Secure ACS System Architecture

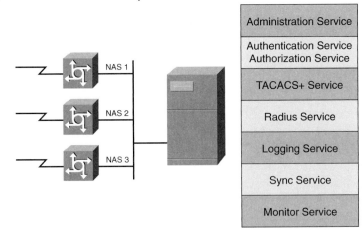

You can start and stop each module individually from within the Microsoft Services Control Panel or as a group from within the Cisco Secure ACS HTML interface.

How Cisco Secure ACS Authenticates Users

Using either the RADIUS or TACACS+ protocol, the NAS directs all dial-in user access requests to Cisco Secure ACS for authentication and authorization of privileges, which verifies the username and password, as shown in Figure 5-7. The following service and ACS user database interaction occurs:

- The TACACS+ or RADIUS service directs the request to the Cisco Secure ACS authentication and authorization service, where the request is authenticated against the Cisco Secure ACS user database, associated authorizations are assigned, and accounting information is logged to the Cisco Secure ACS logging service.

- The Windows 2000 user database does not authenticate and grant dial permission as a local user. The user may log in to Windows 2000 after the dialup AAA process is complete.

Figure 5-7   Using the ACS Database Alone

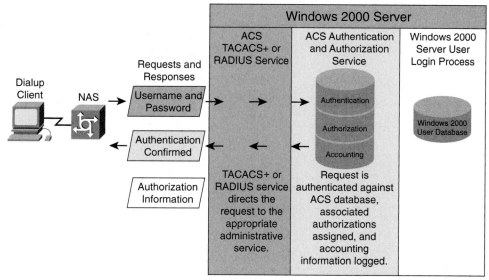

Using a Windows Database

When Cisco Secure ACS uses the Windows 2000 Server user database for AAA, the following service and database interaction occurs (see Figure 5-8):

1. TACACS+ or RADIUS service directs the request to the Cisco Secure ACS Authentication and Authorization service, where the username and password are sent to the Windows 2000 user database for authentication.

2. If approved, Windows 2000 Server grants dial permission as a local user.

3. A response is returned to Cisco Secure ACS, and authorizations are assigned.

4. Confirmation and associated authorizations assigned in Cisco Secure ACS for that user are sent to the NAS. Accounting information is logged.

Using the Windows 2000 user database makes single login for dial-in and network login possible, because the username and password used for authentication are the same used for network login.

Figure 5-8   Using a Windows Database

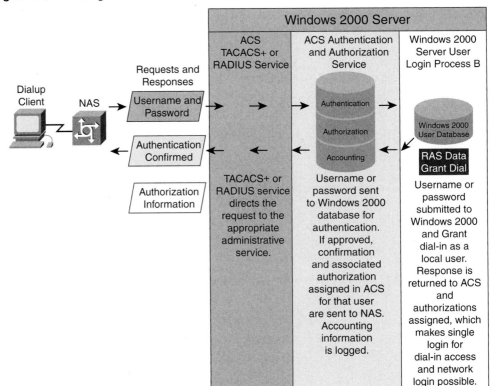

Using an External User Database

You can configure Cisco Secure ACS to forward authentication of users to one or more external user databases, as shown in Figure 5-9. In organizations in which a substantial user database already exists, Cisco Secure ACS can leverage the work already invested in building the database without any additional input.

Figure 5-9   Using an External User Database

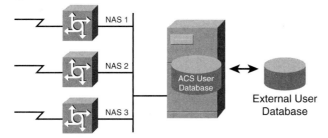

For Cisco Secure ACS to interact with an external user database, Cisco Secure ACS requires an application programming interface (API) for third-party authentication. Cisco Secure ACS communicates with the external user database using the API. For Windows user databases and Generic LDAP, the program interface for the external authentication is local to Cisco Secure ACS. In these cases, no further components are required. For other third-party authentication sources, additional components might be required.

In addition to performing authentication for network access, Cisco Secure ACS can perform authentication for TACACS+ enable privileges using external user databases.

Using Token Cards

Cisco Secure ACS supports several third-party token servers, including the following:

- LEAP proxy RADIUS servers
- RSA SecurID token servers
- RADIUS-based token servers, including these:
  — ActivCard token servers
  — CRYPTOCard token servers
  — Vasco token servers
  — PassGo token servers
  — SafeWord token servers
  — Generic RADIUS token servers

For some token servers, Cisco Secure ACS acts as a client to the token server. For others, it uses the RADIUS interface of the token server for authentication requests. As with the Windows 2000 database, after the username is located in the Cisco Secure ACS user database, CSAuth can check the selected token server to verify the username and token card password. The token server then provides a response approving or denying validation. If the response is approval, CSAuth knows that authentication should be granted for the user.

Cisco Secure ACS can support token servers using the RADIUS server built in to the token server. Instead of using the proprietary API of the vendor, Cisco Secure ACS sends standard RADIUS authentication requests to the RADIUS authentication port on the token server.

Cisco Secure ACS supports any token server that is RADIUS-server compliant with Internet Engineering Task Force (IETF) RFC 2865. So, in addition to the RADIUS-enabled token server vendors explicitly supported, you can use any token server that supports RADIUS-based authentication.

You can create multiple instances of each of these token server types in Cisco Secure ACS for Windows Server.

Figure 5-10 illustrates how token cards function in a Cisco Secure ACS environment.

Figure 5-10   Using Token Cards

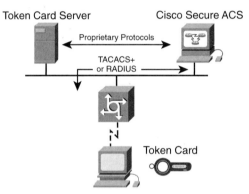

User-Changeable Passwords

Starting with Cisco Secure ACS for Windows Server Version 3.2, system administrators can enable User-Changeable Password (UCP) (see Figure 5-11). UCP is an application that enables users to change their Cisco Secure ACS passwords with a web-based utility. A web server that runs Microsoft Internet Information Server (IIS) 5.0 or later is required to install UCP.

When users need to change passwords, they can access the UCP server web page using a supported web browser. The UCP web page requires users to log in. The password required is the PAP password for the user account. UCP authenticates the user with Cisco Secure ACS and then allows the user to specify a new password. UCP changes both the PAP and CHAP passwords for the user to the password submitted.

Communication between the UCP server and the Cisco Secure ACS system is protected with 128-bit encryption. To further increase security, it is recommended to implement Secure Sockets Layer (SSL) to protect communication between user web browsers and the UCP server.

The SSL protocol provides security for remote-access data transfer between the UCP web server and the user's web browser. Because users change their Cisco Secure ACS database passwords over a connection between their web browsers and Microsoft IIS, user and password data are vulnerable. The SSL protocol encrypts data transfers, including passwords, between web browsers and Microsoft IIS.

Figure 5-11   User-Changeable Passwords

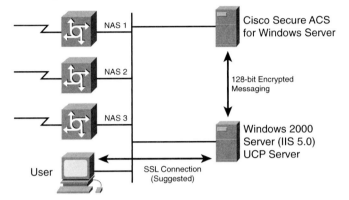

Configuring RADIUS and TACACS+ with Cisco Secure ACS

This section covers all aspects of configuring RADIUS and TACACS+ with the Cisco Secure ACS, including the following:

- Installation steps

- Administering Cisco Secure ACS for Windows

- Troubleshooting

- Enabling TACACS+

- Verifying TACACS+

- Configuring RADIUS

Installation Steps

During new Cisco Secure ACS installations, or upgrades and reinstallations that do not preserve the existing configuration, the installation requires specific information about the computer that Cisco Secure ACS will be installed on and an AAA client on the network. To facilitate the installation, collect the applicable information before beginning the installation.

Note

If Cisco Secure ACS is being upgraded or reinstalled and the existing configuration and database are to be kept, you do not have to perform the following procedure, which requires information already recorded in the original Cisco Secure ACS installation.

To collect information that is required during the installation of Cisco Secure ACS, follow these steps:

Step 1.   Determine whether the computer that Cisco Secure ACS will be installed on is a domain controller or a member server. If Cisco Secure ACS is going to be used to authenticate users with a Windows domain user database, be aware that after Cisco Secure ACS is installed additional Windows configuration is necessary.

Step 2.   For the first AAA client that will be configured to use AAA services provided by Cisco Secure ACS, determine which AAA protocol and vendor-specific attribute to implement:

- TACACS+ (Cisco IOS)
- RADIUS (Cisco Aironet)
- RADIUS (Cisco BBSM)
- RADIUS (Cisco IOS/PIX)
- RADIUS (Cisco VPN 3000)
- RADIUS (Cisco VPN 5000)
- RADIUS (IETF)
- ADIUS (Ascend)
- RADIUS (Juniper)
- RADIUS (Nortel)
- RADIUS (iPass)

Step 3.   Record the name of the AAA client.

Step 4.   Record the IP address of the AAA client.

Step 5.   Record the IP address of the computer where Cisco Secure ACS will be installed.

Step 6.   Record the TACACS+ or RADIUS key.

The Cisco Secure ACS installation can be condensed to the following steps:

Step 1.   Preconfigure the Windows 2000 Server system.

Step 2.   Verify a basic network connection between the Windows 2000 Server and the router or routers using ping and Telnet.

Step 3.   Install Cisco Secure ACS for Windows Server on the Windows 2000 Server system.

Step 4.   Initially configure Cisco Secure ACS for Windows Server via the web browser interface.

Step 5.   Configure the router or routers for AAA.

Step 6.   Verify correct installation and operation.

Lab 5.2.1 Install and Configure CSACS 3.3 for Windows

In this lab, you install Cisco Secure ACS for Windows 2000. Students then examine the features of Cisco Secure ACS for Windows.

Administering Cisco Secure ACS for Windows

The Cisco Secure ACS for Windows Server web browser interface, as shown in Figure 5-12, makes administration of AAA features easy.

Figure 5-12   Administering Cisco Secure ACS for Windows

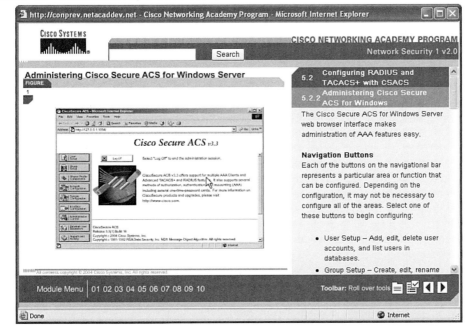

Navigation Buttons

Each of the buttons on the navigational bar represents a particular area or function that you can configure. Depending on the configuration, it might not be necessary to configure all the areas. Select one of these buttons to begin configuring:

- **User Setup**—Add, edit, delete user accounts, and list users in databases.

- **Group Setup**—Create, edit, rename groups, and list all users in a group.

- **Shared Profile Components**—Develop and name reusable, shared sets of authorization components that may be applied to one or more users or groups of users and referenced by name within their profiles. Components include network access restrictions (NARs), command authorization sets, and downloadable PIX Security Appliance access control lists (ACLs).

- **Network Configuration**—Configure and edit AAA clients and server parameters, add and delete network access clients and servers, and configure AAA server distribution parameters.

- **System Configuration**—Start and stop Cisco Secure ACS services, configure logging, control database replication, and control RDBMS Synchronization.

- **Interface Configuration**—Configure user-defined fields that will be recorded in accounting logs, configure TACACS+ and RADIUS options, and control display of options in the user interface.

- **Administration Control**—Control administration of Cisco Secure ACS from any workstation on the network.

- **External User Databases**—Configure the unknown user policy, configure authorization privileges for unknown users, and configure external database types.

- **Reports & Activity**—Select **Reports & Activity** in the navigational bar to view the following information. These files can be imported into most database and spreadsheet applications. The following is a partial list of the types of reports available when accessing Reports & Activity:

  — **TACACS+ Accounting Report**—Lists when sessions stop and start, records NAS messages with username, provides caller line identification information, and records the duration of each session

  — **RADIUS Accounting Report**—Lists when sessions stop and start, records NAS messages with username, provides caller line identification information, and records the duration of each session

  — **Failed Attempts Report**—Lists authentication and authorization failures with an indication of the cause

  — **Logged-In Users**—Lists all users currently receiving services for a single network access server or all network access servers with access to Cisco Secure ACS

  — **Disabled Accounts**—Lists all user accounts that are currently disabled

  — **Admin Accounting Reports**—Lists configuration commands entered on a TACACS+ (Cisco) NAS

- **Online Documentation**—Provides more detailed information about the configuration, operation, and concepts of Cisco Secure ACS.

Troubleshooting

Start troubleshooting Cisco Secure ACS-related AAA problems by examining the Failed Attempts Report under Reports and Activity, as shown in Figure 5-13. The report shows several types of failures and provides a valuable source of troubleshooting information.

Figure 5-13 Troubleshooting

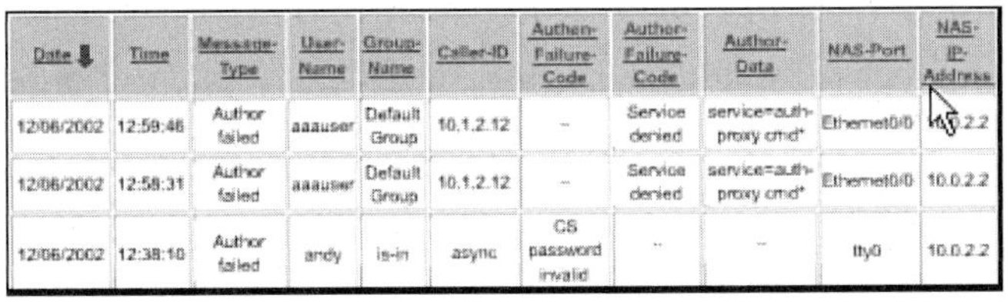

Date ↓	Time	Message-Type	User-Name	Group-Name	Caller-ID	Authen-Failure-Code	Author-Failure-Code	Author-Data	NAS-Port	NAS-IP-Address
12/06/2002	12:59:46	Author failed	aaauser	Default Group	10.1.2.12	–	Service denied	service=auth-proxy cmd*	Ethernet0/0	10.0.2.2
12/06/2002	12:58:31	Author failed	aaauser	Default Group	10.1.2.12	–	Service denied	service=auth-proxy cmd*	Ethernet0/0	10.0.2.2
12/06/2002	12:38:10	Author failed	andy	is-in	async	CS password invalid	–	–	tty0	10.0.2.2

Authentication Failure

Assuming that Cisco Secure ACS and the router are communicating, you can check the following.

If authenticating against the Windows 2000 user database, check these items:

- Are the username and password being entered correctly? The password is case sensitive.

- Do the username and password exist in the Windows 2000 user database? Check for these in the User Manager.

- Is the dial-in interface on the network access server configured with the **ppp authentication pap** command?

- Is the User Must Change Password at Next Login check box checked in Windows 2000 Server? Deselect it if so.

- Does the username have the rights to log on locally in the Windows 2000 Server window (Trust Relationship/Domain)?

- Is Cisco Secure ACS configured to authenticate against the Windows 2000 user database?

- Is Cisco Secure ACS configured to reference the Grant Dial-In Permission to User setting (trust relationship/domain)?

- If the username was able to authenticate before and cannot now, is the account disabled on Windows 2000 Server or Cisco Secure ACS?

- Has the password expired on Windows 2000 Server?

- Does the username contain an illegal character?

- Windows 2000 Server sends domain name and username for authentication if using dialup networking.

Authorization Failure

If the dial-in user is authenticating, but authorization is failing, check the following:

- Are the proper network services checked in the Group Settings area?

- If IP is checked, how is the dial-in user obtaining an IP address?

- Is there an IP pool configured on the NAS?

- Is the name of the IP pool entered in the Group Settings area? (Leave blank if a default IP pool has been configured.)

- If authorizing commands, has the **aaa authorization commands 1 tacacs+** command been entered in to the Cisco IOS Software configuration? The **1** can be substituted for any privilege level from 0 through 15.

- Has the Permitted radio button for the command been selected?

- Has the Permitted radio button for the argument been selected?

Enabling TACACS+

Note

When using the Cisco IOS **aaa new-model** command, always provide for an enable password login method. This guards against the risk of being locked out of the router should the administrative session fail while enabling AAA, or if the TACACS+ server becomes unavailable.

The first steps in configuring the router are as follows:

Step 1.   Enable TACACS+.

Step 2.   Specify the list of Cisco Secure ACS servers that will provide AAA services for the router.

Step 3.   Configure the encryption key that is used to encrypt the data transfer between the router and the Cisco Secure ACS server.

The configuration mode command **aaa new-model** forces the router to override every other authentication method previously configured for the router lines. If an administrative Telnet or console session is lost while enabling AAA on a Cisco router, and no enable password is specified, the administrator might be locked out of the router.

At a minimum, you should enter the following commands in the order shown:

```
router(config)#aaa new-model
router(config)#aaa authentication login default group tacacs+ enable
```

Specifying the **enable** authentication method enables the administrator to reestablish a Telnet or console session and use the enable password to access the router. If this is not done, and the administrator is locked out of the router, physical access to the router is required, with a minimum of having to perform a password-recovery sequence. At worst, the entire configuration saved in nonvolatile random-access memory (NVRAM) can be lost.

To begin global configuration, enter the following commands, using the correct IP address of the Cisco Secure ACS servers and your own encryption key:

```
router(config)#tacacs-server key keystring
router(config)#tacacs-server host ip-address
```

For example:

```
router(config)#tacacs-server key 2bor!2b@?
router(config)#tacacs-server host 10.1.2.4
```

You can use these two commands to share the key with all servers. For a single server, you use the following command:

```
router(config)#tacacs-server host ip-address key keystring
```

For example:

```
router(config)#tacacs-server host 10.1.2.4 key 2bor!2b@?del
```

The **2bor!2b@?** global key is the encryption key shared between the router and the two Cisco Secure ACS servers. The encryption key should be kept secret to protect the privacy of passwords that are sent between the Cisco Secure ACS servers and the router during the authentication process.

The **tacacs-server key** command is used when two or more TACACS+ servers share the same key. You can specify multiple Cisco Secure ACS servers, each with its own key, by using a **tacacs-server host** command for each server, as follows:

```
router(config)# tacacs-server host 10.1.2.4 key keyforTACACS1
router(config)# tacacs-server host 10.1.2.5 key i
```

After enabling AAA globally on the access server, define the authentication method lists and apply them to lines and interfaces. These authentication method lists are security profiles that indicate the protocol or login and authentication method used.

To define an authentication method list using the **aaa authentication** command, complete the following steps:

Step 1. Specify the dial-in protocol, such as AppleTalk Remote Access Protocol (ARAP), PPP, or NetWare Access Server Interface (NASI), or login authentication.

Step 2. Identify a list name or default. A list name can be any alphanumeric string. You can assign different authentication methods to different named lists. You can specify only one dial-in protocol per authentication method list. However, you can create multiple authentication method lists with each of these options. Each list must have a different name.

Specify the authentication method, such as TACACS+, followed by local in case a TACACS+ server is not available on the network. You can specify up to four multiple methods.

After defining these authentication method lists, apply them to one of the following:

- **Lines**—tty lines or the console port for login and asynchronous lines, in most cases, for AppleTalk Remote Access (ARA)

- **Interfaces**—Interfaces, either synchronous or asynchronous, that are configured for PPP

Use the following command in global configuration mode to enable AAA authentication processes:

```
Router(config)#aaa authentication {login | enable default | arap | ppp | nasi} {default |
list-name} method1 [method2 [method3 [method4]]]
```

The syntax for the **aaa authentication login** command is as follows:

```
aaa authentication login {default | list-name} method1 [method2...]
```

where:

- **default**—Uses the listed authentication methods that follows this argument as the default list of methods when a user logs in

- *list-name*—Defines the character string used to name the list of authentication methods activated when a user logs in

- *method*—Specifies at least one of the following keywords:

  — **enable**—Uses the enable password for authentication

  — **krb5**—Uses Kerberos 5 for authentication

  — **krb5-telnet**—Uses Kerberos 5 Telnet authentication protocol when using Telnet to connect to the router

  — **line**—Uses the line password for authentication

  — **local**—Uses the local username database for authentication

  — **local-case**—Uses case-sensitive local username database for authentication

  — **none**—Uses no authentication

  — **group radius**—Uses the list of all RADIUS servers for authentication

  — **group tacacs+**—Uses the list of all TACACS+ servers for authentication

  — **group** *group-name*—Uses a subset of RADIUS or TACACS+ servers for authentication as defined by the **aaa group server radius** or **aaa group server tacacs+** commands

Verifying TACACS+

When TACACS+ is used on a router, you can use the **debug tacacs** command for more detailed debugging information.

To trace TACACS+ packets, enter the following command on the router:

```
debug tacacs
```

Use the following **debug** command to display information from the TACACS+ helper process:

```
debug tacacs events
```

Example 5-1 shows part of the **debug aaa authentication** command output for a TACACS login attempt that succeeded. The information indicates that TACACS+ is the authentication method used.

```
Example 5-1    The debug aaa authentication Command
14:01:17:  AAA/AUTHEN  (567936829) :
Method=TACACS+
14:01:17:  TAC+:   send AUTHEN/CONT packet
14:01:17:  TAC+:  (567963829):   received authen
Response status = PASS
14:01:17:  AAA/AUTHEN  (567963829):   status = PASS
```

Also, note that the AAA/AUTHEN status indicates that the authentication has passed.

There are three possible results of an AAA session:

- PASS
- FAIL
- ERROR

Failure

Example 5-2 shows part of the **debug tacacs** command output for a TACACS login attempt that was unsuccessful, as indicated by the status FAIL. The status fields are probably the most useful part of the **debug tacacs** command.

```
Example 5-2     debug tacacs Command Example Output: Failure
13:53:35: TAC+:  Opening TCP/IP connection to 10.1.1.4/49
13:53:35: TAC+:  Sending TCP/IP packet number 416942312-1 to
10.1.1.4/49(AUTHEN/START)
13:53:35: TAC+:  Receiving TCP/IP packet number 416942312-2 from
10.1.1.4/49
13:53:35: TAC+:  (416942312):  received authen response status =
GETUSER
13:53:37: TAC+:  send AUTHEN/CONT packet
13:53:37: TAC+:  Sending TCP/IP packet number 416942312-3 to
10.1.1.4/49(AUTHEN/CONT)
13:53:37: TAC+:  Receiving TCP/IP packet number 416942312-4 from
10.1.1.4/49
13:53:37: TAC+:  (416942312):  received authen response status =
GETPASS
13:53:38: TAC+:  send AUTHEN/CONT packet
13:53:38: TAC+:  Sending TCP/IP packet number 416942312-5 to
10.1.1.4/49(AUTHEN/CONT)
13:53:38: TAC+:  Receiving TCP/IP packet number 416942312-6 from
10.1.1.4/49(AUTHEN/CONT)
13:53:38: TAC+:  (416942312):  received authen response status = FAIL
13:53:40: TAC+:  Closing TCP/IP connection to 10.1.1.4/49
```

Pass

Example 5-3 shows part of the **debug tacacs** command output for a TACACS login attempt that succeeded, as indicated by the status PASS.

```
Example 5-3     TACACS+ Authentication Pass
14:00:09: TAC+:  Opening TCP/IP connection to 10.1.1.4/49
14:00:09: TAC+:  Sending TCP/IP packet number 383258052-1 to
10.1.1.4/49(AUTHEN/START)
14:00:09: TAC+:  Receiving TCP/IP packet number 383258052-2 from
10.1.1.4/49
14:00:09: TAC+:  (383258052):  received authen response status =
GETUSER
14:00:10: TAC+:  send AUTHEN/CONT packet
14:00:10: TAC+:  Sending TCP/IP packet number 383258052-3 to
10.1.1.4/49  (AUTHEN/CONT)
14:00:10: TAC+:  Receiving TCP/IP packet number 383258052-4 from
10.1.1.4/49
14:00:37: TAC+:  (383258052):  received authen response status =
GETPASS
14:00:14: TAC+:  send AUTHEN/CONT packet
```

Example 5-3   TACACS+ Authentication Pass   *continued*

```
14:00:14: TAC+:  Sending TCP/IP packet number 383258052-5 to
10.1.1.4/49(AUTHEN/CONT)
14:00:14: TAC+:  Receiving TCP/IP packet number 383258052-6 from
10.1.1.4/49
14:00:14: TAC+:  (383258052):  received authen response status = PASS
14:00:14: TAC+:  Closing TCP/IP connection to 10.1.1.4/49
```

Example 5-4 shows sample **debug tacacs events** output.

Example 5-4   **debug tacacs events** Command Output

```
router#debug tacacs events
%LINK-3-UPDOWN: Interface Async2, changed state to up
00:03:16:  TAC+:  Opening TCP/IP to 10.1.1.4/49 timeout=15
00:03:16:  TAC+:  Opened TCP/IP handle 0x48A87C to 10.1.1.4/49
00:03:16:  TAC+:  periodic timer started
00:03:16:  TAC+:  10.1.1.4 req=3BD868 id=1242409656 ver=193 handle=0x48AB87C (ESTAB)
expire=14 AUTHEN/START/SENDAUTH/CHAP queued
00:03:17:  TAC+:  10.1.1.4  ESTAB 3BD868 worte 46 of 46 bytes
00:03:22:  TAC+:  10.1.1.4  CLOSEWAIT read=12 wanted=12 alloc=12 got=12
00:03:22:  TAC+:  10.1.1.4  CLOSEWAIT read=61 wanted=61 alloc=61 got=49
00:03:22:  TAC+:  10.1.1.4  received 61 byte reply for 3BD868
00:03:22:  TAC+:  req=3BD868 id=-1242409656 ver=193 handle=0x48A87C (CLOSEWAIT)
  expire=9
AUTHEN/START/SENDAUTH/CHAP processed
00:03:22:  TAC+:  periodic timer stopped (queue empty)
00:03:22:  TAC+:  Closing TCP/IP 0x48A87C connection to 10.1.1.4/49
00:03:22:  TAC+:  Opening TCP/IP to 10.1.1.4/49 timeout=15
00:03:22:  TAC+:  Opened TCIP/IP handle 0x489F08 to 10.1.1.4/49
00:03:22:  TAC+:  periodic timer started
00:03:22:  TAC+:  10.1.1.4 req=3BD868 id=299214410 ver=192 handle=0x489F08 (ESTAB)
expire=14 AUTHEN/START/SENDAUTH/CHAP queued
00:03:23:  TAC+:  10.1.1.4  ESTAB 3BD868 wrote 41 of 41 bytes
00:03:23:  TAC+:  10.1.1.4  CLOSEWAIT read=12 wanted=12 alloc=12 got=12
00:03:23:  TAC+:  10.1.1.4  CLOSEWAIT read=21 wanted=21 alloc=21 got=9
00:03:23:  TAC+:  10.1.1.4  received 21 byte reply for 3BD868
00:03:23:  TAC+:  req=3BD868 id=299214410 ver=192 handle=0x489F08 (CLOSEWAIT)
  expire=13
AUTHEN/START/SENDAUTH/CHAP processed
00:03:23:  TAC+:  periodic timer stopped (queue empty)
```

In this example, the opening and closing of a TCP connection to a TACACS+ server are shown, as are the bytes read and written over the connection and the connection's TCP status.

The TACACS messages are intended to be self-explanatory or for consumption by service personnel only. However, the messages shown are briefly explained in the following text:

This message indicates that a TCP open request to host 10.1.1.4 on port 49 will time out in 15 seconds if it gets no response:

```
00:03:16: TAC+: Opening TCP/IP to 10.1.1.4/49 timeout=15
```

This message indicates a successful open operation and provides the address of the internal TCP "handle" for this connection:

```
00:03:16: TAC+: Opened TCP/IP handle 0x48A87C to 10.1.1.4/49
```

For more detailed information, refer to the Debug Command Reference at Cisco.com.

You can obtain more meaningful output from **debug** commands if the router is configured using the following command:

```
service timestamps type [uptime] datetime [msec] [localtime] [show-timezone]
```

where:

- *type*—Indicates the type of message to time-stamp: debug or log

- **uptime**—Optional keyword that creates a time stamp with the time since the system was rebooted

- **datetime**—Creates a time stamp with the date and time

- **msec**—Optional keyword that includes the milliseconds in the date and time stamp

- **localtime**—Optional keyword that creates a time stamp relative to the local time zone

- **show-timezone**—Optional keyword that includes the time zone name in the time stamp

Configuring RADIUS

RADIUS configuration is a three-step process:

Step 1.   Configure communication between the router and the RADIUS server.

Step 2.   Use the AAA global configuration commands to define method lists containing RADIUS to define authentication and authorization methods. Method lists include the following keywords:

- **enable**—Uses the enable password for authentication

- **line**—Uses the line password for authentication

- **local**—Uses local username database for authentication

- **none**—Uses no authentication

- **radius**—Uses RADIUS authentication

— **tacacs+**—Uses TACACS+ authentication

Step 3.   AAA accounting for RADIUS connections can be created.

Use **line** and **interface** commands to cause the defined method lists to be used.

Use the **radius-server** command to configure router-to-RADIUS server communication. The **radius-server** global command is analogous to **tacacs server** global commands.

To begin global configuration, enter the following commands, using the correct IP address of the Cisco Secure ACS servers and your own encryption key:

```
router(config)#radius-server key keystring
router(config)#radius-server host ip-address
```

For example:

```
router(config)#radius-server key 2bor!2b@?
router(config)#radius-server host 10.1.2.4
```

You can use these two commands to share the key with all servers. For a single server, you use the following command:

```
router(config)#radius-server host ip-address key keystring
```

For example:

```
router(config)#tacacs-server host 10.1.2.4 key 2bor!2b@?del
```

Summary

This chapter covered Cisco Secure ACS for Windows Server and how to configure it to provide AAA services for a typical network. The chapter first gave an introduction into Cisco Secure ACS for Windows, describing the features, functions, architecture, and supported protocols and databases. It then detailed these same objects and the services installed as part of Cisco Secure ACS. The module then covered the installation and configuration of a new installation of Cisco Secure ACS for Windows Server. Administration and troubleshooting of the ACS was then covered, after which AAA configuration on the router was discussed (including configuration for TACACS+ and RADIUS). Troubleshooting and debugging AAA were also covered.

Check Your Understanding

Complete all the review questions listed here to test your understanding of the topics and concepts in this chapter. Answers are listed in Appendix A, "Check Your Understanding Answer Key."

1. Which three protocols does Cisco Secure ACS support for user-to-NAS authentication? (Choose three.)

   a. CHAP

   b. IPsec

   c. L2TP

   d. MS-CHAP

   e. PAP

   f. PPP

2. Which Microsoft Windows platform meets the minimum requirement to install Cisco Secure ACS Version 3.3?

   a. Windows 98

   b. Windows XP Professional

   c. Windows 2000 Server

   d. Windows 2000 Professional

3. Which utility provides database backup and restore functionality to Cisco Secure ACS?

   a. CSUtil

   b. CSAccupdate

   c. CSDBSync

   d. CSAdmin

4. Which Cisco Secure ACS Windows service checks a selected token server to verify the username and token card password and then provides a response approving or denying validation?

   a. CSAdmin

   b. CSAuth

   c. CSLog

   d. CSMon

   e. CSTacacs

5. Which three database types does Cisco Secure ACS for Windows support for user authentication? (Choose three.)

   a. RSA SecureID token server database

   b. Windows NT/2000 user database

   c. Certificate authority database

   d. Cisco Secure ACS database

   e. Flat-file database

6. Cisco Secure ACS can authenticate clients using a number of different databases. Which user database makes single login for both dial-in and network authentication possible?

   a. The ACS database

   b. A Windows database

   c. An external user database

   d. A token server database

7. Which situation is an example of an authorization failure?

   a. A user tries to log in to a server and is denied access.

   b. A user tries to open a spreadsheet file but is denied access.

   c. A user tries to log in to an account but has forgotten the password.

   d. A user tries to log in to an application, but there is no record of the user using it.

CHAPTER 6

Configure Trust and Identity at Layer 3

Upon completion of this chapter, you should be able to answer the following questions:

- What is the Cisco IOS Firewall authentication proxy?

- What are some of the PIX Security Appliance AAA features?

- How do I configure AAA on the PIX Security Appliance?

Key Terms

This chapter uses the following key terms. You can find the definitions in the glossary at the end of the book.

Authentication proxy   page 274

Dynamic access control entries (ACEs)   page 274

Authentication proxy provides dynamic, per-user authentication and authorization, authenticating users against industry-standard TACACS+ and RADIUS authentication protocols. Authenticating and authorizing connections by users provides more robust protection against network attacks. In this module, you learn how to configure a Cisco router to authenticate using authentication proxy. This module then examine how to configure, monitor, and troubleshoot authentication, authorization, and accounting (AAA) configurations on the PIX Security Appliance.

Cisco IOS Firewall Authentication Proxy

The Cisco IOS Firewall *authentication proxy* feature enables network administrators to apply specific security policies on a per-user basis. Users can be identified and authorized on the basis of their per-user policy, and access privileges can be tailored on an individual basis, as opposed to a general policy applied across multiple users.

With the authentication proxy feature, users can log in to the network or access the Internet via HTTP, HTTPS, FTP, or Telnet, and their specific access profiles are automatically retrieved and applied from a Cisco Secure Access Control Server (ACS) or other authentication server. The user profiles are active only when there is active traffic from the authenticated users.

The authentication proxy is compatible with other Cisco IOS security features such as Network Address Translation (NAT), Context-Based Access Control (CBAC), IPsec encryption, and the Cisco VPN Client.

Authentication Proxy Operation

When a user initiates an HTTP, HTTPS, FTP, or Telnet session through the firewall, it triggers the authentication proxy, as shown in Figure 6-1. The authentication proxy first checks to determine whether the user has been authenticated. If a valid authentication entry exists for the user, the session is allowed and no further intervention is required by the authentication proxy. If no entry exists, the authentication proxy responds to the connection request by prompting the user for a username and password.

Users must successfully authenticate with the authentication server by entering a valid username and password. If the authentication succeeds, the user's authorization profile is retrieved from the AAA server. The authentication proxy uses the information in this profile to create *dynamic access control entries (ACEs)-*and add them to the inbound access control list (ACL) of an input interface, and to the outbound ACL of an output interface if an output ACL exists at the interface. By doing this, the firewall allows authenticated users access to the network as permitted by the authorization profile.

If the authentication fails, the authentication proxy reports the failure to the user and prompts the user for a configurable number of retries.

The authentication proxy sets up an inactivity, or idle, timer for each user profile. So long as there is activity through the firewall, new traffic initiated from the user's host does not trigger the authentication proxy, and all authorized user traffic is permitted access through the firewall.

If the idle timer expires, the authentication proxy removes the user's profile information and dynamic ACL entries. When this happens, traffic from the client host is blocked. The user must initiate another HTTP, HTTPS, FTP, or Telnet connection to trigger the authentication proxy.

Figure 6-1   Authentication Proxy Request from a Remote User

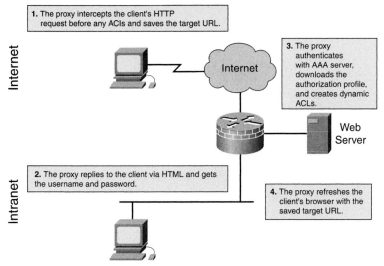

Supported AAA Servers

The Cisco IOS Firewall authentication proxy supports the following AAA protocols and servers, as shown in Figure 6-2:

Figure 6-2   Supported AAA Servers

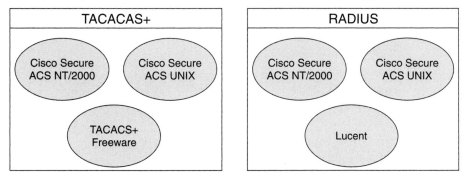

- TACACS+

  — Cisco Secure ACS for Windows 2000 Server

  — Cisco Secure ACS for UNIX

  — TACACS+ Freeware

- RADIUS

  — Cisco Secure ACS for Windows 2000 Server

  — Cisco Secure ACS for UNIX

  — Lucent

  — Other standard RADIUS servers

AAA Server Configuration

The authentication proxy is applied in the inward direction at any interface on the router where per-user authentication and authorization occurs, as shown in Figure 6-3. Applying the authentication proxy inward at an interface causes it to intercept a user's initial connection request before that request is subjected to any other processing by the firewall. If the user fails to authenticate with the AAA server, the connection request is dropped.

How the authentication proxy is applied depends on the security policy. For example, all traffic through an interface can be blocked, and then the authentication proxy feature can be enabled to require authentication and authorization for all user-initiated HTTP, HTTPS, FTP, or Telnet connections. Users are authorized for services only after successful authentication with the AAA server. The authentication proxy feature also enables administrators to use standard ACLs to specify a host or group of hosts whose initial HTTP, HTTPS, FTP, or Telnet traffic triggers the proxy.

Figure 6-3   Authentication Proxy Configuration

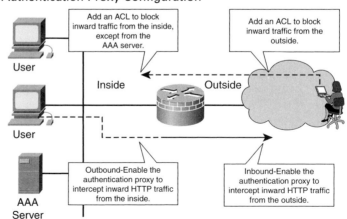

You can configure the Cisco Secure ACS for Windows Server AAA server to support authentication proxy by configuring the AAA authorization auth-proxy service, as demonstrated in Figure 6-4. This creates a new section in the Group Setup frame in which user profiles can be created. This does not interfere with other types of services that the AAA server might have.

Figure 6-4   Create auth-proxy service in the Cisco Secure ACS

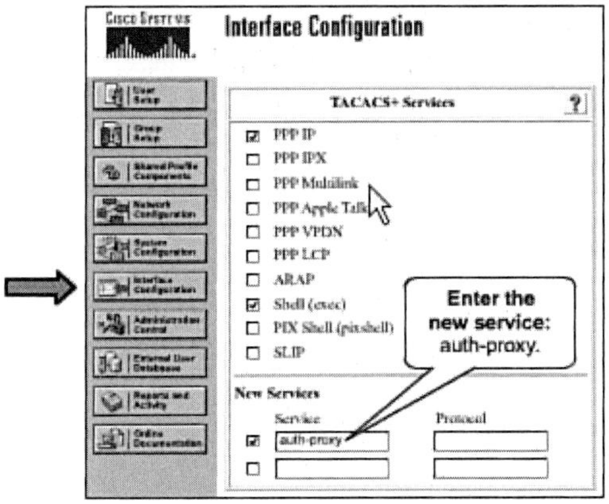

AAA Configuration

Use the **aaa new-model** global configuration command to enable the AAA access control system. Use the **no** form of this command to disable AAA. By default, **aaa new-model** is not enabled. The syntax for this command is as follows:

```
Router (config)#[no] aaa new-model
```

Specify Authentication

To set AAA authentication, use the **aaa authentication login** global configuration command, the syntax for which is as follows:

```
Router(config)#[no] aaa authentication login default method1 [method2]
```

where *method1* [*method2*] can be **group tacacs+**, **group radius**, or both.

Specify Authorization

To set AAA authorization, use the following global configuration command:

```
Router(config)#[no] aaa authorization auth-proxy default method1 [method2]
```

The **aux-proxy** keyword enables authorization proxy for AAA methods.

Again, *method1* [*method2*] can be **group tacacs+**, **group radius**, or both.

Note

After AAA is enabled, TACACS and extended TACACS commands are no longer available. If AAA functionality is initialized and a decision is made later to use TACACS or extended TACACS, issue the no version of this command and then enable the version of TACACS to be used.

Define a TACACS+ Server

To specify the IP address of a TACACS+ server, use the following global configuration command:

```
Router(config)#[no] tacacs-server host ip-addr
```

where *ip-addr* is the IP address of the TACACS+ server.

You can use multiple **tacacs-server host** commands to specify additional servers. The servers are used in the order in which they are specified.

To set the authentication encryption key used for all TACACS+ communications between the Cisco IOS Firewall router and the AAA server, use the following global configuration command:

```
Router(config)#[no] tacacs-server key string
```

where *string* is the key used for authentication and encryption.

Define a RADIUS Server

To specify the IP address of a RADIUS server, use the following global configuration command:

```
Router(config)#[no] radius-server host ip-addr
```

where *ip-addr* is the IP address of the RADIUS server.

You can use multiple **radius-server host** commands to specify additional servers. The servers are used in the order in which they are specified.

Note

The key entered for either the **tacacs-server key** or the **radius-server key** command must match the key used on the AAA server. All leading spaces are ignored, but spaces within and at the end of the key are not. If spaces are used in the key, do not enclose the key in quotation marks unless the quotation marks themselves are part of the key.

To set the authentication encryption key used for all RADIUS communications between the Cisco IOS Firewall router and the AAA server, use the following global configuration command:

```
Router(config)#[no] radius-server key string
```

where *string* is the key used for authentication and encryption.

 Lab 6.1.3   Configure Local AAA on a Cisco Router

In this lab, you secure and test access to the EXEC mode, vty lines, and the console. You configure local database authentication using AAA. You then verify and test the AAA configuration.

Allow AAA Traffic to the Router

All traffic requiring authentication and authorization should be denied by the router using extended ACLs, as shown in Example 6-1. Upon successful authentication, dynamic ACEs are inserted into the ACLs to permit only the traffic authorized by the user profile. The authentication proxy customizes each of the ACEs in the user profile by replacing the source IP addresses in the downloaded ACL with the source IP address of the authenticated host.

An extended ACL should be applied to the inbound direction of the interface that is configured for proxy authentication. All other ACLs that restrict traffic in the direction of authenticated traffic flow should be extended ACLs so that proxy authentication can dynamically update the ACEs as necessary to permit authorized traffic to pass.

Example 6-1   Allow AAA Traffic to the Router

```
Router(config)#access-lists 111 permit tcp host 10.9.9.2 eq tacacs host 10.0.0.1
Router(config)#access-list 111 permit icmp any any
Router(config)#access-list 111 deny ip any any
Router(config)#interface ethernet0/0
Router(config-if)#ip access-group 111 in
```

If the AAA server resides on the same interface where proxy authentication is configured, you must configure an ACL to permit TACACS+ or RADIUS traffic from the AAA server to the firewall.

Use the following guidelines when writing the extended ACL:

- To permit AAA server communication, create an ACE where the source address is the AAA server and destination address is the interface where the AAA server resides.

- Some traffic might need to be permitted without requiring authentication, such as Internet Control Message Protocol (ICMP) or routing updates.

- Deny all other traffic.

- Apply the extended ACL to the inbound direction of the interface where proxy authentication is configured.

To use the authentication proxy with HTTP, use the **ip http server** command to enable the HTTP server on the router. Then, use the **ip http authentication aaa** command to require the HTTP server to use AAA for authentication:

```
Router(config)#ip http server
Router(config)#ip http authentication aaa
```

The HTTPS feature requires a Cisco IOS crypto image. Enabling this feature supports these options:

- HTTP-initiated sessions normally exchange the username and password in clear text. This exchange is encrypted when using HTTPS.

- HTTPS-initiated sessions are proxy authenticated.

To use the authentication proxy with HTTPS, use the **ip http secure-server** command to enable the HTTP server on the router. Then, use the **ip http authentication aaa** command to require the HTTP server to use AAA for authentication.

Note

Proxy authentication does not update ACLs blocking return traffic. If traffic in the opposite direction must be restricted, use static ACLs to manually permit return traffic for authorized traffic. Preferably, use CBAC to dynamically create ACLs to securely permit return traffic for proxy-authenticated sessions.

Lab 6.1.4   Configure Authentication Proxy

In this lab, you first configure Cisco Secure ACS for Windows 2000. You also configure authentication, authorization, and accounting (AAA). You then configure an authentication proxy. Finally, you test and verify the functionality of the authentication proxy.

Authentication Proxy Configuration

This section discusses how to configure the authentication proxy settings on a Cisco router.

Set Global Timers

The inactivity timeout value is the length of time that an authentication cache entry, along with its associated dynamic user ACL, is managed after a period of inactivity. To set the global authentication proxy inactivity timeout value, use the following global configuration command:

```
Router(config)#[no] ip auth-proxy {inactivity-timer min | absolute-timer min}
```

The **inactivity-timer** *min* option specifies the length of time in minutes that an authentication cache entry, along with its associated dynamic user ACL, is managed after a period of inactivity. Enter a value in the range 1 to 35,791. The default value is 60 minutes. This option must be set to a higher value than the idle timeout of any CBAC protocols; otherwise, when the authentication proxy removes the user profile along with the associated dynamic user ACLs, there might be some idle connections monitored by CBAC. Removing these user-specific ACLs could cause those idle connections to hang. If the CBAC idle timeout value is shorter, CBAC resets these connections when the CBAC idle timeout expires, which is before the authentication proxy removes the user profile.

The **absolute-timer** *min* option allows administrators to configure a window during which the authentication proxy on the enabled interface is active. Enter a value in the range 1 to 35,791 minutes (45 and half days). The default value is 0 minutes. After the absolute timer expires, the authentication proxy is disabled regardless of any activity. The global absolute timeout value can be overridden by the local value, which is enabled via the **ip auth-proxy name** command. The absolute timer is turned off by default, and the authentication proxy is enabled indefinitely.

Define and Apply Authentication Proxy Rules

To create an authentication proxy rule, use the following global configuration command:

```
router(config)#[no] ip auth-proxy name auth-proxy-name {ftp | http | telnet}[inactivity-
timer min] [absolute-timer min] [list {acl-num | acl-name}]
```

where:

- *auth-proxy-name*—Associates a name with an authentication proxy rule. Enter a name of up to 16 alphanumeric characters.

- **ftp** | **http** | **telnet**—Selecting one of these three protocols specifies what will trigger the authentication proxy

- **inactivity-timer** *min*—(Optional)Overrides the global authentication proxy cache timer for a specific authentication proxy name, offering more control over timeout values. Enter a value in the range 1 to 2,147,483,647. The default value is equal to the value set with the **ip auth-proxy** command. This argument replaces **auth-cache-time** in previous releases; some versions support both arguments.

- **absolute-timer** *min*—(Optional)Specifies a window in which the authentication proxy on the enabled interface is active. Enter a value in the range 1 to 65,535 minutes (45 and a half days). The default value is 0 minutes.

- **list**—(Optional)Specifies a standard (1–99), extended(100–199), or named IP ACL to use with the authentication proxy. With this option, the authentication proxy is applied only to those hosts in the ACL. If no list is specified, all connections initiating HTTP, FTP, or Telnet traffic arriving at the interface are subject to authentication.

To apply an authentication proxy rule at a firewall interface, use the following interface configuration command:

```
router(config-if)#[no] ip auth-proxy auth-proxy-name
```

The *auth-proxy-name* argument specifies the name of the authentication proxy rule to apply to the interface configuration. The authentication proxy rule is established with the authentication proxy name command.

Example 6-2 demonstrates configuring an authentication proxy rule.

> **Example 6-2**   Authentication Proxy Rule
>
> ```
> router(config)#ip auth-proxy name aprule http
> router(config)#interface ethernet0
> router(config-if)#ip auth-proxy aprule
> ```

Note

A proxy authentication rule can consist of multiple statements, each specifying a different authentication type. This configuration supports proxy authentication for multiple applications, using a combination of HTTP, HTTPS, FTP, or Telnet authentication at the same time.

Authentication Proxy Rules with ACLs

An authentication proxy rule can be associated with an ACL, providing control over which hosts use the authentication proxy. To create an authentication proxy rule with ACLs, use the following global configuration command:

```
router(config)#[no] ip auth-proxy name auth-proxy-name list {acl-num | acl-name}
```

where:

- *auth-proxy-name*—Associates a name with an authentication proxy rule. Enter a name of up to 16 alphanumeric characters.

- **list** {*acl-num* | *acl-name*}—(Optional) Specifies a standard (1–99), extended (100–199), or named IP access list to sue with the authentication proxy. With this option, the authentication proxy is applies only to those hosts in the ACL. If no list is specified, all connections initiating HTTP, FTP, or Telnet traffic arriving at the interface are subject to authentication.

Example 6-3 demonstrates configuring an authentication proxy rule with ACLs.

Example 6-3   Authentication Proxy Rules with ACLs

```
router(config)#ip auth-proxy name aprule http list 10
router(config)#access-list 10 permit 10.0.0.0 0.0.0.255
router(config)#interface ethernet0
router(config-if)#ip auth-proxy aprule
```

Test and Verify Authentication Proxy

You can use the following commands in privileged EXEC mode to test and verify the authentication proxy configuration:

- **show ip auth-proxy**

- **debug ip auth-proxy**

- **clear ip auth-proxy cache**

Use the **show ip auth-proxy** command to display the authentication proxy entries, the running authentication proxy configuration, or the authentication proxy statistics. The syntax of the **show ip auth-proxy** command is as follows:

```
show ip auth-proxy {cache | configuration | statistics}
```

where:

- **cache**—Lists the host IP address, the source port number, the timeout value for the authentication proxy, and the state for connections using authentication proxy. If the authentication proxy stat is HTTP_ESTAB, the user authentication was successful.

- **configuration**—Displays all authentication proxy rules configured on the router.

- **statistics**—Displays all router statistics related to the authentication proxy.

The **debug ip auth-proxy** is another useful command, the syntax for which is as follows:

```
debug ip auth-proxy {ftp | function-trace | http | object-creation | object-deletion | tcp |
telnet | timer}
```

where:

- **ftp**—Displays FTP events related to the authentication proxy

- **function-trace**—Displays the authentication proxy functions

- **http**—Displays HTTP events related to the authentication proxy

- **object-creation**—Displays additional entries to the authentication proxy cache

- **object-deletion**—Displays deletion of cache entries for the authentication proxy

- **tcp**—Displays TCP events related to the authentication proxy

- **telnet**—Displays Telnet-related authentication proxy events

- **timer**—Displays authentication proxy timer-related events

The **clear ip auth-proxy cache** command clears authentication proxy entries from the router. The syntax of the **clear ip auth-proxy cache** command is as follows:

```
clear ip auth-proxy cache {* | ip_addr}
```

where:

- *—Clears all authentication proxy entries, including user profiles and dynamic ACLs

- *ip_addr*—Clears the authentication proxy entry, including user profiles and dynamic ACLs, for the specified IP address

Introduction to PIX Security Appliance AAA Features

This section examines PIX Security Appliance AAA features and AAA server support.

PIX Security Appliance Authentication

Three types of authentication are available on the PIX Security Appliance:

- Access authentication

- Cut-through proxy authentication

- Tunnel access authentication

PIX Security Appliance access authentication enables the administrator to require authentication verification to access the PIX. The following access authentication service options are available:

- Enable password

- Serial

- SSH

- HTTP

- Telnet

In the example in Figure 6-5, a remote administrator is attempting to access the PIX Security Appliance via Secure Shell (SSH) from a home office while a local administrator is attempting to access the security appliance via Telnet. Both must be authenticated before they are permitted to access the PIX.

For cut-through proxy authentication, you can configure the PIX Security Appliance to require user authentication for a session through the PIX, as specified in the **aaa authentication** command.

Only Telnet, FTP, HTTPS, and HTTP sessions can be intercepted to authenticate users. In the example in Figure 6-5, a remote user is attempting an HTTP session with the web server. If the user is authenticated by the PIX, the HTTP session to the web server is connected, or cut through. The PIX then shifts the session flow and all traffic flows directly between the server and the client while maintaining session state information.

For tunnel access authentication, you can configure the PIX Security Appliance to require a remote tunnel user to authentication prior to full tunnel establishment. In the example in Figure 6-5, a remote user establishes an IPsec tunnel with the home office to gain access to the corporate web server. Before the tunnel is fully established, the PIX prompts the remote user for a username and password. The credentials are verified before the remote user tunnel is fully established and the user is allowed to access the corporate web server.

Figure 6-5   Types of Authentication

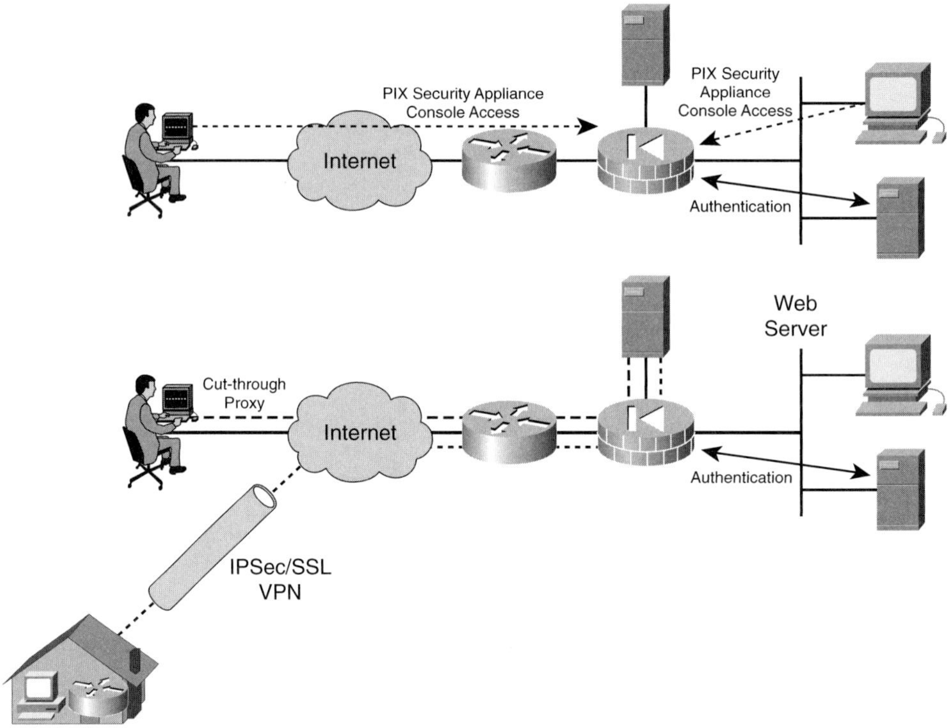

PIX Security Appliance Authorization

PIX Security Appliance access authorization is a way of facilitating and controlling administration, who can access the security appliance and which commands they can execute. The administrator assigns commands to a privilege level. The administrator creates user accounts and links a privilege level to each user. When a console user attempts to access the security appliance console, the user is prompted for a username and password. When authenticated, the console user is granted the access-level privileges assigned to their user account.

If the administrator wants to allow all authenticated users to perform HTTP, HTTPS, FTP, and Telnet through the PIX Security Appliance, authentication is sufficient, and authorization is not needed. If there is reason to allow only some subset of users, or to limit users to certain sites and protocols, however, authorization is needed. The PIX supports two basic methods of user authorization:

- The PIX Security Appliance is configured with rules specifying which connections need to be authorized by the AAA server. When the first packet of a traffic flow matches a predefined rule, the AAA server is consulted by the PIX for access rights. The AAA server returns a permit or deny authorization message.

- The PIX Security Appliance is configured with rules specifying which connections need to be authenticated by the AAA server. The AAA server is configured with authorization rules assigned to the authenticating user. The authorization rules come in the form of ACLs. An ACL is attached to the user or group profile, on the AAA server. When the first packet of a traffic flow matches a predefined rule, The AAA server is consulted by the PIX to determine whether to permit or deny the traffic. During the authentication process, if the end user is authenticated, the Cisco ACS server downloads an ACL to the PIX. The ACL is applied to the traffic flow. Cisco ACS can store ACLs and download them to the PIX. When a remote user attempts to establish a tunnel to the PIX, the administrator can force the tunnel user to authenticate before granting access to the security appliance. When a tunnel user authenticates, the PIX retrieves tunnel information for the defined user, or group. The tunnel authorization information can include such information as virtual private network (VPN) access hours, simultaneous logins, client block rules, personal computer firewall type, idle timeout, and so on. The tunnel group information is applied to the tunnel before the tunnel is fully established.

PIX Security Appliance Accounting

An administrator can configure the PIX Security Appliance to enable accounting for specific network services. Accounting records are generated to track the initiation and termination of predefined sessions. The PIX can be configured to generate accounting records for configuration changes. For example, accounting records can track when a Telnet user logged in to the PIX, at what privilege level, what configuration commands were entered, and when they terminated the session. Accounting records can track the beginning and end of a web session between a remote user and the corporate demilitarized zone (DMZ) web server. Accounting records can also be used to track the start and finish of remote tunnel access sessions. These records are kept on the designated AAA server or servers.

AAA Server Support

The PIX Security Appliance supports authentication and authorization using its own local server, an internal database, or an external AAA server. Accounting is tracked on an external accounting server.

The protocol for communications between the PIX Security Appliance and an external AAA sever varies by AAA feature. Table 6-1 presents a graphic representation of the AAA features, functions, and supported protocols. Across the top are the three AAA features:

- Authentication
- Authorization
- Accounting

Within each AAA feature are the three functions that can use the AAA features:

- Tunnel access
- Console access
- Cut-through proxy

Along the left side are the supported AAA protocols:

- Local, referring to the PIX Security Appliance internal database
- RADIUS
- TACACS+
- NT
- Kerberos
- Lightweight Directory Access Protocol (LDAP)

Table 6-1   AAA Server Support

Protocol	Authentication			Authorization			Accounting		
	Tunnel Access	Console Access	Cut-Through Proxy	Tunnel Access	Console Access	Cut-Through Proxy	Tunnel Access	Console Access	Cut-Through Proxy
Local	✓	✓	✓	✓	✓				
RADIUS	✓	✓	✓	✓		✓	✓	✓	✓
TACACS+	✓	✓	✓		✓	✓	✓	✓	✓
SDI	✓								
NT	✓								
Kerberos	✓								
LDAP				✓					

Configure AAA on the PIX Security Appliance

This section looks at all the aspects of configuring AAA on the PIX Security Appliance. These aspects include PIX Security Appliance access authentication, interactive user authentication, and the local user database. The "PIX Security Appliance Access Authentication" subsection explores prompts and timeouts, cut-through proxy authentication, and authentication of non-Telnet, -FTP, or -HTTP traffic. This section also looks at authorization configurations, to include downloadable ACLs. The section ends with accounting configurations and how to troubleshoot AAA configurations.

PIX Security Appliance Access Authentication

The **aaa authentication serial console** command enables administrators to require authentication verification to access the PIX Security Appliance console. Authenticated access to the PIX console involves different types of prompts, depending on the option that is chosen with the **aaa authentication [serial | enable | telnet | ssh] console** command.

The **enable** and **ssh** options allow three tries before stopping access attempts with an access denied message. The **enable** option requests a username and password before accessing privileged mode for serial, Telnet, or SSH connections. The **ssh** option requests a username and password before the first command-line prompt on the SSH console connection.

The **serial** option requests a username and password before the first command-line prompt on the serial console connection.

The **telnet** option forces the user to specify a username and password before the first command-line prompt of a Telnet console connection.

By default, both the **serial** and **telnet** options cause the user to be prompted continually until that user successfully logs in. The administrator might choose to configure a maximum failed attempts value for local database users.

Telnet access to the Security Appliance console is available from any internal interface and requires previous use of the **telnet** command. Telnet access to the outside interface is only available though an IPsec tunnel. SSH access to the Security Appliance console is available from any interface and requires previous use of the **ssh** command. An IPsec tunnel is not required for SSH access to the outside interface.

Interactive User Authentication

Configuring interactive user authentication is a three-step process, as follows:

Step 1.   Specify a AAA server group. The administrator defines a group name and the authentication protocol:

```
pixfirewall(config)# radius-server key string
```

Step 2.   Designate an authentication server. The administrator defines the location of the AAA server and a key:

```
pixfirewall(config)# aaa-server server-tag [{if_name}] host ip_address
```

Step 3.   Enable user authentication. The administrator defines a rule to specify which security appliance access method to authenticate and which authentication server to reference:

```
pixfirewall(config)#aaa authentication [serial | enable | telnet |ssh | http]
console server_tag [local]
```

Specify a AAA Server Group

Use the **aaa-server** command to specify AAA server groups. For PIX Security Appliance access authentication, the PIX supports TACACS+, RADIUS, and local database authentication. Separate groups of TACACS+ or RADIUS servers for specifying different types of traffic can be defined, such as a TACACS+ server for inbound traffic and another for outbound traffic. The **aaa** command references the server tag to direct AAA traffic to the appropriate AAA server.

You can configure up to 15 single-mode server groups, and each group can have up to 16 AAA servers, for a total of up to 240 TACACS+ or RADIUS servers. When a user logs in, the servers are accessed one at a time starting with the first server in the server group configuration, until a server responds.

The default configuration provides the following two **aaa-server** entries:

```
aaa-server tacacs+ protocol tacacs+
aaa-server radius protocol radius
```

Note

The Security Appliance listens for RADIUS on ports 1645 and 1646. If the RADIUS server uses ports 1812 and 1813, it must be configured to use ports 1645 and 1646.

Designate an Authentication Server

The next step is to define the AAA server and the AAA server attributes, using the following command:

```
pixfirewall(config)#aaa-server server_tag (if_name) host ip_address key timeout seconds
```

where:

- *server_tag*—Specifies a case-sensitive alphanumeric string that is the name of the server group. Use the *server_tag* in the **aaa** command to associate **aaa authentication, aaa authorization,** and **aaa accounting** command statements with a AAA server.

- *if_name*—Specifies the interface name on the side where the AAA server resides.

- **host** *ip_address*—Specifies the IP address of the TACACS+ or RADIUS server.

- *key*—Specifies the case-sensitive, alphanumeric keyword of up to 127 characters that is the same value as the key on the TACACS+ server. Any characters entered past the limit of 127 are ignored. The key is used for encrypting data between the client and server. The key must be the same on both the client and server systems. Spaces are not permitted in the key, but other special characters are allowed. If a key is not specified, encryption does not occur.

- **timeout** *seconds*—Indicates a retransmit timer that specifies the duration of the period during which the Security Appliance retries access. The Security Appliance retires access to the AAA server four times, each time for the length of this period, before choosing the next AAA server. The default is 5 seconds. The maximum time is 30 seconds. For example, if the timeout value is 10 seconds, the Security Appliance retransmits for 10 seconds; and if no acknowledgment is received, tries 3 times more, for a total of 40 seconds, to retransmit data before the next AAA server is selected.

For example, in Figure 6-6, there is a AAA server that belongs to the NY_ACS group. It is located out the inside interface and has an IP address of 10.0.0.2. The encryption key is **secretkey**, and the request timeout is 10 seconds, based on the following configuration:

```
pixfirewall(config)#aaa-server NY_ACS (inside) host 10.0.0.2 secretkey timeout 10
```

Figure 6-6   Specifying a AAA Server Group

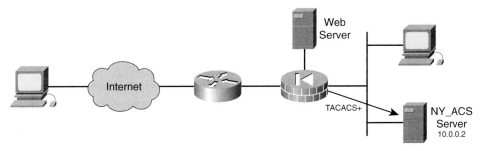

Enable User Authentication

To require authentication verification to access the console of the PIX Security Appliance, use the following command:

```
aaa authentication [serial | enable | telnet | ssh | http] console server_tag LOCAL
```

where:

- **serial**—Specifies access verification for the Security Appliance's serial console.
- **enable**—Specifies access verification for the Security Appliance's privilege mode.
- telnet—Specifies access verification for Telnet access to the Security Appliance console.
- **ssh**—Specifies verification for SSH access to the Security Appliance console.
- **http**—Specifies verification for HTTP access to the Security Appliance (via PDM).
- **console**—Specifies that access to the Security Appliance console requires authentication.
- *server_tag*—Specifies the server tag set with the **aaa-server** command. To use the local Security Appliance user authentication database, enter **LOCAL** for this parameter.

Authenticated access to the PIX Security Appliance console involves different types of prompts, depending on the option used with the **aaa authentication console** command.

To configure administrative authentication to support fallback to the local user database if all servers in the specified server group or groups are disabled, use the **aaa authentication command** with the **local** option specified. This feature is disabled by default. Referring to back to example in Figure 6-6, each access method authenticates using the NY_ACS server. In the event the NY_ACS server is no longer accessible, the PIX Security Appliance is configured to access the local database for console access authentication.

The Local User Database

An administrator can configure a local database in the PIX Security Appliance. The local database can be the primary means for authenticating console access or as a fallback database when the AAA server is no longer accessible. Use the following command to create user accounts in the local user database:

```
username name {nopassword | password password}
```

You can create a password for the user or create a user account with no password using the **nopassword** keyword. Use the **encrypted** keyword if the password is already encrypted, and use the **privilege** keyword to assign a privilege level to the user.

To delete an existing user account, use the **no username** command. To remove all the entries from the user database, enter the **clear config username** command.

In the example in Figure 6-7, the administrator defines a user **admin** with a password of **cisco123** in the PIX local database, using the following configuration:

```
pixfirewall(config)#username admin password cisco123
pixfirewall(config)#aaa authentication telnet console LOCAL
```

When Telnet access to the PIX is attempted, the user is authenticated using the PIX local internal database.

Figure 6-7   How to Add Users to the Local Database

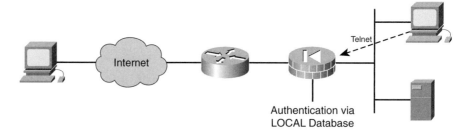

The **aaa local authentication attempts max-fail** *fail-attempts* command enables the administrator to set a limit on the number of retries for serial and Telnet access users. After the limit is exceeded, the users are locked out. The administrator can use the **show aaa local user** command to view the local user lock-time, failed-attempts, and locked status.

In Example 6-4, the access limit is set to 3.The admin1 user attempts to gain console access to the PIX Security Appliance. After three failed attempts, the admin1 user is locked out.

```
Example 6-4      Maximum Failed Attempts
pixfirewall(config)#aaa local authentication attempts max-fail 3
pixfirewall(config)#show aaa local user
Lock-time   Failed-attempts  Locked   User
15:34:56    3                 Y          admin1
```

To clear the failed-attempts counter or lockout status for a specific user or for all users, the administrator can use the following command:

```
clear aaa local user {fail-attempts | lockout} {all | username name}
```

The administrator can view the statistics associated with the local users and the local server. With the **show local user** command, the administrator can view the lock-time, failed-attempts, and locked status of each user in the local database. With the **show aaa-server local** command, the administrator can view the status of the local server.

Authentication Prompts and Timeout

Authentication prompts use the following command to change the AAA challenge text for HTTP, FTP, and Telnet access through the PIX Security Appliance:

```
pixfirewall(config)#auth-prompt [accept | reject | prompt] string
```

The value supplied for the string *argument* is text that appears above the username and password prompts that display when a user is logging in, as shown in Figure 6-8, based on the following configuration:

```
pixfirewall(config)#auth-prompt prompt Please Authenticate
pixfirewall(config)#auth-prompt reject Authentication Failed, Try Again
pixfirewall(config)#auth-prompt accept You've Been Authenticated
```

Figure 6-8   Authentication Prompts

```
Please Authenticate
Username: asjdkl
Password:
Authentication Failed, Try Again
Please Authenticate to the Firewall
Username: asjikl
Password:
You've Been Authenticated
```

Authentication timeouts use the following command to specify how long the cache should be kept after the user connections become idle:

```
pixfirewall(config)#timeout uauth hh:mm:ss [absolute | inactivity]
```

where:

- *hh:mm:ss*—Sets the time interval (in hours, minutes, and seconds) before users will be required to re-authenticate

- **absolute**—Specifies that the time interval starts at user login

- **inactivity**—Specifies the time interval for inactive sessions (no traffic)

The **timeout** command value must be at least 2 minutes. Use the **clear uauth** command to delete all authorization caches for all users, which causes them to re-authenticate the next time they create a connection.

The **inactivity** and **absolute** qualifiers cause users to re-authenticate after either a period of inactivity or an absolute duration. The inactivity timer starts after a connection becomes idle. If a user establishes a new connection before the duration of the inactivity timer, the user is not required to re-authenticate. If a user establishes a new connection after the inactivity timer expires, the user must re-authenticate.

The absolute timer runs continuously, but waits and prompts the user again when the user starts a new connection, such as clicking a link after the absolute timer has elapsed. The user is then prompted to re-authenticate. The absolute timer must be shorter than the xlate timer; otherwise, a user could be prompted again after the session has ended.

Both an inactivity timer and an absolute timer can operate at the same time, but the absolute timer duration should be set for a longer period than the inactivity timer. If the absolute timer is set at less than the inactivity timer, the inactivity timer is never invoked. For example, if the absolute timer is set to 10 minutes and the inactivity timer to an hour, the absolute timer prompts the user every 10 minutes, and the inactivity timer will never be started.

Note

Do not set the **timeout uauth** duration to 0 seconds when using the virtual HTTP option or passive FTP.

If the inactivity timer is set to some duration, but the absolute timer is set to 0, users are re-authenticated only after the inactivity time elapses. If both timers are set to 0, users have to re-authenticate on every new connection.

Cut-Through Proxy Authentication

The PIX Security Appliance gains dramatic performance advantages because of the cut-through proxy, as shown in Figure 6-9. This is a method of transparently verifying the identity of users at the firewall and permitting or denying access to any TCP- or UDP-based application. This method eliminates the price and performance impact that UNIX system-based firewalls impose in similar configurations and leverages the authentication and authorization services of the Cisco Secure ACS.

Figure 6-9   Cut-Through Proxy Operation

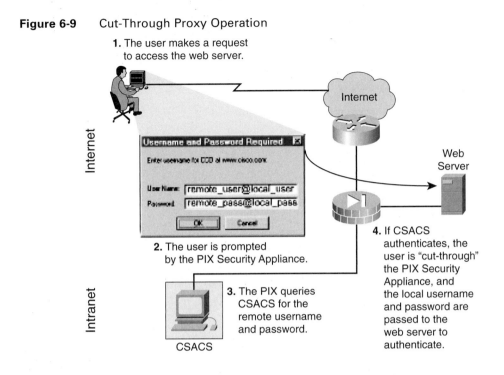

1. The user makes a request to access the web server.

Internet

Web Server

Username and Password Required

Enter username for CCD at www.cisco.com.

User Name: remote_user@local_user

Password: remote_pass@local_pass

OK   Cancel

2. The user is prompted by the PIX Security Appliance.

4. If CSACS authenticates, the user is "cut-through" the PIX Security Appliance, and the local username and password are passed to the web server to authenticate.

3. The PIX queries CSACS for the remote username and password.

CSACS

The PIX Security Appliance cut-through proxy challenges a user initially at the application layer, and then authenticates against standard TACACS+, RADIUS, or local databases. After the policy is checked, the PIX shifts the session flow, and all traffic flows directly between the server and the client while maintaining session state information.

To authenticate a cut-through proxy user, only FTP, Telnet, HTTP, and HTTPS sessions can be intercepted. More information on the four authentication sessions is as follows:

- **Telnet**—The user gets a prompt generated by the PIX Security Appliance. The user has up to four chances to log in. If the username or password fails after the fourth attempt, the PIX drops the connection.

- **FTP**—The user gets a prompt from the FTP program. If the user enters an incorrect password, the connection is dropped immediately.

- **HTTP**—The user sees a window generated by the web browser. If the user enters an incorrect password, the user is prompted again.

- **HTTPS**—The user gets a prompt generated by the PIX Security Appliance. The user has up to three chances to log in. If the username or password fails after the third attempt, the PIX drops the connection.

Keep in mind that browsers cache usernames and passwords. If the PIX Security Appliance should be timing out an HTTP/HTTPS connection but it is not, re-authentication might actually be taking place, with the web browser sending the cached username and password back to the

PIX. If Telnet and FTP seem to work normally, but HTTP/HTTPS connections do not, this is usually the reason.

Authentication of Non-Telnet, -FTP, or -HTTP Traffic

The PIX Security Appliance authenticates users via Telnet, FTP, HTTP, or HTTPS. But, what if users need to access a Microsoft file server on port 139 or a Cisco IP/TV server for instance? How will they be authenticated? Whenever users are required to authenticate to access services other than by Telnet, FTP, HTTP, or HTTPS, they need to do one of the following:

- Authenticate first by accessing a Telnet, FTP, HTTP, or HTTPS server before accessing other services.

- Authenticate to the PIX Security Appliance virtual Telnet or virtual HTTP service before accessing other services, as shown in Figure 6-10. When there are no Telnet, FTP, HTTP, or HTTPS servers with which to authenticate, or just to simplify authentication for the user, the PIX allows a virtual Telnet or virtual HTTP authentication option. This option permits the user to authenticate directly with the PIX using the virtual Telnet or virtual HTTP IP address.

Figure 6-10   Authentication of Non-Telnet, -FTP, or -HTTP Traffic

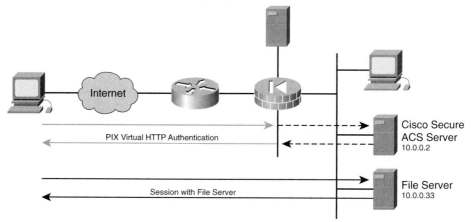

Virtual Telnet

The virtual Telnet option provides a way to pre-authenticate users who require connections through the PIX Security Appliance using services or protocols that do not support authentication. The virtual Telnet IP address is used both to authenticate in and authenticate out of the PIX.

When an unauthenticated user establishes a Telnet session to the virtual IP address, the user is challenged for the username and password, and then authenticated with the TACACS+ or RADIUS server. After authentication, the user sees the message "Authentication Successful," and the authentication credentials are cached in the PIX Security Appliance for the duration of the user authentication, or uauth, timeout.

If a user wants to log out and clear the entry in the PIX Security Appliance uauth cache, the user can again access the virtual address via Telnet. The user is prompted for a username and password, the PIX removes the associated credentials from the uauth cache, and the user receives a "Logout Successful" message.

In Figure 6-11, the user wants to establish a NetBIOS session on port 139 to access the file server. The user accesses the virtual Telnet address at 192.168.0.10, and is immediately challenged for a username and password before being authenticated with the RADIUS AAA server. After the user is authenticated, the PIX Security Appliance allows that user to connect to the file server without re-authentication. This authentication is made possible with the following configuration:

```
pixfirewall(config)#static (inside,outside) 192.168.0.10 10.0.0.33 netmask
255.255.255.255 0 0
pixfirewall(config)#access-list 120 permit tcp host 192.168.9.10 host 192.168.0.10
pixfirewall(config)#aaa-server authin protocol radius
pixfirewall(config)#aaa-server authin (inside) host 10.0.0.2
pixfirewall(config-aaa-server)#key cisco123
pixfirewall(config)#aaa authentication match 120 outside authin
pixfirewall(config)#virtual telnet 192.168.0.10
```

Figure 6-11   Authentication via Virtual Telnet

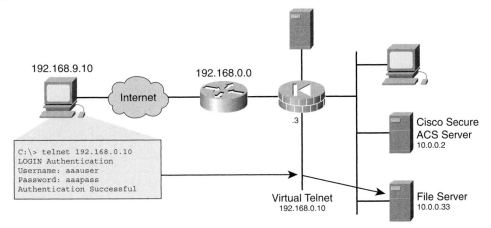

Virtual HTTP

With the virtual HTTP option, web browsers work correctly with the PIX Security Appliance HTTP authentication. The PIX assumes that the AAA server database is shared with a web server and automatically provides the AAA server and web server with the same information. The virtual HTTP option works with the PIX to authenticate the user, separate the AAA server information from the web client's URL request, and direct the web client to the web server. The virtual HTTP option works by redirecting the initial web browser connection to an IP address, which resides in PIX, authenticating the user, and then redirecting the browser back to the URL that the user originally requested. This option is so named because it accesses a virtual HTTP server on the PIX, which in reality does not exist.

This option is especially useful for PIX Security Appliance interoperability with Microsoft Internet Information Server (IIS), but it is useful for other authentication servers. When using HTTP authentication to a site running Microsoft IIS that has Basic text authentication or Windows NT Challenge/Response authentication enabled, users might be denied access from the Microsoft IIS server because the browser appends the string: "Authorization: Basic=Uuhjksdkfhk==" to the HTTP **GET** commands. This string contains the PIX authentication credentials. Windows NT IIS servers respond to the credentials and assume that a Windows NT user is trying to access privileged pages on the server. Unless the PIX username and password combination is exactly the same as a valid Windows NT username and password combination on the Microsoft IIS server, the HTTP **GET** command is denied.

To solve this problem, the PIX Security Appliance redirects the initial browser connection to the virtual HTTP IP address, authenticates the user, and then redirects the browser to the URL that the user originally requested. Virtual HTTP is transparent to the user. Users enter actual destination URLs in their browsers as they normally would. Figure 6-12 depicts authentication with the virtual HTTP option.

Note

Do not set the timeout uauth duration to 0 seconds when using the virtual HTTP option. Doing this prevents HTTP connections to the real web server.

Figure 6-12   Authentication via Virtual HTTP

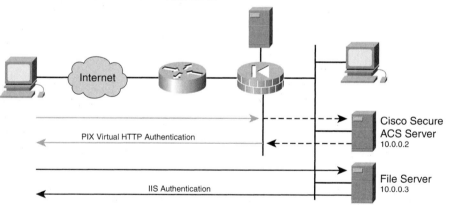

Tunnel User Authentication

For tunnel access authentication, you can configure the PIX Security Appliance to require a remote tunnel user to authenticate prior to gaining access to the corporate services. The PIX will prompt users for a username and password, as shown in Figure 6-13. The PIX can authenticate the user before fully establishing the tunnel.

Figure 6-13   Tunnel User Authentication

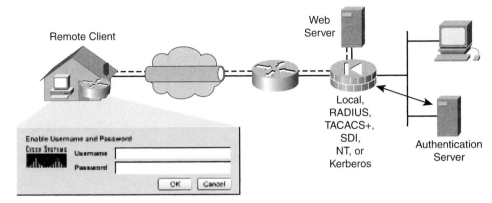

Each remote VPN user belongs to a specific VPN group, or a default group. As users establish VPN tunnels to the central-site PIX Security Appliance, they authenticate. Through the authentication process, the PIX identifies which group the remote user belongs to. The PIX responds by pushing the appropriate VPN group policy to the remote user. For example, there are three VPN group policies configured: engineering, marketing, and training. Each VPN client belongs to one group. As the remote users establish VPN tunnels, they authenticate. When they authenticate, the PIX identifies which VPN group they belong to. The central-site PIX pushes a specific policy to each remote user.

Authorization Configuration

If all authenticated users are allowed to perform all operations—HTTP, HTTPS, FTP, and Telnet—through the PIX Security Appliance, authentication is sufficient, and authorization is not needed. If there is reason to allow only some subset of users or to limit users to certain sites, authorization is needed. The PIX supports the following two basic methods of user authorization when per-user access rules are specified in the context of AAA:

- **Classic user authorization**—The access rules are configured on the TACACS+ AAA server and consulted on demand. With classic authorization, the PIX Security Appliance is configured with rules specifying which connections need to be authorized by the AAA server. The AAA server is consulted for access rights on demand.

- **Download of per-user ACLs**—PIX Security Appliance Software Version 6.2 introduced the ability to store full ACLs on a AAA server and download them to the PIX. An ACL is attached to the user or group profile on the AAA server. During the authentication process, after the user's credentials have been authenticated, the AAA server returns the ACL to the PIX. The returned ACL is modified based on the source IP address of the authenticated user. This functionality is supported only with RADIUS.

User authorization is a two-step process. The administrator identifies the traffic flow to authorize such as all FTP traffic flows. The administrator configures the command authorization in the AAA server. The administrator can refine by group which set of can access what corporate resources. The configuration steps are as follows:

Step 1.   Configure the PIX Security Appliance for authorization. The administrator can use the older form of the **aaa authorization** {**include** | **exclude**} command or the newer version, the **aaa authorization match** command.

Step 2.   Define the TACACS+ AAA server group parameters. The **per-group** command authorization parameters include commands and arguments.

Note

It is assumed that **aaa authentication** configuration was already completed.

Enable Authorization Match

The administrator can define ACLs, based on identified traffic flows, on the PIX Security Appliance, and then apply the ACLs to the **aaa authorization match** command, the syntax for which is as follows:

```
pixfirewall(config)#aaa authorization match acl_name if_name server_tag
```

Any sessions matching the ACL must be authorized by the defined TACACS+ server. In Example 6-5, the three ACL statements are for any-to-any FTP, Telnet, and HTTP traffic. The ACLs are applied to the outside interface. Any traffic matching these characteristics inbound on the outside interface must be authorized by authenticating TACACS+ server.

Example 6-5   Enable Authorization Match

```
pixfirewall(config)#access-list 101 permit tcp any any eq telnet
pixfirewall(config)#access-list 101 permit tcp any any eq ftp
pixfirewall(config)#access-list 101 permit tcp any any eq www
pixfirewall(config)#aaa authorization match 101 outside authin
```

Authorization of Non-Telnet, -FTP, -HTTP, or -HTTPS Traffic

The authorization of non-Telnet, -FTP, -HTTP, or -HTTPS is a two-step process:

Step 1.   Identify the traffic flows to be authorized.

Step 2.   Define the group attributes in the TACACS+ AAA server.

The command for AAA **authorization** of non-Telnet, non-FTP, or non-HTTP commands is as follows:

```
aaa authorization {include | exclude} author_service {inbound | outbound | if_name }
local_ip_local_mask foreign_ip_foreign_mask server_tag
```

where:

- **include** *author_service*—Specifies the services that require authorization. Use a protocol and port number. Services not specified are authorized implicitly. Services specified in the

aaa authentication command do not affect the services that require authorization. Use port number of 0 to specify all ports.

- **exclude** *author_service*—Creates an exception to a previously stated rule by excluding the specified service from authorization to the specified host or networks.

- *if_name*—Specifies the interface name from which users require authentication. Use *if_name* in combination with the *local_ip* address and the *foreign_ip* address to determine where access is sought and from whom.

- *local_ip*—Specifies the IP address of the host or network of hosts that you want to be authenticated or authorized. You can set this address to 0 to mean all hosts and to let the authentication server decide which hosts are authenticated.

- *local_mask*—Specifies the network mask of *local_ip*. Always specify a specific mask value. Use 0 if the IP address is 0. Use 255.255.255.255 for a host.

- *foreign_ip*—Specifies the IP address of the hosts you want to access the *local_ip* address. Use 0 to mean all hosts.

- *foreign_mask*—Specifies the network mask of *foreign_ip*. Always specify a specific mask value. Use 0 if the IP address is 0. Use 255.255.255.255 for a host.

- *server_tag*—Specifies the server tag set with the **aaa-server** command.

Downloadable ACLs

The PIX Security Appliance Software can store ACLs on a AAA server and download them to the PIX as a user is authenticated. The PIX will permit or deny the user access based on the authentication of the user's credentials and the downloaded ACL. A user is authorized to do only what is permitted in the user's individual or group ACL entries. Only authentication needs to be configured on the PIX, and an ACL attached to the user, or group, profile on the AAA server. The PIX supports per-user or per-group ACL authorization.

Downloadable ACLs enable the administrator to enter an ACL one time, in Cisco Secure ACS, and then load that ACL to any number of PIX Security Appliances. Downloadable ACLs work in conjunction with ACLs that are configured directly on the PIX and applied to its interfaces.

Neither type of ACL takes precedence over the other. To pass through the PIX Security Appliance, traffic must be permitted by both the interface ACL and the dynamic ACL if both are applicable. If either ACL denies the traffic, the traffic is prohibited.

Downloadable ACLs are applied to the interface from which the user is prompted to authenticate. They expire when the uauth timer expires and can be removed by entering the **clear uauth** command.

The sequence of events shown in Figure 6-14, takes place when named downloadable ACLs are configured and a user attempts to establish a connection through the PIX Security Appliance.

Note

Downloadable ACLs are supported with RADIUS only. They are not supported with TACACS+.

Figure 6-14 PIX Downloadable ACL Authorization

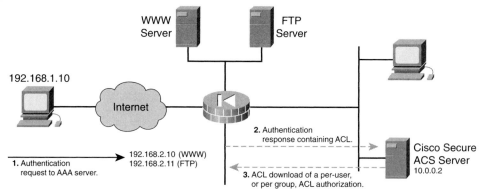

In the example shown in Figure 6-15, the PIX Security Appliance forwards the connection request to the web server. The downloaded ACL appears on the PIX as shown here:

```
access-list#ACSACL #-PIX-acs_ten_acl -3b5385f7 permit ftp any host 172.26.26.50
access-list#ACSACL# -PIX-acs_ten_acl -3b5385f7 permit http any host 172.26.26.50
```

The ACL name is the name for the ACL as defined in the Shared Profile Component (SPC), and 3b5385f7 is a unique version identification.

Figure 6-15 Downloadable ACLs

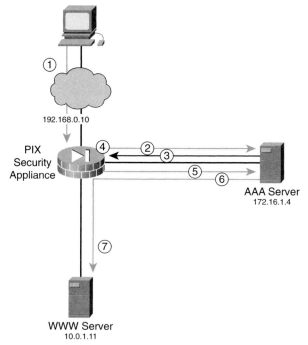

The steps depicted in Figure 6-15 are as follows:

1. The user initiates a connection to the web server at the global address 192.168.0.10. The application connection request is intercepted by the PIX Security Appliance, which then interacts with the user to obtain the username and password.

2. The PIX builds sends a request containing the user identification and password to the AAA server.

3. The AAA server authenticates the user and retrieves the ACL name associated with the user from its configuration database. The AAA server then sends the ACL named to the PIX.

4. The PIX checks to determine whether it already has the named ACL. A downloadable ACL is not downloaded again as long as it exists on the PIX.

5. If the named ACL is not present, the PIX uses the name as a user identification and a null password to build a RADIUS access request. The PIX then sends the RADIUS access request to the AAA server.

6. The AAA server retrieves the ACL associated with the ACL name from its configuration database and sends it to the PIX.

7. The PIX applies the dynamic ACL to the interface. The decision to forward or drop the packet is based on reviewing both the interface and dynamic ACLs. The user then connects and interacts with the web server.

There are two methods of configuring downloadable ACLs on the AAA server:

■   The first method, downloading named ACLs, is to configure the SPC to include both the ACL name and the actual ACL and then configure a user, or group, authentication profile to include the SPC. If a downloadable ACL is configured as a named SPC, that ACL can be applied to any number of Cisco Secure ACS user, or group, profiles. This method should be used when there are frequent requests for downloading a large ACL.

■   The second method is to configure on the AAA server a user authentication profile that includes the actual PIX ACL. In this case, the ACL is not identified by a name. Each ACL entry must be defined in the user profile. This method should be used when there are not frequent requests for the same ACL. For instructions on downloading ACLs without names, refer to the documentation at Cisco.com.

Accounting Configuration

To enable, disable, or view user accounting on a server designated by the **aaa-server** command, use the following command:

```
pixfirewall(config)#aaa accounting match acl_name interface_name server_tag
```

Accounting is provided for all services, or it can be limited to one or more services. The user accounting services keep a record of which network services a user has accessed. These records are kept on the designated AAA server or servers. Accounting information is sent only to the active server in a server group unless simultaneous accounting is enabled. The **aaa accounting** command applies only to TACACS+ and RADIUS servers.

To enable the generation of an accounting record, the administrator identifies a traffic flow with an ACL and applies the ACL to the **aaa accounting match** command. Consider the following configuration for the network in Figure 6-16:

```
pixfirewall(config)#access-list 110 permit tcp any host 192.168.2.10 eq ftp
pixfirewall(config)# access-list 110 permit tcp any host 192.168.2.10 eq www
pixfirewall(config)#aaa accounting match 110 outside NY_ACS
```

The ACL 110 identifies the FTP and HTTP traffic flow from any host to the WWW server at IP address 192.168.2.10. The **match** *acl_name* option in the **aaa accounting match** command instructs the PIX Security Appliance to generate an accounting record when the action the user is trying to perform matches the actions specified in the ACL. Therefore, any time a user tries to access WWW server via FTP or HTTP, an accounting record is generated and sent to the accounting server NY_ACS.

Figure 6-16   Enable Accounting Match

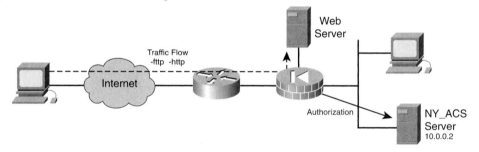

User accounting records are configured to be kept on a AAA server using the following command:

```
pixfirewall(config)#aaa accounting {include | exclude} acctg_service if_name local_ip
local_mask foreign_ip foreign_mask server_tag
```

where:

- **include** *acctg_service*—Specifies the accounting service. Accounting is provided for al services, or you can limit it to one or more services. Possible values are **any**, **ftp**, **http**, **telnet**, or **protocol/port**. Use **any** to provide accounting for all TCP services. To provide accounting for UDP services, use the **protocol/port** form.

- **exclude** *acctg_service*—Creates an exception to a previously stated rule by excluding the specified service from authentication, authorization, or accounting to the specified host. The **exclude** parameter allows the user to specify a port to exclude to a specific host or hosts.

- *if_name*—Specifies the interface name from which users require authentication. Use *if_name* in combination with the *local_ip* address and the *foreign_ip* address to determine where access is sought from and from whom.

- *local_ip*—Specifies the IP address of the host or network of hosts that you want to be authenticated or authorized. You can set this address to 0 to mean all hosts and to let the authentication server decide which hosts are authorized.

- *local_mask*—Specifies the network mask of *local_ip*. Always specify a specific mask value. Use 0 if the IP address is 0. Use 255.255.255.255 for a host.

- *foreign_ip*—Specifies the IP address of the hosts you want to access the *local_ip* address. Use 0 to mean all hosts.

- *foreign_mask*—Specifies the network mask of *foreign_ip*. Always specify a specific mask value. Use 0 if the IP address is 0. Use 255.255.255.255 for a host

- *server_tag*—Specifies the server tag set with the **aaa-server** command.

Traffic that is not specified by an **include** statement is not processed.

Consider the following configuration for the network in Figure 6-17:

```
pixfirewall(config)#aaa accounting include any inside 0.0.0.0 0.0.0.0 0.0.0.0 0.0.0.0
NY_ACS
pixfirewall(config)#aaa accounting exclude any inside 10.0.0.34 255.255.255.255 0.0.0.0
0.0.0.0 NY_ACS
```

Accounting records are kept on the AAA server for all outbound connections except for those connections originating from host 10.0.0.34.

Figure 6-17   Enable Accounting Include | Exclude

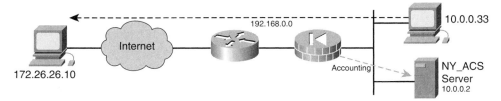

Console Session Accounting

The administrator can enable the generation of accounting records to mark the establishment and termination of PIX Security Appliance console access with the following command:

```
pixfirewall(config)#aaa accounting {http | serial | telnet | ssh | enable} console
server_tag
```

Valid server group protocols are RADIUS and TACACS+.

Consider the following configuration for the network in Figure 6-18:

```
pixfirewall(config)#username student1 password cisco123
pixfirewall(config)#aaa authentication telnet console LOCAL
pixfirewall(config)#aaa accounting telnet console NY_ACS
```

The username and password for student1 are added to the PIX local database. Next, the administrator configures the PIX to authenticate all Telnet access sessions using the local database to authenticate users. Finally, an accounting record is generated for each Telnet session. The record is sent to the NY_ACS server.

Figure 6-18   Admin Accounting

Command Accounting

Each command entered by a user is recorded and sent to the accounting server or servers when you use the following command:

```
pixfirewall(config)#aaa accounting command [privilege level] server-tag
```

The optional **privilege** specification indicates the minimum privilege level that must be associated with a command for an accounting record to be generated. This command applies only to TACACS+ servers. The name of the server or server group to which this command applies must be specified.

As a result of the following command, the PIX Security Appliance records all changes to the configuration by users accessing the PIX with privilege level 15 and lower:

```
pixfirewall(config)#aaa accounting command privilege 15 mytacacs
```

Lab 6.3.9   Configure Local AAA on the PIX Security Appliance

In this lab, you configure a local user account. You then configure and test inbound and outbound authentication, Telnet and HTTP console access, and virtual Telnet authentication. Finally, you change and test authentication timeouts and prompts.

Troubleshooting the AAA Configuration

Use the **show uauth** command to display one or all currently authenticated users, the host IP to which they are bound, and any cached IP and port authorization information. In the example in

Figure 6-19, aaauser with an IP address of 192.168.2.10 is authenticated as the output from show uauth reveals:

```
pixfirewall(config)#show uauth
                                 Current            Most Seen
Authenticated Users                 1                  1
Authentication in Progress          0                  1
user 'aaauser' at 192.168.2.10, authenticated
   absolute timeout:    0:05:00
   inactivity timeout:  0:00:00
```

Figure 6-19   Displaying an Authenticated User

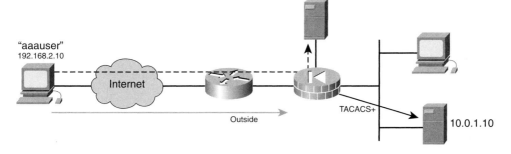

To display AAA server statistics for all configured server groups, or for a particular group, use the **show aaa-server** command. In Example 6-6, for the network in Figure 6-20, the top portion the **show aaa-server statistic** displays the server statistics. The bottom portion displays the server messaging statistics. The server group is NY_ACS, which uses the TACACS+ protocol, has an IP address of 10.0.1.10, uses server port number 49 for messaging, and is active. There are two requests, two challenges, and two accept messages.

```
Example 6-6     Displaying AAA Server Statistics
pixfirewall#show aaa-server ny_acs
Server Group:     ny_acs
Server Protocol:  tacacs+
Server Address:   10.0.1.10
Server port:      49
Server status:    ACTIVE, Last transaction at 16:17:23 UTC Mon Nov 29 2004
Number of pending requests          0
Average round trip time             3ms
Number of authentication requests   2
Number of authorization requests    0
Number of accounting requests       0
Number of retransmissions           0
Number of accepts                   2
Number of rejects                   0
Number of challenges                2
```

Figure 6-20   Determining the TACACS+ Server Statistics

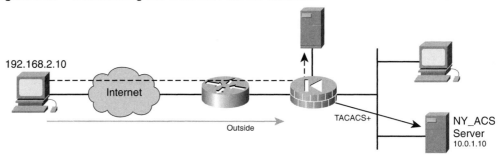

The administrator can also view the AAA server messaging statistics. In Example 6-7, there was an authentication request, a challenge, and an accept message. There were no rejects or retransmissions.

```
Example 6-7    Displaying AAA Server Messaging Statistics
pixfirewall#show aaa-server
Server Group:    myradius
Server Protocol: radius
Server Address:  10.0.0.2
Server port:     1645(authentication), 1646(accounting)
Server status:   ACTIVE, Last transaction at 14:33:13 utc Thu Aug 26 2004
Number of pending requests         0
Average round trip time            30ms
Number of authentication requests  1
Number of authorization requests   0
Number of accounting requests      0
Number of retransmissions          0
Number of accepts                  1
Number of rejects                  0
Number of challenges               1
Number of malformed responses      0
Number of bad authenticators       0
Number of timeouts                 0
Number of unrecognized responses   0
```

After a user has been authenticated, the administrator can view the downloaded ACL using the **show access-list** command. In Figure 6-21, the user at 192.168.1.10 attempts to gain access to web server at 192.168.2.10. After an end user enters his username and password, the PIX Security Appliance forwards the user credentials to the ACS server. If the end user is authenticated, the ACS server downloads a preconfigured ACL, #ACSACL#-IP- RADIUSAUTH-3ddb8ab6, to the PIX. The ACL name is the name for the ACL as defined in the SPC, #ACSACL#-IP- RADIUSAUTH, and the unique version identification, 3ddb8ab6. In this example, the end user is authorized to access 192.168.2.10 using HTTP. Example 6-8 shows the output from the **show access-list** command for this scenario.

Figure 6-21   Downloaded ACL Scenario

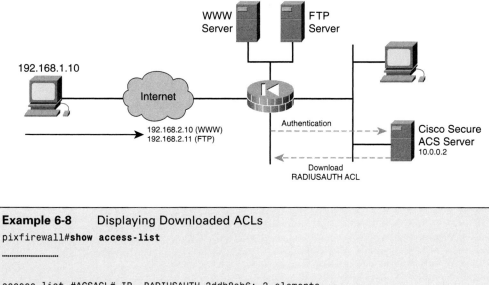

Example 6-8   Displaying Downloaded ACLs

```
pixfirewall#show access-list

...........................

access-list #ACSACL#-IP- RADIUSAUTH-3ddb8ab6; 3 elements
access-list #ACSACL#-IP- RADIUSAUTH-3ddb8ab6 line 1 extended
  permit tcp any host 192.168.2.10 eq www (hitcnt = 5)
access-list #ACSACL#-IP- RADIUSAUTH-3ddb8ab6 line 2 extended
  permit tcp any host 192.168.2.10 eq ftp (hitcnt = 0)
access-list #ACSACL#-IP- RADIUSAUTH-3ddb8ab6 line 3 extended
  deny ip any any (hitcnt = 0)
```

You can use the **show uauth** command to view the authenticated end user, their IP address, and the matching downloaded ACL.

 Lab 6.3.10   Configure AAA on the PIX Security Appliance Using Cisco Secure ACS for Windows 2000

In this lab, you configure and test inbound and outbound authentication, console access, and virtual Telnet authentication, and authorization and accounting. You also learn to change and test authentication timeouts and prompts.

Summary

This chapter discussed the Cisco IOS Firewall authentication proxy feature. You should be able to configure authentication proxy on a Cisco IOS router to apply specific security policies on a per-user basis.

You should also understand how the PIX Security Appliance supports AAA services. This understanding should include the ability to configure, monitor, and troubleshoot AAA on the PIX. The discussion included how to set usernames and passwords in the PIX local user database, so that these entries can be used for authentication. Authentication against an external AAA server was also discussed. Students should now be able to configure downloadable per-user ACLs to accomplish authorization. You should also understand user, administration, and command accounting on the PIX.

Check Your Understanding

Complete all the review questions listed here to test your understanding of the topics and concepts in this chapter. Answers are listed in Appendix A, "Check Your Understanding Answer Key."

1. Users must successfully authenticate with the authentication server by entering a valid username and password. If the authentication succeeds, what happens?

    a. The user is allowed on the network.

    b. The user has to provide an additional MD5 key.

    c. The user must input an ACE entry.

    d. The user's authorization profile is retrieved from the AAA server.

2. To use the authentication proxy with HTTP, what must you do?

    a. Use the **ip http server** command to enable the HTTP server on the router.

    b. Use the **http server** command to enable the HTTP server on the router.

    c. Use the **ip http authentication aaa** command to enable the HTTP server on the router.

    d. Use the **http authentication aaa** command to enable the HTTP server on the router.

3. Which command displays the authentication proxy entries, the running authentication proxy configuration, or the authentication proxy statistics?

    a. firewall(config)# **show aaa all**

    b. firewall(config)# **show aaa server**

    c. firewall(config)# **show ip auth-proxy**

    d. firewall(config)# **show ip auth-proxy all**

4. Which three types of authentication are available on the PIX Security Appliance? (Choose three.)

    a. Access authentication

    b. IP FTP authentication

    c. Cut-through proxy authentication

    d. Tunnel access authentication

    e. Crossover authentication

5. What is the first step in configuring interactive user authentication?

    a. Specify a AAA server group

    b. Designate an authentication server

    c. Enable user authentication

    d. Specify authentication proxy

7. What is the default timeout (in minutes) for the inactivity timer of the **auth-proxy** command?

   a. 10

   b. 30

   c. 40

   d. 60

8. After configuring the RADIUS server authentication encryption key to SecUrity66, what command would be needed on the Cisco router to communicate with the RADIUS server?

   a. Router (config)# **radius-server key SecUrity66**

   b. Router (config)# **radius-server host SecUrity66**

   c. Router (config)# **radius-server key SecUrity66 client**

   d. Router (config)# **radius-server host SecUrity66 client**

9. On a PIX Security Appliance, you can download per-user ACLs from which type of AAA server?

   a. Kerberos

   b. TACACS+

   c. RADIUS

   d. LDAP

   e. Microsoft

CHAPTER 7

Configure Trust and Identity at Layer 2

Upon completion of this chapter, you should be able to answer the following questions:

- What is the Identity Based Networking Services (IBNS)?

- How do I configure 802.1x port-based authentication?

Key Terms

This chapter uses the following key terms. You can find the definitions in the glossary at the end of the book.

Identity Based Networking Services (IBNS)
  page 312

Extensible Authentication Protocol (EAP)
  page 313

802.1x   page 313

Cisco *Identity Based Networking Services (IBNS)* is an integrated solution combining several Cisco products that offer authentication, access control, and user policies to secure network connectivity and resources. The Cisco IBNS solution enables greater security while simultaneously offering cost-effective management of changes throughout the organization. In this chapter, you are introduced to Cisco ISBN. This chapter also discusses 802.1x and EAP as they relate to IBNS. You also learn to configure a Cisco Secure Access Control Server (ACS) to authenticate using EAP-MD5 and RADIUS.

This chapter also discusses the use IEEE 802.1x port-based authentication to prevent unauthorized devices from gaining access to the network. As LANs extend to hotels, airports, and corporate lobbies, insecure environments are created. The IEEE 802.1x standard defines a client/server-based access control and authentication protocol that restricts unauthorized clients from connecting to a LAN through publicly accessible ports. The authentication server authenticates each client connected to a switch port before making available any services offered by the switch or the LAN. You learn the necessary steps to configure 802.1x port-based authentication on a Cisco Catalyst switch.

Identity Based Networking Services (IBNS)

Cisco IBNS provides united control of user identity with enterprise Cisco virtual private network (VPN) concentrators, Cisco IOS routers, and PIX Security Appliances to offer authentication, access control, and user policies to secure network connectivity and resources, as shown in Figure 7-1.

Figure 7-1   Identity Based Networking Services

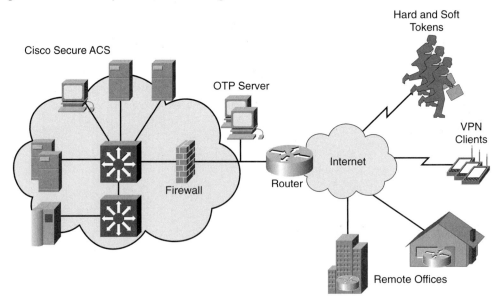

Features and Benefits

The Cisco IBNS solution provides the following benefits:

- **Intelligent adaptability for offering greater flexibility and mobility to users**—Creating user or group profiles with policies that define trust relationships between users and network resources allows organizations to easily authenticate, authorize, and account for all users of wired or wireless networks.

- **A combination of authentication, access control, and user policies to secure network connectivity and resources**—Because policies are associated with users and not physical ports, users obtain more mobility and freedom, and network administration is simplified. Greater scalability and ease of management is achieved through policy enforcement and dynamic provisioning.

- **User productivity gains and reduced operating costs**—Providing security and greater flexibility for wired or wireless network access provides enterprises with the capability to have cross-functional or new project teams form more quickly, enables secure access for trusted partners and vendors and facilitates secure conference-room connectivity. Enabling flexibility with secure network access through centralized policy-based administration decreases the time, complexity, and effort associated with port security techniques at the MAC level.

IEEE 802.1x

802.1x is a standardized framework defined by the IEEE that is designed to provide port-based network access. 802.1x performs port-level authentication of network clients by using information unique to the client and with credentials known only to the client, as depicted in Figure 7-2.

The 802.1x standard is an extremely flexible protocol because it is based on the ***Extensible Authentication Protocol (EAP)***. EAP (Internet Engineering Task Force [IETF] RFC 2284) is a highly pliable standard. 802.1x encompasses the range of EAP authentication methods, including Message Digest 5 (MD5), Transport Layer Security (TLS), Tunneled Transport Layer Security (TTLS), Lightweight Extensible Authentication Protocol (LEAP), Protected Extensible Authentication Protocol (PEAP), SecurID, Subscriber Identity Module (SIM), and Authentication and Key Agreement (AKA).

Figure 7-2 802.1x Roles

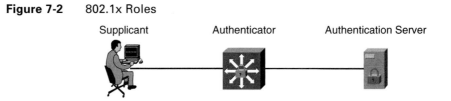

Supplicant   Authenticator   Authentication Server

The 802.1x framework defines three roles in the authentication process:

- **Supplicant**—The endpoint that is seeking network access is known as the supplicant. The supplicant can be an end-user device or a standalone device, such as an IP phone.

- **Authenticator**—The device to which the supplicant directly connects and through which the supplicant obtains network access permission is known as the authenticator.

- **Authentication server**—The authenticator acts as a gateway to the authentication server, which is responsible for actually authenticating the supplicant.

The authentication process consists of exchanges of *Extensible Authentication Protocol (EAP)* messages. This exchange occurs between the supplicant and the authentication server. The authenticator acts as a transparent relay for this exchange and as a point of enforcement for any policy configuration instructions the authentication server sends back as a result of the authentication process.

An alternative wireless LAN (WLAN) security approach focuses on developing a framework for providing centralized authentication and dynamic key distribution. This approach is based on the IEEE 802.11 Task Group end-to-end framework using 802.1x and EAP to provide this enhanced functionality. Cisco has incorporated 802.1x and EAP into its Cisco Wireless Security Suite. The three main elements of an 802.1x and EAP approach are as follows:

- Mutual authentication between the client and the RADIUS authentication server

- Encryption keys dynamically derived after authentication

- Centralized policy control, where session timeout triggers reauthentication and new encryption key generation

When these features are implemented, a wireless client that associates with an access point cannot gain access to the network until the user performs a network logon. After association, the client and the network access point or RADIUS server exchange EAP messages to perform mutual authentication, with the client verifying the RADIUS server credentials, and vice versa. An EAP supplicant is used on the client machine to obtain the user credentials. Upon successful client and server mutual authentication, the RADIUS server and client then derive a client-specific Wired Equivalent Privacy (WEP) key to be used by the client for the current logon session. User passwords and session keys are never sent in the clear over the wireless link.

802.1x Components

You can deploy 802.1x to authenticate users such as desktop users in a corporation or teleworkers accessing the network from a home office. In the home office scenario, access control is required to prevent other residents from the home from gaining access to controlled corporate resources, as shown in Figure 7-3.

Figure 7-3   802.1x Authenticator and Supplicant

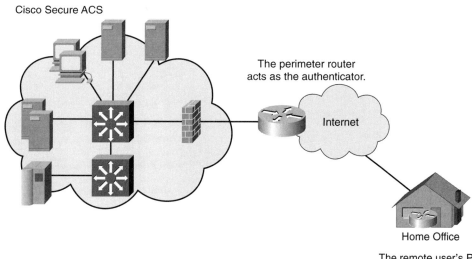

The authenticator and supplicant are the two components used to implement 802.1x functionality. The authenticator is a network component that checks credentials and applies the access policy, usually implemented on a router, switch, or wireless access point. The supplicant is a software component on the user's workstation that answers the challenge from the authenticator. You can also implement supplicant functionality on network devices to authenticate to upstream devices. Mutual authentication functionality can also be used when network devices must restrict access policy to each other. Cisco IOS Software does not currently support mutual authentication.

In the simplest scenario, no traffic is allowed to flow from a client device to the network until the client authenticates. 802.1x frames are the only traffic between the client, or supplicant, and the access control device, or authenticator. A user trying to access network resources must provide access credentials using software on the client workstation. Microsoft Windows XP includes 802.1x supplicant support, whereas an add-on component for Microsoft Windows 2000 is available as a Microsoft hotfix.

When the user provides their credentials, the information is sent to the authenticator by some variant of EAP. The user's information is encrypted in the EAP transfer so that the user's credentials cannot be easily compromised. The authenticator sends the credentials to the authentication, authorization, and accounting (AAA) server, which verifies the user credentials against its database. If the AAA server is configured to return a network access policy, it returns the policy associated with the user or their corresponding group. The authenticator applies the network policy to the user's connection, allowing traffic to flow according to the policy. The policy may include traffic engineering values, VLAN information for user connection, and IP address information.

You can configure the authenticator with default access policies to offer restricted connectivity for client devices that do not have supplicant support. This setup allows unauthenticated users to have limited network access, but they must provide credentials in some other fashion if access to restricted resources is needed. Default policy provision for IP phones, for instance, may be required, because IP phones do not yet include supplicant capability.

802.1x Applications with Cisco IOS Software

Cisco IOS Software support for 802.1x functionality can be leveraged to improve security on teleworker connections, where remote workers have single or multiple computers in the home, and the user needs to prevent his or her spouse or children from gaining access to the corporate network. Through the application of default user policy, the spouse and children have access to the public Internet but not the business network.

Extranet VPN offers another application for 802.1x access control, in which users at partner facilities are not allowed to access corporate resources until their controlled credentials are provided, ensuring that unauthorized users cannot access the network and that traffic from network attacks does not cross into the partner's network.

You can leverage 802.1x technology inside the enterprise to ensure that only permitted users are allowed access to network connectivity resources. You could integrate this capability with other workstation software components to ensure that users' computers have all required software updates, such as operating system service packs or antivirus software signature files. This prevents users who represent a security risk from accessing restricted network resources.

802.1x makes unauthorized access to protected resources more difficult through the requirement of valid access credentials. By deploying 802.1x, administrators effectively eliminate the possibility of users deploying unauthorized wireless access points, resolving one of the biggest issues of easy-to-deploy wireless network equipment.

Several components of 802.1x support in Cisco IOS Software offer capability for increased security on access router platforms.

With 802.1x port-based authentication, the devices in the network have specific roles, as shown in Figure 7-4.

Figure 7-4   802.1x Components

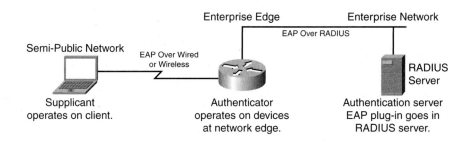

- **Client**—The device, such as a workstation, that requests access to the LAN and switch services and responds to the requests from the switch. The workstation must be running 802.1x-compliant client.

- **Authentication server**—Performs the actual authentication of the client. The authentication server validates the identity of the client and notifies the switch whether the client is authorized to access the LAN and switch services. Because the switch acts as the proxy, the authentication service is transparent to the client. In this release, the RADIUS security system with EAP extensions is the only supported authentication server. It is available in Cisco Secure ACS Version 3.0 and later. RADIUS operates in a client/server model in which secure authentication information is exchanged between the RADIUS server and one or more RADIUS clients.

- **Switch**—Controls the physical access to the network based on the authentication status of the client. The switch can be a Catalyst 3550 switch, a Catalyst 2950 switch, or wireless access point. The switch acts as an intermediary between the client and the authentication server, requesting identity information from the client, verifying that information with the authentication server, and relaying a response to the client. The switch includes the RADIUS client, which is responsible for encapsulating and decapsulating the EAP frames and interacting with the authentication server.

When the switch receives EAP over LAN (EAPOL) frames and relays them to the authentication server, the Ethernet header is stripped and the remaining EAP frame is re-encapsulated in the RADIUS format. The EAP frames are not modified or examined during encapsulation, and the authentication server must support EAP within the native frame format. When the switch receives frames from the authentication server, the server's frame header is removed, leaving the EAP frame, which is then encapsulated for Ethernet and sent to the client.

How 802.1x Works

802.1x works on a complex series of challenges and responses. This topic covers the authentication initiation, message exchanges, and port states.

Authentication Initiation and Message Exchange

The switch or the client can initiate authentication. If authentication on a port is enabled by using the **dot1x port-control auto** interface configuration command, the switch must initiate authentication when it determines that the port link state transitions from down to up. It then sends an EAP-request/identity frame to the client to request its identity. Upon receipt of the frame, the client responds with an EAP-response/identity frame.

If during boot the client does not receive an EAP-request/identity frame from the switch, the client can initiate authentication by sending an EAPOL-start frame. This prompts the switch to request the identity of the client.

When the client supplies its identity, the switch begins its role as the intermediary, passing EAP frames between the client and the authentication server until authentication succeeds or fails. If the authentication succeeds, the switch port becomes authorized.

The specific exchange of EAP frames depends on the authentication method being used. Figure 7-5 and Figure 7-6 show a message exchange initiated by the client using the one-time password (OTP) authentication method with a RADIUS server. The actual authentication conversation occurs between the client and the authentication server using EAP. The authenticator is aware of this activity, but it is just a middleman.

Figure 7-5   How 802.1x Works: Summary View

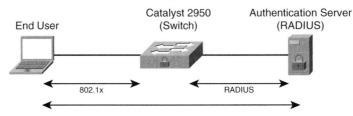

Ports in Authorized and Unauthorized States

The switch port state determines whether the client is granted access to the network. The port starts in the unauthorized state. While in this state, the port disallows all ingress and egress traffic except for 802.1x packets. When a client is successfully authenticated, the port transitions to the authorized state, allowing all traffic for the client to flow normally.

If a client that does not support 802.1x is connected to an unauthorized 802.1x port, the switch requests the identity of the client. In this situation, the client does not respond to the request, the port remains in the unauthorized state, and the client is not granted access to the network.

In contrast, when an 802.1x-enabled client connects to a port that is not running 802.1x, the client initiates the authentication process by sending the EAPOL-start frame. When no response is received, the client sends the request for a fixed number of times. Because no response is received, the client begins sending frames as if the port is in the authorized state.

Figure 7-6   How 802.1x Works: Detailed View

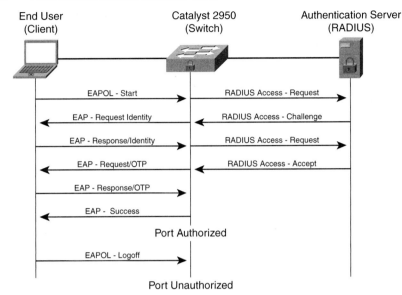

You can manually configure the port authorization state by using the **dot1x port-control** interface configuration command, the syntax of which follows:

```
[no] dot1x port-control {auto | force-authorized | force-unauthorized}
```

where:

- **auto**—Enables 802.1x authentication on the interface and causes the port to transition to the authorized or unauthorized state based on the 802.1s authentication exchange between the switch and the client.

- **force-authorized**—Disables 802.1x authentication on the interface and causes the port to transition to the authorized state without any authentication exchange required. The port sends and receives normal traffic without 802.1x-based authentication of the client.

- **force-unauthorized**—Denies all access through this interface by forcing the port to transition to the unauthorized state, ignoring all attempts by the client to authenticate. The switch cannot provide authentication services to the client through the interface.

If the client is successfully authenticated, the port state changes to authorized, and all frames from the authenticated client are allowed through the port. If the authentication fails, the port remains in the unauthorized state, but authentication can be retried. If the authentication server cannot be reached, the switch can resend the request. If no response is received from the server after the specified number of attempts, authentication fails, and network access is not granted.

When a client logs off, it sends an EAPOL-logoff message, causing the switch port to transition to the unauthorized state.

If the link state of a port transitions from up to down, or if an EAPOL-logoff frame is received, the port returns to the unauthorized state.

Selecting the Correct EAP

EAP, based on IETF 802.1x, is an end-to-end framework that allows the creation of authentication types without changing AAA client configurations. The characteristics of EAP are as follows:

- Extension of PPP to provide additional authentication features.

- A flexible protocol used to carry arbitrary authentication information.

- Typically rides on top of another protocol such as 802.1x or RADIUS. EAP can also be used with TACACS+.

- Specified in RFC 2284.

- Supports multiple authentication types:

    — EAP-MD5: Plain Password Hash (CHAP over EAP)

    — EAP-TLS (based on X.509 certificates)

    — LEAP (EAP-Cisco Wireless)

    — PEAP (Protected EAP)

The varieties of EAP supported by the Cisco Secure ACS are as follows:

- **EAP-MD5**—An EAP protocol that does not support mutual authentication

- **EAP-TLS**—EAP incorporating Transport Layer Security (TLS)

- **LEAP**—An EAP protocol used by Cisco Aironet wireless equipment; LEAP supports mutual authentication

- **PEAP**—Protected EAP, which is implemented with EAP—Generic Token Card (GTC) and EAP-MSCHAPv2 protocols

- **EAP-FAST**—EAP Flexible Authentication via Secured Tunnel (EAP-FAST), a faster means of encrypting EAP authentication, supports EAP-GTC authentication

Table 7-1 compares the EAP types.

Table 7-1   EAP Comparison

	LEAP	MS PEAP	CISCO PEAP	EAP-TLS
Static: Password support	✓	✓	✓	N/A
One-time password support	N/A	N/A	✓	N/A
Microsoft Windows password change	N/A	✓	✓	N/A
Requires server certificate	N/A	✓	✓	✓
Requires client certificate	N/A	N/A	N/A	✓
LDAP/NDS database support	N/A	✓	✓	LDAP Only
Multiple operating system support	✓	Microsoft operating systems	N/A	N/A
Single sign-on for Windows	✓	N/A	N/A	✓

N/A means not applicable in the preceding table

Cisco LEAP

Cisco LEAP, an enhancement to IEEE 802.11b WEP encryption, is a widely deployed EAP type in use today in WLANs, as shown in Figure 7-7. LEAP derives a per-user, per-session key that relies on mutual authentication, where both the user and the access point must be authenticated. The RADIUS server sends an authentication challenge to the client. The client uses a one-way hash of the user-supplied password to create a response to the challenge and then sends that response to the RADIUS server. Using information from its user database, the RADIUS server creates its own response and compares that to the response from the client. When the RADIUS server authenticates the client, the process repeats in reverse, enabling the client to authenticate the RADIUS server. When this is complete, an EAP-success message is sent to the client, and both the client and the RADIUS server derive the dynamic WEP key.

Figure 7-7   Cisco LEAP

EAP-TLS

EAP-TLS is an IETF standard, defined in RFC 2716, that is based on the Transport Layer Security (TLS) protocol, as shown in Figure 7-8. EAP-TLS uses Public Key Infrastructure (PKI) digital certificates (X.509) rather than username/password for both user and server authentication. The RADIUS server sends its certificate to the client in Phase 1 of the authentication sequence. This is known as server-side TLS. The client validates the RADIUS server certificate by verifying the certificate authority that issued the certificate and the contents of the digital certificate. When this is complete, the client sends its certificate to the RADIUS server in Phase 2 of the authentication sequence. This is known as client-side TLS. The RADIUS server validates the client's certificate by verifying the issuer of the certificate and the contents of the digital certificate. When this is complete, an EAP-success message is sent to the client, and both the client and the RADIUS server derive the dynamic WEP key. Note that certificate management is both complex and costly.

Figure 7-8   EAP-TLS

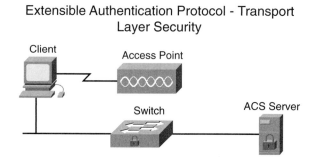

PEAP

PEAP is an IETF draft RFC authored by Cisco Systems, Microsoft, and RSA Security, as shown in Figure 7-9. An enhancement to EAP-TLS, PEAP uses a digital certificate for server authentication. For user authentication, PEAP supports various EAP-encapsulated methods within a protected TLS tunnel. Phase 1 of the authentication sequence is the same as that for EAP-TLS. At the end of Phase 1, an encrypted TLS tunnel is created between the user and the RADIUS server for transporting EAP authentication messages. In Phase 2, the RADIUS server authenticates the client through the encrypted TLS tunnel via another EAP type. When this is complete, an EAP-success message is sent to the client, and both the client and the RADIUS server derive the dynamic WEP key. PEAP is available for use with both Microsoft and Cisco products.

Figure 7-9   PEAP

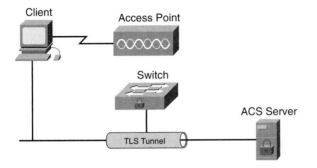

Protected Extensible Authentication Protocol

EAP Type Configuration

The important policy decision regarding authentication in a Cisco Catalyst switch environment is which EAP authentication type to deploy. You have two choices: EAP-MD5 and EAP-TLS. This choice is likely to be influenced by which database is in use and by security implications.

IBNS and Cisco Secure ACS

Historically, Ethernet networks offered few capabilities for the authentication of devices or users to the network. When originally developed, the protocols underpinning TCP/IP over Ethernet, such as Address Resolution Protocol (ARP) and Dynamic Host Configuration Protocol (DHCP), simply did not address user authentication, authorization, or accounting. The key challenge at the time was connectivity. Advanced security concerns were issues for the future. It is still true today that in the vast majority of organizations any person who can physically attach a computer to the LAN will automatically be granted TCP/IP connectivity to the network without further checks concerning whether such connectivity is appropriate. With the security focus of most organizations having been on the external risks posed by connection to the Internet, relatively uncontrolled IP access has been available on the LAN. With the wider deployment of networks and the accompanying vulnerabilities, most organizations are becoming concerned about this reliance on crude physical security to limit access to their networks.

The addition of RADIUS support to Cisco Catalyst switches means that the user-based access control schemes that have been available to control remote user access are now available on the links of Cisco Catalyst switches. This represents a fundamental breakthrough in the access control schemes that can now be achieved on broadcast or switch-based Ethernet networks. One example of configuration data that an organization might want delivered by RADIUS is the VLAN identification for each user.

EAP represents the technology framework that makes it possible to deploy RADIUS into Ethernet network environments. It also allows for the adoption of AAA schemes and the security advantages that are available when using AAA servers. The 802.1x standard, also known as

EAPOL, concerns that part of the wider EAP standard that relates to broadcast media networks. Upon connection, EAPOL provides a communications channel between an end user on a client LAN device to the AAA server through the LAN switch. Conceptually, the functionality is similar to that provided by PPP servers on point-to-point links. With the addition of AAA support for user access control, all Ethernet LAN connections can be authenticated against the individual user requesting it. Network connectivity is provided only if valid credentials are supplied. In addition, the RADIUS protocol provides for delivery of granular control of the network connectivity to be supplied by switch to the user. Finally, RADIUS provides for the collection of a user's usage statistics of network resources, as shown in Figure 7-10 where the switch detects the 802.1x compatible client, forces authentication, and then acts as a middleman during the authentication. Upon successful authentication, the switch sets the port to forwarding and applies the designated policies.

Figure 7-10   How Does Basic Port-Based Network Access Work?

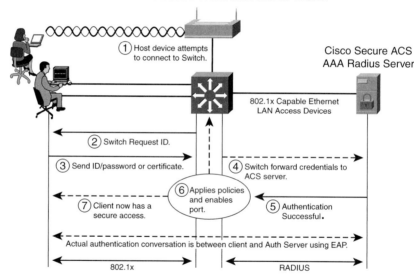

By supporting complex challenge-response dialogues, EAP facilitates the user-based authentication demands of both conventional one-way hashed password authentication schemes such as Challenge Handshake Authentication Protocol (CHAP) and more advanced authentication schemes such as TLS or digital certificates. The flexible capabilities provided by EAP thus allow deploying organizations to start with less-secure but simple-to-implement authentication protocols and then move to more secure but more complex protocols as requirements dictate. For a more complete explanation of EAP and a discussion of the capabilities and security attributes of the different password protocol schemes supported, do a search at Cisco.com.

Network access policy is a broad concept. In general, it defines how users can connect to the network and what services they will be provided when connected to it.

Cisco Secure ACS-based access policy enforcement provides control by using central authentication and authorization of network users. The Cisco Secure ACS database maintains all user IDs, passwords, and privileges in the form of a RADIUS access profile. Upon receipt of a RADIUS access-request packet from the switch on behalf of a user, the Cisco Secure ACS first determines which authentication method will be used for that request and then processes it.

ACS Deployment Considerations

How an enterprise network is configured is probably the most important factor in deciding how and where to deploy Cisco Secure ACS. Cisco Secure ACS deployment varies widely depending on the network topology in which it serves.

Small LAN Environment

In the small LAN environment, a single Cisco Secure ACS is usually located close to the switch. In this environment, the user database is usually small because few switches require access to the Cisco Secure ACS for AAA. A single Cisco Secure ACS can handle the modest workload. A second server can be deployed for redundancy. The second server should be set up as a replication partner to the primary server because losing the Cisco Secure ACS would prevent users from gaining access to the network. Figure 7-11 illustrates an example of a Cisco Secure ACS deployment in a small LAN.

Figure 7-11   ACS Deployment in a Small LAN

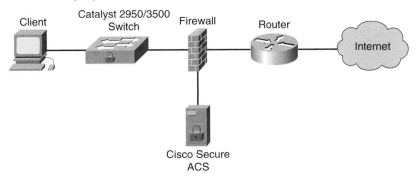

Access to the system hosting the Cisco Secure ACS should be limited to as small a number of users and devices as necessary. In Figure 7-11, this is achieved by connecting the Cisco Secure ACS host through to a private LAN segment on the firewall. Access to this segment would be limited only to the Cisco Catalyst switch client and those user machines that require HTTP access to the Cisco Secure ACS for administrative purposes. Normal LAN users should not be able to see the Cisco Secure ACS at all.

Large Network Environment

In a larger network that is geographically dispersed, speed, redundancy, and reliability are important in determining whether to use a centralized Cisco Secure ACS service or a number of geographically dispersed Cisco Secure ACS servers. Network speed can be important in deciding how Cisco Secure ACS should be deployed because delays in authentication introduced by the network can result in timeouts at the client side or the switch.

A useful approach in large extended networks, such as for a globally dispersed corporation, is to have at least one Cisco Secure ACS deployed in each major geographical region. Depending upon the quality of the WAN links, these can act as backup partners to servers in other regions to protect against failure of the Cisco Secure ACS in any particular region. In Figure 7-12, Switch 1 is configured with Cisco Secure ACS 1 as its primary AAA server but with Cisco Secure ACS 2 of Region 2 as its secondary. Switch 2 is configured with Cisco Secure ACS 2 as its primary but with Cisco Secure ACS 3 as its secondary. Likewise, Switch 3 uses Cisco Secure ACS 3 as its primary, but Cisco Secure ACS 1 as its secondary. In this way, AAA WAN traffic is minimized by using a local Cisco Secure ACS as the primary AAA server, and the number of Cisco Secure ACS units required is also minimized by using the primary Cisco Secure ACS from another region as the secondary when necessary.

The model can be extended further down to campus or even individual site level if reliable high-speed connections between locations are not available, or if the performance requirements of the individual sites call for local servers. The same issue can be applied to an external database used by the Cisco Secure ACS. The database should be deployed near enough to the Cisco Secure ACS installation to ensure reliable and timely access.

Figure 7-12   ACS Deployment in a Global Network

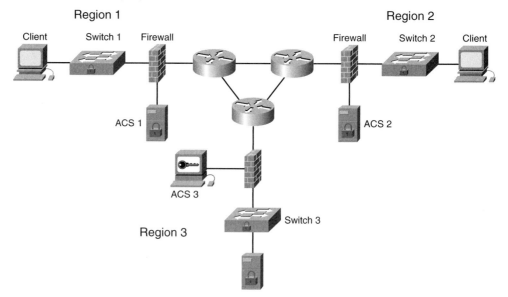

Cisco Secure ACS RADIUS Profile Configuration

After a user successfully completes the EAP authentication process of whatever type, the Cisco Secure ACS responds to the switch with a RADIUS authentication-accept packet granting that user access to the network, as depicted in Figure 7-13. This packet is a fairly standard RADIUS authentication-accept packet and can carry a variety of the usual RADIUS attributes that may be communicated and that will be understood by the Cisco Catalyst switch. Taken as a whole, the attributes that compose the access-accept packet constitute an access profile. When received by the switch, the attributes are then processed in compliance with the RADIUS RFC and whatever logic is implemented above the level of the protocol. The access profile generally contains user-specific authorization information, such as access control lists (ACLs) to be applied or the VLAN ID to be assigned.

Figure 7-13   Cisco Secure ACS RADIUS Response

End User   Cisco Catalyst Switch   Cisco Secure ACS

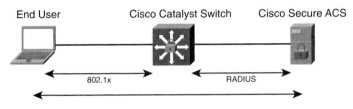

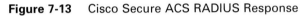

Configuration of the RADIUS profile is performed on the Cisco Secure ACS under the Group Setup section or the User Setup section. For attributes to show up in the Group and User sections, they first have to be configured as required in the Interface Configuration section. The following attributes are required:

- [064] Tunnel-Type
- [081] Tunnel-Private-Group-ID

These attributes can be found under the IETF RADIUS Settings section of Interface Control. Checking these boxes causes the appropriate fields to appear on the Group and User pages.

For reasons of administrative scalability, RADIUS profiles are usually configured at the group level rather than one for each user. To configure a VLAN ID to be assigned to all users belonging to a specific group accessing the network through a Cisco Catalyst 4000, 5000, or 6000 switch, navigate to that page for the group within Cisco Secure ACS and locate the IETF RADIUS settings section. If the attributes have been configured in the Interface Configuration, the attributes Tunnel-Type [# 64] and Tunnel-Private-Group-ID [# 81] will appear there for configuration.

To configure these, check the check box on the left of both attributes. For the Tunnel-Type attribute, ensure the first Tag list is set to 1 and the corresponding value is set to VLAN. Make sure that the second Tag list is set to 0. For the Tunnel-Private-Group-ID, again make sure the first Tag list value is set to 1 and then set the corresponding value field to the appropriate num-

Note

Because RADIUS VLAN ID assignment is not supported by Cisco Catalyst 2950 and 3550 switches, assignment of it by the Cisco Secure ACS using RADIUS should not be attempted. Support for VLAN ID to Cisco Catalyst 6000 switches by RADIUS requires Cisco Catalyst Operating System Version 7.2 or later.

ber for the VLAN to be assigned. Again, make sure that the second Tag list is set to 0. In normal usage, RADIUS supports multiple tunnel attribute support tags. When assigning VLAN IDs to a Cisco Catalyst switch, remember that the switch ignores anything with a tag other than 1. Only a single VLAN ID may be supplied in each RADIUS response packet to a Cisco Catalyst switch.

 Lab 7.1.9   Configure EAP on Cisco ACS for Windows

In this lab, you configure EAP with Cisco Secure ACS for Windows.

Configuring 802.1x Port-Based Authentication

The tasks involved with configuring 802.1x port-based authentication on a switch are as follows:

Step 1.   Enable 802.1x authentication (Required).

Step 2.   Configure the switch-to-RADIUS server communication (Required).

Step 3.   Enable periodic reauthentication (Optional).

Step 4.   Manually reauthenticate a client connected to a port (Optional).

Step 5.   Reset the 802.1x configuration to the default values (Optional).

Step 6.   Change the quiet period (Optional).

Step 7.   Change the switch-to-client retransmission time (Optional).

Step 8.   Change the switch-to-client frame-retransmission number (Optional).

Step 9.   Enable multiple hosts (Optional).

Step 10. Reset the 802.1x configuration to the default values (Optional).

Table 7-2 describes the default 802.1x configuration on a switch.

Table 7-2   Default 802.1x Configuration

Feature	Default Setting
AAA	Disabled.
RADIUS server	IP address: None specified. UDP authentication port in: 1812. Key: None specified.
Per-interface 802.1x enable state	Disabled (Force-authorized). The port sends and receives normal traffic without 802.1x-based authentication of the client.

Table 7-2   Default 802.1x Configuration   *continued*

Feature	Default Setting
Periodic reauthentication	Disabled.
Number of seconds between reauthentication attempts	3600 seconds.
Quiet period	60 seconds. This is the number of seconds that the switch remains in the quiet state following a failed authentication exchange with the client.
Retransmission time	30 seconds. This is the number of seconds that the switch should wait for a response to an EAP request/identity frame from the client before rescinding the request.
Maximum retransmission number	2 times. This is the number of times that the switch sends an EAP-request/identity frame before restarting the authentication process.
Multiple host support	Disabled.
Client timeout period	30 seconds. When relaying a request from the authentication server to the client, the amount of time the switch waits for a response before resending the request to the client.
Authentication server timeout period	30 seconds. When relaying a response from the client to the authentication serve, the amount of time the switch waits for a reply before resending the response to the server. This setting is not configurable.

When 802.1x is enabled, ports are authenticated before any other Layer 2 features are enabled. The 802.1x protocol is supported on Layer 2 static-access ports, but it is not supported on the following port types:

- **Trunk port**—If an administrator attempts to configure 802.1x on a trunk port, an error message appears, and 802.1x is not enabled. If an administrator attempts to change the mode of an 802.1x-enabled port to trunk, the port mode is not changed.

- **Dynamic ports**—A port in dynamic mode can negotiate with its neighbor to become a trunk port. If an administrator attempts to enable 802.1x on a dynamic port, an error message appears, and 802.1x is not enabled. If an administrator attempts to change the mode of an 802.1x-enabled port to dynamic, the port mode is not changed.

- **Dynamic-access ports**—If an administrator attempts to enable 802.1x on a dynamic-access (VLAN Query Protocol [VQP]) port, an error message appears, and 802.1x is not enabled. If an administrator attempts to change an 802.1x-enabled port to dynamic VLAN assignment, an error message appears, and the VLAN configuration is not changed.

- **EtherChannel port**—Before enabling 802.1x on the port, you must first remove it from the EtherChannel. If an administrator attempts to enable 802.1x on an EtherChannel or on an active port in an EtherChannel, an error message appears, and 802.1x is not enabled. If 802.1x is enabled on a not-yet-active port of an EtherChannel, the port does not join the EtherChannel.

- **Secure port**—A secure port cannot be configured as an 802.1x port. If an administrator attempts to enable 802.1x on a secure port, an error message appears, and 802.1x is not enabled. If an administrator attempts to change an 802.1x-enabled port to a secure port, an error message appears, and the security settings are not changed.

- **Switched Port Analyzer (SPAN) destination port**—802.1x can be enabled on a port that is a SPAN destination port. However, 802.1x is disabled until the port is removed as a SPAN destination. 802.1x can be enabled on a SPAN source port.

The 802.1x protocol is not supported on an LRE switch interface that has a Cisco 585 Long-Reach Ethernet (LRE) customer premises equipment (CPE) connected to it.

Enabling 802.1x Authentication

To enable 802.1x port-based authentication, AAA must be enabled and an authentication method list must be specified. A method list describes the sequence and authentication methods to be queried to authenticate a user.

The software uses the first method listed to authenticate users. If that method fails to respond, the software selects the next authentication method in the list. This process continues until there is successful communication with a listed authentication method or until all defined methods are exhausted. If authentication fails at any point in this cycle, the authentication process stops, and no other authentication methods are attempted.

Beginning in privileged EXEC mode, the following steps are used to configure 802.1x port-based authentication:

Step 1. Enter global configuration mode.

Step 2. Enable AAA.

Step 3.   Create an authentication method list with the **aaa authentication dot1x {default}
method1 [method2...]** command. To create a default list that is used when a named
list is not specified in the authentication command, use the default keyword followed
by the methods that are to be used in default situations. The default method list is
automatically applied to all interfaces. At least one of the following keywords must
be entered:

- **group radius**—Use the list of all RADIUS servers for authentication.

- **none**—Use no authentication. The client is automatically authenticated by the
  switch without using the information supplied by the client.

Step 4.   Enter interface configuration mode, and specify the interface connected to the client
that is to be enabled for 802.1x authentication.

Step 5.   Enable 802.1x authentication on the interface.

The port authorization state is controlled by using the **dot1x port-control** interface
configuration command and the following keywords:

- **force-authorized**—Disables 802.1x and causes the port to transition to the
  authorized state without any authentication exchange required. The port sends
  and receives normal traffic without 802.1x-based authentication of the client.
  This is the default setting.

- **force-unauthorized**—Causes the port to remain in the unauthorized state,
  ignoring all attempts by the client to authenticate. The switch cannot provide
  authentication services to the client through the interface.

- **auto**—Enables 802.1x authentication and causes the port to begin in the unauthorized state, allowing only EAPOL frames to be sent and received through
  the port. The authentication process begins when the link state of the port transitions from down to up, or when an EAPOL-start frame is received. The
  switch requests the identity of the client and begins relaying authentication
  messages between the client and the authentication server. Each client attempting to access the network is uniquely identified by the switch by using the
  client's MAC address.

Step 6.   Return to privileged EXEC mode.

Step 7.   Verify the configuration.

To disable 802.1x AAA authentication, use the **no aaa authentication dot1x {default ı list-
name} method1 [method2...]** global configuration command. To disable 802.1x authentication,
use the **dot1x port-control force-authorized** or the **no dot1x port-control** interface configuration command.

Example 7-1 demonstrates how to enable AAA and 802.1x on Fast Ethernet port 0/12.

```
Example 7-1      Enabling AAA and 802.1x
Switch# configure terminal
Switch(config)# aaa new-model
Switch(config)# aaa authentication dot1x default group radius
Switch(config)# interface fastethernet0/12
Switch(config-if)# dot1x port-control auto
Switch(config-if)# end
```

Configuring the Switch-to-RADIUS Server Communication

RADIUS security servers are identified by host name or IP address, host name and specific UDP port numbers, or IP address and specific UDP port numbers. The combination of the IP address and UDP port number creates a unique identifier, which enables RADIUS requests to be sent to multiple UDP ports on a server at the same IP address. If two different host entries on the same RADIUS server are configured for the same service, such as authentication, the second host entry configured acts as the failover backup to the first one. The RADIUS host entries are tried in the order that they are configured.

Beginning in privileged EXEC mode, follow these steps to configure the RADIUS server parameters on the switch:

Step 1.   Enter global configuration mode.

Note

Always configure the key as the last item in the **radius-server host** command syntax because leading spaces are ignored, but spaces within and at the end of the key are used. If spaces are used in the key, do not enclose the key in quotation marks unless the quotation marks are part of the key.

If multiple RADIUS servers are to be used, reenter this command.

Step 2.   Configure the RADIUS server parameters on the switch with the **radius-server host** {*hostname* ı *ip-address*} **auth-port** *port-number* **key** *string* command:

For *hostname* ı *ip-address*, specify the host name or IP address of the remote RADIUS server. For **auth-port** *port-number*, specify the UDP destination port for authentication requests. The default is 1812. For **key** *string*, specify the authentication and encryption key used between the switch and the RADIUS server. The key is a text string that must match the encryption key used on the RADIUS server.

Step 3.   Return to privileged EXEC mode.

Step 4.   Verify the configuration.

To delete the specified RADIUS server, use the **no radius-server host** {*hostname* ı *ip-address*} global configuration command.

To specify the server with IP address 172.20.39.46 as the RADIUS server, to use port 1612 as the authorization port, and to set the encryption key to rad123, matching the key on the RADIUS server, you enter the following:

```
Switch(config)# radius-server host 172.120.39.46 auth-port 1812 key rad123
```

You can globally configure the timeout, retransmission, and encryption key values for all RADIUS servers by using the **radius-server host** global configuration command. To configure these options on a per-server basis, use the **radius-server timeout**, **radius-server resend**, and the **radius-server key** global configuration commands.

Some settings on the RADIUS server need to be configured, too. These settings include the IP address of the switch and the key string to be shared by both the server and the switch.

Enabling Periodic Reauthentication

Periodic 802.1x client reauthentication, and how often it occurs, can be configured. If a time period before enabling reauthentication is not specified, the number of seconds between reauthentication attempts is 3600.

Automatic 802.1x client reauthentication is a global setting and cannot be set for clients connected to individual ports.

Beginning in privileged EXEC mode, the following steps are used to enable periodic reauthentication of the client and to configure the number of seconds between reauthentication attempts:

Step 1. Enter global configuration mode.

Step 2. Enable periodic reauthentication of the client, which is disabled by default, with the **dot1x re-authentication** command.

Step 3. Set the number of seconds between reauthentication attempts with the **dot1x timeout re-authperiod** *seconds* command. The range is 1 to 4294967295, and the default is 3600 seconds. This command affects the behavior of the switch only if periodic reauthentication is enabled.

Step 4. Return to privileged EXEC mode.

Step 5. Verify the configuration.

To disable periodic reauthentication, use the **no dot1x re-authentication** global configuration command. To return to the default number of seconds between reauthentication attempts, use the **no dot1x timeout re-authperiod** global configuration command.

To enable periodic reauthentication and set the number of seconds between reauthentication attempts to 4000, enter the following:

```
Switch(config)# dot1x re-authentication
Switch(config)# dot1x timeout re-authperiod 4000
```

Manually Reauthenticating a Client Connected to a Port

You can manually reauthenticate a client connected to a specific port at any time by entering the **dot1x re-authenticate interface** *interface-id* privileged EXEC command.

To manually reauthenticate the client connected to Fast Ethernet port 0/12, enter the following:

```
Switch(config)# dot1x re-authenticate interface fastethernet0/12
```

Enabling Multiple Hosts

You can attach multiple hosts to a single 802.1x-enabled port. In this mode, only one of the attached hosts must be successfully authorized for all hosts to be granted network access. If the port becomes unauthorized, such as in the case that reauthentication fails or an EAPOL-logoff message is received, all attached clients are denied access to the network.

Beginning in privileged EXEC mode, follow these steps to allow multiple hosts on an 802.1x-authorized port that has the **dot1x port-control** interface configuration command set to **auto**:

Step 1. Enter global configuration mode.

Step 2. Enter interface configuration mode and specify the interface to which multiple hosts are indirectly attached.

Step 3. Allow multiple hosts on an 802.1x-authorized port with the **dot1x multiple-hosts** command. Make sure that the **dot1x port-control** interface configuration command set is set to **auto** for the specified interface.

Step 4. Return to privileged EXEC mode.

Step 5. Verify the configuration with the **show dot1x interface** *interface-id* command.

To disable multiple hosts on the port, use the **no dot1x multiple-hosts** interface configuration command.

To enable 802.1x on FastEthernet interface 0/1 and to allow multiple hosts, enter the following:

```
Switch(config)# interface fastethernet0/1
Switch(config-if)# dot1x port-control auto
Switch(config-if)# dot1x multiple-hosts
```

Resetting the 802.1x Configuration to the Default Values

Beginning in privileged EXEC mode, follow these steps to reset the 802.1x configuration to the default values:

Step 1. Enter global configuration mode.

Step 2. Reset the configurable 802.1x parameters to the default values with the **dot1x default** command.

Step 3.   Return to privileged EXEC mode.

Step 4.   Verify the configuration with the **show dot1x** command.

Displaying 802.1x Statistics and Status

To display 802.1x statistics for all interfaces, use the **show dot1x statistics** privileged EXEC command. To display 802.1x statistics for a specific interface, use the **show dot1x statistics interface** *interface-id* privileged EXEC command.

To display the 802.1x administrative and operational status for the switch, use the **show dot1x** privileged EXEC command. To display the 802.1x administrative and operational status for a specific interface, use the **show dot1x interface** *interface-id* privileged EXEC command.

 Lab 7.2.8   Configure 802.1x Port-Based Authentication

In this lab, students configure 802.1x port-based authentication on a Catalyst 2950 switch.

Summary

This chapter discussed the use of Cisco IBNS to enhance Layer 2 security. You should now be able to explain how Cisco IBNS improves the security of physical and logical access of LANs. Students will also be able to describe how 802.1x provides port-based identity network access control. You should also be able to define the role of each 802.1x component. This chapter also included a discussion that described how 802.1x uses EAP. You should now be able to select the appropriate EAP type to meet a given set of network requirements. You should also be able to describe how Cisco Secure ACS provides RADIUS-based AAA services for use with 802.1x.

This chapter also introduced the tasks involved in configuring 802.1x port-based authentication on a Catalyst switch. You should now be able to enable 802.1x authentication and configure the RADIUS server parameters on the switch. You should also be able to enable periodic reauthentication of the client. This chapter discussed the reauthentication of the client connected to a specific port at any time. You should be able to demonstrate the configuration of a switch to allow multiple hosts. You should be able to discuss the steps that are necessary to reset the 802.1x configuration to the default values.

Check Your Understanding

Complete all the review questions listed here to test your understanding of the topics and concepts in this chapter. Answers are listed in Appendix A, "Check Your Understanding Answer Key."

1. What three roles are defined by the 802.1x authentication process?

    a. Supplicant

    b. Authorizer

    c. Authenticator

    d. Authentication server

2. The authentication process consists of exchanges of Extensible Authentication Protocol (EAP) messages. This exchange occurs between whom?

    a. The supplicant and the authenticator

    b. The supplicant and the authentication server

    c. The supplicant and the authorizer

    d. The supplicant and the authorization server

3. Which of the following best describes the role of an authenticator?

    a. Network component usually implemented on a router, switch, or wireless access point

    b. Software component usually implemented on a router, switch, or wireless access point

    c. Software component usually on user's workstation

    d. Network component usually on user's workstation

4. IEEE 802.1x can be used to authenticate users for wireless access to network resources. Which protocol has Cisco incorporated into its Cisco Wireless Security Suite to provide authentication between client and authentication server?

    a. CHAP

    b. PAP

    c. EAP

    d. WEP

5. What varieties of EAP are supported by the Cisco Secure ACS?

    a. EAP-MD5

    b. EAP-TLS

    c. LEAP

    d. PEAP

    e. EAP-FAST

    f. All the above

6. EAP-TLS is an IETF standard that uses which of the following?

   a. Digital certificates for server authentication

   b. Digital certificates for user authentication

   c. Digital certificates for both user and server authentication

   d. MD5 key for server authentication

   e. MD5 key for user authentication

   f. MD5 key for both user and server authentication

7. PEAP is an IETF draft RFC authored by which of the following? (Choose three.)

   a. Cisco Systems

   b. Microsoft

   c. Symantec

   d. Sun Systems

   e. RSA Security

8. Which two policy choices do you have regarding authentication in a Cisco Catalyst Switch environment?

   a. EAP-MD5

   b. EAP-TLS

   c. LEAP

   d. PEAP

   e. EAP-FAST

   f. All the above

CHAPTER 8

Configure Filtering on a Router

Upon completion of this chapter, you should be able to answer the following questions:

- What are the various filtering technologies?

- What is Cisco IOS Firewall Context-Based Access Control?

- How do I configure Cisco IOS Firewall Context-Based Access Control?

Key Terms

This chapter uses the following key terms. You can find the definitions in the glossary at the end of the book.

Access control lists (ACLs)   page 340

Stateful packet filtering   page 342

URL filtering   page 344

Context-Based Access Control (CBAC)   page 344

This chapter discusses, in detail, how routers are used to secure a network through the use the Context-Based Access Control (CBAC) component of the Cisco IOS Firewall feature set.

Filtering and Access Lists

Access control lists (ACLs) are used to filter and secure network traffic. ACLs filter network traffic by controlling whether routed or switched packets are forwarded or blocked at the interface. Each packet is examined to determine how that packet should be handled based on the criteria specified within the ACL. One particular type of ACL implementation, CBAC, is discussed in detail. CBAC provides a greater level of security among the ACLs by inspecting traffic at Layers 3 and higher. Information gathered by CBAC is used to create temporary openings in the firewall ACLs. You will learn the steps required to create and establish CBAC:

Step 1. Pick an interface, internal or external.

Step 2. Configure IP ACLs at the interface.

Step 3. Set audit trails and alerts.

Step 4. Set global timeouts and thresholds.

Step 5. Define port-to-application mapping (PAM).

Step 6. Define inspection rules.

Step 7. Apply inspection rules and ACLs to interfaces.

Step 8. Test and verify.

In addition to applied ACLs, CBAC has several other uses. Packets entering the firewall are only inspected by CBAC if they first pass the inbound ACL at the interface. If a packet is denied by the ACL, the packet is simply dropped and not inspected by CBAC.

Packet Filtering

A firewall can use packet filtering to limit information entering a network, or information moving from one segment of a network to another. Packet filtering uses ACLs, which allow a firewall to accept or deny access based on packet types and other variables.

This method is effective when a protected network receives a packet from an unprotected network. Any packet that is sent to the protected network and does not fit the criteria defined by the ACLs is dropped.

However, there are problems with packet filtering:

- Arbitrary packets can be sent that fit the ACL criteria and, therefore, pass through the filter.

- Packets can pass through the filter by being fragmented.

- Complex ACLs are difficult to implement and maintain correctly.

- Some services cannot be filtered. For example, FTP uses the command session to negotiate which ports will be used for the data session. Because you have no fixed FTP data ports to work with (active FTP uses a fixed source port but negotiates the destination port), all possibilities must be opened up. This is a poor security posture because it can allow other services to be accessed. If you want to support active FTP, you must permit in all TCP traffic with a source port of 20 and a destination port of greater than 1023. The problem is this would allow any service listening above 1023 to be accessed (like X Window System). Although you could specifically block these ports and open all others above 1023, you will experience intermittent problems with FTP.

You will experience similar problems with other complex protocols such as Distributed Component Object Model (DCOM), which negotiates the ports to use through Remote Procedure Call (RPC). With DCOM, however, you can usually configure the server to only use a limited number of ports. For example, we could configure our Exchange server to only negotiate TCP ports 20001 through 20010 for use with DCOM.

In a similar manner, packet filtering has trouble dealing with certain Internet Control Message Protocol (ICMP) traffic. For example, time exceeded in transit and host and network unreachable packets store the first 64 bits of the original packet header in their payload. Because filtering has no way of analyzing the payload or maintaining state on a connection, it has no way of distinguishing between legitimate ICMP errors or crafted ones. With this in mind, you have to choose to either block all packets or let them all through.

Figure 8-1 depicts the packet-filtering process.

Figure 8-1   Packet Filtering

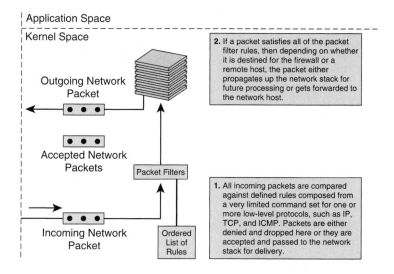

Stateful Filtering

A stateful packet filter is simply a static packet filter that has the additional ability of maintaining connection state. This might not sound like much, but it is actually a powerful capability. By remembering the state of a connection, a stateful filter can make intelligent decisions about which packets are true reply traffic and which packets have been crafted. The real replies can be allowed through while the crafted packets are filtered out. Most stateful filters try to match all traffic against an existing state table entry. If a match is found, the traffic is passed through. If no match is found, the packet is evaluated against the firewall rule base. This is an extremely efficient method of dealing with traffic because most packets will be part of an existing session.

Stateful packet filtering maintains complete session state information for each connection, as shown in Figure 8-2. Each time a TCP, as shown in Figure 8-3, or UDP, as shown in Figure 8-4, connection is established for inbound or outbound connections, the information is logged in a stateful session flow table.

Figure 8-2   Stateful Packet Filtering

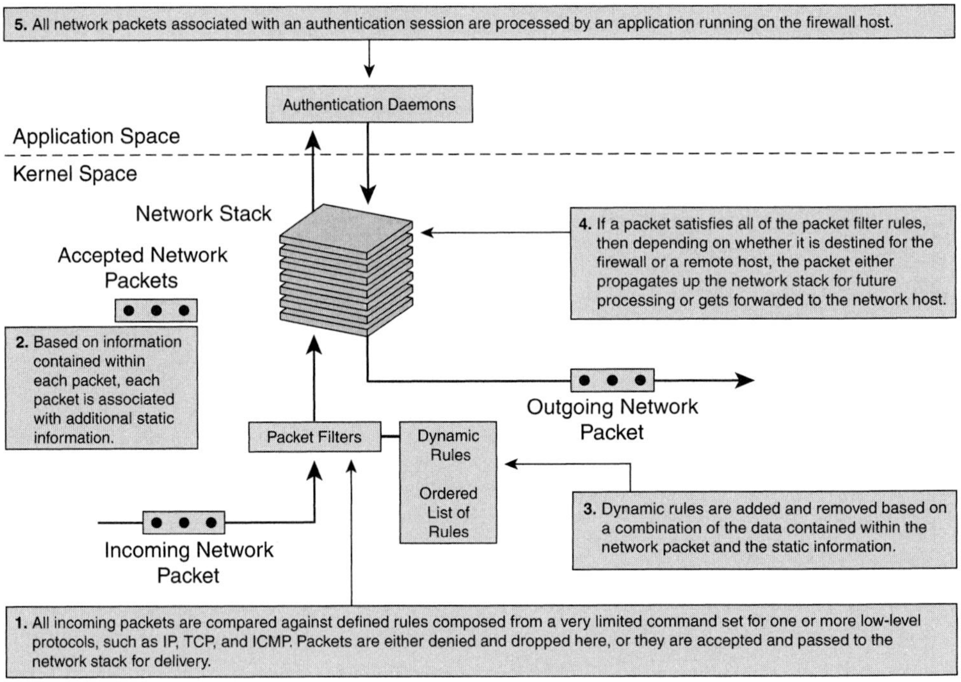

Figure 8-3 TCP Connections

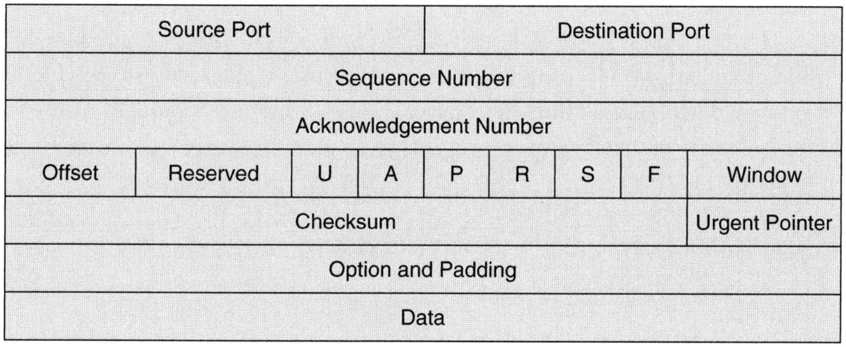

Source Port				Destination Port			
Sequence Number							
Acknowledgement Number							
Offset	Reserved	U	A	P	R	S	F	Window
Checksum						Urgent Pointer	
Option and Padding							
Data							

Figure 8-4 UDP Connections

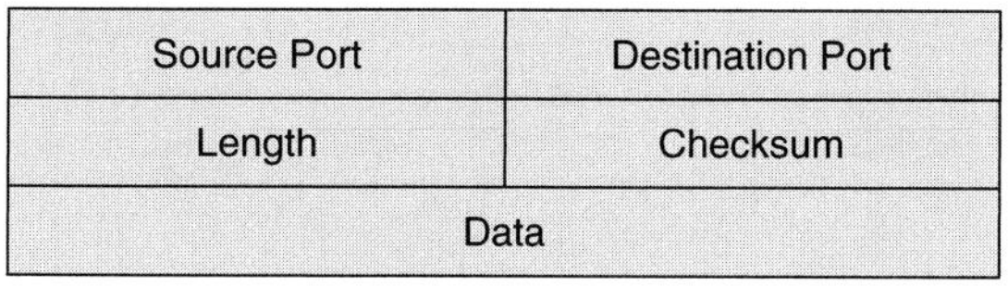

Source Port	Destination Port
Length	Checksum
Data	

The additional flags and fields in TCP packets allow TCP to ensure reliable transport between hosts. These connections are easily monitored because each connection can be examined for its current state. A TCP connection can be flagged as already established or as newly forming. The firewall can use this connection information to accept or reject traffic.

Whereas TCP packets have fields and flags that allow inspection by the firewall to determine connection state, UDP connections do not have this additional information. This lack of state information makes UDP much harder to secure. Domain Name System (DNS) is a common service that uses UDP.

The stateful session flow table contains the source and destination addresses, port numbers, TCP sequencing information, and additional flags for each TCP or UDP connection associated with that particular session. This information creates a connection object and, consequently, all inbound and outbound packets are compared against session flows in the stateful session flow table. Data is permitted through the firewall only if an appropriate connection exists to validate its passage.

This method is effective because of the following:

- It works on packets and connections.

- It operates at a higher performance level than packet filtering or using a proxy server.

- It records data in a table for every connection or connectionless transaction. This table serves as a reference point to determine whether packets belong to an existing connection or are from an unauthorized source.

URL Filtering

URL filtering services provide URL filtering for a firewall, enabling network administrators to effectively monitor and control network traffic. URL-filtering applications are used to block specific URLs on the basis of a defined policy, as shown in Figure 8-5. This is useful because between the hours of 9 a.m. and 5 p.m.

- 30 percent to 40 percent of Internet surfing is not business related.

- 70 percent of all Internet porn traffic occurs.

- More than 60 percent of online purchases are made.

Figure 8-5   URL-Filtering Topology

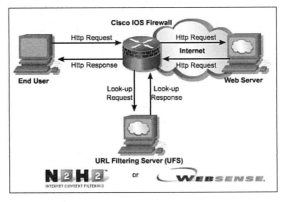

When the firewall receives a request to access a URL from users, it queries the URL-filtering server to determine whether to return or block the requested web page. The URL-filtering server checks its configurations to determine whether the URL should be blocked. If the URL should be blocked, URL-filtering applications can display blocking messages or direct the user requesting the URL to a specified website.

Two common URL-filtering applications are Websense and N2H2.

Cisco IOS Firewall Context-Based Access Control

Context-Based Access Control (CBAC) intelligently filters TCP and UDP packets based on application layer protocol session information. CBAC can inspect traffic for sessions that originate on any interface of the router. CBAC inspects traffic that travels through the firewall to discover and manage state information for TCP and UDP sessions. This state information is used to create temporary openings in the ACLs that are configured on the router. These temporary openings allow return traffic and additional data connections for permissible sessions.

CBAC Packets

Inspecting packets at the application layer and maintaining TCP and UDP session information provides CBAC with the ability to detect and prevent certain types of network attacks, such as SYN flooding. CBAC also inspects packet sequence numbers in TCP connections to determine whether they are within expected ranges. CBAC drops any suspicious packets. In addition, CBAC can detect unusually high rates of new connections and issue alert messages. CBAC inspection can help protect against certain denial-of-service (DoS) attacks involving fragmented IP packets, as shown in Figure 8-6.

Figure 8-6   Cisco IOS Firewall CBAC

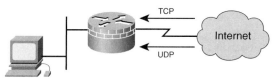

Keep in mind the following CBAC features:

- Packets are inspected upon entering the firewall by CBAC if they are not specifically denied by an ACL.

- CBAC permits or denies specified TCP and UDP traffic through a firewall.

- A state table is maintained with session information.

- ACLs are dynamically created or deleted.

Cisco IOS ACLs

Before delving into CBAC, you need to understand some basic ACL concepts. The following are general statements about traditional ACLs:

- ACLs end in an implied deny any statement.

- If ACLs are not configured on an interface, all connections are permitted by default.

- ACLs provide traffic filtering at the network layer by utilizing the following:

  — Source and destination IP addresses

  — Source and destination ports

- ACLS can be used to implement a filtering firewall.

- ACLs open ports permanently to allow traffic, creating a security vulnerability.

- ACLs do not work with applications that negotiate ports dynamically.

Without CBAC, traffic filtering is limited to ACL implementations that examine packets at the network layer, or at most, the transport layer.

How CBAC Works

CBAC specifies which protocols are to be inspected, the interface, interface direction (either in or out), and where the inspection originates, as shown in Figure 8-7. CBAC inspect only specified protocols. For these protocols, packets flowing through the firewall in any direction are inspected, as long as they flow through the interface where inspection is configured. Packets entering the firewall are inspected by CBAC only if they first pass the inbound ACL at the interface. If a packet is denied by the ACL, the packet is simply dropped and not inspected by CBAC.

Figure 8-7   How CBAC Works I

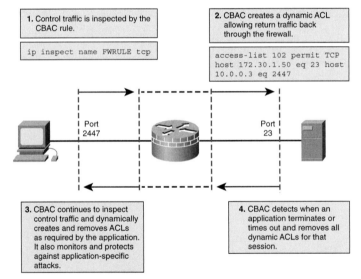

CBAC inspects and monitors only the control channels of connections. The data channels are not inspected. CBAC software analyzes the FTP commands and responses. For example, during FTP sessions both the control and data channels, which are created when a data file is transferred, are monitored for state changes. CBAC only inspects the control channel.

CBAC inspection recognizes application-specific commands in the control channel. CBAC tracks the sequence numbers in all TCP packets and drops the packets with sequence numbers that are not within expected ranges. CBAC inspection recognizes application-specific commands such as illegal Simple Mail Transfer Protocol (SMTP) in the control channel. CBAC inspection also detects and prevents certain application-level attacks. When CBAC suspects an attack, the DoS feature can take the following actions:

- Generate alert messages
- Protect system resources that could impede performance
- Block packets from suspected attackers

CBAC uses timeout and threshold values to manage session state information. It uses this information to help determine when to drop sessions that do not become fully established. Setting timeout values for network sessions helps prevent DoS attacks by freeing system resources. They accomplish this by dropping sessions after a specified amount of time. Setting threshold values for network sessions helps prevent DoS attacks by controlling the number of half-open sessions, which limits the amount of system resources applied to half-open sessions. When a session is dropped, CBAC sends a reset message to the devices at both endpoints, source and destination, of the session. When the system under DoS attack receives a reset command, it releases or frees processes and resources related to that incomplete session.

CBAC provides three thresholds against DoS attacks:

- The total number of half-open TCP or UDP sessions
- The number of half-open sessions based on time
- The number of half-open TCP-only sessions per host

If a threshold is exceeded, CBAC has two options:

- Send a reset message to the endpoints of the oldest half-open session, making resources available to service newly arriving SYN packets.
- In the case of half-open TCP-only sessions, CBAC blocks all SYN packets temporarily for the duration configured by the threshold value. When the router blocks a SYN packet, the TCP three-way handshake is never initiated. This prevents the router from using memory and processing resources needed for valid connections.

DoS detection and prevention requires the creation of a CBAC inspection rule, which is applied to an interface. The inspection rule must include the protocols that will be monitored against DoS attacks. For example, if TCP inspection is enabled on the inspection rule, CBAC can track all TCP connections to watch for DoS attacks. If the inspection rule includes FTP protocol inspection but not TCP inspection, CBAC tracks only FTP connections for DoS attacks.

A state table maintains session state information. Whenever a packet is inspected, a state table is updated to include information about the state of the packet connection. Return traffic is permitted back through the firewall only if the state table contains information indicating that the packet belongs to a permissible session. Inspection controls the traffic that belongs to a valid session and forwards the traffic it does not recognize. When return traffic is inspected, the state table information is updated as necessary.

UDP sessions are approximated. With UDP, there are no actual sessions. The software approximates sessions by examining the information in the packet and determining whether the packet is similar to other UDP packets, such as having similar source or destination addresses and port numbers. The software also checks whether the packet is within the configurable UDP idle timeout period.

ACL entries are dynamically created and deleted. CBAC dynamically creates and deletes ACL entries at the firewall interfaces, according to the information maintained in the state tables. These ACL entries are applied to the interfaces to examine traffic flowing back into the internal network. These entries create temporary openings in the firewall to permit only traffic that is part of a permissible session, as shown in Figure 8-8. The temporary ACL entries are never saved to nonvolatile RAM (NVRAM).

Figure 8-8   How CBAC Works II

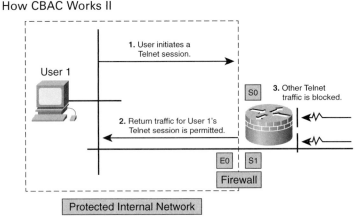

CBAC-Supported Protocols

CBAC is a powerful tool for controlling traffic flows. One of the reasons for this is that CBAC supports traffic inspection at both the session and application layers of the OSI model. Traffic inspection at both of these levels is discussed in the following subsections.

Inspecting the Session Layer

It is possible to configure CBAC to inspect all TCP sessions, regardless of the application layer protocol. This is sometimes called single-channel or generic TCP inspection. CBAC can also be configured to inspect UDP sessions, regardless of the application layer protocol. This is sometimes called single-channel or generic UDP inspection.

Inspecting Application Layer Protocols

It is also possible to configure CBAC to inspect specific application layer protocols. Table 8-1 lists the application layer protocols that can be configured for CBAC. CBAC filters based on OSI Layers 5 and 7.

Table 8-1   CBAC-Supported Protocols

OSI Layer	Protocols
Application	VDOLiveRPC (Sun RPC, not DCE RPC)
	Microsoft RPC
	FTP
	TFTP
	UNIX R-commands (for example, rlogin, rexec, and rsh)
	SMTP
	Java
	SQL*Net
	RTSP (for example, RealNetworks)
	H.323 (for example, NetMeeting, ProShare, CUSeeMe [only the White Pine version])
Session	All TCP sessions, regardless of the application layer protocol; sometimes called single-channel or generic TCP inspection
	All UDP sessions, regardless of the application layer protocol; sometimes called single-channel or generic UDP inspection

The traffic from a protocol configured for CBAC is inspected and state information is maintained. In general, packets are allowed back through the firewall only if they belong to a permissible session.

Configuring Cisco IOS Firewall Context-Based Access Control

This section concentrates on the tasks involved in configuring the CISCO IOS Firewall CBAC on Cisco routers.

CBAC Configuration Tasks

The following tasks enable you to configure CBAC:

Step 1.   Pick an interface, internal or external.

Step 2.   Configure IP ACLs at the interface.

Step 3.   Set audit trails and alerts.

Step 4.   Set global timeouts and thresholds.

Step 5.   Define PAM.

Step 6.   Define inspection rules.

Step 7.   Apply inspection rules and ACLs to interfaces.

Step 8.   Test and verify.

Prepare for CBAC

For CBAC to work properly, you must configure IP ACLs appropriately at the interface. When evaluating IP ACLs at the firewall, use the following three general rules:

- **Start with a basic configuration**—If ACL configuration is attempted without a good understanding of how ACLs work, security risks might inadvertently be introduced to the firewall and to the protected network.

  A basic initial configuration allows all network traffic to flow from the protected networks to the unprotected networks, while blocking network traffic from any unprotected networks.

- **Permit CBAC traffic to leave the network through the firewall**—All ACLs that evaluate traffic leaving the protected network should permit traffic that will be inspected by CBAC. For example, if Telnet will be inspected by CBAC, Telnet traffic should be permitted on all ACLs that apply to traffic leaving the network.

- **Use extended ACLs to deny CBAC return traffic entering the network through the firewall**—For temporary openings to be created in an ACL, the ACL must be an extended ACL. So, wherever there are ACLs that will be applied to returning traffic, you must use extended ACLs. The ACLs should deny CBAC return traffic, because CBAC will open up temporary holes in the ACLs.

Traffic should normally be blocked when it enters your network.

Note

If the firewall only has two connections, one to the internal network and one to the external network, using an inbound ACL works well because packets are stopped before they get a chance to affect the router itself.

Basic Configuration

When CBAC is configured for the first time, it is helpful to start with a basic ACL configuration that makes the operation of the firewall easy to understand without compromising security. The basic configuration allows all network traffic from the protected networks access to the unprotected networks, while blocking all network traffic, with some exceptions, from the unprotected networks to the protected networks.

When configuring the initial firewall ACLs, follow these guidelines:

- **Do not configure an ACL for traffic from the protected networks to the unprotected networks. All traffic from the protected networks is allowed to flow through the interface**—This helps to simplify firewall management by reducing the number of ACLs applied at the interfaces. This assumes a high level of trust for the users on the protected networks, and it assumes there are no malicious users on the protected networks who might launch attacks from the inside. Network access for users on the protected networks can be fine-tuned as necessary.

- **Configure an ACL that includes entries permitting certain ICMP traffic from unprotected networks**—Although an ACL that denies all IP traffic not part of a connection inspected by CBAC seems most secure, it is not practical for normal operation of the router. The router expects to see ICMP traffic from other routers in the network. In addition, ICMP traffic is not inspected by CBAC, meaning specific entries are needed in the ACL to permit return traffic for ICMP command. For example, a user on a protected network could use the ping command to get the status of a host on an unprotected network. Without entries in the ACL that permit echo reply messages, the user on the protected network gets no response to the ping command.

- **Add an ACL entry denying any network traffic from a source address matching an address on the protected network**—This is know as antispoofing protection because it prevents traffic from an unprotected network from assuming the identity of a device on the protected network.

- **Add an entry denying broadcast messages with a source address of 255.255.255.255**—This entry helps to prevent broadcast attacks.

- **By default, the last entry in an extended ACL is an implicit denial of all IP traffic not specifically allowed by other entries in the ACL**—Although this is the default setting, this final deny statement is not shown by default in an ACL. Optionally, you can add an entry to the ACL denying IP traffic with any source or destination address with no undesired effects.

External Interface

The following guidelines apply to ACLs when CBAC is configured on an external interface:

- If there is an outbound IP ACL configured at the external interface, the ACL can be a standard or extended ACL. This outbound ACL should permit traffic that is to be inspected by CBAC. If traffic is not permitted, it will not be inspected by CBAC and will be dropped.

- The inbound IP ACL at the external interface must be an extended ACL. This inbound ACL should deny traffic that is to be inspected by CBAC. CBAC will create temporary openings in this inbound ACL as appropriate to permit only return traffic that is part of a valid, existing session.

Internal Interface

The following guidelines apply to ACLs when CBAC is configured on an internal interface:

- If there is an inbound IP ACL at the internal interface or an outbound IP ACL at external interfaces, these ACLs can be either standard or extended ACLs. These ACLs should permit traffic that is to be inspected by CBAC. If traffic is not permitted, it will not be inspected by CBAC and will be dropped.

- The outbound IP ACL at the internal interface and the inbound IP ACL at the external interface must be extended ACLs. These outbound ACLs should deny traffic that is to be inspected by CBAC. CBAC will create temporary openings in these outbound ACLs as appropriate to permit only return traffic that is part of a valid, existing session. It is not necessary to configure an extended ACL at both the outbound internal interface and the inbound external interface, but at least one is necessary to restrict traffic flowing through the firewall into the internal protected network.

Setting Audit Trails and Alerts

A useful feature of CBAC is its ability to generate alerts and audit trails. This makes monitoring and tracking predefined security events much more efficient and effective. The alert and audit trail process works as follows:

- CBAC generates real-time alerts and audit trails based on events tracked by the firewall, including illegitimate access attempts, and inbound and outbound services.

- Enhanced audit trail features use syslog to track all network transactions, while recording time stamps, source host, destination host, ports used, and the total number of transmitted bytes for advanced session-based reporting.

- Real-time alerts send syslog error messages to central management consoles upon detecting suspicious activity.

Note that when using CBAC inspection rules, it is possible to configure alerts and audit trail information on a per-application protocol basis. For example, to generate audit trail information for HTTP traffic, just specify that in the CBAC rule covering HTTP inspection.

To disable CBAC alert messages, which display on the console, use the **ip inspect alert off** command in global configuration mode. To enable CBAC alert messages, use the **no** form of this command:

```
ip inspect alert-off
no ip inspect alert-off
```

To turn on CBAC audit trail messages, which display on the console after each CBAC session closes, use the **ip inspect audit trail** command in global configuration mode. Use the **no** form of this command to turn off CBAC audit trail messages:

```
ip inspect audit trail
no ip inspect audit trail
```

The syntax for the **ip inspect audit-trail** and the **ip inspect alert-off** commands follows:

```
Router (config)# logging on
Router (config)# logging 10.0.0.3
Router (config)# ip inspect audit-trail
Router (config)# no ip inspect alert-off
```

No other arguments or keywords are used with either command.

Setting Global Timeouts

CBAC uses timeouts and thresholds to determine how long to manage state information for a session and to determine when to drop sessions that do not become fully established. These timeouts and thresholds apply globally to all sessions.

The default timeout and threshold values can be used or they can be changed to values more suitable to the network security requirements. You should make any changes to the timeout and threshold values before continuing with the CBAC configuration.

TCP SYN and FIN Wait Times

Use the **ip inspect tcp synwait-time** global configuration command to define how long the software will wait for a TCP session to reach the established state before dropping the session. The default is 30 seconds. Use the **no** form of this command to reset the timeout to the default. The syntax of the **ip inspect tcp synwait-time** command follows:

```
ip inspect tcp synwait-time seconds
no ip inspect tcp synwait-time
```

Use the **ip inspect tcp finwait-time** global configuration command to define how long a TCP session will still be managed after the firewall detects a FIN exchange. The default is 5 seconds. Use the **no** form of this command to reset the timeout to default. The syntax of the **ip inspect tcp finwait-time** command follows:

```
ip inspect tcp finwait-time seconds
no ip inspect tcp finwait-time
```

TCP, UDP, and DNS Idle Times

Use the **ip inspect tcp idle-time** global configuration command to specify the TCP idle timeout (the length of time a TCP session will still be managed after no activity). Use the **no** form of this command to reset the timeout to default.

Use the **ip inspect udp idle-time** global configuration command to specify the UDP idle timeout (the length of time a UDP session will still be managed after no activity). Use the **no** form of this command to reset the timeout to default. The syntax for the **ip inspect {tcp | udp} idle-time** commands follows, where *seconds* specifies the length of time a TDP or a UDP session will still be managed after no activity. For TCP sessions, the default is 3600 seconds (1 hour). For UDP sessions, the default is 30 seconds.

```
ip inspect {tcp | udp} idle-time seconds
no ip inspect {tcp | udp} idle-time
```

Use the **ip inspect dns-timeout** global configuration command to specify the DNS idle time-out. Use the **no** form of this command to reset the timeout to the default. The syntax for the **ip inspect dns-timeout** command follows, where *seconds* specifies the length of time a DNS name lookup session will still be managed after no activity. The default is 5 seconds.

```
ip inspect dns-timeout seconds
no ip inspect dns-timeout
```

Setting Global Thresholds

An unusually high number of half-open sessions could indicate that a denial-of-service (DoS) attack is occurring. For TCP, half-open means that the three-way handshake has not yet been completed, so the session has not reached the established state. For UDP, half-open means that the firewall has detected no return traffic.

CBAC measures both the total number of existing half-open sessions and the rate of session establishment attempts. Both TCP and UDP half-open sessions are counted in the total number and rate measurements. Measurements are made one time each minute.

When the number of existing half-open sessions rises above a threshold, the **max-incomplete high** *number*, CBAC goes into aggressive mode and deletes half-open sessions as required to accommodate new connection requests. The software continues to delete half-open requests as necessary, until the number of existing half-open sessions drops below another threshold, the **max-incomplete low** *number*.

Use the **ip inspect max-incomplete high** command in global configuration mode to define the number of existing half-open sessions that will cause CBAC to start deleting half-open sessions. Use the **no** form of this command to reset the threshold to default. The syntax for the **ip inspect max-incomplete high** command follows, where *number* defines the number of existing half-open sessions that cause the software to start deleting half-opened sessions (aggressive mode). The default is 500 half-opened sessions.

```
ip inspect max-incomplete high number
no ip inspect max-incomplete high
```

Use the **ip inspect max-incomplete low** command in global configuration mode to define the number of existing half-open sessions that will cause CBAC to stop deleting half-open sessions. Use the **no** form of this command to reset the threshold to default. The syntax for the **ip inspect max-incomplete low** command follows. The default number is 400 half-opened sessions.

```
ip inspect max-incomplete low number
no ip inspect max-incomplete low
```

When the rate of new connection attempts rises above a threshold, the **one-minute high** *number*, CBAC deletes half-open sessions as required to accommodate new connection attempts. The software continues to delete half-open sessions as necessary, until the rate of new connection attempts drops below another threshold, the **one-minute low** *number*. The rate thresholds are measured as the number of new session connection attempts detected in the last one-minute sample period. CBAC reviews the one-minute rate on an ongoing basis, meaning that CBAC reviews the rate more frequently than one minute and does not keep deleting half-open sessions for one minute after a DoS attack has stopped. This means that CBAC will stop deleting sessions sooner than one minute after the attack has stopped.

Use the **ip inspect one-minute high** command in global configuration mode to define the rate of new un-established sessions that will cause the software to start deleting half-open sessions. The default is 500 half-opened sessions. Use the **no** form of this command to reset the threshold to default. The syntax for the **ip inspect one-minute high** command follows:

```
ip inspect one-minute high number
no ip inspect one-minute high
```

Use the **ip inspect one-minute low** command in global configuration mode to define the rate of new unestablished TCP sessions that will cause the software to stop deleting half-open sessions. The default is 400 half-opened sessions. Use the **no** form of this command to reset the threshold to the default. The syntax for the **ip inspect one-minute low** command follows.

```
ip inspect one-minute low number
no ip inspect one-minute low
```

Half-Open Connection Limits by Host

An unusually high number of half-open sessions with the same destination host address could indicate that a DoS attack is being launched against the host. Whenever the number of half-open sessions with the same destination host address rises above the threshold configured by the **max-incomplete host** *number* command, CBAC deletes half-open sessions according to one of the following methods:

- If the **block-time** *minutes* timeout is 0, the default value, CBAC deletes the oldest existing half-open session for the host for every new connection request to the host. This ensures that the number of half-open sessions to a given host never exceeds the threshold.

- If the **block-time** *minutes* timeout is greater than 0, CBAC deletes all existing half-open sessions for the host, and then blocks all new connection requests to the host. CBAC continues to block all new connection requests until the block time expires.

CBAC also sends syslog messages whenever the **max-incomplete host** *number* is exceeded, and when blocking of connection initiations to a host starts or ends.

The global values specified for the threshold and blocking time apply to all TCP connections inspected by CBAC.

Use the **ip inspect tcp max-incomplete host** global configuration command to specify threshold and blocking time values for TCP host-specific DoS detection and prevention. Use the **no** form of this command to reset the threshold and blocking time to the default values. The syntax for the **ip inspect tcp max-incomplete host** command follows. *number* specifies how many half-opened TCP sessions with the same host destination address can exist at a time before the software starts deleting half-opened sessions to the host. Use a number from 1 to 250. The default is 50 half-opened sessions. *minutes* specifies how long the software will continue to delete new connection requests to the host. The default is 0 minutes.

```
ip inspect tcp max-incomplete host number block-time minutes
no ip inspect tcp max-incomplete host
```

System-Defined Port-to-Application Mapping

Port-to-application mapping (PAM) enables administrators to customize TCP or UDP port numbers for network services or applications. PAM uses this information to support network environments that run services using ports that differ from the registered or well-known ports associated with an application.

Using the port information, PAM establishes a table of default port-to-application mapping information at the firewall. The information in the PAM table enables CBAC supported services to run on nonstandard ports. PAM also supports host- or subnet-specific port mapping, which enables administrators to apply PAM to a single host or subnet using standard ACLs. Host- or subnet-specific port mapping is done using standard ACLs.

PAM creates a table, or database, of system-defined mapping entries using the well-known or registered port mapping information set up during the system startup. The system-defined entries comprise all the services supported by CBAC, which requires the system-defined mapping information to function properly.

The system-defined mapping information cannot be deleted or changed. Therefore, it is impossible to map HTTP services to port 21, the system-defined port for FTP, or FTP services to port 80, the system-defined port for HTTP.

Table 8-2 shows the default system-defined services and applications found in the PAM table.

Table 8-2   Default PAM Table Listings

Application	Port
cuseeme	7648
exec	512
ftp	21
http	80
h323	1720

Table 8-2   Default PAM Table Listings

Application	Port
login	512
mgcp	2427
msrpc	135
netshow	1755
realmedia	7070
rtsp	554
rtsp-alt	8554
shell	514
sip	5060
smtp	25
sql-net	1521
streamworks	1558

User-Defined PAM

Network services or applications that use nonstandard ports require user-defined entries in the PAM table. For example, the network might run HTTP services on the nonstandard port 8080 rather than on the system-defined default port 80. In this case, PAM can be used to map port 8080 with HTTP services. If HTTP services run on other ports, use PAM to create additional port mapping entries. After a port mapping entry is defined, you can overwrite that entry later just by mapping that specific port with a different application.

User-defined port mapping information can also specify a range of ports for an application by establishing a separate entry in the PAM table for each port number in the range.

User-defined entries are saved with the default mapping information when the router configuration is saved.

Use the **ip port-map** configuration command to establish PAM. Use the **no** form of this command to delete user-defined PAM entries. The following **ip port-map** command syntax maps a port number to an application:

```
router(config)#ip port-map appl_name port port_num
```

User-defined entries in the mapping table can include host- or network-specific mapping information, which establishes port mapping information for specific hosts or subnets. In some environments, it might be necessary to override the default port mapping information for a specific host or subnet.

Note

If an attempt is made to map an application to a system-defined port, a message appears warning the administrator of a mapping conflict.

With host-specific port mapping, you can use the same port number for different services on different hosts. This means that port 8000 can be mapped to HTTP services for one host, while port 8000 can be mapped to Telnet services for another host.

Host-specific port mapping also enables administrators to apply PAM to a specific subnet when that subnet runs a service that uses a port number that is different from the port number defined in the default mapping information. For example, hosts on subnet 192.168.0.0 might run HTTP services on nonstandard port 8000, whereas other traffic through the firewall uses the default port 80 for HTTP services.

Host- or network-specific port mapping enables administrators to override a system-defined entry in the PAM table. For example, if CBAC finds an entry in the PAM table that maps port 25, the system-defined port for SMTP, with HTTP for a specific host, CBAC identifies port 25 as HTTP protocol traffic on that host.

Use the **list** option for the **ip port-map** command to specify an ACL for a host or subnet that uses PAM. Use the **show ip port-map** privileged EXEC command to display the PAM information.

The following command syntax maps a port number to an application for a given host:

```
Router(config)#access-list permit acl_num ip_addr ip port-map appl_name port port_num
list acl_num
```

The following command syntax maps a port number to an application for a given network:

```
Router(config)#access-list permit acl_num ip_addr wildcard_mask ip port-map appl_name
port port_num list acl_num
```

The following command shows all port mapping information:

```
router#show ip port-map
```

The following command syntax shows port mapping information for a given application:

```
router#show ip port-map appl_name
```

The following command syntax shows port mapping information for a given application on a given port:

```
router#show ip port-map port port_num
```

For example:

```
Router# show ip port-map ftp
Default mapping: ftpport 21    system defined
Host specific:   ftpport 1000 in list 10 user
```

Defining Inspection Rules for Applications

Inspection rules must be defined to specify what IP traffic and which application layer protocols will be inspected by CBAC at an interface. Normally, only one inspection rule is defined.

Note

If the host-specific port mapping information is the same as existing system- or user-defined default entries, host-specific port changes have no effect.

The only exception might occur if CBAC is enabled in two directions at a single firewall interface. In this case, two rules must be configured, one for each direction.

An inspection rule should specify each desired application layer protocol and, if desired, generic TCP or generic UDP. The inspection rule consists of a series of statements, each listing a protocol and specifying the same inspection rule name.

Inspection rules include options for controlling alert and audit trail messages and for checking IP packet fragmentation.

Use the **ip inspect name** command in global configuration mode to define a set of inspection rules. Use the **no** form of this command to remove the inspection rule for a protocol or to remove the entire set of inspection rules. The syntax for the **ip inspect name** command follows:

```
router (config)#ip inspect name inspection-name protocol [alert {on | }] [audit-trail {on
| off}] {timeout seconds]
```

This command defines the application protocols to inspect and will be applied to an interface. Available protocols include **tcp**, **udp**, **cuseeme**, **ftp**, **http**, **h323**, **netshow**, **rcmd**, **realaudio**, **rpc**, **smtp**, **sqlnet**, **streamworks**, **tftp**, and **vdolive**. **alert**, **audit trail**, and **timeout** are configurable per protocol and override global settings.

For example:

```
Router(config)# ip inspect name FWRULE smtp alert on audit-trail on timeout 300
Router(config)# ip inspect name FWRULE ftp alert on audit-trail on timeout 300
```

Java Inspection

Java inspection enables Java applet filtering at the firewall. Java applet filtering distinguishes between trusted and untrusted applets by relying on a list of external sites designated as friendly. If an applet is from a friendly site, the firewall allows the applet through. If the applet is not from a friendly site, the applet is blocked. Alternatively, applets from all sites could be permitted except for sites specifically designated as hostile. The following syntax for the **ip inspect name** command controls Java blocking with a standard ACL:

```
router (config)# ip inspect name inspection-name http java-list acl-num [alert {on |
off}] [audit-trail {on | off}] [timeout seconds]
```

For example:

```
Router (config)# ip inspect name FWRULE http java-list 10 alert on audit-trial on
timeout 300
Router(config)# access-list 10 deny 172.26.26.0 0.0.0.255
Router(config)# access-list 10 permit 172.27.27.0 0.0.0.255
```

Note

CBAC does not detect or block encapsulated Java applets. Therefore, Java applets that are wrapped or encapsulated, such as applets in .zip or .jar format, are not blocked at the firewall. CBAC also does not detect or block applets loaded via FTP, gopher, or HTTP on a nonstandard port.

Remote Procedure Call (RPC) Inspection

Before looking at how and why Remote Procedure Call (RPC) application inspection is necessary, it is necessary to have a basic understanding of the protocol. RPC is an independent set of functions used for accessing remote nodes on a network. Using RPC network services, you can create applications in much the same way a programmer writes software for a single computer using local procedure calls. The RPC protocols extend the concept of local procedure calls across the network, which means that administrators can develop distributed applications for transparent execution across a network.

RPC inspection enables the specification of various program numbers. It is possible to define multiple program numbers by creating multiple entries for RPC inspection, each with a different program number. If a program number is specified, all traffic for that program number is permitted. If a program number is not specified, all traffic for that program number is blocked. For example, if an RPC entry is created with the NFS program number, all NFS traffic is allowed through the firewall. The syntax of the **ip inspect name** command for RPC applications follows. This syntax allows given RPC program number's wait-time and keeps the connection open for a specified number of minutes.

```
router (config)#ip inspect name inspection-name rpc program-number number [wait-time
minutes] [alert {on | off}] [audit-trail {on | off}] [timeout seconds]
```

For example:

```
Router (config)# ip inspect name FWRULE rpc program-number 100022 wait-time 0 alert off
audit-trail on
```

SMTP Inspection

SMTP inspection causes SMTP commands to be inspected for illegal commands. Any packets with illegal commands are dropped, and the SMTP session hangs and eventually times out. An illegal command is any command *except* for the following legal commands: **DATA**, **EXPN**, **HELO**, **HELP**, **MAIL**, **NOOP**, **QUIT**, **RCPT**, **RSET**, **SAML**, **SEND**, **SOML**, and **VRFY**. The syntax for the **ip inspect name** command for SMTP application inspection follows:

```
router (config) #ip inspect name inspection-name smtp [alert {on | off}] [audit-trail
{on | off}] [timeout seconds]
```

If disabled, all SMTP commands are allowed through the firewall, and potential mail server vulnerabilities are exposed.

Defining Inspection Rules for IP Fragmentation

CBAC inspection rules can help protect hosts against certain DoS attacks involving fragmented IP packets. Even though the firewall keeps an attacker from making actual connections to a given host, the attacker might still be able to disrupt services provided by that host.

Recall that sometimes packets are fragmented for transmission. The initial packet is flagged for identification, and the remaining fragmented packets are flagged according to their original order. If an initial packet is filtered by an ACL, the other associated packets are dropped.

Problems might arise when some of the noninitial packets show up at the receiving interface before their initial packet. These fragments must be queued until the initial packet arrives and things can get sorted out. It is possible to mount a DoS attack by sending many noninitial IP fragments, or by sending complete fragmented packets through a router with an ACL that filters the first fragment of a fragmented packet. These fragments can tie up resources on the target host as it tries to reassemble the incomplete packets.

Using fragmentation inspection, the firewall maintains an interfragment state, or structure, for IP traffic. Noninitial fragments are discarded unless the corresponding initial fragment was permitted to pass through the firewall. Noninitial fragments received before the corresponding initial fragments are discarded.

Because routers running Cisco IOS Software are used in a large variety of networks, and because the CBAC feature is often used to isolate parts of internal networks from one another, the fragmentation inspection feature is not enabled by default. Fragmentation detection must be explicitly enabled for inspection rules using the **ip inspect name** global command. Unfragmented traffic is never discarded, because it lacks a fragment state. Even when the system is under heavy attack with fragmented packets, legitimate fragmented traffic, if any, stills get some fraction of the fragment state resources of the firewall, and legitimate, unfragmented traffic can flow through the firewall unimpeded.

The syntax of the **ip inspect name** command for IP packet fragmentation follows:

```
router (config)#ip inspect name inspection-name fragment max number timeout seconds
```

where:

- **max number** refers to unassembled fragmented IP packets.

- **timeout** *seconds* is when the unassembled fragmented IP packets begin to be discarded.

For example:

```
Router(config)# ip inspect name FWRULE fragment max 254 timeout 4
```

Defining Inspection Rules for ICMP

Although ICMP is a useful tool for debugging network connectivity issues, intruders can use it to map private networks. Armed with the information provided by ICMP replies, intruders might attempt targeted attacks on critical network resources. For this reason, many network administrators configure routers and firewalls to block all ICMP packets from entering the private network. The downside to blocking all ICMP packets is that although it keeps intruders from using ICMP, it also takes away a valuable network troubleshooting tool.

Cisco routers using Cisco IOS Software Releases 12.2(11)YU and later with the Cisco IOS Firewall feature set can perform stateful inspection of ICMP packets. This feature enables the router to trust ICMP packets generated from inside the private network and permit their associated replies while blocking other possibly malicious ICMP packets.

Although Cisco IOS routers can be configured to selectively allow certain ICMP packets through the router, the network administrator must still determine which messages are potentially malicious and which are not.

Stateful inspection of ICMP packets is limited to the most common types of ICMP messages used by network administrators to debug network connectivity issues. ICMP messages that do not provide useful troubleshooting services are not allowed. Table 8-3 identifies the Cisco IOS Firewall-supported ICMP packet types.

Table 8-3   ICMP Packet Types Supported by CBAC

ICMP Packet Type	Name	Description
0	Echo reply	Reply to echo request (type 8).
3	Destination unreachable	Possible reply to any request. Note: This packet is included because it is a possible response to any ICMP packet request.
8	Echo request	Ping or traceroute request.
11	Time exceeded	Reply to any request if the time to live (TTL) packet is 0.
13	Time stamp request	Request.
14	Time stamp reply	Reply to time stamp request (type 13).

ICMP packet types 0 and 8 are used for pinging; the source sends out an echo request packet, and the destination responds with an echo reply packet. ICMP packet types 0, 8, and 11 are used for ICMP traceroute; echo request packets are sent out starting with a time-to-live (TTL) packet of 1, and the TTL is incremented for each hop. The intermediate hops respond to the echo request packet with a time exceeded packet and the final destination responds with an echo reply packet.

ICMP stateful inspection is explicitly enabled using the **ip inspect name** *inspection-name* **icmp** (global) command. The syntax of the **ip inspect name** *inspection-name* **icmp** command for ICMP packet inspection follows:

```
ip inspect name inspection-name icmp [alert {on | off}] [audit-trail {on | off}] [timeout
seconds]
no ip inspect name inspection-name icmp
```

where:

- *inspection-name*—Names the set of inspection rules. To add a protocol to an existing set of rules, use the same inspection name as the existing set of rules. The inspection name cannot exceed 16 characters. If the name is longer then 16 characters, the name is truncated to the 16-character limit.

- **icmp**—Specifies ICMP inspection for the named rule.

- **alert** {**on** ǀ **off**}—(Optional) For ICMP inspection, the generation of alert messages can be set to on or off. If no option is selected, alerts are generated on the basis of the setting of the **ip inspect alert-off** command.

- **audit-trail** {**on** ǀ **off**}—(Optional) For ICMP inspection, audit trail can be set on or off. If no option is selected, audit trail messages are generated on the basis of the setting of the **ip inspect audit-trail** command.

- **timeout** *seconds*—(Optional) Specifies the number of seconds for an ICMP idle timeout.

To troubleshoot ICMP inspection, use the following optional commands.

The following optional command displays existing sessions that are currently being tracked and inspected by Cisco IOS Firewall. The optional **detail** keyword causes additional details about these sessions to be shown:

```
router #show ip inspect session [detail]
```

The following optional command displays the contents of all current IP ACLs:

```
router #show ip access-list
```

The following optional command displays the operations of the ICMP inspection engine for debugging purposes:

```
router #debug ip inspect icmp
```

Applying Inspection Rules and ACLs to Interfaces

Now that inspection rules and how to configure them have been discussed, it is important to understand how they are applied to interfaces on the router. Remember, no inspection rule or ACL can become effective until it is applied to a router interface. Use the **ip inspect** interface configuration command to apply a set of inspection rules to an interface. Use the **no** form of this command to remove the set of rules from the interface. The syntax for the **ip inspect** command follows:

```
router (config)#ip inspect name inspection-name {in ǀ out}
```

where:

- *inspection-name*—Names the set of inspection rules

- **in**—Applies the inspection rules to inbound traffic

- **out**—Applies the inspection rules to outbound traffic

For example, the following applies the inspection rule to interface e0/0 in the inward direction:

```
Router(config)# interface e0/0
Router(config)# ip inspect FWRULE in
```

General Rules

For the Cisco IOS Firewall to be effective, both inspection rules and ACLs must be strategically applied to all the interfaces on the router. The following is the general rule of thumb for applying inspection rules and ACLs on the router:

- On the interface where traffic initiates:

    — Apply the ACL on the inward direction that only permits wanted traffic.

    — Apply the rule on the inward direction that inspects wanted traffic.

- On all other interfaces apply the ACL on the inward direction that denies all traffic, except traffic that is not inspected by CBAC, such as ICMP.

Two-Interface Firewall

Now that you know how to configure one interface with inspection rules, it is time to learn how to configure multiple interfaces like this. As an example, configure the router to be a Cisco IOS Firewall between two networks, inside and outside, as shown in Figure 8-9.

Figure 8-9   Two-Interface Firewall

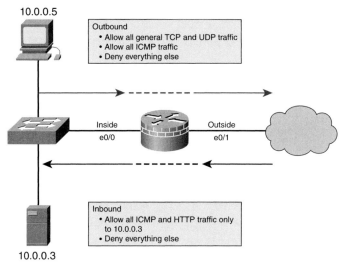

Implementing the following security policy will allow all general TCP and UDP outbound traffic initiated on the inside, from network 10.0.0.0 to access the Internet, as shown in Figure 8-10. ICMP traffic will also be allowed from the same network. Other networks on the inside, which are not defined, must be denied.

Figure 8-10   Outbound Traffic

Use the following syntax to configure CBAC to inspect TCP and UDP traffic:

```
Router (config)#ip inspect name OUTBOUND tcp
Router (config)#ip inspect name OUTBOUND upd
```

Use the following syntax to permit inside-initiated traffic from the 10.0.0.0 network:

```
Router (config)#access-list 101 permit ip 10.0.0.0.0.0.0.255 any
Router (config)#access-list 101 deny ip any any
```

Use the following syntax to apply an ACL and inspection rule to the inside interface in an inward direction:

```
Router (config)#interface e0/0
Router (config-if)#ip inspect OUTBOUND in
Router (config-if)#ip access-group 101 in
```

For inbound traffic initiated on the outside, allow everyone to access only ICMP and HTTP to host 10.0.0.3, as shown in Figure 8-11. Deny all other traffic.

Figure 8-11   Inbound Traffic

Use the following syntax to configure CBAC to inspect TCP traffic:

```
Router (config)#ip inspect name INBOUND tcp
```

Use the following syntax to permit outside-initiated ICMP and HTTP traffic to host 10.0.0.3:

```
Router (config)#access-list 102 permit icmp any host 10.0.0.3
Router (config)#access-list 102 permit tcp any host 10.0.0.3 eq www
Router (config)#access-list 102 deny ip any any
```

Use the following syntax to apply an ACL and inspection rule to outside interface in inward direction:

```
Router (config)#interface e0/1
Router (config-if)#ip inspect INBOUND in
Router (config-if)#ip access-group 102 in
```

Three-Interface Firewall

Multiple interfaces can be configured, as depicted in Figure 8-12. As an example, configure the router to act as a Cisco IOS Firewall between three networks: inside, outside, and demilitarized zone (DMZ). Implement by a security policy allowing all general TCP and UDP outbound traffic initiated on the inside from network 10.0.0.0 to access the Internet and the DMZ host 172.16.0.2. ICMP traffic will also be allowed from the same network to the Internet and the DMZ host. Other networks on the inside, which are not defined, must be denied. For inbound traffic initiated on the outside, allow everyone to only access ICMP and HTTP to DMZ host 172.16.0.2. Deny all other traffic.

Figure 8-12   Three-Interface Firewall

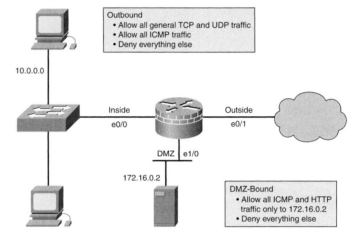

For outbound traffic on a three-interface firewall, use the following syntax to configure CBAC to inspect TCP and UDP traffic:

```
Router (config)#ip inspect name OUTBOUND tcp
Router (config)#ip inspect name OUTBOUND upd
```

Use the following syntax to permit inside-initiated traffic from the 10.0.0.0 network:

```
Router (config)#access-list 101 permit ip 10.0.0.0.0.0.0.255 any
Router (config)#access-list 101 deny ip any any
```

Use the following syntax to apply an ACL and inspection rule to the inside interface in an inward direction:

```
Router (config)#interface e0/0
Router (config-if)#ip inspect OUTBOUND in
Router (config-if)#ip access-group 101 in
```

For inbound traffic on a three-interface firewall, use the following syntax to configure CBAC to inspect TCP traffic:

```
Router (config)#ip inspect name INBOUND tcp
```

Use the following syntax to permit outside-initiated ICMP and HTTP traffic to host 172.16.0.2:

```
Router (config)#access-list 102 permit icmp any host 172.16.0.2
Router (config)#access-list 102 permit tcp any host 172.16.0.2 eq www
Router (config)#access-list 102 deny ip any any
```

Use the following syntax to apply an ACL and inspection rule to outside interface in inward direction:

```
Router (config)#interface e0/1
Router (config-if)#ip inspect INBOUND in
Router (config-if)#ip access-group 102 in
```

To permit only ICMP traffic initiated in the DMZ, use the following syntax:

```
Router (config)#access-list 103 permit icmp host 172.16.0.2 any
Router (config)#access-list 103 deny ip any any
```

To permit only outward ICMP and HTTP traffic to host 172.16.0.2, use the following syntax:

```
Router (config)#access-list 104 permit icmp any host 172.16.0.2
Router (config)#access-list 104 permit tcp any host 172.16.0.2 eq www
Router (config)#access-list 104 deny ip any any
```

To apply proper ACLs and an inspection rule to the interface, use the following syntax:

```
Router (config)#interface e1/0
Router (config-if)#ip access-group 103 in
Router (config-if)#ip access-group 104 out
```

Testing and Verifying CBAC

Administrators can use the **show ip inspect** command family to test and verify a CBAC installation, as shown in Table 8-4.

Table 8-4 Verifying CBAC

Command	Purpose
show ip inspect name *inspection-name*	Shows a particular configured inspection rule
show ip inspect config	Shows the complete CBAC inspection configuration
show ip inspect interfaces	Shows interface configuration with regard to applied inspection rules and ACLs
show ip inspect session [**detail**]	Shows existing sessions that are currently being tracked and inspected by CBAC
show ip inspect all	Shows all CBAC configuration and all existing sessions currently being tracked and inspected by CBAC

Example 8-1 displays the **show ip inspect name FWRULE** and **show ip inspect config** output.

```
Example 8-1      Displaying Inspection Rule and CBAC Inspection Configurations
R1# show ip inspect name FWRULE
Inspection name FWRULE
        rpc program-number 100022 wait-time 0 alert is off
audit trail is on timeout
  30
        smtp alert is on audit-trail is on timeout 200


R1#show ip inspect config
Session audit trail is disabled
Session alert is enabled
one-minute (sampling period) thresholds are [400:500] connections
max-incomplete sessions thresholds are [400:500]
max-incomplete tcp connection per host is 50. Block-time 0 minute.
tcp synwait-time is 30 sec -- tcp finwait-time is 5 sec
tcp idle-time is 3600 sec — udp idle-time is 30 sec
dns-timeout is 5 sec
Inspection Rule Configuration
  Inspection name FWRULE
```

Example 8-2 shows the **show ip inspect session** command output.

```
Example 8-2      The show ip inspect session Command Output
Router# show ip inspect session
Established Sessions
  Session 6155930C (10.0.0.3:35009)=>(172.30.0.50:34233) tcp SIS_OPEN
  Session 6156F0CC (10.0.0.3:35011)=>(172.30.0.50:34234) tcp SIS_OPEN
  Session 6156AF74 (10.0.0.3:35010)=>(172.30.0.50:5002) tcp SIS_OPEN
```

debug Commands

To display messages about CBAC events, use the **debug ip inspect** EXEC command. The **no** form of this command disables debugging output. The following syntax for the **debug ip inspect** command shows a protocol-specific **debug**:

```
router (config)#debug ip inspect protocol
```

The following are general **debug** commands:

```
Router# debug ip inspect function-trace
Router# debug ip inspect object-creation
Router# debug ip inspect object-deletion
Router# debug ip inspect events
Router# debug ip inspect timers
```

Removing the CBAC Configuration

Use the **no ip inspect** command to remove the entire CBAC configuration, as follows. This command also resets all global timeouts and thresholds to their defaults, deletes all existing sessions, and removes all associated dynamic ACLs. This command has no other arguments, keywords, default behavior, or values:

```
router (config)#no ip inspect
```

 Lab 8.3.13   Configure Cisco IOS Firewall CBAC

In this lab, you learn how CBAC enables a router-based firewall. You configure a simple firewall including CBAC using the Security Device Manager (SDM). You then learn to configure a simple firewall including CBAC and RFC filtering using the Cisco IOS CLI. You also test and verify CBAC operation.

Configuring a Cisco IOS Firewall Using SDM

You can configure two types of Cisco IOS Firewall with the Security Device Manager (SDM):

- **Basic Firewall**—Choose this option to create a firewall using SDM default rules. This one-step Firewall Wizard configures only one outside interface and one or more inside interfaces. It does not support configuring a DMZ or custom inspection rules. The Use Case Scenario diagram in the Firewall Wizard (see Figure 8-13) represents a typical network configuration for this type of firewall. This basic firewall could be used in telecommuter or small office/home office scenarios.

- **Advanced Firewall**—Choose this option to be led through the configuration of a firewall with a DMZ interface by the SDM Wizard. This wizard enables the administrator to configure the router to connect to the Internet and configure hosts off a DMZ interface to be accessible to outside users. This wizard also allows for specification of an inspection rule for the firewall.

The one-step Firewall Wizard is available from the Firewall and ACL page, as shown in Figure 8-13.

Figure 8-13   Firewall Wizard

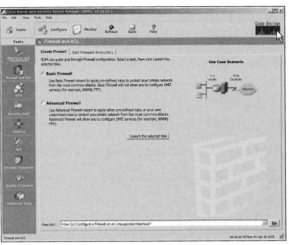

Summary

This chapter discussed CBAC for Cisco routers. CBAC was shown to be a more specific, security-minded implementation of ACLs. ACLs are used to filter and secure network traffic. Although ACLs filter network traffic by controlling whether routed or switched packets are forwarded or blocked at the interface, CBAC is used to create temporary openings in the firewall ACLs. You should understand the steps required for configuring CBAC:

Step 1. Pick an interface, internal or external.

Step 2. Configure IP ACLs at the interface.

Step 3. Set audit trails and alerts.

Step 4. Set global timeouts and thresholds.

Step 5. Define PAM.

Step 6. Define inspection rules.

Step 7. Apply inspection rules and ACLs to interfaces.

Step 8. Test and verify.

By understanding the tasks required to configure CBAC, you should understand the following concepts:

- What CBAC is, how it works, and how to configure and test the different components

- How and why inspection rules are used with Java, RPC applications, SMTP, and IP fragmentation; and how they are applied to router interfaces

- The different configuration requirements for a two-interface solution compared to a multi-interface solution

Check Your Understanding

Complete all the review questions listed here to test your understanding of the topics and concepts in this chapter. Answers are listed in Appendix A, "Check Your Understanding Answer Key."

1. What is the first step required to create and establish CBAC?

   a. Pick an interface

   b. Configure IP ACLs

   c. Set audit trails and alerts

   d. Set global timeouts an alerts

   e. Define PAM

   f. Apply inspection rules

   g. Test and verify

2. Context-Based Access Control (CBAC) intelligently filters TCP and UDP packets based on what?

   a. Application layer protocol session information

   b. Presentation layer protocol session information

   c. Network layer protocol session information

   d. Physical layer protocol session information

3. CBAC suspects an attack. The DoS feature can take which of the following actions? (Choose three.)

   a. Generate alert messages

   b. Reset system resources

   c. Protect system resources that could impede performance

   d. Block packets from suspected attackers

   e. Re-allocate and redirect incoming traffic

4. DoS detection and prevention requires the creation of a CBAC inspection rule which

   a. Is applied to an interface and must include the protocol that will be monitored.

   b. Is not applied to an interface and must include the protocol that will be monitored.

   c. Is applied to an interface and does not include the protocol that will be monitored.

   d. Is not applied to an interface and does not include the protocol that will be monitored.

5. It is good practice to not configure an access list for traffic from the protected network to the unprotected network.

   a. True

   b. False

6. To turn on CBAC audit trail messages, which display on the console after each CBAC session closes, you use which of the following commands?

a. **ip inspect audit trail**

b. **ip inspect audit trail enable**

c. **set ip inspect audit trail**

d. **ip inspect audit trail inspect**

7. Which of the following global configuration commands is used to define how long the software will wait for a TCP session to reach the established state before dropping the session?

a. **ip inspect tcp synwait-time enable**

d **ip inspect tcp synwait-time**

c **ip inspect tcp finwait-time**

d. **ip inspect tcp finwait-time enable**

8. What is port-to-application mapping (PAM) used for?

a. Enables administrators to close well-known TCP or UDP ports.

b. Enables administrators to customize TCP or UDP port numbers for network services or applications

c. Has nothing to do with TCP or UDP ports

d. Enables administrators to apply access lists to interfaces based on TCP or UDP well-known port associations

9. What command do you use to remove the CBAC configuration?

a. **ip no cbac**

b. **no ip cbac**

c. **no ip inspect cbac**

d. **no ip inspect**

10. The timeout value in the **ip inspect name** command is configured in what units?

a. Microseconds

b. Milliseconds

c. Seconds

d. Minutes

CHAPTER 9

Configure Filtering on a PIX Security Appliance

Upon completion of this chapter, you should be able to answer the following questions:

- How do I configure ACLs and content filters?

- What is object grouping?

- How do I configure a Security Appliance modular policy?

- How do I configure advanced protocol inspection?

Key Terms

This chapter uses the following key terms. You can find the definitions in the glossary at the end of the book.

Modular Policy Framework (MPF)   page 374

Adaptive Security Algorithm (ASA)   page 375

Access control element (ACE)   page 377

This chapter covers access control lists (ACLs) and how they are handled by the PIX Security Appliance. The first part of this chapter focuses on configuring ACLs and knowing how and when to use ACLs in different network environments. This section also discusses applet filtering and URL filtering. You learn when to use this technology and why it is necessary.

This chapter also introduces you to the concept of object grouping, which puts ACLs into object and nested object groups. To simplify the task of creating and applying ACLs, administrators can group network objects, such as hosts, and services, such as FTP and HTTP. Grouping ACLs can drastically reduce the number of separate access lists.

Modular policy provides greater granularity and more flexibility when configuring network policies. The *Modular Policy Framework (MPF)* provides a consistent and flexible way to configure PIX Security Appliance features. One case where MPF could be used is to create a timeout configuration specific to a particular TCP application, as opposed to one that applies to all TCP applications.

This chapter concludes with a discussion of advanced protocol handling and inspection, and how you can tune it to fit the PIX Security Appliance operation. This chapter moves on to discuss the advanced protocols used for multimedia support, including real-time streaming protocols. The protocols required to support IP telephony are covered, too.

Configuring ACLs and Content Filters

The configuration of every PIX Security Appliance defaults to an inside interface with a security level of 100 and an outside interface with a security level of 0. Nothing is more secure than the internal network, and nothing less secure than the external network. By default, after address translation is configured, all communications are permitted in an outbound direction, from a more-secure to a less-secure level. By default, all communications are prohibited in an inbound direction, from a less-secure to a more-secure level.

PIX Security Appliance ACLs

ACLs are used to allow traffic arriving at a PIX Security Appliance to flow from a lower-security network to a higher-security network. The interface ACL permits or denies the initial packet incoming on that interface; furthermore, the ACL needs to describe only the initial packet of the application and does not need to consider the return traffic. Figure 9-1 depicts where the ACL can be configured on the PIX Security Appliance. ACLs are configured on the PIX Security Appliance in almost the exact same manner as they are for Cisco routers. This means that a network administrator who is already familiar with how to the configure ACLs on routers can now apply that knowledge to the PIX Security Appliance, too.

Figure 9-1   PIX Security Appliance ACL Configuration

The *Adaptive Security Algorithm (ASA)* check applies to every packet of a communication. ACLs are only evaluated one time per connection. ACLs can work in both directions. After an ACL is configured, you can activate it with the **access-group** command. If no ACL is attached to an interface, the following default ASA policy applies:

- Outbound permitted by default unless explicitly denied

- Inbound denied by default unless explicitly permitted

The **access-list** command is used to permit or deny traffic. When configuring ACLs on the PIX Security Appliance to permit and deny traffic, a network administrator should follow certain basic principles and guidelines, as further depicted in Figure 9-2:

- Higher to lower security:

    — The ACL is used to restrict outbound traffic.

    — The source address argument of the **access-list** command is the actual address of the host or network.

- Lower to higher:

    — The ACL is used to restrict inbound traffic.

    — The destination address argument of the **access-list** command is the translated global IP address.

Figure 9-2   Implementing ACLs

Note

ACLs are always checked before translation is performed on the PIX Security Appliance.

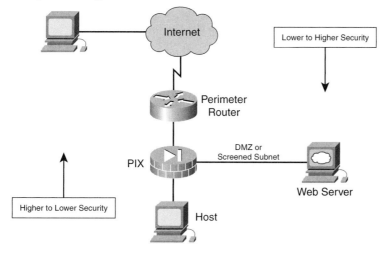

Configuring ACLs

The actual configuration of the ACL on a PIX Security Appliance is relatively simple. An ACL is implemented using the following commands:

```
pixfirewall (config)#access-list acl_ID deny | permit protocol source_addr source_mask
[operator port[port]] destination_addr destination mask operator port [port]
pixfirewall (config)#access-group acl_ID in interface interface_name
```

The **access-list** command is used to create an ACL, and the **access-group** command binds the ACL to the specific interface on the PIX. Keep in mind that only one ACL can be bound to an interface at a time using the **access-group** command.

For example, to create an ACL that denies access from the 192.168.1.0 network to TCP ports less than 1025 on host 192.168.0.1, you enter the following:

```
pixfirewall (config)#access-list DMZ1 deny tcp 192.168.0 255.255.255.0 host 192.168.0.1
lt 1025
```

To bind this ACL, DMZ1, to interface dmz, you enter the following:

```
pixfirewall (config)#access-group DMZ1 in interface dmz
```

PIX ACLs differ from ACLs on Cisco IOS routers in that the PIX does not use a wildcard mask like Cisco IOS routers do. It uses a regular subnet mask in the ACL definition. As with Cisco IOS routers, the PIX ACL has an implicit deny all at the end of the ACL.

In addition, use the following command to allow an ACL to define traffic to be excluded from the Network Address Translation (NAT) process:

```
pixfirewall (config)#nat [(if_name)] 0 access-list acl_name [outside]
```

For example:

```
pixfirewall (config)#access-list NONAT permit ip host 10.0.0.11 host 10.2.1.3
pixfirewall (config)#nat (inside) 0 access-list NONAT
```

It is important to realize that there is more to configuring ACLs on the PIX Security Appliance than just creating and applying the configuration. ACLs are a powerful tool that can create many network issues if the network administrator does not plan their use well. Before the administrator can begin to configure an ACL on the PIX, it is necessary to have a thorough understanding of the traffic that will be filtered and the user requirements of the network. If the appropriate preparation is not done, it is extremely easy to accidentally disallow business-critical traffic. To specify a source, local, or destination address, use the following guidelines:

- Use a 32-bit address in four-part, dotted-decimal format.

- Use the keyword **any** as an abbreviation for an address and mask of 0.0.0.0 0.0.0.0. This keyword is normally not recommended for use with IPsec.

- Use the **host** keyword as an abbreviation for a mask of 255.255.255.255.

When specifying a network mask, follow these guidelines:

- Do not specify a mask if the address is for a host if the destination address is for a host, use the **host** keyword before the address, as shown in the following example:

  ```
  access-list acl_grp permit tcp any host 192.168.1.1
  ```

- If the address is a network address, specify the mask in 32-bit, four-part, dotted format. Place zeros in the bit position that should be ignored.

- Remember that the network mask differs from the mask used in the Cisco IOS Software **access-list** command. With the PIX Security Appliance, use 255.0.0.0 for a Class A address, 255.255.0.0 for a Class B address, and 255.255.255.0 for a Class C address. If using a subnetted network address, use the appropriate network mask, as shown in the following example:

  ```
  access-list acl_grp permit tcp any 209.165.201.0 255.255.255.224
  ```

The **show access-list** command lists the **access-list** command statements in the configuration. The **show access-list** command also lists a hit count that indicates the number of times an element has been matched during an **access-list** command search.

The **clear access-list** command is used to clear an access list counter. If no ACL is specified, all the ACL counters are cleared. If the **counters** option is specified, it clears the hit count for the specified ACL. If no ACL is specified, all the ACL counters are cleared.

The **no access-list command** removes an **access-list** command from the configuration. If all the **access-list** command statements in an ACL group are removed, the **no access-list** command also removes the corresponding **access-group** command from the configuration.

To specify whether the defined ACL should be active immediately or when specified, use the following command:

```
pixfirewall(config)#access-list mode {auto-commit | manual-commit}
```

Specifying the **auto-commit** option indicates that any ACL will take effect immediately.

Specifying the **manual-commit** option indicates that any ACL will not take effect until the following command is issued:

```
pixfirewall(config)#access-list commit
```

This command compiles and applies/activates previously created ACLs.

ACL Line Numbers

To view the configured ACLs, use the **show access-list** command. The **access-list** commands are listed by ACL line number in the command output. The line number was not part of the original command line, but was added by the operating system. Each individual *access control element (ACE)* is given a single line number. All ACEs pertaining to an object group are given the same line number. Object groups are covered later in this module.

Line numbers enables the administrator to insert, or delete, ACEs at any position within a list of existing ACEs. Use the following command to insert an **access-list** command statement:

```
access-list id [line line-number] [extended] {deny | permit} {object-group
network_obj_grp_id | tcp | udp} source_address mask [operator port] dest_address mask
[operator port]
```

Use the **no** form of this command to delete an **access-list** command statement. Line numbers are maintained internally in increasing order, starting from 1. A user can insert a new entry between two consecutive ACEs by choosing the line number of the ACE with the higher line number. An ACE cannot be inserted in the middle of object group ACEs. Line numbers are displayed by the **show access-list** command, but are not shown in the actual configuration.

Example 9-1 shows the currently applied access lists and where the administrator wants to add an ACE.

Example 9-1   ACL Line Numbers

```
pixfirewall (config) # show access-list
access-list aclout line 2 extended permit tcp any host 192.168.0.7 ew www (hitcnt=0)
access-list aclout line 3 extended permit tcp any host 192.168.0.8 eq www hitcnt=0)
! Insert
access-list aclout line 4 extended permit tcp any host 192.168.0.10 eq www (hitcnt=0)
access-list aclout line 5 extended permit tcp any host 192.168.1.11 eq www (htcnt=0)
```

To insert the ACE, the administrator enters the following:

```
pixfirewall (config)#access-list aclout line 4 permit tcp any host 192.168.0.9 eq www
```

Entering **line 4** in the **access-list** command line inserts this command into the fourth position in the ACL. This forces the existing line 4 ACE down one position in the ACL. The **line 4 access-list** command line becomes the new number 4 ACE. The current number 4 ACE becomes the new number 5 ACE.

The icmp Command

Pinging to the PIX Security Appliance interface can be enabled or disabled. With pinging disabled, the PIX cannot be detected on the network. The following command implements this feature, which is also referred to as configurable proxy pinging:

```
pixfirewall(config)#icmp {permit | deny} src_addr src_mask [icmp type] if_name
```

By default, pinging through the PIX to a PIX interface is not allowed. Pinging an interface from a host on that interface is allowed. To deny all ping requests at the outside interface and permit all unreachable messages at the outside interface, you enter the following:

```
pixfirewall(config)#icmp deny any echo outside
pixfirewall(config)#icmp permit any unreachable outside
```

Figure 9-3 depicts the end results.

Figure 9-3   Enabling/Disabling Pings

To use the **icmp** command, configure an **icmp** command statement that permits or denies ICMP traffic that terminates at the PIX Security Appliance. If the first matched entry is a **permit** entry, the ICMP packet continues to be processed. If the first matched entry is a **deny** entry or an entry is not matched, the PIX discards the ICMP packet and generates the "%PIX-3-313001 Syslog" message. An exception is when an **icmp** command statement is not configured; in which case, **permit** is assumed.

The **clear icmp** command removes **icmp** command statements from the configuration.

nat 0 ACLs

The **nat 0** command enables a host or network to be exempt from NAT. The following command takes this a step further by enabling administrators to exempt from NAT any traffic that is matched by an **access-list** entry:

```
pixfirewall(config)#nat [(if_name)] 0 access-list acl_name [outside]
```

where:

- *if_name* is the internal network interface name. If the interface is associated with an ACL, the **if_name** is the higher security level interface name.

- **access-list** associates an **access-list** command with the **nat 0** command.

- *acl_name* is the name you use to identify the **access-list** command statement.

- **outside** specifies that the **nat** command apply to the outside interface address.

Destination-sensitive **nat 0 access-list** is usually used in virtual private network (VPN) scenarios.

In Figure 9-4, the users in the corporate office want to communicate with the branch site over a VPN tunnel. To accomplish this, the administrator uses **nat 0 access-list**. The IP source network, 10.0.0.0/24, and IP destination network, 10.200.0.0/24, are defined in the ACL:

```
pixfirewall(config)#access-list VPN-NO-NAT permit ip 10.0.0.0 255.255.255.0 10.200.0.0
255.255.255.0
```

The ACL is applied to the **nat 0** command:

```
pixfirewall(config)#nat (inside) 0 access-list VPN-NO-NAT
```

Any VPN traffic originating at 10.0.0.0/24 and destined for 10.200.0.0/24 is not translated by the PIX. For example, the internal host 10.0.0.11 will be permitted to bypass NAT when con-

Note

Cisco recommends that permission is granted for the ICMP unreachable message type, ICMP type 3. Denying ICMP unreachable messages disables ICMP Path MTU Discovery, which can halt IPsec and PPTP traffic. See RFC 1195 and RFC 1435 for details about Path MTU Discovery.

Note

PIX Release 6.3(2) correctly executes **nat 0** address translation rules entered in the configuration terminal or stored in the startup configuration. However, such commands are not recorded in the running configuration. If the running configuration is then written to the startup configuration and the unit is rebooted, all traces of **nat 0** address translation rules are lost. This bug does not affect **nat 0 access-list** configurations, which are commonly used in IPsec VPNs. Inbound static translation rules from one address or network to the same address or network are not affected either. Only **nat 0** translation rules, also known as *identity NAT rules*, are affected.

necting to outside host 10.200.0.3. The **nat 0 access-list** supports both inbound and outbound connections with no restrictions.

Figure 9-4   The **nat 0 access-list** Command

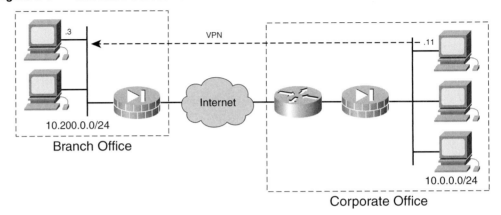

In Figure 9-5, the small office/home office worker wants to access the corporate network via VPN without local translation, and the Internet with a translated address. To access the corporate network, **nat 0 access-list** is configured. The following access list defines both the source network of the traffic, 10.100.1.0, and the destination network, 10.10.0.0:

```
SOHO(config)#access-list VPN-NO-NAT permit ip 10.100.1.0 255.255.255.0 10.10.0.0
255.255.255.0
SOHO(config)#nat (inside) 0 access-list VPN-NO-NAT
SOHO(config)#nat (inside) 1 10.100.1.0 255.255.255.0
SOHO(config)#global (outside) 1 interface
```

Any traffic that matches the **access-list** statement is not translated. Corporate traffic is not translated by the PIX.

Figure 9-5   Home Office: **nat 0** Access Control List Scenario

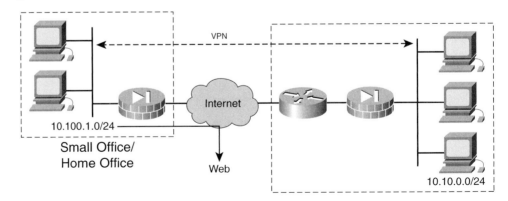

The second scenario is to translate any traffic bound for the Internet. The **nat (inside) 1** statement defines the source network, 10.100.1.0. The global address is based on the IP address of the outside interface. The **nat 0** command takes precedence over the **nat (inside) 1** command. Any packets that match the ACL are transmitted without translation. Any 10.100.1.0 network packets that do not match the VPN-NO-NAT access list are translated by the PIX.

Turbo ACLs

An ACL typically consists of multiple ACL entries, which are organized internally by the PIX Security Appliance as a linked list. As Figure 9-6 illustrates, when a packet is subjected to access list control, the PIX searches this linked list in a linear way to find a matching element. The matching element is then examined to determine whether the packet is to be transmitted (permitted) or dropped (denied). The disadvantage to this method is that with a linear search, the average search time increases proportionally to the size of the ACL.

Figure 9-6   Regular ACL Processing

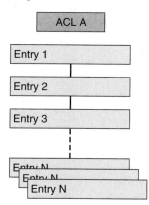

Turbo ACLs were created to improve the average search time for ACLs containing a large number of entries. They do this by causing the PIX Security Appliance to compile sets of lookup data tables for ACLs, as shown in Figure 9-7. This feature can be enabled globally and then disabled for specific ACLs. It can also be enabled only for the specific ACLs. For short ACLs, the Turbo ACL feature does not improve performance. A Turbo ACL search of an ACL of any length requires about the same amount of time as a regular search of an ACL consisting of approximately 12 to 18 entries. For this reason, even when enabled, the Turbo ACL feature is only applied to ACLs with 19 or more entries.

Figure 9-7   Turbo ACL Processing

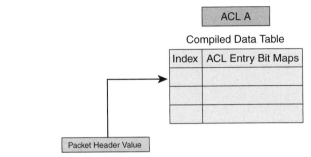

The Turbo ACL feature requires significant amounts of memory and is most appropriate for high-end PIX Security Appliance models, such as the PIX 525 or 535. The minimum memory required for Turbo ACL support is 2.1 MB, and approximately 1 MB of memory is required for every 2000 ACL elements. The actual amount of memory required depends not only on the number of ACL elements but also on the complexity of the entries. Furthermore, when adding or deleting an element from a Turbo ACL, the internal data tables associated with the ACL must be regenerated. This produces an appreciable load on the PIX CPU.

Turbo ACLs can be configured globally or on a per-ACL basis. Use the **access-list compiled** command to configure Turbo ACLs on all ACLs having 19 or more entries. This command causes the Turbo ACL process to scan through all existing ACLs. During the scanning, it marks every ACL to be Turbo configured, and compiles any ACL that has 19 or more ACEs and has not yet been compiled.

You can apply the Turbo ACL feature to individual ACLs with the **access-list** *acl_ID* **compiled** command. The **no** form of this command disables the Turbo ACL feature for specific ACLs after Turbo ACLs are globally configured.

The command **no access-list compiled**, which is the default, causes the PIX Security Appliance Turbo ACL process to scan through all compiled ACLs and mark each one as non-Turbo. It also deletes all existing Turbo ACL structures.

Using ACLs

Example 9-2 shows access lists that restrict internal users from establishing outside web connections, while still allowing other IP traffic from internal users to the Internet, as depicted in Figure 9-8.

Example 9-2   Restricting Web Access with ACLs

```
pixfirewall#write terminal
...
access-list acl_inside deny tcp any any eq www
access-list acl_inside permit ip any any
access-group acl_inside in interface inside
nat (inside) 1 10.0.0.0 255.255.255.0
global (outside) 1 192.168.0.20-192.168.0.254 netmask
255.255.255.0
...
```

Figure 9-8   Deny Web Access to the Internet

The ACL **acl_inside** is applied to the inside interface. The ACL **acl_inside** denies HTTP connections from an internal network, but lets all other IP traffic through. Applying an ACL to the inside interface restricts internal users from establishing outside web connections.

In Example 9-3, the IP address of the web server is translated to an outside IP address of 192.168.0.11. The ACL acl_outside is applied to traffic inbound to the outside interface. The ACL acl_outside permits HTTP connections from the Internet to a public Internet web server, 192.168.0.11. All other IP traffic is denied access to the demilitarized zone (DMZ) or inside networks. Figure 9-9 depicts the results of the ACL actions.

Note

The internal network addresses, 10.0.0.0, are dynamically translated to the range 192.168.0.20 through 192.168.0.254 to allow outbound connections.

Example 9-3   Directing Outside Traffic to the DMZ

```
pixfirewall#write terminal
...
static (dmz, outside) 192.168.0.11
172.16.0.2
access-list acl_outside permit tcp any
host 192.168.0.11 eq www access-group
acl_outside in interface outside
...
```

Figure 9-9   Permit Web Access to the DMZ

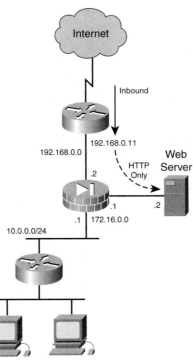

In Figure 9-10, the web server is statically translated from 172.16.0.2 to 172.18.0.17. In Example 9-4, the ACL acl_partner is applied to traffic inbound to the partnernet interface. The ACL acl_partner permits web connections from the hosts on network 172.18.0.0/24 to the DMZ web server via its statically mapped address, 172.18.0.17. All other traffic from the Partner network is denied.

In the second scenario in Figure 9-10, the client on the DMZ is trying to connect to the mail server on the inside network. The mail server IP address is statically translated to 172.16.0.11 by the PIX Security Appliance. In Example 9-4, the ACL acl_dmz is applied to traffic inbound to the DMZ interface. The ACL acl_dmz permits the host 172.16.0.4 mail access to the internal mail server on the inside interface via the statically mapped address of the mail server, 172.16.0.11. All other traffic originating from the DMZ network is denied.

Figure 9-10 Partner Web Access to DMZ and DMZ Access to Internet Mail

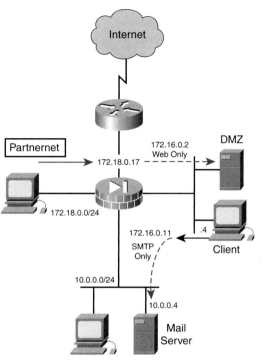

Example 9-4 Directing Outside Web Traffic to the DMZ and Denying All Other IP Traffic

```
pixfirewall#write terminal
...
nameif ethernet2 dmz sec50
nameif ethernet3 partnernet sec40
static (dmz,partnernet) 172.18.0.17
172.16.0.2
access-list acl_partner permit tcp
172.18.0.0 255.255.255.0 host
172.18.0.17 eq www
access-group acl_partner in interface
partnernet
static (inside,dmz) 172.16.0.11
10.0.0.4
access-list ack_dmz permit tcp host
172.16.0.4 host 172.16.0.11 eq smtp
access-group acl_dmz in interface dmz
...
```

Lab 9.1.7a   Configure Access Through the PIX Security Appliance Using ASDM

In this lab, you use Cisco Adaptive Security Device Manager (ASDM) to verify the starting configuration. You then configure the PIX Security Appliance to allow inbound traffic to the bastion host using ASDM. You also configure the PIX Security Appliance to allow inbound traffic to the inside host using ASDM. Finally, you test and verify correct PIX Security Appliance operation using ASDM.

 Lab 9.1.7b   Configure Access Through the PIX Security Appliance Using CLI

In this lab, you configure the PIX Security Appliance to allow inbound traffic to both the inside host and the bastion host. You then test and verify correct PIX Security Appliance operation.

 Lab 9.1.7c   Configure Multiple Interfaces Using the CLI—Challenge Lab

In this lab, you complete the objective of configuring three PIX interfaces and configure access through the PIX Security Appliance.

Malicious Code Filtering

Applets are programs executed from within another program. One common form of network attack is to embed a malicious or destructive applet inside of an apparently nonthreatening application. Because the applet is embedded in what appears to the firewall as an allowed application, it is allowed into the network. When a user unknowingly activates the downloaded applet, the malicious code is already inside the network and can potentially do a great deal of damage.

Although it is difficult to stop these types of attacks, one option that the administrator has is to allow the PIX Security Appliance to filter applications that could potentially be hiding malicious applets. By doing so, the administrator eliminates any potential threat that they might pose. The downside to this solution is that users can no longer use any of the applications that are filtered out.

Java Filtering

As the name suggests, Java filtering enables an administrator to prevent Java applets from being downloaded by an inside system, as shown in Figure 9-11. Java applets may be downloaded when administrators permit access to port 80 (HTTP). The PIX Security Appliance Java applet filter can stop Java applications on a per-client or per-IP address basis. When Java filtering is enabled, the PIX searches for the programmed "cafe babe" string. If the string is found, the PIX drops the Java applet. A sample Java class code snippet looks like the following:

```
00000000: café babe 003 002d 0099 0900 8345 0098
```

Figure 9-11   Malicious Applet Filtering

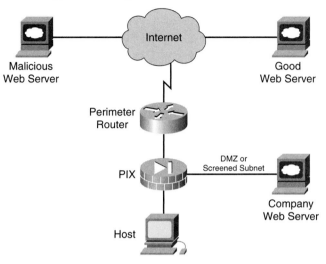

ActiveX Filtering

Another application that can be filtered by the PIX Security Appliance to protect against malicious applets is ActiveX. ActiveX controls are applets that can be inserted in web pages or other applications. They were formerly known as Object Linking and Embedding (OLE) or Object Linking and Embedding Controls (OCX). ActiveX controls create a potential security problem because they provide a way for someone to attack servers. Because of this security threat, administrators have the option of using the PIX to block all ActiveX controls.

The **filter** {**activex** ı **java**} command filters out ActiveX or Java usage from outbound packets. In the example in Figure 9-12, the following command specifies that ActiveX is being filtered on port 80 from any internal host and for connections to any external host:

```
pixfirewall#filter activex 80
0.0.0.0.0.0.0.0 0.0.0.0.0.0.0.0
```

Figure 9-12　ActiveX Filtering

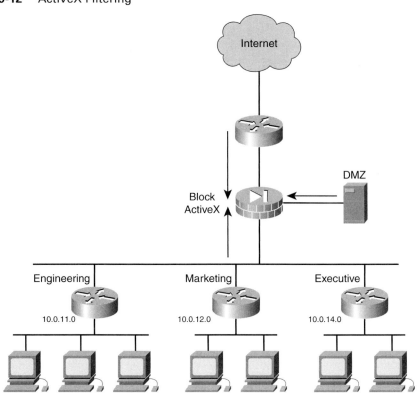

URL Filtering

The PIX Security Appliance can be enabled to work with a Websense or N2H2 URL-filtering application, as shown in Figure 9-13. When the PIX receives a request to access a URL from users, it queries the URL-filtering server to determine whether to return, or block, the requested web page.

Before URL filtering can begin, at least one server on which a Websense or N2H2 URL-filtering application will run must be designated. The limit is 16 URL servers. You can use only one URL-filtering application at one time, either N2H2 or Websense. In addition, changing the configuration on the PIX Security Appliance does not update the configuration on the application server. This configuration must be done separately, according to the vendor instructions.

Figure 9-13   URL Filtering with a URL-Filtering Server

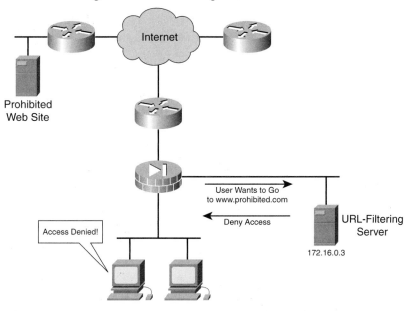

Use the **url-server** command to designate the server on which the URL-filtering application runs, and then enable the URL-filtering service with the **filter url** command, as demonstrated here for the network in Figure 9-13:

```
pixfirewall(config)#url-server (dmz) host 172.16.0.3
  timeout 10 protocol TCP version 4
pixfirewall(config)#filter url http 0 0 0 0 allow
```

PIX Security Appliance Software Versions 6.1 and earlier do not support the filtering of URLs longer than 1159 bytes. PIX Version 6.2 supports the filtering of URLs up to 6 KB for the Websense filtering server. The maximum allowable length of a single URL can be increased by entering the **url-block** *url-size* command. This option is available with Websense URL filtering only.

HTTPS and FTP filtering extends web-based URL filtering to HTTPS and FTP, with the following command, which was added in PIX Security Appliance Software Version 6.3:

```
pixfirewall(config)#filter [https | ftp | dest-port local_ip local_mask]
  foreign_ip foreign_mask [allow]
```

The **ftp** command option enables FTP filtering, and the **https** command option enables HTTPS filtering. Both command options are available with Websense URL filtering only.

The rest of the command syntax is explained as follows:

- *dest-port*—The destination port number
- *local_ip*—The IP address of the host from which access is sought

- *local_mask*—Network mask of *local_ip*

- *foreign_ip*—The IP address of the host to which access is sought

- *foreign_mask*—Network mask of *foreign_ip*

- **allow**—Enables outbound connections to pass through the PIX Firewall without filtering when the URL-filtering server is unavailable

The following command instructs the PIX Security Appliance to send all URL requests to the URL-filtering server to be filtered:

```
pixfirewall(config)#filter https 0 0 0 0 allow
```

The **allow** option in the filter command is crucial to the use of the PIX URL-filtering feature. If the **allow** option is used and the URL-filtering server goes offline, the PIX lets all FTP and HTTPS URL requests continue without filtering. If the **allow** option is not specified, all FTP and HTTPS URL requests are stopped until the server is back online. Figure 9-14 depicts the results of HTTPS and FTP filtering.

Figure 9-14   HTTPS and FTP Filtering

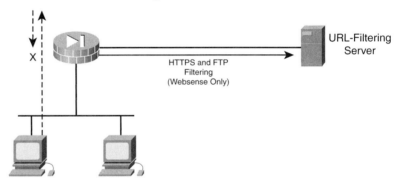

  Lab 9.1.9   Configure ACLs in the PIX Security Appliance Using the CLI

In this lab activity, you learn to disable pinging from an interface. You then configure inbound and outbound access control lists (ACLs).

Object Grouping

An ACL can cause the PIX Security Appliance to allow a designated client to access a particular server for a specific service. When there is only one client, one host, and one service, only a minimum number of lines in an ACL are needed. However, as the number of clients, servers, and services increases, the number of lines in an ACL required increases exponentially.

To simplify the task of creating and applying ACLs, administrators can group network objects, such as hosts, and services, such as FTP and HTTP. This reduces the number of ACLs required to implement complex security policies. For example, a security policy that normally requires 3300 lines in an ACL might require only 40 lines after hosts and services are properly grouped.

Object grouping provides a way to group objects of a similar type so that a single ACL can apply to all the objects in the group. The following types of object groups can be created:

- **Network**—Used to group client hosts, server hosts, or subnets For example: subnet 10.0.0.0/24, 10.0.1.11, 10.0.2.11 (inside hosts).

- **Protocol**—Used to group protocols. It can contain one of the keywords **icmp**, **ip**, **tcp**, or **udp**, or an integer in the range 1 to 254 representing an IP protocol number. Use the keyword **ip** to match any Internet protocol, including ICMP, TCP, and UDP. For example: TCP, UDP (inside protocols).

- **Service**—Used to group TCP or UDP port numbers assigned to a different service. For example: HTTP, HTTPS, FTP (DMZ services).

- **ICMP-type**—Used to group ICMP message types that are permitted or denied access. For example: echo and echo reply (ping).

Applying a PIX Security Appliance object group to a command is the equivalent of applying every element of the object group to the command. The following example shows the group DMZ_Servers contains servers 192.168.0.10, 192.168.0.11, and 192.168.0.12.

The command

```
pixfirewall(config)#access-list outside permit tcp any object-group DMZ_Servers object-
group DMZ_Services
```

is equivalent to the following:

```
pixfirewall(config)#access-list outside permit tcp any host 192.168.0.10 eq http
pixfirewall(config)#access-list outside permit tcp any host 192.168.0.10 eq https
pixfirewall(config)#access-list outside permit tcp any host 192.168.0.10 eq ftp
pixfirewall(config)#access-list outside permit tcp any host 192.168.0.11 eq http
pixfirewall(config)#access-list outside permit tcp any host 192.168.0.11 eq https
pixfirewall(config)#access-list outside permit tcp any host 192.168.0.11 eq ftp
pixfirewall(config)#access-list outside permit tcp any host 192.168.0.12 eq http
pixfirewall(config)#access-list outside permit tcp any host 192.168.0.12 eq https
pixfirewall(config)#access-list outside permit tcp any host 192.168.0.12 eq ftp
```

The group DMZ_Services supports HTTP, HTTPS, and FTP protocols. Applying the groups DMZ_Servers and DMZ_Services to an ACE is the same as applying all the hosts and protocols individually.

Getting Started with Object Groups

Complete the following steps to configure an object group and to use it in the configuration of ACLs:

Step 1.   Use the **object-group** command to enter the appropriate subcommand mode for the type of group to be configured. All subcommands entered from the subcommand prompt apply to the object group identified by the **object-group** command.

Step 2.   In subcommand mode, define the members of the object group. In subcommand mode, object grouping subcommands and all other PIX Security Appliance commands can be entered, including **show** commands and **clear** commands. Enter a question mark (**?**) in the subcommand mode to view the permitted subcommands.

Step 3.   (Optional) Use the **description** subcommand to describe the object group.

Step 4.   Return to configuration mode by entering the **exit** command or the **quit** command. When any valid configuration command other than one designed for object grouping is entered, the subcommand mode is terminated.

Step 5.   (Optional) Use the **show object-group** command to verify that the object group has been configured successfully. This command displays a list of the currently configured object groups of the specified type. Without a parameter, the command displays all object groups.

Step 6.   Apply the object group to the **access-list** command. Replace the parameters of the **access-list** command with the corresponding object group.

Step 7.   (Optional) Use the **show access-list** command to display the expanded ACEs.

Configuring Object Groups

This section examines the specific commands used to configure object groups. It focuses on the first two steps of the process: configuring the **object-group** command, and defining the object group in subcommand mode.

The first command to look at is the **object-group** command. This command defines which type of object group will be created. The types of object groups are as follows:

- Network groups
- Service groups
- Protocol groups
- ICMP-type groups

After the **object-group** command is entered, the object group subcommand mode that corresponds to the object group type that is being used displays. For example, if a network object group is to be configured, the administrator defines a network object group. This then takes the administrator to the network object group subcommand prompt. Here, the hosts and or networks that were to be part of the object group are defined.

Alternatively, if a services object group were being used, the administrator would enter that subcommand mode and define the TCP or UDP port numbers that were to be part of the object group.

Network Object Groups

To configure a network object group, you use the following commands:

```
pixfirewall(config)#object-group network grp_id
! Assigns a name to the group and enables the network sub-command mode
pixfirewall(config-network)#network-object host {host_addr | host_name}
! Assigns an IP or hostname to the network object group
pixfirewall(config-network)#network-object net_addr netmask
! Defines a subnet object that is part of the network object group
```

For example, to create a network object group named CLIENT that consists of host 10.0.1.11 and network 10.0.0.0, you enter the following:

```
pixfirewall(config)# object-group network CLIENTS
pixfirewall(config-network)#network-object host 10.0.1.11
pixfirewall(config-network)#network-object 10.0.0.0 255.255.255.0
```

Service Object Groups

To configure a service object group, you use the following commands:

```
pixfirewall(config)#object-group service grp_id {tcp | udp| tcp-udp}
! Assigns a name to a service group and enables the service subcommand mode
pixfirewall(config-service)#port-object eq service
! Assigns a single TCP or UDP port number to the service object group
pixfirewall(config-service)#network-object net_addr netmask
! Assigns a range of TCP or UDP port numbers to the service object group
```

For example, to create a service group named MYSERVICES, that contains HTTP and FTP, you enter the following:

```
pixfirewall(config)#object-group service MYSERVICES tcp
pixfirewall(config-service)#port-object eq http
pixfirewall(config-service)#port-object eq ftp
```

Protocol Object Groups

To configure a protocol object group, you use the following commands:

```
pixfirewall(config)#object-group protocol grp_id
! Assigns a name to a protocol object group and enables the protocol sub-command mode
```

```
pixfirewall(config-protocol)#protocol-object protocol
! Assigns a protocol to the protocol object group
```

For example, to create a protocol group named MYPROTOCOLS, which contains ICMP and TCP, you enter the following:

```
pixfirewall(config)#object-group protocol MYPROTOCOLS
pixfirewall(config-protocol)#protocol-object icmp
pixfirewall(config-protocol)#protocol-object tcp
```

ICMP-Type Object Groups

To configure an ICMP-type object group, you use the following commands:

```
pixfirewall(config)#object-group icmp-type grp_id
! Assigns a name to an ICMP-type object group and enables the icmp-type sub-command mode
pixfirewall(config-protocol)#icmp-object icmp-type
! Assigns an ICMP message type to the object group
```

For example, to create an ICMP-type group named PING that contains echo and echo-reply message types, you enter the following:

```
pixfirewall(config)#object-group icmp-type PING
pixfirewall(config-icmp-type)#icmp-object echo
pixfirewall(config-icmp-type)#icmp-object echo-reply
```

Lab 9.2.3   Configure Service Object Groups Using ASDM

In this lab, you configure an inbound access control list (ACL) with object groups. You also learn to configure a service object group. You then configure web and ICMP access to the inside host. Finally, you test and verify the inbound ACL.

Nested Object Groups

In addition to grouping individual objects, it is also possible to group objects within a nested group. An object can be a member of a group. For object groups to be nested, they must be of the same type. For example, two or more Network object groups can be grouped together but a Protocol group and a Network group cannot be grouped together. In the example shown in Figure 9-15, the administrator configured hosts from the 10.0.0.0/24 network to form the Inside_Eng object group. The administrator added hosts from the 10.0.1.0/24 network to form the Inside_Mktg object group. For some ACLs, the administrator found it advantageous to combine the Inside_Eng and Inside_Mktg object groups to form the nested object group Inside_Networks and apply the nested object group, Inside_Networks to selected ACLs. Hierarchical object grouping can achieve greater flexibility and modularity for specifying access rules.

Figure 9-15   Nested Object Groups

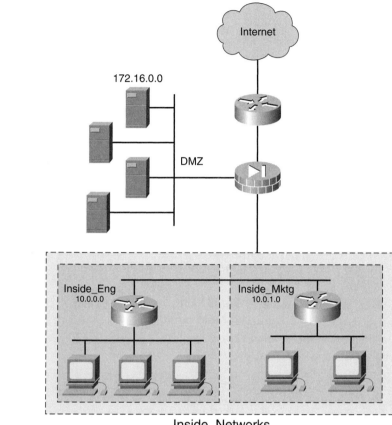

The following command is used to construct hierarchical, or nested, object groups:

```
pixfirewall(config-group-type)#group-object object_group_id
```

The **group-object** command, which is not to be confused with the **object-group** command, places one object group into another, as demonstrated in Example 9-5.

Example 9-5   Nesting Object Groups

```
pixfirewall(config)#object-group service SERVICEA tcp
pixfirewall(config-service)#port-object eq smtp
pixfirewall(config-service)#port-object eq ftp
pixfirewall(config-service)#exit
pixfirewall(config)#object-group service SERVICE tcp
pixfirewall(config-protocol)#group-object SERVICESA
```

The difference in object groups and group objects is as follows:

- An object group is group consisting of objects.

- A group object is an object in a nested group and is itself a group.

Duplicated objects are allowed in an object group if it is due to the inclusion of group objects. For example, if object 1 is in both group A and group B, a group C can be defined that includes both A and B. A group object that causes the group hierarchy to become circular is not allowed. For example, if group A includes group B, group B cannot include group A.

Complete the following steps to configure nested object groups:

Step 1.   Create an object group to be nested within another object group, such as Inside_Eng.

Step 2.   Add the appropriate type of objects to the object group, such as 10.0.1.0/24.

Step 3.   Assign an identity to the object group within which other object groups will be nested, such as Inside_Networks.

Step 4.   Add the first object group to the second object group.

Step 5.   Add any other objects that are required to the group, such as Inside_Mktg.

In Example 9-6, the access list named ALL enables all hosts in HOSTGROUP1 and HOSTGROUP2 to make outbound FTP connections. Without nesting, all the IP addresses in HOSTGROUP1 and HOSTGROUP2 would have to be redefined in the ALLHOSTS group. With nesting, however, the duplicated definitions of the hosts are eliminated.

Example 9-6   Eliminating Access List Redundancy with Group Objects

```
pixfirewall(config)#object-group network HOSTGROUP1
pixfirewall(config-network)#network-object host 10.0.0.11
pixfirewall(config-network)#network-object host 10.0.0.12
pixfirewall(config-network)#exit
pixfirewall(config)#object-group network HOSTGROUP2
pixfirewall(config-network)#network-object host 10.0.0.13
pixfirewall(config-network)#network-object host 10.0.0.14
pixfirewall(config-network)#exit
pixfirewall(config)#object-group network ALLHOSTS
pixfirewall(config-network)#group-object HOSTGROUP1
pixfirewall(config-network)#group-object HOSTGROUP2
pixfirewall(config-network)#exit
pixfirewall(config)#access-list ALL permit tcp object-group ALLHOSTS any eq ftp
pixfirewall(config)#access-group ALL in interface inside
```

Example 9-7 illustrates multiple nested object groups configured so that one ACL entry enables remote hosts 172.26.26.50 and 172.26.26.51 (see Figure 9-16) to initiate FTP and SMTP connections to all local hosts in the ALLHOSTS group. Note that with object grouping configured, only one ACL entry is required.

Example 9-7   Nesting Multiple Object Groups to Enable Permission

```
pixfirewall(config)#show static
static (inside,outside) 192.168.1.10
10.0.1.11 netmask 255.255.255.255
static (inside,outside) 192.168.1.12
10.0.1.12 netmask 255.255.255.255
static (inside,outside) 192.168.2.10
10.0.2.11 netmask 255.255.255.255
static (inside,outside) 192.168.2.12
10.0.2.12 netmask 255.255.255.255

pixfirewall(config)#show object-group
object-group network REMOTES
network-object host 172.26.26.51
network-object host 172.26.26.51
object-group network LOCALS1
network-object host 192.160.1.11
network-object host 192.160.1.11
object-group network LOCALS2
network-object host 192.160.2.11
network-object host 192.160.2.11
object-group network ALLLOCALS
group-object LOCALS1
group-object LOCALS2
object-group service BASIC
port-object eq ftp
port-object eq smtp

pixfirewall(config)#access-list
INBOUND permit tcp object-group
REMOTES object-group ALLLOCALS
object-group BASIC
```

Figure 9-16   Multiple Object Groups in ACLs Example

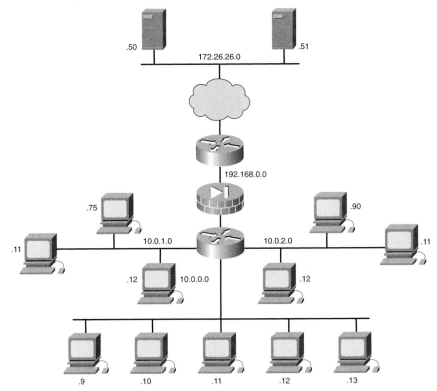

Managing Object Groups

After object groups have been put in place, it is important for network administrators to be able to monitor and modify them as necessary. This section looks at the following three commands that are used for these purposes:

- **show object-group**

- **no object-group**

- **clear object-group**

Viewing Object Groups

To easily review object groups that are currently configured on a PIX Security Appliance, use the following command:

```
pixfirewall(config)#show object-group [protocol | service | icmp-type | network]
```

This enables the administrator to view the object groups based on several criteria. The PIX displays defined object groups by their *grp_id* when the **show object-group id** *grp_id* command is entered. The PIX also displays defined object groups by group type when the show **object-**

group command is entered with the **protocol**, **service**, **icmp-type**, or **network** option. When the **show object-group** command is entered without a parameter, all defined object groups are shown, as demonstrated in Example 9-8.

Example 9-8   Displaying Configured Object Groups

```
pixfirewall(config)#show object-group
object-group network HOSTGROUP1
    network-object host 10.0.0.11
    network-object host 10.0.0.12
object-group network HOSTGROUP2
    network-object host 10.0.0.13
    network-object host 10.0.0.14
object-group network ALLHOSTS
    group-object HOSTGROUP1
    group-object HOSTGROUP2
```

Removing Object Groups

Two commands are used to maintain object groups on a PIX Security Appliance: the **no object-group** and **clear object-group** commands. The **no object-group** command removes a single object group from the configuration, whereas the **clear object-group** command is used to erase all object groups from the PIX.

To remove a specific service object group, you use the following command:

```
pixfirewall(config)#no object-group service grp_id {tcp | udp |tcp-udp}
```

To remove a specific protocol, network, or ICMP-type object group, you use the following command:

```
pixfirewall(config)#no object-group {protocol | network |icmp-type grp_id}
```

To remove all object groups or all object groups of a specific type, you use the following command:

```
pixfirewall(config)#clear object-group [protocol | service | icmp-type | network]
```

For example to remove the object group ALLHOSTS and all protocol object groups, you enter the following:

```
pixfirewall(config)#no object-group network ALLHOSTS
pixfirewall(config)#clear object-group protocol
```

 Lab 9.2.5   Configure Object Groups and Nested Object Groups Using the CLI

In this lab, you learn to configure a service, ICMP-type, and nested server object group. You also learn to configure an inbound access control list (ACL) with object groups. You then configure web and ICMP access to the inside host. Finally, you test and verify the inbound ACL.

Configure a Security Appliance Modular Policy

There is a growing need to provide greater granularity and flexibility in configuring network policies, such as the following:

- The capability to identify and prioritize voice traffic

- The capability to rate limit remote access VPN connections

- The capability to perform deep packet inspection on specific flows of traffic

- The capability to set connection values

The PIX Security Appliance Software Release 7.0 provides this functionality with the introduction of Modular Policy Framework (MPF). MPF is a framework in which administrators can define traffic classes at the desired granularity and apply actions, or policies, to them. Figure 9-17 show a basic overview of modular policy, which serves the following functions:

- Defines flows of traffic

- Associates a security policy to traffic flows

- Enables a set of security policies on an interface or globally

Figure 9-17   Modular Policy Overview

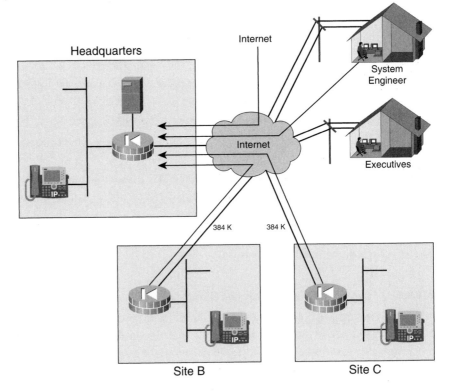

MPF is configured using three main commands:

- **class-map**—This command is used to identify a traffic flow. A traffic flow is a set of traffic that is identifiable by its packet content. In Figure 9-18, voice traffic between Site B and Headquarters is an example of a traffic flow, as are remote-access VPNs that allow the system engineers and executives to access network resources at the headquarters.

- **policy-map**—This command is used to associate one or more actions with a class of traffic. For example, in Figure 9-18, all voice traffic between Site B and Headquarters is provided low-latency queuing.

- **service-policy**—This command is used to enable a set of policies on an interface. In the example in Figure 9-18, the voice priority queuing policy is applied to the outside interface.

In the example in Figure 9-18, a network administrator identified five traffic flows:

- Internet traffic

- System engineer remote VPN traffic

- Executive remote VPN traffic

- Two site-to-site VPN tunnels to Site B and Site C with voice

After the traffic flows are identified, security policies are mapped to each flow. The policy for traffic from the Internet is to perform deep packet inspection and inline intrusion prevention system (IPS). For both the system engineers and the executive remote VPN traffic, the administrator will police the amount of bandwidth used by each group. For site-to-site traffic over a VPN, all voice connection traffic is given higher-priority queuing. The last class is the default inspection class. All traffic is subject to the default inspection policy. After the classes and policies are defined, policies are assigned to a specific interface, or assigned globally. In the example in the Figure 9-18, the **Global_Policy** is assigned globally. The **Outside_Policy** is assigned to the outside interface.

Figure 9-18   Modular Policy

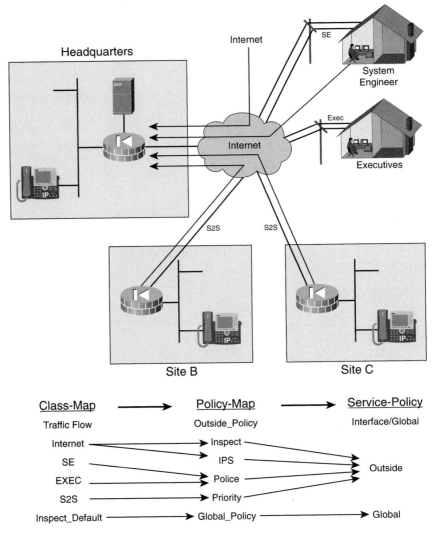

Configuring a Class Map

The **class-map** command is used to classify a set of traffic with which security actions may be associated. The syntax of the **class-map** commands is as follows:

```
class-map class_map_name
```

Configuring a class map is a two-step process:

Step 1.   Name a class of traffic

Step 2.   Define the attributes of the traffic.

A name is assigned to each individual class of traffic. For example, for the network shown previously in Figure 9-18, four traffic classes are named:

```
pixfirewall(config)#class-map se
pixfirewall(config)#class-map exec
pixfirewall(config)#class-map s2s
pixfirewall(config)#class-map internet
```

The **class-map se** command identifies the system engineer remote VPN traffic from the system engineers. The **class-map s2s** command identifies the remote VPN traffic from the system engineers.

After you name a class of traffic, the next step is to identify the characteristics of the traffic flow. To be considered part of a named class, a traffic flow must match a defined set of attributes. There are various types of match criteria in a class map. One example of match criteria is an ACL that defines all traffic from the Internet to the DMZ. Another match is VPN tunnel group. This includes all members of the SE and EXEC tunnel groups for the network shown in Figure 9-18. Another such match is a TCP or UDP port number. This could be used to define all HTTP or FTP traffic.

The following list provides some examples of class-matching criteria:

- **match access-list**—This keyword specifies to match an entry in an ACL.

- **match any**—This keyword specifies that all traffic is to be matched. Match any is used in the class default class map.

- **match dcsp**—This keyword specifies to match the Internet Engineering Task Force (IETF)-defined Differentiated Service Code Point (DSCP) value in the IP header. This allows the administrator to define classes based on the DCSP values defined within the Type of Service (TOS) byte in the IP header.

- **match flow**—This keyword specifies to match each IP flow within a tunnel group. This match command must be used in conjunction with the **match tunnel-group** command.

- **match port**—This keyword specifies to match traffic using a TCP or UDP destination port.

- **match precedence**—This keyword specifies to match the precedence value represented by the TOS byte in the IP header. This allows the administrator to define classes based on the precedence defined within the TOS byte in the IP header.

- **match rtp**—This keyword specifies to match Real-Time Transport Protocol (RTP) destination port. This allows the administrator to match on a UDP port number within the specified range. The allowed range is targeted at capturing applications likely to be using RTP.

- **match tunnel-group**—This keyword specifies to match tunnel traffic.

A traffic class is a set of traffic identifiable by its packet content. For example, TCP traffic with a port value of 21 and 80 can be classified as an Internet traffic class.

Configure a Policy Map

The **policy-map** command is used to configure various policies. The syntax of the **policy-map** commands is as follows:

```
policy-map policymap_name
description text
class classmap_name
```

A policy map consists of a **class** command and its associated actions. The PIX Security Appliance supports one policy per interface and one global policy. Each policy map can support multiple classes and policy actions.

Figure 9-19   Policy Map Overview

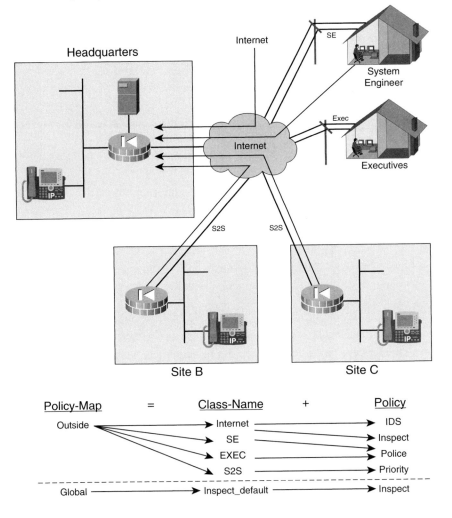

Use the following steps to define a policy map:

Step 1.   Name the policy.

Step 2.   Identify a class of traffic covered by this policy.

Step 3.   Associate an action or actions with each traffic flow.

In the example in Figure 9-19, there are two policy maps:

- **Outside policy map**—Supports four class maps: the Internet, SE, EXEC, and S2S class maps. Intrusion detection, inspect, police, and priority actions are associated with the aforementioned classes.

- **Global policy map**—Supports default inspection criteria for all traffic.

The first step is to define the policy maps. In the example in Figure 9-19, there are two policy maps, outside and global.

The next step is to identify which traffic flows, or classes, are specified in a policy map. Each traffic flow is identified by a class map name. The following commands identify the outside policy map and assign the Internet class traffic flow to the outside policy map:

```
pixfirewall(config)#policy-map outside
pixfirewall(config-pmap)#class internet
```

The last step is to associate actions with specific traffic flows within a policy map. After identifying the outside policy map and assigning the Internet class traffic flow to the outside policy map, the administrator must next associate actions with this traffic flow. Some of the policy action options, as demonstrated in Example 9-9, are as follows:

- Forward traffic to the intrusion detections system (IDS)

- Perform specified protocol inspections

- Police the bandwidth used by the specified flow

- Direct the flow to the low-latency queue

- Set connection parameters on these flows

Example 9-9   Determining Which Actions to Associate with a Policy Map

```
pixfirewall(config)# policy-map outside
pixfirewall(config-pmap)# class internet
pixfirewall(config-pmap-c)# ?
MPC policy-map     class configuration
  exit              Exit from MPC close action configuration mode
  help              Help for MPC policy-map configuration mode
  ids               Intrusion detection services
  inspect           Protocol inspection services
  no                Negate or set default values of a command
  police            Police
  priority          Strict scheduling priority for this close
  set               Set QoS values or connection values
```

To display all the policy map configurations or the default policy map configuration, use the **show running-config policy-map** command.

Configuring a Service Policy

To activate a policy map globally on all interfaces or on a single interface, use the following command:

```
pixfirewall(config)#service-policy policymap_name [ global | interface intf]
```

The interface can be a VLAN interface or a physical interface. In general, a **service-policy** command can be applied to any interface that can be defined by the **nameif** command. To disable, use the **no** form of this command.

To display all currently running service policy configurations, use the following command:

```
pixfirewall(config)#show running-config service-policy
```

To display the configured service policies, use the **show service-policy** command in global configuration mode, as demonstrated in Example 9-10.

Example 9-10   Show Service-Policy Statistics

```
pixfirewall(config)#show service-policy
Interface outside:
   Service-policy: outside
     Class-map: se
       police:
             cir 56000 bps, be 1000 bytes
           conformed 0 packets, 0 bytes, actions:
               transmit
           exceed 0 packets, 0 bytes, actions:
               drop
           conformed 0 bps, exceed 0 bps
     Class-map: exec
       police:
             cir 56000 bps, be 1000 bytes
           conformed 0 packets, 0 bytes, actions:
               transmit
           exceed 0 packets, 0 bytes, actions:
               drop
           conformed 0 bps, exceed 0 bps
     Class-map: s2s
     Class-map: internet
       IDS: mode inline, packet 0
```

Configuring Advanced Protocol Inspection

Today, corporations that use the Internet for business transactions want to keep their internal networks secure from potential threats. These corporations usually implement firewalls as part of their network-defense strategy. Firewalls can help protect their networks, but some firewalls might cause problems, too. For example, applications such as FTP, HTTP, multimedia, and SQL*Net require their communications protocols to dynamically negotiate source or destination ports or IP addresses. Some firewalls cannot participate in these dynamic protocol negotiations, resulting in either the complete blockage of these corporate services or the need to pre-configure static holes in the firewall to allow these services.

A good firewall has to inspect packets above the network layer and do the following as required by the protocol or application:

- Securely open and close negotiated ports or IP addresses for legitimate client/server connections through the firewall

- Use Network Address Translation (NAT)-relevant instances of an IP address inside a packet

- Use Port Address Translation (PAT)-relevant instances of ports inside a packet

- Inspect packets for signs of malicious application misuse

You can configure the PIX Security Appliance to inspect the required protocols, or applications, and permit them to traverse the PIX with dynamic, stateful adjustments to the security policy of the PIX. This enables the corporate networks to remain secure while still being able to continue conducting day-to-day business.

The Adaptive Security Algorithm (ASA), used by the PIX Security Appliance for stateful application inspection, ensures the secure use of applications and services. Some applications require special handling by the PIX application-inspection function. Applications that require special application-inspection functions are those that embed IP addressing information in the user data packet or that open secondary channels on dynamically assigned ports.

The application-inspection function works with NAT to help identify the location of embedded addressing information. This allows NAT to translate these embedded addresses and to update any checksum or other fields that are affected by the translation.

The application-inspection function also monitors sessions to determine the port numbers for secondary channels. Many protocols open secondary TCP or UDP ports. The initial session on a well-known port is used to negotiate dynamically assigned port numbers. The application-inspection function monitors these sessions, identifies the dynamic port assignments, and permits data exchange on these ports for the duration of the specific session.

In the example in Figure 9-20, the FTP client is shown in active mode opening a control channel between its port 2008 and the FTP server port 21. When data is to be exchanged, the FTP client alerts the FTP server through the control channel that it expects the data to be delivered back from FTP server port 20 to its port 2010. If FTP inspection is not enabled, the return data from FTP server port 20 to FTP client port 2010 is blocked by the Security Appliance. With FTP inspection enabled, however, the Security Appliance inspects the FTP control channel to recognize that the data channel will be established to the new FTP client port 2010 and temporarily creates an opening for the data channel traffic for the life of the session.

Default Traffic Inspection and Port Numbers

By default, protocol inspection is enabled on the PIX Security Appliance. In Example 9-11, by default, the PIX is configured to inspect the listed protocols on the specified TCP or UDP port numbers. For example, the PIX inspects HTTP traffic on TCP port 80. The PIX inspects FTP traffic on TCP port 20. There is more on modifying port numbers or adding additional inspection port numbers later in the lesson.

Figure 9-20   Inspect Command

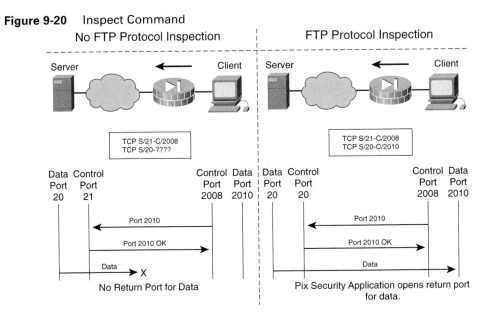

Example 9-11   Default Traffic Inspection and Port Numbers

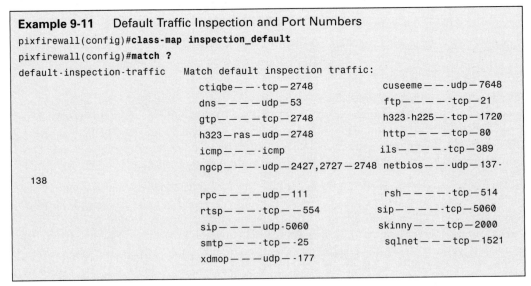

Default Protocol Inspection Policy

By default, protocol inspection is enabled globally in Example 9-12. The class map **inspection_default** identifies a class of traffic matching the TCP/UDP port numbers delineated under the **default-inspection-traffic** parameter. The **asa_global_fw_policy** policy map associates which protocol inspections are performed on the **inspection_default** class of traffic. Finally, the **asa_global_fw_policy** service policy is applied globally. No intervention is required by the administrator to enable default inspections on the PIX Security Appliance. The administrator can choose to modify the default class map, policy map, or service policy.

Example 9-12   Default Protocol-Inspection Policy

```
! Class Map
class-map inspection_default
    match default-inspection traffic

! Policy Map
policy-map asa_global_fw_policy
class inspection default
  inspect ctiqbe
  inspect dns
  inspect ftp
  inspect h323 h225
  inspect http
  inspect ils
  inspect ngop
  inspect netbios
  inspect rpc
  inspect rtsp
  inspect sip
  inspect skinny
  inspect smtp
  inspect snmp
  inspect sqlnet
  inspect tftp
  inspect xdmop
  inspect icmp

! Service Policy
service-policy asa_global_fw_policy global
```

Disabling Inspection for a Protocol

In the **asa_global_fw_policy** policy map (see Example 9-12), there is a default list of protocols that are inspected by the PIX Security Appliance. The administrator can choose to disable inspection of specific protocols by issuing the **no** form of the **inspect** *protocol* command. In Example 9-13, CTIQBE and CUSEEME protocol inspection is disabled.

Example 9-13   Disabling Inspection for a Protocol

```
pixfirewall(config)#policy-map asa_global_fw_policy
pixfirewall(config-pmap)#class inspection_default
pixfirewall(config-pmap-c)#no inspect ctiqbe
pixfirewall(config-pmap-c)#no inspect cuseeme
pixfirewall(config-pmap-c)#exit
pixfirewall(config-pmap)#exit
```

Add a Protocol-Inspection Port Number

The administrator can also choose to enable protocol inspection on an additional destination port number, such as HTTP inspection on port TCP port 8080. Adding protocol inspection to an additional port number is a two-step process:

Step 1.   Identify traffic using a specific TCP/UDP destination port number in the **class-map** command, such as TCP port 8080.

Step 2.   In a policy map, associate a policy with a class of traffic.

In Example 9-14, HTTP inspection is applied to traffic with TCP destination port 8080. These commands enable the PIX Security Appliance to recognize that connections to port 8080 should be treated in the same manner as connections to HTTP port 80.

Example 9-14   Add a Protocol-Inspection Port Number

```
pixfirewall(config)#class-map 8080_inspect_traffic
pixfirewall(config-ftp-map)#match port tcp eq 8080
pixfirewall(config-ftp-map)#exit
pixfirewall(config)#policy-map asa global_fw_policy
pixfirewall(config-pmap)#class 8080_inspect_traffic
pixfirewall(config-pmap-c)#inspect http
pixfirewall(config-pmap-c)#exit
pixfirewall(config-pmap)#exit
```

FTP Inspection

The PIX Security Appliance supports application inspection for a large number of protocols, including FTP. FTP applications require special handling by the PIX application-inspection function. FTP applications embed data channel port information in the control channel traffic. The FTP-inspection function monitors the control channel, identifies the data port assignment, and permits data exchange on the data port for the duration of the specific session. In the example in Figure 9-21, the FTP client is shown opening a control channel between itself and the FTP server. When data is to be exchanged, the FTP client alerts the FTP server through the control channel that it expects the data to be delivered back from FTP server port another a different port. If FTP inspection is not enabled, the return data from FTP server port is blocked by the PIX. With FTP inspection enabled, however, the PIX inspects the FTP control channel to recognize that the data channel will be established to the new FTP client port and temporarily creates an opening for the data channel traffic for the life of the session. By default, the PIX inspects port 21 connections for FTP traffic. The FTP application inspection inspects the FTP sessions and performs the following four tasks:

- Prepares dynamic secondary data connections

- Tracks **ftp** command-response sequence

- Generates an audit trail

- NATs embedded IP addresses

Figure 9-21   FTP Inspection

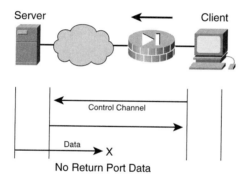

If the **inspect ftp strict** option is enabled, each **ftp** command and response sequence is tracked for anomalous activity, such as the following:

- **Truncated command**—Number of commas in the **PORT** and **PASV** reply command is checked to determine whether it is five. If it is not five, the PORT command is assumed to be truncated, and the TCP connection is closed.

- **Incorrect command**—Checks the **ftp** command to determine whether it ends with <CR><LF> characters, as required by the RFC. If it does not, the connection is closed.

- **Size of RETR and STOR commands**—These are checked against a fixed constant. If the size is greater, an error message is logged, and the connection is closed.

- **Command spoofing**—The **PORT** command should always be sent from the client. The TCP connection is denied if a **PORT** command is sent from the server.

- **Reply spoofing**—PASV reply command (227) should always be sent from the server. The TCP connection is denied if a **PASV** reply command is sent from the client. This prevents the security hole when the user executes **"227 xxxxx a1, a2, a3, a4, p1, p2"**.

- **TCP stream editing**.

- **Invalid port negotiation**—The negotiated dynamic port value is checked to determine whether it is less than 1024. Because port numbers in the range from 1 to 1024 are reserved for well-known connections, if the negotiated port falls in this range, the TCP connection is freed.

- **Command pipelining**—The number of characters present after the port numbers in the **PORT** and **PASV** reply command is cross-checked with a constant value of 8. If it is more than 8, the TCP connection is closed.

Administrators can further enhance inspection on FTP traffic to improve security and to control the service going through the PIX by filtering FTP request commands.

Active Mode FTP Inspection

Active mode FTP uses two channels for communications. When a client starts an FTP connection, it opens a TCP channel from one of its high-order ports to port 21 on the server. This is referred to as the *command channel*. When the client requests data from the server, it tells the server to send the data to a given high-order port. The server acknowledges the request and initiates a connection from its own port 20 to the high-order port that the client requested. This is referred to as the *data channel*.

Because the server initiates the connection to the requested port on the client, it was difficult in the past to have firewalls allow this data channel to the client without permanently opening port 20 connections from outside servers to inside clients for outbound FTP connections. This created a potential vulnerability by exposing clients on the inside of the firewall. Protocol inspections have resolved this problem.

For outbound FTP traffic, when the client requests data, the PIX opens a temporary inbound opening for the data channel from the server. This opening is torn down after the data is sent.

For inbound FTP traffic, the PIX handles it differently, depending on the type of ACL in place:

- If an ACL exists allowing inbound connections to an FTP server, and if all outbound traffic is implicitly allowed, no special handling is required, because the server initiates the data channel from the inside

- If an ACL exists allowing inbound connections to an FTP server, and if all outbound traffic is not implicitly allowed, the PIX opens a temporary connection for the data channel from the server. This opening is torn down after the data is sent.

Figure 9-22 depicts how the PIX Security Appliance handles outbound and inbound FTP traffic using active mode FTP inspection.

Figure 9-22   Active Mode FTP Inspection

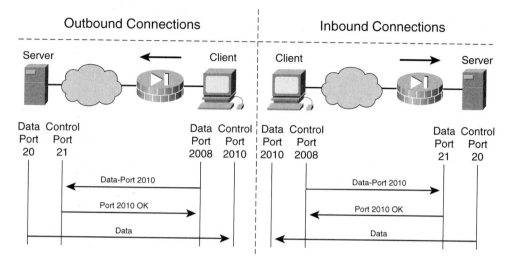

Passive Mode FTP Inspection

Passive mode FTP (PFTP) also uses two channels for communications. The command channel works the same as in a active mode FTP connection, but the data channel setup works differently. When the client requests data from the server, it asks the server whether it accepts PFTP connections. If the server accepts PFTP connections, it sends the client a high-order port number to use for the data channel. The client then initiates the data connection from its own high-order port to the port that the server sent.

Because the client initiates both the command and data connections, early firewalls could easily support outbound connections without exposing inside clients to attack. Inbound connections, however, proved more of a challenge. The FTP-inspection protocol resolved this issue.

For outbound FTP traffic, the PIX handles it differently, depending on the type of ACL in place:

- If an ACL exists implicitly allowing outbound FTP traffic, no special handling is required because the client initiates both the command and data channels from the inside.

- If an ACL exists that does not allow outbound FTP traffic, the PIX opens a temporary connection for the data channel from the client. This opening is torn down after the data is sent.

For inbound FTP traffic, if an ACL exists allowing inbound connections to a PFTP server, when the client requests data, the PIX opens a temporary inbound connection for the data channel initiated by the client. This opening is torn down after the data is sent.

FTP Deep Packet Inspection

The existing FTP inspection allows traffic by default and restricts traffic that fails security checks. FTP deep packet inspection enables the administrator to block specific FTP request commands through the PIX Security Appliance, such as renaming a file. When an FTP request command is filtered, the connection is closed. The administrator can define which FTP commands should be blocked with the **ftp-map** command. The FTP commands that can be blocked are as follows:

- **appe**—Append to a file
- **cdup**—Change to a parent of current directory
- **help**—Access remote help information from server
- **mfr**—Rename a file
- **mfo**—Rename a file
- **site**—Specify a server-specific command
- **store**—Store a file
- **stou**—Store a file with a unique name

Use the following four steps to filter FTP commands:

Step 1. Define which FTP commands to filter in the **ftp-map** command.

Step 2. Identify a traffic flow in the **class-map** command.

Step 3. Configure a policy that associates the FTP commands to be filtered, in an FTP map, with the traffic flow identified in a class map.

Step 4. Apply the policy on an interface, or on a global basis.

Use the **ftp-map** command to define which FTP commands should be blocked. After the administrator enters the **ftp-map** command and a map name, the system enters the FTP map configuration mode. Use the following command to list which FTP request commands should be blocked:

```
pixfirewall(config)#deny-request-cmd {cdup | retr | stor | stou | appe | rnfr | rnto | site |
help}
```

For example, the following commands define the inbound_ftp FTP map and which commands should be filtered:

```
pixfirewall(config)#ftp-map inbound_ftp
pixfirewall(config-ftp-map)#deny-request-cmd cdup rnfr rnto site stor stou
```

In Example 9-15, the **ftp-map inbound_ftp** command identifies six FTP request commands to filter. The class map inbound_ftp_traffic matches traffic defined by access-list 101, as well as FTP traffic between any host and host 192.168.1.11—the FTP server. In the inbound policy map, the FTP command request restrictions defined in the **ftp-map inbound_ftp** command are associated with the inbound_ftp_traffic class of traffic. Finally, the inbound policy is enabled on the outside interface.

Example 9-15   FTP Inspection Example

```
pixfirewall(config)#ftp-map inbound_ftp
pixfirewall(config-ftp-map)#deny-request-cmd cdup rnfr rnto site stor stou
pixfirewall(config)#access-list 101 permit tcp any host 192.168.1.11 eq ftp
pixfirewall(config)#class-map inbound_ftp_traffic
pixfirewall(config-ftp-map)#match access-list 101
pixfirewall(config-ftp-map)#exit
pixfirewall(config)#policy-map inbound
pixfirewall(config-pmap)#class inbound_ftp_traffic
pixfirewall(config-pmap-c)#inspect ftp strict inbound_ftp
pixfirewall(config-pmap-c)#exit
pixfirewall(config-pmap)#exit
pixfirewall(config)#service-policy inbound outside
```

HTTP Inspection

The **inspect http** command protects against specific attacks and other threats associated with HTTP traffic. HTTP inspection performs the following functions:

- HTTP inspection

- URL screening through N2H2 or Websense

- Java and ActiveX filtering

By default, HTTP inspection is enabled globally. Inspection of HTTP port 80 traffic is defined in the inspection_default class map. In the asa_global_fw_policy policy map (refer to Example 9-14 in the section "Add a Protocol Inspection Port Number" earlier in this module), HTTP inspection is associated with the inspection_default class of traffic, HTTP port 80. HTTP inspection is enabled globally in the asa_global_fw_policy service policy. To remove HTTP inspection, use the **no inspect http** command in the policy map.

Enhanced HTTP Inspection

Enhanced HTTP inspection verifies that HTTP messages conform to RFC 2616, use RFC-defined methods or supported extension methods, and comply with various other criteria. In many cases, these criteria and the system response when the criteria are not met can be configured. The criteria that can be applied to HTTP messages, beyond those already mentioned, are as follows:

- Specify maximum header length for HTTP request and response messages

- Specify maximum and minimum content length

Note

The last two features are configured in conjunction with the **filter** command. The **no inspect http** command statement also disables the **filter url** command.

- Confirm content type in the message header is the same as the body of the HTTP message

- Specify maximum URI length in request message

- Specify supported HTTP transfer-encoding type

- Specify supported MIME types

To enable enhanced HTTP inspection, use the **inspect http** *http-map* command. The enhanced rules that apply to HTTP traffic are defined via the **http-map** command.

Enhanced HTTP Inspection Configuration

Configuring enhanced HTTP inspection is a four-step process, as follows:

Step 1. Configure the **http-map** command to define the enhanced HTTP inspection parameters and the action taken when a parameter in the configured category is detected.

Step 2. Identify the flow of traffic using the **class-map** command. The administrator can use the default class map, inspection_default. The administrator can also define a new traffic flow; for example, any hosts trying to access the corporate web server from the Internet.

Step 3. Associate the HTTP map with a class of traffic with the **policy-map** command. The administrator can use the default policy map, asa_global_fw_policy. The administrator can also define a new policy, such as an inbound traffic policy for any hosts trying to access the corporate web server from the Internet.

Step 4. Apply the policy to an interface, or globally, using the **service-policy** command. The administrator can use the default service policy, asa_global_fw_policy. The administrator can also define a new service policy, such as a policy for all inbound Internet-sourced traffic, and apply the service policy to the outside interface.

In Example 9-16, the administrator created a new modular policy for HTTP traffic from the Internet to the corporate web server with an IP address of 192.168.1.11, instead of modifying the existing default global modular policy. To accomplish this, the administrator configured a new HTTP map, class map, policy map, and service policy. The administrator created an HTTP map, inbound_http. In the HTTP map, the administrator restricted RPC request methods, defined message criteria, and restricted HTTP applications. In the class map, the administrator identified the traffic flow with a matching ACL, access-list 102. In a new policy map, the administrator associated the actions in the new HTTP map with traffic identified in the ACL. Finally, the new service policy is enabled on the outside interface.

Example 9-16   Configuring Enhanced HTTP Inspection

```
pixfirewall(config)#http-map inbound_http
pixfirewall(config-http-map)#request-method rfc delete action reset log
pixfirewall(config-http-map)#request-method rfc post action reset log
pixfirewall(config-http-map)#request-method rfc put action reset log
pixfirewall(config-http-map)#content-type-verification match-req-rsp action reset log
pixfirewall(config-http-map)#port-misuse p2p action reset log
pixfirewall(config-http-map)#exit
pixfirewall(config)#access-list 102 permit TCP any host 192.168.1.11 eq www
pixfirewall(config)#class-map inbound_http_traffic
pixfirewall(config-ftp-map)#match access-list 102
pixfirewall(config-ftp-map)#exit
pixfirewall(config)#policy-map inbound
pixfirewall(config-pmap)#class inbound_http_traffic
pixfirewall(config-pmap-c)#inspect http inbound_http
pixfirewall(config-pmap-c)#exit
pixfirewall(config-pmap)#exit
pixfirewall(config)#service-policy inbound outside
```

Protocol Application Inspection

This section discusses the configuration and handling of the RSH, SQL, SMTP, ICMP, and SNMP protocols.

Remote Shell

Remote Shell (RSH) uses two channels for communications. When a client first starts an RSH connection, it opens a TCP channel from one of its high-order ports to port 514 on the server. The server opens another channel for standard error output to the client.

For RSH traffic, the PIX Security Appliance behaves as follows:

- **Outbound connections**—When standard error messages are sent from the server, the PIX opens a temporary inbound opening for this channel. This opening is torn down when no longer needed.

- **Inbound connections**:

  — If an ACL exists allowing inbound connections to an RSH server, and if all outbound TCP traffic is implicitly allowed, no special handling is required because the server initiates the standard error channel from the inside.

  — If an ACL exists allowing inbound connections to an RSH server, and if all outbound TCP traffic is not implicitly allowed, the PIX opens a temporary inbound opening for the standard error channel from the server. This opening is torn down after the messages are sent.

Figure 9-23 depicts this process.

Figure 9-23   Remote Shell Inspection

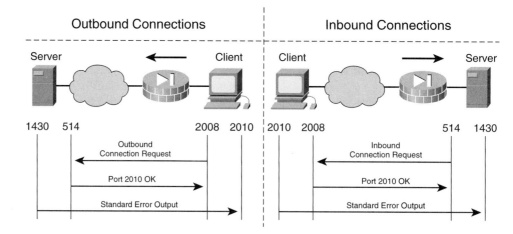

By default, the Security Appliance inspects port 514 connections for RSH traffic. If RSH servers are using ports other than port 514, you can use the **class-map** command to identify these other traffic flows with their different RSH TCP port numbers. To enable RSH application inspection, use the **inspect rsh** command in a policy map, class configuration mode. To remove the RSH inspection, use the **no** form of this command. If the **inspect rsh** command is not enabled

- Outbound RSH will not work properly on that flow of traffic.

- Inbound RSH will work properly on that port if an ACL to the inside server exists.

SQL*Net

SQL*Net uses only one channel for communications, but it could be redirected to a different port, and even more commonly to a different secondary server altogether. When a client starts an SQL*Net connection, it opens a standard TCP channel from one of its high-order ports to port 1521 on the server. The server then proceeds to redirect the client to a different port or IP address. The client tears down the initial connection and establishes the second connection.

For SQL*Net traffic, the PIX Security Appliance behaves as follows:

- **Outbound connections**:

  — If all outbound TCP traffic is implicitly allowed, no special handling is required because the client initiates all TCP connections from the inside.

  — If all outbound TCP traffic is not implicitly allowed, the PIX opens a connection for the redirected channel between the server and the client.

■ **Inbound connections**—If an ACL exists allowing inbound connections to a SQL*Net server, the PIX opens an inbound connection for the redirected channel.

Figure 9-24 depicts this process.

Figure 9-24  SQL*Net Inspection

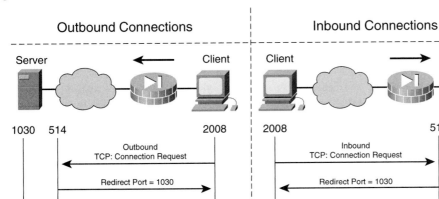

By default, the PIX Security Appliance inspects port 1521 connections for SQL*Net traffic. If SQL*Net servers are using ports other than port 1521, you can use the **class-map** command to identify these other traffic flows with their different SQL*Net port numbers. To enable SQL*Net application inspection, use the **inspect sqlnet** command in a policy map, class configuration mode. To remove the SQL*Net inspection, use the **no** form of this command. If the **inspect sqlnet** command is not enabled

■ Outbound SQL*Net will work properly on that port so long as outbound traffic is not explicitly disallowed.

■ Inbound SQL*Net will not work properly on that port.

ESMTP

Extended SMTP (ESMTP) is an enhancement to Simple Mail Transfer Protocol (SMTP) and is similar is most respects to SMTP. ESMTP application inspection provides improved protection against SMTP-based attacks by restricting the types of SMTP commands that can pass through the PIX Security Appliance. ESMTP application inspection supports the following commands:

■ Seven minimum SMTP commands: **HELO, MAIL, RCPT, DATA, RSET, NOOP**, and **QUIT** (RFC 821)

■ Eight ESTMP commands: **AUTH, DATA, EHLO, ETRN, SAML, SEND, SOML**, and **VRFY**

To enable ESMTP inspection, use the **inspect esmtp** command. You can define the ports on which to activate ESMTP inspection (default port is 25). If you disable the **inspect esmtp** command, all SMTP commands are allowed through the PIX, potentially exposing mail servers to attacks.

ICMP

Without Internet Control Message Protocol (ICMP) stateful inspection, ICMP can be used to attack the network. ICMP inspection enables the PIX Security Appliance to track ICMP traffic so that it can be inspected like TCP and UDP traffic. For any single request, there will always be a single reply. When ICMP inspection is enabled, the ICMP payload is scanned to retrieve the pertinent information (source IP address, destination IP address, protocol, identification number, and sequence number) from the original packet. The idea is to match this session information in the PIX for each ICMP request and response pair. ICMP inspection allows replies only when the ICMP reply session information matches a request. The ICMP inspection ensures that there is only one response for each request. Figure 9-25 provides an example of ICMP inspection.

Figure 9-25   ICMP Inspection

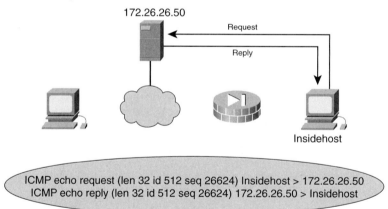

In Figure 9-25, Insidehost is sending an ICMP request packet to the server at destination IP address 172.26.26.50. With ICMP inspection enabled, the PIX tracks the information in the ICMP echo request, source, destination, protocol, identification number, and sequence number. ICMP inspection allows the ICMP reply from the server at 172.26.26.50 when it matches the original request.

To configure the ICMP inspection engine, use the **inspect icmp** command in policy map class configuration mode.

SNMP

By default, the PIX Security Appliance performs no inspection of Simple Network Management Protocol (SNMP). You can use the **snmp-map** and **inspect snmp** commands to filter out SNMP traffic based on the SNMP protocol version field in the packets. To configure SNMP version blocking, first define an SNMP map and then apply the SNMP map to a SNMP inspection policy.

Use the **snmp-map** command to identify the SNMP protocol version or versions to deny. When the administrator enters this command, the PIX Security Appliance enters the SNMP map configuration mode. From the SNMP map configuration mode, the administrator can define which SNMP protocol version to deny, version 1, 2, 2c, or 3. After defining the SNMP map, the administrator can apply the map parameters using the **inspect snmp** *map_name* command. The PIX inspects the SNMP traffic based on the contents of the SNMP map configuration.

To identify a specific map for defining the parameters for SNMP inspection, use the **snmp-map** *map_name* command. To remove the map, use the **no** form of this command. To enable SNMP inspection, use the **inspect snmp** *map_name* command in a policy map. To remove the configuration, use the **no** form of this command.

Example 9-17 demonstrates how to configure SNMP inspection and Figure 9-26 depicts the results.

Example 9-17   Configuring SNMP Inspection

```
pixfirewall(config)#snmp-map snmp_deny_v1
pixfirewall(config-snmp-map)#deny version 1 rnto site stor
pixfirewall(config-snmp-map)#exit
pixfirewall(config)#policy-map asa_global_fw_policy
pixfirewall(config-pmap)#class snmp-port
pixfirewall(config-pmap-c)#inspect snmp snmp_deny_v1
pixfirewall(config-pmap-c)#exit
pixfirewall(config-pmap)#exit
pixfirewall(config)#service-policy asa_global_fw_policy global
```

Multimedia Support

Multimedia applications might transmit requests on TCP, get responses on UDP or TCP, use dynamic ports, use the same port for source and destination, and so on. Every application behaves in a different way, and the PIX Security Appliance must dynamically open and close ports for secure multimedia connections using a single secure method without vulnerability, which is difficult, as depicted in Figure 9-27.

Figure 9-26   SNMP Inspection

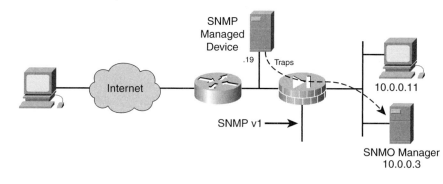

Figure 9-27   Why Multimedia Is an Issue

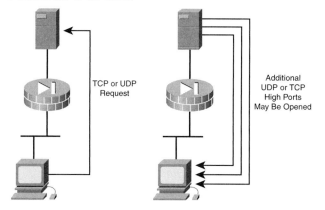

Consider the following two examples of multimedia applications:

- **RealAudio**—Sends the originating request to TCP port 7070. The RealAudio server replies with multiple UDP streams anywhere from UDP port 6970 through 7170 on the client machine.

- **CUseeMe client**—Sends the originating request from TCP port 7649 to TCP port 7648. The CUseeMe datagram is unique in that it includes the legitimate IP address in the header and in the payload and sends responses from UDP port 7648 to UDP port 7648.

The PIX Security Appliance dynamically opens and closes UDP ports for secure multimedia connections. Administrators do not need to open a large range of ports, which creates a security risk, or have to reconfigure any application clients.

Also, the PIX Security Appliance supports multimedia with or without NAT. Many firewalls that cannot support multimedia with NAT limit multimedia usage to only registered users, or require exposure of inside IP addresses to the Internet. Lack of support for multimedia with NAT often forces multimedia vendors to join proprietary alliances with firewall vendors to accomplish compatibility for their applications.

Real-Time Streaming Protocol (RTSP)

Real-Time Streaming Protocol (RTSP) is a real-time audio and video delivery protocol used by many popular multimedia applications. When establishing a control channel, RTSP uses one TCP channel and up to two additional UDP channels. The TCP port used to establish the control channel is the well-known port 554. This TCP control channel is then used to negotiate the other two UDP channels depending on the transport mode that is configured on the client.

Although UDP is occasionally used to setup the control channel for RTSP applications, RFC 2326 specifies only TCP. Therefore, the PIX provides support only for TCP. The first UDP channel that is established is the data connection and can use one of the following transport modes:

- Real-Time Transport Protocol (RTP)
- Real Data Transport Protocol (RDT), which is not supported by the PIX Security Appliance

The second UDP channel that is established is another control channel, which can use one of the following modes:

- Real-Time Control Protocol (RTCP)
- UDP Resend

RTSP also supports a TCP-only mode. This mode contains only one TCP connection, which is used as the control and data channels. Because this mode contains only one constant standard TCP connection, no special handling by the PIX Security Appliance is required.

The PIX Security Appliance supports two types of RTSP:

- Standard RTP Mode
- RealNetworks RDT mode

Together these modes are used to support applications such as Cisco IP/TV, Apple QuickTime 4, and the RealNetworks suite of applications. The RealNetworks suite includes RealAudio, RealPlayer, and RealServer. The sections that follow examine both standard RTP mode and RealNetworks RDT mode.

Standard RTP Mode

In standard RTP mode, the following three channels are used by RTSP:

- TCP control channel is the standard TCP connection initiated from the client to the server.
- RTP data channel is the simplex (unidirectional) UDP session used for media delivery using the RTP packet format from the server to the client. The client's port is always an even-numbered port.

- RTCP reports is the duplex (bidirectional) UDP session used to provide synchronization information to the client and packet-loss information to the server. The RTCP port is always the next consecutive port from the RTP data port.

For standard RTP mode RTSP traffic, the PIX Security Appliance behaves in the following manner:

- **Outbound connections**—After the client and the server negotiate the transport mode and the ports to use for the sessions, the Security Appliance opens temporary inbound dynamic openings for the RTP data channel and RTCP report channel from the server.

- **Inbound connections**:

   — If an ACL exists allowing inbound connections to an RTSP server, and if all outbound UDP traffic is implicitly allowed, no special handling is required because the server initiates the data and report channel from the inside.

   — If an ACL exists allowing inbound connections to an RTSP server, and if all outbound TCP traffic is not implicitly allowed, the Security Appliance opens temporary dynamic openings for the data and report channels from the server.

Figure 9-28 illustrates how a client and server using an RTSP application communicate in standard RTP mode. The initial TCP connection uses known port 554. The second UDP channel is set up by the server and is bidirectional, for it to provide synchronization information to the client and packet-loss information to the server.

Figure 9-28   Standard RTP Mode

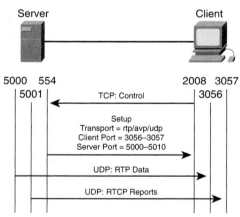

RealNetworks RDT Mode

In RealNetworks RDT mode, the following three channels are used by RTSP:

- TCP control channel is the standard TCP connection initiated from the client to the server.

- UDP data channel is the simplex, or unidirectional, UDP session used for media delivery using the standard UDP packet format from the server to the client.

- UDP resend is the simplex, or unidirectional, UDP session used for the client to request that the server resend lost data packets.

For RealNetworks RDT mode RTSP traffic, the PIX Security Appliance behaves in the following manner:

- **Outbound connections**:

  — If outbound UDP traffic is implicitly allowed, and after the client and the server negotiate the transport mode and the ports to use for the session, the Security Appliance opens temporary inbound openings for the UDP data channel from the server.

  — If outbound UDP traffic is not implicitly allowed, and after the client and the server negotiate the transport mode and the ports to use for the session, the Security Appliance opens a temporary inbound opening for the UDP data channel from the server and a temporary outbound opening for the UDP resend channel from the client.

- **Inbound connections**:

  — If an ACL exists allowing inbound connections to an RTSP server, and if all outbound UDP traffic is implicitly allowed, the Security Appliance opens a temporary inbound opening for the UDP resend from the client.

  — If an ACL exists allowing inbound connections to an RTSP server, and if all outbound TCP traffic is not implicitly allowed, the Security Appliance opens temporary opening for the UDP data and UDP resend channels from the server and client, respectively.

Figure 9-29 illustrates how a client and server using an RTSP application communicate in RealNetworks RDT mode. Notice that unlike standard mode RTP, the second RDP channel is not bidirectional. Instead, it is unidirectional and simply allows the client to request the server to resend lost packets.

Figure 9-29   RealNetworks RDT Mode

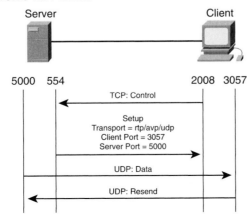

Protocols Required to Support IP Telephony

Voice over IP (VoIP) and multimedia standards supported by the PIX Security Appliance include H.323 Version 4, Session Initiation Protocol (SIP), Cisco Skinny Client Control Protocol (SCCP), and Media Gateway Control Protocol (MGCP), helping businesses secure deployments of a wide range of current and next-generation VoIP and multimedia applications.

The PIX Security Appliance also provide security services for Telephony Application Programming Interface (TAPI)-based and Java TAPI (JTAPI)-based applications when these applications use Computer Telephony Interface Quick Buffer Encoding (CTIQBE) as the network transport mechanism, such as the Cisco IP SoftPhone.

H.323

H.323 is more complicated than other traditional protocols because it uses two TCP connections and four to six UDP sessions for a single "call." Only one of the TCP connections goes to a well-known port. All the other ports are negotiated and are temporary. Furthermore, the content of the streams is far more difficult for firewalls to understand than with many other protocols because H.323 encodes packets using Abstract Syntax Notation (ASN.1).

By default, the PIX Security Appliance inspects port 1720 connections for H.323 traffic. If there are network devices using ports other than the default ports, the **class-map** command is used to identify these other traffic flows with their different port numbers. Use the **no inspect h323** command to disable the inspection of traffic for H.323 connections. Supported H.323 applications are as follows:

- Cisco Multimedia Conference Manager

- Microsoft NetMeeting

- Intel Video Phone

- Intel Internet Phone

- CUseeMe Networks:

    — Meeting Point

    — CUseeMe Pro

- VocalTec Communications:

    — Internet Phone

    — Gatekeeper

SIP

Session Initiation Protocol (SIP) is an application layer control protocol used to set up and tear down multimedia sessions. These multimedia sessions include Internet telephony and similar applications. SIP uses RTP for media transport and RTCP for providing a quality of service (QoS) feedback loop. Using SIP, the PIX Security Appliance can support any SIP VoIP gateways and VoIP proxy servers.

To support SIP calls through the PIX Security Appliance, signaling messages for the media connection addresses, media ports, and embryonic connections for the media must be inspected, because although the signaling is sent over a well-known destination port (UDP/TCP 5060), the media streams are dynamically allocated. You can use the **inspect sip** command to enable or disable SIP support. SIP is a text-based protocol and contains IP addresses throughout the text. With the SIP inspection enabled, the PIX inspects the packets, and both NAT and PAT are supported.

By default, the PIX Security Appliance inspects port 5060 connections for SIP traffic. If there are network devices using ports other than the default ports, you can use the **class-map** command to identify these other traffic flows with their different port numbers. Use **no inspect sip** command to disable the inspection of traffic for SIP connections. You can use the **show conn state sip** command to display all active SIP connections.

SCCP

In PIX Security Appliance Software Versions 6.0 and later, application handling supports Skinny Client Control Protocol (SCCP), also known as skinny protocol. SCCP is used by Cisco IP Phones for VoIP call signaling. SCCP defines the set of messages needed for a Cisco IP Phone to communicate with the Cisco CallManager for call setup. The IP Phone uses a randomly selected TCP port to send and receive SCCP messages. Call Manager listens for SCCP messages at TCP port 2000. SCCP uses RTP and RTCP for media transmissions. The media ports are randomly selected by the IP Phones.

Skinny protocol inspection enables the PIX Security Appliance to dynamically open negotiated ports for media sessions. SCCP support allows an IP Phone and Cisco CallManager to be placed on separate sides of the Security Appliance.

Skinny protocol inspection is enabled by default to listen for SCCP messages on port 2000. If there are network devices using ports other than the default ports, you can use the **class-map** command to identify these other traffic flows with their different port numbers. Use the **no inspect skinny** command to disable the inspection of skinny protocol traffic.

CTIQBE

The TAPI and JTAPI are used by many Cisco VoIP applications. Cisco PIX Security Appliance Software Version 6.3 introduces support for a specific protocol, Computer Telephony Interface Quick Buffering Code (CTIQBE), which is used by Cisco TAPI Service Provider (TSP) to communicate with Cisco Call Manager. Support for this protocol is enabled by default.

By default, the PIX Security Appliance inspects port 2748 connections for CTIQBE traffic. If there are network devices using ports other than the default ports, you can use the **class-map** command to identify these other traffic flows with their different port numbers. Use **no inspect ctiqbe** command to disable the inspection of traffic for CTIQBE connections.

MGCP

Cisco PIX Security Appliance Software Version 6.3 introduces support for application inspection of Media Gateway Control Protocol (MGCP). MGCP is used for controlling media gateways from external call control elements called media gateway controllers or call agents. A media gateway is typically a network element that provides conversion between the audio signals carried on telephone circuits and data packets carried over the Internet or over other packet networks. Examples of media gateways are as follows:

- **Trunking gateway**—Provides an interface between the telephone network and a VoIP network. Such gateways typically manage a large number of digital circuits.

- **Residential gateway**—Provides a traditional analog (RJ-11) interface to a VoIP network. Examples of residential gateways include cable modem/cable set-top boxes, xDSL devices, and broadband wireless devices.

- **Business gateway**—Provides a traditional digital PBX interface or an integrated soft PBX interface to a VoIP network. MGCP messages are transmitted over UDP.

To use MGCP, at least two ports typically need to be configured, one on which the gateway receives commands and one for the port on which the call agent receives commands. Normally, a call agent sends commands to port 2427, whereas a gateway sends commands to port 2727. Audio packets are transmitted over an IP network using RTP. MGCP inspection enables the Security Appliance to securely open negotiated UDP ports for legitimate media connections through the Security Appliance. Neither NAT nor PAT is supported by Cisco PIX Security Appliance Software Version 6.3 or earlier.

DNS Inspection

The PIX Security Appliance knows that Domain Name System (DNS) queries are a one-request, one-answer conversation, so the connection slot is released immediately after a DNS answer is received. When the DNS A record is returned, the PIX applies address translation not only to the destination address, but also to the embedded IP address of the web server, as shown in Figure 9-30. This address is contained in the user data portion of the DNS reply packet. As a result, a web client on the inside network gets the address it needs to connect to the web server on the inside network. Prior to PIX Security Appliance Software Version 6.2, the PIX translated the embedded IP address with the help of the **alias** command. In PIX Security Appliance Software Version 6.2 or later, the PIX has full support for NAT of embedded IP addresses within a DNS response packet.

Figure 9-30   DNS Inspection

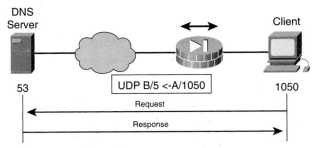

The PIX Security Appliance features full support for NAT of DNS messages originating from either inside or outside interfaces. This means that if a client on an inside network requests DNS resolution of an inside address from a DNS server on an outside interface, the DNS A record is translated correctly. It is no longer necessary to use the **alias** command to perform DNS doctoring.

In Figure 9-31, the following transactions occur:

1. The client on the inside network issues an HTTP request to server 10.0.0.10, using the hostname cisco.com.

2. The PIX Security Appliance translates the nonroutable source address of the web client in the IP header and forwards the request to the DNS server on its outside interface.

3. When the DNS A record is returned, the PIX applies address translation not only to the destination address, but also to the embedded IP address of the web server. This address is contained in the user data portion of the DNS reply packet.

4. As a result, the web client on the inside network gets the address it needs to connect to the web server on the inside network.

NAT of DNS messages is implemented in both the **nat** and **static** commands, as demonstrated in Example 9-18.

Figure 9-31   DNS Record Translation

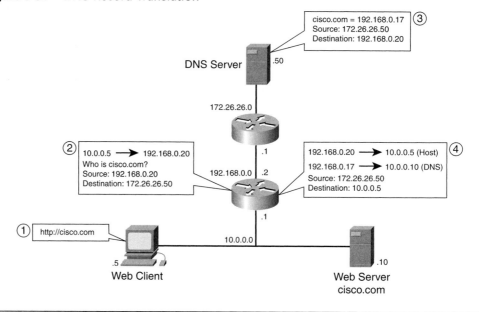
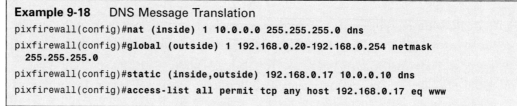

```
Example 9-18    DNS Message Translation
pixfirewall(config)#nat (inside) 1 10.0.0.0 255.255.255.0 dns
pixfirewall(config)#global (outside) 1 192.168.0.20-192.168.0.254 netmask
  255.255.255.0
pixfirewall(config)#static (inside,outside) 192.168.0.17 10.0.0.10 dns
pixfirewall(config)#access-list all permit tcp any host 192.168.0.17 eq www
```

Lab 9.4.10   Configure and Test Advanced Protocol Handling on the Cisco PIX Security Appliance

In this lab, you complete the objective of configuring three PIX interfaces and configure access through the PIX Security Appliance.

Summary

You should now understand how the PIX Security Appliance supports ACL use. This includes understanding how to configure standard and Turbo ACLs on the PIX and knowing how to use ACLs in a variety of network environments. Furthermore, you should understand ACL-related topics such as filtering malicious applets and using object groups and nested object groups to simplify complex ACLs.

You should now be able to discuss how modular policy provides greater granularity and more flexibility when configuring network policies. You should be able to configure a class map by identifying a class and defining a class of traffic. You should be able to configure a policy map by identifying a class and defining a policy for the class of traffic. You should also be able to configure a service policy by identifying a policy name and applying the policy globally or to an interface.

The chapter included a discussion of advanced protocol handling, and how you can configure the PIX Security Appliance to support specific protocols. Among these protocols are the advanced protocols used for multimedia support, real-time streaming protocols, and the protocols required to support IP telephony. These protocols include RTP and H.323. Some of these protocols operate over two channels, each of which has different access requirements.

Check Your Understanding

Complete all the review questions listed here to test your understanding of the topics and concepts in this chapter. Answers are listed in Appendix A, "Check Your Understanding Answer Key."

1. The Adaptive Security Algorithm (ASA) check applies to every packet of a communication. Access control lists (ACLs) are evaluated how many times per connection?

   a. 1

   b. 2

   c. A random number of times

   d. Never

2. When configuring ACLs on the PIX Security Appliance to permit and deny traffic, what are certain basic principles and guidelines that a network administrator should follow? (Choose two.)

   a. Higher to lower security: The ACL is used to restrict outbound traffic, and the source address argument of the **access-list** command is the actual address of the host or network.

   b. Higher to lower security: The ACL is used to restrict inbound traffic, and the source address argument of the **access-list** command is the actual address of the host or network.

   c. Lower to higher security: The ACL is used to restrict inbound traffic, and the source address argument of the **access-list** command is the actual address of the host or network.

   d. Lower to higher security: The ACL is used to restrict outbound traffic, and the destination address argument of the **access-list** command is the translated global IP address.

3. PIX ACLs differ from ACLs on Cisco IOS routers in that the PIX does not use a wildcard mask like Cisco IOS routers. It uses a regular subnet mask in the ACL definition.

   a. True

   b. False

4. To insert an **access-list** command statement, you would use which of the following commands?

   a. **access-list new-line** *line-num* command

   b. **access-list id line** *line-num* command

   c. **line-num** *line-num* command

   d. **line-num id line** *line-num* command

5. What types of object groups can be created?

    a. IP object group

    b. Network, Protocol, Service and ICMP type object group

    c. Turbo and non-Turbo object group

    d. Data link, Network, transport object group

6. Modular Policy Framework (MPF) is configured using which three basic commands?

    a. **class-map**, **policy-map**, and **service-policy**

    b. **network-map**, **protocol-map**, and **service-policy**

    c. **class-map**, **policy-map**, and **icmp-type**

    d. **class-map**, **network-map**, and **service-policy**

7. The **inspect http** command protects against specific attacks and other threats associated with HTTP traffic. HTTP inspection performs which of the following functions? (Choose three.)

    a. HTTP inspection

    b. URL screening through N2H2 or Websense

    c. Java and ActiveX filtering

    d. Virus checking

    e. Adware/pop-up filtering

8. H.323 is more complicated than other traditional protocols because it uses two TCP connections and four to six UDP sessions for a single "call." Only one of the TCP connections goes to a well-known port. All the other ports are negotiated and are temporary.

    a. True

    b. False

9. SIP is a/an _____ control protocol used to set up and tear down multimedia sessions. These multimedia sessions include Internet telephony and similar applications.

    a. Transport layer

    b. Application layer

    c. Network layer

    d. Session layer

10. The PIX Security Appliance features full support for NAT of DNS messages originating from either inside or outside interfaces.

    a. True

    b. False

Upon completion of this chapter, you should be able to answer the following questions:

- What are some Layer 2 attacks?

- What are some MAC address, ARP, and DHCP vulnerabilities?

- What are some VLAN vulnerabilities?

- What are some spanning-tree vulnerabilities?

Key Terms

This chapter uses the following key terms. You can find the definitions in the glossary at the end of the book.

Address Resolution Protocol (ARP)   page 441

Gratuitous ARP (GARP)   page 441

Dynamic ARP Inspection (DAI)   page 444

Like routers, both Layer 2 and Layer 3 switches have their own sets of network security requirements. Unlike routers, however, not much public information discusses the network security risks in switches and how to mitigate those risks. This module covers Layer 2 attacks and how to use Cisco IOS features to mitigate such threats to the network. This module covers several types of Layer 2 attacks and strategies to mitigate these attacks.

Introduction to Layer 2 Attacks

Upon completing this chapter, you will be able to mitigate network Layer 2 attacks, including content-addressable memory (CAM) table overflow, VLAN hopping, Spanning Tree Protocol (STP) manipulation, MAC address spoofing, and DHCP starvation.

Like routers, both Layer 2 and Layer 3 switches have their own sets of network security requirements. Often, little consideration is given to the network security risks in switches and what can be done to mitigate those risks. Switches are susceptible to many of the same Layer 3 attacks as routers. Most of the network security techniques detailed in the section of the SAFE Enterprise whitepaper titled "Routers Are Targets" also applies to switches. However, switches, and Layer 2 of the OSI reference model in general, are subject to network attacks in unique ways. These attacks include the following:

- CAM table overflow
- MAC address spoofing
- DHCP starvation
- VLAN hopping
- STP manipulation

MAC Address, ARP, and DHCP Vulnerabilities

In Figure 10-1, the machine that belongs to the attacker is on VLAN 10. The attacker floods MAC addresses to port 3/25 on the switch. When the CAM table threshold is reached, the switch operates as a hub and simply floods traffic out all ports. This flooding also occurs on adjacent switches configured with VLAN 10, but flooding is limited to only the source VLAN and does not affect other VLANs.

Figure 10-1   CAM Table Overflow Attack

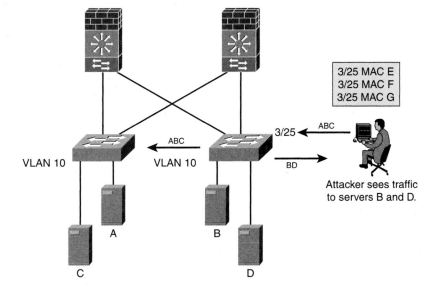

MAC flooding is an attempt to exploit the fixed hardware limitations of the CAM table of a switch. The Catalyst switch CAM table stores the source MAC address and the associated port of each device connected to the switch. The CAM table on the Catalyst 6000 can contain 128,000 entries. These 128,000 entries are organized as 8 pages that can store approximately 16,000 entries. A 17-bit hash algorithm is used to place each entry in the CAM table. If the hash results in the same value, each entry is stored on separate pages. When these eight locations are full, the traffic is flooded out all ports on the same VLAN on which the source traffic is being received.

CAM tables are limited in size. If enough entries are entered into the CAM table before other entries are expired, the CAM table fills up to the point that no new entries can be accepted. Typically, a network intruder floods the switch with a large number of invalid-source MAC addresses until the CAM table fills up. When that occurs, the switch floods all ports with incoming traffic because it cannot find the port number for a particular MAC address in the CAM table. The switch, in essence, acts like a hub. If the intruder does not maintain the flood of invalid-source MAC addresses, the switch eventually times out older MAC address entries from the CAM table and begins to act like a switch again. CAM table overflow only floods traffic within the local VLAN, so the intruder sees only traffic within the local VLAN to which he or she is connected.

In May 1999, the tool macof was released. It was written in approximately 100 lines of Perl code and was later ported to C language code and incorporated into the dsniff package. This tool floods a switch with packets containing randomly generated source and destination MAC and IP addresses. When the CAM table of the switch fills up with these addresses, the switch begins to forward all frames it receives to every port. In Figure 10-1, the attacker is sending out multiple packets with various-source MAC addresses. Over a short period, the CAM table in the switch fills up until it cannot accept new entries. As long as macof is left running, the CAM table on the switch remains full. When this happens, the switch begins to broadcast all packets that it receives out of every port, so packets sent from server B to server D are also broadcast out of port 3/25 on the switch to which the attacker is attached.

Mitigating CAM Table Overflow Attacks

You can mitigate CAM table overflow attacks by configuring port security on the switch, as Example 10-1 demonstrates. This option provides for either the specification of the MAC addresses on a particular switch port or the specification of the number of MAC addresses that can be learned by a switch port. When an invalid MAC address is detected on the port, the switch can either block the offending MAC address or shut down the port.

Example 10-1   Configuring Port Security on a Switch

```
! Enable port security on interface
Switch(config-if)# switchport port-security
! Enable port security and set specific MAC address
Switch(config-if)# switchport port-security [mac_addr]
```

Specifying MAC addresses on switch ports is far too unmanageable a solution for a production environment. Limiting the number of MAC addresses on a switch port is manageable. A more administratively scalable solution is the implementation of dynamic port security at the switch. To implement dynamic port security, specify a maximum number of MAC addresses that will be learned, as demonstrated in Example 10-2.

Example 10-2   Configuring Dynamic Port Security on a Switch

```
! Set maximum number of MAC addresses
Switch(config-if)# switchport port-security maximum (1-132)
! Set action on violation
Switch(config-if)# switchport port-security violation shutdown [protect | restrict |
  shutdown]
```

Port Security

Port security allows administrators to specify MAC addresses for each port or to permit a limited number of MAC addresses. When a secure port receives a packet, the source MAC address of the packet is compared to the list of secure source addresses that were manually configured or learned on the port. If a MAC address of a device attached to the port differs from the list of secure addresses, the port shuts down permanently, shuts down for a specified period of time, or drops incoming packets from the insecure host. The behavior of the port depends on how it is configured to respond to a security violator. The default behavior is to shut down permanently.

Cisco recommends to configure the port security feature to issue a **shutdown** instead of dropping packets from insecure hosts through the **restrict** option. The **restrict** option might fail under the load of an attack, and the port is disabled anyway.

To restrict traffic through a port by limiting and identifying MAC addresses of the stations allowed to access the port, perform the following tasks:

Step 1.   Enter interface configuration mode for the physical interface where port security is to be configured:

```
Switch(config)# interface interface_id
```

Step 2.   Set the interface mode as access. An interface in the default mode, dynamic desirable, cannot be configured as a secure port:

```
Switch(config-if)# switchport mode access
```

Step 3.   Enable port security on the interface:

```
Switch(config-if)# switchport port-security
```

Step 4.   (Optional) Set the violation mode and the action to be taken when a security violation is detected:

```
Switch(config-if)# switchport port-security violation [protect | restrict |
    shutdown]
```

Step 5.   (Optional) Enter a secure MAC address for the interface. You can use this command to enter the maximum number of secure MAC addresses. If fewer secure MAC addresses than the maximum are configured, the remaining MAC addresses are dynamically learned:

```
Switch(config-if)# switchport port-security mac-address mac_address
```

Step 6.   Return to privileged EXEC mode:

```
Switch(config-if)# end
```

Verify the Port Security Configuration

You can use two different commands to check the port security configuration:

```
switch#show port-security interface interface_id
switch#show port-security address
```

The first command displays port security settings for the switch or for the specified interface, including the maximum allowed number of secure MAC addresses for each interface, the number of secure MAC addresses on the interface, the number of security violations that have occurred, and the violation mode.

The second command displays port security settings for the switch or for the specified interface, including the maximum allowed number of secure MAC addresses for each interface, the number of secure MAC addresses on the interface, the number of security violations that have occurred, and the violation mode.

MAC Spoofing: Man-in-the-Middle Attacks

MAC spoofing attacks involve the use of a known MAC address of another host to attempt to make the target switch forward frames destined for the targeted host to the network attacker. By sending a single frame with the source MAC address of the targeted host, the network attacker overwrites the CAM table entry so that the switch forwards packets destined for the targeted host to the network attacker. The targeted host does not receive any traffic until it sends traffic. When the targeted host sends out traffic, the CAM table entry is rewritten once more so that it associates the MAC address back to the original port.

Figure 10-2 shows how MAC spoofing works. In the beginning, the switch has learned that Host A is on port 1, Host B is on port 2, and Host C is on port 3. Host B sends out a packet identifying itself with the IP address of Host B but with MAC address of Host A. This traffic causes the switch to move the location of Host A in its CAM table from port 1 to port 2. Traffic from Host C destined to Host A is now visible to Host B.

Figure 10-2   MAC Spoofing—Man-in-the-Middle Attacks

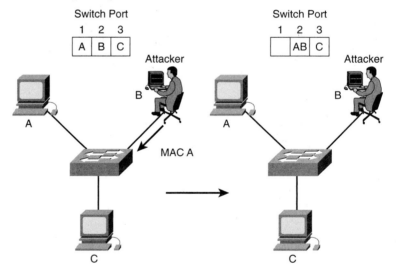

Mitigating MAC Spoofing Attacks

Use the **port security** interface configuration command to mitigate MAC spoofing attacks. The **port security** command enables you to specify the MAC address of the system connected to a particular port. The command also enables you to specify an action to take if a port security violation occurs. However, as with CAM table overflow attack mitigation, specifying a MAC address on every port is an unmanageable solution. You can use hold-down timers in the interface configuration menu to mitigate Address Resolution Protocol (ARP) spoofing attacks by setting the length of time an entry will stay in the ARP cache. However, hold-down timers by themselves do not suffice. Modification of the ARP cache expiration time on all end systems would be required, as would static ARP entries. Even in a small network, this approach does not scale well. One solution is to use private VLANs to help mitigate these network attacks. Example 10-3 shows the steps to configure the switch to mitigate MAC spoofing attacks.

Example 10-3   Configuring a Switch to Mitigate MAC Spoofing Attacks

```
Switch(config-if)# port security max-mac-count (1-132)
! Enable port security and set maximum MAC address
Switch(config-if)# port security action [shutdown | trap]
! Specify action to take when violation occurs
Switch(config-if)# arp timeout seconds
! Specify ARP timeout
```

Lab 10.2.4   Mitigate Layer 2 Attacks

In this lab activity, you configure network switches and routers to mitigate Layer 2 attacks. After completing this activity, you will be able to mitigate CAM table overflow attacks, MAC spoofing attacks, and DHCP starvation attacks.

Using Dynamic ARP Inspection to Mitigate MAC Spoofing Attacks

Address Resolution Protocol (ARP) is used to map IP addressing to MAC addresses in a LAN segment where hosts of the same subnet reside. Normally, a host sends out a broadcast ARP request to find the MAC address of another host with a particular IP address, and an ARP response comes from the host whose address matches the request. The requesting host then caches this ARP response.

ARP Spoofing

ARP inherently makes a provision for hosts to perform unsolicited ARP replies. An unsolicited ARP reply is called a *gratuitous ARP (GARP)*. GARP can be exploited maliciously by an attacker to spoof the identity of an IP address on a LAN segment. Typically, this is used to spoof the identity between two hosts or all traffic to and from a default gateway in a man-in-the-middle attack.

By crafting an ARP reply, a network attacker can make his system appear to be the destination host sought by the sender, as shown in Figure 10-3. The ARP reply causes the sender to store the MAC address of the attacking system in the ARP cache. This MAC address is also stored by the switch in its CAM table. In this way, the network attacker has inserted the MAC address of his system into both the CAM table of the switch and the ARP cache of the sender. This allows the network attacker to intercept frames destined for the host that is being spoofed.

Figure 10-3   ARP Spoofing

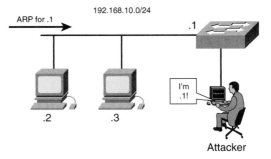

DHCP Snooping

A solution that you can use to mitigate various ARP-based network exploits is DHCP snooping, as demonstrated in Example 10-4. DHCP snooping provides security by filtering trusted DHCP messages and then using these messages to build and maintain a DHCP snooping binding table. DHCP snooping considers DHCP messages originating from any user-facing port that is not a DHCP server port or an uplink to a DHCP server as untrusted. From a DHCP snooping perspective, these untrusted, user-facing ports should not send DHCP server type responses such as DHCPOffer, DHCPAck, or DHCPNak.

Example 10-4   Using DHCP Snooping to Mitigate ARP-Based Network Attacks

```
Switch(config)# ip dhcp snooping
! Enable DHCP snooping
Switch(config)# ip dhcp snooping vlan vlan_id {,vlan_id}
! Enable DHCP snooping for specific VLANs.
Switch(config-if)# ip dhcp snooping trust
! Configure an interface as trusted for DHCP snooping purposes
Switch(config-if)# ip dhcp snooping limit rate rate
! Set rate limit for DHCP snooping
```

DHCP snooping acts like a firewall between untrusted hosts and DHCP servers. It also gives the administrator a way to differentiate between untrusted interfaces connected to the end user and trusted interfaces connected to the DHCP server or another switch.

DHCP Snooping Configuration Guidelines

The configuration guidelines for DHCP snooping are as follows:

- DHCP snooping must be enabled globally on the switch.

- DHCP snooping is not active until DHCP snooping is enabled on a VLAN.

- Before configuring the DHCP information option on the switch, make sure to configure the device that is acting as the DHCP server. For example, you must specify the IP addresses that the DHCP server can assign, or you must specify **exclude**, or you must configure DHCP options for devices.

The steps to configure DHCP snooping are as follows:

Step 1. Enable DHCP snooping globally:

```
Switch(config)# ip dhcp snooping
```

Step 2. Enable DHCP snooping on a VLAN or range of VLANs. A single VLAN can be identified by VLAN ID number, or start and end VLAN IDs can be used to specify a range of VLANs. The range is 1 to 4094:

```
Switch(config-if)# ip dhcp snooping vlan vlan_id {, vlan_id}
```

Step 3. Enter interface configuration mode and specify the interface to be configured:

```
Switch(config-if)# interface interface-id
```

Step 4. (Optional) Configure the interface as trusted or untrusted. You can use the **no** keyword to configure an interface to receive messages from an untrusted client. The default is untrusted:

```
Switch(config-if)# ip dhcp snooping trust
```

Step 5. (Optional) Configure the number of DHCP packets per second that an interface can receive. The range is 1 to 4294967294. The default is no rate limit:

```
Switch(config-if)# ip dhcp snooping limit rate rate
```

Step 6. Display the switch DHCP snooping configuration:

```
Switch(config-if)# show ip dhcp snooping
```

Note

Recommended practice is that you use an untrusted rate limit of not more than 100 packets per second. Normally, the rate limit applies to untrusted interfaces. If you configure rate limiting for trusted interfaces, you need to adjust the rate limit to a higher value because trusted interfaces might aggregate DHCP traffic in the switch.

The DHCP Snooping Binding Table

The DHCP snooping binding table contains the MAC address, IP address, lease time, binding type, VLAN number, and interface information corresponding to the local untrusted interfaces of a switch. The table does not have information about hosts interconnected with a trusted port because each interconnected switch has its own DHCP snooping binding table.

An untrusted interface is an interface configured to receive messages from outside the network or firewall. A trusted interface is an interface configured to receive only messages from within the network. The DHCP snooping binding table can contain both dynamic and static MAC address to IP address bindings.

The **show ip dhcp snooping binding** command displays the DHCP snooping binding entries for a switch, as shown in Example 10-5.

Example 10-5 DHCP Snooping Binding Entries

```
Switch(config)# show ip dhcp snooping binding
                                  Lease
MacAddress           IpAddress     (sec)   Type      VLAN   Interface
_____.     _____       __ _.   ____.     __     _____
00:30:94:C2:EF:35    41.0.0.51     286     dynamic   41     FastEthernet0/3
00:D0:B7:1B:35:DE    41.0.0.52     237     dynamic   41     FastEthernet0/3
00:00:00:00:00:01    40.0.0.46     286     dynamic   40     FastEthernet0/9
00:00:00:00:00:03    42.0.0.33     286     dynamic   42     FastEthernet0/9
00:00:00:00:00:02    41.0.0.53     286     dynamic   41     FastEthernet0/9
```

Dynamic ARP Inspection

Dynamic ARP Inspection (DAI) determines the validity of an ARP packet based on the valid MAC address-to-IP address bindings stored in a DHCP snooping database. In addition, DAI can validate ARP packets based on user-configurable access control lists (ACLs). This allows for the inspection of ARP packets for hosts using statically configured IP addresses. DAI allows for the use of per-port and VLAN ACLs (VACLs) to limit ARP packets for specific IP addresses to specific MAC addresses.

Note

DAI is not available on the Cisco Catalyst 2950 switch. DAI is available on Catalyst models 3550 and higher.

DHCP Starvation Attacks

A DHCP starvation attack works by broadcasting DHCP requests with spoofed MAC addresses, as shown in Figure 10-4, something easily achieved with attack tools such as gobbler. If enough requests are sent, the network attacker can exhaust the address space available to the DHCP servers for a period of time. This is a simple resource-starvation attack, similar to how a SYN flood is a starvation attack. The network attacker can then set up a rogue DHCP server on his system and respond to new DHCP requests from clients on the network.

Figure 10-4 DHCP Snooping Binding Entries

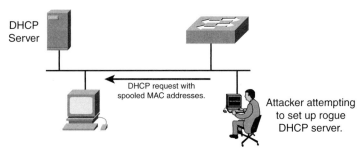

Exhausting all the DHCP addresses is not required to introduce a rogue DHCP server, as stated in RFC 2131:

The client collects DHCPOFFER messages over a period of time, selects one DHCPOFFER message from the (possibly many) incoming DHCPOFFER messages (for example, the first DHCPOFFER message or the DHCPOFFER message from the previously used server) and extracts the server address from the 'server identifier' option in the DHCPOFFER message. The time over which the client collects messages and the mechanism used to select one DHCPOFFER are implementation dependent.

By placing a rogue DHCP server on the network, a network attacker can provide clients with addresses and other network information. Because DHCP responses typically include default gateway and Domain Name System (DNS) server information, the network attacker can supply his own system as the default gateway and DNS server, resulting in a man-in-the-middle attack.

You can use the same techniques as used to mitigate CAM table flooding to mitigate DHCP starvation by limiting the number of MAC addresses on a switch port. As implementation of RFC 3118, *Authentication for DHCP Messages*, increases, DHCP starvation attacks will become more difficult to instigate.

You can use additional features in the Catalyst family of switches, such as the DHCP snooping feature, to help guard against a DHCP starvation attack. DHCP snooping is a security feature that filters untrusted DHCP messages and builds and maintains a DHCP snooping binding table. The binding table contains information such as the MAC address, IP address, lease time, binding type, VLAN number, and the interface information corresponding to the local untrusted interfaces of a switch. Untrusted messages are those received from outside the network or firewall, and untrusted switch interfaces are those configured to receive such messages from outside the network or firewall.

You can use the following commands to mitigate DHCP starvation attacks using DHCP snooping:

```
switch(config)#ip dhcp snooping
switch(config)#ip dhcp snooping vlan vlan_id {,vlan_id}
switch(config-if)#ip dhcp snooping trust
switch(config-if)#ip dhcp snooping limit rate rate
```

VLAN Vulnerabilities

This section looks at two VLAN vulnerabilities: VLAN hopping attacks and private VLAN vulnerabilities. This section also explains how to mitigate VLAN hopping attacks and defend private VLANs.

VLAN Hopping Attacks

VLAN hopping is a network attack whereby an attacking system sends out packets destined for a system on a different VLAN that cannot normally be reached by the attacker. This traffic is tagged with a VLAN ID for a VLAN other than the one on which the attacking system belongs. The attacking system can also attempt to behave like a switch and negotiate trunking so that the attacker can send and receive traffic between multiple VLANs.

Switch Spoofing

In a switch spoofing attack, the network attacker configures a system to spoof itself as a switch. This requires that the network attacker be capable of emulating either Inter-Switch Link (ISL) or 802.1Q signaling along with Dynamic Trunking Protocol (DTP) signaling. Using this method, a network attacker can make a system appear to be a switch with a trunk port. If successful, the attacking system then becomes a member of all VLANs.

Note

This attack works only if the trunk is configured with the native VLAN of the network attacker. The attack works for unidirectional traffic only and works even if the trunk ports are set to off.

Double Tagging

Another VLAN hopping attack involves tagging the sent frames with two 802.1Q headers to forward the frames to the wrong VLAN. The first switch that encounters the double-tagged frame strips the first tag off the frame and then forwards the frame, as shown in Figure 10-5.

Figure 10-5   Double 802.1Q Encapsulation VLAN Hopping Attack—Step 1

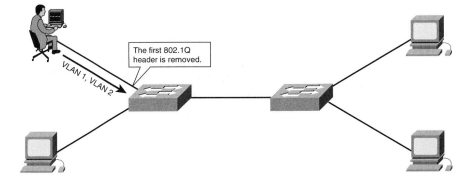

The result is that the frame is forwarded with the inner 802.1Q tag out all the switch ports, including trunk ports, configured with the native VLAN of the network attacker, as shown in Figure 10-6.

The second switch then forwards the packet to the destination based on the VLAN identifier in the second 802.1Q header, as shown in Figure 10-7.

Figure 10-6   Double 802.1Q Encapsulation VLAN Hopping Attack—Step 2

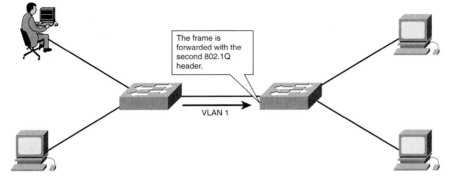

Figure 10-7   Double 802.1Q Encapsulation VLAN Hopping Attack—Step 3

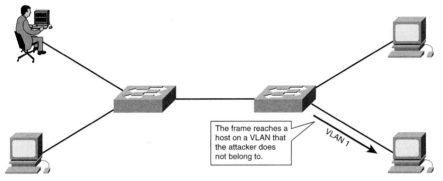

Mitigating VLAN Hopping Attacks

Mitigating VLAN hopping attacks requires several modifications to the VLAN configuration. One of the more important elements is to use dedicated VLAN IDs for all trunk ports. Also, disable all unused switch ports and place them in an unused VLAN. Set all user ports to non-trunking mode by explicitly turning off DTP on those ports. You can do so on Cisco IOS switches by setting the switch port mode to access with the **switchport mode access** interface configuration command.

Security best practices for VLANs and trunking include the following:

- Always use a dedicated VLAN ID for all trunk ports.

- Disable unused ports and put them in an unused VLAN.

- Be paranoid: Do not use VLAN 1 for anything.

- Disable auto-trunking on user-facing ports (DTP off).

- Explicitly configure trunking on infrastructure ports.

- Use all tagged mode for the native VLAN on trunks.

Private VLAN Vulnerabilities

Private VLANs are a common mechanism to restrict communications between systems on the same logical IP subnet. Private VLANs work by limiting the ports within a VLAN that can communicate with other ports in the same VLAN. Isolated ports within a VLAN can communicate only with promiscuous ports. Community ports can communicate only with other members of the same community and promiscuous ports. Promiscuous ports can communicate with any port. One network attack that can bypass the network security of private VLANs involves the use of a proxy to bypass access restrictions to a private VLAN.

In this network attack against private VLANs, frames are forwarded to a host on the network connected to a promiscuous port, such as on a router. In Part A of Figure 10-8, the network attacker sends a packet with the source IP and MAC address of his device, a destination IP address of the target system, but a destination MAC address of the router. The switch forwards the frame to the router. The router routes the traffic, rewrites the destination MAC address as that of the target, and sends the packet back out. Now the packet has the proper format, as shown in Part B of Figure 10-8, and is forwarded to the target system. This network attack allows only for unidirectional traffic because any attempt by the target to send traffic back is blocked by the private VLAN configuration. If both hosts are compromised, static ARP entries could be used to allow bidirectional traffic. This scenario is not a private VLAN vulnerability because all the rules of private VLANs were enforced. However, the network security was bypassed.

Note

Private VLANs are not configurable on the Cisco Catalyst 2950 switch.

Figure 10-8   Private VLAN Proxy Attack

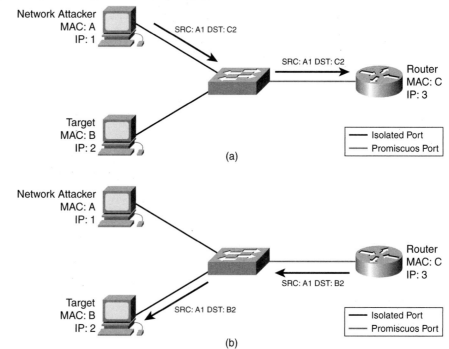

Defending Private VLANs

You can configure ACLs on the router port to mitigate private VLAN attacks. You can also use VACLs to help mitigate the effects of private VLAN attacks. Consider this example of using ACLs on the router port: If a server farm segment is 172.16.34.0/24, configuring the ACLs shown in the Example 10-6 on the default gateway mitigates the private VLAN proxy attack.

Example 10-6   Configuring ACLs to Mitigate Private VLAN Proxy Attacks

```
Router(config)# access-list 101 deny ip 172.16.34.0 0.0.0.255 172.16.34.0 0.0.0.255
  log
Router(config)# access-list 101 permit ip any any
Router(config)# interface fastethernet 0/1
Router(config-if)# ip access-group 101 in
```

Spanning Tree Protocol Vulnerabilities

This section discusses Spanning Tree Protocol (STP) vulnerabilities and how to prevent STP manipulation.

Another attack against switches involves intercepting traffic by attacking the Spanning Tree Protocol. STP is used in switched networks to prevent the creation of bridging loops in an Ethernet network topology. Upon boot, the switches begin a process of determining a loop-free topology. The switches identify one switch as a root bridge and block all other redundant data paths.

By attacking STP, the network attacker hopes to spoof his system as the root bridge in the topology. This attack requires the attacker to be connected to two different switches, which can be done with either multiple network interface cards (NICs) or with a hub. To perform this attack, the network attacker broadcasts out STP configuration/topology change bridge protocol data units (BPDUs) in an attempt to force spanning-tree recalculations. The BPDUs sent out by the attacking system announce that the attacking system has a lower bridge priority. If successful, the network attacker can see a variety of frames.

Figure 10-9 illustrates how a network attacker can use STP to change the topology of a network so that it appears that the attacking host is a root bridge with a higher priority. By sending spoofed BPDUs, the network attacker causes the switches to initiate spanning-tree recalculations. The two switches then forward frames through the attacking system after it has become the root bridge, which opens the door for man-in-the-middle and denial-of-service (DoS) attacks.

Figure 10-9   Spanning Tree Protocol Vulnerabilities

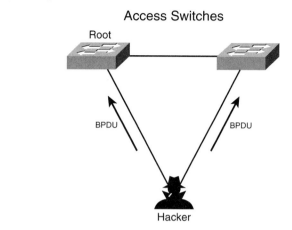

Preventing Spanning Tree Protocol Manipulation

To mitigate STP manipulation, use the root guard and the BPDU guard features to enforce the placement of the root bridge in the network and enforce the STP domain borders. The root guard feature is designed to provide a way to enforce the root bridge placement in the network. The STP BPDU guard is designed to allow network administrators to keep the active network topology predictable. Although BPDU guard may seem unnecessary given that the administrator can set the bridge priority to zero, there is still no guarantee that it will be elected as the root bridge, because there might be a bridge with priority zero and a lower bridge ID. BPDU guard is best deployed toward user-facing ports to prevent rogue switch network extensions by an attacker.

Spanning Tree Protocol Guard

Use the **spanning-tree guard** interface configuration command to enable root guard or loop guard on all the VLANs associated with the selected interface. Root guard restricts which interface is allowed to be the spanning-tree root port or the path to the root for the switch. Loop guard prevents alternate or root ports from becoming designated ports when a failure creates a unidirectional link. Use the **no** form of this command to return to the default setting. The syntax for the **spanning-tree guard** command is as follows:

```
[no] spanning-tree guard [loop | none | root]
```

where:

- **loop**—Enables loop guard
- **none**—Disables root guard or loop guard
- **root**—Enables root guard

Spanning Tree Protocol BPDU Guard

Use the **spanning-tree portfast** global configuration command to globally enable BPDU filtering on PortFast-enabled ports, the BPDU guard feature on PortFast-enabled ports, or the PortFast feature on all nontrunking ports. The BPDU filtering feature prevents the switch port from sending or receiving BPDUs. The BPDU guard feature puts PortFast-enabled ports that receive BPDUs in an error-disabled state. Use the **no** form of this command to return to the default setting. The syntax for the **spanning-tree portfast** command is as follows:

```
[no] spanning-tree portfast [bpdufilter default | bpduguard default | default]
```

where:

- **bpdufilter default**—Globally enables BPDU filtering on PortFast enabled ports and prevent the switch port connected to end stations from sending or receiving BPDUs.

- **bpduguard default**—Globally enables the BPDU guard feature on PortFast enabled ports and place the ports that receive BPDUs in an error-disabled state.

- **default**—Globally enables the PortFast feature on all nontrunking ports. When the PortFast feature is enabled, the port changes directly from a blocking state to a forwarding state without making the intermediate spanning-tree state changes.

Summary

This chapter discussed vulnerabilities and attacks specific to Layer 2 of the OSI model. The chapter introduced several types of Layer 2 attacks along with steps that enable you to mitigate them. You should now be able to discuss the types of Layer 2 network attacks that can be mitigated using Cisco IOS commands. You should be able to describe how CAM table overflow is used in a network attack and how to prevent CAM table overflow. You should understand MAC spoofing attacks and how to prevent them. You should also be able to explain how attackers use DHCP in a network attack.

Poor network design and misconfiguration account for more intrusions than VLAN implementation flaws. To solve misconfiguration issues, here are some best practices to consider when using VLAN switches:

- Determine the role of the switch. Is it switching frames or routing IP traffic? Are you applying security measures (MAC access controls, IP packet filtering policy) using switch software features?

- Document how these services are intended to interact.

- Understand how your switch implements DTP(virtual trunk) and STP.

- Use MAC-level security features where possible. Many VLAN switches provide administrative means to disable switch ports, limit the number of MAC addresses that can connect to a port, and lock down a specific MAC address (or addresses).

■ Isolate switch ports so that no traffic from other ports can be delivered to an isolated or *private VLAN* port. This feature proves particularly useful if you intend to operate a publicly accessible VLAN (for example, a demilitarized zone [DMZ] with web servers) off a VLAN switch alongside trusted VLANs.

■ Consider VLAN switches that provide IEEE 802.1x authentication. 802.1x is not exclusively for wireless networks. You can use 802.1x to deliver VLAN tags based on authenticated identity.

■ Use a secure method for management access (Secure Sockets Layer [SSL], Secure Shell [SSH]).

Check Your Understanding

Complete all the review questions listed here to test your understanding of the topics and concepts in this chapter. Answers are listed in Appendix A, "Check Your Understanding Answer Key."

1. In May 1999 the tool macof was released. This tool is used to initiate which type of Layer 2 attack?

   a. CAM table overflow

   b. MAC address spoofing

   c. DHCP starvation

   d. VLAN hopping

   e. STP manipulation

2. You can mitigate a CAM table overflow attack by which of the following?

   a. Enabling port security

   b. Enabling ARP proxy

   c. Disabling STP

   d. Disabling port security

3. Dynamic port security is an administratively scalable solution for the switch.

   a. True

   b. False

4. Which of the following commands enable you to enter the optional secure MAC address for an interface?

   a. switch(config)# **switchport port-security mac-address** *mac_address*

   b. switch(config-if)# **switchport port-security mac-address** *mac_address*

   c. switch(config-if)# **port-security mac-address** *mac_address*

   d. switch(config-if)# **switchport mac-address** *mac_address*

5. What are the two ways to check port security configuration? (Choose two.)

   a. switch#**show port-security interface** *interface_id*

   b. switch#**show port-security** *address interface_id*

   c. switch#**show port-security** *address*

   d. switch#**show port-security** *interface address*

6. Attackers can maliciously exploit GARP to do what?

a. Spoof the identity of a spanning-tree BPDU on a LAN segment.

b. Spoof the identity of an SNMP object on a LAN segment

c. Spoof the identity of an IP address on a LAN segment

d. Spoof the identity of an MAC address on a LAN segment

7. The DHCP snooping binding table contains which of the following?

a. The MAC address, IP address, lease time, binding type, dhcp pool name, VLAN number, and interface information corresponding to the local untrusted interfaces of a switch

b. The MAC address, IP address, lease time, binding type, dhcp pool name, VLAN number, and interface information corresponding to the local trusted interfaces of a switch

c. The MAC address, IP address, lease time, binding type, VLAN number, and interface information corresponding to the local trusted interfaces of a switch

d. The MAC address, IP address, lease time, binding type, VLAN number, and interface information corresponding to the local untrusted interfaces of a switch

8. Dynamic ARP Inspection (DAI) determines the validity of an ARP and GARP packet based on the valid MAC address-to-IP address bindings stored in an ARP/GARP database.

a. True

b. False

9. Which of the following is not a security best practice for VLANs and trunking?

a. Always use a dedicated VLAN ID for all trunk ports.

b. Disable unused ports and put them in an unused VLAN.

c. Be paranoid: Do not use VLAN 1 for anything.

d. Enable auto-trunking on user-facing ports (DTP on).

e. Explicitly configure trunking on infrastructure ports.

f. Use all tagged mode for the native VLAN on trunks.

10. To mitigate Spanning Tree Protocol manipulation, use the root guard and the BPDU guard features to enforce the placement of the root bridge in the network and enforce the Spanning Tree Protocol domain borders.

a. True

b. False

CHAPTER 1

Intrusion Detection and Prevention Technology

Upon completion of this chapter, you should be able to answer the following questions:

- What are the basics of intrusion detection and prevention?

- What is an inspection engine?

- What are IDS and IPS devices?

Key Terms

This chapter uses the following key terms. You can find the definitions in the glossary at the end of the book.

Intrusion detection   page 456

Intrusion prevention   page 456

Host-based intrusion   page 457

Network intrusion detection   page 458

Signature-based detection   page 460

Anomaly detection   page 462

Intrusion detection is the ability to detect attacks against a network. *Intrusion prevention* takes this ability further by stopping attacks against the network. This chapter introduces the basic concepts of intrusion prevention and detection. The basic types of inspection engines used in an intrusion detection system (IDS) and an intrusion prevention system (IPS) are discussed, too. The chapter concludes with an introduction to the IDS and IPS devices that are part of the Cisco Self-Defending Network solution.

Introduction to Intrusion Detection and Prevention

Intrusion detection is the ability to identify malicious attacks on network and host resources and send logs to a management console.

An IDS is similar to a generic packet sniffer. It reads all the packets off of the wire, but it also compares these packets against known attack patterns. These patterns are known as *signatures*.

On the other hand, intrusion prevention is the ability to stop attacks against the network and should provide the following active defense mechanisms:

- **Detection**—Identifies malicious attacks on network and host resources
- **Prevention**—Stops the detected attack from executing
- **Reaction**—Immunizes the system from future attacks from a malicious source

You can implement either technology at a network level, host level, or both for maximum protection.

When a signature match is found, the IDS or IPS can perform the following actions:

- **Alarm**—Sends alarms to an internal or external log and then forwards the packet through
- **Reset**—Sends packets with a reset flag to both session participants if TCP forwards the packet
- **Drop**—Immediately drops the packet
- **Block**—Denies traffic from the source address of the attack

Note

Recommended practice is to use the drop and reset actions together to ensure that the attack is terminated.

Network Based Versus Host Based

Two basic types of IDSs in the market today are as follows:

- Host-based IDSs (HIDS)
- Network-based IDSs (NIDS)

Host-Based Intrusion Technology

Host-based intrusion response is typically implemented as inline or passive technology depending on the vendor. The passive technology, which was the first-generation technology, is called host-based intrusion detection system (HIDS), which basically sends logs after the attack has occurred and the damage is done. The inline technology, called host-based intrusion prevention system (HIPS), actually stops the attack and prevents damage and propagation of worms and viruses.

Active detection can be set to shut down the network connection or to stop the impacted services automatically. This has the benefit of being able to quickly analyze an event and take corrective action. Cisco provides HIPS via the Cisco Security Agent software.

Current HIPS software requires agent software to be installed on each host, either server or desktop, to monitor activity performed on and against the host. The agent software performs the intrusion detection analysis and prevention. The agent software also sends logs and alerts to a centralized management/policy server.

HIDS is software that you run on each host you want to protect. The software then watches system logs, processes in memory, file changes, and so on for signs of an intrusion. A HIDS tends to be more work, and more expensive, because there are more pieces to deploy. They also tend to be more accurate because they have the benefit of watching more than just traffic on the wire. HIDS also proves useful in a switched environment when network monitoring is not possible. HIDS is also highly recommended for those systems that you really want to secure as tightly as possible.

The advantage of HIPS is that it can monitor operating system processes and protect critical system resources, including files that might exist only on that specific host. This means it can notify network managers when some external process tries to modify a system file in a way that may include a hidden backdoor program.

Figure 1-1 illustrates a typical HIPS deployment. Agents are installed on publicly accessible servers and corporate mail and application servers. The agents report events to a central console server, such as CiscoWorks VPN/Security Management Solution (VMS), located inside the corporate firewall or can e-mail an administrator.

Vendors of host security include Cisco Systems, Symantec, Internet Security Systems (ISS), and Enterasys.

Figure 1-1   Host-Based Intrusion Detection

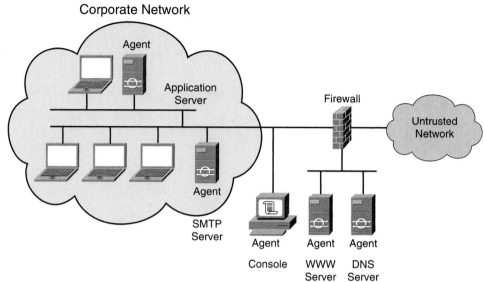

Network-Based Intrusion Technology

Just like host-based intrusion technology, a ***network intrusion detection*** system can be based on active or passive detection. Figure 1-2 illustrates a typical network deployment of intrusion technology. Sensors are deployed at network entry points that protect critical network segments. The network segments have both internal and external corporate resources. Sensors capture and analyze the traffic as it traverses the network. Sensors are typically tuned for intrusion detection analysis. The underlying operating system is stripped of unnecessary network services, and essential services are secured. The sensors report to a central director server located inside the corporate firewall.

Types of Alarms

By definition, every IDS must generate some type of alarm to signal when intrusive activity has been detected on the network. No IDS, however, is 100 percent accurate. This inaccuracy means that an IDS will generate some alarms that do not correspond to actual intrusive activity, and potentially fail to alarm when an actual attack occurs. IDS alarms fall into the two categories: false alarms and true alarms.

Figure 1-2   Network-Based Intrusion Detection

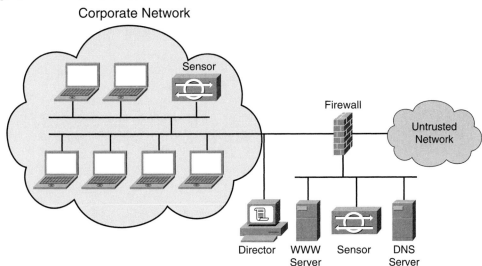

False Alarms

The first broad category of IDS alarms is known as false alarms. These alarms represent situations in which the IDS fails to accurately indicate what is happening on the network. False alarms fall into two major categories: false positives and false negatives.

False Positives

One of the most common terms associated with IDS alarms is a false positive. False positives occur when the IDS generates an alarm based on normal network activity. False positives force administrators to waste time and resources analyzing phantom attacks. Over time, these false positives can also desensitize security personnel so that when a real alarm comes in, it is ignored or slowly processed. A good analogy is a home burglar alarm that goes off accidentally. Each time it goes off, the police respond. If too many false alarms occur, the police might impose a fine. Also, after numerous false alarms, police response time could diminish significantly.

False Negatives

When the IDS fails to generate an alarm for known intrusive activity, it is called a false negative. False negatives represent actual attacks that the IDS missed even though it is programmed to detect the attack. Most IDS developers tend to design their systems to prevent false negatives. It is difficult, however, to totally eliminate false negatives. Nevertheless, false negatives represent a serious risk to network security because they enable an attacker to launch an attack against the network undetected.

A situation in which a specific attack does not generate the appropriate alarm usually represents a software bug. Before reporting this to the vendor using their reporting policy, the administrator needs to make sure that the false negative was not generated because the IDS is saturated with traffic and dropping packets.

True Alarms

The second broad category of IDS alarms is known as true alarms. These alarms represent situations in which the IDS accurately indicates what is happening on the network. True alarms also fall into two major categories: true positives and true negatives.

True Positives

The opposite of a false negative alarm is a true positive alarm. In the case of true positives, the IDS generates an alarm correctly in response to actually detecting the attack traffic that a signature is designed to detect. In an ideal world, 100 percent of the alarms generated by an IDS would be true positives, meaning that every alarm corresponds to an actual attack against the network. To be effective, the number of attacks missed by an IDS should be extremely low. In most cases, it is preferable to have a signature generate a small number of false positives instead of letting any actual attacks get through undetected.

True Negatives

The last alarm classification is a true negative. Like false negatives, true negatives do not represent actual alarms that are generated by the IDS. Instead, a true negative represents a situation in which an IDS signature does not alarm when it is examining normal user traffic. This is the correct behavior. This makes a true negative the opposite of a false positive. When IDS signatures are well written, they do not frequently generate alarms on normal user activity. On the other hand, poorly written or poorly tuned signatures can lead to numerous false positives. Again, in an ideal world, normal user traffic would not cause an IDS to generate an alarm, but false positives do occur. If the IDS generates too many false positives, its credibility begins to suffer.

Inspection Engines

This section looks at signature-based detection, types of signatures, and anomaly-based detection.

Signature-Based Detection

At a basic level, *signature-based detection* can be compared to virus-checking programs (see Figure 1-3). IDS vendors produce and build signatures that the IDS system uses to compare against activity on the network or host. When a match is found, the IDS takes action. The actions taken could include logging the event or sending an alarm to a management console. Although many vendors allow users to configure existing signatures and create new ones, customers are primarily dependent on the vendors to provide the latest signatures to keep the IDS current.

Signature-based detection can also produce false positives, because certain normal network activity can appear to be malicious. For example, some network applications or operating systems might send out numerous Internet Control Message Protocol (ICMP) messages, which a signature-based detection system might interpret as an attempt by an attacker to map out a network segment.

Figure 1-3   IDS Signature Match

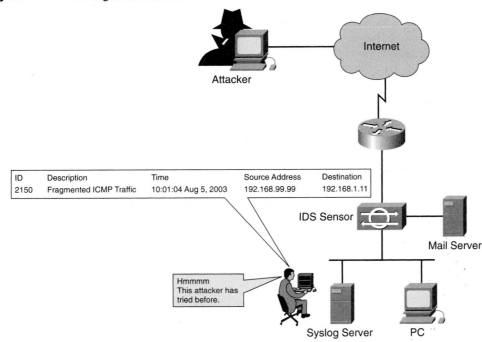

Types of Signatures

IDS signatures can be classified by how many packets it takes for the sensor to positively identify an alarm condition on the network. The two classifications are atomic signatures and compound signatures. Atomic signatures require only one packet to be inspected to identify an alarm condition. Composite signatures require multiple packets to be inspected to identify an alarm condition. The storage of state information between the multiple packets is required to analyze traffic for compound signatures.

IDS signatures can also be categorized as either info or attack signatures. An info signature detects information-gathering activity, such as a port sweep. An attack signature detects attacks attempted into the protected network, such as denial-of-service attempts or the execution of illegal commands during an FTP session.

Anomaly-Based Detection

Anomaly detection is also sometimes referred to as profile-based detection. With anomaly detection, the administrator must build profiles for each user group on the system. This profile incorporates typical user habits, the services normally used, and other relevant information. This profile defines the behavior characteristics for a user group, in essence establishing a baseline for the activities that a normal user routinely does to perform the job. Whenever a user deviates too far from the profile, the IDS generates an alarm.

Building and updating these profiles represents a significant portion of the work required to deploy an anomaly-based IDS. The quality of the profiles directly relates to how successful an IDS will be at detecting attacks against the network.

Anomaly detection provides the following advantages:

- Enables tunable control over false positives

- Detects previously unpublished attacks

The main advantage of anomaly detection is that the alarms are not based on signatures for specific known attacks. Instead, they are based on a profile that defines normal user activity. Therefore, an anomaly-based IDS can generate alarms for previously unpublished attacks, as long as the new attack deviates from normal user activity. This results in the anomaly-based IDS being capable of detecting new attacks the first time that they are used.

The main problem with an anomaly-based IDS is that people tend to vary their activities. They do not always follow the same exact patterns repeatedly. When users deviate from the normal routine, the IDS generates an alarm if this activity falls to far away from normal. The IDS generates this alarm even though no intrusive activity actually takes place.

The definition of *normal* also changes over the life of the network. As the network changes, the traffic considered normal can also change. If this happens, you must update the user profiles to reflect those changes. For a network that changes constantly, updating user profiles can become a major challenge.

Cisco IDS and IPS Devices

This section provides a quick look at some Cisco IDS and IPS devices, some Cisco integrated solutions, and the Cisco IPS 4200 series sensors.

Cisco Integrated Solutions

Cisco intrusion detection and prevention solutions are part of the Cisco Self-Defending Network. Designed to identify and stop worms, network viruses, and other malicious traffic, these solutions can help protect the network. Cisco provides a broad array of solutions for intrusion detection and prevention at both the network and at the endpoint.

Cisco IOS Intrusion Prevention System (IPS)

Cisco IOS Intrusion Prevention System (IPS) is an inline, deep-packet inspection-based solution that helps enable Cisco IOS Software to effectively mitigate a wide range of network attacks without compromising router performance, as shown in Figure 1-4. With the intelligence and performance to accurately identify, classify, and stop malicious or damaging traffic in real time, Cisco IOS IPS is a core component of the Self-Defending Network, enabling the network to defend itself. The alarms from the Cisco IOS Firewall router can be sent to multiple destinations. The logs can be sent to the router's internal buffer, a syslog server, or a Cisco IDS director server.

Figure 1-4   Cisco IOS Firewall IPS

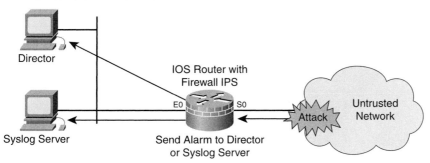

Although it is common practice to defend against head-end attacks by inspecting traffic and installing firewalls, it is also critical to stop malicious traffic close to its entry point by protecting the branch offices. Deploying inline Cisco IOS IPS at the branch enables gateways to drop traffic, send an alarm, or reset the connection as needed to stop attacking traffic at the point of origination and quickly remove unwanted traffic from the network.

PIX and ASA Security Appliances

The PIX Security Appliance and Adaptive Security Appliances are a key element in the overall Cisco end-to-end security solution. The Cisco Security Appliances provide integrated inline intrusion detection and prevention. PIX Software Version 5.2 and later support intrusion detection. The intrusion detection and prevention capabilities of the Adaptive Security Appliance 5500 series can be increased through the addition of a Cisco ASA Advanced Inspection and Prevention Security Services Module (AIP-SSM).

Cisco IDS Network Module

The Cisco IDS Network Module for the Cisco 2600XM, 3600, and 3700 series routers is part of the Cisco IDS Family sensor portfolio and the Cisco Intrusion Protection System, as shown in Figure 1-5. These IDS sensors work in concert with the other IDS components, including Cisco IDS Management Console, CiscoWorks VMS, and Cisco IDS Device Manager, to efficiently protect the data and information infrastructure. Cisco IDS network modules fit into a single network module slot on the Cisco 2600XM series, Cisco 3600, and Cisco 3700 series platforms. The IDS Network Module includes a 20-gigabyte hard disk for logging and storage of events. The external Ethernet port is used for command and control to enable a secure outbound port for management. This setup also allows for both security operations and network operations to have their own command and control interfaces. Each sensor addresses the bandwidth requirements of different routers up to 10 Mbps in the Cisco 2600XM and up to 45 Mbps in the Cisco 3700 series.

Figure 1-5   Cisco IDS Network Module

Intrusion Detection System Services Module (IDSM-2)

The Cisco IDSM-2 protects switched environments by integrating full-featured IPS functions directly into the network infrastructure through the Cisco Catalyst chassis, as shown in Figure 1-6. This integration enables the user to monitor traffic directly off the switch backplane. The IDSM-2 is a one-rack-unit module that you can install in any one slot in the Cisco Catalyst 6500/7600 chassis.

Figure 1-6   Intrusion Detection System Services Module (ISDM-2)

Cisco IPS 4200 Series Sensors

Cisco IPS 4200 series IPS sensors are an important component of the Cisco Self-Defending Network, as shown in Figure 1-7. Cisco IPS sensors offer significant protection to the network by helping to detect, classify, and stop threats, including worms, spyware/adware, network viruses, and application abuse. Administrators can stop more threats with greater confidence with the help of the following elements:

- **Multivector threat identification**—Detailed inspection of Layer 2 through 7 traffic protects the network from policy violations, vulnerability exploitations, and anomalous activity.

- **Accurate prevention technologies**—The Cisco innovative Risk Rating feature and Meta Event Generator provide the confidence to take preventive actions on a broader range of threats without the risk of dropping legitimate traffic.

- **Unique network collaboration**—Network collaboration provides enhanced scalability, up to 8 Gbps, and resiliency, including efficient traffic-capture techniques, load-balancing capabilities, and visibility into encrypted traffic.

- **Comprehensive deployment and management solutions**—Cisco IPS 4200 series sensors are purpose-built IPS appliances that provide the following:

  — Protection of multiple network subnets through the use of up to eight interfaces

  — Simultaneous, dual operation in both promiscuous and inline modes

  — A wide array of performance options, from 80 Mbps to multiple gigabits

  — Embedded web-based management solutions packaged with the sensor

Figure 1-7   Cisco IPS 4240

Summary

This chapter introduced the concepts of intrusion detection and prevention. You should now understand the basic differences between an IDS and an IPS. The basic types of inspection engines were also introduced in this chapter. The chapter concluded with an introduction to the IDS and IPS devices that are part of the Cisco Self-Defending Network solution.

Check Your Understanding

Complete all the review questions listed here to test your understanding of the topics and concepts in this chapter. Answers are listed in Appendix A, "Check Your Understanding Answer Key."

1. Intrusion detection and intrusion prevention can be implemented at what level(s)?

   a. Network level

   b. Host level

   c. Both levels

   d. Neither level

2. When a signature match is found, the IDS or IPS may perform which of the following actions?

   a. Alarm, reset, ignore, or queue

   b. Alarm, reset, drop, or block

   c. Alarm, ignore, drop, or block

   d. Combine, ignore, drop, or block

3. By definition, every IDS must generate some type of alarm to signal when intrusive activity has been detected on the network. What are the two categories of alarms?

   a. True and false

   b. Critical and noncritical

   c. Audio and visual

   d. Single and recurring

4. IDS signatures can be classified by how many packets it takes for the sensor to positively identify an alarm condition on the network. What are the two classifications?

   a. Atomic signatures and compound signatures

   b. Mandatory signatures and optional signatures

   c. True signatures and false signatures

   d. Single signatures and multiple signatures

5. Anomaly detection is also sometimes referred to as profile-based detection. With anomaly detection, the administrator must build profiles for each user group on the system.

   a. True

   b. False

CHAPTER 2

Configure Network Intrusion Detection and Prevention

Upon completion of this chapter, you should be able to answer the following questions:

- What are the basics of the Cisco IOS Intrusion Prevention System?

- How do you configure attack guards on the PIX Security Appliance?

- How do you configure intrusion prevention on the PIX Security Appliance?

- How do you configure shunning on the PIX Security Appliance?

Key Terms

This chapter uses the following key terms. You can find the definitions in the glossary at the end of the book.

Cisco IOS Intrusion Prevention System (IPS)
  page 470

Attack guards   page 470

Intrusion detection   page 470

Shunning   page 470

Signature definition file (SDF)   page 473

Signature micro-engines (SMEs)   page 474

The Security Wheel not only requires the application of security measures on the network; most important, it provides a continual process for monitoring, testing, and improving security measures. The security policy is the centerpiece of the Security Wheel. One method to assist administrators with this cycle is the proper implementation and configuration of the *Cisco IOS Intrusion Prevention System (IPS)*.

The current Cisco IOS IPS monitors and detects more than 1600 of the most common attacks using signatures to detect patterns of misuse in network traffic. The IPS can automatically reset, drop, or alert an administrator about a suspicious packet. In addition, IPS enables you to configure, disable, and exclude signatures.

This chapter also discusses a series of *attack guards* that are part of the PIX Security Appliance feature set. These special techniques can prevent many problems that surround popular services such as mail (Simple Network Management Protocol [SMTP]) and Domain Name Service (DNS).

PIX Security Appliance *intrusion detection* functionality is also discussed. The system of intrusion detection signatures is examined, and the methods of configuration for PIX Security Appliances are explained. The process of dropping attacking packets and potentially threatening packets is called *shunning*. Shunning is discussed, along with configuration examples.

Cisco IOS Intrusion Prevention System (IPS)

The Cisco IOS IPS with inline intrusion capabilities provides an inline, deep-packet-inspection-based IPS solution that helps enable Cisco routers to effectively mitigate a wide range of network attacks without compromising traffic forwarding performance. Cisco IOS IPS can accurately identify, classify, and stop malicious or damaging traffic in real time and is a core component of the Cisco Self-Defending Network.

Cisco IOS IPS capabilities include the ability to dynamically load and enable selected IPS signatures in real time, support for more than 1600 signatures supported by Cisco IPS sensor platforms, and the ability for an administrator to modify an existing signature or create a new signature to address newly discovered threats.

The Cisco IOS IPS acts as an inline IPS sensor, watching packets and sessions as they flow through the router and scanning each packet to match any of the Cisco IOS IPS signatures. When it detects suspicious activity, it responds before network security can be compromised and logs the event through syslog or Security Device Event Exchange (SDEE). The network administrator can configure the Cisco IOS IPS to choose the appropriate response to various threats, as depicted in Figure 2-1.

Figure 2-1   Cisco IOS Intrusion Prevention System

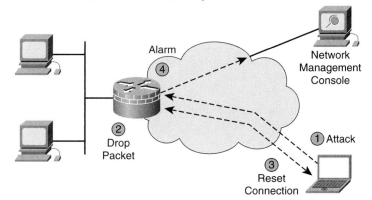

When packets in a session match a signature, the Cisco IOS IPS can take any of the following actions, as appropriate:

- Send an alarm to a syslog server or a centralized management interface
- Drop the packet
- Reset the connection

The features and benefits of the Cisco IOS IPS are as follows:

- **Uses the underlying routing infrastructure**—Provides an additional layer of security with investment protection.

- **Ubiquitous protection of network assets**—Cisco IOS IPS is supported on a broad range of Cisco routers, enabling the administrator to protect network users and assets deep into the network architecture. The router is a security enforcer.

- **Inline deep packet inspection**—Cisco IOS IPS enables administrators to stop known network attacks. By alerting the router to an event, Cisco IOS IPS will intercept intrusion attempts as they traverse the router. Cisco IPS uses deep packet inspection to get into the payload of a packet and uncover the known malicious activity.

- **IPS signature support**—Cisco IOS IPS can now be enabled with any of the more than 1600 IPS signatures supported by the Cisco IDS sensors to mitigate today's know network attacks. As attacks are identified in the Internet, these signatures are updated and posted to Cisco.com so that they can be downloaded to the Cisco router.

- **Customized signature support**—Cisco IOS IPS can now customize existing signatures, while also creating new ones. This Day 1 capability mitigates attacks that try to capitalize on slight deviations of known or newly discovered attacks. Newly discovered attacks are known as zero-day attacks.

- **Parallel signature scanning**—Cisco IOS IPS uses a Parallel Signature Scanning Engine to scan for multiple patterns within a signature micro-engine (SME) at any given time. IPS signatures are no longer scanned on a serial basis.

- **Named and numbered extended ACL support**—Prior to Cisco IOS Software Release 12.3(8)T, only standard, numbered access control lists (ACLs) were supported. Cisco IOS IPS now supports both named and numbered extended ACLs by using one of the **ip ips** *ips-name* **list** *access-list* or **ip ips signature** *signature-id* **list** *acl-list* commands.

Cisco developed the Cisco IOS Software-based IPS capabilities and Cisco IOS Firewall with flexibility in mind, so that individual signatures could be disabled in case of false positives. Generally, it is preferable to enable both the Cisco IOS Firewall and Cisco IOS IPS to support network security policies. However, firewall and IPS capabilities may be enabled independently and on different router interfaces.

Origin of Cisco IOS IPS

Cisco IOS IPS restructures the existing Cisco IOS Software Intrusion Detection System (IDS). The primary difference between Cisco IOS Software IDS and the new, enhanced Cisco IOS IPS is that an intrusion detection system monitors traffic and sends an alert when suspicious patterns are detected; whereas an intrusion prevention system can drop traffic, send an alarm, or reset the connection, enabling the router to mitigate and protect against threats in real time. Cisco IOS IPS inherited the built-in 132 signatures from Cisco IOS Software IDS technology. With the introduction of inline IPS capability, new signatures can be added by downloading a signature definition file (SDF) into the Flash memory of the router, or administrators can specify the location of the SDF in the Cisco IOS IPS configuration on the router.

Router Performance

The performance impact of intrusion prevention depends on the number of signatures enabled, the level of traffic on the router, the router platform, and other individual features enabled on the router, such as encryption. Because the router is being used as a security device, no packet is allowed to bypass the security mechanisms. The IPS process in the router sits directly in the packet path and searches each packet for signature matches. In some cases, the entire packet needs to be searched, and state information and even application state and awareness must be maintained by the router.

Cisco IOS IPS Signatures

The Cisco IOS IPS now identifies more than 700 of the most common attacks using signatures to detect patterns of misuse in network traffic. The intrusion prevention signatures were chosen from a broad cross-section of intrusion prevention signatures. The signatures represent severe breaches of security and the most common network attacks and information-gathering scans.

Signatures

As of Release 12.3(8)T, Cisco IOS IPS has 132 built-in signatures available in the Cisco IOS Software image. The built-in signatures are hard-coded into the Cisco IOS Software image for backward compatibility. Each signature can be set to send an alarm, drop the connection, or reset the connection:

- **Alarm**—This option sends a notification about the attack via syslog, post office, or SDEE protocol.

- **TCP reset**—This option is effective for TCP-based connections and sends a reset to both the source and destination addresses. For example, in case of a half-open SYN attack, Cisco IOS IPS can reset the TCP connections.

- **Drop**—This option discards the packet without sending a reset. By default, the 132 built-in signatures are set to alarm only.

Each action is enabled on a per-signature basis. Each signature has an action assigned by default, based on the severity of the signature.

In addition, Cisco IOS IPS can download IPS signatures without the need for a Cisco IOS Software image update. At the time of this writing, Cisco IOS IPS supports more than 740 signatures. Typically, new signatures are released every two weeks, with emergency signature updates posted as needed. The signatures are posted to Cisco.com. A valid CCO login is required to access the site.

The Nimda virus, for example, can be detected by loading and enabling the following signatures:

Signature ID: 5081:0 WWW WinNT cmd.exe access

Signature ID: 5114:2 WWW IIS Unicode attack

Signature ID: 5326:0 root.exe access

The Signature Definition File

The *signature definition file (SDF)* is integral to Cisco IOS IPS. The SDF is an Extensible Markup Language (XML) file with a definition of each signature along with relevant configurable actions. Cisco IOS IPS reads in the SDF, parses the XML, and populates its internal tables with the information necessary to detect each signature. The SDF contains the signature definition and configuration. Actions such as alarm, drop, or reset can be selected for individual signatures within the SDF. You can modify the SDF so that the router detects only specific signatures. As a result, it can contain all or a subset of the signatures supported in Cisco IOS IPS. The administrator specifies the location of the SDF. The SDF can reside on the local Flash file system (the recommended option or on a remote server. Remote servers can be accessed via TFTP, FTP, Secure Copy Protocol (SCP), or Remote Copy Protocol (RCP). After signatures are loaded and complied onto a router running Cisco IOS IPS, the IPS can begin detecting the new signatures immediately.

Signature Micro-Engines

Cisco IOS IPS uses *signature micro-engines (SMEs)* to load the SDF and scan signatures. Each engine categorizes a group of signatures, and each signature detects patterns of misuse in network traffic. For example, all HTTP signatures are grouped under the HTTP engine. Currently, Cisco IOS IPS supports more than 740 signatures. These signatures are part of the common set of signatures that Cisco IDS sensors support, helping to ensure that all Cisco products use a common resource and are available for download from Cisco.com.

Signatures contained within the SDF are handled by a variety of SMEs. The SDF typically contains signature definitions for multiple engines. The SME typically corresponds to the protocol in which the signature occurs and looks for malicious activity in that protocol. A packet is processed by several SMEs. Each SME scans for various conditions that can lead to a signature pattern match. When an SME scans the packets, it extracts certain values, searching for patterns within the packet via the regular expression engine.

attack-drop.sdf

The attack-drop.sdf file is available in Flash on all Cisco access routers shipped with Cisco IOS Release 12.3(8)T or later. The attack-drop.sdf file can then be loaded directly from Flash into the Cisco IOS IPS system. If Flash is erased, the attack-drop.sdf file might have also been erased (which might happen when erasing the contents of Flash memory before copying a new Cisco IOS image to Flash). If this occurs, the router refers to the built-in signatures within the Cisco IOS image.

Cisco IOS IPS Configuration Tasks

To configure the Cisco IOS IPS on a router and to have it report alarms to a syslog server or using SDEE, complete the following tasks:

Step 1.   Install Cisco IOS IPS on the router.

a. Specify the location of the SDF.

b. Create an IPS rule.

c. (Optional) Attach a policy to a signature.

d. Apply the IPS rule at an interface.

Step 2.   Configure logging using syslog or SDEE.

Step 3.   Verify the configuration. This includes using the available **show**, **clear**, and **debug** commands for the Cisco IOS IPS.

Install the Cisco IOS IPS

This section describes the procedure used to install the Cisco IOS IPS.

Use this procedure to install the latest Cisco IOS IPS signatures on a router for the first time. This procedure enables the administrator to load the default built-in signatures or the attack-drop.sdf file, but not both. To merge the two signature files, the administrator must load the default built-in signatures as described in this procedure. Then, the default signatures can be merged with the attack-drop.sdf file. For example, to specify location of SDF, use the following:

```
Router(config)# ip ips sdf location url
*(Optional) Specifies the location in which the router will load the SDF, attack-drop.sdf
*If this command is not issued, the router will load the default, built-in signatures.
Router(config)# ip ips sdf location disk2:attack-drop.sdf
```

Step 1. Create a named IPS rule that will be applied to an interface later:

```
Router(config)# ip ips name ips-name [list acl]
*creates an IPS rule
Router(config)# ip ips name MYIPS
*Creates an IPS rule named MYIPS that will be applied to an interface.
```

Step 2. Attach the policy to a given signature if desired:

```
Router(config)# ip ips signature signature-id [:sub-signature-id] {delete |
disable | list acl-list}
*attaches a policy to a given signature
Router(config)# ip ips signature 1000 disable
*Disables signature 1000 in the signature definition file.
```

Step 3. At this point, interface configuration mode is entered for the interface where the Cisco IOS IPS will be implemented:

```
router(config)# interface fastethernet 0/1
```

Step 4. The **ip ips** *ips-name* {**in** | **out**} command applies an IPS rule at an interface. This command automatically loads the signatures and builds the signature engines:

```
Router(config-if)# ip ips ips-name [in | out]
*Applies an IPS rule at an interface.
Router(config-if)# ip ips MYIPS in
```

Upgrade to the Latest SDF

An important part of IPS is keeping up with the latest attack signatures. The attack signatures in the router should be kept current with the latest IPS signature file, attack-drop.sdf. The following example shows the commands involved:

```
Router(config)# ip ips name ips-name
*creates an IPS rule
Router(config)# no ip ips sdf builtin
*Instructs the router not to load the built-in signatures
```

Note

Whenever signatures are replaced or merged, the router prompt is suspended while the signature engines for the newly added or merged signatures are being built. The router prompt is available again after the engines have been built. Depending on the platform and how many signatures are being loaded, building the engine can take up to several seconds. It is recommended that logging messages are enabled to monitor the engine building status.

```
Router(config)# ip ips fail closed
```
*instructs the router to drop all packets until the signature engine is built and ready
to scan traffic
```
Router(config-if)# ip ips ips-name {in | out} [list acl]
```
*Applies an IPS rule at an interface. This command automatically loads the signatures
and builds the signature engines.

Support for ip audit Commands

The latest IPS image reads and converts all commands that begin with the words **ip audit** to **ip ips**. For example, the **ip ips** notify command replaces the **ip audit notify** command. If the **ip audit notify** command is part of an existing configuration, the IPS interprets it as the **ip ips notify** command. Although IPS accepts the **audit** keyword, it generates the **ips** keyword when the configuration is shown. Also, if the help character (?) is issued, the command-line interface (CLI) displays the **ips** keyword rather than the **audit** keyword, and the Tab key used for command completion will not recognize the **audit** keyword.

Configure Logging Using Syslog or SDEE

As of Cisco IOS Software Release 12.3(11)T, Cisco IOS IPS provides two methods to report IPS intrusion alerts: Cisco IOS logging (syslog) and Security Device Event Exchange (SDEE), as shown in Figure 2-2.

Figure 2-2   Monitoring Cisco IOS IPS Signatures

Note

Effective Cisco IOS Software Release 12.3(11)T, the Post Office Protocol is no longer supported.

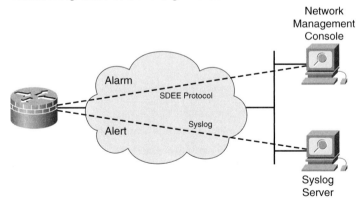

SDEE is a new standard that specifies the format of messages and protocol used to communicate events generated by security devices, such as the exchange of IPS messages between IPS clients and IPS servers. Some of the benefits of SDEE are as follows:

- **Vendor interoperability**—SDEE will become the standard format for all vendors to communicate events to a network management application. This lowers the cost of supporting proprietary vendors' formats and potentially multiple network management platforms.

- **Secured transport**—The use of HTTP over SSL instead of HTTP ensures that data is secured as it traverses the network.

SDEE is flexible, which means all vendors can support address compatibility. This flexibility allows mixed IPS vendor environments to have one network management alert interface. ICSA is currently proposing as the unified industry protocol format for all vendors to communicate with network management applications. SDEE uses a pull mechanism, meaning that requests come from the network management application and the IPS/IPS router responds. SDEE uses HTTP and XML to provide a standardized interface. The Cisco IOS IPS router will still send IPS alerts via syslog.

SDEE is always running, but it does not receive and process events from IPS unless SDEE notification is enabled. If it is not enabled and a client sends a request, SDEE responds with a fault response message, indicating that notification is not enabled.

Storing SDEE Events in the Buffer

When SDEE notification is enabled using the **ip ips notify sdee** command, two hundred events can automatically be stored in the buffer. When SDEE notification is disabled, all stored events are lost. A new buffer is allocated when the notifications are reenabled.

When specifying the size of an events buffer, note the following functionality:

- It is circular. When the end of the buffer is reached, the buffer starts overwriting the earliest stored events. If overwritten events have not yet been reported, a buffer overflow notice is received.

- If a new, smaller buffer is requested, all events stored in the previous buffer are lost.

- If a new, larger buffer is requested, all existing events are saved.

SDEE Prerequisites

To use SDEE, the HTTP server must be enabled with the **ip http server** command. If the HTTP server is not enabled, the router cannot respond to the SDEE clients because it cannot not see the requests.

To specify the method of event notification, use the **ip ips notify** command in global configuration mode. To disable event notification, use the **no** form of this command, as shown here:

```
Router(config)#ip ips notify [log | sdee]
*Sets notification type
Router(config)# ip ips notify sdee
Router(config)#ip ips notify log
Router(config)# ip sdee events num_of_events
*Sets the maximum number of SDEE events that can be stored in the event buffer.
```

The default number of events is 100. Raising the number of events past 100 might cause memory and performance impacts because each event in the event queue requires 32 KB of memory.

Verify the IPS Configuration

This section covers the commands that enable the administrator to verify that the configuration is correct. These include the **show**, **clear**, and **debug** commands.

show Commands

To display IPS information such as configured sessions and signatures, use the **show ip ips** command in privileged EXEC mode. Use the **show ip ips configuration** command to display additional configuration information, including default values that might not be displayed using the **show run** command.

Use the **show ip ips interface** command to display the interface configuration. The following are examples of the **show** command:

```
Router# show ip ips configuration
* verifies that Cisco IOS IPS is properly configured.
Router# show ip ips signature [detailed]
*verifies signature configuration, such as signatures that have been disabled
Router# show ip ips interface
*display the interface configuration
```

clear Commands

To disable Cisco IOS IPS, remove all intrusion detection configuration entries and release dynamic resources, use the **clear ip ips configuration** command in EXEC mode.

Use the **clear ip ips statistics** to reset statistics on packets analyzed and alarms sent.

To clear SDEE events or subscriptions, use the **clear ip sdee** command in EXEC configuration mode. The following are some examples in the use of the **clear** commands:

```
Router# clear ip ips configuration
*remove all intrusion prevention configuration entries, and release dynamic resources.
Router# clear ip ips statistics
*reset statistics on packets analyzed and alarms sent
Router# clear ip sde [events | subscriptions]
*clear SDEE events or subscriptions
```

debug Commands

Many **debug** commands are available to troubleshoot and test Cisco IOS IPS configurations. Use the **no** form of the commands to disable debugging a given option. Instead of **no**, you can use **undebug**. The available **debug** commands are as follows:

```
Router# debug ip ips timer
Router# debug ip ips object-creation
Router# debug ip ips object-deletion
Router# debug ip ips function trace
```

```
Router# debug ip ips detailed
Router# debug ip ips ftp-cmd
Router# debug ip ips ftp-token
Router# debug ip ips icmp
Router# debug ip ips ip
Router# debug ip ips rpc
Router# debug ip ips smtp
Router# debug ip ips tcp
Router# debug ip ips tftp
Router# debug ip ips udp
```

 Lab 12.1.6   Configure a Router with the Cisco IOS Intrusion Prevention System

In this lab activity, you learn how to initialize IPS on the router. You also disable and exclude signatures. You then create and apply audit rules. After the IPS configuration is complete, you verify the IPS configuration on the router and generate a test message.

Configure Attack Guards on the PIX Security Appliance

This section looks at how to configure attack guards, such as Mail Guard, DNS Guard, FragGuard and Virtual Reassembly, AAA Flood Guard, SYN Flood Guard, and connection limits on the PIX Security Appliance.

Mail Guard

Mail Guard provides a safe conduit for SMTP connections from the outside to an inside e-mail server. Mail Guard enables a mail server to be deployed within the internal network without it being exposed to known security problems with some mail server implementations.

When configured, Mail Guard allows only seven SMTP commands as specified in RFC 821 section 4.5.1: HELO, MAIL, RCPT, DATA, RSET, NOOP, and QUIT. Other commands, such as KILL, WIZ, and so forth, are intercepted by the PIX Security Appliance and are never sent to the mail server inside the network. The PIX responds with an OK even to denied commands, so that attackers will not know that their attempts are being thwarted.

By default, the PIX Security Appliance inspects port 25 connections for SMTP traffic. If there are SMTP servers on the network that are using ports other than port 25, you must use the **fixup protocol smtp** command to have the PIX inspect these other ports for SMTP traffic.

Use the **no fixup protocol smtp** command to disable the inspection of traffic on the indicated port for SMTP connections. If the **fixup protocol smtp** command is not enabled for a given port, potential mail server vulnerabilities are exposed.

Using the **no fixup protocol smtp** command without any arguments causes the PIX Security Appliance to clear all previous **fixup protocol smtp** assignments and set port 25 back as the default.

Version 7 of the Finesse (PIX) Software uses the **ip inspect** function rather than **fixup protocol**.

DNS Guard

In an attempt to resolve a name to an IP address, a host may query the same DNS server multiple times. The DNS Guard feature of the PIX Security Appliance, the mechanics of which Figure 2-3 shows, protects the network from UDP session hijacking attacks, and certain types of denial-of-service (DoS) attacks, by making sure that the appropriate UDP conduit is closed after a client has received a response from the DNS server. DNS Guard is always on by default.

Figure 2-3   DNS Guard

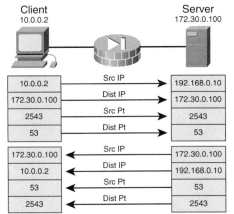

The DNS Guard feature recognizes an outbound DNS query from a client and allows only the first answer from the server back through the PIX. All other replies from the same source are discarded. DNS Guard closes the UDP dynamic conduit opened by the DNS request after the first DNS reply and does not wait for the normal UDP timeout, which by default is 2 minutes.

A host can also query several different DNS servers. The connection to each server is handled separately because each request is sent separately. For example, if the DNS resolver sends three identical queries to three different servers, the PIX Security Appliance creates three different connections. As the PIX receives a reply through each connection, it shuts down that one connection. It does not tear down all three connections because of the first reply. The DNS responses of all servers queried are allowed through the PIX.

FragGuard and Virtual Reassembly

FragGuard and Virtual Reassembly is a PIX Security Appliance feature that provides IP fragment protection. Virtual reassembly is the process of gathering a set of IP fragments, verifying integrity and completeness, tagging each fragment in the set with the transport header, and not combining the fragments into a full IP packet. Virtual reassembly provides the benefits of full reassembly by verifying the integrity of each fragment set and tagging it with the transport header. It also minimizes the buffer space that must be reserved for packet reassembly. Full reassembly of packets is expensive in terms of buffer space that must be reserved for collecting and combining the fragments. Because combining of fragments is not performed with virtual reassembly, no pre-allocation of the buffer is needed.

FragGuard and Virtual Reassembly performs full reassembly of all Internet Control Message Protocol (ICMP) error messages and virtual reassembly of the remaining IP fragments that are routed through the Pix Security Appliance. They use syslog to log any fragment overlapping and small fragment offset anomalies, especially those caused by a Teardrop.c attack.

By default, the PIX Security Appliance accepts up to 24 fragments to reconstruct a full IP packet. Based on the network security policy, an administrator should consider configuring the PIX to prevent fragmented packets from traversing the PIX by entering the **fragment chain 1** interface command on each interface. Setting the limit to 1 means that all packets must be unfragmented.

Note the following regarding fragment configuration:

- The default values limit DoS attacks caused by fragment flooding.

- If an interface is not specified, the command applies to all interfaces.

The **fragment** command provides management of packet fragmentation and improves the compatibility of the PIX Security Appliance with the Network File System (NFS). NFS is a client/server application that enables a computer user to view and optionally store and update files on a remote computer as though they were on the user's own computer. In general, the default values of the **fragment** command should be used. However, if a large percentage of the network traffic through the PIX is NFS, additional tuning might be necessary to avoid database overflow. The general syntax of the **fragment** command is as follows:

```
Pixfirewall(config)# fragment {size | chain | timeout} limit [interface]
```

The syntax that follows demonstrates how to use the **size, chain,** and **timeout** options of the **fragment** command to disallow all fragments through the PIX:

```
Pixfirewall(config)# fragment size database-limit [interface]
*sets the maximum number of packets in the fragment database.
Pixfirewall(config)# fragment chain chain-limit [interface]
*specifies the maximum number of packets into which a full IP packet can be fragmented.
Pixfirewall(config)# fragment timeout seconds [interface]
*specifies the maximum number of seconds that the firewall appliance waits before discarding a packet that is waiting to be reassembled.
```

```
Pixfirewall(config)# fragment size 100 outside
Pixfirewall(config)# fragment chain 20 outside
```

In an environment where the maximum transmission unit (MTU) between the NFS server and client is small, such as a WAN interface, the **chain** option might require additional tuning. In this case, NFS over TCP is highly recommended to improve efficiency.

Setting the *database-limit* of the **size** option to a large value can make the PIX Security Appliance more vulnerable to a DoS attack by fragment flooding. Do not set the *database-limit* equal to or greater than the total number of blocks in the PIX 1550 or 16384 memory pool. See the **show blocks** command for more details.

The **show fragment** command displays the states of the fragment databases. If the interface name is specified, only the database residing at the specified interface displays.

Example 2-1 demonstrates some sample output from the show fragment command.

Example 2-1   The show fragment Command

```
Pixfirewall#show fragment
Interface:  inside
    Size:  200, Chain:  24, Timeout:  5, Threshold:  133
    Queue:  0, Assembled:  0, Fail:  0, Overflow:  0
Interface:  outside
    Size:  200, Chain:  24, Timeout:  5, Threshold:  133
    Queue:  0, Assembled:  0, Fail:  0, Overflow:  0
Interface:  dmz
    Size:  200, Chain:  24, Timeout:  5, Threshold:  133
    Queue:  0, Assembled:  0, Fail:  0, Overflow:  0
```

The following list explains the output of the **show fragment** command:

- **Chain**—Maximum fragments for a single packet set by the **chain** option

- **Timeout**—Maximum seconds set by the **timeout** option

- **Queue**—Number of packets currently awaiting reassembly

- **Assemble**—Number of packets successfully reassembled

- **Fail**—Number of packets that failed to be reassembled

- **Overflow**—Number of packets that overflowed the fragment database

Use the **clear fragment** command to reset the fragment databases and defaults. This causes the PIX Security Appliance to discard all fragments currently waiting for reassembly and to reset the size, chain, and timeout options to their default values.

AAA Flood Guard

DoS attacks are based on the premise of using the resources of a device so extensively that other legitimate traffic is crowded out. For example, when AAA is being used in a network for authentication, a common DoS attack is to send many forged authentication requests to the PIX Security Appliance, thus overwhelming authentication, authorization, and accounting (AAA) resources.

The **floodguard** command enables the PIX Security Appliance to reclaim resources if the user authentication, or uauth, subsystem runs out of resources. If an inbound or outbound uauth connection is being attacked or overused, the PIX actively reclaims TCP resources. When the resources are depleted, the PIX shows messages indicating that it is out of resources or out of TCP users. If the PIX uauth subsystem is depleted, TCP user resources in different states are reclaimed, depending on urgency, in the following order:

1. Timewait

2. FinWait

3. Embryonic

4. Idle

The **floodguard** command is enabled by default:

```
Pixfirewall(config)# floodguard {enable | disable}

*reclaims attacked or overused AAA resources to help prevent DoS attacks on AAA services
(default = enabled).

Pixfirewall(config)# floodguard enable
```

SYN Flood Guard

Protection against various DoS attacks has increased through newer versions of PIX Security Appliance operating systems. Beginning in Version 5.2, TCP Intercept provided for proxy resets of sessions without any knowledge or interference from the destination station. Version 6.2 introduced SYN cookies, which is another proxy verification tool that the PIX operating system uses to validate a new session.

SYN flood attacks, also known as TCP flood or half-open connections attacks, are common DoS attacks perpetrated against IP servers, as shown in Figure 2-4. The attacker spoofs a non-existent source IP address and floods the target with SYN packets pretending to come from the spoofed host. SYN packets to a host are the first step in the three-way handshake of a TCP-type connection. Therefore, the target responds to the SYN packets, as expected, with SYN-ACK packets destined to the spoofed host or hosts. Because these SYN-ACK packets are sent to hosts that do not exist, the target sits and waits for the corresponding ACK packets that never show up. This causes the target to overflow its port buffer with half-open, or embryonic, connections and stop responding to legitimate requests.

Figure 2-4   SYN Flood Attack

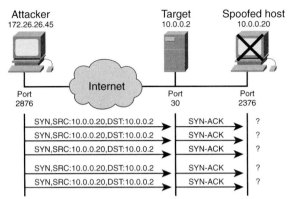

In PIX Security Appliance Software Version 5.2, the SYN Flood Guard feature of the **static** command offers an improved mechanism for protecting systems reachable via a static ACL from TCP SYN attacks. Previously, if an embryonic connection limit was configured in a **static** command statement, the PIX simply dropped new connection attempts when the embryonic threshold was reached. This could allow even a modest attack to stop the web traffic of an organization. For **static** command statements without an embryonic connection limit, the PIX passes all traffic. If the target of an attack has no TCP SYN attack protection or insufficient protection, like most operating systems, the embryonic connection table overloads and all traffic stops.

TCP Intercept

With the TCP Intercept feature available in Versions 5.2 and later, when the optional embryonic connection limit is reached, and until the embryonic connection count falls below this threshold, every SYN bound for the affected server is intercepted, as shown in Figure 2-5. For each SYN, the PIX Security Appliance responds on behalf of the server with an empty SYN/ACK segment. The PIX retains pertinent state information, drops the packet, and waits for the acknowledgment from the client. If the ACK is received, a copy of the client SYN segment is sent to the server, and the TCP three-way handshake is performed between the PIX and the server. Only if this three-way handshake completes will the connection be allowed to resume as normal. This enables the PIX to effectively counter DoS SYN attacks without shutting down all web traffic.

The TCP Intercept feature requires no special configuration. The embryonic connection limits on both the **static** and **nat** commands include the new behavior.

Figure 2-5   TCP Intercept

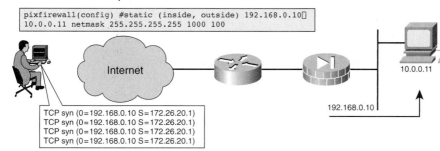

```
pixfirewall(config) #static (inside, outside) 192.168.0.10□
10.0.0.11 netmask 255.255.255.255 1000 100
```

TCP syn (0=192.168.0.10 S=172.26.20.1)
TCP syn (0=192.168.0.10 S=172.26.20.1)
TCP syn (0=192.168.0.10 S=172.26.20.1)
TCP syn (0=192.168.0.10 S=172.26.20.1)

SYN Cookies

PIX Security Appliance Software Version 6.2 introduced SYN cookies. The SYN cookies feature represents a less-CPU-intensive method of verifying incoming TCP sessions for validity. SYN cookies are an implementation of TCP in which servers respond to a TCP SYN request with a cookie. In the original TCP implementation, when a server received a SYN packet, it responded with a SYN-ACK, and entered the half-open state to wait for the ACK that would complete the handshake. Too many half-open connections can result in full buffers.

In the SYN cookies implementation of TCP, when the server receives a SYN packet, it responds with a SYN-ACK packet where the ACK sequence number is calculated from the source address, source port, source sequence number, destination address, destination port, and a secret key. The cookie is a hash of parts of the TCP header and a secret key.

Then, the server releases all states. If an ACK returns from the client, the server can recalculate it to determine whether it is a response to a previous SYN-ACK. If so, the server can directly enter the TCP_ESTABLISHED state and open the connection. In this way, the server avoids managing a batch of potentially useless half-open connections, as shown in Figure 2-6.

Figure 2-6   SYN Cookies

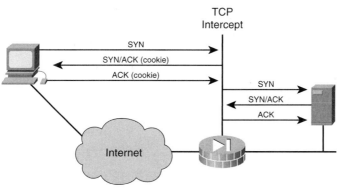

The PIX Security Appliance, rather than the protected server, can respond using SYN cookies. The basic process where the PIX responds is as follows:

1. The PIX responds to the SYN, which includes a cookie in the TCP header of the SYN/ACK. The cookie is a hash of parts of the TCP header and a secret key. The PIX keeps no state information.

2. A legitimate client completes the handshake by sending the ACK back with the cookie.

3. If the cookie is authentic, the firewall appliance proxies the TCP session.

This feature replaces TCP Intercept and is more scalable in terms of performance.

Connection Limits

Use the **static** command to limit the number of embryonic connections allowed to the server to protect internal hosts against DoS attacks. Use the *em_limit* argument to limit the number of embryonic or half-open connections that the server or servers to be protected can handle. A value of zero disables protection. When the embryonic connection limit value is exceeded, all connections are proxied.

Use the **nat** command to protect external hosts against DoS attacks and to limit the number of embryonic connections from the external host. Use the *em_limit* argument to limit the number of embryonic or half-open connections that the server or servers to be protected can handle.

Use the **udp** *udp_max_conns* field to set the maximum number of simultaneous UDP connections the *local_ip* hosts are each allowed to use. Idle connections are closed after the time specified by the **timeout connection** command expires.

In both the **nat** and **static** statements, the *udp_max_conns* field is applicable even when the TCP *max_conns* limit is not set, by using the keyword **udp**. This allows the two limits to be exclusively configured.

Configuring Intrusion Prevention on the PIX Security Appliance

This section explores intrusion detection and the PIX Security Appliance, including how to configure intrusion detection and configure IDS policies.

Intrusion Detection and the PIX Security Appliance

The PIX Security Appliance performs intrusion detection by using intrusion detection signatures. With intrusion detection enabled, the PIX can detect signatures and generate a response when a set of rules is matched to network activity. It can monitor packets for more than 55 intrusion detection signatures and can be configured to send an alarm to a syslog server or a server running Cisco Security Monitor, drop the packet, or reset the TCP connection. The signatures supported by the PIX are a subset of the signatures supported by the Cisco IDS product family.

The PIX Security Appliance can detect two different types of signatures: informational signatures and attack signatures. Information-class signatures are signatures triggered by normal network activity that in itself is not considered to be malicious, but can be used to determine the validity of an attack or for forensics purposes. Attack-class signatures are signatures triggered by an activity known to be, or that could lead to, unauthorized data retrieval, system access, or privileged escalation.

Table 2-1 lists examples of the IDS signatures supported by the PIX Security Appliance.

Table 2-1   Informational and Attack Intrusion Detection Signatures

Message#	Signature ID	Signature Title	Signature Type
400000	1000	IP options-Bad Option List	Informational
400001	1001	IP options-Record Packet Route	Informational
400002	1002	IP options-Timestamp	Informational
400003	1003	IP Options-Security	Informational
400007	1100	IP Fragment Attack	Attack
400010	2000	ICMP Echo Reply	Informational
400011	2001	ICMP Host Unreachable	Informational
400013	2003	ICMP Redirect	Informational
400014	2004	ICMP Echo Request	Informational
400023	2150	Fragmented ICMP Traffic	Attack
400024	2151	Large ICMP Traffic	Attack
400032	4051	UDP Snork Attack	Attack
400035	6051	DNS Zone Transfer	Attack
400041	6103	Proxied RPC Request	Attack

IDS syslog messages all start with %PIX-4-4000nn and have the following format:

```
%PIX-4- 4000nn IDS: sig_num sig_msg from ip_addr to ip_addr on interface int_name
```

For example:

```
%PIX-4-400013 IDS:2003 ICMP redirect from 10.4.1.2 to 10.2.1.1 on interface dmz, and
%PIX-4-400032 IDS:4051 UDP Snork attack from 10.1.1.1 to 192.168.1.1 on interface outside.
```

Configuring Intrusion Detection

You can enable intrusion prevention, or auditing, on the PIX Security Appliance with the **ip audit** commands. Using the **ip audit** commands, you can create audit policies to specify the traffic to be audited or to designate actions to be taken when a signature is detected. After you create a policy, you can apply it to any PIX interface.

Each interface can have two policies, one for informational signatures and one for attack signatures. If both policies are going to be active simultaneously, they should share the same policy name. When a policy for a given signature class is created and applied to an interface, all supported signatures of that class are monitored unless they are disabled with the **ip audit signature disable** command.

The PIX Security Appliance supports both inbound and outbound auditing. Auditing is performed by looking at the IP packets as they arrive at an input interface. For example, if an attack policy is applied to the outside interface, attack signatures are triggered when attack traffic arrives at the outside interface in an inward direction, either as inbound traffic or as return traffic from an outbound connection.

In Figure 2-7, the PIX Security Appliance has an attack policy, which contains the alarm and drop actions applied to its outside interface. Therefore, the following series of events takes place:

1. The intruder attempts to transfer a DNS zone from the DNS server on the demilitarized zone (DMZ).

2. The PIX Security Appliance detects an attack.

3. The PIX Security Appliance drops the connection and sends an IDS syslog message to the syslog server at 10.0.0.11.

Figure 2-7   Intrusion Detection in the PIX Security Appliance

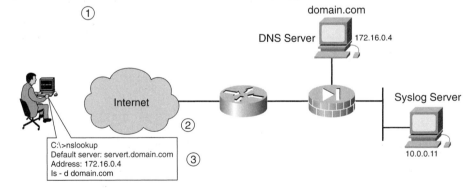

The **ip audit attack** command specifies the default actions to be taken for attack signatures, as illustrated in Figure 2-8.

Figure 2-8   Specify Default Policy Actions

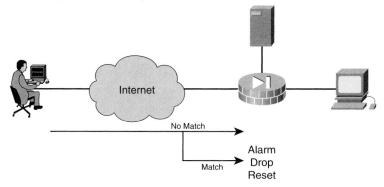

The **no ip audit attack** command resets the action to be taken for attack signatures to the default action. The **show ip audit attack** command displays the default attack actions. The **ip audit info**, **no ip audit info**, and **show ip audit info** commands perform the same functions for signatures classified as informational. Specify the **ip audit info** command without an action option to cancel event reactions.

The command syntax for the **ip audit attack** and **ip audit info** commands are as follows:

```
ip audit attack [action [alarm] [drop] [reset]]
ip audit info [action [alarm] [drop] [reset]]
```

Configuring IDS Policies

Use the **ip audit** command to override the IDS signature defaults, as illustrated in Figure 2-9.

First create a policy with the **ip audit name** command, and then apply the policy to an interface with the **ip audit interface** command, as demonstrated here:

```
pixfirewall(config)#ip audit name outside_policy info
pixfirewall(config)#ip audit name outside_policy attack action alarm drop
```

Figure 2-9   Configure IDS Policies

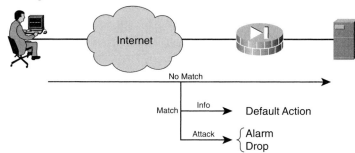

There are two variations of the **ip audit name** command:

```
pixfirewall(config)#ip audit name audit_name info [action [alarm] [drop] [reset]]
pixfirewall(config)#ip audit name audit_name attack [action [alarm] [drop] [reset]]
```

The **ip audit name info** command enables you to create policies for signatures classified as informational. All informational signatures, except those disabled or excluded by the **ip audit signature** command, become part of the policy. The **ip audit name attack** command performs the same function for signatures classified as attack signatures.

The **ip audit name** command also enables the administrator to specify actions to be taken when a signature is triggered. If a policy is defined without actions, the default actions take effect. The default action for both attack and info signatures is alarm.

You can use the **no ip audit name** command to remove an audit policy. The **show ip audit name** command displays audit policies. Use the **no ip audit interface** command to remove a policy from an interface. Use the **show ip audit interface** command to display the interface configuration.

The next step is to apply the policy to an interface with the **ip audit interface** *if_name audit_name* command. In the example in Figure 2-10, the policy **outside_policy** is being applied to the outside interface with the following commands:

```
pixfirewall(config)#ip audit name outside_policy info
pixfirewall(config)#ip audit name outside_policy attack action alarm drop
pixfirewall(config)#ip audit interface outside outside_policy
```

Figure 2-10   Apply IDS Policy to Interface

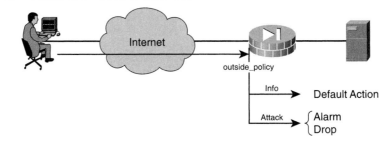

To exclude a signature from auditing, use the following command:

```
pixfirewall(config)#ip audit signature signature_number disable
```

As illustrated in Figure 2-11, to disable signature 6102, you enter the following command:

```
pixfirewall(config)#ip audit signature 6102 disable
```

Use the **no ip audit signature** command to reenable a signature; use the **show ip audit signature** command to display disabled signatures.

Figure 2-11   Disable Intrusion Detection Signatures

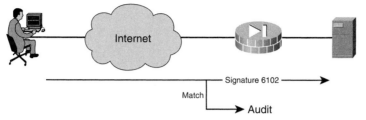

Several **show ip audit** commands are provided to view the current configuration. The **show ip audit count** command proves especially useful for viewing the signatures that have received a hit or match.

Configure Shunning on the PIX Security Appliance

The shun feature of the PIX Security Appliance allows a PIX, when combined with a Cisco IDS sensor, to dynamically respond to an attacking host by preventing new connections and disallowing packets from any existing connection. A Cisco IDS device instructs the PIX to shun sources of traffic when those sources of traffic are determined to be malicious, as illustrated in Figure 2-12.

Figure 2-12   Overview of Shunning

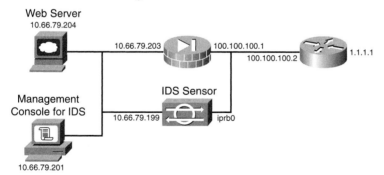

The **shun** command is intended for use primarily by a Cisco IDS device. It applies a blocking function to an interface receiving an attack. The **shun** command is not interface specific. Traffic from the specified source address is dropped no matter which interface it arrives on. Packets containing the IP source address of the attacking host are dropped and logged until the blocking function is removed manually or by the Cisco IDS master unit. No traffic from the IP source address is allowed to traverse the PIX Security Appliance, and any remaining connections time out as part of the normal architecture. The blocking function of the **shun** command is applied whether or not a connection with the specified host address is currently active.

The offending host can be inside or outside of a network protected by the PIX Security Appliance. If the **shun** command is used only with the source IP address of the host, no further traffic from the offending host is allowed.

The **show shun** command displays all shuns currently enabled in the exact format specified. The **no** form of the **shun** command disables a shun based on the IP source address.

In Figure 2-13, host 172.26.26.45 has been attempting a DNS zone transfer from host 192.168.0.10 using a source port other than the well-known DNS port of TCP 53. The offending host (172.26.26.45) has made a connection with the victim (192.168.0.10) with TCP.

The connection in the PIX Security Appliance connection table reads as follows:

```
172.26.26.45, 4000        10.0.0.11 PROT TCP
```

If the **shun** command is applied as shown in Figure 2-13, the PIX Security Appliance deletes the connection from its connection table and prevents packets from 172.26.26.45 from reaching the inside host.

Figure 2-13   Example of Shunning an Attacker

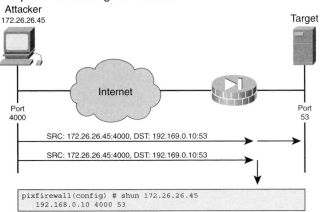

Summary

This chapter expanded upon the idea that network security is a constant cycle of securing, monitoring, testing, and improving, centered on a security policy. This chapter discussed a number of methods that administrators can use to secure a network. The initialization and configuration of a firewall IPS router was discussed, and the student gained hands-on experience by configuring an IPS router through lab activities.

A series of attack guards for the PIX Security Appliance were presented next. These special techniques can prevent many problems that surround popular services such as e-mail and DNS. The methods of intrusion detection available to the PIX Security Appliance were also discussed, and the configuration steps were explained. When a packet must be rejected, the process is called shunning. Shunning was discussed, along with configuration examples.

Check Your Understanding

Complete all the review questions listed here to test your understanding of the topics and concepts in this chapter. Answers are listed in Appendix A, "Check Your Understanding Answer Key."

1. The Cisco IOS Intrusion Prevention System (IPS) cannot accurately do what?

   a. Identify malicious or damaging traffic

   b. Classify malicious or damaging traffic

   c. Stop malicious or damaging traffic

   d. Repair malicious or damaging traffic

2. When packets in a session match a signature, the Cisco IOS IPS cannot take which of the following actions?

   a. Send an alarm to a syslog server or a centralized management interface

   b. Drop the packet

   c. Reset the connection

   d. Rewrite the signature

3. What is the primary difference between Cisco IOS Software Intrusion Detection System (IDS) and the new, enhanced Cisco IOS Intrusion Prevention System (IPS):

   a. IDS monitors traffic and sends an alert when suspicious patterns are detected, whereas IPS can drop traffic, send an alarm, or reset the connection.

   b. IPS monitors traffic and sends an alert when suspicious patterns are detected, whereas IDS can drop traffic, send an alarm, or reset the connection.

   c. IDS and IPS monitor traffic and send an alert when suspicious patterns are detected, whereas IDS can drop traffic, send an alarm, or reset the connection.

   d. IDS monitors traffic and sends an alert when suspicious patterns are detected, whereas neither IPS nor IDS can drop traffic, send an alarm, or reset the connection.

4. The performance impact of intrusion prevention depends on the number of signatures enabled, the level of traffic on the router, the router platform, and other individual features enabled on the router, such as encryption.

   a. True

   b. False

5. Security Device Event Exchange (SDEE) uses which of the following to provide a standardized interface?

    a. XML and HTTP

    b. Java

    c. HXML

    d. Applets

6. To use SDEE, the HTTP server must be enabled with which command?

    a. **ip ips notify** command

    b. **ip http server** command

    c. **ip http notify** command

    d. **ip ips server** command

7. To display IPS information such as configured sessions and signatures, you use which command?

    a. Router# **show ip ips interface** command

    b. Router# **show ip ips** command

    c. Router(int)# **show ip ips interface** command

    d. Router(int)# **show ip ips** command

8. When configured, Mail Guard allows only seven SMTP commands as specified in RFC 821 section 4.5.1. Which commands does Mail Guard allow?

    a. KILL, MAIL, RCPT, DATA, RSET, NOOP, and QUIT

    b. HELO, MAIL, WIZ, DATA, RSET, NOOP, and QUIT

    c. HELO, MAIL, RCPT, DATA, RSET, NOOP, and QUIT

    d. HELO, MAIL, RCPT, DATA, RSET, WIZ, and QUIT

9. FragGuard and Virtual Reassembly perform partial reassembly of all ICMP error messages and virtual reassembly of the remaining IP fragments that are routed through the PIX Security Appliance. They use syslog to log any fragment.

    a. True

    b. False

10. The **shun** feature of the PIX Security Appliance allows a PIX, when combined with a Cisco IDS sensor, to dynamically respond to an attacking host by preventing new connections and disallowing packets from any existing connection.

    a. True

    b. False

CHAPTER 3

Encryption and VPN Technology

Upon completion of this chapter, you should be able to answer the following questions:

- What are encryption basics?
- What are integrity basics?
- How do you implement digital certificates?

- What are VPN topologies?
- What are VPN technologies?
- What is IPsec?

Key Terms

This chapter uses the following key terms. You can find the definitions in the glossary at the end of the book.

Virtual private network (VPN)   page 496

Symmetrical encryption   page 496

Asymmetric encryption   page 497

Diffie-Hellman algorithm   page 499

Message Digest (MD)   page 501

Secure Hash Algorithm (SHA)   page 501

Hashed Message Authentication Code (HMAC)
  page 501

Secure Sockets Layer (SSL)   page 515

Encapsulating Security Payload (ESP)   page 522

Authentication Header (AH)   page 522

This chapter primarily covers the *virtual private network (VPN)* protocols available in Cisco VPN-capable devices. A VPN provides the same network connectivity for remote users over a public infrastructure as they would have over a private network. However, before allowing a user to access a network, certain measures must be taken to ensure authenticity, data integrity, and encryption. In this chapter, you learn about each of these measures and are introduced to the two basic VPN types: site-to-site and remote-access VPNs.

Upon completion of this chapter, you will be able to discuss the protocols and devices used to ensure authenticity, data integrity, and confidentiality with a VPN connection.

Encryption Basics

This section looks at symmetrical and asymmetrical encryption. This section also covers the Diffie-Hellman algorithm.

Symmetrical Encryption

Figure 3-1 shows *symmetrical encryption*, which is also known as secret key encryption. Symmetrical encryption is used for large volumes of data because asymmetrical encryption is much more CPU intensive. The three encryption algorithms available in the Cisco IOS Software include Digital Encryption Standard (DES), Triple DES (3DES), and Advanced Encryption Standard (AES).

Secret key cryptography uses a single key for both encryption and decryption; this key is the shared secret between sender and receiver. Because secret key cryptography uses only one key for both encryption and decryption, it is also called symmetric cryptography.

Figure 3-1   Symmetric Encryption Process

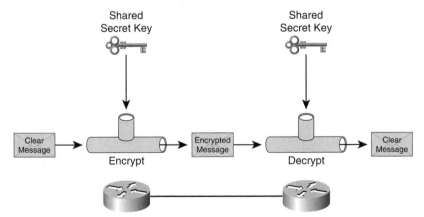

DES is one of the most widely used standards. DES turns clear text into cipher text through an encryption algorithm. The decryption algorithm on the remote end restores clear text from cipher text. Keys enable the encryption and decryption. DES is the most widely used symmetric encryption scheme today. It operates on 64-bit message blocks. The algorithm uses a series of steps to transform 64-input bits into 64-output bits. In the standard form, the algorithm uses 64-bit keys. Fifty-six of these 64-bits, are chosen randomly. The remaining 8 bits are parity bits, one for each 7-bit block of the 56-bit random value.

3DES is an alternative to DES that preserves the existing investment in software but makes a brute-force attack more difficult. 3DES takes a 64-bit block of data and performs the operations of encrypt, decrypt, and encrypt. 3DES can use one, two, or three different keys. The advantage of using one key is that 3DES with one key is the same as standard DES for backward compatibility. However, additional processing time is required with one key. Both the DES and 3DES algorithms are in the public domain and freely available. The U.S. government restricts export of 3DES technology, and many other governments restrict encryption technology within their own boundaries so that they can monitor communications.

AES is a newer encryption algorithm. It currently specifies keys with a length of 128, 192, or 256 bits to encrypt blocks with a length of 128, 192, or 256 bits. All nine combinations of key length and block length are possible. AES is now available in the latest Cisco router images that have IPsec DES/3DES functionality.

The most important feature of a cryptographic algorithm is its security against being compromised. The security of a cryptosystem, or the degree of difficulty for an attacker to determine the contents of the cipher text, is a function of a few variables. In most protocols, the cornerstone to security lies in the secrecy of the key used to encrypt data. Symmetric encryption algorithms are built so that it is extremely difficult for anyone to determine the clear text without having this key. In any cryptosystem, great lengths are taken to protect the secrecy of the encryption key.

Asymmetrical Encryption

Asymmetric encryption is often referred to as public key encryption, as shown in Figure 3-2. It can use either the same algorithm or different but complementary algorithms to scramble and unscramble data. The required public key and a private key are different, but related. The private key is known only to the receiver. The public key is known to the public, and its distribution is not a secret operation.

For example, if Alice and Bob want to communicate using public key encryption, both need a public key and private key pair. Alice has to create her public key/private key pair, and Bob has to create his own public key/private key pair. When communicating with each other securely, Alice and Bob use different keys to encrypt and decrypt data. Asymmetric encryption uses the complementary algorithms to encrypt/decrypt, whereas symmetric encryption uses the same key to encrypt/decrypt.

Figure 3-2   Asymmetric Encryption Process

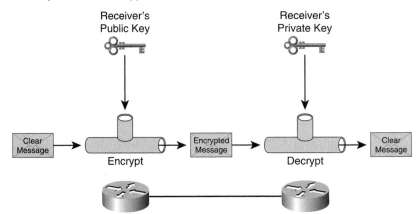

The mechanisms used to generate these public/private key pairs are complex, but they result in the generation of two large random numbers, one of which becomes the public key and the other the private key. Because these numbers, and their product, must adhere to stringent mathematical criteria to preserve the uniqueness of each public/private key pair, generating these numbers is fairly processor intensive.

Some of the more common public key algorithms are the Rivest-Shamir-Adelman (RSA) algorithm and the El Gamal algorithm. Public key encryption algorithms are rarely used for data confidentiality because of their performance constraints. Instead, public key encryption algorithms are typically used in applications involving authentication using digital signatures and key management.

RSA is the public key cryptographic system developed by Ron Rivest, Adi Shamir, and Leonard Adelman. The two methods are RSA signatures and RSA encryption. RSA encryption generates a value known as a nonce. A nonce is temporary random string, which is generated and combined with the peer public key. This method is more secure than the shared key method of authentication. However, it requires more processing power and decreases throughput performance. An RSA signature is the method that uses digital certificates. This method is scalable and typically used by midsize and large corporations. Figure 3-3 illustrates the RSA encryption process.

Nonrepudiation is the ability to prove a transaction occurred, similar to a signed package received from a shipping company. Nonrepudiation is important in financial transactions and similar data transactions. RSA signatures provide nonrepudiation. RSA encryption does not provide nonrepudiation.

Figure 3-3   RSA Encryption Process

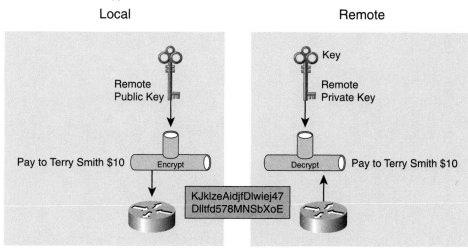

Diffie-Hellman

A critical step in creating a secure VPN involves exchanging the keys. Figure 3-4 shows how the ***Diffie-Hellman algorithm*** provides a way for two parties, Alice and Bob, to establish a shared secret key even though they are communicating over an insecure channel.

Figure 3-4   Diffie-Hellman Algorithm

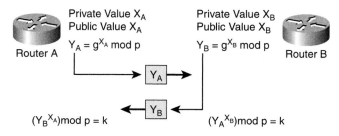

This secret key is used to encrypt data using their favorite secret key encryption algorithm. Two numbers, 'p', a prime, and 'f', a number less than 'p' but with some restrictions, are shared.

Alice and Bob each create a large random number that is kept secret, 'X_A' and 'X_B', as shown in Figure 3-5 The Diffie-Hellman algorithm is now performed, whereby both Alice and Bob carry out some computations and exchange results.

Figure 3-5   Diffie-Hellman Key Exchange

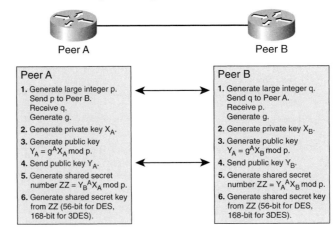

The final exchange results in a common value 'K'. Any party that knows 'p' or 'g' cannot guess or easily calculate the shared secret value, largely because of the difficulty in factoring large prime numbers.

It is important to note that Diffie-Hellman provides for confidentiality but does not provide for authentication. A means for knowing with whom the key is established has not yet been created, so the exchange can be subject to a man-in-the-middle attack. Authentication is achieved via the use of digital signatures in the Diffie-Hellman message exchange.

Diffie-Hellman is used only for key exchange. This method provides a mechanism so that Alice and Bob can determine the same secret key even on a network with someone observing all of their communication.

Integrity Basics

This section looks at hashing, the Hashed Method Authentication Code (HMAC), and digital signatures and certificates.

Hashing

Data integrity is a critical function within a VPN. VPN data is transported over the public Internet. This data could potentially be intercepted and modified. To guard against this, each message has a hash attached to it. A hash is a method of verifying that the contents of a transmission are the same at both ends of the path, similar to a checksum. A hash value is created by a hash function that takes variable input such as a packet and returns a fixed-size string, as shown in Figure 3-6. The hash guarantees the integrity of the original message. If the sent hash matches the received hash, the message has not been tampered with. However, if there is no match, the message was altered. Two common hashing algorithms are *Message Digest (MD)* and *Secure Hash Algorithm (SHA)*. There are several versions of each algorithm.

Figure 3-6   The Hashing Process

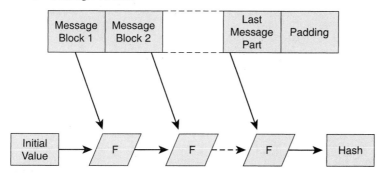

In the example in Figure 3-7, someone is trying to send Terry Smith a check for $10. At the remote end, Alex Jones is trying to cash the check for $100. As the check progressed through the Internet, it was altered. Both the recipient and dollar amounts were changed. In this case, the hashes did not match. The transaction is no longer valid.

Figure 3-7   A Hash Value Is Used to Ensure Data Integrity

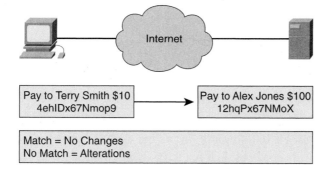

Hashed Method Authentication Code (HMAC)

A *Hashed Message Authentication Code (HMAC)* guarantees the integrity of the message. At the local end, the message and a shared secret key are sent through a hash algorithm, which produces a hash value, as shown in Figure 3-8. This process is similar to the hashing process discussed previously. However, a HMAC combines shared secret key with the message. A hash algorithm is a formula used to develop a fixed-length string of digits that is unique to the contents of the message. A hash is a one-way algorithm. A message can produce a hash, but a hash cannot produce the original message. To send using HMAC, the message and hash are both sent over the network, usually attached to each other.

Figure 3-8 Keyed Hashing Process

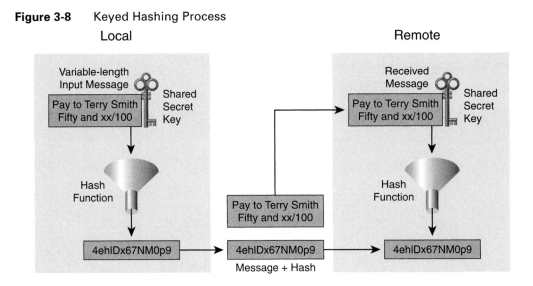

At the remote end, a two-step process occurs. First, the received message and shared secret key are sent through the hash algorithm to recalculate the hash value. Second, the receiver compares the recalculated hash value with the hash that was attached to the message. If the original hash and recalculated hash match, the integrity of the message is guaranteed. If any part of the original message is changed while in transit, the hash values will be different and the modification detected.

There are two common hashing algorithms:

■ **HMAC-MD5 uses a 128-bit shared secret key**—The variable-length message and 128-bit shared secret key are combined and run through the HMAC-MD5 hash algorithm. The output is a 128-bit hash. The hash is appended to the original message and forwarded to the remote end.

■ **HMAC-SHA-1 uses a 160-bit secret key**—The variable-length message and the 160-bit shared secret key are combined and run through the HMAC-SHA-1 hash algorithm. The output is a 160-bit hash. The hash is appended to the original message and forwarded to the remote end. HMAC-SHA-1 is considered cryptographically stronger than HMAC-MD5.

Digital Signatures and Certificates

In paper-based communications, a signed document is notarized with a seal and a signature. With an electronic communication, a document is signed using a digital signature. A digital signature, or digital certificate, is an encrypted hash appended to a document and used to confirm the identity of the sender and the integrity of the document.

Digital signatures are based on a combination of public key encryption and secure one-way hash function algorithms. A digital certificate (shown in Figure 3-9) contains information to identify a user or device, such as the following:

- Serial number

- Validity dates

- Issuer's name

- Subject's name, company, department, or IP address

- Subject's public key info

- Certificate authority signature

Figure 3-9   A Digital Certificate Identifies a User or Device

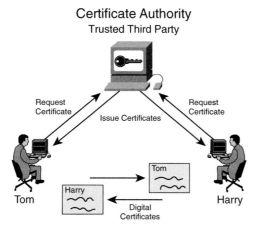

The digital certificate also contains a copy of the entity∞fs public key, as shown in Figure 3-10.

Figure 3-10   Public Key Is Contained in a Digital Certificate

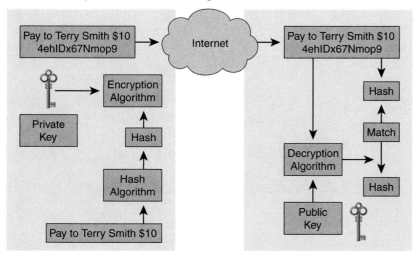

A certificate authority (CA) signs the certificate. The CA is a third party explicitly trusted by the receiver to validate identities and to create digital certificates, as shown in Figure 3-11.

Figure 3-11   Certificate-Based Authentication

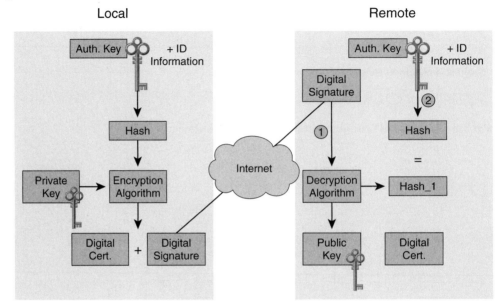

To validate the CA's signature, the receiver must first know the CA's public key. Normally, this is handled out of band or through an operation done at installation. For instance, most web browsers are configured with the public keys of several CAs by default.

In the example in Figure 3-12, the sender derives a hash and encrypts it with its private key.

Figure 3-12   Digital Signatures

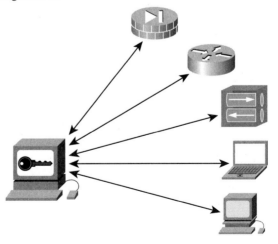

The encrypted hash, which is a digital signature, is attached to the message and forwarded to the remote end. At the receiver end, the encrypted hash is decrypted using the public key of the sender. If the decrypted hash matches the recomputed hash, the signature is genuine. A digital signature ties a message to a sender. The sender is authenticated. The process is summarized as follows:

1. At the sending end, the private key generated by the sender is used to encrypt the hash.

2. At the receiving end:

   The hash is produced by running the original message through a hash algorithm.

   The hash that was appended to the original message is decrypted using the public key from the sender.

3. If the hashes match, the message is signed by private key that was generated by the sender.

   Only a specific private key could have produced the digital signature.

Digital signatures are much more scalable than pre-shared keys. Without digital signatures, keys must be manually shared between each pair of devices. Without certificates, every new device added to the network requires a configuration change on every other device it securely communicates with. However, if you use digital certificates, each device is enrolled with a CA. When two devices want to communicate, they exchange certificates and digitally sign data to authenticate each other. When a new device is added to the network, one simply enrolls that device with a CA, and none of the other devices need modification. When the new device attempts a connection, certificates are automatically exchanged, and the device can be authenticated.

The two common digital signature algorithms are RSA and Directory System Agent (DSA). RSA is used commercially and is the most common. DSA is used mostly by U.S. government agencies.

Implementing Digital Certificates

This section explores certificate authority support, Simple Certificate Enrollment Protocol (SCEP), the Microsoft CA server, and how to enroll a device with a CA.

Certificate Authority Support

Cisco devices support the following open CA standards when implementing IPsec:

- Internet Key Exchange (IKE) is a hybrid protocol that implements Oakley and Skeme key exchanges inside the Internet Security Association and Key Management Protocol (ISAKMP) framework. Although IKE can be used with other protocols, its initial implementation is with the IPsec protocol. IKE provides authentication of the IPsec peers, negotiates IPsec keys, and negotiates IPsec security associations.

- Public-Key Cryptography Standard #7 (PKCS#7) is a standard from RSA Data Security, Inc. used to encrypt, sign, and package certificate enrollment messages.

- Public-Key Cryptography Standard #10 (PKCS#10) A standard syntax from RSA Data Security, Inc. for certificate requests.

- RSA keys come in pairs. Each pair consists of one public key and one private key, as shown in Figure 3-13.

- X.509v3 certificate support allows the IPsec-protected network to scale by providing the equivalent of a digital ID card to each device. When two devices want to communicate, they exchange digital certificates to prove their identity, thus removing the need to manually exchange public keys with each peer or to manually specify a shared key at each peer. These certificates are obtained from a CA. X.509 is part of the X.500 standard.

- CA interoperability permits Cisco IOS devices and CAs to communicate so that Cisco IOS devices can obtain and use digital certificates from the CA. Although you can implement IPsec on a network without the use of a CA, using a CA with SCEP provides manageability and scalability for IPsec.

Figure 3-13 RSA Signature Use in the Network

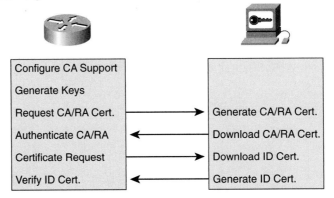

CA Restrictions

The following restrictions apply when configuring a CA:

- This feature should be configured only when both IPsec and ISAKMP are configured in the network.

- The Cisco IOS Software does not support CA server public keys greater than 2048 bits.

CA Prerequisites

A CA must be available to the network before configuring this interoperability feature. The CA must support Cisco Systems public-key infrastructure (PKI) protocol, SCEP (formerly called Certificate Enrollment Protocol [CEP]).

Simple Certificate Enrollment Protocol (SCEP)

SCEP is a Cisco, VeriSign, Entrust, Microsoft, Netscape, and Sun Microsystems initiative that provides a standard way of managing the certificate life cycle. This initiative is important for driving open development for certificate-handling protocols that can be interoperable with devices from many vendors.

SCEP has the following attributes:

- Cisco-sponsored IETF draft

- Lightweight protocol to support certificate life cycle operations on the PIX Security Appliance

- Uses PKC#7 and #10

- Transaction-oriented request and response protocol

- Transport mechanism independent

- Requires manual authentication during enrollment

Two authentication methods that SCEP provides are manual authentication and authentication based on pre-shared secret keys.

The Manual Enrollment Process

In the manual authentication mode, the end entity submitting the request is required to wait until the CA operator using any reliable out-of-band method can verify its identity. An MD5 fingerprint generated on the PKCS#10 requests must be compared out of band between the server and the end entity. SCEP clients and CAs must display this fingerprint to a user to enable this verification if manual mode is used.

Enrollment Using Pre-shared Keys

When using a pre-shared secret scheme, the server should distribute a shared secret key to the end entity, which can uniquely associate the enrollment request with the given end entity. The distribution of the secret must be private. Only the end entity should know this secret. When creating the enrollment request, the end entity is asked to provide a challenge password. When using the pre-shared secret scheme, the end entity must type in the redistributed secret as the password. In the manual authentication case, the challenge password is also required because the server may challenge an end entity with the password before any certificate can be revoked.

Later on, this challenge password is included as a PKCS#10 attribute and is sent to the server as encrypted data. The PKCS#7 envelope protects the privacy of the challenge password with DES encryption.

CA Servers

Several CA vendors interoperate with Cisco IOS Software on Cisco routers. They include Entrust, VeriSign, Baltimore, and Microsoft. Several CA vendors support SCEP for enrolling Cisco routers, as depicted in Figure 3-14.

Figure 3-14 Each IPSEC Peer Enrolls with a CA Server

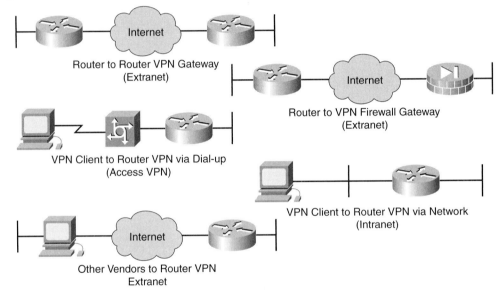

Entrust Technologies

The Entrust CA server is one of several servers interoperable with Cisco. Entrust uses software that is installed and administered by the user. Cisco IOS Software interoperates with the Entrust/PKI 4.0 CA server. Entrust/PKI delivers the ability to issue digital identifications to any device or application supporting the X.509 certificate standard, meeting the need for security, flexibility, and low cost by supporting all devices and applications from one PKI. Entrust/PKI has the following requirements:

- Runs on the Windows NT 4.0 (required for Cisco interoperability), Solaris 2.6, HP-UX 10.20, and AIX 4.3 operating systems

- RSA usage keys on the routers

- Cisco IOS Software Release 11.(3)5T and later

Furthermore, Entrust/PKI supports the following standards:

- CA services
- Registration authority (RA) capability
- SCEP
- PKCS#10

VeriSign OnSite

The VeriSign OnSite CA server is another CA that operates with Cisco routers. VeriSign administers the CA, providing the certificates as a service.

The VeriSign OnSite solution delivers a fully integrated enterprise PKI to control, issue, and manage IPsec certificates for Cisco PIX Security Appliances and Cisco routers. VeriSign OnSite is a service administered by VeriSign. VeriSign OnSite has the following requirements:

- No local server requirements.
- The router must be configured for CA mode with a high (> 60 seconds) retry count.
- Cisco IOS Software Release 12.0(6.0.1)T and later. Cisco IOS Software Release 12.0(5)T is not supported because of a known bug in that release.

Furthermore, VeriSign OnSite supports the following standards:

- SCEP
- X.509 certificate format
- PKCS#7, 10, 11, and 12

Baltimore Technologies

UniCERT is the CA server offered by Baltimore Technologies. Baltimore Technologies has implemented support for SCEP in UniCERT and the PKI Plus toolkit. These make it easy for customers to enable certificate within their environments. The UniCERT CA server has the following requirements:

- The current release of the UniCERT CA module is available for Windows NT.
- Cisco IOS Software Release 12.0(5)T and later.

Furthermore, UniCERT supports the following standards:

X.509v3	DAP
X.9.62	SQL
X.9.92	TCP/IP
X.9.21-2	POP3
CRLv2	SMTP
RFC 2459	HTTP
PKCS#1,7,10,11,12	OCSP
RFC 2510	FIPS 180-1
RFC 2511	FIPS 186-1
SCEP	FIPS 46-3
LDAPv2	FIPS 81CBC
LDAPv3	

Microsoft Windows 2000 Certificate Services

Microsoft has integrated SCEP support into the Windows 2000 CA server through the Security Resource Kit for Windows 2000. This support lets customers use SCEP to obtain certificates and certificate revocation information from Microsoft Certificate Services for all the Cisco VPN security solutions. The requirements are as follows:

- Compatible PC capable of running Windows 2000 Server
- Cisco IOS Software Release 12.0(5)T and later

Furthermore, the SCEP tool for Windows 2000 CA server supports the following standards:

- X.509v3
- CRLv2
- PKCS family (PKCS#7, 10, and 12)
- PKIX
- SSLv3
- Kerberos v5 RFC 1510
- 1964 tokens
- SGC
- IPsec

- PKIINIT

- PC/SC

- IETF 2459

The SCEP tool is not installed by the Windows 2000 Resource Kit setup and must be installed separately.

Enroll a Device with a CA

Figure 3-15 and the list that follows illustrate the typical process for enrolling a device, such as a router or PIX Security Appliance, with a CA.

Figure 3-15   Process of Enrolling a Device with a CA

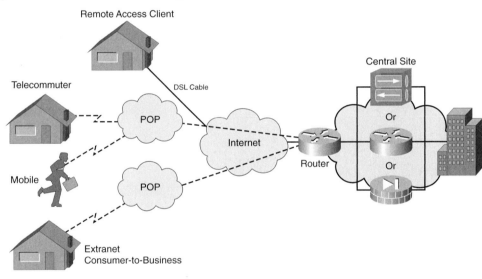

Step 1.   Configure the device for CA support.

Step 2.   Generate a public and private key pair on the device.

Step 3.   The device authenticates the CA server:

— Send the certificate request to the CA/RA.

— Generate a CA/RA certificate.

— Download a CA/RA certificate to the device.

— Authenticate a CA/RA certificate via the CA/RA fingerprint.

Step 4.   The device sends a certificate request to the CA.

Step 5.   The CA generates and signs an identity certificate.

Step 6.   The CA sends the certificates to the device and posts the certificates in its public repository.

Step 7.   The device verifies the identify certificate and posts the certificate.

Most of these steps have been automated by Cisco and the SCEP protocol that is supported by many CA server vendors. Each vendor determines how long certificates are valid.

VPN Topologies

A VPN provides the same network connectivity for remote users over a public infrastructure as they would have over a private network. VPN services for network connectivity include authentication, data integrity, and confidentiality. There are two basic VPN types:

- **Site-to-site VPNs**—There are two common types of site-to-site VPNs, also known as LAN-to-LAN VPNs:

  — Intranet VPNs connect corporate headquarters, remote offices, and branch offices over a public infrastructure.

  — Extranet VPNs link customers, suppliers, partners, or communities of interest to a corporate intranet over a public infrastructure.

- **Remote-access VPNs**—Which securely connect remote users, such as mobile users and telecommuters, to the enterprise.

Site-to-Site VPNs

You can use site-to-site VPNs to connect corporate sites. In the past, a leased line or Frame Relay connection was required to connect sites. Currently, most corporations have Internet access. With Internet access, you can replace expensive leased lines and Frame Relay lines with site-to-site VPNs. You can use site-to-site VPNs to provide the network connection. VPNs can support company intranets and business partner extranets. A site-to-site VPN is an extension of a classic WAN network. You can build site-to-site VPNs using routers, PIX Security Appliances, or VPN concentrators, as shown in Figure 3-16.

Figure 3-16   Site-to-Site VPN

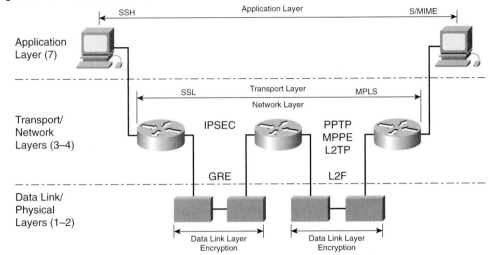

Remote-Access VPNs

A remote-access VPN secures connections for remote users, such as mobile users or telecommuters, to corporate LANs over shared service provider networks. There two types of remote-access VPNs:

- **Client initiated**—Remote users use a VPN client or web browser to establish a secure tunnel across a public network to the enterprise.

- **NAS initiated**—Remote users dial in to an ISP network access server (NAS). The NAS establishes a secure tunnel to the enterprise private network that might support multiple sessions initiated by remote users.

Remote access is targeted to mobile users and home telecommuters. In the past, corporations supported remote users via dial-in networks. This typically required a call to access the corporation. With the advent of VPN, a mobile user can connect to any Internet service provider (ISP) using dial, cable, or Digital Subscriber Line (DSL), and connect to the Internet to access the corporation. This is the evolution of dial networks.

Remote-access VPNs can support the needs of telecommuters, mobile users, consumer-to-business extranets, and so on. A remote-access VPN can be terminated on head-end devices, such as routers, PIX Security Appliances, or VPN concentrators. Remote-access clients can include routers, VPN hardware clients, or VPN software clients, as shown in Figure 3-17.

Figure 3-17   Remote-Access VPN Topology

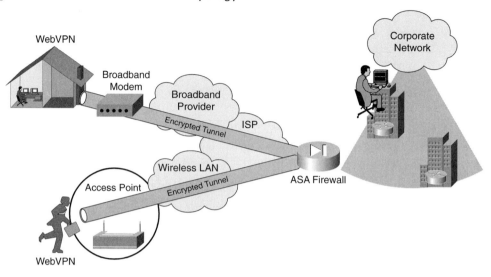

VPN Technologies

This section looks at the different VPN technology options, including WebVPN, the tunneling protocols, and tunnel interfaces.

Figure 3-18 shows the methods of protection implemented on different layers. With implementation of encryption on one layer, this layer and all layers above it are automatically protected. Network layer protection offers one of the most flexible solutions. It is media independent and application independent.

Figure 3-18   VPN Implementations at Different OSI Layers

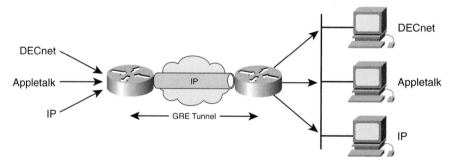

Providing privacy and other cryptographic services at the application layer was also popular in the past. In some situations, it is still heavily used today. However, application layer security is application specific, and protection methods must be re-implemented in every application.

Some standardization has been successful at Layer 4 of the OSI model with protocols such as *Secure Sockets Layer (SSL)* providing privacy, authenticity, and integrity to TCP-based applications. SSL is used heavily in modern e-commerce sites. However, SSL fails to address the issues of flexibility, ease of implementation, and application independence. One of the latest technologies available, Transport Layer Security (TLS), addresses many of the limitations of SSL.

Protection at lower levels of the OSI stack, especially the data link layer, was also used in communication systems of the past. This provided protocol-independent protection on specific untrusted links. However, data link layer protection is expensive to deploy on a large scale because there is a need to protect every single link separately. Data link layer protection allows for man-in-the-middle attacks on intermediate stations, or routers, and is usually proprietary.

Layer 3 is currently the most popular level to apply cryptographic protection to network traffic.

WebVPN

WebVPN lets users establish a secure, remote-access VPN tunnel to a head-end device using a web browser. Users are no longer restricted to a particular PC or workstation, improving mobility and flexibility of access, as shown in Figure 3-19. WebVPN is not a replacement for IPsec, but widens application availability.

Figure 3-19   WebVPN Overview

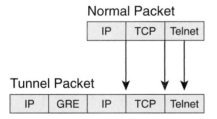

There is no need for either a software or hardware client. WebVPN provides easy access to a broad range of enterprise applications, including web resources, web-enabled applications, NT/Active Directory (AD) file shares that are web enabled, e-mail, and other TCP-based applications from any computer connected to the Internet that can reach HTTP(S) Internet sites.

WebVPN uses the SSL protocol and its successor, TLS, to provide a secure connection between remote users and specific, supported internal resources at a central site.

WebVPN is currently available for VPN 3000 series concentrators, Cisco IOS routers running Cisco IOS Software Release 12.3(14)T and later, and the Adaptive Security Appliance 5500 series.

WebVPN Features

WebVPN features include the following, as illustrated in Figure 3-20:

- Secure access to internal websites via HTTP/HTTPS, including filtering.

- Windows File Access provides access to files on preconfigured file servers, or file browsing on the network.

- TCP port forwarding, or application access, for legacy application support.

- Access to e-mail via Post Office Protocol, Version 3 (POP3S) over SSL, Internet Messages Access Protocol, Version 4 (IMAP4S) over SSL, and Simple Mail Transfer Protocol Secure (SMTPS) over SSL proxies.

Figure 3-20   WebVPN Features

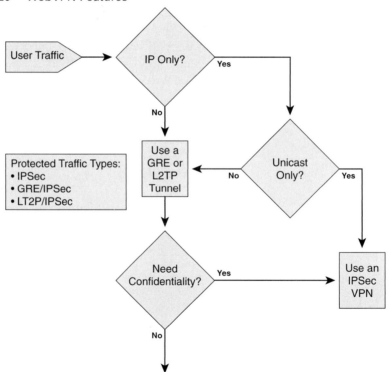

WebVPN is ideal for the following deployments:

- Unmanaged desktops

- Extranets

- Employee-owned computers

- Employees who only need occasional access

- Employees who need access to few applications

- Simple or locked-down access, which provides restricted server and application access by population

WebVPN and IPsec Comparison

Each type of remote access has its own unique set of benefits. WebVPN allows clientless access, but there are possible trade-offs in ease of use and security. You can mitigate many of these trade-offs by properly implementing WebVPN. Note the following additional characteristics of each solution shown in Table 3-1.

Table 3-1   WebVPN and IPsec Comparison

WebVPN	IPsec VPN
Uses a standard web browser to access the corporate network.	Uses purpose-built client software for network access.
SSL encryption native to browser provides transport security.	Client provides encryption and desktop security.
Application accessed through browser portal.	Client establishes seamless connection to network.
Limited client/server application accessed using applets.	All applications are accessible through their native interface.

Tunneling Protocols

A variety of technologies exist to enable tunneling of protocols through networks to create a VPN, as shown in Table 3-2. Prior to the Layer 2 Tunneling Protocol (L2TP) standard established in August 1999, Cisco used Layer 2 Forwarding (L2F) as its proprietary tunneling protocol. L2TP is entirely backward compatible with L2F. L2F is not forward compatible with L2TP. L2TP, defined in RFC 2661, is a combination of Cisco L2F and Microsoft Point-to-Point Tunneling Protocol (PPTP). Microsoft supports PPTP in its earlier versions of Windows and PPTP/L2TP in Windows NT/2000/XP. L2TP is used to create a media-independent, multiprotocol virtual private dial network (VPDN). L2TP enables users to invoke corporate security policies across any VPN or VPDN link as an extension of their internal networks.

Table 3-2   Multiple Choices Choosing a Protocol

Description		Standard
GRE	Generic routing encapsulation	RFCs 1701 and 2784
IPsec	Internet Protocol Security	RFC 2401
L2F	Layer 2 Forwarding	Cisco
L2TP	Layer 2 Tunneling Protocol	RFC 2661
MPLS	Multiprotocol Label Switching	RFC 2547
PPTP	Point-to-Point Tunneling Protocol	Microsoft

The Cisco GRE multiprotocol carrier encapsulates IP, Connectionless-Network Protocol (CLNP), Internetwork Packet Exchange (IPX), AppleTalk, DECnet Phase IV, and Xerox Network Systems (XNS) protocol inside IP tunnels, as shown in Figure 3-21. With GRE tunneling, a router at each site encapsulates protocol-specific packets in an IP header, as shown in Figure 3-22. This creates a virtual point-to-point link between routers across an IP cloud. By connecting multiprotocol subnetworks in a single-protocol backbone environment, IP tunneling allows network expansion across a single-protocol backbone environment. GRE tunneling allows desktop protocols to take advantage of the enhanced route-selection capabilities of IP.

Figure 3-21   Tunneling Protocols

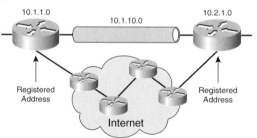

Figure 3-22   GRE Encapsulation Process

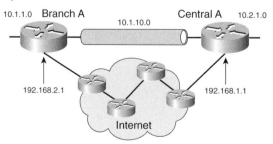

Currently, IPsec is the choice for secure corporate VPNs. However, IPsec supports IP unicast traffic only. Multiprotocol or IP multicast tunneling requires the use of another tunneling protocol. Because of its PPP ties, L2TP is best suited for remote-access VPNs that require multiprotocol support. GRE is best suited for site-to-site VPNs that require multiprotocol support. Also, GRE is typically used to tunnel multicast packets such as routing protocols. Neither of these tunneling protocols supports data encryption or packet integrity. GRE encapsulates all traffic, regardless of its source and destination. Remember to use GRE or L2TP when there is a need to support tunneling packets other than the IP unicast type. In these cases, you can use IPsec in combination with these protocols to provide encryption, such as L2TP/IPsec and GRE/IPsec. In summary, if only IP unicast packets are being tunneled, a simple encapsulation provided by IPsec is sufficient and much less complicated to configure and troubleshoot.

Multiprotocol Label Switching (MPLS) is a VPN technology implemented by ISPs and large corporations. MPLS uses label switching and label switched paths over various link-level technologies. Some examples are Packet-over-SONET, Frame Relay, ATM, and LAN technologies such as all forms of Ethernet and Token Ring. This includes procedures and protocols for the distribution of labels between routers, encapsulations, and multicast considerations.

Currently, many proprietary and standard protocols are used to create a VPN. It is important to understand the proper use and implementation of each type of VPN when deciding on a technology to implement, as shown in Figure 3-23. This chapter provides detailed coverage of IPsec.

Figure 3-23   Selecting VPN Technologies

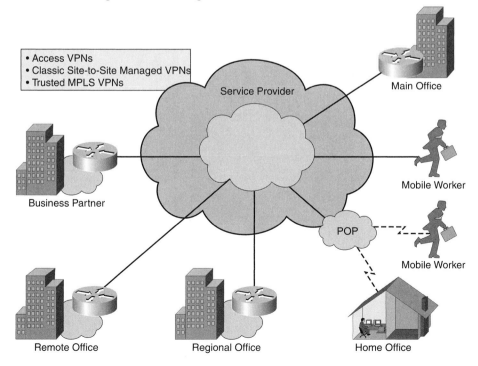

Tunnel Interfaces

Tunnel interfaces provide a point-to-point connection between two routers through a virtual software interface, as shown in Figure 3-24. They also appear as one direct link between routers, hiding the underlying infrastructure, that are connected via a large network, such as the Internet. However, tunnel interfaces should not to be confused with IPsec or L2TP tunnels, which can act as tunnels, but not as true Cisco IOS interfaces.

Figure 3-24   Tunnel Interfaces Act as a Point-to-Point Connection

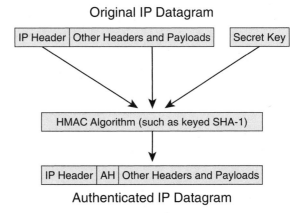

Further tunnel interface configuration information that might prove important is as follows:

- Unnumbered Layer 3 addresses are supported but not allowed for by IPsec.

- Access lists can be applied to the tunnel interface.

- Quality of service (QoS) supports traffic requiring consistent service such as Voice over IP (VoIP).

- Committed access rate (CAR), weighted fair queuing (WFQ), and weighted random early detection (WRED) are not supported on tunnel interfaces at this time.

GRE tunnels provide a designated pathway across the shared WAN and encapsulate traffic with new packet headers, which ensures delivery to specific destinations, as Figure 3-25 and Example 3-1 illustrate.

Figure 3-25   GRE Tunnel Example

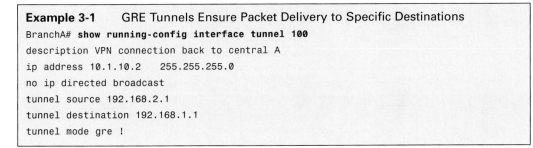

Next Header	Payload Length	RESERVED
Security Parameter Index (SPI)		
Sequence Number		
Authentication Data		

Example 3-1   GRE Tunnels Ensure Packet Delivery to Specific Destinations

```
BranchA# show running-config interface tunnel 100
description VPN connection back to central A
ip address 10.1.10.2   255.255.255.0
no ip directed broadcast
tunnel source 192.168.2.1
tunnel destination 192.168.1.1
tunnel mode gre !
```

The network is private because traffic can enter a tunnel only at an endpoint. Tunnels do not
provide true confidentiality as encryption does, but can carry encrypted traffic. IPsec can be
used to encrypt data before it enters and after it leaves the GRE tunnel.

IPsec

IPsec is a framework of security protocols and algorithms used to secure data at the network
layer, as shown in Table 3-3. Prior to the IPsec standard, Cisco implemented its proprietary
Cisco Encryption Technology (CET) to provide protection at the packet level. RFC 2401
describes the general framework for this architecture. Like all security mechanisms, RFC 2401
helps to enforce a security policy. The policy defines the need for security on various connections, which will be IP sessions. The framework provides data integrity, authentication, confidentiality, and security association and key management.

Table 3-3   Options in an IPsec Framework

IPsec Framework	Choice 1	Choice 2
IPsec protocol	ESP	ESP +AH
Encryption	DES	3DES
Authentication	MD5	SHA
Diffie-Hellman	DH1	DH2

IPsec consists of two protocols:

- *Encapsulating Security Payload (ESP)*—Encapsulates the data but does not provide protection to the outer headers. ESP encrypts the payload for data confidentiality.

- *Authentication Header (AH)*—Provides protection to the entire datagram by embedding the header in the data. The AH verifies the integrity of the IP datagram.

AH and ESP use symmetric secret key algorithms, although public key algorithms are feasible.

The advantages of IPsec displayed in Figure 3-26 allow implementation in a wide range of scenarios, as shown in Table 3-4.

Figure 3-26 Advantages of IPsec

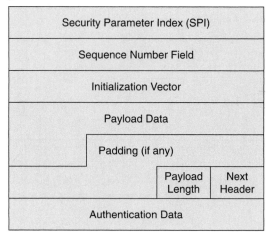

Table 3-4 Common Deployment Scenarios for IPsec

Network Type	Remote Access	Site to Site	Firewall Based
Large enterprise	3080 or 3060 concentrator	VPN routers 71x0	PIX Security Appliance 525 or 535
Medium enterprise	3030 concentrator	Routers 7x00 or 3600	PIX Security Appliance 525 or 515
Small business or branch office	3015 or 3005 concentrator	Routers 3600, 2600, 1700	PIX Security Appliance 506 or 501
Small office/ home office	VPN software client or 3002	DSL router 800 cable router 905	PIX Security Appliance 501

Authentication Header (AH)

The IP AH is used to provide connectionless integrity and data origin authentication for IP datagrams and to provide protection against replays. AH, defined in RFC 2402, provides authentication for as much of the IP header as possible and for upper-level protocol data. However, some IP header fields might change in transit. The value of these fields might not be predictable by the sender, when the packet arrives at the receiver. The values of such fields cannot be protected by AH. AH is defined as IP protocol 51.

AH can be applied alone, in combination with the IP ESP, or in a nested fashion through the use of tunnel mode. Security services can be provided between a pair of communicating hosts, between a pair of communicating security gateways, or between a security gateway and a host. ESP can be used to provide the same security services, and it also provides a confidentiality, or encryption, service. The primary difference between the authentication services provided by ESP and AH is the extent of the coverage. Specifically, ESP does not protect any IP header fields unless ESP encapsulates those fields, or the fields are in tunnel mode, as shown in Figure 3-27.

Figure 3-27   How an AH Is Generated in IPsec

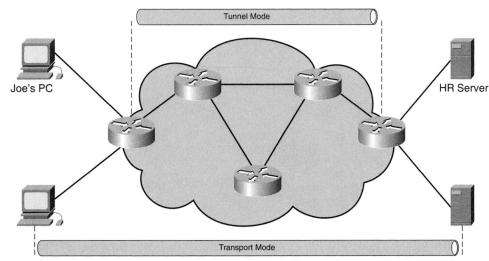

AH provides the packet authentication, integrity assurance, and replay detection/protection via sequence numbers. However, no confidentiality or encryption is provided, as shown in Figure 3-28.

Figure 3-28   AH Fields

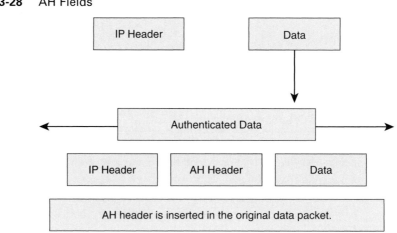

The AH Header structure is as follows:

- A 32-bit Security Parameter Index (SPI) value shows the security association (SA) used for this packet.

- A 64-bit sequence number prevents packet replay.

- Authentication data is an HMAC value of the packet.

The following are reasons to use AH even though ESP seems to do all the security services:

- AH requires less overhead than ESP.

- AH is never export restricted.

- AH is mandatory for IPv6 compliance.

Encapsulating Security Payload (ESP)

ESP, defined in RFC 2406, provides confidentiality, data origin authentication, connectionless integrity, an anti-replay service, and limited traffic flow confidentiality by defeating traffic flow analysis. The set of services provided depends on options selected at the time of SA establishment and on the placement of the implementation. Confidentiality may be selected independent of all other services. However, use of confidentiality without integrity authentication, either in ESP or separately in AH, can subject traffic to certain forms of active attacks that could undermine the confidentiality service. ESP is defined as IP protocol 50.

Data origin authentication and connectionless integrity are joint services and are offered as an option in conjunction with optional confidentiality. The anti-replay service can be selected only if data origin authentication is selected.

Its election is solely at the discretion of the receiver. Although the default calls for the sender to increment the sequence number used for anti-replay, the service is effective only if the receiver checks the sequence number. Traffic flow confidentiality requires selection of tunnel mode. Traffic flow confidentiality is most effective if implemented at a security gateway where traffic aggregation may be able to mask true source-destination patterns. Note that although both confidentiality and authentication are optional, at least one of them must be selected.

Figure 3-29 illustrates the ESP packet header format. One of the most important values is the SPI, which allows the router to keep track of the current SA between two IPsec devices.

Figure 3-29   ESP Header Format

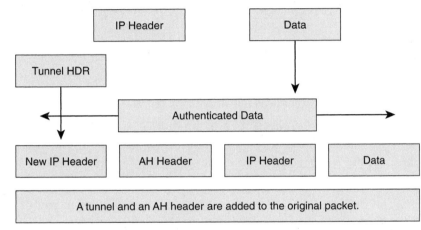

Encryption is done with DES or 3DES. Optional authentication and integrity are provided with HMAC, keyed SHA-1/RFC 2404, or keyed MD5/RFC 2403. Two different key types are contained in the SA:

- Encryption session keys
- HMAC session keys

Tunnel and Transport Modes

Figure 3-30 shows an IPsec-protected path in tunnel and transport mode basic scenarios. In transport mode, each end host does IPsec encapsulation of its own data, host to host. Therefore, IPsec has to be implemented on end hosts. The application endpoint must also be the IPsec endpoint. In tunnel mode, IPsec gateways provide IPsec services to other hosts in peer-to-peer tunnels. End hosts are not aware of IPsec being used to protect their traffic. IPsec gateways provide transparent protection of the traffic of other hosts over untrusted networks.

Figure 3-30   Tunnel Versus Transport Mode

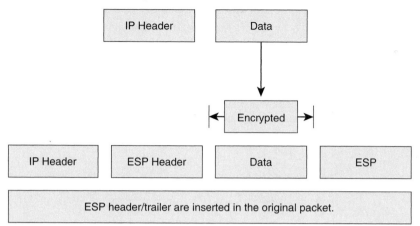

ESP and AH can be applied to IP packets in two different ways:

- **Transport mode**—In transport mode, security is provided only for the transport layer and above. Transport mode protects the payload of the packet but leaves the original IP address in the clear. The original IP address is used to route the packet through the Internet.

- **Tunnel mode**—Tunnel mode provides security for the whole original IP packet. The original IP packet is encrypted. Then, the encrypted packet is encapsulated in another IP packet. The outside IP address is used to route the packet through the Internet.

New AH headers, and optional tunnel headers, are added to the packet. In transport mode, the AH header normally adds 24 bytes to each packet, as in Figure 3-31. In tunnel mode, the tunnel IP and AH headers add 44 bytes to each packet, as in Figure 3-32.

Figure 3-31   AH Header Placement in Transport Mode

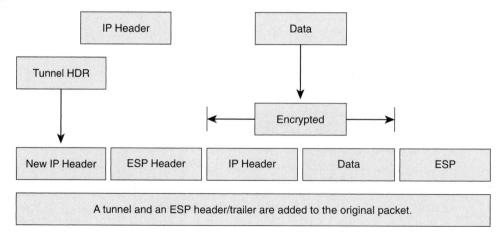

Figure 3-32   AH Header Placement in Tunnel Mode

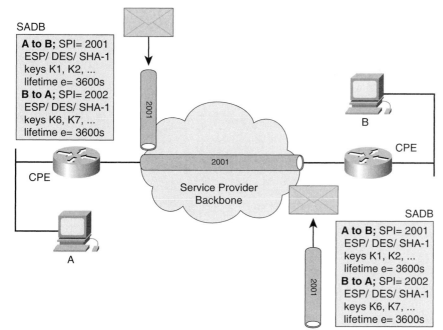

New ESP headers, optional tunnel headers, and a trailer are added to the packet. In transport mode, the ESP header and trailer normally add up to 37 bytes to each packet, as shown in Figure 3-33. In tunnel mode, the tunnel IP and ESP header and trailer add up to 57 bytes to each packet, as shown in Figure 3-34. Using both AH and ESP in tunnel mode can add up to 101 bytes to each packet.

Figure 3-33   ESP Header Placement in Transport Mode

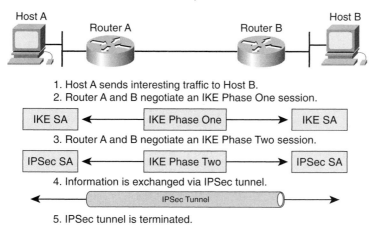

Figure 3-34   ESP Header Placement in Tunnel Mode

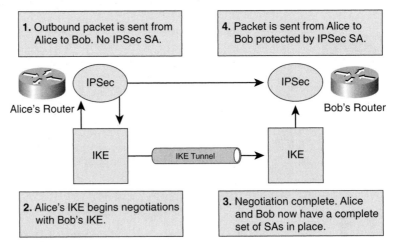

Security Associations

Security associations (SAs) are one of the most basic concepts of IPsec. SAs represent a policy contract between two peers or hosts and describe how the peers will use IPsec security services to protect network traffic. SAs contain all the security parameters needed to securely transport packets between the peers or hosts and practically define the security policy used in IPsec.

Figure 3-35 illustrates the concept of an SA. The routers in the picture use IPsec to protect traffic between hosts A and B. Therefore, each of the routers needs two SAs, which describe traffic protection in both directions. Establishment of SAs is a prerequisite for IPsec traffic protection to work. When relevant SAs are established, IPsec refers to them for all parameters needed to protect a particular traffic flow. For example, an SA might enforce the following policy. For traffic between hosts A and B, use ESP 3DES with keys K1, K2, and K3 for payload encryption, and SHA-1 with K4 for authentication.

SAs always contain unidirectional, or one-way, specifications. SAs are also encapsulation protocol specific. There is a separate SA for each encapsulation protocol, AH and ESP, for a given traffic flow. If two hosts A and B are communicating securely using both AH and ESP, each host builds separate SAs, inbound and outbound, for each protocol. VPN devices store all their active SAs in a local database called the SA database (SADB).

An SA contains the following security parameters:

- Authentication/encryption algorithm, key length, and other encryption parameters, such as key lifetime, used with protected packets

- Session keys for authentication, or HMACs, and encryption, which can be entered manually or negotiated automatically with the help of the IKE protocol, fed to the algorithms

- A specification of network traffic to which the SA will be applied, such as all IP traffic or only Telnet sessions

- IPsec AH or ESP encapsulation protocol and tunnel or transport mode

Figure 3-35   SA Security Parameters

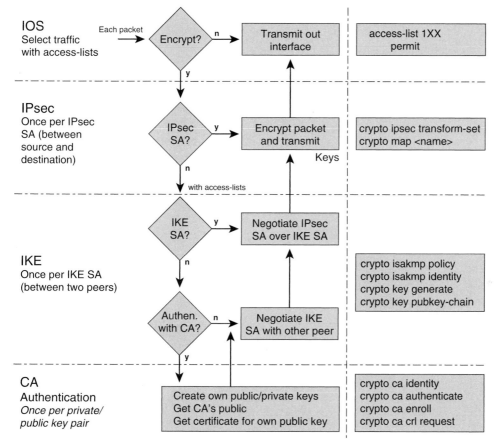

The Security Parameters Index (SPI) is a 32-bit number that identifies each established SA. The SPI uniquely identifies a particular SA in the SADB. Finally, SPIs are written into IPsec packet headers to locate the appropriate SA on the receiving system.

Five Steps of IPsec

The goal of IPsec is to protect the desired data with the necessary security and algorithms, as shown in Figure 3-36.

Figure 3-36   IPsec Process Negotiation

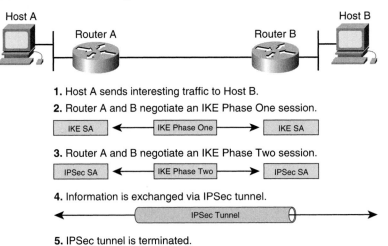

The operation of IPsec can be broken down into five primary steps:

Step 1.   Interesting traffic initiates the IPsec process. Traffic is deemed interesting when a packet triggers an access list that defines traffic to be protected.

Step 2.   During IKE Phase 1, IKE authenticates IPsec peers and negotiates IKE SAs, setting up a secure communications channel for negotiating IPsec SAs in Phase 2.

Step 3.   During IKE Phase 2, IKE negotiates IPsec SA parameters and sets up matching IPsec SAs in the peers. These security parameters are used to protect data and messages exchanged between endpoints.

Step 4.   During the data transfer phase, data is sent between IPsec peers based on the IPsec parameters and keys stored in the SA database.

Step 5.   During IPsec tunnel termination, IPsec SAs terminate through deletion or by timing out.

The events within an IKE session happen in following the order.

1. In IKE Phase 1, in main or aggressive mode, the peers will do the following:

   a. Negotiate an IKE protection suite

   b. Authenticate each other

   c. Exchange keying material to protect the IKE session

   d. Establish the IKE SA

2. Then, in IKE Phase 2, in quick mode, peers do the following:

   a. Negotiate IPsec policies

   b. Exchange keying material of IPsec SAs

   c. Establish IPsec SAs

IKE Phase 1 runs in main or aggressive mode. The mode used is implementation and situation dependent. The purpose of IKE Phase 1 is the negotiation of an IKE protection suite, the authentication of peers, the exchange of keying material to protect the IKE session, and then the establishment of an IKE SA, which defines the parameters of the secure IKE channel.

The IKE main mode is the first mode that negotiates protection suites between peers. ISAKMP uses six messages to establish the IKE SA. These messages include SA negotiation, a Diffie-Hellman key exchange, and the authentication of peers. IKE main mode hides the identity of IKE peers from eavesdroppers and can use the protocol∞fs negotiation capabilities to the fullest.

Like the IKE main mode, the IKE aggressive mode negotiates protection suites between peers. The major difference between the main and the aggressive mode is that the aggressive mode takes half the number of messages as the main mode and consequently offers less negotiating flexibility for the IKE session protection. The initiating peer proposes a list of policies, and the responder accepts a policy or rejects the offers with no further negotiation of protection details. The aggressive mode does protection suite negotiation, authentication of peers, and keying material generating as the main mode does, but because of limited capabilities it does not provide peer identity protection. For example, an eavesdropper can determine the identity of negotiating peers. Because only three messages are needed to establish IKE SA, an IKE aggressive mode exchange is also much faster than an IKE main mode exchange. It is used mainly when security policies are well known on both peers and there is no need to use the full IKE negotiation capabilities to establish an IKE SA as quickly as possible.

IKE Phase 2 is used to negotiate and establish SAs of other protocols, such as AH and ESP for IPsec. Phase 2 needs an established IKE SA, produced in IKE Phase 1, to protect the IKE session, to operate, and only operates in one defined mode, the quick mode. The IKE initiator presents a list of IPsec policy proposals, and the IKE responder chooses an acceptable proposal according to its locally defined policy. When the policy between peers is agreed upon, the keying material is agreed upon, and IPsec SAs are established.

IKE quick mode is quite fast, with almost no noticeable delay associated with it, and no Perfect Forward Secrecy (PFS) functionality is used with IPsec. When an IKE SA is in place, only quick mode exchanges are used to negotiate additional IPsec SAs or to rekey established IPsec SAs when they are about to expire.

Internet Key Exchange (IKE)

IKE enhances IPsec by providing additional features and flexibility and makes IPsec easier to configure. IKE, defined in RFC 2409, is a hybrid protocol that implements the Oakley key exchange and Skeme key exchange inside the ISAKMP framework. ISAKMP is defined in RFC 2408. ISAKMP, Oakley, and Skeme are security protocols implemented by IKE. IKE provides authentication of the IPsec peers, negotiates IPsec keys, and negotiates IPsec SAs.

The IKE tunnel protects the SA negotiations. After the SAs are in place, IPsec protects the data that Alice and Bob exchange, as depicted in Figure 3-37.

Figure 3-37   IKE Use in an IPsec Environment

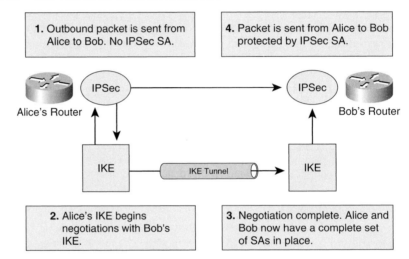

IKE mode configuration allows a gateway to download an IP address, and other network-level configuration, to the client as part of an IKE negotiation. Using this exchange, the gateway gives IP addresses to the IKE client to be used as an inner IP address encapsulated under IPsec. This method provides a known IP address for the client, which can be matched against IPsec policy.

IKE provides the following benefits:

- Eliminates the need to manually specify all the IPsec security parameters in the crypto maps at both peers

- Enables administrators to specify a lifetime for the IPsec SA

- Allows encryption keys to change during IPsec sessions

- Allows IPsec to provide anti-replay services

- Permits CA support for a manageable, scalable IPsec implementation

- Allows dynamic authentication of peers

Table 3-5 describes the component technologies implemented for use by IKE.

Table 3-5   Component Technologies for Use by IKE

Technology	Description
DES	DES is used to encrypt packet data. IKE implements the 56-bit DES-CBC with Explicit IV standard.
3DES	168-bit encryption. 3DES in simple terms is DES performed three times on the same data. The strength of 3DES is approximately twice the strength of DES.
CBC	Cipher Block Chaining (CBC) requires an initialization vector (IV) to start encryption. The IV is explicitly given in the IPsec packet.
Diffie-Hellman	A public key cryptography protocol that allows two parties to establish a shared secret over an unsecured communications channel. Diffie-Hellman is used within IKE to establish session keys, and 768-bit and 1024-bit Diffie-Hellman groups are supported.
MD5	(HMAC variant)—Message Digest 5 (MD5) is a hash algorithm used to authenticate packet data. HMAC is a variant that provides an additional level of hashing.
SHA	(HMAC variant)—Secure Hash Algorithm (SHA) is a hash algorithm used to authenticate packet data. HMAC is a variant that provides an additional level of hashing.

One of the most important factors in the IKE SA negotiation is the mutual authentication of peers. Each peer must be sure that it is talking to the correct peer before negotiating traffic protection IPsec policies with it. This mutual authentication is accomplished using the two-way authentication methods available with IKE. IKE provides three defined methods for two-way authentication:

- Authentication using a pre-shared secret

- Authentication using RSA encrypted nonces

- Authentication using RSA signatures

This book focuses on the pre-shared authentication method and RSA signatures.

IKE and IPsec

IPsec, in Cisco IOS Software, processes packets as shown in Figure 3-38. The PIX Security Appliance processes IPsec traffic in a similar manner.

Figure 3-38 IKE and IPsec Flowchart Used with Cisco IOS Software

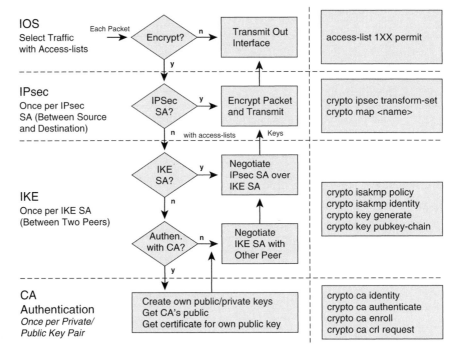

The process shown in Figure 3-38 assumes that public and private keys have already been created and that at least one access list exists.

Step 1. Access lists are used by Cisco IOS Software to select interesting traffic to be encrypted.

a. Cisco IOS Software checks to determine whether IPsec SAs have been established.

b. If the SA has already been established by manual configuration, or set up by IKE, the packet is encrypted based on the policy specified on the router and is sent out the interface.

Step 2. If the SA has not been established, Cisco IOS Software checks to determine whether an ISAKMP SA has been configured and set up. If the ISAKMP SA has been set up, the ISAKMP SA governs negotiation of the IPsec SA as specified in the ISAKMP policy. The packet is then encrypted by IPsec and is sent.

Step 3.   If the ISAKMP SA has not been set up, Cisco IOS Software checks to determine whether certification authority has been configured to establish an ISAKMP policy. If CA authentication is configured, the router will do the following:

   a. Use public/private keys previously configured

   b. Get the public certificate from the CA

   c. Get a certificate for its own public key

   d. Use the key to negotiate an ISAKMP SA

   e. Use the same key, which in turn is used to establish IPsec SA

Step 4.   The router then encrypts and sends the packet.

Cisco VPN Solutions

IPsec VPN capabilities are included in many models of Cisco routers and in the PIX Security Appliance. The products described in the sections that follow also have IPsec capabilities.

VPN 3000 Series Concentrators

The Cisco VPN 3000 series offers best-in-class remote-access VPN devices that provide businesses with flexible, reliable, and high-performance remote-access solutions. The Cisco VPN 3000 series offers solutions for diverse remote-access deployments by offering both IPsec- and SSL-based VPN connectivity on a single platform.

VPN Software Client

The Cisco VPN Client allows organizations to establish end-to-end, encrypted VPN tunnels for secure connectivity for mobile employees or teleworkers. This IPsec client is compatible with all Cisco VPN products.

You can preconfigure the Cisco VPN Client for mass deployments, and initial logins require little user intervention. Cisco VPN Client supports Cisco Easy VPN capabilities, delivering an easy-to-manage remote-access VPN architecture that eliminates the operational costs associated with maintaining a consistent policy and key management method. The Cisco Easy VPN feature allows the Cisco VPN Client to receive security policies upon a VPN tunnel connection from the central site VPN device, configured as the Cisco Easy VPN Server, minimizing configuration requirements at the remote location. This simple and highly scalable solution is ideal for large remote-access deployments where it is impractical to individually configure policies for multiple remote PCs.

The Cisco VPN Client supports Windows 98, Me, NT 4.0, 2000, XP; Linux (Intel); Solaris (UltraSparc 32- and 64-bit); and Mac OS X, 10.1, and 10.2. The Cisco VPN Client is compatible with the following Cisco products:

- Cisco VPN 3000 series concentrators

- Cisco VPN 3000 series concentrator software Version 3.0 and later

- Cisco IOS Software Release 12.2(8)T and later

- Cisco PIX Firewall software Version 6.0 and later

VPN 3002 Hardware Client

The Cisco VPN 3002 Hardware Client combines the ease-of-use and high-scalability features of a software Cisco VPN Client while providing the reliability and stability of a hardware platform. The Cisco VPN 3002 Hardware Client is designed for organizations with many remote-office environments; it easily scales to tens of thousands of devices. The Cisco VPN 3002 Hardware Client is a full-featured VPN client in a hardware platform that supports 56-bit DES, 168-bit 3DES, or up to 256-bit AES encryption.

The Cisco VPN 3002 Hardware Client supports the Cisco Unified Client protocol, allowing it to act as a Cisco Easy VPN Remote device and connect to any Cisco Easy VPN Server, such as a VPN 3000 concentrator, PIX Security Appliance, or Cisco IOS router.

Available in two modes, client and network extension, the Cisco VPN 3002 can be configured to either emulate the operation of the Cisco VPN Client or to establish a secure site-to-site connection with the central site Cisco Easy VPN Server device. Both modes use the Cisco Easy VPN push-policy features and scale to large deployments. The Cisco VPN 3002 Hardware Client is available with or without an eight-port switch.

IPsec VPN Services Module

The Cisco IPsec VPN Services Module is a high-speed module for the Cisco Catalyst 6500 series switch and the Cisco 7600 series Internet router that provides infrastructure-integrated IPsec VPN services to meet the need for ubiquitous connectivity and increased bandwidth requirements.

The IPsec VPN Services Module delivers cost-effective VPN performance on the Cisco Catalyst 6500 series and is suitable for various deployments. For example, in WAN edge deployments, the VPN module provides VPN termination services on the WAN aggregator router.

Summary

This chapter covered the VPN protocols available in Cisco devices. Upon completion of this chapter, you should be to identify the protocols used to ensure authenticity, data integrity, and confidentiality with a VPN connection. You also learned about the protocols that make up the IPsec framework. This chapter also included a discussion of digital certificates and how you can use them to implement VPNs.

Check Your Understanding

Complete all the review questions listed here to test your understanding of the topics and concepts in this chapter. Answers are listed in Appendix A, "Check Your Understanding Answer Key."

1. HMAC-MD5 uses a shared secret key that is how many bits long?

   a. 64

   b. 128

   c. 256

   d. 160

2. HMAC-MD5 uses a 128-bit shared secret key. The variable-length message and 128-bit shared secret key are combined and run through the HMAC-MD5 hash algorithm. The output is a 128-bit hash. The hash is appended to the original message and forwarded to the remote end. The two common digital signature algorithms are which of the following?

   a. RSA and DSA

   b. IKE and IPsec

   c. MD5 and SHA-1

   d. SCEP and CA

3. The two common digital signature algorithms are RSA and DSA. RSA is used commercially and is the most common. DSA is used mostly by U.S. government agencies. SCEP is a Cisco, VeriSign, Entrust, Microsoft, Netscape, and Sun Microsystems initiative that provide a standard way of managing the certificate life cycle.

   a. True

   b. False

4. What are the two types of remote-access VPNs?

   a. Client initiated and NAS initiated

   b. Site-to-site and RA

   c. IKE and IPsec

   d. Telecommuter and mobile user

5. WebVPN enables users to establish a secure, remote-access VPN tunnel to a head-end device using a web browser. What is another characteristic of WebVPN?

   a. There is a need for a software or hardware client.

   b. There is no need for either a software or hardware client.

   c. There is a need for a software but not a hardware client.

   d. There is no need for a software client, but there is a need for a hardware client.

6. Secure access to internal websites via HTTPS; Windows File Access provides access to files on preconfigured file servers, or file browsing on the network; port forwarding, or application access, for legacy application support; e-mail proxies enable e-mail via Post Office Protocol, Version 3 (POP3S) over SSL, Internet Messages Access Protocol, Version 4 (IMAP4S) over SSL, and Simple Mail Transfer Protocol Secure (SMTPS) over SSL proxies are all features of which of the following VPN technologies?

   a. WebVPN

   b. IPsec VPN

   c. VPDN

   d. GRE VPN

7. For multiprotocol or IP multicast tunneling, which tunneling protocol cannot be used?

   a. GRE

   b. IPsec

   c. L2F

   d. L2TP

8. IPsec is a framework of security protocols and algorithms used to secure data at which OSI layer?

   a. Network layer

   b. Data layer

   c. Physical layer

   d. Application layer

9. IPsec consists of which of the following two protocols?

   a. GRE and L2TP

   b. IKE and PPTP

   c. ESP and AH

   d. MD5 and DH1

10. AH may be applied alone, in combination with the IP ESP, or in a nested fashion through the use of tunnel mode.

   a. True

   b. False

CHAPTER 4

Configure Site-to-Site VPN Using Pre-Shared Keys

Upon completion of this chapter, you should be able to answer the following questions:

- How do I prepare a router for site-to-site VPN connectivity using pre-shared keys?

- How do I configure a router for IKE using pre-shared keys?

- How do I configure a router with IPsec using pre-shared keys?

- How do I test and verify IPsec configurations?

- How do I configure a PIX Security Appliance for site-to-site VPN connectivity using pre-shared keys?

Key Terms

This chapter uses the following key terms. You can find the definitions in the glossary at the end of the book.

Virtual private network (VPN)   page 542

Authentication Header (AH)   page 547

Encapsulating Security Payload (ESP)   page 550

Security association (SA)   page 552

This chapter covers the site-to-site *virtual private network (VPN)* configuration for Cisco IOS routers and PIX Security Appliances. A VPN provides the same network connectivity for remote users over a public infrastructure as they would have over a private network. However, before allowing a user to access a network, you must take certain measures to ensure authenticity, data integrity, and encryption.

It is important to realize that a VPN connection can present the biggest hidden hole in a network's perimeter. If you have remote users who access your internal network via VPN software, you take the chance that their system could become compromised and then the attacker would have a encrypted tunnel into your network. Make sure you evaluate the risks of allowing any connection into your network and take steps to mitigate them. For example, supplying all remote users with some form of personal firewall is a good idea. Restricting the amount of access provided to remote users is another. You might trust the user, but do you really trust his system?

Upon completion of this chapter, you will be able to identify and configure the protocols used to ensure authenticity, data integrity, and confidentiality with a site-to-site VPN using pre-shared keys.

IPsec Encryption with Pre-Shared Keys

This section presents an overview of the major IPsec configuration tasks you must complete to build a site-to-site IPsec VPN or a router-to-router IPsec VPN using pre-shared keys. You can establish site-to-site IPsec VPNs between any combination of routers, PIX Security Appliances, VPN concentrators, VPN clients, and other devices that are IPsec compliant, as shown in Figure 4-1.

Figure 4-1   Pre-Shared Keys Used in a VPN

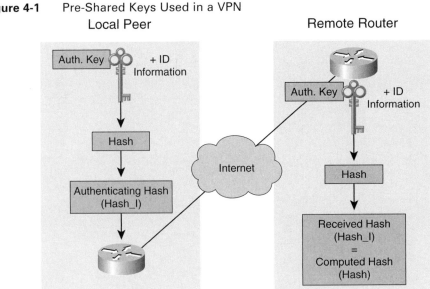

The use of pre-shared keys for authentication of IPsec sessions is relatively easy to configure, but does not scale well for a large number of IPsec clients. The process for configuring IKE pre-shared keys in Cisco IOS Software for Cisco routers consists of the following four major tasks:

- Task 1 is to prepare for IPsec. This task involves determining the detailed encryption policy, identifying the hosts and networks to protect, determining details about the IPsec peers, determining the needed IPsec features, and ensuring existing access control lists are compatible with IPsec.

- Task 2 involves configuring Internet Key Exchange. This task includes enabling IKE, creating the IKE policies, and validating the configuration.

- Task 3 is configuring IPsec. This task includes defining the transform sets, creating crypto access control lists, creating crypto map entries, and applying crypto map sets to interfaces.

- Task 4 is to test and verify IPsec, using **show**, **debug**, and related commands to test and verify that IPsec encryption works. You can also use these commands to troubleshoot problems.

IKE peer authentication using pre-shared secrets is the simplest authentication to configure but has several serious limitations. The authentication is based on a pre-shared secret. Both peers share a secret password string between them. This secret is exchanged securely out of band. During the IKE peer authentication process, peers perform a PPP CHAP-like exchange of random values, hashed with the pre-shared secret key. Authentication via pre-shared secrets uses hashing and is therefore fast. IKE peer authentication using pre-shared secrets works in the following manner (simplified here for clarity):

1. Peer A randomly chooses a string and sends it to peer B.

2. Peer B hashes the received string together with the pre-shared secret and yields a hash value, dependent on the random string and the pre-shared secret.

3. Peer B sends the result of hashing back to peer A.

4. Peer A calculates its own hash of the random string, together with the pre-shared secret, and matches it with the received result from the other peer. If they match, peer B knows the pre-shared secret and is considered authenticated.

5. Now peer B randomly chooses a different random string and sends it to peer A.

6. Peer A also hashes the received string with the pre-shared secret.

7. Peer A sends the authenticated hash back to peer B.

8. Peer B locally hashes the random value and the pre-shared secret and matches it against the received authenticated hash. If they are equal, peer A is also authenticated.

When both peers authenticate each other, the peer authentication procedure is complete. The main limitation of pre-shared secret authentication is the requirement to base the pre-shared secret on the IP address of the remote peer, not its IKE identity. This can impose significant problems in an environment with dynamic peer addresses such as dialup users, DHCP users, and so on.

Planning the IKE and IPsec Policy

It is important to plan IPsec details in advance to minimize configuration errors. You should define the IPsec security policy based on the overall company security policy. Some planning steps are as follows:

Step 1.   **Determine IKE Phase 1 policy**. Determine the IKE policies between IPsec peers based on the number and location of the peers. Some planning steps include the following:

- Determine the key distribution method.
- Determine the authentication method.
- Identify IPsec peer IP addresses and host names.
- Determine ISAKMP policies for peers.

Step 2.   **Determine IKE Phase 2 policy**. Identify IPsec peer details such as IP addresses, IPsec transform sets, and IPsec modes. Crypto maps will be used to gather all IPsec policy details together during the configuration phase.

Step 3.   **Check the current configuration**. Use the **show running-configuration, show isakmp [policy]**, and **show crypto map** commands. You can use other **show** commands to check the current configuration of the router, as covered later in this module.

Step 4.   **Ensure that the network works without encryption**. Do not avoid this step. Ensure that basic connectivity has been achieved between IPsec peers using the desired IP services before configuring IPsec. Use the **ping** command to check basic connectivity.

Step 5.   **Ensure that the ACLs on perimeter devices are compatible with IPsec**. Ensure that perimeter routers and the IPsec peer router interfaces permit IPsec traffic. Use the **show access-lists** command for this step.

Step 1: Determine ISAKMP (IKE Phase 1) Policy

The IKE policy details to enable the selected authentication method need to be determined and then configured. Having a detailed plan lessens the chances of improper configuration. Some planning steps include the following:

- **Determine the key distribution method**—Determine the key distribution method based on the numbers and locations of IPsec peers. For a small site-to-site VPN networks, it might be best to manually distribute keys. For larger networks, you might need to use a certificate authority (CA) server to support scalability of IPsec peers. Internet Security Association Key Management Protocol (ISAKMP) must be configured to support the selected key distribution method.

- **Determine the authentication method**—Choose the authentication method based on the key distribution method. Cisco IOS Software supports either pre-shared keys, RSA encrypted nonces, or RSA signatures to authenticate IPsec peers. This lesson focuses on using pre-shared keys.

- **Identify IP addresses and host names of the IPsec peers**—Determine the details of all the IPsec peers that will use ISAKMP and pre-shared keys for establishing security associations (SAs). This information will be used to configure IKE.

- **Determine ISAKMP policies for peers**—An ISAKMP policy defines a combination or suite of security parameters to be used during the ISAKMP negotiation. Each ISAKMP negotiation begins by each peer agreeing on a common, or shared, ISAKMP policy. The ISAKMP policy suites must be determined in advance of configuration. IKE must then be configured to support the policy details that have been determined. Some ISAKMP policy details include the following:

  — Encryption algorithm

  — Hash algorithm

  — IKE SA lifetime

The goal of this planning step is to gather the precise data that will be needed in later steps to minimize configuration errors.

An IKE policy defines a combination of security parameters used during the IKE negotiation. A group of policies makes up a protection suite of multiple policies that enable IPsec peers to establish IKE sessions and establish SAs with a minimal configuration.

Create IKE Policies for a Purpose

IKE negotiations must be protected, so each IKE negotiation begins by each peer agreeing on a shared IKE policy. This policy states which security parameters will be used to protect subsequent IKE negotiations.

After the two peers agree upon a policy, an SA established at each peer identifies the security parameters of the policy. These SAs apply to all subsequent IKE traffic during the negotiation.

Multiple, prioritized policies can be created at each peer to ensure that at least one policy will match a policy configured on a remote peer.

Define IKE Policy Parameters

Specific values for each IKE parameter can be selected, as outlined in the IKE standard. Choose one value over another based on the security level desired and the type of IPsec peer to which it will be connected.

You must define five parameters in each IKE policy, as outlined in Table 4-1 and Table 4-2. Table 4-1 shows the relative strength of each parameter, and Table 4-2 shows the default values.

Table 4-1   IKE Phase 1 Policy Parameters

Parameter	Strong	Stronger
Encryption algorithm	DES	3DES or AES
Hash algorithm	MD5	SHA-1
Authentication method	Pre-shared	RSA encryption
RSA signature		
Key exchange	DH Group	DH Group 2
DH Group 5		
IKE SA lifetime	86,400 seconds	Less than 86,400 seconds

Table 4-2   ISAKMP (IKE Phase 1) Default Values

Parameter	Accepted Values	Keyword	Default
Message encryption algorithm	DES 3DES AES 128, 192, 256	Des 3des aes	DES
Message integrity hash algorithm	SHA-1 (HMAC variant) MD5(HMAC variant)	Sha md5	SHA-1
Peer authentication method	Pre-shared keys RSA encrypted nonces RSA signatures	pre-share rsa-encr rsa-sig	RSA signatures
Key exchange parameters, the Diffie-Hellman group identifier	768-bit Diffie-Hellman 1024-bit Diffie-Hellman 1536-bit Diffie-Hellman	1 2 5	768-bit Diffie-Hellman
ISAKMP (established security association lifetime)	Specify any number of seconds		86,400 seconds (1 day)

Step 2: Determine IPsec (IKE Phase 2) Policy

An IPsec policy defines a combination of IPsec parameters used during the IPsec negotiation. Planning for IPsec, also known as IKE Phase 2, is another important step that you should complete before actually configuring IPsec on a Cisco router. Policy details to determine at this stage include the following:

- **Select IPsec algorithms and parameters for optimal security and performance**— Determine what type of IPsec security to use when securing interesting traffic. Some IPsec algorithms require trade-offs between high performance and stronger security. Some algorithms have import and export restrictions that can delay or prevent implementation of the network.

- **Select transforms and, if necessary, transform sets**—Use the IPsec algorithms and parameters previously decided upon to help select IPsec transforms, transform sets, and modes of operation.

- **Identify IPsec peer details**—Identify the IP addresses and host names of all IPsec peers to be connected.

- **Determine IP address and applications of hosts to be protected**—Decide which hosts IP addresses and applications should be protected at the local peer and remote peer.

- **Select manual or IKE-initiated SAs**—Choose whether SAs are manually established or are established through IKE.

The goal of this planning step is to minimize misconfiguration (that is, gather the precise data needed for later steps).

Cisco IOS Software supports the IPsec transforms shown in the following example:

```
RouterA(config)# crypto ipsec transform-set
Stransform-set-name ?
ah-md5-hmac    AH-HMAC-MD5 transform
ah-sha-hmac    AH-HMAC-SHA transform
comp-lzs       IP compression using LZS compression algorithm
esp-3des       ESP transform using 3DES(EDE) cipher (168 bits)
esp-aes        ESP transform using AES cipher
esp-des        ESP transform using DES cipher (56 bits)
esp-md5-hmac   ESP transform using HMAC-MD5 auth
esp-null       ESP transform w/o cipher
esp-seal       ESP transform using SEAL cipher (160 bits)
esp-sha-hmac   ESP transform using HMAC-SHA auth
```

Authentication Header (AH) is rarely used because authentication is now available with the **esp-sha-hmac** and **esp-md5-hmac** transforms. AH is also not compatible with Network Address Translation (NAT) or Port Address Translation (PAT).

The Cisco IOS command parser prevents invalid combinations from being entered. For example, after an AH transform is specified, it does not allow another AH transform to be specified for the current transform set.

Step 3: Check the Current Configuration

You should check the current Cisco router configuration to determine whether there are any IPsec policies already configured that are useful for, or might interfere with, the planned IPsec policy configurations. Use previously configured IKE and IPsec policies and details, if possible, to save configuration time. However, previously configured IKE and IPsec policies and details can make troubleshooting more difficult if problems arise.

To check whether IKE policies have previously been configured, start with the **show running-config** command. You can also use a variety of **show** commands specific to IPsec. For example, you can use the **show crypto isakmp policy** command to examine default and any configured IKE Phase 1 policies, as demonstrated in Example 4-1.

The default protection suite seen in Example 4-1 is available for use without modification. You can also use other available **show** commands to view IKE and IPsec configuration.

```
Example 4-1      Check Current Configuration
RouterA#show crypt isakmp policy
Default protection suite
    encryption algorithm:   DES - Data Encryption Standard (56 bit keys)
    hash algorithm:         Secure Hash Standard
    authentication method: Rivest-Shamir-Adleman Signature
    Diffie-Hellman Group:   #1 (768 bit)
  Lifetime:                 86400 seconds, no volume limit
```

The **show crypto map** command, demonstrated in Example 4-2 for the network topology depicted in Figure 4-2, proves useful for viewing any previously configured crypto maps. Crypto maps are covered in detail later in this lesson. You can (and should) use previously configured maps to save configuration time. However, previously configured crypto maps can interfere with the planned IPsec policy configuration.

Example 4-2   Displaying Configured Crypto Maps

```
RouterA#show crypto map
Crypto Map "mymap" 10 ipsec-isakmp
        Peer = 172.30.2.2
        Extended IP access list 102
            access-list 102 permit ip host 172.30.2.2
host 172.30.2.2
        Current peer: 172.30.2.2
        Security association lifetime:   4608000
kilobytes/3600 seconds
        PFS (Y/N):  N
        Transform sets={ mine, }
```

Figure 4-2   View Configured Crypto Maps

You can use the **show crypto ipsec transform-set** command to view previously configured transform sets, as demonstrated here:

RouterA#**show crypto ipsec transform-set mine**
```
Transform set mine:  { esp-des }
   Will negotiate = { Tunnel },
```

You can (and should) use previously configured transforms to save configuration time.

Step 4: Ensure the Network Works Without Encryption

You must check basic connectivity between peers before IPsec configuration can begin.

Use the router **ping** command to test basic connectivity between IPsec peers. Although a successful ICMP echo, or ping, verifies basic connectivity between peers, you should verify that the network works with any other protocols or ports that are to be encrypted, such as Telnet or FTP, before beginning IPsec configuration.

After IPsec is activated, basic connectivity troubleshooting can be difficult because the security configuration might mask a more fundamental networking problem. Previous security settings could result in no connectivity.

Step 5: Ensure ACLs Are Compatible with IPsec

You need to check existing ACLs on perimeter routers, PIX Security Appliances, or other routers to ensure that they do not block IPsec traffic, as demonstrated in Figure 4-3 and Example 4-3. Perimeter routers typically implement a restrictive security policy with ACLs, where only specific traffic is permitted and all other traffic is denied. Such a restrictive policy blocks IPsec traffic, so specific **permit** statements need to be added to the ACL to allow IPsec traffic.

Figure 4-3   Ensure that ACLs Are Compatible with IPsec

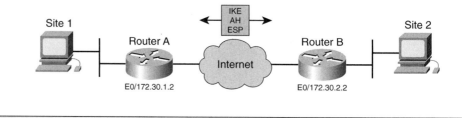

Example 4-3   Verifying That ACLs Do Not Block IPsec Traffic

```
RouterA#show access-lists
access-list 102 permit ahp host 172.30.1.2 host 172.30.2.2
access-list 102 permit esp host 172.30.1.2 host 172.30.2.2
access-list 102 permit udp host 172.30.1.2 host 172.30.2.2 eq isakmp


RouterB#show access-lists
access-list 102 permit ahp host 172.30.2.2 host 172.30.1.2
access-list 102 permit esp host 172.30.2.2 host 172.30.1.2
access-list 102 permit udp host 172.30.2.2 host 172.30.1.2 eq isakmp
```

Ensure that the ACLs are configured so that ISAKMP, *Encapsulating Security Payload (ESP)*, and AH traffic is not blocked at interfaces used by IPsec. ISAKMP uses UDP port 500. ESP is assigned IP protocol number 50, and AH is assigned IP protocol number 51. In some cases, you might need to add a statement to router ACLs to explicitly permit this traffic. You can add ACL statements to the perimeter router as follows:

Step 1.   Examine the current ACL configuration at the perimeter router and determine whether it will block IPsec traffic:

        RouterA#**show access-lists**

Step 2.   Add ACL entries to permit IPsec traffic. To do this, modify the existing ACL as follows:

        a.   Copy the existing ACL configuration and paste it into a text editor.

        b.   Add the ACL entries to the top of the list in the text editor.

c. Delete the existing ACL with the **no access-list** *access-list number* command.

d. Enter configuration mode and copy and paste the new ACL into the router.

e. Verify that the ACL is correct with the **show access-lists** command.

Configure a Router for IKE Using Pre-Shared Keys

Configuring a router for IKE using pre-shared keys requires completion of a four-step process:

Step 1.   Enable or disable IKE.

Step 2.   Create IKE policies.

Step 3.   Configure pre-shared keys.

Step 4.   Verify the IKE configuration.

This section looks at each of these steps in detail.

Step 1: Enable or Disable IKE

IKE is enabled by default. IKE does not have to be enabled for individual interfaces, but it is enabled globally for all interfaces at the router.

If IKE is not used with an IPsec implementation, you can disable it at all IPsec peers.

If IKE is disabled, the following concessions must be made at the peers:

- All the IPsec SAs in the crypto maps at all peers must be manually specified.
- The IPsec SAs of the peers will never time out for a given IPsec session.
- During IPsec sessions between the peers, the encryption keys will never change.
- Anti-replay services will not be available between the peers.
- CA support cannot be used.

To disable IKE, use the **no isakmp enable** command in global configuration mode. To reenable IKE use the **isakmp enable** command.

Step 2: Create IKE Policies

You must create IKE policies at each peer. An IKE policy defines a combination of security parameters to be used during the IKE negotiation. An IKE policy is created with the following command:

```
Router(config)#crypto isakmp policy priority
```

This command invokes the **config-isakmp** command mode.

Note

The protocol keyword of **esp** equals the ESP protocol number 50, the keyword of **ahp** equals the AH protocol number 51, and the **isakmp** keyword equals UDP port 500 when used in an extended access list.

Note

ISAKMP can be blocked on interfaces not used for IPsec to prevent possible denial-of-service attacks. You can do this by using an ACL statement that blocks UDP port 500 on the interfaces.

Why Must These Policies Be Created?

IKE negotiations must be protected, so each IKE negotiation begins by agreement of both peers on a common shared IKE policy. This policy states which security parameters will be used to protect subsequent IKE negotiations and mandates how the peers are authenticated.

After the two peers agree upon a policy, the security parameters of the policy are identified by a *security association (SA)* established at each peer, and these security associations apply to all subsequent IKE traffic during the negotiation.

Multiple, prioritized policies must be created at each peer to ensure that at least one policy will match the policy of a remote peer.

Parameters Defined in a Policy

You must define five parameters in each IKE policy, as explained previously in Tables 4-1 and 4-2. These parameters apply to the IKE negotiations when the IKE SA is established.

Multiple IKE policies can be created, each with a different combination of parameter values. A unique priority number is assigned to each created policy. At least one of these policies must contain exactly the same encryption, hash, authentication, and Diffie-Hellman parameter values as one of the policies on the remote peer.

If no policies are configured, the router uses the default policy, which is always set to the lowest priority and which contains the default value of each parameter. To configure a policy, use the commands shown in Table 4-3, beginning in global configuration mode, as demonstrated in Example 4-4 and Figure 4-4. If a value for a parameter is not specified, the default value is assigned.

Table 4-3   IKE Policy Commands

Step	Command	Default
Step 1	`Router(config)#`**`crypto isakmp`** **`policy`** `priority`	Identifies the policy to create. Each policy is uniquely identified by the assigned priority number. This command puts the administrator into the **config-isakmp** command mode.
Step 2	`Router(config-isakmp)#` `encryption {des	3des}`	Specifies the encryption algorithm.
Step 3	`Router(config-isakmp)#`**`hash`** **`{sha	md5}`**	Specifies the hash algorithm.
Step 4	`Router(config-isakmp)#authentication` `{rsa-sig ¦ rsa-encr ¦ pre-share}`	Specifies the authentication method.

Table 4-3   IKE Policy Commands   *continued*

Step	Command	Default
Step 5	`Router(config-isakmp)#` `group {1	2	5}`	Specifies the Diffie-Hellman group identifier.
Step 6	`Router(config-isakmp)#` `lifetime seconds`	Specifies the lifetime of the SA.
Step 7	`Router(config-isakmp)#exit`	Exits config-isakmp command mode.
Step 8	`Router(config)#exit`	Exits global configuration mode.
Step 9	`Router#show crypto isakmp policy`	(Optional) Displays all existing IKE policies. (Use this command in EXEC mode.)

Example 4-4   Create IKE Policies with the **crypto isakmp** Command

```
RouterA(config)#crypto isakmp policy 110
RouterA(config-isakmp)#authentication pre-share
RouterA(config-isakmp)#encryption des
RouterA(config-isakmp)#group1
RouterA(config-isakmp)#hash md5
RouterA(config-isakmp)#lifetime 86400
```

Figure 4-4   IKE Policy

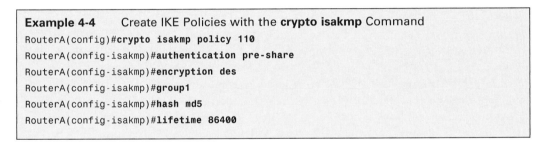

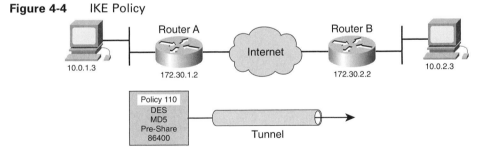

Note

The default policy and the default values for configured policies do not show up in the configuration when a **show running configuration** command is issued. Instead, to see the default policy and any default values within configured policies, use the **show crypto isakmp policy** command, as you will learn in the section "Step 4: Verify the IKE Configuration."

ISAKMP Policy Negotiation

ISAKMP peers negotiate acceptable ISAKMP policies before agreeing upon the SA to be used for IPsec. When the ISAKMP negotiation begins in IKE Phase 1 main mode, ISAKMP looks for an ISAKMP policy that is the same on both peers. The peer that initiates the negotiation sends all its policies to the remote peer, and the remote peer tries to find a match with its policies. The remote peer looks for a match by comparing its own highest-priority policy against the policies received from the peer. The remote peer checks each of its policies in order of its priority, checking the highest priority first, until a match is found.

A match is made when both policies from the two peers contain the same encryption, hash, authentication, and Diffie-Hellman parameter values, and when the remote peer's policy specifies a lifetime less than or equal to the lifetime in the policy being compared. If the lifetimes are not identical, the shorter lifetime from the remote peer's policy is used. Assign the most secure policy the lowest priority number so that the most secure policy will find a match before any less-secure policies configured.

If no acceptable match is found, ISAKMP refuses negotiation, and IPsec is not established. If a match is found, ISAKMP completes the main mode negotiation, and IPsec SAs are created during IKE Phase 2 quick mode.

ISAKMP Identity

The ISAKMP identity should be set for each peer that uses pre-shared keys in an IKE policy, as demonstrated in Example 4-5.

```
Example 4-5      ISAKMP Policy Negotiation
RouterA(config)#                        RouterB(config)#
crypto isakmp policy 100                crypto isakmp policy 100
  hash md5                                hash md5
  authentication pre-share                authentication pre-share
crypto isakmp policy 200                crypto isakmp policy 200
  authentication rsa-sig                  authentication rsa-sig
  hash sha                                hash sha
crypto isakmp policy 300                crypto isakmp policy 300
  authentication pre-share                authentication pre-share
```

When two peers use IKE to establish IPsec SAs, each peer sends its identity to the remote peer. Each peer sends either its host name or its IP address, depending on how the ISAKMP identity of the router has been set up, using the following command:

```
Router(config)#crypto isakmp identity {address | hostname}
```

where:

- *address*—Sets the ISAKMP identity to the IP address of the interface that is used to communicate to the remote peer during negotiations. The keyword is typically used when there is only one interface that will be used by the peer for ISAKMP negotiations and the IP address is known.

- *hostname*—Sets the ISAKMP identity to the host name, concatenated with the domain name (for example, myhost.domain.com). The keyword should be used if there is more than one interface on the peer that might be used for ISAKMP negotiations or if the interface's IP address is unknown (such as with dynamically assigned IP addresses).

By default, a peer's ISAKMP identity is the IP address of the peer. If appropriate, the identity could be changed to be the peer's host name instead. As a general rule, set the identities of all peers the same way. Either all peers should use their IP addresses or all peers should use their host names. If some peers use their host names and some peers use their IP addresses to identify themselves to each other, IKE negotiations could fail if the identity of a remote peer is not recognized and a Domain Name System (DNS) lookup cannot resolve the identity.

Step 3: Configure Pre-Shared Keys

To configure pre-shared keys, perform these tasks at each peer that uses pre-shared keys in an IKE policy, as shown in Figure 4-5:

1. Set the ISAKMP identity of each peer. The identity of each peer should be set to either its host name or by its IP address. By default, the peer identity is set to its IP address.

2. Specify the shared keys at each peer. Note that a given pre-shared key is shared between two peers. A given peer could be specified to use the same key to share with multiple remote peers. A more secure approach is to specify different keys to share between different pairs of peers.

Figure 4-5   Configure Pre-Shared Keys

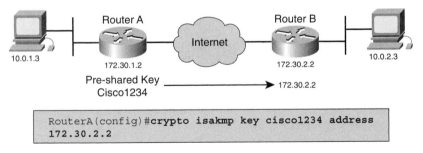

To specify pre-shared keys at a peer, use the commands shown in Table 4-4 in global configuration mode.

Table 4-4   Pre-Shared Key Configuration Commands

Step	Command	Purpose
Step 1	Router(config)#**crypto isakmp key** *keystring* **address** *pee-address* or Router(config)#**crypto isakmp key** keystring **hostname** peer-hostname	At the local peer: Specifies the shared key to be used with a particular remote peer. If the remote peer specified its ISAKMP identity with an address, use the **address** keyword in this step; otherwise, use the **hostname** keyword in this step.
Step 2	Router(config)#**crypto isakmp key** *keystring* **address** peer-address or Router(config)#**crypto isakmp key** *keystring* hostname peer-**hostname**	At the remote peer: Specifies the shared key to be used with the local peer. This is the same key you just specified at the local peer. If the local peer specified its ISAKMP identity with an address, use the **address** keyword in this step; otherwise, use the **hostname** keyword in this step.
Step 3	Repeat Steps 1 and 2 for each remote peer.	

Step 4: Verify the IKE Configuration

Use the **show crypto isakmp policy** command to display configured and default policies. Example 4-6 shows the resultant ISAKMP policy for RouterA from Figure 4-5. RouterB's configuration is identical.

```
Example 4-6    Verify the ISAKMP Configuration
RouterA#show crypto isakmp policy
Protection suite of priority 110
  encryption algorithm:        DES - Data Encryption Standard
                (56 bit keys).
  hash algorithm:              Message Digest 5
  authentication method:       Pre-shared Key
  Diffie-Hellman-group:        1 (768 bit)
  lifetime:                    86400 seconds, no volume limit
Default protection suite
  encryption algorithm:        DES - Data Encryption Standard
                (56 bit keys).
  hash algorithm:              Secure Hash Standard
  authentication method:       Rivest-Shamir-Adleman
Signature
  Diffie-Hellman-group:        1 (768 bit)
  lifetime:                    86400 seconds, no volume limit
```

Configure a Router with IPsec Using Pre-Shared Keys

The general tasks and commands used to configure IPsec encryption on Cisco routers are summarized as follows. Subsequent topics of this section discuss each configuration step in detail.

Step 1.   Configure transform set suites with the **crypto ipsec transform-set** command.

Step 2.   Determine the IPsec (IKE Phase 2) policy.

Step 3.   Configure crypto ACLs with the **access-list** command.

Step 4.   Configure crypto maps with the **crypto map** command.

Step 5.   Apply the crypto maps to the terminating/originating interface with the **interface** and **crypto map** commands.

Step 1: Configure Transform Set Suites

A transform set represents a certain combination of security protocols and algorithms that enact a security policy for traffic. During the IPsec SA negotiation, the peers agree to use a particular transform set for protecting a particular data flow.

You can specify multiple transform, and then specify one or more of these transform sets in a crypto map entry. The transform set defined in the crypto map entry is used in the IPsec SA negotiation to protect the data flows specified by the ACL in that crypto map entry.

During IPsec SA negotiations with IKE, the peers search for a transform set that is the same at both peers. When such a transform set is found, it is selected and will be applied to the protected traffic as part of the IPsec SAs of both peers.

With manually established SAs, there is no negotiation with the peer, so both sides must specify the same transform set. Transform sets are limited to one AH and up to two ESP transforms.

If a transform set definition is changed, the change is only applied to crypto map entries that reference the transform set. The change is not applied to existing SAs, but is used in subsequent negotiations to establish new SAs. To force the new settings to take effect sooner, you can clear all or part of the SA database by using the **clear crypto sa** command.

To define a transform set, use the commands shown in Table 4-5 starting in global configuration mode.

Table 4-5   Transform Set Commands

Step	Command	Purpose
Step 1	Router(config)#**crypto ipsec transform-set** *transform-set-name tranfrom1* [*transform2* [*transform3*]]	Defines a transform set. Complex rules define which entries you can use for the transform arguments. These rules are explained in the command description for the **crypto ipsec transform-set** command. This command puts you into the crypto transform configuration mode.
Step 2	Router(cfg-crypto-tran)# **mode** [**tunnel** ¦ **transport**]	(Optional)Changes the mode associated with the transform set. The transport mode setting is only applicable to traffic whose source and destination addresses are the IPsec peer addresses. It is ignored for all other traffic. Default mode is tunnel.
Step 3	Router(cfg-crypto-tran)#**exit**	Exits the crypto transform configuration mode.

For the network illustrated in Figure 4-6, you might define the transform set as follows:

```
RouterA(config)#crypto ipsec transform-set MINE esp-des esp-md5-hmac
```

Figure 4-6   Configure Transform Sets

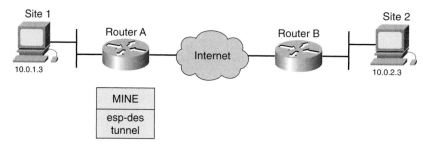

To edit a transform set, follow these steps:

Step 1.   Configure transform set suites.

Step 2.   Delete the transform set from the crypto map.

Step 3.   Delete the transform set from global configuration.

Step 4.   Reenter the transform set with corrections.

Step 5.   Assign the transform set to a crypto map.

Step 6.   Clear the SA database.

Step 7.   Observe the SA negotiation and ensure it works properly.

Transform sets are negotiated during quick mode in IKE Phase 2 using the previously configured transform sets. Configure the transforms from most to least secure as dictated by the security policy. The transform set defined in the crypto map entry is used in the IPsec SA negotiation to protect the data flows specified by the ACL in that crypto map entry.

During the negotiation, the peers search for a transform set that is the same at both peers. For example, each transform set on Router A is compared against each transform set on Router B in succession. The transform sets 10, 20, and 30 on Router A are compared with the transform set 40 on Router B. The result is no match. All the transform sets on Router A are then compared to the transform on Router B. Ultimately, the transform set 30 on Router A matches the transform set 60 on Router B. When such a transform set is found, it is selected and applied to the protected traffic as part of the IPsec SA of both peers. IPsec peers agree on one transform proposal per SA in unidirectional manner.

Step 2: Determine the IPsec (IKE Phase 2) Policy

An IPsec policy defines a combination of IPsec parameters used during the IPsec negotiation. Planning for IPsec, also known as IKE Phase 2, is another important step that you should complete before actually configuring IPsec on a Cisco router. Policy details to determine at this stage include the following:

- **Select IPsec algorithms and parameters for optimal security and performance—**
  Determine what type of IPsec security to use when securing interesting traffic. Some IPsec algorithms require trade-offs between high performance and stronger security. Some algorithms have import and export restrictions that might delay or prevent implementation of the network.

- **Select transforms and, if necessary, transform sets—**Use the IPsec algorithms and parameters previously decided upon to help select IPsec transforms, transform sets, and modes of operation.

- **Identify IPsec peer details—**Identify the IP addresses and host names of all IPsec peers to be connected.

- **Determine IP address and applications of hosts to be protected—**Decide which hosts IP addresses and applications should be protected at the local peer and remote peer.

- **Select manual or IKE-initiated SAs—**Choose whether SAs are manually established or are established through IKE.

The goal of this planning step is to gather the precise data required in later steps to minimize misconfiguration.

Authentication Header (AH) is rarely used because authentication is now available with the **esp-sha-hmac** and **esp-md5-hmac** transforms. AH is also not compatible with NAT or PAT.

The Cisco IOS command parser prevents invalid combinations from being entered. For example, after an AH transform is specified, it does not allow another AH transform to be specified for the current transform set.

Step 3: Create Crypto ACLs

Crypto access lists are used to define which IP traffic will be and which will not be protected by IPsec, as illustrated by Figure 4-7. These access lists are not the same as regular access lists, which determine what traffic to forward or block at an interface. For example, you can create a crypto access list to protect all IP traffic between two subnets or Telnet traffic between two individual hosts.

Figure 4-7   Purpose of Crypto ACLs

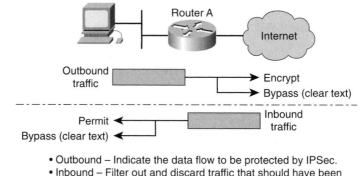

• Outbound – Indicate the data flow to be protected by IPSec.
• Inbound – Filter out and discard traffic that should have been protected by IPSec.

The access lists themselves are not specific to IPsec. It is the crypto map entry referencing the specific access list that defines whether IPsec processing is applied to the traffic matching a **permit** statement in the access list.

If certain traffic is to receive one combination of IPsec protection, such as authentication only, and other traffic is to receive a different combination of IPsec protection, such as both authentication and encryption, you must create two different crypto access lists to define the two different types of traffic. These different access lists are then used in different crypto map entries that specify different IPsec policies.

To create crypto access lists, use the following command in global configuration mode:

```
access-list access-list-number [dynamic dynamic-name [timeout minutes]] {deny | permit}
protocol source source-wildcard destination destination-wildcard [precedence precedence]
[tos tos] [log]
```

Although the ACL syntax is unchanged, the meanings differ slightly for crypto ACLs. The **permit** keyword specifies that matching packets must be encrypted. The **deny** keyword specifies that matching packets need not be encrypted. Any unprotected inbound traffic that matches a **permit** entry in the crypto ACL for a crypto map entry flagged as IPsec will be dropped, because this traffic was expected to be protected by IPsec.

Cisco recommends that you avoid the **any** keyword. The **permit any any** statement is strongly discouraged, too, because this statement causes all outbound traffic to be protected and requires protection for all inbound traffic. All inbound packets that lack IPsec protection will be silently dropped, including packets for routing protocols, Network Time Protocol (NTP), echo, echo response, and so on.

Try to be as restrictive as possible when defining the traffic to protect in a crypto ACL. If you must use the **any** keyword in a **permit** statement, you must preface that statement with a series of **deny** statements to filter out any traffic that should not be protected that would otherwise fall within that **permit** statement.

In a later step, the crypto ACL is applied to a crypto map, which in turn is assigned to a specific interface.

Cisco recommends that for every crypto access list specified for a static crypto map entry that is defined at the local peer a symmetrical, or mirror image, crypto access list be configured at the remote peer. This symmetrical crypto access list ensures that traffic that has IPsec protection applied locally can be processed correctly at the remote peer. The crypto map entries themselves must also support common transforms and must refer to the other system as a peer.

Both inbound and outbound traffic is evaluated against the same outbound IPsec ACL. The criteria of the ACL are applied in the forward direction to traffic when exiting a router, and the reverse direction to traffic when entering a router. When a router receives encrypted packets back from an IPsec peer, it uses the same ACL to determine which inbound packets to decrypt by viewing the source and destination addresses in the ACL in reverse order.

The example shown in Figure 4-8 illustrates why symmetrical ACLs are recommended. For site 1, IPsec protection is applied to traffic between hosts on the 10.0.1.0 network as the data exits the interface of Router A when the destination is one of the site 2 hosts on the 10.0.2.0 network. For traffic from site 1 hosts on the 10.0.1.0 network to site 2 hosts on the 10.0.2.0 network, the ACL entry on Router A is evaluated as follows:

- Source = hosts on 10.0.1.0 network.

- Destination = hosts on 10.0.2.0 network.

Figure 4-8   Configure Symmetrical Peer Crypto ACLs

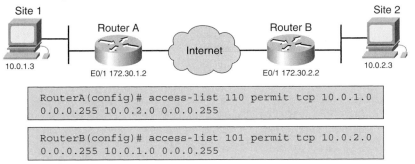

For incoming traffic from site 2 hosts on the 10.0.2.0 network to site 1 hosts on the 10.0.1.0 network, that same ACL entry on Router A is evaluated as follows:

- Source = hosts on 10.0.2.0 network.

- Destination = hosts on 10.0.1.0 network.

Step 4: Create Crypto Maps

Crypto map entries created for IPsec set up SA parameters, tying together the various parts configured for IPsec, including the following:

- Which traffic should be protected by IPsec, as defined in crypto ACL

- The peer where IPsec-protected traffic should be sent

- The local address to be used for the IPsec traffic

- Which IPsec type should be applied to this traffic

- Whether SAs are established, either manually or using IKE

- Other parameters needed to define an IPsec SA

Crypto map entries with the same crypto map name but different map sequence numbers are grouped into a crypto map set. These crypto map sets are applied to interfaces. Then, all IP traffic passing through the interface is evaluated against the applied crypto map set. If a crypto map entry sees outbound IP traffic that should be protected and the crypto map specifies the use of IKE, an SA is negotiated with the remote peer according to the parameters included in the crypto map entry. If the crypto map entry specifies the use of manual SAs, an SA should have already been established in the configuration. If a dynamic crypto map entry sees outbound traffic that should be protected and no SA exists, the packet is dropped.

The policy described in the crypto map entries is used during the negotiation of SAs. If the local router initiates the negotiation, it uses the policy specified in the static crypto map entries to create the offer to be sent to the specified IPsec peer. If the IPsec peer initiates the negotiation, the local router checks the policy from the static crypto map entries, and any referenced dynamic crypto map entries, to decide whether to accept or reject the request of the peer.

When two IPsec peers try to establish an SA, they must each have at least one crypto map entry that is compatible with one of the crypto map entries on the other peer. For two crypto map entries to be compatible, they must at least meet the following criteria:

- The crypto map entries must contain compatible crypto access lists, such as mirror image access lists. In the case where the responding peer is using dynamic crypto maps, the entries in the local crypto access list must be permitted by the crypto access list of the remote peer.

- The crypto map entries must each identify the other peer, unless the responding peer is using dynamic crypto maps.

- The crypto map entries must have at least one transform set in common.

You can apply only one crypto map set to a single interface. The crypto map set can include a combination of Cisco Encryption Technology (CET), IPsec using IKE, and IPsec with manually configured SA entries. Multiple interfaces can share the same crypto map set so that the same policy can be applied to multiple interfaces.

If more than one crypto map entry is created for a given interface, use the sequence number of each map entry to rank the map entries. The lower the sequence number, the higher the priority. At the interface that has the crypto map set, traffic is evaluated against higher-priority map entries first.

You can create multiple crypto map entries for a given interface if any of the following conditions exist:

- If different data flows are to be handled by separate IPsec peers.

- If different IPsec security needs to be applied to different types of traffic, either to the same or separate IPsec peers. Consider, for example, that traffic between one set of subnets needs to be authenticated, and traffic between another set of subnets needs to be both authenticated and encrypted. In this case, the different types of traffic should have been defined in two separate ACLs, and a separate crypto map entry must be created for each crypto ACL.

- If IKE is not being used to establish a particular set of SAs, multiple ACL entries need to be specified, separate ACLs must be created, one per permit entry, and a separate crypto map entry for each ACL must be specified.

Use the **crypto map** global configuration command to create or modify a crypto map entry and enter the crypto map configuration mode:

```
crypto map map-name seq-num [ipsec-manual]
crypto map map-name seq-num [ipsec-isakmp] [dynamic dynamic-map-name]
```

Use a different sequence number for each peer. Multiple peers can be specified in a single crypto map for redundancy. Use one crypto map per interface. Set the crypto map entries referencing dynamic maps to be the lowest-priority entries in a crypto map set. Remember that the lowest-priority entries have the highest sequence numbers. Use the **no** form of this command to delete a crypto map entry or set.

Example 4-7 shows a crypto map with two peers specified for redundancy for the network in Figure 4-9. If the first peer cannot be contacted, the second peer is used. No limit applies to the number of redundant peers that you can configure.

Example 4-7   Example Crypto Map Commands

```
RouterA(config)#crypto map MYMAP 110 ipsec-isakmp
RouterA(config-crypto-map)#match address 110
RouterA(config-crypto-map)#set peer 172.30.2.2
RouterA(config-crypto-map)#set peer 172.30.3.2
RouterA(config-crypto-map)#set pfs group1
RouterA(config-crypto-map)#set transform-set MINE
RouterA(config-crypto-map)#set security-association lifetime seconds 86400
```

Figure 4-9   Network with Crypto Maps

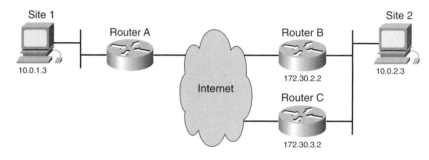

The **crypto map** command has a crypto map configuration mode with the commands and syntax shown in Table 4-6.

Table 4-6   Crypto Map Configuration Commands

Command	Description
set	Used with the **peer**, **pfs**, **transform-set**, and **security-association** commands.
peer [**hostname** | *ip-address*]	Specifies the allowed IPsec peer by IP address or host name.
pfs [*group1* | *group2* | *group5*]	Specifies Diffie-Hellman Group 1, Group 2, or Group 5.
transform-set [*set name(s)*]	Specifies the list of transform sets in priority order. For an **ipsec-manual** crypto map, you can specify only one transform set. For an **ipsec-isakmp** or **dynamic** crypto map entry, you can specify up to six transform sets.
security-association *lifetime*	Sets SA lifetime parameters in seconds or kilobytes.

Table 4-6 Crypto Map Configuration Commands *continued*

Command	Description
match address [access-list-id | name]	Identifies the extended ACL by its name or number. The value should match the **access-list-number** or **name** argument of a previously defined IP-extended ACL being matched.
no	Used to delete commands entered with the **set** command.
exit	Exits crypto map configuration mode.

Step 5: Apply Crypto Maps to Interfaces

You need to apply a crypto map to each interface through which IPsec traffic will flow. Applying the crypto map set to an interface instructs the router to evaluate all the traffic that passes through the interface against the crypto map set and to use the specified policy during connection or SA negotiation on behalf of traffic to be protected by IPsec.

To apply a crypto map set to an interface, use the **crypto map** *map-name* command in interface configuration mode, as follows:

```
Router(config)#interface interface
Router(config-if)#crypto map map-name
```

For redundancy, you can apply the same crypto map to more than one interface. The default behavior is as follows:

- Each interface has its own piece of the SA database.
- The IP address of the local interface is used as the local address for IPsec traffic originating from or destined to that interface.

If you apply the same crypto map set to multiple interfaces for redundancy purposes, you must specify an identifying interface. This has the following effects:

- The per-interface portion of the IPsec SA database is established one time and shared for traffic through all the interfaces that share the same crypto map.
- The IP address of the identifying interface is used as the local address for IPsec traffic originating from or destined to those interfaces sharing the same crypto map set.

One suggestion is to use a loopback interface as the identifying interface.

To specify redundant interfaces and name an identifying interface, use the **crypto map** *map-name* **local-address** *interface-id* command in global configuration mode.

Test and Verify the IPsec Configuration of the Router

You can perform the following actions to test and verify that the IPsec VPN has been configured correctly:

- Display the configured ISAKMP policies using the **show crypto isakmp policy** command.

- Display the configured transform sets using the **show crypto ipsec transform-set** command.

- Display the current state of the IPsec SAs with the **show crypto ipsec sa** command.

- View the configured crypto maps with the **show crypto map** command.

- Debug ISAKMP and IPsec traffic through the Cisco IOS with the **debug crypto ipsec** and **debug crypto isakmp** commands.

Display the Configured ISAKMP Policies

Use the **show crypto isakmp policy** EXEC command to view the parameters for each ISAKMP policy, as demonstrated in Example 4-8.

```
Example 4-8      Displaying ISAKMP Policy Parameters
Router# show crypto isakmp policy
Protection suite of priority 110
    encryption algorithm:     DES - Data Encryption Standard
(56 bit keys).
    hash algorithm            Message Digest 5
    authentication method:    Rivest-Shamir-Adleman
Encryption
    Diffie-Hellman group:     #1 (768 bit)
    lifetime:                 86400 seconds, no volume limit
Default protection suite
    encryption algorithm:     DES - Data Encryption Standard
(56 bit keys)
    hash algorithm:           Secure Hash Standard
    authentication method:    Rivest-Shamir-Adleman
Signature
    Diffie-Hellman group:     #1 (768 bit)
    lifetime:                 86400 seconds, no volume limit
```

Display the Configured Transform Sets

Use the show **crypto ipsec transform-set** [*transform-set-name*] EXEC command to view the configured transform sets as demonstrated in Example 4-9.

Example 4-9   Sample **show crypto ipsec transform-set** Command Output

```
Router#show crypto ipsec transform-set
Transform-set MINE: { esp-des esp-md5-hmac}
   will negotiate = {Tunnel, },
```

This command shows only the transform sets with the specified *transform-set-name*. If no *transform-set-name* is specified, all transform sets configured at the router display.

Display the Current State of IPsec SAs

Use the following EXEC command to view the settings used by current SAs:

`show crypto ipsec sa [map map-name | address | identity | details]`

If no keyword is used, all SAs display. Table 4-7 explains the command syntax for this command, and Example 4-10 demonstrates sample output from the command.

Table 4-7   **show crypto ipsec sa** Command Syntax

Command	Description
map *map-name*	(Optional) Displays any existing SAs created for the crypto map.
address	(Optional) Displays all the existing SAs, sorted by the destination address and then by protocol (AH or ESP).
identity	(Optional) Displays only the flow information. It does not show the SA information.
detail	(Optional) Displays detailed error counters. (The default is the high-level send/receive error counters.)

Example 4-10   Sample **show crypto ipsec sa** Command Output

```
Router A#show crypto ipsec sa
Interface:  Ethernet 0/1
    Crypto map tag: MYMAP, local addr. 172.30.1.2
    local ident (addr/mask/prot/port):
(172.30.1.2/255.255.255.255/0/0)
    remote ident (addr/mask/prot/port):
(172.30.2.2/255.255.255.255/0/0)
    current_peer: 172.30.2.2
      PERMIT, flags={origin_is_acl,}
    #pkts encaps: 21, #pkts encrypt: 21, #pkts digest 0
    #pkts decap:   21, #pkts decrypt: 21, #pkts verify  0
    #send errors 0, #recv errors 0
      local crypto endpt.; 172.30.1.2, remote crypto endpt.;172.30.2.2
      path mtu 1500, media mtu 1500
      current outbound spi: 8AE1C9C
```

Display the Configured Crypto Maps

Use the following EXEC command to view the currently configured crypto map:

```
show crypto map [interface interface ¦ tag map-name]
```

If no keywords are used, all crypto maps configured at the router display.

When the **interface** keyword is used, only the crypto map set applied to the specified interface displays. When the **tag** keyword is used, only the crypto map set with the specified *map-name* displays.

Example 4-11 demonstrates sample output from the **show crypto map** command.

```
Example 4-11    show crypto map Command Output
Router#show crypto map
Crypto Map "MYMAP" 10 ipsec-isakmp
        Peer = 172.30.2.2
        Extended IP access list 102
            access-list 102 permit ip host 172.30.1.2 host 172.30.2.2
        Current peer: 172.30.2.2
        Security association lifetime: 4608000 kilobytes/3600 seconds
        PFS (Y/N): N
        Transform sets={ MINE, }
```

Enable debug Output for IPsec Events

Use the **debug crypto ipsec EXEC** and the **debug crypto isakmp** commands to display IPsec and ISAKMP events. The **no** form of these commands disables debugging output.

These commands generate a significant amount of output for every IP packet processed. You should use them only when IP traffic on the network is low, so that other activity on the router is not adversely affected. For example, to display debug messages about all IPsec actions, enter the following command:

```
Router# debug crypto ipsec
```

To display **debug** messages about all ISAKMP actions, enter the following command:

```
Router# debug crypto isakmp
```

Enable debug Output for ISAKMP Events

To display messages about IKE events, use the **debug crypto isakmp** command in privileged EXEC mode. To disable debugging output, use the **no** form of this command.

Cisco IOS Software can generate many useful system error messages for ISAKMP. Two examples of error messages are as follows:

```
%CRYPTO-6-IKMP_SA_NOT_AUTH: Cannot accept Quick Mode exchange from %15i if SA is not
authenticated!
%CRYPTO-6-IKMP_SA_NOT_OFFERED: Remote peer %15i responded with attribute [chars] not
offered or changed
```

For the first error message, the ISAKMP SA with the remote peer was not authenticated, but even still the peer attempted to begin a quick mode exchange. This exchange must only be done with an authenticated SA. The recommended action is to contact the administrator of the remote peer to resolve the improper configuration.

For the second error message, the ISAKMP peers negotiate policy by the initiator offering a list of possible alternative protection suites. The responder responded with an ISAKMP policy that the initiator did not offer. The recommended action is to contact the administrator of the remote peer to resolve the improper configuration.

Lab 4.4.7   Configure IOS IPsec Using Pre-Shared Keys

In this lab, you prepare to configure virtual private network (VPN) support. You learn to configure Internet Key Exchange (IKE) Phase 1. You also configure IKE parameters and verify IKE and IP Security (IPsec). You then configure the IPsec parameters. Finally, you test and verify the IPsec configuration.

Configure a VPN Using SDM

Security Device Manager (SDM) can guide administrators through a simple VPN configuration. The VPN Wizard is accessible by clicking the VPN icon.

The following two options are available in the wizard:

- **Create a Site-to-Site VPN**—This option enables administrators to create a VPN network connecting two routers.

- **Create a Secure GRE Tunnel (GRE-over-IPsec)**—This option enables administrators to configure a generic routing encapsulation protocol (GRE) tunnel between the router and a peer system.

When using the site-to-site VPN Wizard, SDM can be allowed to use default settings for most of the configuration values, or SDM can be used to guide the administrator in configuring a VPN.

Quick Setup

To quickly configure a site-to-site VPN using SDM-provided defaults, check **Quick setup**, and then click **Next**. SDM automatically provides a default IKE policy to govern authentication, a default transform set to control the encryption of data, and a default IPsec rule that encrypts all traffic between the router and the remote device.

Quick setup is best used when both the local router and the remote system are Cisco routers using SDM.

Quick setup configures 3DES encryption if it is supported by the Cisco IOS image. Otherwise, it configures DES encryption. If AES or SEAL encryption is needed, click **Step-by-step wizard**.

To view the default IKE policy, transform set, and IPsec rule that will be used to configure a one-step VPN, click **View Defaults**.

Step-by-Step Wizard

To configure a site-to-site VPN using specified parameters, check **Step-by-Step wizard**, and then click **Next**. You can create a custom configuration for the VPN. You can use any of the SDM default parameters that you need in the configuration. The Step-by-Step Wizard enables the administrator to specify stronger encryption than the Quick Setup Wizard allows.

Lab 4.4.8a   Configuring Cisco IOS IPsec with Pre-Shared Keys Using SDM

In this lab, you prepare to configure VPN support. You learn to configure a VPN tunnel using the SDM VPN Wizard. You also modify the IKE and IPsec configuration. You then test and verify the IPsec configuration.

Lab 4.4.8b   Configuring Cisco GRE IPsec Tunnel Using SDM

In this lab, you prepare to configure VPN support. You learn to configure a GRE/IPsec tunnel using the SDM VPN Wizard. You also modify the GRE/IPsec configuration. You then test and verify the GRE/IPsec configuration.

Configure a PIX Security Appliance Site-to-Site VPN Using Pre-Shared Keys

The rest of this chapter discusses the configuration of an IPsec-based VPN between two PIX Security Appliances operating as secure gateways using pre-shared keys for authentication. The four overall tasks used to configure IPsec encryption on the PIX are as follows:

- **Task 1**—Prepare to configure VPN support. This task consists of several steps that determine IPsec policies, ensure that the network works, and ensure that the PIX Security Appliance can support IPsec.

- **Task 2**—Configure IKE parameters. This task consists of several configuration steps that ensure that IKE can set up secure channels to desired IPsec peers during IKE Phase 1.

- **Task 3**—Configure IPsec parameters. This task consists of several configuration steps that specify IPsec SA parameters between peers and set global IPsec values. IKE negotiates SA parameters and sets up IPsec SAs during IKE Phase 2.

- **Task 4**—Test and verify VPN configuration. After IPsec is configured, it is necessary to verify that it has been configured correctly and ensure that it works.

Subsequent topics of this lesson discuss each configuration task in greater detail.

Task 1: Prepare to Configure VPN Support

Configuring IPsec encryption can be complicated. Planning in advance of the actual configuration helps the administrator to configure IPsec encryption correctly the first time and minimize configuration errors. You should start this task by defining the overall security needs and strategy based on the overall company security policy. Planning steps include the following:

Step 1. **Determine the IKE (IKE Phase 1) policy**—Determine the IKE policies between peers based on the number and location of IPsec peers.

Step 2. **Determine the IPsec (IKE Phase 2) policy**—Identify IPsec peer details such as IP addresses and IPsec modes. Determine the IPsec policies applied to the encrypted data passing between peers.

Step 3. **Ensure that the network works without encryption**—Ensure that basic connectivity has been achieved between IPsec peers using the desired IP services before configuring firewall appliance IPsec.

Step 4. Implicitly permit IPsec packets to bypass PIX Security Appliance ACLs and access groups. You can do this with the sysopt connection **permit-ipsec** command.

Task 2: Configure IKE parameters

Configuring IKE consists of the following steps:

Step 1. **Enable or disable IKE**—Enable or disable IKE, or ISAKMP, negotiation with the **isakmp enable** *interface-name* command in global configuration mode. This command specifies the PIX Security Appliance interface on which the IPsec peer will communicate. IKE is enabled by default for all PIX interfaces. Use the **no isakmp enable** *interface-name* command to disable IKE on an individual interface.

Note

If the authentication method of pre-shared keys is specified, you must manually configure the pre-shared key.

Step 2.   **Configure IKE Phase 1 policy**—Configure an IKE Phase 1 policy with the **isakmp policy** command to match expected IPsec peers by completing the substeps that follow:

a. Identify the policy with a unique priority designation with the **isakmp policy** *priority* command. Use an integer from 1 to 65,534, with 1 being the highest priority and 65,534 the lowest.

b. Specify the encryption algorithm with the **isakmp policy** *priority* **encryption {des | 3des |aes | aes-192 | aes-256}** command. The default is **des**.

c. Specify the hash algorithm with the **isakmp policy** *priority* **hash {md5 | sha}**. The default is **sha**.

d. Specify the authentication method with the **isakmp policy** *priority* **authentication {pre-share | rsa-sig}** command.

e. Specify the DH group identifier with the **isakmp policy** *priority* **group 1 | 2 | 5 | 7** command. The default is **group 1**.

f. Specify the IKE SA lifetime with the **isakmp policy** *priority* **lifetime** *seconds* command. The default is 86,400 seconds.

Here is a sample IKE Phase 1 policy configuration:

```
pixfirewall(config)#isakmp policy 10 encryption des
pixfirewall(config)#isakmp policy 10 hash share
pixfirewall(config)#isakmp policy 10 authentication pre-share
pixfirewall(config)#isakmp policy 10 group 1
pixfirewall(config)#isakmp policy 10 lifetime 86400
```

Note

The PIX Security Appliance has preset default values. If a default value is entered for a given policy parameter, it will not be written in the configuration. If a value is not specified for a given policy parameter, the default value is assigned. You can view the configured and default values with the **show isakmp policy** command.

Step 3.   **Configure a tunnel group**—A tunnel group is a set of records that contain tunnel connection policies. You can configure a tunnel group to identify authentication, authorization, and accounting (AAA) servers; specify connection parameters; and define a default group policy. The PIX Security Appliance stores tunnel groups internally. There are two default tunnel groups on the PIX: DefaultRAGroup, which is the default IPsec remote-access tunnel group; and DefaultL2Lgroup, which is the default IPsec LAN-to-LAN tunnel group. You can change these groups but not delete them. The PIX uses these groups to configure default tunnel parameters for remote access and LAN-to-LAN tunnel groups when no specific tunnel group is identified during tunnel negotiation. To establish a basic LAN-to-LAN connection, you must set the connection type to IPsec LAN to LAN, and an authentication method must be configured (for example, pre-shared key).

Use the **tunnel-group** *name* **type** *type* global configuration command to configure a tunnel group (the *type* argument defines the type of VPN connection to be established), as demonstrated in Figure 4-10.

Figure 4-10   Configure a Tunnel Group

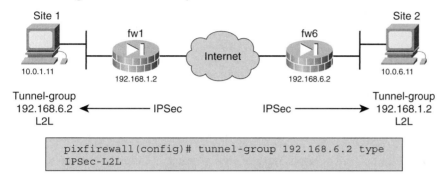

Step 4.   **Configure tunnel group attributes, pre-shared key**—Configure the tunnel group pre-shared key attributes using the following command:

```
Pixfirewall(config)#tunnel-group name [general attributes | ipsec-attributes
    | ppp-attributes]
```

The *name* variable specifies the name of the tunnel group. Executing this command enters tunnel group IPsec-attributes submode in which you can associate a pre-shared key with the connection policy:

```
Pixfirewall(config-ipsec)#pre-shared-key key
```

The **pre-shared-key** *key* command specifies a pre-shared key to support IKE connections based on pre-shared keys. The *key* variable specifies an alphanumeric key between 1 and 127 characters.

Figure 4-11 demonstrates this process.

Figure 4-11   Configure Tunnel Group Attributes, Pre-Shared Key

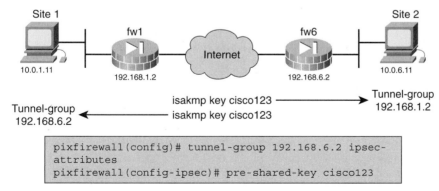

The **tunnel-group** command includes the following variations:

```
Pixfirewall(config)#tunnel-group name general-attributes
Pixfirewall(config-general)#
```

This first mode is used to configure settings common to all supported tunneling protocols.

```
Pixfirewall(config)# tunnel-group name ipsec-attributes
Pixfirewall(config-ipsec)#
```

This second mode is used to configure settings specific to the IPsec tunneling protocol.

```
Pixfirewall(config)# tunnel-group name ppp-attributes
Pixfirewall(config-ppp)#
```

This last mode is used to configure settings specific to the PPP tunneling protocol.

Each of these commands puts the administrator in a configuration mode for configuring the attributes at the level of the configuration mode.

Step 5.   **Verify IKE Phase 1 policies**—The **show run crypto isakmp** command displays configured and default policies, as demonstrated here:

```
Pixfirewall#show run crypto isakmp
isakmp identity address
isakmp enable outside
isakmp policy 10 authentication pre-share
isakmp policy 10 encryption 3des
isakmp policy 10 hash sha
isakmp policy 10 group 2
isakmp policy 10 lifetime 86400
```

The **show run crypto isakmp** command displays configured policies much as they would appear with the **write terminal** command.

The **show run tunnel-group** command displays tunnel group information about all or a specified tunnel group and tunnel group attributes.

Task 3: Configure IPsec Parameters

The steps and commands used to configure IPsec encryption on the PIX Security Appliance are as follows:

Step 1.   **Configure interesting traffic**—Crypto ACLs perform the same function on the PIX Security Appliance and a Cisco IOS router. Crypto ACLs are used to define which IP traffic is interesting and will be protected by IPsec, and which traffic will not be protected by IPsec, as shown in Figure 4-12. Remember that it is recommended to avoid using the **any** keyword to specify source or destination addresses.

Figure 4-12 Configure Interesting Traffic with ACLs

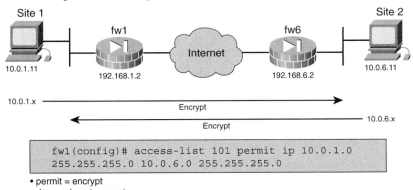

```
fw1(config)# access-list 101 permit ip 10.0.1.0
255.255.255.0 10.0.6.0 255.255.255.0
```

- permit = encrypt
- deny = do not encrypt

Use the **show run access-list** command to display currently configured ACLs. Figure 4-13 contains an example ACL for each of the peer PIX Security Appliances. In the fw1 ACL, the source network is 10.0.1.0, and the destination network is 10.0.6.0. In the fw6 ACL, the source network is 10.0.6.0, and the destination address is 10.0.1.0. The ACLs are symmetrical.

Figure 4-13 Example of Crypto ACLs

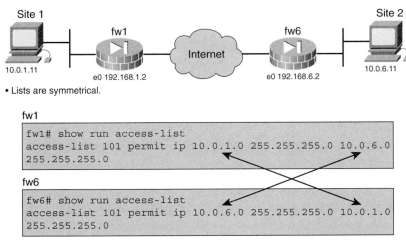

The **nat 0** command instructs the PIX Security Appliance not to use NAT for any traffic deemed interesting traffic for IPsec. In Figure 4-14, traffic matching access-list 101, traffic from 10.0.1.0/24 to 10.0.6.0/24, is exempt from NAT.

Figure 4-14   Exclude Traffic with the **nat 0** Command

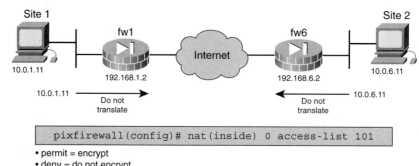

```
pixfirewall(config)# nat(inside) 0 access-list 101
```

• permit = encrypt
• deny = do not encrypt

Note

In PIX Security Appliance Version 6.0 and later, Layer 2 Tunneling Protocol (L2TP) is the only protocol that can use the IPsec transport mode. The PIX discards all other types of packets using IPsec transport mode.

Step 2.   **Configure an IPsec transform set**—To configure the IPsec transform set, use the following command:

```
Pixfirewall(config)#crypto ipsec transform-set transform-set-name transform1
    [transform2]
```

Transforms define the IPsec security protocols and algorithms. Each transform represents an IPsec security protocol, ESP, AH, or both, plus the algorithm to be used. Transform sets are limited to two transforms.

You can specify multiple transform sets, and then you can specify one or more of these transform in a crypto map entry. The transform set defined in the crypto map entry is used in the IPsec SA negotiation to protect the data flows specified by the ACL of that crypto map entry.

During the IPsec SA negotiation, the peers agree to use a particular transform set for protecting a particular data flow.

A transform set equals an AH transform and an ESP transform plus the mode, either transport mode or tunnel mode. Transform sets are limited to one AH and two ESP transforms. The default mode is tunnel. Be sure to configure matching transform sets between IPsec peers.

The PIX Security Appliance supports the following transforms:

- **esp-des**—ESP transform using DES cipher (56 bits)
- **esp-3des**—ESP transform using 3DES cipher (168 bits)
- **esp-aes**—ESP transform using AES-128 cipher
- **esp-aes-192**—ESP transform using AES-192 cipher
- **esp-aes-256**—ESP transform using AES-256 cipher
- **esp-md5-hmac**—ESP transform using HMAC-MD5 auth
- **esp-sha-hmac**—ESP transform using HMAC-SHA auth
- **esp-none**—ESP no authentication
- **esp-null**—ESP null encryption

Choosing IPsec transforms combinations can prove complex. The following tips might help:

- To provide data confidentiality, include an ESP encryption transform.
- Also consider including an ESP authentication transform or an AH transform to provide authentication services for the transform set. To ensure data authentication for the outer IP header and the data, include an AH transform. Choose from the MD5 or SHA authentication algorithm.
- The SHA algorithm is generally considered stronger than MD5, but it is slower.
- Examples of acceptable transform combinations are as follows:
  - **esp-des** for high performance encryption
  - **ah-md5-hmac** for authenticating packet contents with no encryption
  - **esp-3des** and **esp-md5-hmac** for strong encryption and authentication
  - **ah-sha-hmac** and **esp-3des** and **esp-sha-hmac** for strong encryption and authentication

Step 3. **Configure the crypto map**—The syntax for the crypto map command is as follows:

```
Firewall(config)#crypto map map-name seq-num {ipsec-isakmp | ipsec-manual |
  [dynamic dynamic-map-name]}
```

where:

- **ipsec-isakmp**—Indicates that IKE will be used to establish the IPsec SAs for protecting the traffic specified by this crypto map entry.
- **ipsec-manual**—Indicates that IKE will not be used to establish the IPsec SAs for protecting the traffic specified by the crypto map entry. Note that manual configuration of SAs is not supported on the PIX 501
- **map** *map-name*—Indicates the name of the crypto map set.

Configure the crypto map with the **crypto map** command by completing the substeps shown in Table 4-8.

Table 4-8   Configure a Crypto Map Entry

Step	Description
1	Create a crypto map entry in IPsec ISAKMP mode [9] with the **crypto map** *map-name seq-num* **ipsec-isakmp** command. This identifies the crypto map with a unique crypto map name and sequence number.
2	Assign an ACL to the crypto map entry with the **crypto map** *map-name seq-num* **match address** *access-list-name* command.
3	Specify IPsec peer with the **crypto map** *map-name seq-num* **set peer** [*hostname* | *ip-address*] command. This specifies the peer host name or IP address. You can specify multiple peers by repeating this command.
4	Specify which transform sets are allowed for this crypto map entry with the **crypto map** *map-name seq-num* **set transform-set** [*transform-set-name 1-6*] command. If multiple transform sets are used, list them in order of priority, with the highest priority first. You can specify up to six transform sets.

Step 4.   **Apply the crypto map to an interface**—Apply the crypto map to an interface with the following command:

```
pixfirewall(config)#crypto map map-name interface interface-name
```

This activates the IPsec policy.

Step 5.   Use the **show run crypto map** command to verify the crypto map configuration—Consider the following output of the command for a crypto map for the PIX Security Appliance with the name fw1:

```
fw1# show run crypto map
crypto map FW1MAP 10 match address 101
crypto map FW1MAP 10 set peer 192.168.6.2
crypto map FW1MAP 10 set transform-set pix6
crypto map FW1MAP interface outside
```

Task 4: Test and Verify the IPsec Configuration

You can perform the following actions to test and verify that the VPN is configured correctly on the PIX Security Appliance:

- Verify ACLs and select interesting traffic with the **show run access-list** command.

- Verify correct IKE configuration with the **show run isakmp** and **show run tunnel-group** commands.

- Verify correct IPsec configuration of transform sets with the **show run ipsec** command.

- Verify the correct crypto map configuration with the **show run crypto map** command.

- Clear IPsec SAs for testing of SA establishment with the **clear crypto ipsec sa** command.

- Clear IKE SAs for testing of IKE SA establishment with the **clear crypto isakmp sa** command.

Debug IKE and IPsec traffic through the firewall appliance with the **debug crypto ipsec** and **debug crypto isakmp** commands.

Lab 4.5.5a   Configure a PIX Security Appliance Site-to-Site IPsec VPN Tunnel Using the CLI

In this lab exercise, you prepare to configure VPN support. You then configure IKE and IPsec parameters. Finally, you test and verify IPsec configuration.

Lab 4.5.5b   Configure a PIX Security Appliance Site-to-Site IPsec VPN Tunnel Using the ASDM

In this lab exercise, you configure IKE and IPsec parameters using the Adaptive Security Device Manager (ADSM) VPN Wizard. You then test and verify IPsec configuration.

Summary

This chapter covered the configuration of site-to-site VPNs using Cisco IOS routers and PIX Security Appliances. Upon completion of this chapter, you should be able to identify and configure the protocols used to ensure authenticity, data integrity, and confidentiality with a site-to-site VPN using pre-shared keys.

You learned that successful implementation of an IPsec network requires advance planning before beginning configuration of individual devices. The steps that you must follow when configuring an IPsec network were introduced, and you gained hands-on experience with these tasks through the lab activities.

Check Your Understanding

Complete all the review questions listed here to test your understanding of the topics and concepts in this chapter. Answers are listed in Appendix A, "Check Your Understanding Answer Key."

1. What is the main limitation of pre-shared secret authentication?

    a. Pre-shared secret is based on dynamic MAC addressing.

    b. Pre-shared secret is based on the IP address of the remote peer.

    c. Pre-shared secret is not based on the IP address of the remote peer.

    d. Pre-shared secret is based on static MAC addressing.

2. It is important to plan IPsec details in advance to minimize configuration errors. One of the steps is to make sure ACLs on perimeter devices are compatible with IPsec.

    a. True

    b. False

3. Specific values for each IKE parameter can be selected, as outlined in the IKE standard. Which are the stronger combination of encryption and hash algorithms?

    a. DES and MD5

    b. 3DES and MD5

    c. DES and SHA-1

    d. 3DES and SHA-1

4. Authentication Header (AH) is rarely used because authentication is now available with the **esp-sha-hmac** and **esp-md5-hmac** transforms. AH is also compatible with NAT or PAT.

    a. True

    b. False

5. ISAKMP uses which UDP port?

    a. 500

    b. 50

    c. 51

    d. 52

6. ISAKMP peers negotiate acceptable ISAKMP policies before agreeing upon the SA to be used for IPsec. When the ISAKMP negotiation begins in IKE Phase 1 main mode

   a. ISAKMP looks for an ISAKMP policy that is different on both peers, and the peer that initiates the negotiation sends all its policies to the remote peer, and the remote peer tries to find a match with its policies.

   b. ISAKMP looks for an ISAKMP policy that is the same on both peers, and the peer that initiates the negotiation sends all its policies to the remote peer, and the remote peer tries to find a miss match with its policies.

   c. ISAKMP looks for an ISAKMP policy that is the same on both peers, and the peer that initiates the negotiation sends all its policies to the remote peer, and the remote peer tries to find a match with its policies.

   d. ISAKMP looks for an ISAKMP policy that is the different on both peers, and the peer that initiates the negotiation sends some of its policies to the remote peer, and the remote peer tries to find a match with its policies.

7. A match is made when both policies from the two peers contain the same encryption, hash, authentication, and Diffie-Hellman parameter values, and when the remote peer's policy specifies a lifetime less than or equal to the lifetime in the policy being compared.

   a. True

   b. False

8. When designing crypto access lists for a network, it is important to do which of the following?

   a. Remember that a **permit** statements will permit certain protocols and that you define a mirror image crypto access list be configured at the remote peer.

   b. Remember that **permit** statements will permit certain traffic be encrypted and that you define a mirror image crypto access list be configured at the remote peer.

   c. Remember that a permit statements will permit certain protocols and that you not define a mirror image crypto access list be configured at the remote peer.

   d. Remember that a permit statements will permit certain traffic be encrypted and that you not define a mirror image crypto access list be configured at the remote peer.

9. On a single router interface, you can do which of the following?

   a. Apply only one crypto map set

   b. Apply multiple crypto map sets

10. To view the settings used by current security associations, you use which of the following commands?

a. **show crypto ipsec**

b. **show crypto sa**

c. **show crypto isakmp sa**

d. **show crypto ipsec sa**

CHAPTER 5

Configure Site-to-Site VPN Using Digital Certificates

Upon completion of this chapter, you should be able to answer the following questions:

- How do I configure certificate authority support on a Cisco router?

- How do I configure a Cisco IOS router site-to-site VPN using digital certificates?

- How do I configure a PIX Security Appliance site-to-site VPN using digital certificates?

Key Terms

This chapter uses the following key terms. You can find the definitions in the glossary at the end of the book.

Certificate authority (CA)   page 584

Certificate revocation lists (CRLs)   page 585

This chapter guides you through the process of configuring a Cisco router to support certificate authorities (CAs). Included are topics on managing nonvolatile RAM (NVRAM), router date and time settings, and commands to configure RSA keys and CAs. Upon completion of this chapter, you will be able to configure the Cisco IOS router and the PIX Security Appliance for a site-to-site VPN using digital certificates for authentication.

Configure CA Support on a Cisco Router

Configuring Cisco IOS Software *certificate authority (CA)* support is complicated. Having a detailed plan lessens the chances of configuration errors. Some planning steps include the following steps:

Step 1. **(Optional) Manage the nonvolatile RAM (NVRAM) memory usage**—In some cases, storing certificates and CRLs locally does not present a problem. However, in other cases, memory might become an issue, particularly if the CA supports a registration authority (RA) and a large number of CRLs end up being stored on the router.

Step 2. **Set the time and date on the router**—The router must have an accurate time and date to enroll with a CA server.

```
clock timezone
clock set
```

Step 3. **Configure the hostname and domain name of the router**—The hostname is used in prompts and default configuration filenames. The domain name is used to define a default domain name that the Cisco IOS Software uses to complete unqualified hostnames.

```
hostname name
ip domain-name name
```

Step 4. **Generate an RSA key pair**—RSA keys are used to identify the remote VPN peer. One general-purpose key or two special-purpose keys can be generated.

```
crypto key generate rsa usage keys
```

Step 5. **Declare a CA**—To declare the CA that the router should use, use the **crypto pki trustpoint** global configuration command. Use the **no** form of this command to delete all identity information and certificates associated with the CA.

```
crypto pki trustpoint name
```

Step 6. **Authenticate the CA**—The router needs to authenticate the CA it does this by obtaining the self-signed certificate from the CA that contains the public key of the CA.

```
crypto pki authenticate name
```

Step 7.   **Request a certificate for the router**—Complete this step to obtain the identity certificate for the router from the CA.

```
crypto pki enroll name
```

Step 8.   **Save the configuration**—After configuring the router for CA support, the configuration should be saved.

```
crypto running-config startup-config
```

Step 9.   **(Optional) Monitor and maintain CA interoperability.**

```
crypto pki trustpoint name
```

The following substeps are optional, depending on the particular requirements:

- Request a CRL.
- Delete the RSA keys on the router.
- Delete both public and private certificates from the configuration.
- Delete the public keys of IPsec peers.

Step 10.   **Verify the CA support configuration.**

```
show crypto pki certificates
show crypto key mypubkey | pubkey-chain
```

Step 1: Manage the NVRAM

Certificates and *certificate revocation lists (CRLs)* are used by the router when a CA is used. Normally, certain certificates and all CRLs are stored locally in the NVRAM of the router, and each certificate and CRL uses a moderate amount of memory.

The following certificates are normally stored at the router:

- The certificate of the router.
- The certificate of the CA.
- Root certificates obtained from CA servers. All root certificates are saved in RAM after the router has been initialized.
- Two RA certificates, if the CA supports an RA.

In some cases, storing certificates and CRLs locally will not present a problem. However, in other cases, memory might become an issue if a large number of certificates and CRLs end up being stored on the router. These certificates and CRLs can consume a large amount of NVRAM space.

To save NVRAM space, you can configure the router so that certificates and CRLs should not be stored locally, but should be retrieved from the CA when needed. Doing so will save NVRAM space but could produce a slight performance impact.

To specify that certificates and CRLs should not be stored locally on the router, but should be retrieved when required, turn on query mode by using the **crypto ca certificate query** command in global configuration mode.

Note

Query mode might affect availability if the CA is down.

If query mode is not turned on initially, you can turn it on later even if certificates and CRLs have already been stored on the router. In this case, when query mode is turned on, the stored certificates and CRLs are deleted from the router after the configuration is saved. If the configuration is copied to a TFTP site prior to turning on query mode, stored certificates and CRLs are saved at the TFTP site.

If query mode is turned on initially, you can turn it off later. If query mode is turned off later, you can issue the **copy system:running-config nvram:startup-config** command beforehand to save all current certificates and CRLs to NVRAM. Otherwise, they are lost during a reboot and must be retrieved the next time they are needed by the router.

Step 2: Set the Router Time and Date

Ensure that the time zone, time, and date has been accurately set with the **show clock** commands in privileged EXEC mode. The clock must be accurately set before generating RSA key pairs and enrolling with the CA server because certificates are time-sensitive. On certificates, there is a valid from and to date and time. When the certificate is validated by the router, the router determines whether its system clock falls within the validity range. If it does, the certificate is valid. If not, the certificate is deemed invalid or expired.

To specify the time zone of the router, use the **clock timezone** global configuration command. The command sets the time zone and an offset from universal time code (UTC), as shown in the following example:

```
Router(config)#clock timezone zone hours [minutes]
```

The following command sets the router time zone and offset from UTC:

```
Router A(config)# clock timezone cst -6
Router# clock set hh:mm:ss day month year
Router# clock set hh:mm:ss month day year
```

The following command sets the router time and date:

```
routerA# clock set 23:59:59 17 February 2005
```

Note

It is recommended that an NTP server is used to set the time on routers that do not have a clock circuit chip.

You can optionally set the router to automatically update the calendar and time from a Network Time Protocol (NTP) server with the **ntp** series of commands.

Step 3: Add a CA Server Entry to the Router Host Table

The hostname and IP domain name of the router must be configured if this has not already been done. This is required because the router assigns a fully qualified domain name (FQDN) to the keys and certificates used by IPsec, and the FQDN is based on the hostname and IP domain name assigned to the router. For example, a certificate named router20.example.com is based on a router hostname of router20 and a router IP domain name of example.com.

To specify or modify the hostname for the network server, use the **hostname** *name* global configuration command. For Router A in the network in Figure 5-1, for example, you enter the following:

```
router(config)#hostname RouterA
```

The **setup** command facility also prompts for a hostname at startup.

Figure 5-1   Add a CA Server Entry to the Router Host Table

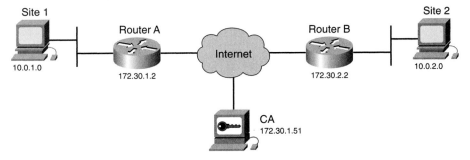

To define a default domain name that the Cisco IOS Software uses to complete unqualified hostnames, use the **ip domain-name** *name global* configuration command. Unqualified names are names without a dotted-decimal domain name. To disable use of the Domain Name System (DNS), use the **no** form of this command. For Router A in the network in Figure 5-1, for example, you could enter the following:

```
RouterA(config)#ip domain-name xyz.com
```

Use the following global configuration command to define a static hostname-to-address mapping in the host cache:

```
ip host name address1 [address2…addressN]
```

For Router A in the network in Figure 5-2, for example, you could enter the following:

```
RouterA(config)#ip host vpnca 172.30.1.51
```

To remove the name-to-address mapping, use the **no** form of this command.

Figure 5-2   Static Name-to-Address Mapping

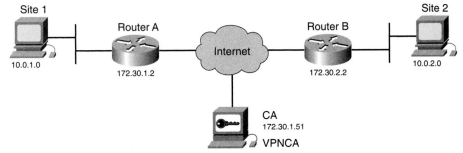

Step 4: Generate an RSA Key Pair

RSA key pairs are used to sign and encrypt Internet Key Exchange (IKE) key management messages and are required before obtaining a certificate for the router.

Use the following global configuration command to generate RSA key pairs, as shown in Figure 5-3:

```
Router(config)#crypto key generate rsa [general-keys | usage-keys]
```

Using the **usage-keys** keyword generates two sets of RSA keys:

- Use one key set for RSA signatures

- Use one key set for RSA-encrypted nonces

Figure 5-3   Generate an RSA Key Pair

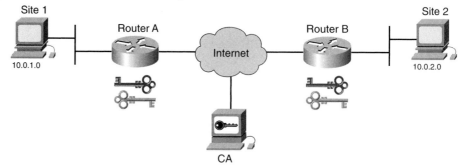

Note

Before issuing the command to generate RSA keys, make sure that the router has a hostname and IP domain name configured. The **crypto key generate rsa** command cannot be completed without a hostname and IP domain name.

By default, RSA key pairs do not exist. If the **usage-keys** option is not used in the command, general-purpose keys are generated. RSA keys are generated in pairs consisting of one public RSA key and one private RSA key. If the router already has RSA keys when this command is issued, the router warns and prompts the administrator to replace the existing keys with new keys.

The keys generated by the **crypto key generate rsa** command are saved in the private configuration in NVRAM, which is never displayed to the administrator or backed up to another device.

There are two mutually exclusive types of RSA key pairs: special-usage keys and general-purpose keys. When RSA key pairs are generated, it can be indicated whether to generate special-usage keys or general-purpose keys.

Special-Usage Keys

If special-usage keys are generated, two pairs of RSA keys are created. One pair is used with any IKE policy that specifies RSA signatures as the authentication method, and the other pair is used with any IKE policy that specifies RSA encrypted nonces as the authentication method.

If both types of RSA authentication methods are present in the IKE policies, special-usage keys might be the preferred option. With special-usage keys, each key is not unnecessarily exposed.

Without special-usage keys, one key is used for both authentication methods, increasing the exposure of that key.

General-Purpose Keys

If general-purpose keys are generated, only one pair of RSA keys is created. This pair is used with IKE policies specifying either RSA signatures or RSA encrypted nonces. Therefore, a general-purpose key pair might get used more frequently than a special-usage key pair.

When RSA keys are generated, the administrator is prompted to enter a modulus length, as shown in Example 5-1. A longer modulus could offer stronger security, but takes longer to generate and takes longer to use. A modulus below 512 is normally not recommended. Cisco recommends using a minimum modulus of 1024.

Example 5-1   Generate RSA Keys: Example Output

```
RouterA(config)#crypto key generate rsa
The name for the keys will be:  router.cisco.com
Choose the size of the key modulus in the range of 360 to 2048 for
your Signature Keys. Choosing a key modulus greater than 512 may take a few minutes.

How many bits in the modulus [512]:   512
Generating RSA keys...
[OK}


RouterA#show crypto key mypubkey rsa
% Key pair was generated at: 23:58:59 UTC Dec 31 2000
Key name:  RouterA.cisco.com
 Usage:  General Purpose Key
 Key Data:
  305C300D 06092A86 4886F70D 01010105 00034B00 30480241 00A9443B
62FDACFB
  CCDB8784 19AE1CD8 95B30953 1EDD30D1 380119D6 4636E015 4D7C6F33
4DC1F6E0
  C929A25E 521688A1 295907F4 E98BF920 6A81CE57 28A21116 E3020301 0001
```

Step 5: Declare a CA

Note that in Cisco IOS Software Release 12.3(7)T, **crypto pki trustpoint** replaces the **crypto ca trustpoint** command from previous Cisco IOS Software releases. The **crypto ca trustpoint** command can be entered, but the command is written in the configuration as **crypto pki trustpoint**.

Use the following global configuration command to declare what CA server the router will use:

`Router(config)#`**`crypto pki trustpoint`** `name`

For the network shown in Figure 5-4, for example, you enter the following:

`RouterA(config)#`**`crypto pki trustpoint vpnca`**

The **crypto pki trustpoint** command allows the router to re-enroll to the CA server automatically when its certificates expire. Use the **no** form of this command to delete all identity information and certificates associated with the CA.

Note

The **crypto pki trustpoint** command is only significant locally. It does not have to match the identity defined on any of the VPN peers.

Figure 5-4   Declaring a CA

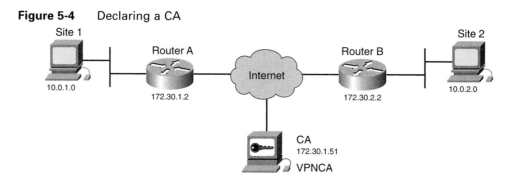

Performing the **crypto pki trustpoint** command puts the prompt into the ca-trustpoint configuration mode, where you can specify characteristics for the CA using the commands shown in the Example 5-2. Table 5-1 shows information about these commands.

```
Example 5-2     Specifying CA Characteristics
RouterA(config)# crypto pki trustpoint vpnca
RouterA(ca-trustpoint)# ?
ca trustpoint configuration commands:
    crl        CRL options
    default      Set a command to its defaults
    enrollment   Enrollment parameters
    exit         Exit from certificate authority identity entry mode
    no         Negate a command or set its defaults
    query        Query parameters
RouterA(ca-trustpoint)# enrollment ?
    http-proxy    HTTP proxy server for enrollment
    mode        Mode supported by the Certificate Authority
    retry        Polling parameters
    url        CA server enrollment URL
```

Table 5-1   Trustpoint Configuration Command Descriptions

Command	Description
enrollment url *url*	Specifies the URL of the CA. This is always required.
enrollment mode	Specifies the RA mode. This is required only if the CA system provides an RA.
query url	Specifies the URL of the LDAP server. This is required only if your CA supports an RA and Lightweight Directory Access Protocol (LDAP).
enrollment retry-period	(Optional) Specifies a period of time the router should wait between sending certificate request entries.
enrollment retry-count	(Optional) Specifies a period of time the router should wait between sending certificate request retries.
query url	(Optional) Specifies how many certificate request retries the router will send before giving up.

Based on the network shown in Figure 5-4, the commands in Example 5-3 declare a CA and identify characteristics of the CA.

Example 5-3   Declaring a CA

```
RouterA(config)#crypto pki trustpoint vpnca
RouterA(ca-trustpoint)#enrollment url http://vpnca/certserv/mscep/mscep.dll
RouterA(ca-trustpoint)#enrollment mode ra
RouterA(ca-trustpoint)#crl optional
```

In this example, the name vpnca is created for the CA, which is located at http://vpnca. The example also declares a CA using an RA. The scripts for the CA are stored in the default location, and the CA uses Simple Certificate Enrollment Protocol (SCEP) rather than LDAP. This is the minimum possible configuration required to declare a CA that uses an RA.

The preceding example declares a Microsoft Windows 2000 CA. Note that the enrollment URL points to the MSCEP dynamic link library (DLL).

Step 6: Authenticate the CA

The router needs to authenticate the CA to verify its validity. The router does this by obtaining the self-signed certificate of the CA that contains the public key of the CA. Because the CA certificate is self-signed, meaning that the CA signs its own certificate, the public key of the CA should be manually authenticated, as shown in Figure 5-5. This is done by contacting the CA administrator to verify the fingerprint of the CA certificate. To get the public key of the CA, use the **crypto pki authenticate** *name* command in global configuration mode. Use the same name that was used when declaring the CA with the **crypto pki trustpoint** command.

Figure 5-5   Authenticate the CA

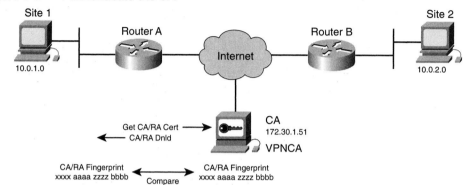

If RA mode is used, using the **enrollment mode ra** command, when the **crypto pki authenticate** command is issued, the RA signing and encryption certificates are returned from the CA and the CA certificate.

Example 5-4 demonstrates a CA authentication.

Example 5-4   CA Authentication

```
RouterA(config)# crypto pki authenticate VPNCA
Certificate has the following attributes:
Fingerprint: 93700C31 4853EC4A DED81400 43D3C82C
% Do you accept this certificate? [yes/no]: y
```

Step 7: Request a Certificate for the Router

A signed certificate must be obtained from the CA for each RSA key pair on the router. If general-purpose RSA keys were generated, the router has only one RSA key pair and needs only one certificate. If special-usage RSA keys were generated, the router has two RSA key pairs and needs two certificates, as shown in Figure 5-6.

To request signed certificates from the CA, use the **crypto pki enroll** *name* command in global configuration mode. For the network in Figure 5-6, you enter the following:

```
RouterA(config)#crypto pki enroll vpnca
```

Figure 5-6   Request a Certificate for the Router

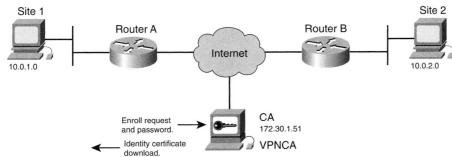

During the enrollment process, a challenge password is created. The CA administrator can use this password to validate the identity of the individual who is requesting the certificate. This password is not saved with the configuration. This password is required in the event that the certificate needs to be revoked, so it must be remembered or stored in a manner consistent with the security policy of the organization.

Technically, enrolling and obtaining certificates are two separate events, but they both occur when the **crypto pki enroll** command is issued.

If a certificate for the keys already exists, this command cannot be completed. Instead, the administrator is prompted to remove the existing certificate first. Existing certificates can be removed with the **no certificate** command.

Step 8: Save the Configuration

Use the **copy running-config startup-config** command to save the configuration. This command includes saving RSA keys to private NVRAM. RSA keys are not saved with the configuration when a **copy system:running-config rcp:** or **copy system:running-config tftp:** command is issued.

Step 9: Monitor and Maintain CA Interoperability

The following steps are optional, depending on the particular requirements:

- Request a CRL.
- Query a CRL.
- Delete RSA keys from the router.
- Delete peer public keys.
- Delete certificates from the configuration.
- View keys and certificates.

Caution

The **crypto pki enroll** command is not saved in the router configuration. If the router reboots after the **crypto pki enroll** command is issued, but before the certificates are received, the command must be reissued.

Request a CRL

A CRL can be requested only if the CA does not support an RA. The following information applies only when the CA does not support an RA.

When the router receives a certificate from a peer, the router downloads a CRL from the CA. The router then checks the CRL to make sure the certificate that the peer sent has not been revoked. If the certificate appears on the CRL, the router does not accept the certificate and does not authenticate the peer.

With CA systems that support RAs, multiple CRLs exist and the certificate of the peer indicates which CRL applies and should be downloaded by the router. If the router does not have the applicable CRL and cannot obtain one, the router rejects the certificate of the peer, unless the **crl optional** command is used in the configuration. If the **crl optional** command is used, the router still tries to obtain a CRL, but if it cannot obtain a CRL, it can still accept the certificate of the peer.

A CRL can be reused with subsequent certificates until the CRL expires, if query mode is off. If the router receives a certificate from a peer after the applicable CRL has expired, the router downloads the new CRL.

When the router receives additional certificates from peers, the router continues to attempt to download the appropriate CRL, even if it was previously unsuccessful, and even if the **crl optional** command is enabled. The **crl optional** command only specifies that when the router cannot obtain the CRL, the router is not forced to reject a certificate of a peer outright.

If the router has a CRL that has not yet expired, but it is suspected that the contents of the CRL are out-of-date, it is possible to request that the latest CRL be downloaded immediately to replace the old CRL. To request immediate download of the latest CRL, use the **crypto pki crl request** *name* command in global configuration mode. This command replaces the CRL currently stored on the router with the newest version of the CRL.

Delete RSA Keys from the Router

Under certain circumstances you might need to delete the RSA keys that were generated for the router. For example, if the RSA keys are believed to be compromised in some way and should no longer be used, you should delete the keys.

To delete all RSA keys from the router, use the **crypto key zeroize rsa** command in global configuration mode. After the RSA keys are deleted, the CA administrator should be asked to revoke certificates for the router at the CA. It will be necessary to supply the challenge password created when the certificates were obtained with the **crypto pki enroll** command. The certificates should also be manually removed from the router configuration.

Delete Certificates from the Configuration

If the need arises, certificates saved on the router can be deleted. The router saves its own certificates, the certificate of the CA, and any RA certificates, unless the router is in query mode.

To delete the certificate of the router or RA certificates from the configuration, use the commands shown in Table 5-2 in global configuration mode.

Table 5-2   Deleting Certificates from the Configuration

Step	Command	Description
Step 1	Router# **show crypto pki certificates**	Displays the certificate stored on your router, note (or copy) the serial number of the certificate you want to delete
Step 2	Router(config)# **crypto pki certificate chain** *name*	Enters certificate chain configuration mode
Step 3	Router(config-cert-cha)# **no certificate** *certificate-serial-number*	Deletes the certificate

Delete Public Keys of Peers

Under certain circumstances, you might need to delete the RSA public keys of peer devices from the router configuration. For example, if the integrity of a peer public key is doubted, you should delete the key. To delete an RSA public key of a peer, use the commands shown in Table 5-3, beginning in global configuration mode.

Table 5-3   Deleting a Peer's Public Keys

Step	Command	Description
Step 1	Router(config)# **crypto key pubkey-chain rsa**	Enters public key configuration mode.
Step 2	Router(config-pubkey-c)# **no named-key** key-name [**encryption** | **signature**] or Router(config-pubkey-c)# **no addressed-key** key-address [**encryption** | **signature**]	Deletes a remote peer's RSA public key. Specify the peer's fully qualified domain name or the remote peer's IP address.
Step 3	**exit**	Returns to global configuration mode.

To delete the CA certificate, the entire CA trustpoint must be removed. This also removes all certificates associated with the CA, including the certificate belonging to the router, the CA certificate, and any RA certificates. To remove a CA trustpoint, use the **no crypto pki trustpoint** *name* command in global configuration mode.

Step 10: Verify the CA Support Configuration

To view any configured CA or RA certificates, use the following command:

router#**show crypto pki certificates**

To view RSA keys for the router and other IPsec peers enrolled with a CA, use the following command:

router#**show crypto key {mypubkey | pubkey-chain} rsa**

Table 5-4 provides more detailed steps for displaying keys and certificates.

Note

You can implement the **show crypto ca roots** command only when multiple CAs are configured in the router.

Table 5-4   show crypto Commands

Step	Command	Description
Step 1	Router# **show crypto key mypubkey rsa**	Displays your router's RSA public keys.
Step 2	Router# **show crypto key pubkey-chain rsa**	Displays a list of all the RSA public keys stored on your router. These include the public keys of peers who have sent your router their certificates during peer authentication for IPsec.
Step 3	Router# **show crypto key pubkey-chain rsa	name** *key-name* **| address** *key-address*	Displays details of a particular RSA public key stored on your router.
Step 4	Router# **show crypto pki certificates**	Displays information about your certificate, the CA's certificate, and any RA certificates.
Step 5	Router# **show crypto ca roots**	Displays the CA roots configured in the router.

Example 5-5 displays the running configuration of a router properly configured for CA support.

Example 5-5   CA Support Configuration on a Router

```
RouterA# show running-config
!
hostname RouterA
!
ip domain-name cisco.com
!
Crypto pki trustpoint VPNCA
 enrollment mode ra
 enrollment url http://vpcna:80
 query url ldap://vpnca
 crl optional
crypto pki certificate chain entrust
 certificate 37C6EAD6
 30820299 30820202 A0030201 02020437 C6EAD630 0D06092A
 864886F7 0D010105
 (certificates concatenated)
```

Configure a Cisco IOS Router Site-to-Site VPN Using Digital Certificates

The configuration of a site-to-site VPN using digital certificates is similar to the configuration that is done when pre-shared keys are used for authentication. This section discusses the configuration tasks and steps in detail. The following tasks are used to configure a site-to-site VPN using digital certificates:

■ **Task 1**: **Prepare for IKE and IPsec**—To prepare for IPsec, determine the following detailed encryption policy:

— Identify the hosts and networks to be protected.

— Determine IPsec peer details.

— Determine the IPsec features that are needed.

— Ensure that the existing access lists are compatible with IPsec.

■ **Task 2: Configure CA support**—To configure CA support, set the router hostname and domain name, generate the keys, declare a CA, authenticate and request network-own certificates.

■ **Task 3: Configure IKE for IPsec**—To configure IKE, enable IKE, create the IKE policies, and validate the configuration.

■ **Task 4: Configure IPsec**—To configure IPsec, define the transform sets, create crypto access lists, create crypto map entries, and apply crypto map sets to the interfaces.

- **Task 5: Test and verify IPsec**—Use **show**, **debug**, and related commands to test and verify that IPsec encryption works and to troubleshoot problems.

Task 1: Prepare for IKE and IPsec

Successful implementation of an IPsec network using digital certificates for authentication requires advance planning before beginning configuration of individual routers. In Task 1, define the IPsec security policy based on the overall company security policy. Some planning steps follow:

Step 1. **Plan for CA support**—Determine the CA server details. This includes variables such as the type of CA server to be used, the IP address, and the CA administrator contact information.

Step 2. **Determine the Internet Security Association and Key Management Protocol (ISAKMP, IKE Phase 1) policy**—Determine the IKE policies between IPsec peers based on the number and location of the peers.

Step 3. **Determine the IPsec (IKE Phase 2) policy**—Identify IPsec peer details such as IP addresses and IPsec modes. Then, configure crypto maps to gather all IPsec policy details together.

Step 4. **Check the current configuration**—Use the **show run**, **show crypto isakmp policy**, and **show crypto map** commands, and the many other **show** commands that are covered later in this module.

Step 5. **Ensure the network works without encryption**—Ensure that testing basic connectivity has been achieved between IPsec peers using the desired IP services before configuring IPsec. You can use the **ping** command to check basic connectivity.

Step 6. **Ensure that access lists are compatible with IPsec**—Ensure that perimeter routers and the IPsec peer router interfaces permit IPsec traffic. Use the **show access-lists** command to view the existing ACLs.

Task 2: Configure CA Support

This section presents the steps necessary to configure CA support on a router:

Step 1. Manage the NVRAM memory usage. (Optional)

Step 2. Set the router time and date.

```
clock timezone
clock set
```

Step 3.   Configure the router hostname and domain name.

```
hostname name
ip domain-name name
```

Step 4.   Generate an RSA key pair RSA keys are used to identify the remote VPN peer.

```
crytpo key generate rsa usage keys
```

Step 5.   Declare a CA.

```
crypto ca trustpoint name
```

Step 6.   Authenticate the CA.

```
crypto ca authenticate name
```

Step 7.   Request a certificate.

```
crypto ca enroll name
```

Step 8.   Save the configuration.

```
copy running-config startup-config
```

Step 9.   Monitor and maintain CA interoperability. (Optional)

```
crypto ca trustpoint name
```

Step 10.   Verify the CA support configuration.

```
show crypto ca certificates
show crypto key mypubkey | pubkey-chain
```

Task 3: Configure IKE

The third task in configuring Cisco IOS IPsec is to configure the IKE parameters. This section presents the steps used to configure IKE policies.

Configuring IKE consists of the following steps and commands:

Step 1.   Enable IKE with the **crypto isakmp enable** command, in case it has been disabled from the default enable condition.

Step 2.   Create IKE policies with the **crypto isakmp policy** command.

Step 3.   Set the IKE identity to address or hostname with the **crypto isakmp identity** command.

Step 4.   Test and verify the IKE configuration with the **show crypto isakmp policy** and **show crypto isakmp sa** commands.

The **crypto isakmp policy** command invokes the ISAKMP policy configuration command mode config-isakmp, which can be used to set ISAKMP parameters, as demonstrated in Example 5-6.

Example 5-6   Creating IKE Policies

```
RouterA(config)#crypto isakmp policy 110
RouterA(config-isakmp)#authentication rsa-sig
RouterA(config-isakmp)#encryption des
RouterA(config-isakmp)#group 1
RouterA(config-isakmp)#hash md5
RouterA(config-isakmp)#lifetime 86400
```

While in the **config-isakmp** command mode, certain keywords are available to specify the parameters in the policy, as shown in Table 5-5. If one of these parameters is not specified, the default value for that parameter is used.

Table 5-5   Configure IKE Parameters

Command	Keyword Accepted	Value	Default Value	Description
encryption	des 3des	56-bit DES-CBC 168-bit DES	des	Message encryption algorithm
hash	sha 3d5	SHA-1 (HMAC variant) md5(HMAC variant)	sha	Message integrity (hash) algorithm
authentication	rsa-sig rsa-encr pre-share	RSA signatures RSA encrypted nonces Pre-shared keys	rsa-sig	Peer authentication method
group	1 2	768-bit Diffie-Hellman or 1024-bit Diffie-Hellman	1	Key exchange parameters (Diffie-Hellman identifier)
lifetime	-	Can specify any number of seconds	86,400 seconds (1 day)	ISAKMP-established security association (SA) lifetime

You can configure multiple ISAKMP policies on each peer participating in IPsec. ISAKMP peers negotiate acceptable ISAKMP policies before agreeing on the SA to be used for IPsec.

Task 4: Configure IPsec

The fourth task in configuring Cisco IOS IPsec is to configure the IPsec parameters that were previously gathered. This section presents the steps used to configure IPsec. The general steps and commands used to configure IPsec encryption on Cisco routers are summarized as follows:

Step 1. Configure transform set suites with the **crypto IPsec transform-set** command.

Step 2. Configure global IPsec security association lifetimes with the **crypto IPsec security-association lifetime** command.

Step 3. Configure crypto access lists with the **access-list** command.

The rest of the steps used to configure IPsec parameters for IKE RSA signature keys are as follows:

Step 4. Configure crypto maps with the **crypto map** command.

Step 5. Apply the crypto maps to the terminating or originating interface with the **interface** and the **crypto map** commands.

Task 5: Test and Verify IPsec

Cisco IOS Software contains a number of **show**, **clear**, and **debug** commands useful for testing and verifying IPsec and ISAKMP. Administrators can perform the following actions to test and verify that they have correctly configured a VPN using Cisco IOS Software:

- Display the configured IKE policies using the **show crypto isakmp policy** command.

- Display the configured transform sets using the **show crypto IPsec transform set** command.

- Display the current state of the IPsec SAs with the **show crypto IPsec sa** command.

- View the configured crypto maps with the **show crypto map** command.

- Debug IKE and IPsec traffic through the Cisco IOS VPN with the **debug crypto ipsec** and **debug crypto isakmp** commands.

- Debug CA events through the Cisco IOS VPN using the **debug crypto key-exchange** and **debug crypto pki** commands.

Use **debug** commands with caution. Enabling debugging can disrupt operation of the router because of the large amount of output. Before starting a **debug** command, always consider the output that this command will generate and the amount of time this might take. Also, look at the CPU load by using the **show processes cpu** command. Verify that you have ample CPU time available before beginning the debugs.

Lab 5.2.6   Configure IPsec Using Digital Certificates

In this lab, you first prepare for IKE and IPsec. You then learn to configure certificate support. You also configure IKE and IPsec. Finally, you test and verify the IPsec configuration.

Configure a PIX Security Appliance Site-to-Site VPN Using Digital Certificates

As discussed previously, the use of pre-shared keys for IKE authentication works well only when there are few IPsec peers. Although there are a number of methods for authentication, using a CA server is the most scalable solution. Other IKE authentication methods require manual intervention to generate and distribute the keys on a per-peer basis. When using the PIX Security Appliance to implement IPsec VPNs using digital certificates, the CA server enrollment process can be largely automated so that it scales well to large deployments. Each PIX that is to be configured as an IPsec peer individually enrolls with the CA server and obtains public and private encryption keys compatible with other peers that are enrolled with the server, as shown in Figure 5-7.

Figure 5-7   CA Server Fulfilling Requests from IPsec Peers

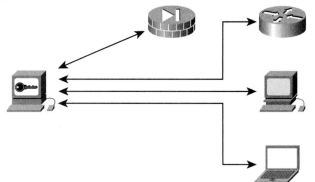

The PIX Security Appliance supports the following CA servers:

- Cisco IOS Certificate Server
- Baltimore Technologies
- Entrust
- Microsoft Certificate Services
- Netscape CMS
- RSA Keon
- VeriSign

Enroll the PIX Security Appliance with a CA

The PIX Security Appliance enrolls with a CA server in a series of steps in which specific keys are generated and then exchanged by the PIX and the CA server to ultimately form a signed certificate.

The enrollment steps can be summarized as follows:

Step 1. The PIX Security Appliance generates an RSA public and private key pair.

Step 2. The PIX Security Appliance obtains a public key and its certificate from the CA server.

Step 3. The PIX Security Appliance requests a signed certificate from the CA using the generated RSA keys and the public key certificate from the CA server.

Step 4. The CA administrator verifies the request and sends a signed certificate.

Generate an RSA Key Pair

RSA key pairs are generated with the **crypto key generate rsa** command. If you do not use additional keywords, this command generates one general purpose RSA key pair. Because the key modulus is not specified, the default key modulus of 1024 is used. Other modulus sizes can be specified with the **modulus** keyword. Use the **show crypto key mypubkey rsa** command to view the created key pair.

To remove RSA key pairs, use the **crypto key zeroize rsa** command in global configuration mode.

Obtain a Public Key and Certificate from the CA Server

Create a trustpoint corresponding to the CA from which the PIX Security Appliance needs to receive its certificate with the **crypto ca trustpoint** *trustpoint* command. Upon entering this command, crypto ca trustpoint configuration mode is entered. To specify SCEP enrollment, use the **enrollment url** command. To specify manual enrollment, use the **enrollment terminal** command. As needed, specify other characteristics for the trustpoint. You can find more information about these command in the Command Reference.

After configuring the trustpoint, obtain the CA certificate for the trustpoint with the **crypto ca authenticate** command. The public key of the CA is included with this certificate.

Request a Signed Certificate from the CA

Enroll the PIX Security Appliance with the trustpoint using the **crypto ca enroll** command. Before entering this command, contact the CA administrator because the administrator might need to authenticate the enrollment request manually before the CA grants its certificates.

Verify That the CA Administrator Has Sent a Signed Certificate

After the enrollment is complete, verify that the enrollment process was successful by using the **show crypto ca certificate** command. The output of this command shows the details of the certificate issued for the PIX Security Appliance and the CA certificate for the trustpoint. Be sure to save the configuration by using the **write memory** command after the certificate has been received.

 Lab 5.3.2   Configure a Site-to-Site IPsec VPN Tunnel with CA Support

In this lab exercise, you prepare for and then configure CA support. You then configure and verify IKE and IPsec parameters. You verify that the VPN connection is up and working properly. Finally, you verify the VPN status and configuration using PIX Device Manager (PDM).

Summary

Upon completing this chapter, you should be able to configure CA support on Cisco routers. You should also be able to configure the Cisco IOS router and the PIX Security Appliance for a site-to-site VPN using digital certificates for authentication.

Check Your Understanding

Complete all the review questions listed here to test your understanding of the topics and concepts in this chapter. Answers are listed in Appendix A, "Check Your Understanding Answer Key."

1. Which of the following certificates are not normally stored at the router?

    a. The certificate of the router

    b. The certificate of the CA

    c. Root certificates obtained from CA servers

    d. Two RA certificates, if the CA supports an RA

    e. The certificate of the remote server

2. To save NVRAM space, the router can be configured so that certificates and CRLs should not be stored locally, but should be retrieved from the CA when needed. To specify that certificates and CRLs should not be stored locally on the router, but should be retrieved when required, turn on query mode by using which of the following commands?

    a. Router # **crypto ca query**

    b. Router # **crypto ca certificate query**

    c. Router (config)# **crypto ca certificate query**

    d. Router (config)# **crypto certificate query**

3. The clock must be accurately set before generating RSA key pairs and enrolling with the CA server because certificates are time sensitive. When a router validates a certificate, it does which of the following?

    a. Checks the CA from and to date and time with its internal clock

    b. Checks the CA from date and time with its internal clock

    c. Checks the CA from time with its internal clock

    d. Checks the CA to time with its internal clock

4. RSA keys are generated in pairs consisting of which of the following?

    a. One public RSA key and one private RSA key

    b. One public RSA key and one public CA key

    c. One private RSA key and one private CA key

    d. Two private RSA keys

5. To request signed certificates from the CA, use the **crypto pki enroll** *name* command in global configuration mode.

   a. True

   b. False

6. Which of the following commands would you use to delete all RSA keys from the router?

   a. **crypto key zeroize rsa** command in interface configuration mode

   b. **crypto zeroize rsa** command in global configuration mode

   c. **crypto key zeroize rsa** command in global configuration mode

   d. **crypto pki unenroll** command in global configuration mode

7. Which of the following are options for configuring IKE parameters?

   a. **1** or **2**

   b. **rsa-sig** or **rsa-enc**

   c. **des** or **3des**

   d. **sha** or **3d5**

8. To display the configured transform set use, you would use which of the following commands?

   a. **show IPsec transform set**

   b. **show crypto IPsec transform set**

   c. **show crypto ike transform set**

   d. **show ike transform set**

9. The PIX Security Appliance generates which of the following?

   a. An RSA public and private key pair

   b. An IKE public and private key pair

   c. An IPsec public and private key pair

   d. An RSA public and an IKE private key pair

10. After the enrollment is complete, you can verify that the enrollment process was successful by using the **show crypto ca certificate** command.

   a. True

   b. False

CHAPTER 6

Configure Remote Access VPN

Upon completion of this chapter, you should be able to answer the following questions:

- What is Cisco Easy VPN?

- How do I configure an Easy VPN server?

- How do I configure an Easy VPN Remote for the Cisco VPN Client 4.x?

- How do I configure a Cisco Easy VPN remote-access router?

- How do I configure the PIX Security Appliance as an Easy VPN server?

- How do I configure a PIX 501 or 506 as an Easy VPN client?

- How do I configure the Adaptive Security Appliance to support WebVPN?

Key Terms

This chapter uses the following key terms. You can find the definitions in the glossary at the end of the book.

Cisco Easy VPN   page 608

Cisco Unity Client Protocol   page 608

Reverse route injection (RRI)   page 613

Dead peer detection (DPD)   page 619

Transparent tunneling   page 626

This chapter introduces the two components of *Cisco Easy VPN*: the Cisco Easy VPN Server and Cisco Easy VPN Remote. Both components work together to provide safe, reliable, and secure remote-access virtual private networks (VPNs) for users. This chapter covers how Easy VPN works and how users and administrators can use it to ease the creation of secure VPNs. The chapter also covers configuration of routers and PIX Security Appliances as Easy VPN Servers. You also learn about configuring Easy VPN Remote with the Cisco VPN Client, Cisco routers, and the PIX 501 and 506/506E models. This chapter also provides an explanation of how to configure WebVPN on an Adaptive Security Appliance (ASA).

Introduction to Cisco Easy VPN

Cable modems, digital subscriber line (DSL) routers, and other forms of broadband access provide high-performance connections to the Internet, but many applications also require the security of VPN connections that perform a high level of authentication and that encrypt the data between two particular endpoints. However, establishing a VPN connection between two routers can be complicated and typically requires tedious coordination between network administrators to configure the VPN parameters of the two routers.

The Cisco Easy VPN Remote feature eliminates much of this tedious work by implementing *Cisco Unity Client Protocol*, which allows most VPN parameters to be defined at a Cisco Easy VPN Server. This server can be a dedicated VPN device, such as a Cisco VPN 3000 concentrator, a PIX Security Appliance, or a Cisco IOS router that supports the Cisco Unity Client Protocol.

After the Cisco Easy VPN Server has been configured, a VPN connection can be created with minimal configuration on an Easy VPN Remote client, such as a Cisco 800 series router or a Cisco 1700 series router. When the Easy VPN Remote initiates the VPN tunnel connection, the Cisco Easy VPN Server pushes the IPsec policies to the Easy VPN Remote and creates the corresponding VPN tunnel connection.

The Cisco Easy VPN Remote feature provides for automatic management of the following details:

- Negotiating tunnel parameters, such as addresses, algorithms, and lifetime

- Establishing tunnels according to the parameters that were set

- Automatically creating the Network Address Translation (NAT) or Port Address Translation (PAT) and associated access control lists (ACLs) that are needed, if any

- Authenticating users; that is, ensuring that users are who they say they are by way of usernames, group names, and passwords

- Managing security keys for encryption and decryption

- Authenticating, encrypting, and decrypting data through the tunnel

Overview of the Easy VPN Server

Easy VPN Server enables Cisco IOS routers, PIX Security Appliances, and Cisco VPN 3000 series concentrators to act as VPN headend devices in site-to-site or remote-access VPNs, where the remote office devices are using the Easy VPN Remote feature. Using this feature, security policies defined at the headend are pushed to the remote VPN device, ensuring that those connections have current policies in place before the connection is established.

In addition, an Easy VPN Server-enabled device can terminate IPsec tunnels initiated by mobile remote workers running VPN Client software on PCs. This flexibility makes it possible for mobile and remote workers, such as salespeople on the road or telecommuters, to access their headquarters intranet where critical data and applications exist.

Overview of Cisco Easy VPN Remote

Easy VPN Remote enables Cisco IOS routers, PIX Security Appliances, and Cisco VPN 3002 hardware clients or software clients to act as remote VPN clients. These devices can receive security policies from an Easy VPN Server, minimizing VPN configuration requirements at the remote location. This cost-effective solution is ideal for remote offices with little IT support or for large customer premises equipment (CPE) deployments where it is impractical to individually configure multiple remote devices. This feature makes VPN configuration as easy as entering a password, which increases productivity and lowers costs because the need for local IT support is minimized.

In the example in Figure 6-1, the VPN gateway is a Cisco IOS router running the Easy VPN Server feature. Remote Cisco IOS routers and VPN software clients connect to the Cisco IOS router Easy VPN Server for access to the corporate intranet.

The Cisco Easy VPN Remote feature requires that the destination peer be a Cisco IOS Easy VPN Server or VPN concentrator that supports the Cisco Easy VPN Server feature. Some of the other restrictions for the Cisco Easy VPN Remote feature are as follows:

- **Only ISAKMP policy group 2 supported on Easy VPN Servers**—The Unity Protocol supports only Internet Security Association Key Management Protocol (ISAKMP) policies that use group 2 (1024-bit Diffie-Hellman) Internet Key Exchange (IKE) negotiation, so the Easy VPN Server being used with the Cisco Easy VPN Remote feature must be configured for a group 2 ISAKMP policy. The Easy VPN Server cannot be configured for ISAKMP group 1 or group 5 when being used with a Cisco Easy VPN client.

- **Transform sets support**—To ensure a secure tunnel connection, the Cisco Easy VPN Remote feature does not support transform sets that provide encryption without authentication, such as ESP-DES and ESP-3DES. Transform sets that provide authentication without encryption, such as ESP-NULL ESP-SHA-HMAC and ESP-NULL ESP-MD5-HMAC, are also not supported.

- **Dial backup for Easy VPN Remotes**—Line-status-based backup is not supported in this feature.

Note

The Cisco Unity Client Protocol does not support Authentication Header (AH) authentication, but Encapsulation Security Protocol (ESP) is supported.

■ **NAT interoperability support**—NAT interoperability is not supported in client mode with split tunneling.

Figure 6-1 Remote Access Using Cisco Easy VPN

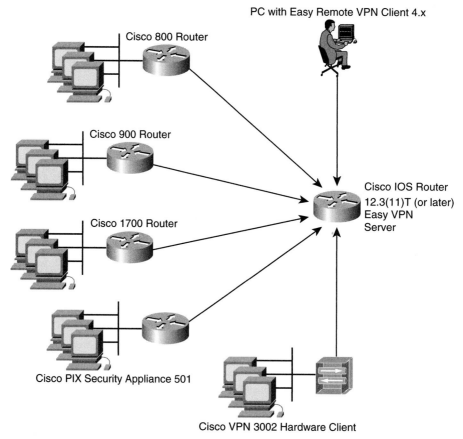

How Cisco Easy VPN Works

When an Easy VPN Remote client initiates a connection with an Easy VPN Server gateway, the conversation that occurs between the peers consists of the following major steps:

1. Device authentication via ISAKMP

2. User authentication using IKE Extended Authentication (XAUTH)

3. VPN policy push, when using mode configuration

4. IPsec security association (SA) creation

The following is a detailed description of the Easy VPN Remote connection process:

1. The VPN client initiates the IKE Phase 1 process, as shown in Figure 6-2.

Because there are two ways to perform authentication, the VPN client must consider the following when initiating this phase.

If a pre-shared key is to be used for authentication, the VPN client initiates aggressive mode (AM). When pre-shared keys are used, the accompanying group name entered in the configuration GUI, ID_KEY_ID, is used to identify the group profile associated with this VPN client.

If digital certificates are to be used for authentication, the VPN client initiates main mode (MM). When digital certificates are used, the organizational unit (OU) field of a distinguished name (DN) is used to identify the group profile.

Because the VPN client can be configured for pre-shared key authentication, which initiates IKE AM, it is recommended that the administrator change the identity of the Cisco IOS VPN device via the **crypto isakmp identity hostname** command. This action does not affect certificate authentication via IKE MM.

Figure 6-2   Step 1: VPN Client Initiates the IKE Phase 1 Process

2. The VPN client attempts to establish an ISAKMP SA between peer IP addresses by sending multiple ISAKMP proposals to the Easy VPN Server, as shown in Figure 6-3.

To reduce the amount of manual configuration on the VPN client, every combination of encryption and hash algorithms, in addition to authentication methods and Diffie-Hellman (DH) group sizes, is proposed.

Figure 6-3   Step 2: VPN Client Establishes an ISAKMP SA

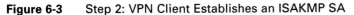

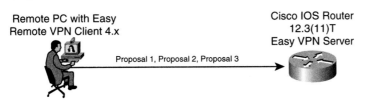

3. The Easy VPN Server accepts the SA proposal, as shown in Figure 6-4.

ISAKMP policy is global for the Easy VPN Server and can consist of several proposals. In the case of multiple proposals, the Easy VPN Server uses the first match. The most-secure policies should always be listed first.

Device authentication ends and user authentication begins at this point.

Figure 6-4   Step 3: Easy VPN Server Accepts the SA Proposal

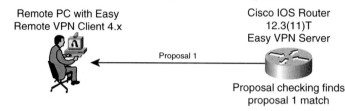

4. The Easy VPN Server initiates a username/password challenge, as shown in Figure 6-5.

The information that is entered is checked against authentication entities using authentication, authorization, and accounting (AAA) protocols such as RADIUS and TACACS+. Token cards can also be used via AAA proxy.

VPN devices configured to handle remote VPN clients should always be configured to enforce user authentication.

Figure 6-5   Step 4: Username/Password Challenge

5. If authentication is successful, the mode configuration process is initiated, as shown in Figure 6-6.

The remaining system parameters, such as IP address, Domain Name System (DNS), and split-tunnel attributes, are pushed to the VPN client at this time using mode configuration. The IP address is the only required parameter in a group profile. All other parameters are optional.

Figure 6-6   Step 5: Mode Configuration Process Is Initiated

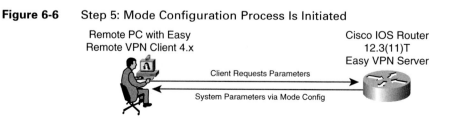

6. The reverse route injection (RRI) process is initiated, as shown in Figure 6-7.

Reverse route injection (RRI) ensures that a static route is created on the Easy VPN Server for the internal IP address of each VPN client.

It is recommended that RRI is enabled on the crypto map, either static or dynamic, for the support of VPN clients, unless the crypto map is being applied to a generic routing encapsulation (GRE) tunnel already being used to distribute routing information.

Figure 6-7   Step 6: RRI Process Is Initiated

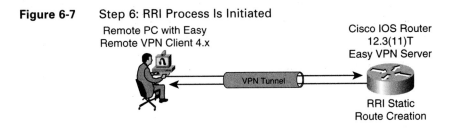

7. IPsec quick mode completes the connection, as shown in Figure 6-8.

After IPsec SAs have been created, the connection is complete.

Figure 6-8   Step 7: Connection Is completed with IPsec Quick Mode

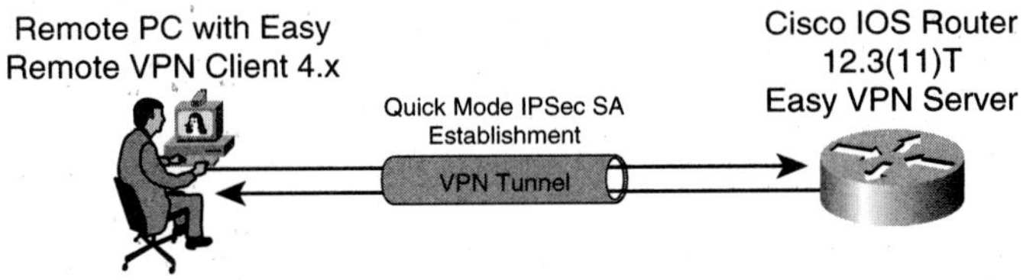

Cisco Easy VPN Server Configuration Tasks

Complete the following tasks to configure an Easy VPN Server for XAUTH with Easy VPN Remote clients:

- **Task 1**—Create an IP address pool.

- **Task 2**—Configure group policy lookup.

- **Task 3**—Create an ISAKMP policy for remote VPN client access.

- **Task 4**—Define a group policy for a mode configuration push.

- **Task 5**—Create a transform set.

- **Task 6**—Create a dynamic crypto map with RRI.

- **Task 7**—Apply a mode configuration to the dynamic crypto map.

- **Task 8**—Apply the crypto map to the router interface.

- **Task 9**—Enable IKE dead peer detection (DPD).

- **Task 10**—Configure XAUTH. XAUTH is not required when using Easy VPN, but it is covered in this lesson as part of this example. This option can be disabled.

- **Task 11**—(Optional) Enable the XAUTH save password feature.

After the VPN server configuration is complete, use the following commands to display the crypto map configuration and verify the running configuration:

```
show crypto map [interface interface ¦ tag map-name]
show running-config
```

Task 1: Create an IP Address Pool

If a local IP address pool is to be used, that pool must first be configured using the **ip local pool** command. The syntax for this command is as follows:

```
ip local pool {default ¦ pool-name low-ip-address [high-ip-address]}
```

For example, to configure the IP address pool depicted in Figure 6-9, you enter the following:

```
vpngate1(config)#ip local pool REMOTE-POOL 10.0.1.100 10.0.1.150
```

Figure 6-9   Creating an IP Address Pool

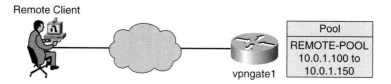

Creating a local address pool is optional if an external DHCP server is in use on the network.

Task 2: Configure Group Policy Lookup

Configuring group policy lookup is completed in two steps:

Step 1.   The first step when preparing the Easy VPN Server router for remote access is to establish a AAA section in the configuration file using the **aaa new-model** command in global configuration mode:

```
router(config)#aaa new-model
```

Step 2.   Enable group policy lookup using the **aaa authorization network** command:

```
router(config)#aaa authorization network list-name local [method1 [method2]]
```

A RADIUS server and the router local database may be used together and will be tried in the order listed.

For example, to create a user group for local AAA policy lookup for the scenario in Figure 6-10, you enter the following:

```
vpngate1(config)#aaa new-model
vpngate1(config)#aaa authorization network VPN-REMOTE-ACCESS local
```

Figure 6-10   Configure Group Policy Lookup

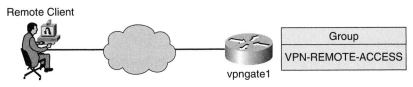

Task 3: Create ISAKMP Policy for Remote VPN Access

Complete this task to configure the ISAKMP policy for all Easy VPN Remote clients attaching to this router. Use the standard ISAKMP configuration commands to accomplish this task. For the scenario depicted in Figure 6-11, a general example of how to configure the ISAKMP policy starting in global configuration mode is as follows:

```
vpngate1(config)#crypto isakmp enable
vpngate1(config)#crypto isakmp policy 1
vpngate1(config-isakmp)#authen pre-share
vpngate1(config-isakmp)#encryption 3des
vpngate1(config-isakmp)#group 2
vpngate1(config-isakmp)#exit
```

Figure 6-11   Create ISAKMP Policy for Remote VPN Client Access

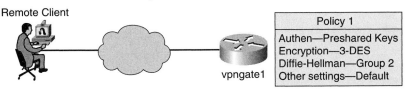

Task 4: Define a Group Policy for a Mode Configuration Push

This task creates a transform set for the Easy VPN Remote clients to use when they attempt to build an IPsec tunnel to the router. Use the standard method for creating a transform set, as shown in the following example.

Step 1.   Add the group profile to be defined.

Use the following command to specify the policy profile of the group that will be defined and enter ISAKMP group configuration mode:

```
crypto isakmp client configuration group {group-name | default}
```

For the scenario depicted in Figure 6-12, you enter the following:

```
vpngate1(config)#crypto isakmp client configuration group VPN-REMOTE-ACCESS
vpngate1(config-isakmp-group)#
```

Note

The crypto isakmp client configuration group command, which specifies group policy information that needs to be defined or changed, must be entered before entering the key, dns, wins, domain, or pool commands.

Figure 6-12   Add the Group Profile to Be Defined

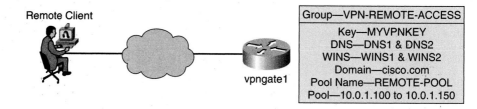

Step 2.   Configure the ISAKMP pre-shared key.

Use the **key** *name* command in ISAKMP group configuration mode to specify the ISAKMP pre-shared key when defining group policy information for the mode configuration push. This command must be used if the VPN client identifies itself to the router with a pre-shared key. For the VPN-REMOTE-ACCESS group profile first defined in Step 1 and depicted in Figure 6-12, you enter the following:

```
vpngate1(config-isakmp-group)#key MYVPNKEY
```

Step 3.   (Optional) Specify the DNS servers.

Specify the primary and secondary DNS servers using the dns primary-server secondary-server command in ISAKMP group configuration mode. For the VPN-REMOTE-ACCESS group profile depicted in Figure 6-12, you enter the following:

```
vpngate1(config-isakmp-group)#dns DNS1 DNS2
vpngate1(config-isakmp-group)#dns 172.26.26.120 172.26.26.130
```

Step 4.   (Optional) Specify the Windows Internet Name Service (WINS) servers.

Specify the primary and secondary WINS servers using the wins primary-server secondary-server command in ISAKMP group configuration mode. For the VPN-REMOTE-ACCESS group profile depicted in Figure 6-12, you enter the following:

```
vpngate1(config-isakmp-group)#wins WINS1 WINS2
vpngate1(config-isakmp-group)#wins 172.26.26.160 172.26.26.170
```

Step 5.   (Optional) Specify the DNS domain.

Specify the DNS domain to which a group belongs by using the **domain** *name* command in ISAKMP group configuration mode. For the VPN-REMOTE-ACCESS group profile depicted in Figure 6-12, you enter the following:

```
vpngate1(config-isakmp-group)#domain cisco.com
```

Step 6.   Specify the local IP address pool.

Use the **pool** *name* command to refer to an IP local address pool, which defines a range of addresses that will be used to allocate an internal IP address to a VPN client. For the VPN-REMOTE-ACCESS group profile depicted in Figure 6-12, you enter the following:

```
vpngate1(config-isakmp-group)#pool REMOTE-POOL
```

Task 5: Create a Transform Set

This task creates a transform set for the Easy VPN Remote clients to use when they attempt to build an IPsec tunnel to this router. Use the standard method for creating a transform set:

```
router(config)#crypto ipsec transform-set transform-set-name transform1 [transform2
[transform3]]
```

To create a transform set named VPNTRANSFORM, for example, you enter the following:

```
vpngate1(config)#crypto ipsec transform-set VPNTRANSFORM esp-3des esp-sha-hmac
vpngate1(config-crypto-trans)#exit
```

Task 6: Create a Dynamic Crypto Map with RRI

This task creates a dynamic crypto map to be used when building IPsec tunnels to Easy VPN Remote clients. In this example, RRI is used to ensure that returning data destined for a particular IPsec tunnel can find that tunnel. RRI ensures that a static route is created on the Easy VPN Server for each client internal IP address.

Complete the following steps to create the dynamic crypto map with RRI:

Step 1. Create a dynamic crypto map.

Create a dynamic crypto map entry and enter the crypto map configuration mode using the **crypto dynamic-map** *dynamic-map-name dynamic-seq-num* command.

A dynamic crypto map entry is essentially a crypto map entry without all the parameters configured. It acts as a policy template where the missing parameters are later dynamically configured, as the result of an IPsec negotiation, to match the requirements of as remote peer. This practice allows remote peers to exchange IPsec traffic with the router even if the router does not have a crypto map entry specifically configured to meet all the requirements of the remote peer.

To create a dynamic crypto map named DYNMAP with a sequence number of 1, for example, you enter the following:

```
vpngate1(config)#crypto dynamic-map DYNMAP1
vpngate1(config-crypto-map)#exit
```

Dynamic crypto maps are

- Not used by the router to initiate new IPsec SAs with remote peers.

- Used when a remote peer tries to initiate an IPsec SA with the router.

- Used in evaluating traffic.

Step 2.   Assign a transform set to the crypto map.

Specify which transform sets are allowed for the crypto map entry by using the following command:

```
router(config-crypto-map)#set transform-set transform-set-name [transform-set-name2…transform-set-
    name6]
```

When using this command, be sure to list multiple transform sets in order of priority, with the highest priority listed first. Note that this is the only configuration statement required in dynamic crypto map entries.

To specify the VPNTRANSFORM transform set originally created in Task 5, for example, you enter the following:

```
vpngate1(config-crypto-map)#set transform-set VPNTRANSFORM
```

Step 3.   Enable RRI.

Enable RRI using the following command:

```
router(config-crypto-map)#reverse-route
router(config-crypto-map)#exit
```

This command has no arguments or keywords.

Task 7: Apply Mode Configuration to the Dynamic Crypto Map

Apply mode configuration to a dynamic crypto map using the following steps in global configuration mode:

Step 1.   Configure the router to respond to mode configuration requests.

Configure the router to initiate or reply to mode configuration requests with the following command:

```
router(config)#crypto map map-name client configuration address {initiate ¦
    respond}
```

Note that VPN clients require the **respond** keyword to be used. The **initiate** keyword was used with older VPN clients and is no longer used with the 3.x or later versions of Cisco VPN Client.

Step 2.   Enable IKE queries for group policy lookup.

Enable ISAKMP querying for group policy when requested by the VPN client with the following command:

```
router(config)#crypto map map-name isakmp authorization list list-name
```

AAA uses the *list-name* argument to determine which method list is used to find the policy, either local or RADIUS, as defined in the **aaa authorization network** command.

For example, to specify the group policy VPN-REMOTE-ACCESS (refer back to Figure 6-12) for lookup, you enter the following:

```
vpngate1(config)#crypto map CLIENTMAP isakmp authorization list VPN-REMOTE-
    ACCESS
```

Step 3.   Apply the dynamic crypto map to the crypto map.

Apply the dynamic crypto map to the crypto map using the following command in global configuration mode:

```
router(config)#crypto map map-name seq-num ipsec-isakmp dynamic dynamic-map-
    name
```

For example:

```
vpngate1(config)#crypto map CLIENTMAP 65535 ipsec-isakmp dynamic DYNMAP
```

Task 8: Apply a Dynamic Crypto Map to the Router Interface

The **crypto map** *map-name* command is used to apply the crypto map to the outside interface of the Easy VPN Server router.

Figure 6-13 shows where a crypto map is applied to the outside interface. The configuration needed to accomplish this is as follows:

```
vpngate1(config)#interface ethernet0/1
vpngate1(config-if)#crypto map CLIENTMAP
vpngate1(config-if)#exit
```

Figure 6-13   Applying the Dynamic Crypto Map to the Crypto Map

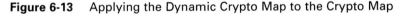
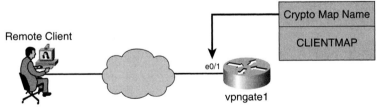

Task 9: Enable IKE Dead Peer Detection

Dead peer detection (DPD) is a keepalive scheme that allows the router to query the liveliness of its IKE peer. There are two options for DPD:

- On-demand DPD—Under the default option, on-demand DPD, messages are sent on the basis of traffic patterns. For example, if a router has to send outbound traffic and the liveliness of the peer is questionable, the router sends a DPD message to query the status of the peer. If a router has no traffic to send, it never sends a DPD message. If a peer is dead, and the router never has any traffic to send to the peer, the router does not find out until the IKE or IPsec SA has to be rekeyed. On the other hand, if the router has traffic to send to the peer, and the peer does not respond, the router initiates a DPD message to determine the state of the peer.

■ Periodic DPD—Functions on the basis of the timer. If the timer is set for 10 seconds, the router sends a hello message every 10 seconds, unless the router receives a hello message from the peer. The benefit of periodic DPD is earlier detection of dead peers. However, periodic DPD relies on periodic messages that have to be sent with considerable frequency. The result of sending frequent messages is that the communicating peers must encrypt and decrypt more packets.

Use the **crypto isakmp keepalive** *secs retries* command in global configuration mode to enable a Cisco IOS VPN gateway, instead of the VPN client, to send DPD messages, as depicted in Figure 6-14.

Figure 6-14   Enable IKE Dead Peer Detection

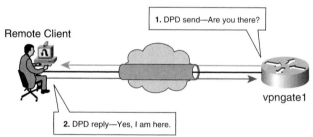

Task 10: (Optional) Configure XAUTH

Complete the following steps to configure XAUTH on the Easy VPN Server router:

Step 1.   Enable AAA login authentication via the following command:

```
router(config)#aaa authentication login list-name method1 [method2...]
```

For the VPN user group VPNUSERS, as depicted in Figure 6-15, you enter the following:

```
vpngate1(config)#aaa authentication login VPNUSERS local
```

Figure 6-15   Enable AAA Login Authentication

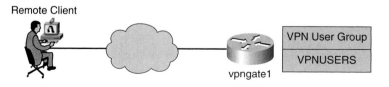

Step 2.   Set the XAUTH timeout value.

Set the XAUTH timeout value using the **crypto isakmp xauth timeout** *seconds* command.

Step 3.   Enable ISAKMP XAUTH for the dynamic crypto map by using the **authentication list** option of the following command:

```
router(config)#crypto map map-name client authentication list list-name
```

For example:

```
vpngate1(config)#crypto map CLIENTMAP client authentication list VPNUSERS
```

Task 11: (Optional) Enable the XAUTH Save Password Feature

Cisco Easy VPN Remote uses one of three available authentication methods:

- **No XAUTH**—When no XAUTH is used, there is no authentication for the user when establishing the VPN tunnels. This is the least secure practice when configuring and using Cisco Easy VPN Remote.

- **XAUTH with no password save feature**—This is better than no XAUTH, but it requires that users reenter the password each time they need to establish the VPN tunnel. This need might occur several times in one VPN session. Although this is the most secure form of authentication for Cisco Easy VPN Remote, it is also the most bothersome to users.

- **XAUTH with password save feature**—Using the password save function, users need only enter their password one time when establishing the VPN tunnel. After that, Cisco Easy VPN Remote automatically reenters the password when required.

Note

Note that the save password feature must be configured for both the Cisco Easy VPN Server and the Cisco Easy VPN Remote.

Enabling the XAUTH save password feature is an optional step. When configured, it allows the Easy VPN Remote to save and reuse the last-validated username and password for reauthentication. This means that a user no longer needs to reenter the information manually. This step could have been done earlier, in Step 1 of Task 4, while performing the **crypto isakmp client configuration group** command.

Use the **save-password** command in ISAKMP group configuration mode as demonstrated here:

```
vpngate1(config)#crypto isakmp client configuration group VPN-REMOTE-ACCESS
vpngate1(config-isakmp-group)#save-password
```

 Lab 6.2.12a   Configure Remote Access Using Cisco Easy VPN

In this lab, you learn to enable policy lookup via authentication, authorization, and accounting (AAA). You then define group policy information for mode configuration push. You also configure and verify the IPsec transforms and crypto maps. You also learn to install and configure the Cisco VPN Client 4.0 or later, and then use the VPN Client to connect to the corporate intranet.

Lab 6.2.12b   Configure Cisco Easy VPN Server with NAT

In this lab, you first verify the Easy VPN Server configuration. You learn to configure and modify PAT using both the Security Device Manager (SDM) and the command-line interface (CLI), and you also test remote connectivity.

Cisco Easy VPN Client 4.x Configuration Tasks

The Cisco VPN Client for Windows, referred to in this lesson as VPN Client, is software that runs on a Microsoft Windows-based PC. The VPN Client on a remote PC, communicating with a Cisco Easy VPN Server on an enterprise network or with a service provider, creates a secure connection over the Internet.

Complete the following tasks to configure the Cisco VPN Client 4.x for Easy VPN Remote access:

- **Task 1**—Install the Cisco VPN Client 4.x on the remote user's PC.
- **Task 2**—Create a new client connection entry.
- **Task 3**—Choose an authentication method.
- **Task 4**—Configure transparent tunneling.
- **Task 5**—Enable and add backup servers.
- **Task 6**—Configure a connection to the Internet through dialup networking.

Task 1: Install the Cisco VPN Client 4.x on the Remote PC

The VPN Client can be installed on a system through either the Microsoft Windows Installer (MSI) or InstallShield, as shown in Figure 6-16. Both applications use installation wizards to walk the user through the installation. Installing the VPN Client through InstallShield includes an Uninstall icon in the program group. MSI installation does not include this icon. In the latter case, to manually remove VPN Client applications, you can use the Microsoft Add/Remove Programs utility.

If a VPN Client has been previously installed, when the **vpnclient_en.exe** command or **vpn-clien_en.msi** is executed, an error message displays, as shown in Figure 6-17. The previously installed VPN Client must be uninstalled before proceeding with the new installation.

Figure 6-16   Install Cisco VPN Client 4.x

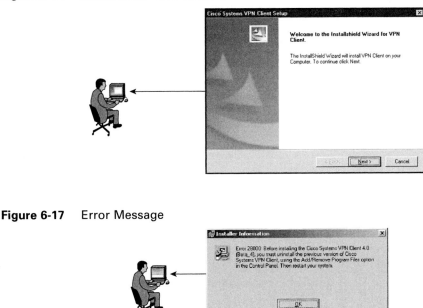

Figure 6-17   Error Message

To remove a VPN Client installed with the MSI installer, use the Windows Add/Remove Programs control panel. To remove a VPN Client installed with InstallShield, choose **Start > Programs > Cisco Systems VPN Client > Uninstall Client**.

Task 2: Create a New Client Connection Entry

To use the VPN Client, at least one connection entry must be created, which identifies the following information:

- The VPN device, also known as the remote server, to access.
- Pre-shared keys. The IPsec group to which the user is assigned to. The group determines how the user can access and use the remote network. For example, the group specifies access hours, number of simultaneous logins, user authentication method, and the IPsec algorithms that the VPN Client uses.
- The name of the certificate that will be used for authentication.
- Optional parameters that govern VPN Client operation and connection to the remote network.

Multiple connection entries can be created if the VPN Client is used to connect to multiple networks, although not simultaneously, or if the remote user belongs to more than one VPN remote-access group, as shown in Figure 6-18.

Figure 6-18   Create a New Client Connection Entry

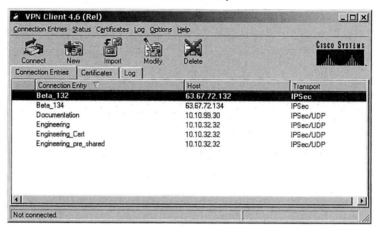

Creating a New Connection Entry

Use the following procedure to create a new connection entry:

Step 1.   Start the VPN Client by choosing **Start > Programs > Cisco Systems VPN Client > VPN Client**.

Step 2.   The VPN Client application starts and displays the advanced mode main window. If necessary, open the Options menu in simple mode and choose **AdvancedMode** or press **Ctrl-M**.

Step 3.   Choose **New** from the toolbar or the Connection Entries menu. The VPN Client displays a form.

Step 4.   Enter a unique name for this new connection. You can use any name to identify this connection. This name can contain spaces, and it is not case sensitive.

Step 5.   Enter a description of this connection. This field is optional, but it helps to further identify this connection.

Step 6.   Enter the hostname or IP address of the remote VPN device that the client will connect to.

Task 3: Choose an Authentication Method

Under the Authentication tab, enter the information for the authentication method that will be used. The VPN Client can connect as part of a group that is configured on the remote VPN device, or by supplying an identity digital certificate (see Figure 6-19).

Figure 6-19   Configure Client Authentication Properties

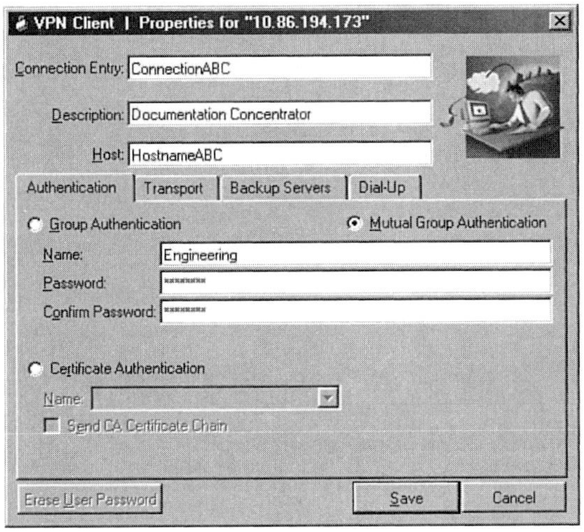

Group Authentication

The network administrator usually configures group authentication for the remote user. If this is not the case, use the following procedure:

Step 1.   Click the **Group Authentication** button.

Step 2.   In the Name field, enter the name of the IPsec group to which the remote user belongs. This entry is case sensitive.

Step 3.   In the Password field, enter the password, which is also case sensitive, for the IPsec group to which the remote user belongs. The field displays only asterisks.

Step 4.   Verify the password by entering it again in the Confirm Password field.

Mutual Group Authentication

Using mutual group authentication requires a root certificate that is compatible with the central-site VPN installed on the system. The network administrator can load a root certificate on the remote user's system during installation of the VPN Client software. When mutual group authentication is used, the VPN Client software verifies whether the remote user has a root certificate installed. If not, it prompts the remote user to install one. Before the user can continue, a root certificate must be imported. When the root certificate has been installed, follow the steps for group authentication.

Certificate Authentication

For certificate authentication, perform the following procedure, which varies according the type of certificate that is being used:

Step 1.   Click the **Certificate Authentication** button.

Step 2.   Choose the name of the certificate that is being used from the menu.

If the field says No Certificates Installed and is shaded, the VPN Client must enroll for a certificate before this feature can be used.

Task 4: Configure Transparent Tunneling

Transparent tunneling allows secure transmission between the VPN Client and a secure gateway through a router serving as a firewall, which may also be performing NAT or PAT. Transparent tunneling encapsulates ESP traffic within UDP packets and can allow for both ISAKMP and ESP to be encapsulated in TCP packets before they are sent through the NAT or PAT devices or firewalls. The most common application for transparent tunneling is behind a home router performing PAT.

The VPN Client also sends keepalives frequently, ensuring that the mappings on the devices are kept active.

Not all devices support multiple simultaneous connections behind them. Some cannot map additional sessions to unique source ports. Be sure to check with the device vendor to verify whether this limitation exists. Some vendors support ESP PAT, also known as IPsec passthrough, which might let the VPN Client operate without enabling transparent tunneling.

To use transparent tunneling, the central-site VPN device must be configured to support it.

This parameter is enabled on the VPN Client by default, as Figure 6-20 shows. To disable this parameter, uncheck the check box. It is recommended to always keep this parameter checked.

Figure 6-20   Task 4: Configure Transparent Tunneling

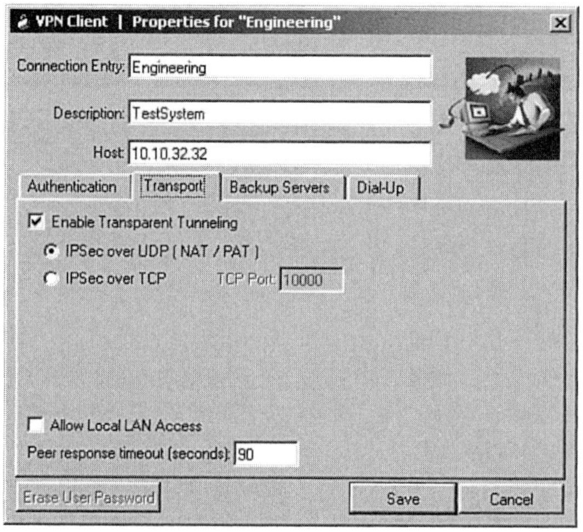

Transparent tunneling can be done over UDP or over TCP. The mode used must match that used by the secure gateway to which the VPN Client is connecting. Either mode operates properly through a PAT device. Multiple simultaneous connections might work better with TCP; and if the VPN Client is in an extranet environment, in general, TCP mode is preferable. UDP does not operate with stateful firewalls; so in this case, TCP should be used.

Using IPsec over UDP (NAT/PAT)

To enable IPsec over UDP (NAT/PAT), click the button. With UDP, the port number is negotiated. UDP is the default mode.

Using IPsec over TCP (NAT/PAT/Firewall)

To enable IPsec over TCP, click the button. When using TCP, the port number for TCP must also be entered in the TCP port field. This port number must match the port number configured on the secure gateway. The default port number is 10000.

Allowing Local LAN Access

In a multiple-NIC (network interface card) configuration, local LAN access pertains only to network traffic on the interface on which the tunnel was established. The Allow Local LAN Access parameter gives remote users access to the resources on their local LAN when they are connected through a secure gateway to a central-site VPN device. The resources could include printers, fax machines, shared files, or other systems. When this parameter is enabled and the central site is configured to permit it, remote users can access local resources while connected. When this parameter is disabled, all traffic from the client system goes through the IPsec connection to the secure gateway.

Note

This feature works only on one NIC, the same NIC as the tunnel.

To enable this feature, check **Allow Local LAN Access** (see Figure 6-20). To disable it, uncheck the check box. If the local LAN that the remote user is on is not secure, you should disable this feature. For example, this feature would be disabled when the local LAN is in a hotel or airport.

A network administrator at the central site configures a list of networks at the client side that the remote users can access. Remote users can access up to 10 networks when this feature is enabled. When Allow Local LAN Access is enabled and the VPN Client is connected to a central site, all traffic from the remote system goes through the IPsec tunnel except traffic to the networks excluded from doing so, as configured in the network list.

When this feature is enabled and configured on the VPN Client and permitted on the central-site VPN device, the remote user can see a list of the local LANs available by looking at the Routes table in the VPN Client statistics.

To display the Routes table, use the following procedure:

Step 1.   Display the Status menu and choose **Statistics**.

Step 2.   Choose **Route Details** from the Statistics dialog box.

The routes table shows local LAN routes, which do not traverse the IPsec tunnel, and secured routes, which do traverse an IPsec tunnel to a central-site device. The routes in the Local LAN Routes column are for locally available resources.

Task 5: Enable and Add Backup Servers

The private network can include one or more backup VPN servers to use if the primary server is not available. The system administrator should tell the remote user whether to enable backup servers. Information on backup servers can download automatically from the VPN concentrator, or this information can be entered manually, as shown in Figure 6-21.

Figure 6-21   Enable and Add Backup Servers

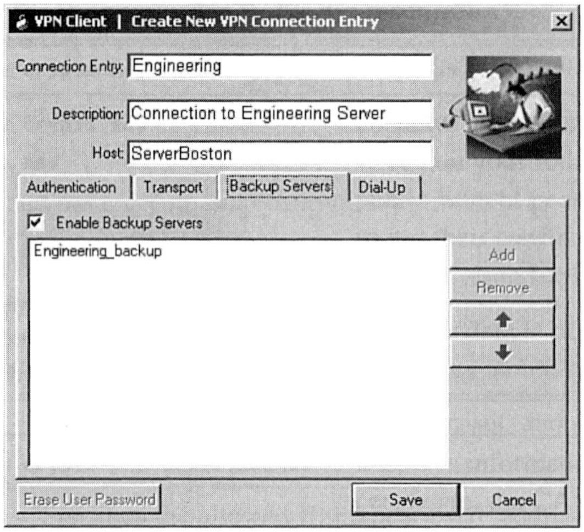

To enable backup servers from the VPN Client, use the following procedure:

Step 1.   Open the Backup Servers tab.

Step 2.   Check **Enable Backup Server(s)**. This is not checked by default.

Step 3.   Click **Add** to enter the address of a backup server.

Step 4.   Enter the hostname or IP address of the backup server. Use a maximum of 255 characters.

Step 5.   To add more backup devices, repeat Steps 2, 3, and 4.

Task 6: Configure Connection to the Internet Through Dialup Networking

To connect to a private network using a dialup connection, perform the following steps:

Step 1.   Use a dialup connection to an Internet service provider (ISP) to connect to the Internet.

Step 2.   Use the VPN Client to connect to the private network through the Internet.

To enable and configure this feature, check the **Connect to the Internet via dial-up** check box. This feature is not checked by default, as shown in Figure 6-22.

Figure 6-22   Configure Connection to the Internet

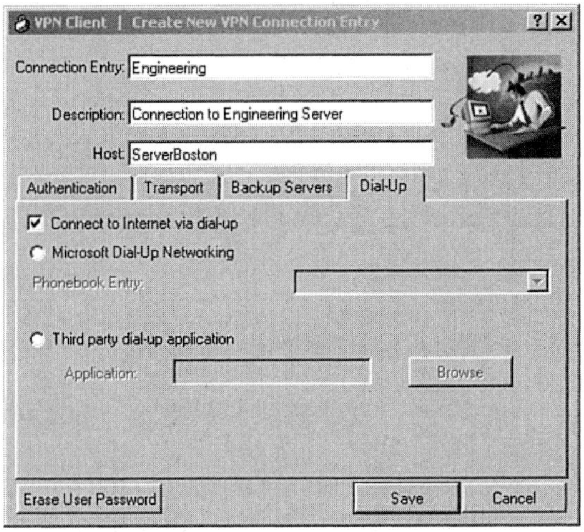

Remote users can connect to the Internet using the VPN Client application using either Microsoft Dial-up Networking (DUN) or a third-party dialup program.

Configure Cisco Easy VPN Remote for Access Routers

The Cisco Easy VPN Remote feature supports the following three modes of operation:

- **Client mode**—This mode specifies the NAT/PAT be configured to allow PCs and hosts on the client side of the VPN connection to form a private network. Their IP address must not use any of the IP addresses of the destination network. Client mode automatically configures the NAT/PAT translation and ACLs that are needed to implement the VPN connection. These configurations are automatically, but temporarily, created when the VPN connection is initiated. When the tunnel is torn down, the NAT/PAT and ACL configurations are automatically deleted. The NAT/PAT configuration is created with the following assumptions:

- The **ip nat inside** command is applied to all inside interfaces, including default inside interfaces. The default inside interface is Ethernet0 for the Cisco 800 and uBR900 series routers. The default inside interface is FastEthernet0 for Cisco 1700 series routers.

- The **ip nat outside** command is applied to the interface that is configured for Easy VPN Remote. On the Cisco uBR905 and Cisco uBR925 routers, this is always the cable-modem0 interface. On the Cisco 800 and 1700 series routers, this is the outside interface configured for Easy VPN Remote. The Cisco 1700 series routers can have multiple outside interfaces configured.

- **Network extension mode**—This mode specifies that the hosts at the client end of the VPN connection use fully routable IP addresses that are reachable by the destination network over the tunneled network. Together they form one logical network. Because PAT is not used, the client PCs and hosts have direct access to the PCs and hosts on the destination network.

- **Network extension plus mode**—Identical to network extension mode with the additional capability of being able to request an IP address via mode configuration and automatically assign it to an available loopback interface. The IPsec SAs for this IP address are automatically created by Easy VPN Remote. The IP address is typically used for troubleshooting using ping, Telnet, and Secure Shell (SSH).

Easy VPN Remote Modes of Operation

All modes of operation also optionally support split tunneling, which allows secure access to corporate resources through the VPN tunnel while also allowing Internet access through a connection to an ISP or other service. Split tunneling eliminates the corporate network from the path for web access.

Client Mode Example

The diagram in Figure 6-23 illustrates the client mode of operation. In this example, the Cisco 831 router provides access to two PCs, which have IP addresses in the 10.0.0.0 private network space. These PCs connect to the Ethernet interface on the Cisco 831 router, which also has an IP address in the 10.0.0.0 private network space. The Cisco 831 router performs NAT or PAT translation over the VPN tunnel so that the PCs can access the destination network.

Figure 6-23   Easy VPN Remote Client Mode

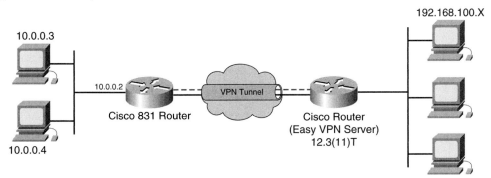

Note

The diagram could also represent a split-tunneling connection, in which the client PCs can access public resources in the global Internet without including the corporate network in the path for the public resources.

Network Extension Mode Example

The diagram in Figure 6-24 illustrates the network extension mode of operation. In this example, the Cisco 831 router acts as Cisco Easy VPN Remote devices, connecting to a router used as a Cisco Easy VPN Server.

The client hosts are given IP addresses that are fully routable by the destination network over the tunnel. These IP addresses could be either in the same subnet space as the destination network, or in separate subnets, assuming that the destination routers are configured to properly route those IP addresses over the tunnel.

In this example, the PCs and hosts attached to the two routers have IP addresses that are in the same address space as the destination enterprise network. The PCs connect to the Ethernet interface of the Cisco 831 router, which also has an IP address in the enterprise address space. This scenario provides a seamless extension of the remote network.

Figure 6-24   Easy VPN Remote Network Extension Mode

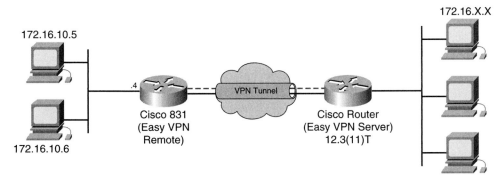

Configuration Tasks for Cisco Easy VPN Remote for Access Routers

Configuring Cisco access routers to act as Easy VPN Remote clients consists of the following tasks:

- **Task 1**—(Optional) Configure the DHCP server pool.

- **Task 2**—Configure and assign the Cisco Easy VPN client profile.

- **Task 3**—(Optional) Configure XAUTH password save.

- **Task 4**—Initiate the VPN tunnel.

- **Task 5**—Verify the Cisco Easy VPN configuration.

Task 1: Configure the DHCP Server Pool

To use the DHCP server of the local router to assign IP addresses to the hosts that are connected to the LAN interface of the router, you must create a pool of IP addresses for the internal DHCP server. The DHCP server then assigns an IP address from this pool to each host when it connects to the router:

```
exit
Router(config)# ip dhcp excluded-address lan-ip-address
```

In a typical VPN connection, the hosts connected to the LAN interface of the router are assigned an IP address in a private address space. The router then uses NAT/PAT to translate those IP addresses into a single IP address that is transmitted across the VPN tunnel connection.

The following steps enable you to create the DHCP server pool:

Step 1.   Create a DHCP server address pool using the **ip dhcp pool pool-name** command. This places the administrator in DHCP pool configuration mode:

```
router(config)# ip dhcp pool pool-name
```

Step 2.   Use the **network** command to specify the IP network and subnet mask of the address pool that will be used by the hosts connected to the local Ethernet interface of the router:

```
router(dhcp-config)#network ip-address [mask ¦ /prefix-length]
```

Step 3.   Use the **default-router** command to specify the IP address of the default router for a DHCP client. At least one address must be specified. You can specify up to eight addresses per command.

```
router(dhcp-config)#default-router address [address2....addressN]
```

Step 4.   Use the **import all** command to ensure that the router is configured with the proper DHCP parameters from the central DHCP server. This option requires a central

DHCP server be configured to provide the DHCP options. This server can be on a different subnet or network:

```
router(dhcp-config)#import all
```

Step 5. The **lease command** is optional. Use this command to specify the duration of the DHCP lease. Use the **exit** command to leave the DHCP pool configuration mode:

```
router(dhcp-config)#lease {days [hours][minutes]¦infinite}
router(dhcp-config)#exit
```

Step 6. Use the **ip dhcp excluded-address** *lan-ip-address* command to exclude the specified address from the DHCP server pool. The *lan-ip-address* should be the IP address assigned to the LAN interface of the router.

Example 6-1 demonstrates a DHCP server pool configuration for the network in Figure 6-25.

Example 6-1   DHCP Server Pool Configuration

```
vpnRemote1(config)#ip dhcp pool CLIENT
vpnRemote1(dhcp-config)#network 10.10.10.0 255.255.255.0
vpnRemote1(dhcp-config)#default-router 10.10.10.1
vpnRemote1(dhcp-config)#import all
vpnRemote1(dhcp-config)#lease 3
vpnRemote1(dhcp-config)#exit
vpnRemote1(config)#ip dhcp excluded-address 10.10.10.1
```

Figure 6-25   DHCP Server Pool

Task 2: Configure and Assign the Cisco Easy VPN Client Profile

The following steps are used to configure the Cisco Easy VPN client profile and to assign the profile to a router interface:

Step 1. Use the **crypto ipsec client ezvpn** *name* command to create a profile. This places the administrator in Cisco Easy VPN Remote configuration mode:

```
router(config)# crypto ipsec client ezvpn name
```

Step 2. Use the **group** *group-name* **key** *group-key* command to specify the IPsec group and IPsec key values to be associated with this profile. The values of *group-name* and *group-key* must match the values assigned in the Easy VPN Server:

```
router(config-crypto-ezvpn)# group group-name key group-key
```

Step 3. Use the **peer** command to specify the IP address or hostname for the destination peer. This is typically the IP address of the outside interface of the Easy VPN Server. If a hostname is used, a DNS server must be configured and available for this to work:

```
router(config-crypto-ezvpn)#peer [ip-address ¦ hostname]
```

Step 4. Use the **mode** command to specify the type of VPN connection that should be made. The options are client mode or network extension mode:

```
router(config-crypto-ezvpn)#mode {client ¦ network-extension ¦ network-plus}
```

Step 5. Enter the **exit** command to leave Easy VPN Remote configuration mode.

Step 6. Use the **crypto ipsec client ezvpn** *name* command in interface configuration mode to assign the Easy VPN client profile to a router interface.

Example 6-2 demonstrates how to assign the Easy VPN client profile to a router interface for the network in Figure 6-26.

Example 6-2   Assigning an Easy VPN Client Profile to a Router Interface

```
vpnRemote1(config)#crypto ipsec client ezvpn VPNGATE1
vpnRemote1(config-crypto-ezvpn)#group VPNREMOTE1 key MYVPNKEY
vpnRemote1(config-crypto-ezvpn)#peer 20.20.20.2
vpnRemote1(config-crypto-ezvpn)#mode client
vpnRemote1(config-crypto-ezvpn)#exit
vpnRemote1(config)#interface ethernet1

vpnRemote1(config-if)#crypto ipsec client ezvpn VPNGATE1

vpnRemote1(config-if)#exit
```

Figure 6-26   Assign Easy VPN Remote to the Interface

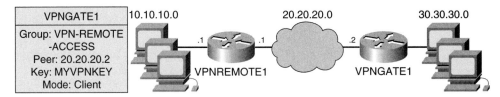

Task 3: (Optional) Configure the XAUTH Save Password Feature

Task 3 is an optional task. If XAUTH is not used, skip this task.

If the save password feature is enabled on the Cisco Easy VPN Server, it must be enabled on the client, too. If both ends of the tunnel do not match, the VPN tunnel will not be established.

You can also complete this task as part of Task 2.

Enter the **username** *aaa-username* **password** *aaa-password* command in ezvpn crypto configuration mode for the specific client profile, as demonstrated here:

```
vpnRemote1(config)#crypto ipsec client ezvpn VPNGATE1
vpnRemote1(config-crypto-ezvpn)#username VPNUSER password VPNPASS
vpnRemote1(config-crypto-ezvpn)#exit
```

This is the AAA username and password used to automatically reauthenticate the user with the XAUTH password save feature enabled in the Cisco Easy VPN Server.

Task 4: (Optional) Initiate the VPN Tunnel (XAUTH)

Task 4 is also optional. If XAUTH is not being used, skip this task.

With XAUTH configured, the VPN tunnel must be initiated manually, for at least the first time. A Cisco IOS Software message appears similar to the following because the software is waiting for a valid XAUTH username and password:

```
01:34:42:  EZVPN: Pending Xauth Request, Please enter the following command:

01:34:42:  EZVPN: crypto ipsec client ezvpn xauth
```

This message displays whenever an administrator logs in to the remote router console port.

Step 1. Enter the **crypto ipsec client ezvpn xauth** command:

```
vpnRemote1#crypto ipsec client ezvpn xauth
```

Step 2. Enter the username and password as prompted:

```
Enter Username and Password: VPNUSER
Password: *******
```

Which of two options happens next is determined by the XAUTH configuration:

- With just the XAUTH feature enabled, when the SA expires, the username and password must be reentered manually. This process is ongoing. The same Cisco IOS message will display and the user must repeat this manual process to reauthenticate each time.

- With the XAUTH password save enabled, when the SA expires, the last valid username and password is reused automatically. This option is the more popular of the two.

Task 5: Verify the Cisco Easy VPN Configuration

Task 5 consists of reviewing the Easy VPN configuration using the **show crypto ipsec client ezvpn** command, as demonstrated in Example 6-3.

Example 6-3   Verify the Cisco Easy VPN Configuration

```
vpnRemote1#show crypto ipsec client ezvpn


Easy VPN Remote Phase: 2


Tunnel name : VPNGATE1
Inside interface list: Ethernet0
Outside interface: Ethernet1
Current State: IPSEC_ACTIVE
Last Event: SOCKET_UP
Address: 30.30.30.24
Mask: 255.255.255.255
DNS Primary: 30.30.30.10
DNS Secondary: 30.30.30.11
NBMS/WINS Primary: 30.30.30.12
NBMS/WINS Secondary: 30.30.30.13
Default Domain: cisco.com
```

Example 6-4 presents an Easy VPN remote-access router configuration.

Example 6-4   Easy VPN Remote Configuration

```
version 12.2
hostname VPNREMOTE1
!
username admin privilege 15 password 7 070E25414707485744
ip subnet-zero
ip domain-name cisco.com
ip dhcp excluded-address 10.10.10.1
!
ip dhcp pool CLIENT
   import all
   network 10.10.10.0 255.255.255.0
   default router 10.10.10.1
   lease 3
!
crypto ipsec client ezvpn VPNGATE1
  connect auto
  group VPNREMOTE1 key 0 MYVPNKEY
  mode client
  peer 20.20.20.2
  username VPNUSER password 0 VPNPASS

interface Ethernet0
  ip address 10.10.10.1 255.255.255.0
```

Example 6-4   Easy VPN Remote Configuration   *continues*

```
  crypto ipsec client ezvpn VPNGATE1 inside
!
interface Ethernet1
  ip address 20.20.20.2 255.255.255.0
  crypto ipsec client ezvpn VPNGATE1
!
ip classless
ip route 0.0.0.0 0.0.0.0 Ethernet1
ip route 30.30.30.0 255.255.255.0 Ethernet1
ip http server
no ip http secure-server
!
line con 0
 no modem enable
 stopbits 1
line aux 0
line vty 0 4
!
end
```

Configure the PIX Security Appliance as an Easy VPN Server

Complete the following tasks to configure the PIX Security Appliance as an Easy VPN Server for XAUTH with Easy VPN Remote clients:

- **Task 1**—Create an ISAKMP policy for remote Cisco VPN Client access.

- **Task 2**—Create an IP address pool.

- **Task 3**—Define a group policy for a mode configuration push.

- **Task 4**—Create a transform set.

- **Task 5**—Create a dynamic crypto map.

- **Task 6**—Assign a dynamic crypto map to a static crypto map.

- **Task 7**—Apply a dynamic crypto map to the PIX Security Appliance interface.

- **Task 8**—Configure XAUTH.

- **Task 9**—Configure NAT and NAT 0.

- **Task 10**—Enable IKE DPD.

Task 1: Create an ISAKMP Policy for Remote VPN Client Access

Complete this task to configure the ISAKMP policy for Easy VPN Server. Use the standard ISAKMP configuration commands to accomplish this task. To configure the ISAKMP policy for the scenario in Figure 6-27, you enter the following:

```
pixfirewall(config)#isakmp enable outside
pixfirewall(config)#isakmp policy 20 authentication pre-share
pixfirewall(config)#isakmp policy 20 encryption des
pixfirewall(config)#isakmp policy 20 hash sha
pixfirewall(config)#isakmp policy 20 group 2
```

Figure 6-27   Create an ISAKMP Policy for Remote VPN Client Access

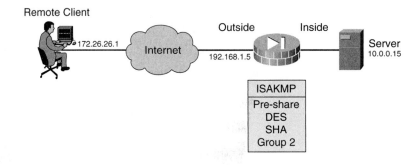

Task 2: Create an IP Address Pool

If you are creating a local IP address pool for when the remote client is using the remote server as an external DHCP server, you need to configure it using the **ip local pool** {*pool-name low-ip-address* [*high-ip-address*]} command. For the scenario in Figure 6-28, you enter the following command:

```
pixfirewall(config)#ip local pool MYPOOL 10.0.11.1-10.0.11.254
```

Figure 6-28   Create an IP Address Pool

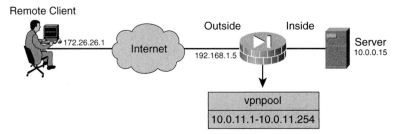

Task 3: Define a Group Policy for Mode Configuration Push

Complete this task to define a group policy to be pushed during mode configuration. Although users can belong to only one group per connection, they can belong to specific groups with different policy requirements.

Use the following steps, beginning in global configuration mode, to define the policy attributes that are pushed to the Cisco VPN Client through mode configuration for the scenario depicted in Figure 6-29.

Figure 6-29   Group Policy for Mode Configuration Push

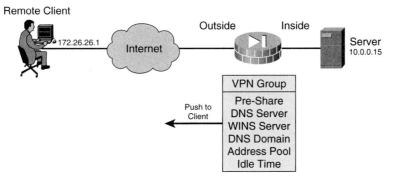

Step 1.   Set the tunnel group type.

To enable remote access, the tunnel group type must be named and set to remote access using the **tunnel-group** *name* **type** *type* command as follows:

```
pixfirewall(config)tunnel-group training type IPSec_RA
```

Step 2.   Configure the IKE pre-shared key.

First, you need to enter tunnel group ipsec-attributes submode to configure the key using the **tunnel-group** *name* [**general-attributes** | **ipsec-attributes**] command. Then, you use the **pre-shared-key** *key* command to specify the IKE pre-shared key when defining group policy information for the mode configuration push. This command must be used if the Cisco VPN Client identifies itself to the router with a pre-shared key. For the network in Figure 6-29, the configuration is as follows:

```
pixfirewall(config)#tunnel-group training ipsec-attributes
pixfirewall(config-ipsec)#pre-shared-key cisco123
```

Step 3.   Specify the local IP address pool.

First, you need to enter tunnel group general-attributes submode to configure the address pool using the **tunnel-group** *name* [**general-attributes** | **ipsec-attributes**] command. Then, you use the **address-pool** command to refer to an IP local pool address, which defines a range of addresses that will be used to allocate an internal IP address to a VPN client. For the network in Figure 6-29, the configuration is as follows:

```
pixfirewall(config)#tunnel-group training general-attributes
pixfirewall(config-general)#address-pool MYPOOL
```

Step 4. Configure the group policy type.

Use the **group-policy** *group-name* [**internal** | **external** | **attributes**] command to create and specify the type of group to be created:

```
pixfirewall(config)#group-policy training internal
```

Step 5. Enter the group policy attributes submode.

Enter the group policy attribute subcommand mode to configure parameters specific to the group created:

```
pixfirewall(config)#group-policy training attributes
pixfirewall(config-group-policy)#
```

Step 6. Specify the DNS servers

For this optional step, specify the primary and secondary DNS servers using the **dns-server value** *dns_ip_prim* [*dns_ip_sec*] command in group-policy configuration mode:

```
pixfirewall(config-group-policy)#dns-server value 10.0.0.15
```

Every time that the **dns-server** command is issued, the existing setting are overwritten. To add a DNS server rather than overwrite previously configured servers, include the IP addresses of all DNS servers when this command is entered.

Step 7. Specify the WINS servers.

For this optional step, specify the primary and secondary WINS servers using the **wins-server value** *dns_ip_prim* [*dns_ip_sec*] command in group-policy configuration mode:

```
pixfirewall(config-group-policy)#wins-server value 10.0.0.15
```

As with DNS servers, every time that the **wins-server** command is issued, the existing settings are overwritten.

Step 8. Specify the DNS domain.

For this optional step, specify the DNS domain to which a group belongs by using the **default-domain** {**value** *domain-name* | **none**} command in group-policy configuration mode:

```
pixfirewall(config-group-policy)#default-domain value cisco.com
```

The PIX Security Appliance passes the default domain name to the IPsec client to append to DNS queries that omit the domain field. This domain name applies only to tunneled packets. When there are no default domain names, users inherit the default domain name in the default group policy.

Step 9.   Specify the idle timeout.

Use the **vpn-idle-timeout** {*minutes* | **none**} command to set the inactivity timeout for a Cisco VPN Client. When the inactivity timeout for a given VPN Client or Easy VPN Remote device expires, the tunnel is terminated. The default inactivity timeout is 30 minutes. For the network in Figure 6-29, the configuration is as follows:

```
pixfirewall(config-group-policy)#vpn-idle-timeout 600
```

Task 4: Create a Transform Set

Specify which transform sets are allowed for the crypto map entry by using the **crypto ipsec transform-set** *transform-set-name* [*transform1* [*transform2*]] command. When using this command, be sure to list multiple transform sets in order of priority, with the highest priority first. Note that this is the only configuration statement required in dynamic crypto map entries. For the network in Figure 6-30, the configuration is as follows:

```
pixfirewall(config)#crypto ipsec transform-set remoteuser1 esp-des esp-sha-hmac
```

Figure 6-30   Transform Set

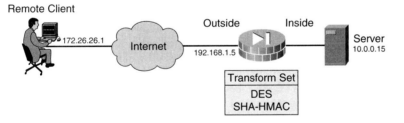

Tasks 5 Through 7: Dynamic Crypto Map

Task 5, 6, and 7 all have to do with creating a dynamic crypto map.

Task 5: Create Dynamic Crypto Map

Create a dynamic crypto map entry and enter the crypto map configuration mode using the following command:

```
pixfirewall(config)#crypto dynamic-map dynamic-map-name dynamic-seq-num set transform-set
transform-set-name1
```

For the network shown previously in Figure 6-30, you enter the following:

```
pixfirewall(config)#crypto dynamic-map rmt-dyna-map 10 set transform-set remoteuser1
```

A dynamic crypto map entry is essentially a crypto map entry without all the parameters configured. It acts as a policy template where the missing parameters are later dynamically configured, as the result of an IPsec negotiation, to match the requirements of a remote peer. This allows remote peers to exchange IPsec traffic with the PIX Security Appliance even if the PIX does not have a crypto map entry specifically configured to meet all the requirements of the remote peer.

Dynamic crypto maps are not used by the PIX Security Appliance to initiate new IPsec SAs with remote peers. Dynamic crypto maps are used when a remote peer tries to initiate an IPsec SA with the PIX. Dynamic crypto maps are also used in evaluating traffic.

Task 6: Assign the Dynamic Crypto Map to a Static Crypto Map

Add the dynamic crypto map to a static crypto map using the following command:

```
pixfirewall(config)#crypto map map-name seq-num ipsec-isakmp dynamic dynamic-map-name
```

For the network shown previously in Figure 6-30, you enter the following:

```
pixfirewall(config)#crypto map rmt-user-map 10 set ipsec-isakmp dynamic rmt-dyna-map
```

Task 7: Apply the Crypto Map to an Interface

Apply the crypto map to the outside interface of the PIX Security Appliance with the **crypto-map** *map-name* **interface** *interface-name* command:

```
pixfirewall(config)#crypto map rmt-user-map interface outside
```

Task 8: Configure XAUTH

Complete the following steps to configure XAUTH on the Easy VPN Server PIX Security Appliance:

Step 1.   Enable AAA login authentication.

Enable AAA login authentication using the **aaa-server** *server_tag* **protocol** *auth_protocol* command as follows:

```
pixfirewall(config)#aaa-server mytacacs protocol tacacs+
```

Step 2.   Define the AAA server IP address and encryption key.

Set the IP address of the AAA server and the encryption key using the following command:

```
pixfirewall(config-aaa-server)#aaa-server server_tag [(if_name)] host server-
    ip [key] [timeout seconds]
```

For the same network shown previously in Figure 6-30, the command is as follows:

```
pixfirewall(config-aaa-server)#aaa-server mytacacs (inside) host 10.0.0.15
    cisco123 timeout 5
```

Step 3.   Enable IKE XAUTH for the crypto map.

Enable IKE XAUTH for the tunnel using the **authentication-server-group** [*inter-face-name*] *server-group* [**LOCAL | NONE**] command in tunnel-group general-attributes configuration mode as demonstrated here:

```
pixfirewall(config)#tunnel-group training general-attributes
pixfirewall(config-general)#authentication-server-group mytacacs
```

Task 9: Configure NAT and NAT 0

The last task is to define which traffic is encrypted and sent down the IPsec tunnel and which traffic is translated and transmitted in clear text. The NAT 0 **access-list** command defines which traffic is encrypted but not translated, as demonstrated in Example 6-5 for the network in Figure 6-31. Traffic sourced from network 10.0.0.0/24 and destined for a host on 10.0.11.0/24 network is encrypted. The remaining traffic is translated, using NAT, to the IP address of the outside interface and then transmitted in clear text.

```
Example 6-5      Easy VPN Remote Configuration Example
pixfirewall(config)#access-list 101 permit 10.0.0.0 255.255.0 10.0.11.0 255.255.255.0
pixfirewall(config)#nat (inside) 0 access-list 101
pixfirewall(config)#nat (inside) 1 0.0.0.0 0.0.0.0
pixfirewall(config)#global (outside) 1 interface
```

Figure 6-31   Effects of NAT and NAT 0 Configuration

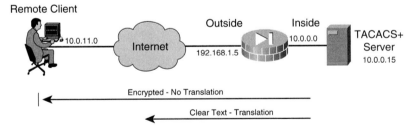

Task 10: Enable IKE DPD

DPD allows two IPsec peers to determine whether the other is still alive during the lifetime of a VPN connection. DPD is useful because a host might reboot, or the dialup link of a remote user might disconnect without notifying the peer that the VPN connection is gone away. When the IPsec host determines that a VPN connection no longer exists, it can notify the user, attempt to switch to another IPsec host, or clean up valuable resources that were allocated for the peer that no longer exists.

A DPD peer can send DPD messages, reply to DPD messages, or both. DPD messages are uni-directional and are automatically sent by Cisco VPN Clients. Unlike the old-style IKE keepalives, DPD is not required on both peers. DPD can be configured on just the remote, just the headend, or both, depending on the requirements. Figure 6-32 demonstrates communication between DPD peers.

Figure 6-32 Enable IKE Dead Peer Detection

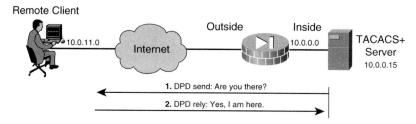

To enable the PIX Security Appliance gateway to send IKE DPD messages, use the following command in tunnelgroup ipsec-attributes configuration mode:

```
Pixfirewall(config-ipsec)#isakmp keepalive [thrshold seconds] [retry seconds] [disable]
```

You can configure the number of seconds between DPD messages. The number of seconds between retries if a DPD message fails can also be configured.

Lab 6.5.9a   Configure a Secure VPN Using IPsec Between a PIX and a VPN Client Using Adaptive Security Device Manger (ASDM)

In this lab exercise, you configure the PIX Easy VPN Server feature using the VPN Wizard. You then install and configure the Cisco VPN Client on the host PC. Finally, you verify and test the Cisco VPN Client remote-access connection.

Lab 6.5.9b   Configure a Secure VPN Using IPsec Between a PIX and a VPN Client Using the CLI

In this lab exercise, you configure and verify the PIX Easy VPN Server feature using the CLI. You then install and configure the Cisco VPN Client on a Microsoft Windows end-user PC. Finally, you verify and test the Cisco VPN Client remote-access connection.

Note

PIX Security Appliance 7.0 software is not available for the 501 and 506E models. The configuration steps covered in this chapter are based on Release 6.3.

Configure a PIX 501 or 506E as an Easy VPN Client

This section focuses on the Easy VPN Remote configuration for the client device on a PIX 501 or 506E security device.

PIX Security Appliance Easy VPN Remote Feature Overview

Any PIX Security Appliance unit running Version 6.2 or later can be configured as a Cisco Easy VPN Server or an Easy VPN Remote. Using the PIX as an Easy VPN Server lets the administrator configure the VPN policy in a single location on the Easy VPN Server. After you configure the VPN policy, Easy VPN Server can push VPN policy configuration to multiple Easy VPN Remote devices, which greatly simplifies configuration and administration.

When using PIX Security Appliance Software Version 6.2 and later, a PIX 501 or PIX 506/506E can be used as an Easy VPN Remote device when connecting to an Easy VPN Server, such as a Cisco VPN 3000 concentrator, Cisco IOS router, or another PIX, as shown in Figure 6-33. Easy VPN Remote device functionality, sometimes called a hardware client, allows the PIX to establish a VPN tunnel to the Easy VPN Server. Hosts running on the LAN behind the PIX can connect through the Easy VPN Remote without individually running any VPN client software.

Each Easy VPN Remote device is assigned to a group. The administrator uses the **vpngroup** command to associate security policy attributes with a VPN group name. As Easy VPN Remote devices establish a VPN tunnel to the Easy VPN Server, the attributes associated with their group are pushed to the Easy VPN Remote device.

Figure 6-33 Implementing PIX Security Appliance Easy VPN Remote

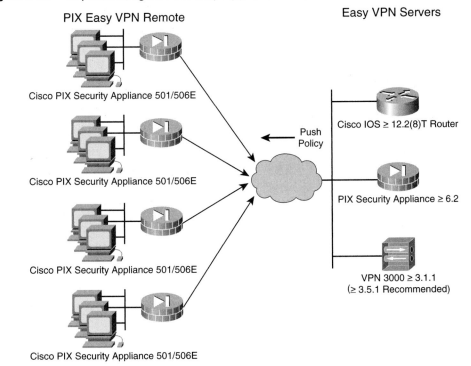

PIX Easy VPN Remote

Easy VPN Servers

Cisco PIX Security Appliance 501/506E

Cisco PIX Security Appliance 501/506E

Cisco PIX Security Appliance 501/506E

Cisco PIX Security Appliance 501/506E

Push Policy

Cisco IOS ≥ 12.2(8)T Router

PIX Security Appliance ≥ 6.2

VPN 3000 ≥ 3.1.1
(≥ 3.5.1 Recommended)

Easy VPN Remote Configuration

The Easy VPN Server controls the policy enforced on the PIX Security Appliance Easy VPN Remote device. However, to establish the initial connection to the Easy VPN Server, some configuration must be completed locally. This configuration can be done by using Cisco PIX Device Manager (PDM) or by using the CLI.

If the Easy VPN Remote uses pre-shared keys, enter the following command:

```
pixfirewall(config)#vpnclient vpngroup {groupname} password {preshared_key}
```

Replace *groupname* with an alphanumeric identifier for the VPN group. Replace *preshared_key* with the encryption key to use for securing communications to the Easy VPN Server.

If the Easy VPN Server uses XAUTH to authenticate the PIX Security Appliance client, enter the following command:

```
pixfirewall(config)#vpnclient username {xauth_username} password {xauth_password}
```

Replace *xauth_username* with the username assigned for XAUTH. Replace *xauth_password* with the password assigned for XAUTH.

Identify the remote Easy VPN Server by entering the following command:

```
pixfirewall(config)#vpnclient server {ip_primary} [ip_secondary_n]
```

Replace *ip_primary* with the IP address of the primary Easy VPN Server. Replace *ip_secondary_n* with the IP address of one or more Easy VPN Servers. A maximum of 11 Easy VPN Servers are supported. The list of servers consists of 1 primary and up to 10 secondary servers.

Easy VPN Client Device Mode and Enabling Easy VPN Remote Clients

Set the Easy VPN Remote device to one of two modes: client mode or network extension mode. In client mode, the remote PIX Security Appliance applies PAT to all client IP addresses connected to the inside interface. In the example in Figure 6-34, when PC 10.1.1.2 attempts connect to the server at the central site, the remote PIX translates the original PC IP address and port number using the IP address and a port number of the outside interface PAT. Because of the translation, the IP address of PC1 is not visible from the central site.

The other option is network extension mode (NEM). With NEM, the IP address of the inside PCs are received without change at the central site. In this instance, the IP address of the PC is visible from the central site. In the example in Figure 6-34, the remote inside PC makes a connection to a server on the central site. The original PC IP address, 10.1.1.2, is not translated by the remote PIX Security Appliance.

Figure 6-34   Easy VPN Client Device Mode

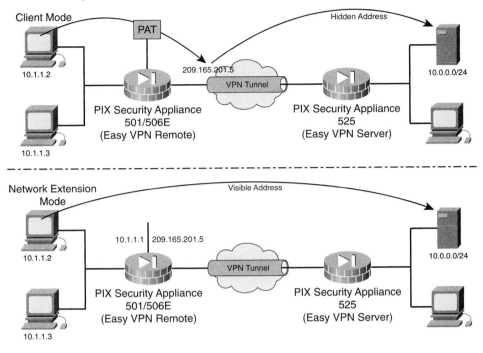

Set the Easy VPN Remote device mode by entering the following command:

`pixfirewall(config)#`**`vpnclient mode {client-mode ¦ network-extension-mode}`**

Client mode applies NAT to all IP addresses of clients connected to the inside (higher-security) interface of the PIX Security Appliance.

The **network-extension-mode** option does not apply NAT to any IP addresses of clients on the inside (higher-security) interface of the PIX Security Appliance.

Finally, enable the Easy VPN Remote device by entering the **vpnclient enable** command.

Easy VPN Remote Authentication

This section introduces two Easy VPN Remote authentication methods:

- Secure Unit Authentication (SUA)

- Individual User Authentication (IUA)

Secure Unit Authentication

SUA is a feature introduced with PIX Security Appliance Software Version 6.3 to improve security when using a PIX as an Easy VPN Remote device. With SUA, one-time passwords, two-factor authentication, and similar authentication schemes can be used to authenticate the remote PIX before establishing a VPN tunnel to an Easy VPN Server. SUA is configured as part of the VPN policy on the Easy VPN Server and cannot be configured directly on the Easy VPN Remote device. After connecting to the Easy VPN Server, the Easy VPN Remote device downloads the VPN policy, which then enables or disables SUA.

When SUA is disabled and the PIX Security Appliance is in network extension mode, a connection is automatically initiated. When SUA is disabled with client mode, the connection is automatically initiated whenever any traffic is sent through the PIX to a network protected by the Easy VPN Server.

When SUA is enabled, static credentials included in the local configuration of the Easy VPN Remote device are ignored. A connection request is initiated as soon as an HTTP request is sent from the remote network to the network protected by the Easy VPN Server. All other traffic to the network protected by the Easy VPN Server is dropped until a VPN tunnel is established. A connection request can also be initiated from the CLI of the Easy VPN Remote device.

After SUA is enabled and before a VPN tunnel is established, any HTTP request to the network protected by the Easy VPN Server is redirected to the URL as follows:

`https://inside-ipaddr/vpnclient/connstatus.html`

Replace *inside-ipaddr* with the IP address of the inside interface of the PIX Security Appliance used as the Easy VPN Remote device. The connection can be activated manually by entering this URL in the Address or Location box of a browser. This URL can also be used to check the status of the VPN tunnel. This URL provides a page containing a Connect link that displays an authentication page. If authentication is successful, the VPN tunnel is established. After the VPN tunnel is established, other users on the network protected by the Easy VPN Remote device can access the network protected by the Easy VPN Server without further authentication.

Enable SUA by entering the following command at the Easy VPN Server:

`pixfirewall(config)#vpngroup` *groupname* `secure-unit-authentication`

Replace *groupname* with an alphanumeric identifier for the VPN group using SUA.

Individual User Authentication

If it is necessary to control access by individual users behind the Easy VPN remote device, IUA can be implemented. IUA causes clients on the inside network of the Easy VPN Remote to be individually authenticated based on the IP address of the inside client. IUA supports authentication with both static and dynamic password mechanisms.

IUA is enabled by means of the downloaded VPN policy, and it cannot be configured locally. When IUA is enabled, each user on the network protected by the Easy VPN Remote device is prompted for a username and password when trying to initiate a connection. A PIX Security Appliance acting as an Easy VPN Server downloads the contact information for the AAA server to the Easy VPN Remote device, which sends each authentication request directly to the AAA server. A PIX Security Appliance Easy VPN Server performs proxy authentication to the

AAA server. The Easy VPN Remote device sends each authentication request to the Easy VPN Server.

IUA supports individually authenticating clients on the inside network of the Easy VPN Remote, based on the IP address of each inside client. IUA supports both static and one-time password (OTP) authentication mechanisms. IUA is enabled by means of the downloaded VPN policy, and it cannot be configured locally. To enable IUA on a PIX Security Appliance used as the Easy VPN Server, enter the following command:

```
pixfirewall(config)#vpngroup groupname user-authentication
```

This command enables individual user authentication for the VPN group identified by *groupname*.

To specify the length of time that a VPN tunnel can remain open without user activity, enter the following command:

```
pixfirewall(config)#vpngroup groupname user-idle-timeout {hh: mm: ss}
```

This command specifies the length of time for the specified VPN group in hours, minutes, and seconds (*hh:mm:ss*).

To specify the AAA server to use for IUA on a PIX Security Appliance being used as the Easy VPN Server, enter the following command:

```
vpngroup groupname authentication-server server_tag
```

This command specifies the AAA server identified by *server_tag* for the VPN group identified by *groupname*.

Configure the Adaptive Security Appliance to Support WebVPN

You can configure the ASA to support a web-based VPN. This sections looks at the WebVPN end-user interface, how to configure WebVPN general parameters, the WebVPN servers and URLs, how to configure WebVPN port forwarding, e-mail proxy, and content filters and ACLs.

WebVPN End-User Interface

This section covers the home page, website access, browsing files, and port forwarding.

Home Page

The administrator designs this page to meet the individual requirements of the end user, as shown in Figure 6-35. Using this interface, the end user can conveniently and securely access the internal network of the organization from any computer that has an Internet connection. The end user can check e-mail, view or transfer files, visit internal corporate websites, or run internal web applications from any web browser. The user navigates using the buttons provided within the WebVPN interface window. The following buttons are available:

- **Help**—The user can click this icon to access this help system.
- **Show Toolbar**—The user can click this icon to show the WebVPN toolbar.
- **Home**—The user can click this icon to return to the home page.
- **Logout**—The user can click this icon to end the remote-access session.

Figure 6-35   Home Page

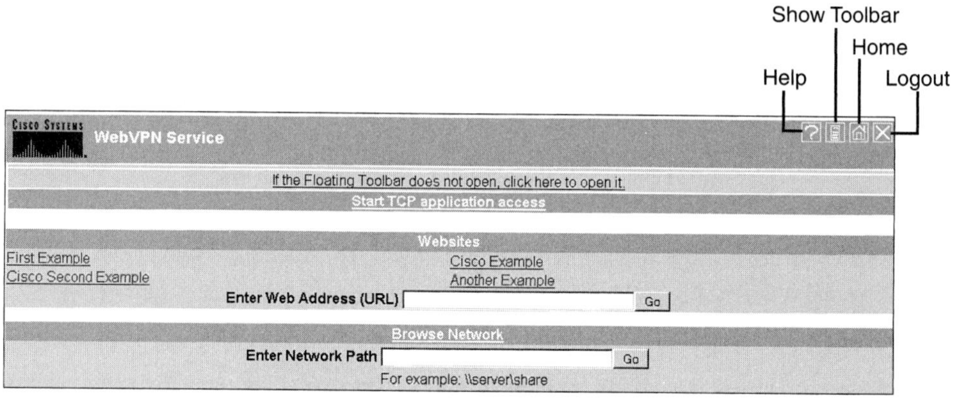

Website Access and Browsing Files

If the administrator sets up end-user accounts to access particular websites or file shares, one or more links appear under Websites on the home page of the end user. To access the website or file share, the end user just clicks the link. If the site is protected, the end user must enter a username and password.

If the administrator has granted end-user access to a server that is not specifically listed, the end user can enter the web address of the server directly in the Enter Web Address (URL) text box or the Enter Network Path text box. Alternatively, the end user can browse the network by clicking the Browse Network link.

When connected to a file share, the end user can upload and download files, creates new folders, and delete and rename files by clicking the appropriate links.

Whenever the end user is visiting a website via a secure remote-access session, a toolbar appears on the web page. The toolbar is to remind the end user that the access is being provided through the corporate network.

Port Forwarding

The administrator can configure certain client/server applications for use by the end user. Starting Application Access, or Port Forwarding, opens a secure connection between the end user computer and the remote server. When the window is open or minimized, the connection is active. If the end user quits the window, the connection closes.

The chart in the Application Access window lists the available applications and key details about the secure connection, as shown in Figure 6-36. This chart is display only. The end user cannot edit it, and clicking on a cell does not start the application.

Note

Port forwarding requires Sun Microsystems Java Runtime Environment Version 1.4 or later to be installed on the end-user system. It can be down-loaded automatically if needed.

Figure 6-36   Port Forwarding

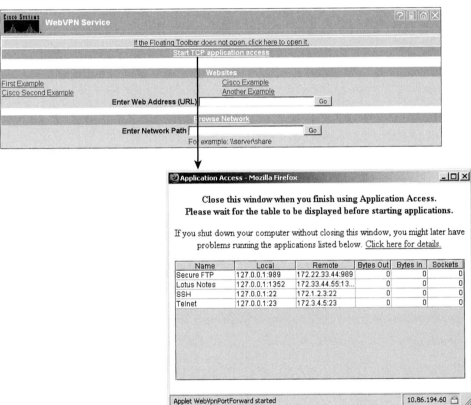

WebVPN provides access to TCP-based applications by mapping application-specific ports on the PC of the end user to application-specific ports on servers behind the ASA. When an end user accesses an application over WebVPN using hostnames to identify the application server, the ASA modifies the Windows Hosts file to include a mapping entry for that application.

The chart has the following fields:

- **Name**—The name of an available client application

- **Local**—The hostname, or IP address, and TCP port to configure on the client application to allow communication with the remote server

- **Remote**—The hostname, or IP address, and TCP port of the remote server

- **Bytes Out/In**—The amount of data that this application receives or sends through the secure connection

- **Sockets**—The number of TCP connections that the application is using

Configure WebVPN General Parameters

WebVPN features must be enabled on an interface-specific basis. On any interface, these features can be configured either singly or in combination. To use the following features on an interface, the administrator must enable them on each individual interface:

- WebVPN (HTTPS) connections

- POP3S, IMAP4S, and SMTPS for e-mail proxy sessions

- HTTPS management sessions

To enable the ASA HTTP server, use the **http server enable** command. To specify hosts that can access the HTTP server internal to the ASA, use the **http** command.

WebVPN Command Submode

The following features are configured in one location and apply to all users accessing the ASA via WebVPN:

accounting-server group	enable
authentication	http-proxy
authentication-server-group	https-proxy
authorization-dn-attributes	login-message
authorization-required	logo
authorization-sever-group	logout-message
accounting-server-group	nbns-server
authentication	password-prompt
authentication-server-group	secondary-color
authentication-dn-attributes	secondary-text-color

authentication-required	text-color
authentication-server-group	title
default-group-policy	title-color
default-idle-timeout	username-prompt

Generally, these features apply to items where the group has not been determined. This configuration is done using a subcommand mode called WebVPN. The **webvpn** command is used to enter the subcommand mode. WebVPN does not need to be configured for the e-mail proxies to be configured.

These WebVPN subcommand mode commands let the administrator configure AAA servers, default group policies, default idle timeout, HTTP and HTTPS proxies, NetBIOS Name Service (NBNS) servers for WebVPN, and the appearance of WebVPN screens that end users see.

The WebVPN subcommand mode configures general WebVPN parameters and the look and feel of the end-user interface.

NBNS Server Configuration

The ASA queries NBNS servers to map NetBIOS names to IP addresses. WebVPN requires NetBIOS to access or share files on remote systems. There is a maximum of three server entries. The first server configured is the primary server, and the others are backups for redundancy.

To add a NBNS server for Common Internet File System (CIFS) name resolution, you enter the following command:

```
ciscoasa(config-webvpn)#nbna-server {ipaddr or hostname} [master] [timeout timeout]
[retry retries]
```

Specifying the **master** option indicates that this is a master browser, rather than just a WINS server. You can enter this command multiple times. The **no** option removes the matching entry from the configuration. The timeout value is in seconds. The default timeout value is 2 seconds, and the range is 1 to 30. The default number of retries is 2, and the range is 0 to 10.

Authentication Server Configuration

To specify the set of authentication servers to use with WebVPN or one of the e-mail proxies, use the **authentication-sever-group** *groupname* command.

For WebVPN, use this command in WebVPN mode. For e-mail proxies, IMAP4S, POP3S, or SMTPS, use this command in the applicable e-mail proxy mode. The default is to not have any authentication servers configured.

Home Page Look-and-Feel Configuration

Many of the commands in the WebVPN subcommand mode control and customize the look and feel of the home page of the end user, as shown in Figure 6-37.

Figure 6-37   Home Page Look-and-Feel Configuration

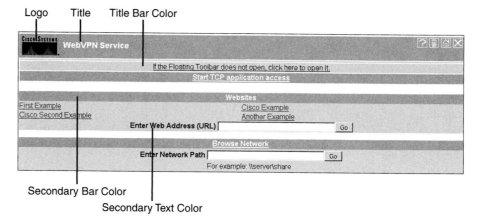

Items that you can configure include the following:

- **HTML title**—The HTML title string that is in the browser title and on the title bar. Limited to 255 characters. The default is WebVPN Service. Specifying no title removes the command from the configuration and resets the value to the default. To have no title, the **title** *titletext* command is issued without a string.

- **Login message**—This is the HTML text that prompts the user to log in. The prompt is limited to 255 characters. The default is "Please enter your username and password." This string is presented to the user before login. Specifying **no login-message** removes the command from the configuration and resets the value to the default. To have no login message, the **login-message** command is issued without a string.

- **Logo**—The **logo** command specifies the custom logo image that displays on the login and home pages. It is a file that can be uploaded by the administrator to the security gateway. The filename is limited to no more than 255 characters. The logo must be a JPG, PNG, or GIF file, and must be less than 100 KB. An error will occur if the file does not exist. If the logo file is subsequently deleted, no logo displays. The default is to use the Cisco logo. Specifying **no logo** removes the command from the configuration and resets the value to the default. To have no logo, specify **logo none**.

- **Title color**—The **title-color** command enables you to set the color of the title bars on the login, home, and file access pages. The value can be a comma-separated RGB value, an HTML color value beginning with a # sign, or the name of the color that is recognized in HTML. The value is limited to 32 characters. The default is one of the Cisco purples, #9999CC. Specifying **no title-color** reverts the value to the default.

- **Secondary color**—The **secondary-color** command enables you to set the color of the secondary title bars on the login, home, and file access pages. The value can be a comma-separated RGB value, an HTML color value beginning with a # sign, or the name of the color that is recognized in HTML. The value is limited to 32. The default is one of the Cisco purples, #CCCCFF. Specifying **no secondary-color** reverts the value to the default.

- **Text color**—The **text-color** command enables you to set the color of the text on the title bars. It is restricted to just two values to limit the number of icons that need to exist for the toolbar. The default value is white. Specifying **no text-color** reverts the value to the default.

- **Secondary text color**—The **secondary-text-color** command enables you to set the color of the text on the secondary bars. It is restricted to be aligned with the title bar text color. The default value is black. Specifying **no secondary-ext-color** reverts the value to the default.

Configure WebVPN Servers and URLs

Use the **vpn-tunnel-protocol** command in group-policy configuration mode or username configuration mode to configure a VPN tunnel type for the user or group using the following command sequence:

```
ciscoasa(config)#group-policy group_name [internal ¦ external ¦ attributes]
ciscoasa(config-group-policy)#vpn-tunnel-protocol {webvpn ¦ ipsec¦ l2tp/ipsec}
```

The following types are available:

- **webvpn**—Provides VPN services to remote users via an HTTPS-enabled web browser and does not require a client.

- **ipsec**—Negotiates an IPsec tunnel between two peers, such as a remote-access client or another secure gateway. Creates SAs that govern authentication, encryption, encapsulation, and key management.

- **l2tp/ipsec**—Provides interoperability with the Microsoft VPN client.

Enable URL Entry for WebVPN Users

Use the **webvpn** command in group-policy configuration mode or in username configuration mode to enter the WebVPN mode. The commands available in WebVPN mode apply to the username or group policy from which they are configured. WebVPN mode commands for group policies and usernames define access to files, messaging application programming interface (MAPI) proxy, URLs, and TCP applications over WebVPN. They also identify ACLs and types of traffic to filter.

WebVPN mode, which is entered from global configuration mode, enables the administrator to configure global settings for WebVPN. Commands in this mode also enable the administrator to customize a WebVPN configuration for specific users or group policies. WebVPN does not need to be configured to use e-mail proxies.

Use the **functions** command in WebVPN mode to enable file access and file browsing, MAPI proxy, and URL entry over WebVPN for this user or group policy:

```
ciscoasa(config-webvpn)#functions {file-access | file-browsing | file-entry | url-entry |
mapi | none}
```

To remove a configured function, use the **no** form of this command. To remove all configured functions, including a null value created by issuing the function's **none** command, use the **no** form of this command without arguments. The **no** option allows inheritance of a value from another group policy. To prevent inheriting function values, use the **functions none** command. Functions are disabled by default.

The **url-entry** option enables or disables user entry of URLs. When enabled, the ASA still restricts URLs with any configured URL or network ACLs. When URL entry is disabled, the ASA restricts WebVPN users to the URLs on the home page. Use the **url-list** command in WebVPN mode, which is entered from group-policy or username mode, to apply a list of WebVPN servers and URLs to a particular user or group policy:

```
ciscoasa(config-webvpn)#url-list {listname displayname url | none}
```

To remove a list, including a null value created by using the **url-list none** command, use the **no** form of this command. The **no** option allows inheritance of a value from another group policy.

To prevent inheriting a URL list, use the **url-list none** command. Before the **url-list** command can be used in WebVPN mode to identify a URL list to display on the WebVPN home page for a user or group policy, the list must be created. Use the **url-list** command in global configuration mode to create one or more lists, as follows:

```
ciscoasa(config)#url-list URLs "Superservers" http://10.0.1.10
ciscoasa(config)#url-list URLs "CIFS SHARE" cifs://10.0.1.11/training
```

Defining URLs with the url-list Command

Use the **url-list** command in global configuration mode to configure a set of URLs for WebVPN users to access, as shown in Figure 6-38. To configure a list with multiple URLs, use this command with the same *listname* multiple times, one time for each URL. To remove an entire configured list, use the **no url-list** *listname* command. To remove a configured URL, use the **no url-list** *listname url* command. To configure multiple lists, use this command multiple times, assigning a unique *listname* to each list. To allow access to the URLs in a list for a specific group policy or user, use the *listname* created here with the **url-list** command in WebVPN mode.

Figure 6-38   Defining URLs

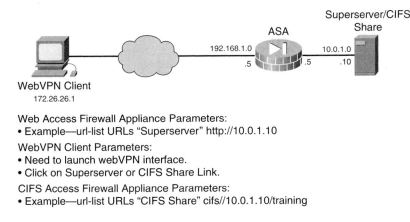

Web Access Firewall Appliance Parameters:
• Example—url-list URLs "Superserver" http://10.0.1.10

WebVPN Client Parameters:
• Need to launch webVPN interface.
• Click on Superserver or CIFS Share Link.

CIFS Access Firewall Appliance Parameters:
• Example—url-list URLs "CIFS Share" cifs//10.0.1.10/training

You must configure the various parameters highlighted in Figure 6-38 on the ASA to enable WebVPN access to the resources on the private network. Files access via CIFS is configured in the same basic manner.

Configure WebVPN Port Forwarding

Use the **port-forward** command in WebVPN mode to enable WebVPN application access for this user or group policy:

```
ciscoasa(config-webvpn)#functions port-forward
ciscoasa(config-group-policy)#port-forward {value listname ¦ none}
```

To remove the port-forwarding attribute from the configuration, including a null value created by issuing the **port-forward none** command, use the **no** form of this command. The **no** option allows inheritance of a list from another group policy. To prevent inheriting a port forwarding list, use the **port-forward none** command.

The *listname* value identifies the list of applications WebVPN users can access. Before the **port-forward** command can be used in WebVPN mode to enable application access, a list of applications that users are able to use in a WebVPN connection must be configured. Use the **port-forward** command in global configuration mode to define this list.

Port forwarding provides mapping information that the ASA adds to the Hosts file on the PC of the end user as the application opens. This mapping information lets the PC connect to the server at the central site that supports the desired application.

Port forwarding can work only if the applications on remote servers are uniquely identified, and therefore reachable, either by hostname or by IP address and port. Keep the following in mind when configuring port forwarding:

■ Hostnames, correctly defined on the ASA, are constant and by definition unique. The use of hostnames is recommended.

- IP addresses change depending on the location of the end user relative to the remote server. If the remote server is identified by IP address, users must reconfigure the application on their PC each time they change location.

Use the **port-forward** command in global configuration mode to configure the set of applications that WebVPN users can access over forwarded TCP ports:

```
ciscoasa(config)#port-forward {listname localport remoteserver remoteport description}
```

This command defines the following:

- The name of the port-forwarding list

- The port for the WebVPN user

- The actual link that the link accesses

- The actual port that the link accesses

To configure access to multiple applications, use this command with the same *listname* multiple times, one time for each application. To remove an entire configured list, use the **no port-forward** *listname* command. To remove a configured application, use the **no port-forward** *listname localport* command. The *remoteserver* and *remoteport* parameters do not need to be included in the command.

To allow access to particular TCP port-forwarding applications for a specific user or group policy, use the created *listname* with the **port-forward** command in WebVPN mode.

The example in Figure 6-39 contrasts configuring port forwarding using DNS names versus IP addresses.

Figure 6-39   Port-Forwarding Configuration Example: DNS vs. IP Addresses

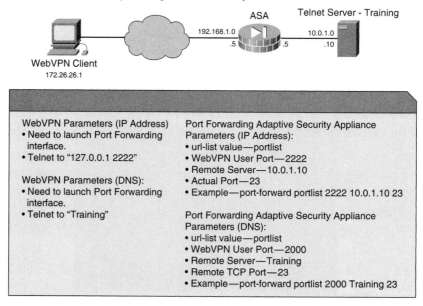

Keep the following in mind:

- If IP addresses are used, users need to have client applications point to a 127.0.0.1 address and local port that can vary from location to location when connecting over WebVPN. They must reconfigure applications to a real IP address and port when they connect locally.

- If hostnames are used, users can set their client applications to connect to the real hostname and TCP port for both remote WebVPN and directly connected sessions.

Configure WebVPN E-Mail Proxy

The **functions mapi** command enables or disables Microsoft Outlook/Exchange port forwarding at the group or user level and is only necessary if this feature is to be used.

Proxy servers are defined by entering the appropriate subcommand mode in global configuration mode with the **pop3a**, **smtps**, and **imap4s** commands. Proxy servers are available for POP3S, SMTPS, and IMAP4S.

Use the **server** {*ipaddr or hostname*} command in the applicable e-mail proxy mode to specify a default e-mail proxy server. The ASA sends requests to the default e-mail server when the user connects to the e-mail proxy without specifying a server. If a default server is not configured, and a user does not specify a server, the security appliance returns an error.

Use the **authentication-server-group** *group tag* command in the applicable e-mail proxy mode to specify the set of authentication servers to use with the e-mail proxy.

Use the **authentication** {**aaa** | **certification** | **mailhost** | **piggyback**} command in the applicable e-mail proxy mode to configure authentication methods for the e-mail proxy. The options for this command result in the following:

- **aaa**—Use previously configured AAA server for authentication

- **certificate**—Use certificate for authentication

- **mailhost**—Authenticate via the remote mail server (SMTPS only)

- **piggyback**—Requires the use of an established HTTPS WebVPN session

To restore the default, **aaa**, use the **no** form of this command.

Figure 6-40 illustrates the various parameters that must be configured on each device. The main items of interest are the e-mail server address and port assignments entered on the e-mail client. These must match the ones configured on the ASA, not those configured on the e-mail server. In this example, the username and password on the e-mail server and the ASA are the same, so no special delimiters need to be used on the e-mail client

Figure 6-40   E-Mail Proxy Configuration Example

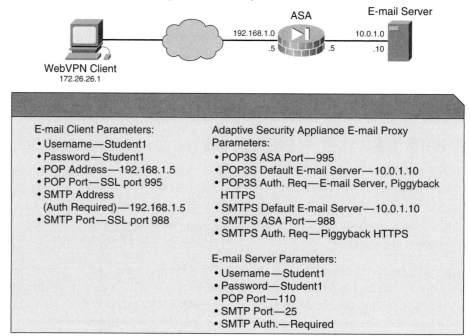

E-mail Client Parameters:
- Username—Student1
- Password—Student1
- POP Address—192.168.1.5
- POP Port—SSL port 995
- SMTP Address
  (Auth Required)—192.168.1.5
- SMTP Port—SSL port 988

Adaptive Security Appliance E-mail Proxy
Parameters:
- POP3S ASA Port—995
- POP3S Default E-mail Server—10.0.1.10
- POP3S Auth. Req—E-mail Server, Piggyback
  HTTPS
- SMTPS Default E-mail Server—10.0.1.10
- SMTPS ASA Port—988
- SMTPS Auth. Req—Piggyback HTTPS

E-mail Server Parameters:
- Username—Student1
- Password—Student1
- POP Port—110
- SMTP Port—25
- SMTP Auth.—Required

Configure WebVPN Content Filters and ACLs

WebVPN content filters and ACLs are configured in the group-policy attributes in the WebVPN subcommand mode by entering the following:

```
ciscoasa(config)#group-policy group_name attributes
ciscoasa(config-group-policy)#webvpn
```

Use the following command to configure WebVPN content filtering, which enables the administrator to block or remove the parts of websites that use Java or ActiveX or scripts, that display images, and that deliver cookies:

```
ciscoasa(config-group-policy)#html-content-filter {cookies | images | java | none |
scripts}
```

Where:

- **cookies**—Removes cookies from the images, providing limited ad filtering and privacy.

- **images**—Removes references to images (removes <IMG> tags).

- **java**—Removes references to Java and ActiveX (removes <EMBED>, <APPLET>, and <OBJECT> tags).

- **none**—Indicates that there is no filtering. Set a null value, thereby disallowing filtering. Prevents inheriting filtering values.

- **scripts**—Removes references to scripting (removes <SCRIPT> tags).

By default, these parameters are disabled, which means that no filtering occurs.

WebVPN ACLs are used to permit or deny various types of traffic for a user or group policy. These are filters that permit or deny user access to specific networks, subnets, hosts, and web servers.

Use the **filter** command in WebVPN mode to specify the name of the access list to use for WebVPN connections for this group policy or username:

```
ciscoasa(config-webvpn)#filter {value ACLname ¦ none}
```

To remove the access list, including a null value created by issuing the **filter none** command, use the **no** form of this command. The **no** option allows inheritance of a value from another group policy. To prevent inheriting filter values, use the **filter value none** command.

To add an access list to the configuration that supports filtering for WebVPN, use the **access-list webtype** command in global configuration mode:

```
ciscoasa(config)#access-list id webtype {deny ¦ permit} url [url_string ¦ any] [log
[[disable ¦ default] ¦ level] [interval secs] [time_range name]]
```

The **filter** command is then used to apply those ACLs for WebVPN traffic.

Summary

This chapter primarily covered the configuration of Cisco Easy VPN Server and Cisco Easy VPN Remote. Cisco Easy VPN Server configuration on routers and PIX Security Appliances was discussed. Configuring Easy VPN Remote with the Cisco VPN Client, Cisco routers, and the PIX 501 and 506/506E models was also covered. This chapter also explained how to configure WebVPN on an ASA.

Check Your Understanding

Complete all the review questions listed here to test your understanding of the topics and concepts in this chapter. Answers are listed in Appendix A, "Check Your Understanding Answer Key."

1. Which of the following details is not provided for in the Cisco Easy VPN Remote feature?

   a. Negotiating tunnel parameters, such as addresses, algorithms, and lifetime

   b. Automatically creating the NAT or PAT and associated access lists that are needed, if any

   c. Managing security keys for encryption and decryption

   d. Authenticating, encrypting, and decrypting data through the tunnel

   e. Providing username and login information to servers

2. Cisco Easy VPN consists of the Cisco Easy VPN Server and the Cisco Easy VPN Remote.

   a. True

   b. False

3. The Unity Protocol supports only Internet Security Association Key Management Protocol (ISAKMP) policies that use which of the following?

   a. Group 1 IKE negotiation

   b. Group 2 IKE negotiation

   c. Group 3 IKE negotiation

   d. Group 4 IKE negotiation

4. The first step when preparing the Easy VPN Server router for remote access is to establish what?

   a. AAA by using the **aaa new-model** command

   b. AAA by using the **aaa enable** command

   c. Encryption by using the **encryption enable** command

   d. Ensure CDP is running by using the **CDP enable** command

5. Which of the following global commands do you use to enable reverse route injection (RRI)?

   a. **reverse-route**

   b. **reverse-route enable**

   c. **ip reverse-route**

   d. **ip reverse-route enable**

6. Dead peer detection (DPD) is a keepalive scheme that allows the router to query the liveliness of its IKE peer. There are three options for DPD: periodic, on-demand, and random.

  a. True

  b. False

7. Which of the following is *not* a Cisco Easy VPN Remote mode of operation?

  a. Client mode

  b. Network extension mode

  c. Network extension plus mode

  d. Node use mode

8. Which of the following commands would you use to check or review your Easy VPN configuration?

  a. **show crypto client ezvpn** command

  b. **show crypto ipsec client ezvpn** command

  c. **show ipsec client ezvpn** command

  d. **show crypto ipsec client** command

9. When using the **crypto ipsec transform-set** command, be sure to list multiple transform sets in order of priority, with the highest priority first.

  a. True

  b. False

10. The NAT 0 **access-list** command defines which traffic is encrypted but not translated.

  a. True

  b. False

CHAPTER 7

Secure Network Architecture and Management

Upon completion of this chapter, you should be able to answer the following questions:

- What are the Layer 2 security best practices?

- What is a Security Device Manager (SDM) audit?

- How do I create a Router Management Center (MC)?

- How do I configure Simple Network Management Protocol (SNMP)?

Key Terms

This chapter uses the following key terms. You can find the definitions in the glossary at the end of the book.

Security Device Manager (SDM)   page 666

Router Management Centers (MCs)   page 666

Simple Network Management Protocol (SNMP) page 666

Security zone   page 667

DHCP snooping   page 668

Dynamic ARP inspection   page 669

Port security   page 673

Private VLANs (PVLANs)   page 674

Building blocks   page 695

Jobs   page 686

Chapter contribution by Belle Woodward

This chapter begins with a discussion of best practices for Layer 2 security. You are introduced to multiple physical network scenarios, and then given vulnerabilities and mitigation techniques for each.

First you learn about the *Security Device Manager (SDM)* and how its Security Audit Wizard can provide a comprehensive router security audit. SDM uses security configurations from Cisco Technical Assistance Center, TAC, and International Computer Security Association, ICSA, as a baseline for comparisons and default settings.

You also learn how to manage large site-to-site and remote-access virtual private networks (VPNs) through the use of *Router Management Centers (MCs)*. We also go into more detail in understanding VPNs.

Finally, you learn about *Simple Network Management Protocol (SNMP)* and how network administrators use it to manage network performance, monitor network infrastructure devices, rectify network problems, and plan for future network growth. Within its simplicity, SNMP uses little to no security. However, when used properly, the information gathered by SNMP queries can effectively assist the administrator with security.

Factors Affecting Layer 2 Mitigation Techniques

The information in this chapter is applicable to many different situations; however, the cases are meant to highlight implementation of Layer 2 mitigation techniques in specific scenarios. The scenarios can be broken down into eight total cases, as shown in Table 7-1, and which depend on the following three separate factors:

- The number of security zones in the network design

- The number of user groups in the network design

- The number of switch devices in the network design

Table 7-1   Typical Cases

Case #	Security Zones	Number of User Groups	Number of Switch Devices
1	Single	Single	Single
2	Single	Single	Multiple
3	Single	Multiple	Single
4	Single	Multiple	Multiple
5	Multiple	Single	Single

Table 7-1   Typical Cases   *continued*

Case #	Security Zones	Number of User Groups	Number of Switch Devices
6	Multiple	Single	Multiple
7	Multiple	Multiple	Single
8	Multiple	Multiple	Multiple

As you can see from Table 7-1, case 1 involves a network design using one physical switch, with a single *security zone* of trust containing a single user group. Case 8 involves a network design using multiple physical switches, with multiple security zones of trust containing multiple user groups. An example of case 1 is a small business network using a broadband connection behind a digital subscriber line (DSL) router or firewall. An example of case 8 is a large application service provider data center. The sections that follow discuss these cases in further detail.

Single Security Zone, One User Group, and One Physical Switch

This design uses a single physical switch containing a single zone of trust. Only traffic belonging to the user group within the security zone traverses the switch. The example in Figure 7-1 could be a demilitarized zone (DMZ) network switch lying between the edge router and corporate firewall. This design assumes the systems within the security zone are contained within the same VLAN.

Figure 7-1   Single Security Zone, One User Group, One Physical Switch

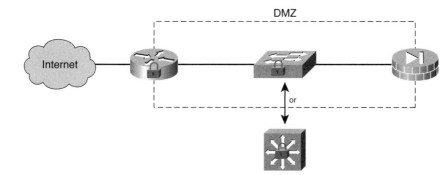

Vulnerabilities

Some of the Layer 2 vulnerabilities in this design include the following:

- **MAC spoofing**—MAC spoofing attacks involve the use of a known MAC address of another host to attempt to make the target switch forward frames destined for the remote host to the network attacker. By sending a single frame with the other host's source Ethernet address, the network attacker overwrites the CAM table entry so that the switch forwards packets destined for the host to the network attacker.

■ **CAM table overflow**—The CAM table in a switch contains information such as the MAC addresses available on a given physical port of a switch and the associated VLAN parameters. CAM tables are limited in size. Typically, a network intruder floods the switch with a large number of invalid-source MAC addresses until the CAM table fills up. When that occurs, the switch floods all ports with incoming traffic because it cannot find the port number for a particular MAC address in the CAM table.

Mitigation

You will use the mitigation techniques shown in the following examples to secure the Layer 2 environment from Figure 7-1.

To mitigate MAC spoofing using Cisco IOS Software, you can use the following commands:

```
switch(config-if)# switchport port-security maximum value
```

The preceding command sets the maximum number of secure MAC addresses for the interface.

```
Switchport port-security violation {protect | restrict | shutdown}
```

The preceding command sets the violation mode and the action to be taken.

```
switch(config-if)# arp timeout seconds
```

The preceding command configures the timeout, in seconds that an entry remains in the Address Resolution Protocol (ARP) cache.

To mitigate MAC spoofing using the Catalyst operating system, you can use the following commands:

```
Switch> set port security mod/port enable [mac_addr]
```

The preceding command enables port security.

```
Switch>set port security mod/port mac_addr
```

The preceding command enables port security for specific MAC address.

```
Switch> set port security mod/port violation {shutdown | restrict}
```

The preceding command sets actions on violation.

To configure *DHCP snooping* using Cisco IOS Software, you can use the following commands:

```
Switch(config)# ip dhcp snooping
```

The preceding command enables DHCP snooping globally.

```
Switch(config)#ip dhcp snooping vlan vlan_id {,vlan_id}
```

The preceding command enables DHCP snooping on VLANs.

```
Switch(config-if)# ip dhcp snooping trust
```

The preceding command configures the interface as trusted or untrusted.

```
Switch(config-if)# ip dhcp snooping limit rate rate
```

The preceding command configures the number of DHCP packets per second (pps) that an interface can receive.

Because this design is so small, port security is actually administratively feasible. Layer 2 switches are part of the security perimeter between zones of trust. As such, they should be managed securely through the use of Secure Shell (SSH) and SNMPv3. Of course, configuration audits and penetration testing including exploiting Layer 2 vulnerabilities should be done regularly with tools such as Meta-sploit, Ettercap, and Nessus. An equally effective administrative approach is shown in the following example, in which dynamic port security is used through the application of DHCP snooping and dynamic ARP inspection.

To configure *dynamic ARP inspection*, you can use the following commands:

```
Switch(config)#ip arp inspection vlan_id{,vlan_id}
```

The preceding command enables ARP inspection per VLAN.

```
Switch(config)# ip arp inspection validate [src-mac] [dst-mac] [ip]
```

The preceding command performs specific checks for ARP inspection.

```
Switch(config-if)#ip arp inspection trust
```

The preceding command sets a per-port configurable trust state.

Single Security Zone, One User Group, and Multiple Physical Switches

This design uses multiple physical switches containing a single zone of trust. Only traffic belonging to the user group within the security zone traverses the switches. The example in Figure 7-2 could be a large DMZ or a DMZ with multiple VLANs all existing within a single security zone of trust. This could even be interpreted as a Layer 3 switch providing inter-VLAN routing throughout the DMZ.

Vulnerabilities

Layer 2 vulnerabilities in this design include the following:

- **MAC spoofing**.

- **CAM table overflow**.

- **VLAN hopping**—VLAN hopping is a network attack whereby an end system sends out packets destined for a system on a different VLAN that cannot normally be reached by the end system. This traffic is tagged with a different VLAN ID to which the end system belongs. Or, the attacking system might be trying to behave like a switch and negotiate trunking so that the attacker can send and receive traffic between other VLANs.

■ **Spanning-tree attacks, in networks with multiple switches**—By attacking the Spanning Tree Protocol (STP), the network attacker hopes to spoof his or her system as the root bridge in the topology. To do this, the network attacker broadcasts out STP configuration/topology change bridge protocol data units (BPDUs) in an attempt to force spanning-tree recalculations. The BPDUs sent out by the network attacker's system announce that the attacking system has a lower bridge priority. If successful, the network attacker can see a variety of frames.

Figure 7-2   Single Security Zone, One User Group, and Multiple Physical Switches

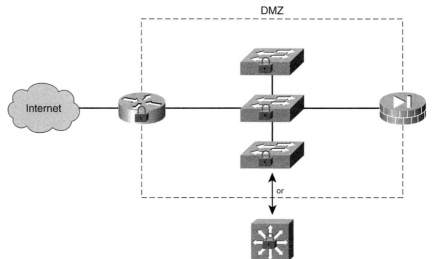

Mitigation

Should the security zone be small enough, using port security will help mitigate the CAM table overflow vulnerability and the MAC spoofing vulnerability. When multiple switches are involved, you can use BPDU guard and root guard to protect the integrity of STP.

As with the previous cases, the switches should be managed as securely as possible and tested on a regular basis.

Single Security Zone, Multiple User Groups, and One Physical Switch

Figure 7-3 shows a design where VLANs are used to separate traffic of multiple user groups within a single physical network. A practice of this design would be an application service provider, data center, or different departments within a single corporate enterprise requiring data segregation.

Figure 7-3   Single Security Zone, Multiple User Groups, and One Physical Switch

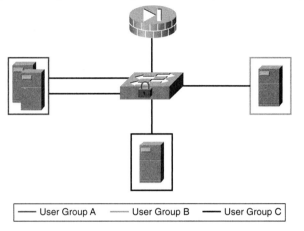

| User Group A | User Group B | User Group C |

Vulnerabilities

Layer 2 vulnerabilities in this design include the following:

- MAC spoofing
- CAM table overflow
- VLAN hopping

Mitigation

Should the security zone be small enough, using port security will help mitigate the CAM table overflow vulnerability and the MAC spoofing vulnerability. Using the list that follows, you can hope to mitigate VLAN hopping attacks on the networks:

- Use dedicated VLAN IDs for all trunk ports.
- Disable all unused switch ports and place them in an unused VLAN.
- Set all user ports to nontrunking mode by explicitly turning off DTP on those ports.

As with the previous cases, the switches must be managed as securely as possible and tested on a regular basis.

Single Security Zone, Multiple User Groups, Multiple Physical Switches

This scenario represents a slightly more complex case than the previous ones. The design shown in Figure 7-4 represents a network using high availability and trunking between switches. The direction of network traffic as determined by STP will make mitigating some of the attacks much more difficult.

Figure 7-4   Single Security Zone, Multiple User Groups, Multiple Physical Switches

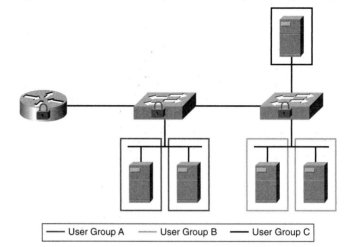

| —— User Group A | —— User Group B | —— User Group C |

Vulnerabilities

Layer 2 vulnerabilities in this design include the following:

- MAC spoofing
- CAM table overflow
- VLAN hopping
- STP attacks

Mitigation

Should the security zone be small enough, using port security will help mitigate the CAM table overflow vulnerability and the MAC spoofing vulnerability. By using the list in the preceding "Mitigation" section for "Single Security Zone, Multiple User Groups, and One Physical Switch," you can try to mitigate VLAN-hopping techniques. To protect from attackers who might physically plug into switches within a security zone, you might need to implement 802.1x authentication.

Multiple Security Zones, One User Group, and One Physical Switch

This design provides for a single physical switch existing in two security zones of trust. Only traffic from one user group traverses the switch. An example of such a design is a switch configured for double-duty on both DMZ and internal interfaces of a firewall. VLANs separate traffic on a single physical LAN into multiple logical LANs through the use of VLAN tags. The use of VLANs can be considered as a possible way of segmenting multiple interfaces of a firewall on a single switch, as shown in Figure 7-5.

Figure 7-5   Multiple Security Zones, One User Group, and One Physical Switch

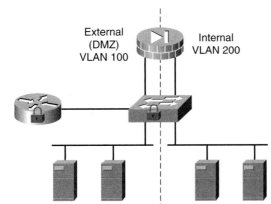

In this example, the external network, the DMZ, and the internal network use the same switch for Layer 2 connectivity. The external network traffic is tagged as VLAN ID 100; the internal network traffic is tagged with VLAN ID 200. Although it is technically feasible to make this design secure, there are significant ramifications should the switch be compromised.

Vulnerabilities

Layer 2 vulnerabilities of this design include the following:

- MAC spoofing, within VLANs
- CAM table overflow, through per VLAN traffic flooding
- VLAN hopping

Mitigation

If the security zones are small enough, use ***port security*** to help mitigate the CAM table overflow vulnerability and the MAC spoofing vulnerability. In addition, you can accomplish mitigation of VLAN hopping by following the VLAN best practices outlined in this chapter. As with the previous cases, the switches must be managed as securely as possible and tested on a regular basis.

In the design shown in Figure 7-6, another mitigation approach is to split the Layer 2 functionality of the switch to two separate physical switches. If this is done, the mitigation techniques described in case 1 would apply to both distinct security zones.

Figure 7-6 Multiple Switch Network Separation

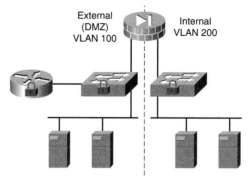

If *private VLANs (PVLANs)* are used in any of the VLANs, consideration must be given to the possibility of PVLAN attacks. If the VLANs use DHCP for address assignment, DHCP starvation by an attacker and needs to be considered.

Multiple Security Zones, One User Group, Multiple Physical Switches

This design, shown in Figure 7-7, represents a large data center within a single enterprise. However, the need to segregate traffic and data for various groups or departments within the enterprise is reflected by the separation of the data center into security zones. This can be accomplished securely through the use of VLANs within the data center, but there are considerations that must be evaluated regarding some of the potential vulnerabilities. In Figure 7-7, the two switches have a trunk between carrying all the VLAN traffic between the switches.

Figure 7-7 Multiple Switch Network Separation

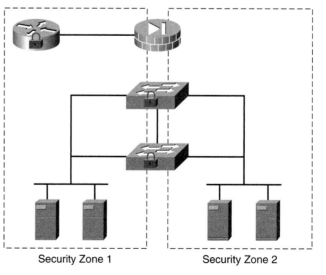

Vulnerabilities

Primary Layer 2 vulnerabilities of this design include the following:

- MAC spoofing, within VLANs
- CAM table overflow, through per-VLAN traffic flooding
- VLAN hopping
- STP attacks

Mitigation

If the security zones are small enough, use port security to help mitigate CAM table overflow vulnerabilities and the MAC spoofing vulnerability. In addition, you can accomplish mitigation of VLAN hopping by following the VLAN best practices outlined in this chapter. If necessary, deploy 802.1x authentication to prevent unauthorized access to each of the security zones from an attacker who might physically connect to a switch in the design. Another possible mitigation method would be to add a firewall within the design, or add a Layer 3 switch with an integrated firewall, as shown in Figure 7-8. The firewall enforces additional Layer 3 traffic segregation. As with the previous cases, the switches must be managed as securely as possible and be tested on a regular basis.

Figure 7-8   Alternative Network Topology

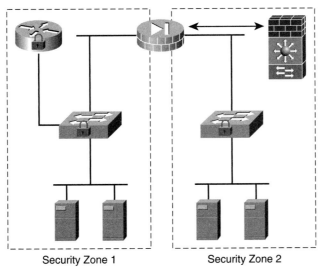

Security Zone 1   Security Zone 2

Multiple Security Zones, Multiple User Groups, Single Physical Switch

The design shown in Figure 7-9 is similar to the previous scenario by having multiple user groups within the data center, each requiring its own level of security for its systems. However in this case, all the user groups connect to a single central switch. VLANs can be used to provide traffic segregation between the security zones.

Figure 7-9   Multiple Security Zones, Multiple User Groups, Single Physical Switch

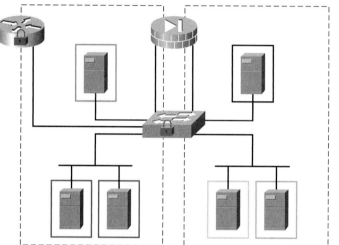

Vulnerabilities

Primary Layer 2 vulnerabilities of this design include the following:

- **MAC spoofing, within VLANs**

- **CAM table overflow, through per VLAN traffic flooding**

- **VLAN hopping**

- **Private VLAN attacks, on a per-VLAN basis**—Private VLAN is a Layer 2 feature and therefore it is supposed to isolate traffic only at Layer 2. On the other hand, a router works at Layer 3, and when it is attached to a PVLAN promiscuous port it is supposed to forward Layer 3 traffic received on that port to whatever destination it is meant to, even if it is in the same subnet. Therefore, it is absolutely normal for two hosts in an isolated VLAN to fail to communicate with each other through direct Layer 2 communication and instead to succeed to talk to each other by using the router as a packet relay.

Mitigation

If the security zones are small enough, use port security to help mitigate CAM table overflow vulnerabilities and the MAC spoofing vulnerability. In addition, you can accomplish mitigation of VLAN hopping by following the VLAN best practices outlined within this chapter. If necessary, deploy 802.1x authentication to prevent unauthorized access to each of the security zones from an attacker who might physically connect to a switch in the design. Another possible mitigation method is to add a firewall within the data center design and integrate it into the central switch similar to that used in the previous design. The firewall enforces additional Layer 3 traffic segregation between the various user groups. As with the previous cases, the switches must be managed as securely as possible and tested on a regular basis.

Multiple Security Zones, Multiple User Groups, Multiple Physical Switches

The design shown in Figure 7-10 represents the most complex of the series. It is similar to the previous scenario by having multiple user groups within the data center each requiring their own level of security for their systems. Instead of all the user groups connecting to a single central switch, multiple switches operate at both Layer 2 and Layer 3 throughout the design. VLANs can be used to provide traffic segregation between the security zones. The need to provide high security in some of the zones might require additional measures.

Figure 7-10   Multiple Security Zones, Multiple User Groups, Multiple Physical Switches

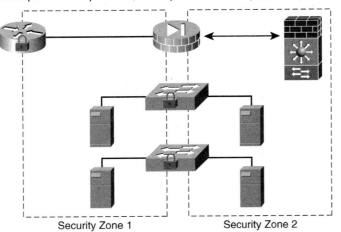

Security Zone 1   Security Zone 2

Vulnerabilities

Primary layer 2 vulnerabilities of this design include the following:

- MAC spoofing, within VLANs
- CAM table overflow, through per VLAN traffic flooding
- VLAN hopping
- STP attacks
- VTP attacks

If private VLANs are implemented within each VLAN, this design might also be vulnerable to a private VLAN proxy attack. In addition, if one of the VLANs is large and DHCP is used for address management, this design might be vulnerable to DHCP starvation attacks.

Mitigation

If the security zones are small enough, use port security to help mitigate CAM table overflow vulnerabilities and the MAC spoofing vulnerability. In addition, you can accomplish mitigation of VLAN hopping by following the VLAN best practices outlined within this chapter. If necessary, deploy 802.1x authentication to prevent unauthorized access to each of the security zones from an attacker who might physically connect to a switch in the design. Another possible mitigation method is to add a firewall within the data center design and integrate it into the one or more of the switches, similar to that employed in the case 6 design. The firewall enforces additional Layer 3 traffic segregation between the various user groups. As with the previous cases, the switches must be managed as securely as possible and tested on a regular basis.

Layer 2 Security Best Practices

Although security attacks on networks are not new events, attacks that use Layer 2 to bypass VLAN restrictions are quickly gaining sophistication and popularity. To mitigate the effects of these attacks as much as possible, the following precautions are recommended:

- Manage switches as securely as possible. Use SSH if possible, or an out-of-band management system. Avoid the use of clear-text management protocols such as Telnet or SNMP Version 1.
- Use IP permit lists to restrict access to management ports.
- Selectively use SNMPv3 and treat community strings like root passwords.
- When SNMPv3 is used as a management protocol, restrict management access to the VLAN so that entities on untrusted networks cannot access management interfaces or protocols. Consider using DHCP snooping and IP source guard to mitigate DHCP starvation attacks.

- Always use a dedicated VLAN ID for all trunk ports.

- Avoid using VLAN 1.

- Set all user ports to nontrunking mode.

- Deploy port security where possible for user ports. When feasible, configure each port to associate a limited number of MAC addresses. Approximately two to three MAC addresses should be adequate in most situations. This will mitigate MAC flooding and other network attacks. Alternatively, deploy dynamic port security using DHCP snooping along with DAI.

- Have a plan for the ARP security issues in the network. Consider using DHCP snooping along with DAI and IP source guard to protect against MAC spoofing and IP spoofing on the network.

- Use VLAN ACLs (VACLs) to prevent rogue DHCP servers by limiting replies to DHCP clients to valid DHCP servers on the network. A more flexible approach is to use DHCP snooping to block unauthorized DHCP servers from responding to DHCP request packets.

- Enable STP attack mitigation with BPDU guard and root guard.

- Use PVLANs where appropriate to further divide Layer 2 networks.

- Use Cisco Discovery Protocol (CDP) only where appropriate.

- Disable all unused ports and put them in an unused VLAN. This setup prevents network intruders from plugging into unused ports and communicating with the rest of the network.

- Use Cisco IOS Software access control lists (ACLs) on IP-forwarding devices to protect Layer 2 proxy on private VLANs.

- Eliminate native VLANs from 802.1q trunks.

- Use Virtual Terminal Protocol (VTP) passwords to authenticate VTP advertisements.

- Consider using Layer 2 port authentication, such as 802.1x, to authenticate clients attempting connectivity to a network.

- Procedures for change control and configuration analysis must be in place to ensure that changes result in a secure configuration. This is especially valuable in cases where several organizational groups may control the same switch, and even more valuable in network security deployments where even greater care must be taken.

Many of the preceding features are available in Cisco Catalyst switches. Table 7-2 details the availability of some the features discussed in this chapter in the switches listed across the top row.

Table 7-2   Cisco Switch Security Features

	Catalyst 2900 XL	Catalyst 3500 XL	Catalyst 2950	Catalyst 3550 CatOS	Catalyst 4000 CatOS	Catalyst 5000 CatOS	Catalyst 6000 IOS	Catalyst 4000 IOS	Catalyst 6000
Port security	✓	✓	✓	✓	✓	✓	✓	✓	✓
PVLANs	✓	✓	✓	✓	✓		✓	✓	✓
STP BDPU guard			✓	✓	✓	✓	✓	✓	✓
STP root guard	✓	✓	✓	✓	✓		✓	✓	✓
SSH support		✓	✓	✓		✓	✓	✓	
VMPS client	✓	✓	✓	✓	✓	✓	✓		
VMPS server			✓	✓	✓	✓	✓		
802.1x authentication			✓	✓	✓		✓	✓	✓
Wire-rate ACLs			✓	✓	✓		✓	✓	✓
DHCP snooping								✓	
ARP inspection							✓		
Dynamic ARP inspection				✓			✓	✓	✓

SDM Security Audit

The SDM security audit feature compares router configurations to a predefined checklist of best practices using ICSA and Cisco TAC recommendations.

Examples of the audit actions include, but are not limited to, the following:

- Shuts down unneeded servers on the router. These servers include BOOTP, finger, TCP/UDP small servers.

- Shuts down unneeded services on the router. These services include CDP, ip source-route, ip classless.

- Applies a firewall to the outside interfaces.

- Disables SNMP or enables it with hard-to-guess community strings.

- Shuts down unused interfaces using no ip proxy-arp.

- Forces passwords for the router console and vty lines.

- Forces an enable secret password.

- Enforces the use of ACLs.

The security audit, as shown in Figure 7-11, contains two modes:

- **Security audit**—Examines router configuration and displays the Report Card screen, which shows a list of possible security problems. The administrator can then pick and choose which vulnerability to lock down.

- **One-step lockdown**—Initiates the automatic lockdown using recommended settings.

Figure 7-11   Security Audit Main Window

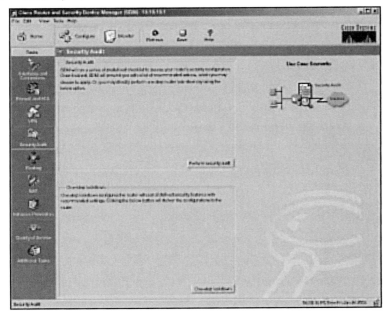

In monitor mode, Cisco SDM provides a quick, graphical status of key router resources and performance measurements such as the interface status, CPU, and memory usage. Cisco SDM takes advantage of integrated routing and security features on routers to provide in-depth diagnostics and troubleshooting of WAN and VPN connections. For example, while troubleshooting a failed VPN connection, the Cisco SDM verifies the router configurations and connectivity from the WAN interface layer to the IPsec crypto map layer. While testing configuration and remote peer connectivity at each layer, Cisco SDM provides pass or fail status, possible reasons of failure, and Cisco TAC-recommended actions for recovery.

Cisco SDM Monitor mode also allows administrators to view the number of network access attempts that were denied by the Cisco IOS Firewall, and it provides easy access to the firewall log. Administrators can also monitor detailed VPN status, such as the number of packets encrypted or decrypted by IPsec tunnels, and Easy VPN client session details.

Figure 7-12 Monitor Mode

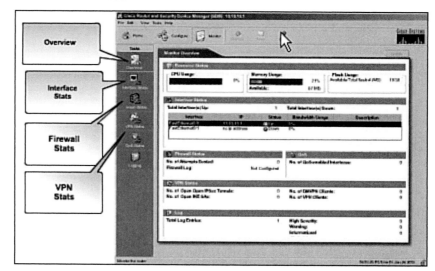

The monitor function as shown in Figure 7-12 includes the following elements:

- **Overview**—Displays the router status including a list of the error log entries

- **Interface Status**—Used to select the interface to monitor and the conditions (for example, packets and errors, in or out) to view

- **Firewall Status**—Displays a log showing the number of entry attempts that were denied by the firewall

- **VPN Status**—Displays statistics about active VPN connections on the router

- **QoS Status**—Displays statistics on quality of service (QoS) configured on router

- **Logging**—Displays an event log categorized by severity level

Router Management Center (MC)

This section introduces and explains the Management Center for VPN routers also known as the Router Management Center. The CiscoWorks Router Management Center (Router MC), a component of the CiscoWorks VPN/Management Solution (VMS), is a web-based application designed for large-scale management of VPN and firewall configurations on Cisco routers, as depicted in Figure 7-13. One of the greatest challenges in implementing large site-to-site and remote-access VPNs is management. The primary role of the Router MC is to manage site-to-site VPNs.

Figure 7-13   Router MC

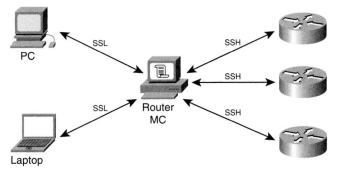

The Router MC can be defined as follows:

- A web-based application for the setup and maintenance of VPN connections using Cisco VPN routers

- Centralizes the configuration of IKE and tunnel policies for multiple devices

- Scalable to a large number of VPN routers

- A web-based application designed for large-scale management of VPN and firewall configurations on Cisco routers, as depicted in Figure 7-14

Figure 7-14   What Is a Router Management Center (MC)?

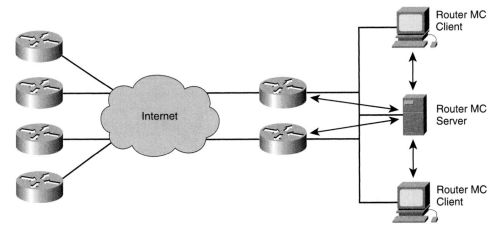

Router MC 1.2.1 provides the following features:

- Enables the setup and maintenance of VPN connections among multiple Cisco VPN routers, in a hub-and-spoke topology

- Enables the provisioning of the critical connectivity, security, and performance parameters of a site-to-site VPN, quickly and easily

- Allows for efficient migration from leased line connections to Internet or intranet-based VPN connections

- Allows for the overlay of a VPN over a Frame Relay network for added security

- Enables the configuration of Cisco IOS routers to function as firewalls

Router MC is scalable to a large number of routers. Its hierarchical router grouping and policy inheritance features enable the configuration of multiple like routers simultaneously, instead of having to configure each router individually. Router MC enables deployment of VPN or firewall configurations to groups of routers or individual routers. It translates the configurations into command-line interface (CLI) commands and either deploys them directly to the routers in the network or to a configuration file for each router. It also uses reusable policy components that can be referenced across multiple connections.

Router MC is integrated with CiscoWorks Common Services, which supplies core server-side components required by Router MC, such as Apache Web server, Secure Sockets Layer (SSL) libraries, SSH libraries, embedded SQL database, Tomcat servlet engine, the CiscoWorks desktop, and others.

Note

These functions are not performed from within the Router MC user interface, but are accessed using the CiscoWorks user interface.

Before installing Router MC 1.2.1, CiscoWorks Common Services 2.2 must be installed and operational. CiscoWorks Common Services provides centralized management of certain functions for all the CiscoWorks VMS products that are installed. These functions include the following:

- Backup and restore of data

- Integration with Access Control Server (ACS) or Common Management Framework (CMF) for user authentication and permissions

- Licensing

- Starting/stopping the database

- Logging of administration tasks

After CiscoWorks Common Services 2.2 is installed, the Router MC 1.2.1 VMS module, or any of the other VMS modules as shown in Figure 7-15, can be installed.

Figure 7-15   Router Management Center (MC) Component

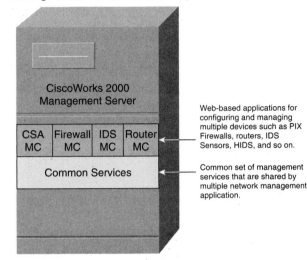

The sections that follow cover topics key to understanding the Router MC.

Hub-and-Spoke Topology

In a hub-and-spoke VPN topology, multiple remote devices, or spokes, communicate securely with a central device, or a hub. A separate, secured tunnel extends between the centralized hub and each of the individual spokes.

VPN Settings and Policies

In the Router MC, VPN configurations are divided into the following items:

- **VPN settings**—VPN configurations that provide a framework for network behavior and VPN policy implementation. Settings include selection of failover method and routing protocols, packet fragmentation settings, specification of internal network and inside interfaces for hubs and spokes, and hub assignment for spokes.

- **IKE policies**—Define the combination of security parameters to be used during IKE negotiation between two IPsec peers, including the encryption and authentication algorithms, the Diffie-Hellman group identifier, and the lifetime of the security association.

- **Tunnel policies**—Define what data will be securely transmitted via the tunnel, crypto ACL, and which authentication and encryption algorithms will be applied to the data to ensure its authenticity, integrity, and confidentiality.

- **Transform sets**—A combination of security protocols, algorithms, and other setting that specify exactly how the data in the IPsec tunnel will be encrypted and authenticated.

- **Network groups**—Named collections of networks/hosts. A network group name can be referenced during the definition of VPN settings and policies, instead of having to specify each network or host individually for each policy definition.

- **Network Address Translation (NAT) policies**—Enable the devices in the secured private network to access outside networks for nonconfidential purposes without monopolizing the resources required for VPN connections.

Device Hierarchy and Inheritance

The Router MC provides a default two-level device hierarchy in which all devices are contained within a global group. The Router MC provides for the creation of device groups, which makes management of a large number of devices easier. VPN configurations can be defined on multiple devices simultaneously.

Policy inheritance in the device hierarchy is implemented in a top-down fashion. The global group is the highest-level object.

All devices in the device inventory inherit VPN configurations defined on the global level. All the groups inherit VPN configurations defined on a device group level and devices contained within that group and override any global configurations inherited from higher-level for those devices. VPN configurations defined on an individual device level apply to that device only and override any configurations inherited from higher-level objects in the hierarchy.

Activities

An activity is a temporary context, within which VPN configuration changes are made to specific objects. These can be global, device groups, or devices. The activity must be approved before its configuration changes are committed to the Router MC database, at which point they are ready for deployment to the relevant devices or files. Before making any configuration changes, administrators must create a new activity or open an existing activity. An activity can be opened by only one person at a time, but can be accessed by several people in sequence. Therefore, before the activity is approved, another user can open it and make further configuration changes to the selected objects.

Jobs

A *job* is a deployment task in which administrators specify the devices to which VPN configurations should be deployed. The Router MC generates the CLI commands for the devices specified in the job, based on the defined VPN policies. These commands can be previewed before deployment takes place. Within the context of the job, administrators can specify whether to deploy the commands directly to the devices in the network or to a file.

Building Blocks

Building blocks in the Router MC refer to network groups and transform sets. Building blocks are reusable, named, global components that can be referenced by multiple policies. When referenced, a building block is incorporated as an integral component of the policy. If a change is made to the definition of a building block, this change is reflected in all policies that reference that building block. Building blocks aid in policy definition by eliminating the need to define that component each time a policy is defined. For example, although transform sets are integral to tunnel policies, administrators can define several transform sets independently of the tunnel policy definitions. These transform sets are always available for selection when creating tunnel policies, on the object on which they were defined and its descendants.

Supported Tunneling Technologies

The Router MC supports the following tunneling technologies:

- **IPsec**—IPsec is a framework of open standards that provides data confidentiality, data integrity, and data origin authentication between peers that are connected over unprotected networks, such as the Internet.

- **IPsec with GRE**—Generic routing encapsulation (GRE) is a tunneling protocol that can encapsulate a variety of protocol packet types inside IP tunnels. GRE accomplish this by creating a virtual point-to-point link to devices at remote points over an IP internetwork.

- **IPsec with GRE over a Frame Relay network**—This option provides all the advantages of using IPsec with GRE and the ability to create secure VPN tunnels over a Frame Relay network. Router MC supports a Frame Relay topology in which the hub acts only as a VPN endpoint, while each spoke acts as both a VPN endpoint and a Frame Relay endpoint. This means that there must be a router in the hub subnet before the VPN endpoint at the hub that acts as the second Frame Relay endpoint.

- **IPsec with GRE and DMVPN**—Dynamic Multipoint VPN (DMVPN) combines GRE tunnels, IPsec encryption, and Next Hop Resolution Protocol (NHRP). It allows for the management of devices with dynamically assigned IP addresses. It also enables direct spoke-to-spoke communication, without the need to go through the hub.

Table 7-3 illustrates a summary of the properties of IPsec versus IPsec with GRE.

Table 7-3   Comparing IPsec Versus IPsec with GRE

Feature	IPsec	IPsec with GRE
Ability to secure protocols other than IP	No	Yes
Spoke-to-spoke connectivity	Yes	No
Dynamic tunneling	Yes	No
Split tunneling	Fine-grained using extended ACL	Network-based granularity
Resilience	Low as it uses IKE keepalive	High as it uses routing protocol
NAT	Yes	Yes

Router MC Installation

The Router MC requires VMS 2.1 Common Services or CiscoWorks 2000. VMS Common Services provides the CiscoWorks 2000 Server-based components, software libraries, and software packages developed for the Router MC.

Before beginning the installation of the Router MC, verify that the server meets the following requirements:

- Hardware:
    - IBM PC-compatible computer with 1 GHz or faster CPU
    - Color monitor capable of viewing 256 colors
    - CD-ROM drive
    - 10BASE-T or faster network connection
- Memory: 1 GB of RAM minimum
- Disk drive space:
    - 9 GB minimum
    - FAT32 or NTFS file system
    - 2 GB of virtual memory
- Software:
    - Windows 2000 Server with Service Pack 2
    - ODBC Driver Manager 3.510 or later

Also, verify that the client machine being used meets the following requirements:

- Hardware:
  - IBM PC-compatible computer with 300 MHz or faster CPU
  - 10BASE-T or faster network connection
- Software:
  - Windows 98, or
  - Windows NT 4.0, or
  - Windows 2000 with Service Pack 2
- Memory: 256 MB of RAM minimum
- Disk drive space: 400 MB virtual memory
- Browser: Internet Explorer 5.5 or 6.0

The Router MC is automatically installed in the CiscoWorks Common Services installation folder. The default folder location is C:\Program Files\CSCOpx\MDC\iosmdc, where C:\ is the drive of installation. A typical installation of the Router MC takes approximately 10 minutes.

Complete the following steps to install the Router MC:

Step 1. Insert the Cisco Router MC CD into the CD-ROM drive. If autorun is enabled, the CD should start the installation process automatically. If autorun is not enabled, locate the setup.exe file on the CD-ROM and execute it.

Step 2. The Extracting Files dialog box appears. After the progress bar indicates that all appears files have been extracted, the InstallShield Wizard preparation dialog box appears.

Step 3. Click **Next**. The Router MC Installation window displays, requesting a password for the Router MC database.

Step 4. Enter a password in the Password field, and confirm the password in the Confirm Password field.

Step 5. Click **Next**. The Start Copying Files window displays.

Step 6. Click **Next**. The Setup Status window displays with an installation status bar that shows the installation progress. After the installation completes, the InstallShield Wizard Complete window displays.

Step 7. Select the **Yes, I want to restart my computer now** button and click **Finish**. The computer restarts to complete the installation of the Router MC.

On all routers that will be managed by the Router MC, complete the following mandatory steps to configure the routers to support SSH:

Step 1.   Configure a unique router hostname.

Step 2.   Configure a domain name.

Step 3.   Generate RSA usage keys.

Step 4.   Ensure that the RSA keys use a modulus size that is greater than 1024.

Getting Started with the Router MC

This section explains how to start using the Router MC. When administrators are logged in to CiscoWorks, they can create accounts based upon the authorization roles that CiscoWorks uses and then launch the Router MC.

Log in to the CiscoWorks web page, shown in Figure 7-16, and launch the Router MC by opening a browser and pointing the browser to the IP address of the CiscoWorks server with a port number of 1741. If the CiscoWorks server is local, enter the following address in the browser: **http://127.0.0.1:1741**.

If this is the first time that CiscoWorks has been used, enter the username **admin** and the password **admin**.

Figure 7-16   Launch the Router MC from the CiscoWorks 2000 Web Page

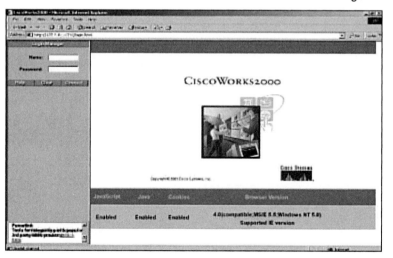

Router MC interface

The Router MC main window is the first window that is encountered in the Router MC user interface. The Router MC user interface contains five tabs, as shown in Figure 7-17:

- **Devices**—Use this tab to import and manage the inventory of routers to be configured using Router MC.

- **Configuration**—Use this tab to define and manage the VPN and firewall settings and policies that will be downloaded to the managed routers.

- **Deployment**—Use this tab to create and manage deployment jobs to deploy the policy definitions to specific routers. When creating a job, the committed configurations for the specified routers are translated into CLI commands, which can then be deployed to the routers or to configuration file.

- **Reports**—Use this tab to view reports on Router MC functions, including activity, deployment, hub-spoke assignment, and audit trail reports.

- **Admin**—Use this tab to modify Router MC application settings, including activity and job approval settings.

Figure 7-17   Router MC Main Window

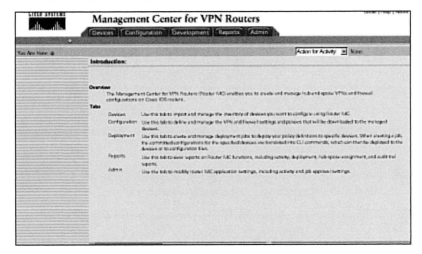

The Router MC interface, as shown in Figure 7-18, is the environment administrators work with when using the Router MC application.

Figure 7-18   Router MC Administrator Interface

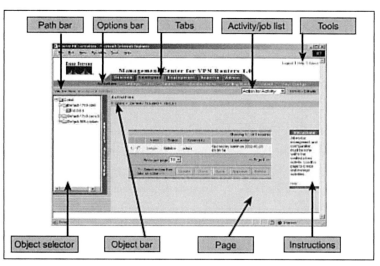

The common elements of the Router MC interface are as follows:

- **Path bar**—Provides a context for the displayed page. Shows the selected tab, option, and then the current page.

- **Options bar**—Displays the options available for the selected tab.

- **Tabs**—Provides access to the Router MC features:

  — **Devices**—Displays options for importing and managing devices and device groups in the Router MC inventory.

  — **Configure**—Displays options for defining connectivity and security between devices, such as IKE and tunnel policies.

  — **Deployment**—Displays options for creating jobs, deploying VPN configurations, and viewing the CLI commands to be deployed to the devices.

  — **Reports**—Displays options for viewing reports, such as a report on activities.

  — **Admin**—Displays options that are used by administrators, such as application settings, timeout values, and stored policies.

- **Activity/job list**—Allows administrators to manage individual Router MC activities when selecting either the Configure tab or the Devices tab, or to manage individual Router MC jobs when selecting the Deployment tab.

- **Tools**—Contains the Logout, Help, and About buttons:

  — **Logout**—Exits Router MC and ends the CiscoWorks session.

— **Help**—Opens a new window that displays context-sensitive help for the displayed page. The window also contains buttons to access the overall help contents, index, and search tools.

— **About**—Displays the Router MC version and copyright.

■ **Instructions**—Provides a brief overview of how to use the page.

■ **Page**—Displays the area used to perform application tasks.

■ **Object bar**—Displays the object or objects selected in the Object selector.

■ **Object selector**—Shows a hierarchy of objects, such as devices and device groups, and lets administrators select the objects to configure.

Router MC Tabs

The Devices tab, as shown in Figure 7-19, is used to import and manage the inventory of routers to be configured using the Router MC.

Figure 7-19 Devices Tab

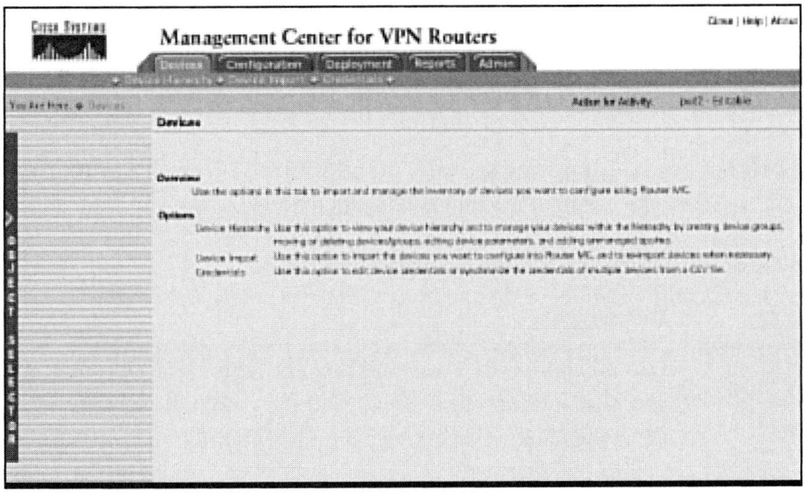

The options provided by the Devices tab are as follows:

■ **Device hierarchy**—Use this option to view the device hierarchy and to manage the routers within the hierarchy by creating device groups, moving or deleting devices/groups, editing router parameters, and adding unmanaged spokes.

■ **Device import**—Use this option to import the routers to be configured into Router MC, and to re-import routers when necessary.

- **Credentials**—Use this option to edit router credentials or synchronize the credentials of multiple routers from a comma-separated value (CSV) file. Device credentials include the username, password, and enable password.

Use the options in the Configuration tab, shown in Figure 7-20, to configure VPN and firewall settings and policies for deployment to the routers.

Figure 7-20   Configuration Tab

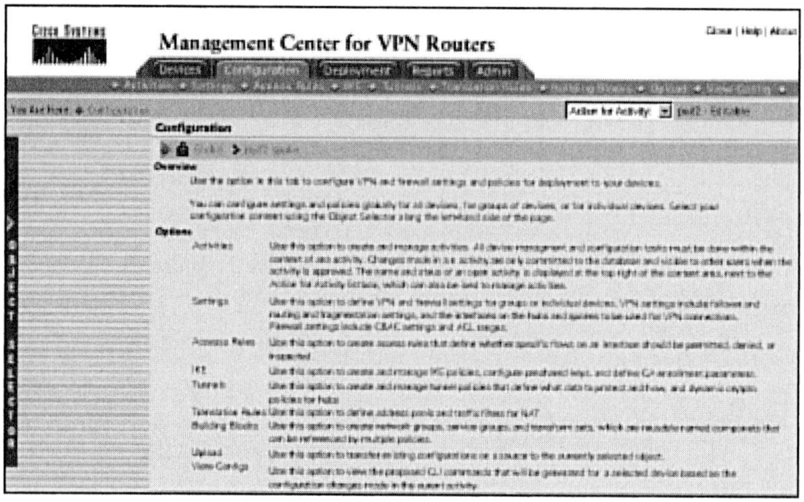

Settings and policies can be configured globally for all routers, for groups of routers, or for individual routers. Select the configuration context using the Object Selector, shown in Table 7-4.

Table 7-4   Configuration Tab Object Selectors

Object Selector	Description
Activities	Use this option to create and manage activities. All router management and configuration tasks must be done within the context of an activity. Changes made in an activity are only committed to the database and visible to other users when the activity is approved. The name and status of an open activity display at the top right of the context area, next to the action for Activity list box, which can also be used to manage activities.
Settings	Use this option to define VPN and firewall settings for groups or individual routers. VPN settings include failover and routing and fragmentation settings, and interfaces on the hubs and spokes to be used for VPN connections. Firewall settings include Context-Based Access Control (CBAC) settings and ACL ranges.

Table 7-4   Configuration Tab Object Selectors   *continued*

Object Selector	Description
Access Rules	Use this option to create access rules that define whether specific traffic flows on an interface should be permitted, denied, or inspected.
IKE	Use this option to create and manage Internet Key Exchange (IKE) policies, configure pre-shared keys, and define certificate authority (CA) enrollment parameters.
Tunnels	Use this option to create and manage tunnel policies that define what data to protect and how, and dynamic crypto policies for hubs.
Translation Rules	Use this option to define address pools and traffic filters for Network Address Translation (NAT).
Building Blocks	Use this option to create network groups, service groups, and transform sets, which are reusable named components that can be referenced by multiple policies.
Upload	Use this option to transfer existing configurations on a source router to the current selected object.
View Configs	Use this option to view the proposed CLI commands that will be generated for a selected router based on the configuration changes made in the current activity.

Deployment of VPN and firewall configurations is always done within the context of a deployment job, as shown in Figure 7-21.

Figure 7-21   Deployment Tab

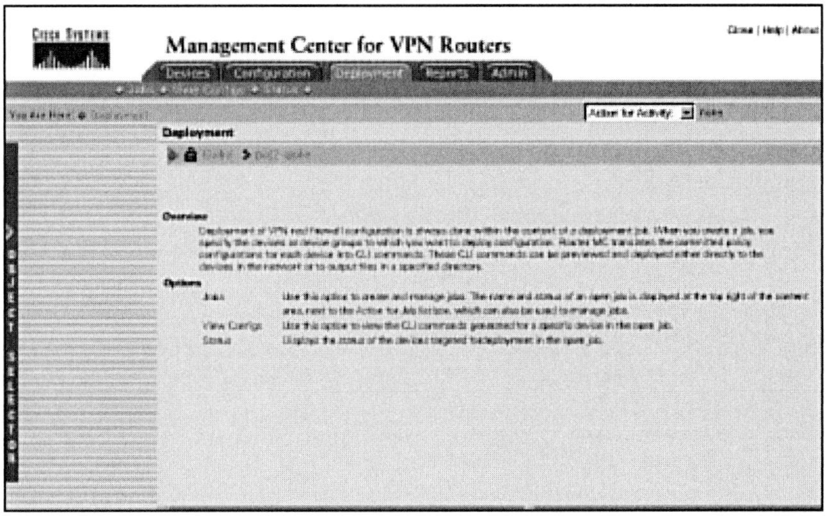

When a job is created, the routers or router groups to which the configurations are to be deployed are specified. Router MC translates the committed policy configurations for each router into CLI commands. These CLI commands can be previewed and deployed either directly to the routers in the network or to output files in a specified directory. The Deployment tab offers the administrator the options listed in Table 7-5.

Table 7-5   Deployment Tab Options

Deployment Tab Option	Description
Jobs	Use this option to create and manage jobs. The name and status of an open job display at the top right of the context area, next to the Action for Job list box, which can also be used to manage jobs.
View Configs	Use this option to view the CLI commands generated for a specific router in the open job.
Status	Displays the status of the routers targeted for deployment in the open job.

The Reports tab, shown in Figure 7-22, is used to view reports on various Router MC functions.

Figure 7-22   Reports Tab

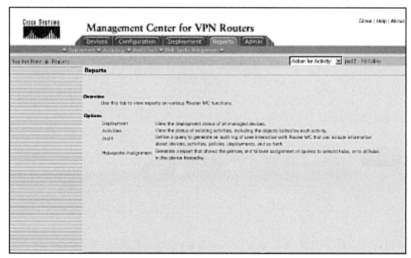

This tab presents the options outlined in Table 7-6.

Table 7-6   Reports Tab Options

Reports Tab Option	Description
Activities	Use this option to view the status of existing activities, including the objects locked by each activity. The Router MC uses a locking model, in which the objects for which policies are being defined and all their descendants in the object hierarchy are locked to other users until the activity is approved or deleted. This is important in large networks where several people have the authority to configure routers. It prevents a potential situation where two or more people are making configuration changes to the same objects at the same time.
Audit	Use this option to define a query to generate an audit log of user interaction with the Router MC that can include information about routers, activities, policies, deployments, and so forth.
Hub-Spoke Assignment	Use this option to generate a report that shows the primary and failover assignment of spokes to selected hubs, or to all hubs in the device hierarchy.

Administrators use the Admin tab, shown in Figure 7-23, to define various Router MC application settings and to define Auto Update Server (AUS) settings.

Figure 7-23   Admin Tab

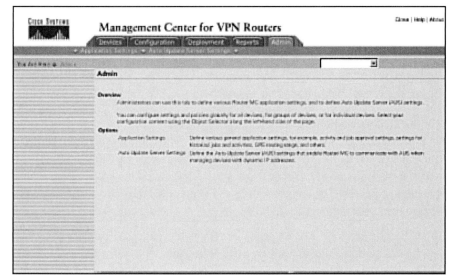

Basic Workflow and Tasks

The Router MC has an inherent basic user workflow. Most Router MC tasks are ordered as follows:

- **Task 1: Create an activity**—All router management and VPN configuration must be done within the context of an activity. When an activity is created, a proposal to create or change VPN or firewall configurations on specific routers is prepared. This proposal must be approved before configurations can be deployed to the routers.

- **Task 2: Create device groups**—Organize the routers in a hierarchy. When device groups are created, the router inventory is strategically divided to facilitate management and deployment. All routers within a device group can share common policies, which can be deployed to a set of routers at the same time, rather than individually. Device groups help to keep a clear picture of the relationships between the routers in the network.

- **Task 3: Import devices**—When devices are imported, the router information is brought into the device inventory, enabling administrators to manage the routers using Router MC. Router information can be imported by having Router MC query the routers directly or by importing router information that is contained in a file.

- **Task 4: Define VPN/firewall settings**—There are two ways to complete this task:

  — If a VPN is being configured, the inside interfaces and internal networks on the hub and spoke must be specified, and the VPN interface on the spokes and the hubs to which the spokes are assigned. The method to be used for resiliency, either IKE keepalive or GRE, can be specified. Additional VPN settings not covered in the basic user workflow include more-advanced configurations for GRE, and packet fragmentation.

  — If firewall policies to be deployed to the routers are being configured, the parameters required for implementing CBAC and for defining access rules, such as fragmentation, timeouts, half-open connections, logging, and ACL ranges, must be defined.

- **Task 5: Define VPN policies/firewall ACLs**—There are two ways to complete this task:

  — For VPN policy configuration, an IKE policy and a tunnel policy must be defined. The IKE policy defines a combination of security parameters to be used during IKE negotiation and authentication of peers. A tunnel policy defines the VPN connection from a spoke to its assigned hub. Tunnel policies are defined on the spoke are then implemented on the hub. The authentication and encryption algorithms that will be used to secure the traffic can be selected.

  — To define the network security policy for firewall policy configuration, ACLs must be used. ACLs provide traffic filtering by enabling the implementation of ACLs and CBAC inspection rules on the interfaces of the managed routers.

- **Task 6: Approve the activity**—Upon completing the VPN or firewall configurations, the activity must be approved before the configurations are committed to the database and can be deployed.

■ **Task 7: Create and deploy a job**—When a job is created, the devices or device groups to which the configurations will be deployed are specified. Administrators have the option to deploy directly to the routers or to files. CLI commands are generated according to the configurations. These commands can be reviewed before deployment. Common configuration tasks include the following:

— Configuring general Cisco IOS Firewall settings

— Building access rules

— Using building blocks

— Using upload

Simple Network Management Protocol (SNMP)

Another technique that the administrator can use to manage and monitor the network is to use SNMP. SNMP is an application layer protocol that facilitates the exchange of management information between network devices. It is part of the TCP/IP protocol suite. SNMP enables network administrators to manage network performance, find and solve network problems, and plan for network growth. SNMP can be used to manage Cisco routers, switches, wireless access points, firewalls, printers, servers, and other SNMP-capable devices.

SNMP Introduction

There are three versions of SNMP, as shown in Table 7-7. SNMPv1 and SNMPv2 have features in common, but SNMPv2 offers enhancements, such as additional protocol operations. SNMPv3 adds administration and security features. This section provides descriptions of the SNMPv3 protocol operations. Cisco recommends disabling SNMP if not in use or to use SNMPv3.

Table 7-7   SNMP Versions

Version	RFCs	Adopted by IETF
SNMPv1	1157–1162	1989
SNMPv2	1901–1908	1993
SNMPv3	3410–3418	2002

SNMP Key Terms

To understand SNMP support in Cisco devices, it is important to understand the SNMP-related terminology discussed in Table 7-8.

Table 7-8   SNMP Key Terms

Terms	Description
Managed devices	Hardware devices such as computers, routers, and terminal servers that are connected to networks.
Agents	Software modules that reside in managed devices. Agents collect and store management information such as the number of error packets received by a network element.
Managed object	A manageable component of a managed device. A managed object might be hardware, configuration parameters, or performance statistics of a device. For example, a list of currently active TCP circuits in a particular host computer is a managed object. Managed objects differ from variables, which are particular object instances. Whereas a managed object might be a list of currently active TCP circuits in a particular host, and object instance is a single active TCP circuit in a particular host. Managed objects have object identifiers (OIDs).
Managed Information Base (MIB)	A collection of managed objects. A MIB can be depicted as an abstract tree with an unnamed root. Individual data items make up the leaves of the tree. These leaves have OIDs that uniquely identify or name them. OIDs are like telephone numbers; they are organized hierarchically with specific digits assigned by different organizations. An OID is written as a sequence of subidentifiers, starting with the tree root in dotted-decimal notation.
Network management stations (NMSs)	A device that executes management applications that monitor and control network elements. The NMS is the console through which the network administrator performs network management functions. It is usually a computer with a fast CPU, mega-pixel color display, substantial memory, and abundant disk space.
Trap	An event notification sent from an agent to the NMS. A trap is one of four types of interaction between an NMS and a managed device. Traps are unsolicited comments from a managed device to the NMS for certain events, such as link up, link down, and generated syslog events.
Community	A string value that provides a simple kind of password protection for communications between an SNMP agent and the SNMP NMS. The common default string is "public".

SNMP Basic Components

An SNMP managed network consists of three key components:

- Managed devices
- Agents
- NMSs

A managed device is a network node that contains an SNMP agent and resides on a managed network. Managed devices collect and store management information and make this information available to NMSs using SNMP. Information is structured as per Structure of Management Information (SMI) standards. Object definitions are provided in many MIBs. Managed devices, sometimes called network elements, can be routers, switches, wireless access points, firewalls, printers, servers, and other SNMP-capable devices.

An agent is a network management software module that resides in a managed device, as shown in Figure 7-24. An agent has local knowledge of management information and translates that information into a form compatible with SNMP.

Figure 7-24   SNMP Agent

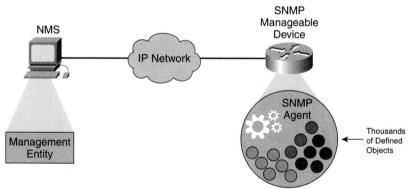

An NMS executes applications that monitor and control managed devices as follows:

1. Management entity collects date by generating requests. This causes in-band traffic coexisting with production traffic.

2. Management entity receives notifications of network alarms or events. This can be forwarded to the manager through e-mail or SMS.

3. Management entity runs applications to analyze or interpret management data.

NMSs provide the bulk of the processing and memory resources required for network management. One or more NMSs must exist on any managed network. SNMP management applications, such as CiscoWorks 2000, communicate with agents to get statistics and alerts from the managed devices.

SNMP Basic Commands

Managed devices are monitored and controlled using basic SNMP commands, as shown in
Figure 7-25:

- The **read** command is used by an NMS to monitor managed devices. The NMS examines
  different variables that are maintained by managed devices. GetRequests are used to read
  the value of an object.

- The **write** command is used by an NMS to control managed devices. The NMS changes
  the values of variables stored within managed devices. SetRequests are used to modify the
  value of an object.

- Managed devices to asynchronously report events to the NMS use the **trap** command.
  When certain types of events occur, a managed device sends a trap to the NMS. Traps provide asynchronous event notification.

- Traversal operations are used by the NMS to determine which variables a managed device
  supports and to sequentially gather information in variable tables, such as a routing table.

Figure 7-25   SNMP Device Management

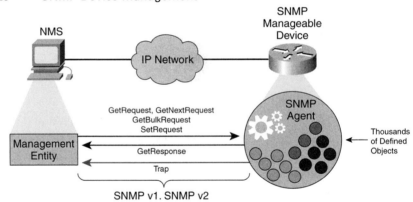

SNMP Security

SNMP is often used to gather statistics and remotely monitor network infrastructure devices. It
is a simple protocol which contains inadequate security in early versions. In SNMPv1, community strings, or passwords, are sent in clear text and can easily be stolen by someone eavesdropping on the wire. These community strings are used to authenticate messages sent between the
SNMP manager and the agent.

SNMPv2 addresses some of the known security weaknesses of SNMPv1. Specifically, version 2
uses the MD5 algorithm to authenticate messages between the SNMP server and the agent.

SNMPv1 lacks any authentication capabilities, which results in vulnerability to a variety of security threats. These include the following:

- **Masquerading**—Consists of an unauthorized entity attempting to perform management operations by assuming the identity of an authorized management entity

- **Modification of information**—Involves an unauthorized entity attempting to alter a message generated by an authorized entity so that the message results in unauthorized accounting management or configuration management operations

- **Message sequence and timing modifications**—Occur when an unauthorized entity reorders, delays, or copies, and later replays a message generated by an authorized entity

- **Disclosure**—Occurs when an unauthorized entity extracts values stored in managed objects, or learns of notifiable events by monitoring exchanges between managers and agents

Because SNMP does not implement authentication, many vendors do not implement set operations, thereby reducing SNMP to a monitoring facility. Whenever possible, configure filters or access lists to allow only specified hosts to have SNMP access to devices, as demonstrated in Figure 7-26 and the commands that follow. If SNMP is not in use, disable the service.

Figure 7-26   Securing SNMP Access

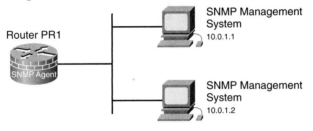

```
router(config)#snmp-server community string [ro | rw] [number]
```

For example:

```
PR1(config)#snmp-server community readSNMP ro
PR1(config)#snmp-server community ReadWritesnmp ro
PR1(config)#access-list 10 permit 10.0.1.1
PR1(config)#access-list 10 permit 10.0.1.2
PR1(config)#snmp-server community RWSNMP rw 10
```

SNMP Version 3 (SNMPv3)

SNMPv3 is an interoperable standards-based protocol for network management. SNMPv3 provides secure access to devices by a combination of authenticating and encrypting packets over the network. The security features provided in SNMPv3 are as follows:

- **Message integrity**—Ensuring that a packet has not been tampered with in transit

- **Authentication**—Determining the message is from a valid source

- **Encryption**—Scrambling the contents of a packet prevent it from being seen by an unauthorized source

SNMPv3 provides for both security models and security levels. A security model is an authentication strategy that is set up for a user and the group in which the user resides. A security level is the permitted level of security within a security model. A combination of a security model and a security level will determine which security mechanism is employed when handling an SNMP packet. Three security models are available: SNMPv1, SNMPv2c, and SNMPv3. Table 7-9 identifies what the combinations of security models and levels mean.

Table 7-9   SNMP Key Terms

Level	Auth	Encryption	What Happens
SNMPv1	noAuthNoPriv	Community String	Uses a community string match for authentication
SNMPv2c	noAuthNoPriv	Community String	Uses a community string match for authentication
SNMPv3	noAuthNoPriv	Username	Uses a username string match for authentication
SNMPv3	AuthNoPriv	MD5 or SHA	Provides authentication based on HMAC-MD5 or HMAC-SHA algorithms
SNMPv3	AuthPriv	MD5 or SHA DES	Adds DES 56-bit encryption in addition to authentication based on DES-56

The benefits of SNMPv3 include the following:

- Data can be collected securely from SNMP devices without fear of the data being tampered with or corrupted.

- Confidential information, for example, SNMP **Set** command packets that change a router's configuration, can be encrypted to prevent its contents from being exposed on the network.

Cisco devices such as router and switches support SNMPv3 message types, as shown in Figure 7-27, and the increased security capabilities, but many management software applications do not support SNMPv3. Applications that support SNMPv3 include MG-Soft MIB Browser, depicted by Figure 7-29, and SNMP Research International's CiAgent or Enterpol. HP OpenView can support SNMPv3 with the help of SNMP Research International extensions.

Figure 7-27   SNMPv3 Message Format

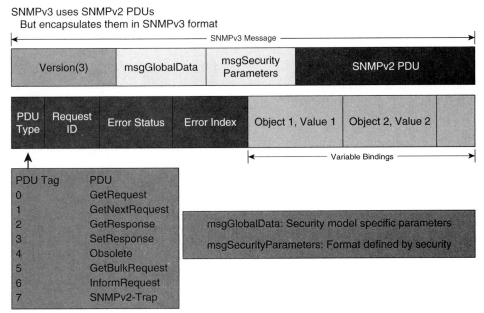

Figure 7-28   MG-Soft MIB Browser

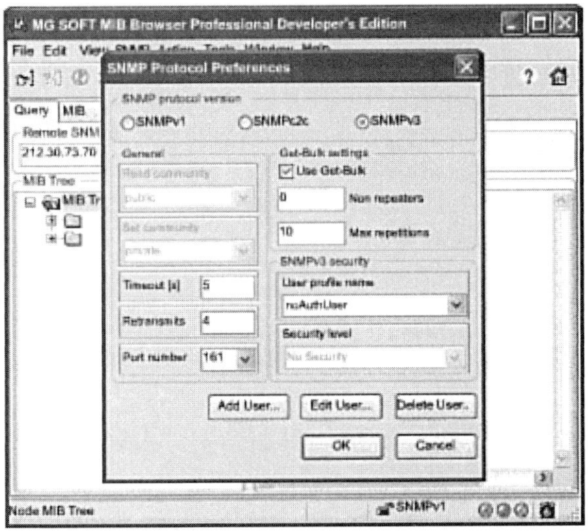

SNMP Management Applications

SNMP is a distributed management protocol. A system can operate exclusively as either an NMS or an agent, or it can perform the functions of both. When a system operates as both an NMS and an agent, another NMS might require that the system query managed devices and provide a summary of the information learned, or that it reports locally stored management information.

CiscoView is a graphical SNMP-based device management tool that provides real-time views of networked Cisco devices. These views deliver a continuously updated physical picture of device configuration and performance conditions, with simultaneous views available for multiple device sessions. In addition, CiscoView is designed for integration with leading network management platforms, such as HP OpenView Network Node Manager, to provide seamless and powerful methods of managing Cisco devices such as routers, switches, hubs, concentrators, and adapters.

To start CiscoView from a third-party NMS requires that the Integration utility has been installed. The following is a list of applications that manage SNMP:

- Windows:
  - 3COM Transcend Network supervisor
  - BTT Software SNMP Trap Watcher
  - Accton AccView/Open (SW6102)
  - Loriot
- Macintosh:
  - Dartware SNMP Watcher
- Linux:
  - snmptraplogd 1.0-6.1
  - NET-SNMP
  - Multi Router Traffic Grapher (MRTG)
- Also, a wide variety of retail packages include the following:
  - CiscoWorks (CiscoView)
  - SolarWinds Professional
  - HP OpenView

Some of these applications may not support SNMPv3. Figure 7-29 shows SNMP TrapWatcher, a downloadable freeware application.

Figure 7-29   SNMP Trap Watcher

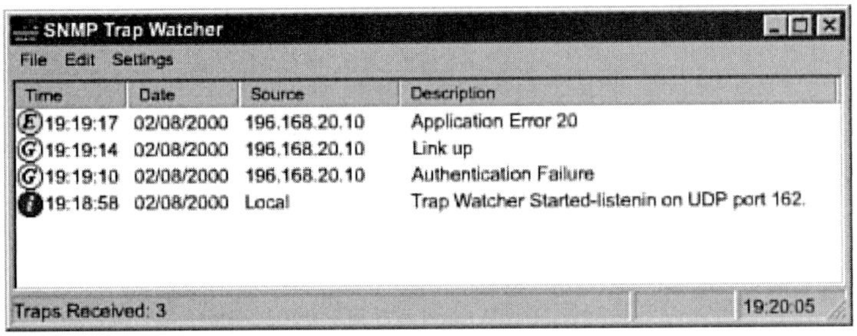

Configure SNMP Support on a Cisco IOS Router

SNMP can form the backbone of a network monitoring system and be an important tool for network security. There are four basic tasks to configure Cisco IOS SNMPv3.

Step 1.   Configure SNMP-Server EngineID using the following command:

```
Router(config)#snmp-server engineID [local engineid-string] | [remote ip-
    address udp-port port-number engineid-string]
```

The preceding command configures a name for either the local or remote SNMP engine on the router. Use the **no** form of this command to remove a specified SNMP group.

The parameters for this command serve the following functions:

— **local**—(Optional) Specifies the local copy of SNMP on the router.

— *engineid-string*—(Optional) Specifies the name of a copy of SNMP.

— **remote**—(Optional) Specifies the remote copy of SNMP on the router.

— *ip-address*—(Optional) Specifies the IP address of the device that contains the remote copy of SNMP.

— **udp-port**—(Optional) Specifies a UDP port of the host to use.

— *port-number*—(Optional) Specifies the socket number on the remote device that contains the remote copy of SNMP. The default is 161.

Step 2.   Configure SNMP-Server Group Names using the following command:

```
Router(config)#snmp-server group [groupname {v1 | v2c | v3 {auth | noauth |
    priv}}] [read readview] [write writeview] [notify notifyview] [access
    access-list]
```

The preceding command configures a new SNMP group, or a table that maps SNMP users to SNMP.

The parameters for this command are described as follows:

— *groupname*—Specifies the name of the SNMP group.

— **v1**—(Optional) The least secure of the possible security models.

— **v2c**—(Optional) The second least secure of the possible security models. It allows for the transmission of informs and counter 64, which allows for integers twice the width of what is normally allowed.

— **v3**—(Optional) The most secure of the possible security models.

— **auth**—(Optional) Specifies authentication of a packet without encrypting it.

— **noauth**—(Optional) Specifies no authentication of a packet.

— **priv**—(Optional) Specifies authentication of a packet and then scrambles it.

— **read**—(Optional) The option that allows you to specify a read view.

— *readview*—(Optional) A string (not to exceed 64 characters) that is the name of the view that enables you only to view the contents of the agent.

— **write**—(Optional) The option that allows you to specify a write view.

— *writeview*—(Optional) A string (not to exceed 64 characters) that is the name of the view that enables you to enter data and configure the contents of the agent.

— **notify**—(Optional) The option that allows you to specify a notify view.

— *notifyview*—(Optional) A string (not to exceed 64 characters) that is the name of the view that enables you to specify a notify, inform, or trap.

— **access**—(Optional) The option that enables you to specify an access list.

— *access-list*—(Optional) A string (not to exceed 64 characters) that is the name of the access list.

Step 3.   Configure SNMP-Server Hosts using the following command:

```
Router(config)#snmp-server host [host {traps | informs}] [version {1 | 2c | 3
[ {auth | noauth | priv}]] community-string [udp-port port] [notification-
type]
```

The preceding command configures the recipient of an SNMP trap operation. To remove the specified host, use the **no** form of this command.

The parameters for this command are described as follows:

— *host*—The address of the recipient for which the traps are targeted.

— **traps**—(Optional) Specifies the type of notification being sent should be a trap.

— **informs**—(Optional) Specifies the type of notification being sent should be an inform.

— **version**—(Optional) Specifies the security model to use.

— **1**—(Optional) The least secure of the possible security models.

— **2c**—(Optional) The second least secure of the possible security models. It allows for the transmission of inform and counter 64, which allows for integers twice the width of what is normally allowed.

— **3**—(Optional) The most secure of the possible security models.

— **auth**—(Optional) Specifies authentication of a packet without encrypting it.

— **noauth**—(Optional) Specifies no authentication of a packet.

— **priv**—(Optional) Specifies authentication of a packet and then scrambles it.

— *community-string*—A string that is used as the name of the community; acts as a password by controlling access to the SNMP community. This string can be set using the **snmp-server host** command, but it is recommended that you set the string using the **snmp-server community** command before using the **snmp-server host** command.

— **udp-port**—(Optional) Specifies a UDP port of the host to use.

— *port*—(Optional) A UDP port number that the host uses. The default is 162.

— *notification-type*—(Optional) Type of trap to be sent to the host. If no type is specified, all traps are sent.

Step 4.   Configure SNMP-Server Users using the following command:

```
Router(config)#snmp-server user username [groupname remote ip-address [udp-
    port port] {v1 | v2c | v3 [encrypted] [auth {md5 | sha} auth-password [priv
    des56 priv password]] [access access-list]
```

The preceding command configures a new user to an SNMP group. To remove a user from an SNMP group, use the **no** form of the command.

The parameters for this command are described as follows:

— *username*—The name of the user on the host that connects to the agent.

— *groupname*—(Optional) The name of the group to which the user is associated.

— **remote**—(Optional) Specifies the remote copy of SNMP on the router.

— *ip-address*—(Optional) The IP address of the device that contains the remote copy of the SNMP.

— **udp-port**—(Optional) Specifies a UDP port of the host to use.

— *port*—(Optional) A UDP port number that the host uses. The default is 162.

— **v1**—(Optional) The least secure of the possible security models.

— **v2c**—(Optional) The second least secure of the possible security models. It allows for the transmission of informs and counter 64, which allows for integers twice the width of what is normally allowed.

— **v3**—(Optional) The most secure of the possible security models.

— **encrypted**—(Optional) Specifies whether the password appears in encrypted format (a series of digits, masking the true characters of the string).

— **auth**—(Optional) Initiates an authentication level setting session.

— **md5**—(Optional) The HMAC-MD5-96 authentication level.

— **sha**—(Optional) The HMAC-SHA-96 authentication level.

— *auth-password*—(Optional) A string (not to exceed 64 characters) that enables the agent to receive packets from the host.

— **priv**—(Optional) The option that initiates a privacy authentication level setting session.

— **des56**—(Optional) The CBC-DES privacy authentication algorithm.

— *priv password*—(Optional) A string (not to exceed 64 characters) that enables the host to encrypt the contents of the message it sends to the agent.

— **access**—(Optional) The option that enables you to specify an access list.

— *access-list*—(Optional) A string (not to exceed 64 characters) that is the name of the access lists.

To display information about SNMP commands, use one of the following commands in EXEC mode:

```
show snmp engineID [local | remote]
show snmp groups
show snmp user
```

 Lab 7.4.5   Configure SNMP Messages on a Cisco Router

In this lab, you learn to configure SNMP. You install SNMP trap watcher and enable SNMP community strings. You then establish the contact and location of the SNMP agent. You also test the configuration. You then learn to limit SNMP to the inside server. Finally, you disable SNMP traps, and then disable SNMP and the associated ACL.

Configure SNMP Support on a PIX Security Appliance

The PIX Security Appliance provides support for network monitoring using SNMPv1 and SNMPv2c. The PIX supports traps and SNMP read access, but does not support SNMP write access.

SNMP Example

In Figure 7-30, the NMS uses a Get operation to request management information contained in an agent on host 172.18.0.15. Within the Get request, the NMS includes a complete object identifier (OID) so that the agent knows exactly what is being sought. The response from the agent contains a variable binding containing the same OID and the data associated with it. The NMS then uses a Set request to tell the agent to change a piece of information. In an unrelated communication, host 172.16.0.2 sends a trap to the NMS because some urgent condition has occurred.

Figure 7-30   Managing and Monitoring Network Devices from the Management Station Using SNMP

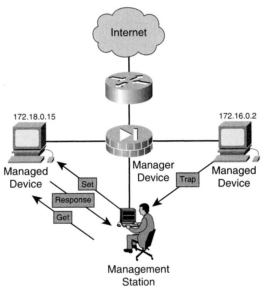

Enabling SNMP

The SNMP agent that runs on the PIX Security Appliance performs two functions:

■ Replies to SNMP requests from NMSs

■ Sends traps to NMSs

To enable the SNMP agent and identify an NMS that can connect to the PIX Security Appliance, follow these steps:

Step 1.   Identify the IP address of the NMS that can connect to the PIX Security Appliance using the following global configuration command:

```
snmp-server host interface_name ip_address [trap | poll] [community text]
  [version {1 | 2c}] [udp-port port].
```

Specify **trap** or **poll** to limit the NMS to receiving traps only or browsing only. By default, the NMS can use both functions.

SNMP traps are sent on UDP port 162 by default. The port number can be changed by using the **udp-port** keyword.

Step 2.   Specify the community string with the following global configuration command:

```
snmp-server community key
```

The SNMP community string is a shared secret between the PIX Security Appliance and the NMS. The *key* is a case-sensitive value up to 32 characters in length. Spaces are not permitted.

Step 3.   (Optional) Set the SNMP server location or contact information with the following global configuration command:

```
snmp-server {contact | location} text
```

Step 4.   Enable the PIX Security Appliance to send traps to the NMS with the following global configuration command:

```
snmp-server enable [traps [all | feature [trap1] [trap2]] [...]]
```

By default, SNMP core traps are enabled. If a trap type is not entered in the command, **syslog** is the default. To enable or disable all traps, enter the **all** option. For SNMP, each trap type can be identified separately.

Step 5.   Enable system messages to be sent as traps to the NMS with the following global configuration command:

```
logging history level
```

Syslog traps must also be enabled using the preceding **snmp-server enable traps** command.

Step 6.   Enable logging, so that system messages are generated and can then be sent to an NMS, with the **logging on** global configuration command.

 Lab 7.4.5   Configure SNMP Monitoring of the PIX Security Appliance Using ASDM

In this lab exercise, you enable the SNMP community string. You also establish the contact and location of the SNMP agent. You then learn to limit SNMP to the inside server. Finally, you test the configuration.

Summary

Upon completing this chapter, you should be able to recommend an appropriate approach to threat mitigation for network topologies containing either single or multiple switches. You should also be able to discuss the use of the SDM Security Audit Wizard to provide a comprehensive router security audit.

This chapter covered the enterprise management of VPNs. One of the greatest challenges to implementing large site-to-site and remote-access VPNs is management. The primary role of the Router MC is to manage site-to-site VPNs. The key topics associated with VPNs were explored, to give you a broad understanding of how Router MC operates to better manage large VPNs.

Finally, you learned about the SNMP. You learned how SNMP enables network administrators to manage network performance, find and solve network problems, and plan for network growth. You learned how SNMP, although simple, can be used effectively to assist the administrator in monitoring the network through its information-gathering capabilities.

Check Your Understanding

Complete all the review questions listed here to test your understanding of the topics and concepts in this chapter. Answers are listed in Appendix A, "Check Your Understanding Answer Key."

1. Give two different ways you can secure SNMP.

   a. Using community strings as root passwords

   b. Encapsulating the traffic in IPsec

   c. Using community strings as user passwords

   d. Removing the default community string from your router's configuration

2. Define and describe the Router MC.

   a. Router MC is a web-based application designed for large-scale management of virtual private network and firewall configurations on Cisco routers.

   b. Scalable to a small number of routers. Its hierarchical router grouping and policy inheritance features disable the configuration of multiple like routers simultaneously.

   c. Decentralizes the configuration of PKE and tunnel policies for multiple devices.

   d. Router MC enables deployment of VTP domains on groups of routers or individual routers.

3. Give two different ways to secure management of network infrastructure devices.

   a. Using SSH for management

   b. Using out-of-band management

   c. Using MD5 authentication on all host machines

   d. Using PGP when communicating to infrastructure devices

4. What are building blocks within the Router MC?

   a. Building blocks in the Router MC refer to network devices with transform sets.

   b. Building blocks are reusable, named, global components that can be referenced by multiple policies.

   c. Building blocks are local policies set by management.

   d. Building blocks aid in policy definition by increasing the need to define that component each time a policy is defined.

5. What are the two different security audit modes in SDM?

   a. One-step teardown

   b. Security Edit

   c. Security audit

   d. One-step lockdown

6. How many security models are available within SNMP?

   a. 3

   b. 2

   c. 1024

   d. 32

7. When should port security be used to mitigate the CAM table overflow?

   a. If the security zones are small enough

   b. When creating multiple VTP domains

   c. When BPDU guard is not effective

   d. If the security zones are large enough

8. Which of the following is not a primary Layer 2 vulnerability of the single security zone, one user group, multiple physical switches design?

   a. MAC spoofing

   b. CAM table overflow

   c. IP spoofing

   d. Spanning-tree attacks, in networks with multiple switches

9. Attacks that use Layer 2 to bypass VLAN restrictions are quickly gaining popularity. To lessen the effects of these attacks as much as possible, which of the following preventive measure is not recommended?

   a. Use IP permit lists to restrict access to management ports.

   b. Selectively use SNMPv3 and treat community strings like root passwords.

   c. Consider using DHCP snooping and IP source guard to mitigate DHCP starvation attacks.

   d. Never use a dedicated VLAN ID for trunk ports.

10. Which of the following is not a security threat to SNMPv1?

   a. Disclosure

   b. Modification of information

   c. Disclosure

   d. Port redirection

Upon completion of this chapter, you should be able to answer the following questions:

- How do I configure a Pix Security Appliance to perform in multiple context mode?

- How do I configure a PIX Security Appliance failover?

- How do I configure transparent firewall mode?

- What is PIX Security Appliance management?

Key Terms

This chapter uses the following key terms. You can find the definitions in the glossary at the end of the book.

security contexts   page 718

failover protection   page 718

transparent firewall mode   page 718

Secure Shell (SSH)   page 741

This chapter provides an overview and explanation of *security contexts*. You can partition a single PIX Security Appliance into multiple virtual firewalls, known as security contexts. Each context is an independent firewall, with its own security policy, interfaces, and administrators. Multiple contexts are similar to having multiple standalone firewalls. This chapter continues with a discussion of configuring and managing of security contexts.

A firewall system working properly provides network protection against many threats. What happens when a power loss occurs, or some other problem, to the firewall? Is network protection to be sacrificed to preserve network availability, or should the network be protected by cutting links until the problem is fixed? Fortunately, you can avoid these situations by establishing *failover protection* to keep the system going in the event of a firewall failure.

This chapter introduces you to the two methods of PIX Security Appliance failover: hardware failover and stateful failover. Instructions are given on how to configure each one of these in a network environment.

This chapter also provides a discussion of *transparent firewall mode*. A transparent firewall is a Layer 2 firewall that is not seen as a router hop to connected devices. Because the PIX Security Appliance is not a routed hop, a transparent firewall can easily be introduced into an existing network.

The last topic covered in this chapter is PIX Security Appliance management. You learn how to conduct system management via remote access, how to configure a PIX Security Appliance to support command authorization, and how to perform image and activation key upgrades on PIX Security Appliances. Because password recovery is important to the management of PIX Security Appliances, this chapter includes step-by-step instructions on how to accomplish password recovery.

Configure a PIX Security Appliance to Perform in Multiple Context Mode

You can partition a single PIX Security Appliance into multiple virtual firewalls, known as security contexts, as shown in Figure 8-1. Each context is an independent firewall, with its own security policy, interfaces, and administrators. Multiple contexts are similar to having multiple standalone PIX Security Appliances.

Each context has its own configuration that identifies the security policy, interfaces, and almost all the options that can be configured on a standalone PIX Security Appliance. If desired, individual context administrators can be allowed to implement the security policy on the context. Some resources are controlled by the overall system administrator, such as VLANs and system resources, so that one context cannot affect other contexts inadvertently.

Figure 8-1   Security Contexts

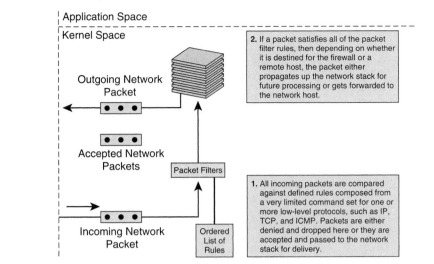

The system administrator adds and manages contexts by configuring them in the system configuration, which identifies basic settings for the PIX Security Appliance. The system administrator has privileges to manage all contexts. The system configuration does not include any network interfaces or network settings for itself. Instead, when the system needs to access network resources, such as downloading the contexts from the server, it uses one of the contexts that is designated as the admin context.

The admin context is just like any other context, except that when a user logs in to the admin context, for example, over an Secure Shell (SSH) connection, that user has system administrator rights and can access the system execution space and all other contexts. Typically, the admin context provides network access to networkwide resources, such as a syslog server or context configuration server.

Just a few situations that call for the consideration of using multiple security contexts are as follows:

- A service provider wanting to sell firewall services to many customers
- A large enterprise or a college campus wanting to keep departments completely separate

In the example in Figure 8-2, a service provider is using a single PIX Security Appliance divided into multiple contexts to deliver the same service as multiple standalone small PIX units. By enabling multiple security contexts on the PIX, the service provider can implement a cost-effective, space-saving solution that keeps all customer traffic separate and secure (and also eases configuration).

Figure 8-2   Multiple Contexts Example

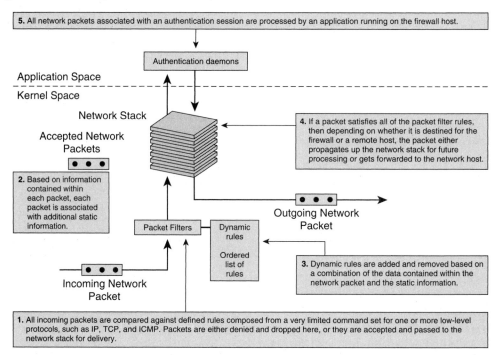

Each context has its own configuration file that identifies the security policy, interfaces, and almost all the options that you can configure on a standalone PIX Security Appliance. The firewall appliance also includes a system configuration that identifies basic setting for the appliance, including a list of contexts, as shown in Figure 8-3. Context configurations can be stored on the local disk partition on the Flash memory card or they can be downloaded from a TFTP, FTP, or HTTP(S) server.

Figure 8-3   Context Configuration Files

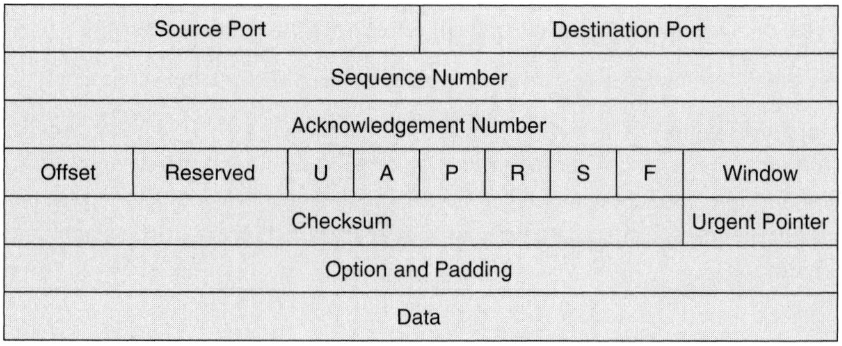

Source Port							Destination Port	
Sequence Number								
Acknowledgement Number								
Offset	Reserved	U	A	P	R	S	F	Window
Checksum							Urgent Pointer	
Option and Padding								
Data								

In addition to individual security contexts, the firewall appliance also includes a system configuration that identifies basic settings for the firewall appliance, including a list of contexts. Like the single-mode configuration, this configuration resides as the "startup" configuration in the Flash partition.

Each packet that enters the PIX Security Appliance must be classified so that the PIX can determine to which context to send a packet. The PIX checks for the following characteristics:

- Source interface, the source VLAN

- Destination address

The PIX Security Appliance uses the characteristic that is unique and not shared across contexts. For example, if a VLAN is shared across contexts, the classifier uses the IP address. A VLAN interface can be shared as long as each IP address space on that VLAN is unique, or overlapping IP addresses can be used as long as the VLANs are unique. The example in Figure 8-4 shows multiple contexts sharing an outside VLAN, while the inside VLANs are unique, allowing overlapping IP address.

Figure 8-4   Packet Classification

Source Port	Destination Port
Length	Checksum
Data	

Enabling Multiple Context Mode

When the PIX Security Appliance is changed from single mode to multiple mode, the PIX converts the running configuration into two files:

- A new startup configuration, stored in Flash, that comprises the system configuration

- admin.cfg, stored in the disk partition, that comprises the admin context, as shown in Figure 8-5

The original running configuration is saved to disk as old_running.cfg. The original startup configuration is not saved; so if it differs from the running configuration, you should back it up before proceeding.

Figure 8-5 Backing Up the Single-Mode Configuration

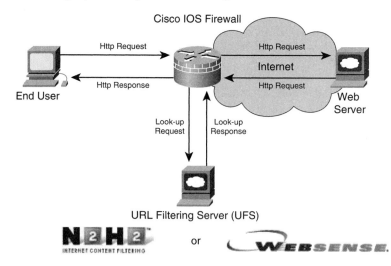

The Admin Context

The system configuration does not include any network interfaces or network settings for itself. When the system needs to access the network, it uses the designated admin context. If the system is already in multiple context mode, or if it is converted from single mode, the admin context is created automatically as a file on the disk partition called admin.cfg.

The admin context has the following characteristics (represented graphically in Figure 8-6):

- The system execution space has no traffic-passing interfaces and uses the policies and interfaces of the admin context to communicate with other devices.

- Used to fetch configurations for other contexts and send system-level syslogs.

- Users logged in to the admin context can change to the system context and create new contexts.

- Because the admin context is special, it does not count against the licensed context count.

- Aside from the significance to the system, it could be used as a regular context.

Setting the Security Context Mode

Use the **show mode** command in privileged EXEC mode to display the security context mode for the running software image and for any image in Flash memory. The mode will be either of the following:

- **Single**—Multiple mode disabled

- **Multiple**—Multiple mode enabled

Figure 8-6   Admin Context

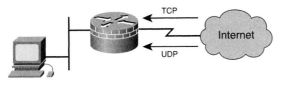

To set the security context mode to single or multiple, use the **mode** command in global configuration mode. In single mode, the PIX Security Appliance has a single configuration and behaves as a single device. In multiple mode, multiple contexts, each with its own configuration, can be created. The number of contexts allowed depends on the license.

When converting from multiple mode to single mode, an administrator might want to first copy a full startup configuration, if one is available, to the PIX Security Appliance. The system configuration inherited from multiple mode is not a complete functioning configuration for a single-mode device.

Configuring a Security Context

Use the **context** command in global configuration mode to create a security context in the system configuration and enter context configuration mode. The security context definition in the system configuration identifies the context name, configuration file URL, VLAN, and interfaces that a context can use.

If an admin context is not present—for example, if the configuration has been cleared—the first context that is added must be the admin context. After the admin context is specified, you can use the **context** command to configure the admin context.

Allocating Interfaces

To allocate interfaces to a security context, use the **allocate-interface** command in context configuration mode. You can enter this command multiple times to specify different ranges. For transparent firewall mode, you can use only two interfaces per context. If the PIX Security Appliance model includes a management interface, you can configure that interface for management traffic in addition to the two network interfaces. The same interfaces can be assigned to multiple contexts in routed mode, if desired. Transparent mode does not allow shared interfaces.

If you specify a range of subinterfaces, you can also specify a matching range of mapped names. Follow these guidelines for ranges:

- The mapped name must consist of an alphabetic portion followed by a numeric portion. The alphabetic portion of the mapped name must match for both ends of the range. For example, enter the following range: **int0-int10**.

- The numeric portion of the mapped name must include the same quantity of numbers as the subinterface range. For example, if both ranges include 100 interfaces, enter the following range: **gigabitethernet0/ 0.100-gigabitethernet0/ 0.199 int1-int100**.

Context Configuration Files

Note

Enter the **allocate-interface** command or commands before entering the **config-url** command. The PIX Security Appliance must assign interfaces to the context before it loads the context configuration. The context configuration might include commands that refer to interfaces, such as **interface**, **nat**, or **global** commands. If the **config-url** command is entered first, the PIX loads the context configuration immediately. If the context contains any commands that refer to interfaces, those commands fail.

Each context on the PIX Security Appliance has its own configuration file, which is specified using the **config-url** command. Until you enter this command, the context is not operational. As soon as you enter the **config-url** command, the context becomes operational.

The configuration files can be stored in a variety of locations. Note that HTTP(S) locations are read-only. Also, all remote URLs must be accessible from the admin context.

To identify the URL from which the system downloads the context configuration, use the **config-url** command in context configuration mode. Note the following:

- When a context URL is added, the system immediately loads the context so that it is running.

- The admin context file must be stored on the Flash memory dual in-line memory module (DIMM).

- If the system cannot retrieve the context configuration file because the server is unavailable, or the file does not yet exist, the system creates a blank context that is ready to be configured with the command-line interface.

- To change the URL, reenter the **config-url** command with a new URL.

  The PIX Security Appliance merges the new configuration with the current running configuration. Reentering the same URL also merges the saved configuration with the running configuration. A merge adds any new commands from the new configuration to the running configuration. If the configurations are the same, no changes occur. If commands conflict or if commands affect the running of the context, the effect of the merge depends on the command. Errors or unexpected results might occur. If the running configuration is blank, as in the case that the server was unavailable and the configuration was never downloaded, the new configuration is used.

  To avoid merging the configurations, clear the running configuration, which disrupts any communications through the context, and then reload the configuration from the new URL.

The running configuration that is edited in configuration mode, or that is used in the **copy** or **write** commands, depends on the location. When in the system execution space, the running configuration consists only of the system configuration. When in a context, the running configuration consists only of that context.

After you activate the context, you configure it much the same as PIX Security Appliance standalone device. Individual device configuration changes made in the context are stored in the configuration specified by the **config-url** command. You cannot change or view the location of the startup configuration file from within the context.

Managing Security Contexts

You can remove a context only by editing the system configuration. To remove a context, use the **no** form of the **context** command. The current admin context cannot be removed unless all other contexts are removed. To clear all context configurations in the system configuration, use the **clear configure context** command in global configuration mode. You can create or remove contexts without a reboot.

Use the **admin-context** command in global configuration mode to set the admin context for the system configuration. Any context can be set to be the admin context, as long as the context configuration resides on the Flash memory DIMM.

As an administrator, when you are logged in to the system execution space or the admin context, you can change between contexts and perform configuration and monitoring tasks within each context. Use the **changeto** command in privileged EXEC mode to change between security contexts and the system context.

Use the **show context** command to display all contexts. From the system execution space, you can view a list of contexts including the name, interfaces, and configuration file. In the system execution space, the PIX Security Appliance displays all contexts if you do not specify a context name.

The **show context detail** command reveals additional details about the context(s), including the running state and information for internal use.

Use the **show context count** command to list the number of contexts configured.

> **Note**
>
> If failover is used, a delay occurs between when the context is removed on the active unit and when the context is removed on the standby unit. An error message indicating that the number of interfaces on the active and standby units are not consistent might display. This error is temporary and can be ignored.

Configure PIX Security Appliance Failover

The failover function for the PIX Security Appliance provides a safeguard in case a PIX fails. Specifically, when one PIX fails, another immediately takes its place. In the failover process, there are two PIX units: the primary PIX and the secondary PIX. The primary PIX functions as the active PIX, performing normal network functions. The secondary PIX functions as the standby PIX, ready to take control should the active PIX fail to perform. When the primary PIX fails, the secondary PIX becomes active while the primary PIX goes on standby. This entire process is called *failover*.

Understanding Failover

There are two types of hardware failover:

- **Active/standby**—In active/standby, one PIX Security Appliance is the actively processing traffic while the other is a hot standby. All traffic flows through the active PIX. In the example in Figure 8-7, the active/standby scenario consists of two PIX units, the primary and secondary. When the primary fails, the secondary becomes active and processes all the traffic. The primary PIX becomes the standby unit.

■ **Active/active**—In active/active, an administrator logically divides a PIX Security Appliance into multiple contexts. Each PIX can process traffic and serve as backup units. In the example in Figure 8-7, each PIX is composed of two contexts. Under normal conditions, each PIX has one active and one standby context. The active context processes approximately 50 percent on the traffic load, while the other context is a standby unit for the other PIX.

In the active/active example in Figure 8-8, the primary PIX Security Appliance on the left fails, so the standby context in the secondary PIX becomes active. In the secondary PIX, both contexts are active, active/active. The PIX on the right handles 100 percent of the traffic using both contexts.

Figure 8-7   Hardware Failover: Active/Standby and Active/Active

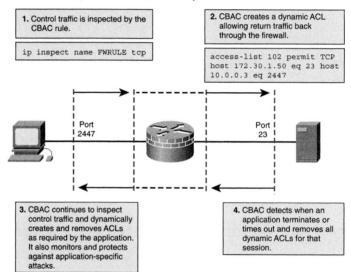

A failover occurs when one of the following situations takes place:

■ A power-off or a power-down condition occurs on the active PIX Security Appliance.

■ The active PIX Security Appliance is rebooted.

■ A link goes down on the active PIX Security Appliance for more than 30 seconds.

■ The command **failover active** is typed on the standby PIX Security Appliance, which forces control back to that unit.

■ Block memory exhaustion occurs for 15 consecutive seconds or more on the active PIX Security Appliance.

There are two types of failover:

- **Hardware failover**—Hardware failover provides hardware redundancy. When the active PIX Security Appliance fails, the standby PIX becomes active. All connections are lost, and client applications must perform a new connection to restart communication through the PIX. The disconnection happens because the active PIX does not pass the stateful connection information to the standby PIX. Failover messages are exchanged over a serial failover cable or a LAN-based failover connection.

- **Stateful failover**—The stateful failover feature passes per-connection stateful information to the standby unit. After a failover occurs, the same connection information is available at the new active unit. End-user applications are not required to do a reconnect to keep the same communication session. The state information passed to the standby unit includes information such as the global pool addresses and status, connection and translation information and status, the negotiated H.323 UDP ports, the port allocation map for Port Address Translation (PAT), and other details necessary to let the standby unit take over processing if the primary unit fails.

Depending on the failure, the PIX Security Appliance switchover takes from 15 to 45 seconds. Applications not handled by stateful failover then require time to reconnect before the active unit becomes fully functional.

Failover Requirements

The Cisco PIX Security Appliance 515/515E, 525, 535 and the Adaptive Security Appliance 5510, 5520, and 5540 can be used for failover. For failover to work, a pair of devices must be identical in the following requirements:

- Model number

- Software version

- Activation keys (DES or 3DES)

- Amount of Flash memory and RAM

- Proper licensing

One important factor for the PIX Security Appliance is failover licensing. The primary failover units must have an unrestricted (UR) license, whereas the secondary can have an UR or a failover (FO) license. The PIX failover (FO) license can be either an active/standby only or an active/active failover only. To perform active/active failover on a PIX with a failover license, the failover license must be an active/active-only failover license. A restricted license cannot be used for failover, and two units with FO licenses cannot be used in a single failover pair.

Note

Neither the Security Appliance 501 nor the Security Appliance 506E can be used for failover.

Failover Interface Test

Both the primary and secondary PIX Security Appliances send special failover hello packets to each other over all network interfaces and the failover cable every 15 seconds to make sure that everything is working. When a failure occurs in the active PIX, and it is not because of a loss of power in the standby PIX, failover begins a series of tests to determine which security appliance has failed. The purpose of these tests is to generate network traffic to determine which, if either, security appliance has failed.

At the start of each test, each PIX clears its received packet count for its interfaces. At the conclusion of each test, each PIX looks to determine whether it has received any traffic. If it has, the interface is considered operational. If one PIX receives traffic for a test and the other PIX does not, the PIX that did not receive traffic is considered failed. If neither PIX has received traffic, the tests then continue.

The following are the four different tests used to test for failover:

- **LinkUp/Down**—This is a test of the network interface card (NIC) itself. If an interface card is not plugged into an operational network, it is considered failed. For example, the hub or switch has failed, has a failed port, or a cable is unplugged. If this test does not find anything, the network activity test begins.

- **Network Activity**—This is a received network activity test. The PIX Security Appliance counts all received packets for up to 5 seconds. If any packets are received at any time during this interval, the interface is considered operational and testing stops. If no traffic is received, the Address Resolution Protocol (ARP) test begins.

- **ARP**—The ARP test consists of reading the ARP cache of the PIX Security Appliance for the 10 most recently acquired entries. The PIX sends ARP requests one at a time to these machines, attempting to stimulate network traffic. After each request, the PIX counts all received traffic for up to 5 seconds. If traffic is received, the interface is considered operational. If no traffic is received, an ARP request is sent to the next machine. If at the end of the list no traffic has been received, the ping test begins.

- **Broadcast ping**—The ping test consists of sending out a broadcast ping request. The PIX Security Appliance then counts all received packets for up to 5 seconds. If any packets are received at any time during this interval, the interface is considered operational and testing stops. If no traffic is received, the testing starts over again with the ARP test.

Failover Cabling

The failover PIX Security Appliances communicate failover information between the PIX units. The communications identifies the unit as primary or secondary, identifies the power status of the other unit, and serves as a link for various failover communications between the two units.

The majority of the failover communications are passed over dedicated failover links. There are three types of failover links, as shown in Figure 8-8:

- **Serial failover cable**—The serial failover cable is a modified RS-232 serial link cable that transfers data at 115 Kbps.

- **LAN-based failover cable**—PIX Security Appliance Software Version 6.2 introduced support for LAN-based failover, so a special serial failover cable is no longer required to connect the primary and secondary units. LAN-based failover overcomes the distance limitations imposed by the 6-foot length of the serial failover cable. With LAN-based failover, failover messages are transmitted over Ethernet connections. LAN-based failover provides message encryption and authentication using a manual pre-shared key for added security. LAN-based failover requires an Ethernet connection to be used exclusively for passing failover communications between two PIX units.

- **Stateful cable**—The stateful failover cable passes per-connection stateful information to the standby unit. Stateful failover requires an Ethernet interface with a minimum speed of 100 Mbps full duplex to be used exclusively for passing state information between the two PIX Security Appliance units. The stateful failover interface can be connected to either a 100BASE-TX or 1000BASE-TX full duplex on a dedicated switch or dedicated VLAN of a switch.

Data is passed over the dedicated interface using IP Protocol 8. No hosts or routers should be on this interface.

Figure 8-8   Types of Failover Cabling

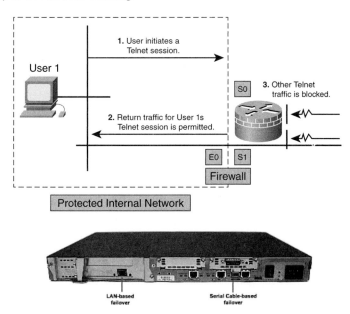

Serial Cable-Based Failover Configuration

In serial cable-based active/standby failover, two PIX Security Appliances are interconnected with a serial failover cable. One unit is the primary unit, the other is the secondary unit. In the top example in Figure 8-9, the primary PIX is active and passes traffic. The IP addresses of the outside and inside interfaces are 192.168.2.2 and 10.0.2.1. The secondary unit is standby and has interface IP addresses of 192.168.2.7 and 10.0.2.7.

In the bottom example in Figure 8-9, notice the primary PIX failed. In active/standby applications, the type of failover unit did not change. The primary unit is still the primary unit. What changed are the roles, active and standby, and the interface IP addresses. The secondary unit is now the active unit passing the traffic. The interface IP addresses were swapped. The secondary unit inherited the IP addresses of the primary unit, 192.168.2.2 and 10.0.2.1.

Figure 8-9   Serial Cable: Active/Standby Failover

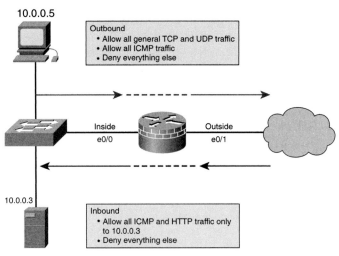

Complete the following steps to configure failover with a serial failover cable. Before starting this procedure, if the standby PIX Security Appliance is powered on, power it down and leave it off until instructed to power it on.

Step 1.   Attach a network cable for each network interface that is planned to be used.

Step 2.   Connect the failover cable between the primary PIX Security Appliance and the secondary PIX.

Step 3.   Configure the following failover parameters on the PIX Security Appliance:

- Failover

- Standby IP addresses

- Stateful failover interface (This is optional, for use with stateful failover.)

- Failover poll time (Optional)

When this configuration is finished, save it to the Flash memory of the primary unit.

Step 4.   Power on the secondary PIX Security Appliance.

Active/Standby LAN-Based Failover Configuration

LAN-based failover overcomes the distance limitations imposed by the 6-foot failover cable. With LAN-based failover, an Ethernet cable can be used to replicate configuration from the primary PIX Security Appliance to the secondary PIX. The special failover cable is not required. Instead, LAN-based failover requires a dedicated LAN interface and a dedicated switch, hub, or VLAN. You should not use a crossover Ethernet cable to connect the two units.

The same LAN interface used for LAN-based failover can also be used for stateful failover. However, the interface needs enough capacity to handle both the LAN-based failover and stateful failover traffic. If the interface does not have the necessary capacity, use two separate, dedicated interfaces.

LAN-based failover allows traffic to be transmitted over Ethernet connections that are relatively less secure than the special failover cable. To secure failover transmissions, LAN-based failover provides message encryption and authentication using a manual pre-shared key.

Complete the following steps to configure LAN-based failover:

Step 1.   Install a LAN-based failover connection between the two PIX Security Appliances. Verify that any switch port that connects to a PIX interface is configured to support LAN-based failover. Disconnect the secondary PIX.

Step 2.   Configure the primary PIX Security Appliance for failover.

Step 3.   Save the configuration of the primary unit to Flash memory.

Step 4.   Power on the secondary PIX Security Appliance.

Step 5.   Configure the secondary PIX Security Appliance with the LAN-based failover command set.

Step 6.   Save the configuration of the secondary unit to Flash memory.

Step 7.   Connect the PIX Security Appliance LAN-based failover interface to the network.

Step 8.   Reboot the secondary unit.

Active/Active Failover

Previously, under the active/standby failover model, only one PIX Security Appliance could be actively processing user traffic (while the other unit acted as a hot standby and prepared to take over if the active unit failed). Cisco PIX and ASA Security Appliances Software Release 7.0 adds the capability of active/active failover. When two devices are configured to function in active/active failover, both units can actively process traffic while at the same time serving as a backup for their peer unit.

The active/active failover feature leverages the virtual context feature. In the example in Figure 8-10, two PIX Security Appliances are configured for active/active failover, Unit A and Unit B. Each PIX is partitioned into two contexts, ctx1 and ctx2. In the two-unit active/active scenario, under normal conditions, there is one active context and one standby context per unit. In Unit A, ctx1 is active and passing traffic. Ctx1 in Unit B is in standby state. In Unit B, ctx2 is active and passing traffic while ctx2 in Unit A is in standby state. Under normal conditions, each unit handles 50 percent of the traffic. The PIX active/active cluster itself does not perform load balancing. It is the administrator's responsibility to engineer the network to route 50 percent of the traffic to each unit. This can be accomplished either statically or with the use of an upstream router to do load balancing on the traffic.

Figure 8-10   Active/Active Failover - 1

In Figure 8-10, Unit A ctx1 was active while ctx2 was standby. Unit B ctx1 was standby while ctx2 was active. Active/active failover logic enables each PIX Security Appliance to determine whether a failure is a context-based or unit-based failure. If an active context fails, the active context transitions to a failed state. In the peer PIX, the standby context changes from standby to active. For example in Figure 8-11, if Unit A interface e0 fails, the Unit A can determine the failure is a context-based failure. The Unit A can place ctx1 in a failed state. Unit A can communicate with Unit B the change in state of ctx1. Unit B can change the state of its ctx1 to active. After the state change, both contexts on Unit B are active and passing traffic. Failover can be context based or unit based. When a failure affects the whole unit, the peer unit can take over by activating any standby contexts and start processing 100 percent of the traffic.

Figure 8-11   Active/Active Failover - 2

Configure Transparent Firewall Mode

The PIX Security Appliance can run in two firewall settings:

- The routed setting based on IP address

- The transparent setting based on MAC address

Traditionally, a firewall is a routed hop and acts as a default gateway for hosts that connect to one of its screened subnets. A transparent firewall, on the other hand, is a Layer 2 firewall that acts like a bump in the wire, or a stealth firewall, and is not seen as a router hop to connected devices, as shown in Figure 8-12.

Figure 8-12   Transparent Versus Router Firewall

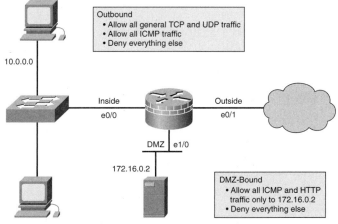

Transparent Firewall Mode Overview

The PIX Security Appliance connects the same network on the inside and outside ports, but each interface resides on a different VLAN.

Note the following:

- Transparent mode supports only two interfaces, typically an inside interface and an outside interface.

- Transparent mode can run both in single and multiple mode.

- The PIX Security Appliance bridges packets from one VLAN to the other instead of routing them.

- MAC lookups are performed instead of routing table lookups.

Because the PIX Security Appliance is not a routed hop, it is easy to introduce a transparent firewall into an existing network. IP readdressing is unnecessary. Maintenance is facilitated because there are no complicated IP routing patterns to troubleshoot and no Network Address Translation (NAT) configuration.

Even though transparent mode acts as a bridge, Layer 3 traffic, such as IP traffic, cannot pass through the PIX Security Appliance. The transparent firewall, however, can allow any traffic through using either an extended access list, for IP traffic, or an EtherType access list, for non-IP traffic. The only traffic allowed through the transparent firewall without an access list is ARP traffic. ARP traffic can be controlled by ARP inspection.

Note

The transparent PIX Security Appliance does not pass Cisco Discovery Protocol (CDP) packets.

Because the PIX Security Appliance is now acting a bridge, device IP addressing should be configured as if the PIX in not in the network. Layer 3 traffic must be explicitly permitted. Each directly connected network must be on the same subnet. A management IP address is required for connectivity to and from the PIX itself. The management IP address must be on the same subnet as the connected network as shown in Figure 8-13. Keep in mind that as a layer 2 device the PIX interfaces must be on different VLANs to differentiate the traffic flow. Do not specify the PIX Security Appliance management IP address as the default gateway for connected devices, because devices need to specify the router on the other side of the PIX Security Appliance as the default gateway.

Figure 8-13   Transparent Firewall Guidelines

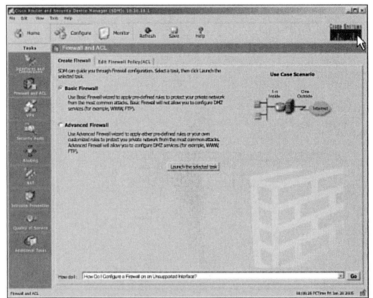

The following features are not supported in transparent mode:

- **NAT**—NAT is performed on the upstream router.

- **Dynamic routing protocols**—The administrator can, however, add static routes for traffic originating on the PIX Security Appliance. Dynamic routing protocols can be allowed through the PIX using an extended access list.

- **IPv6**—There is no fix for this limitation.

- **DHCP relay**—The transparent firewall can act as a DHCP server, but it does not support the DHCP **relay** commands. DHCP relay is not required because DHCP traffic can be allowed to pass through using an extended access list.

- **Quality of service**—QoS must be performed by upstream router.

- **Multicast**—The administrator can, however, allow multicast traffic through the PIX Security Appliance by allowing it in an extended access list.

- **VPN termination for through traffic**—The transparent firewall supports site-to-site VPN tunnels for management connections only. It does not terminate VPN connections for traffic through the PIX Security Appliance. VPN traffic cannot pass through the PIX using an extended access list, but it does not terminate nonmanagement connections.

Enable Transparent Firewall Mode

To view the current firewall mode, enter the **show firewall** command as follows:

```
Pixfirewall(config)#show firewall
Firewall mode: transparent
```

The mode will either be routed or transparent.

To set the firewall mode to transparent mode, use the **firewall transparent** command in global configuration mode as follows:

```
Pixfirewall(config)#firewall transparent
Switched to transparent mode
```

To restore routed mode, use the no form of this command.

For multiple context mode, only one firewall mode can be used for all contexts. The mode must be set in the system configuration. The **firewall transparent** command also appears in each context configuration for informational purposes only. This command cannot be entered in a context.

When the mode is changed, the PIX Security Appliance clears the configuration because many commands are not supported for both modes.

If a text configuration that changes the mode with the **firewall transparent** command is downloaded to the PIX Security Appliance, be sure to put the command at the top of the configuration. The PIX changes the mode as soon as it reads the command, and then continues reading the configuration that was downloaded. If the command is later in the configuration, the PIX clears all the preceding lines in the configuration.

A transparent firewall does not participate in IP routing. The only IP configuration required for the PIX Security Appliance is to set the management IP address. This address is required because the PIX uses this address as the source address for traffic originating on the PIX, such as system messages or communications with authentication, authorization, and accounting (AAA) servers. This address can also be used for remote management access. This address must be on the same subnet as the upstream and downstream routers. For multiple context mode, set the management IP address within each context.

Note

If a configuration already exists, be sure to back up the configuration before changing the mode. You can use this backup for reference when creating a new configuration.

ACLs

The transparent firewall as shown in Figure 8-14 can allow any traffic through using either an extended access control list (ACL), for IP traffic, or an EtherType access list, for non-IP traffic. For example, routing protocol adjacencies can be established through a transparent firewall. Open Shortest Path First (OSPF), Routing Information Protocol (RIP), Extended Interior Gateway Routing Protocol (EIGRP), or Border Gateway Protocol (BGP) traffic can be allowed through based on an extended access list. Protocols such as Hot Standby Router Protocol (HSRP) or Virtual Router Redundancy Protocol (VRRP) can also pass through the PIX Security Appliance. Remember that by default, no traffic is allowed through the firewall, regardless of the security level assigned to the interface.

To specify the traffic that should be allowed to pass through the firewall, use the following command:

```
pixfirewall(config)#access-list id [line line-number] [extended] {deny | permit} {object-
group network_obj_grp_id | protocol} source_address mask dest_address mask
```

For the transparent firewall in Figure 8-14, for example, you might enter the following:

```
Pixfirewall (config)#access-list ACLIN permit icmp 10.0.1.0 255.255.255.0.0 10.0.1.0
255.255.255.0
Pixfirewall(config)#access-group ACLIN in interface inside
Pixfirewall(config)#access-group ACLIN in interface outside
```

Figure 8-14   Configure ACLs to Permit Traversal Through the Transparent Firewall

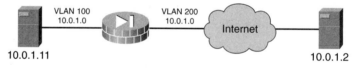

For features that are not directly supported on the transparent firewall, traffic can be allowed to pass through so that upstream and downstream routers can support the functionality. For example, by using an extended access list, DHCP traffic, instead of the unsupported DHCP relay feature, or multicast traffic such as that created by IP/TV can be allowed.

To configure an access list that controls traffic based on its EtherType, use the following command in global configuration mode:

```
Pixfirewall(config)#access-list id ethertype {deny | permit} {ipx | bpdu | mpls-unicast |
mpls-multicast | any | hex_number}
```

For instance, to allow IPX packets through the firewall, you would enter the following:

```
Pixfirewall(config)#access-list ETHER ethertype permit ipx
Pixfirewall(config)#access-group ETHER in interface inside
Pixfirewall(config)#access-group ETHER in interface outside
```

Because EtherTypes are connectionless, you must apply the ACL to both interfaces for traffic to pass in both directions.

The PIX Security Appliance can control any EtherType identified by a 16-bit hexadecimal number. EtherType ACLs support Ethernet V2 frames. 802.3-formatted frames are not handled by the ACL because they use a length field as opposed to a type field. Bridge protocol data units, which are handled by the ACL, are the only exception. They are (SNAP) encapsulated, and the PIX is designed to specifically handle bridge protocol data units (BPDUs).

Only one ACL of each type, extended and EtherType, can be applied to each direction of an interface. The same ACLs can be applied on multiple interfaces.

Predefined EtherTypes are as follows:

- IPX.

- BPDU.

- MPLS.

- Other Ethernet V2/DIX-encapsulated frames can be allowed based on their 2-byte EtherType.

- 802.3-encapsulated frames cannot pass through the firewall at this time.

ARP Inspection

ARP inspection prevents malicious users from impersonating, or spoofing, other hosts or routers. ARP spoofing can enable a man-in-the-middle attack. Configure static ARP entries using the **arp** command before enabling ARP inspection. When ARP inspection is enabled, the PIX Security Appliance compares the MAC address, IP address, and source interface in all ARP packets to static entries in the ARP table and takes the following actions:

Note

The management-specific interface, if present, never floods packets even if this parameter is set to flood.

- If the IP address, MAC address, and source interface match an ARP entry, the packet is passed through.

- If there is a mismatch between the MAC address, the IP address, or the interface, the PIX Security Appliance drops the packet.

- If the ARP packet does not match any entries in the static ARP table, the PIX Security Appliance can be set to either flood the packet out all interfaces or to drop the packet.

Monitor and Maintain a Transparent Firewall

The PIX Security Appliance learns and builds a MAC address table in a similar way as a normal bridge or switch. When a device sends a packet through the PIX, it adds the MAC address to its table, as shown in Figure 8-15. The table associates the MAC address with the source interface so that the PIX knows to send any packets addressed to the device out the correct interface.

Figure 8-15   MAC Address Table

Because the PIX Security Appliance is a firewall, if the destination MAC address of a packet is not in the table, the PIX does not flood the original packet on all interfaces as a normal bridge does. Instead, it generates the following packets for directly connected devices or for remote devices:

- **Packets for directly connected devices**—The PIX Security Appliance generates an ARP request for the destination IP address so that PIX can learn which interface receives the ARP response.

- **Packets for remote devices**—The PIX Security Appliance generates a ping to the destination IP address so that the PIX can learn which interface receives the ping reply.

The Original Packet Is Dropped

By default, each interface automatically learns the MAC addresses of entering traffic, and the PIX Security Appliance adds corresponding entries to the MAC address table. MAC address learning can be disabled if desired; however, unless MAC addresses are statically added to the table, no traffic can pass through the PIX. To disable MAC address learning, enter the following command:

```
Pixfirewall(config)#mac-learn interface_name disable
```

To reenable MAC address learning, use the **no** form of this command:

```
Pixfirewall(config)#no mac-learn interface_name disable
```

By default, each interface automatically learns the MAC addresses of entering traffic, and the PIX Security Appliance adds corresponding entries to the MAC address table.

Normally, MAC addresses are added to the MAC address table dynamically as traffic from a particular MAC address enters an interface. If desired, you can add static MAC addresses to the MAC address table by using the following command:

```
Pixfirewall(config)# mac-address-table static interface_name mac_address
```

One benefit to adding static entries is to guard against MAC spoofing. If a client with the same MAC address as a static entry attempts to send traffic to an interface that does not match the static entry, PIX Security Appliance drops the traffic and generates a system message.

You can view the entire MAC address table, including static and dynamic entries for both interfaces, or you can view the MAC address table for just a single interface can.

Two new **debug** commands have been introduced with regard to transparent firewall mode:

- **debug arp inspection**—Displays debug messages for ARP inspection

- **debug mac-address-table**—Displays debug messages for the MAC address table

Lab 8.3.3   Configure a PIX Security Appliance as a Transparent Firewall

In this lab activity, you configure a PIX Security Appliance is transparent mode.

PIX Security Appliance Management

This section deals with the management of the PIX Security Appliance. You examine managing Telnet and SSH access, command authorization, PIX Security Appliance password recovery, and Adaptive Security Appliance password recovery. This section ends with a discussion on file management and image upgrade and activation keys.

Managing Telnet Access

The serial console permits a single user to configure the PIX Security Appliance, but often this is not convenient for a site with more than one administrator. By configuring console access using Telnet, a maximum of 5 concurrent Telnet connections per context can be allowed, if available, with a maximum of 100 connections divided between all contexts.

Telnet access to the PIX Security Appliance can be enabled on all interfaces; however, the PIX requires that all Telnet traffic to the outside interface be IPsec protected. To enable a Telnet session to the outside interface, configure IPsec on the outside interface to include IP traffic generated by the PIX, and enable Telnet on the outside interface.

The following are the Telnet configuration commands:

- **telnet**—Specifies which hosts can access the PIX Security Appliance console using Telnet. Up to 16 hosts or networks can be specified. The syntax for this command is as follows:

```
Pixfirewall# telnet {{hostname | IP_address mask interface_name} {IPv6_address
    interface_name} | {timeout number}}
```

- **telnet timeout**—Sets the maximum time a console Telnet session can be idle before being logged off by the PIX Security Appliance. The default is 5 minutes. The syntax for this command is as follows:

```
Pixfirewall(config)#telnet timeout minutes
```

- **passwd**—Sets the password for Telnet access to the PIX Security Appliance. The default value is **cisco**. The syntax for this command is as follows:

```
Pixfirewall(config)#{passwd | password} password [encrypted]
```

For the network in Figure 8-16, host 10.0.0.11 on the internal interface is allowed to access the PIX Security Appliance console using Telnet with the password telnetpass. If the Telnet session is idle more than 15 minutes, the PIX closes it. The command sequence to enable this is as follows:

```
Pixfirewall(config)#telnet 10.0.0.11 255.255.255.255 inside
Pixfirewall(config)#telnet timeout 15
Pixfirewall(config)#passwd telnetpass
```

Figure 8-16   Configure Telnet Access

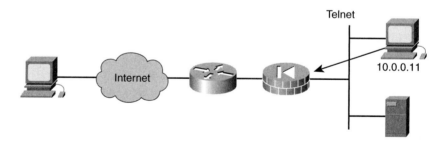

The following commands enable the administrator to view and clear Telnet configuration and Telnet sessions:

- **show running-config telnet**—Displays the current list of IP addresses authorized to access the PIX Security Appliance using Telnet. This command can also be used to display the number of minutes that a Telnet session can remain idle before being closed by the PIX.

- **clear configure telnet**—Removes the Telnet connection and the idle timeout from the configuration.

- **who**—Enables the administrator to view the IP addresses that are currently accessing the PIX Security Appliance console using Telnet.

- **kill**—Terminates a Telnet session. When a Telnet session is killed, the PIX Security Appliance lets any active commands terminate and then drops the connection without warning the user.

Managing SSH Access

Secure Shell (SSH) provides another option for remote management of the PIX Security Appliance. SSH provides a higher degree of security than Telnet, which provides lower-layer encryption and application security. The PIX supports the SSH remote functionality, which provides strong authentication and encryption capabilities. SSHv1 server was introduced in the PIX Security Appliance Software Version 5.2 and SSHv2 server was introduced in the PIX Security Appliance Software Version 7.0. SSH, an application running on top of a reliable transport layer such as TCP, supports logging on to another computer over a network, executing commands remotely, and moving files from one host to another.

Both ends of an SSH connection are authenticated, and passwords are protected by being encrypted. Because SSH uses Rivest, Shamir, and Adleman (RSA) public key cryptography, an Internet encryption and authentication system, an RSA key pair must be generated for the PIX Security Appliance before clients can connect to the PIX console. The PIX must also have an Advanced Encryption Standard (AES) or Triple Data Encryption Standard (3DES) activation key.

The PIX Security Appliance allows up to five SSH clients to simultaneously access the console. Specific hosts or networks that are authorized to initiate an SSH connection to the PIX can be defined, and how long a session can remain idle before being disconnected.

To establish an SSH connection to the PIX Security Appliance console, enter the username **pix** and the Telnet password at the SSH client. When starting an SSH session, the PIX displays a dot (.) on the console before the SSH user authentication prompt appears, as follows:

```
pixfirewall(config)# .
```

The display of the dot does not affect the functionality of SSH. The dot appears at the console when generating a server key or decrypting a message using private keys during SSH key exchange before user authentication occurs. These tasks can take up to 2 minutes or longer. The dot is a progress indicator that verifies that the PIX Firewall is busy and has not hung.

Note

The PIX Security Appliance SSH implementation provides a secure remote shell session without IPsec, and only functions as a server, which means that the PIX cannot initiate SSH connections.

In Example 8-1, an RSA key pair is generated for the PIX Security Appliance using the default key modulus size of 1024. Host 172.26.26.50 is authorized to initiate an SSH connection to the PIX.

Example 8-1   Generation of RSA Key Pair

```
pixfirewall(config)# crypto key zeroize rsa
pixfirewall(config)# write memory
pixfirewall(config)# domain-name cisco.com
pixfirewall(config)# crypto key generate rsa modulus 1024
pixfirewall(config)# write memory
pixfirewall(config)# ssh 172.26.26.50 255.255.255.255 outside
pixefirewall(config)# ssh timeout 30
```

Use the **show ssh sessions** command to list all active SSH sessions on the PIX Security Appliance. The **ssh disconnect** command enables the administrator to disconnect a specific session. Use the **clear configure ssh** command to remove all **ssh** command statements from the configuration, and use the **no ssh** command to remove selected **ssh** command statements. The **debug ssh** command displays information and error messages associated with the **ssh** command.

Command Authorization

Command authorization is a way of facilitating and controlling administration of the PIX Security Appliance. You can use three types of command authorizations to control which users execute certain commands:

- Enable-level command authorization with passwords
- Command authorization using the local user database
- Command authorization using Access Control Server (ACS)

The first type of command authorization, enable-level with passwords, allows the administrator to use the **enable** command with the *priv_level* option to access a PIX Security Appliance privilege level, and then use any command assigned to that privilege level or a lower privilege level. To configure this type of command authorization, the administrator must create and password-protect the privilege levels, assign privilege levels to commands, and enable the command-authorization feature.

The PIX Security Appliance supports up to 16 privilege levels, levels 0 through 15. You can create and secure privilege levels by using the following command:

```
pixfirewall(config)#enable password password [level level] [encrypted]
```

Access to a particular privilege level can be gained from the > prompt by entering the **enable** *level* command with a privilege-level designation and entering the password for that level when prompted.

The following command sequence shows how to create and access a privilege for the network displayed in Figure 8-17:

```
pixfirewall(config)#enable password Passw0rd level 10


pixfirewall> enable 10
Password: Passw0rd
pixfirewall#
```

Figure 8-17   Creating and Accessing Password-Protect Privilege Levels

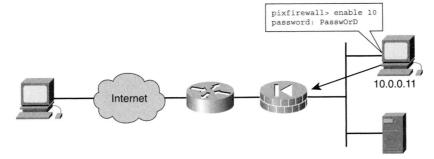

When inside a privilege level, the commands assigned to that level and commands assigned to lower privilege levels can be executed. For example, from privilege level 15, every command can be executed because this is the highest privilege level. If a privilege level is not specified when entering enable mode, the default of 15 is used. Therefore, creating a strong password for level 15 is important.

To assign commands to privilege levels, use the **privilege** command. Replace the level argument with the privilege level, and replace the command argument with the command to assign to the specified level. The **show**, **clear**, or **configure** parameter can be used to optionally set the privilege level for the **show**, **clear**, or **configure** command modifiers of the specified command. The **privilege** command can be removed by using the **no** keyword.

To configure user-defined privilege levels for PIX Security Appliance commands, use the following command:

```
pixfirewall(config)#privilege [show | clear | configure] level level [mode {enable |
configure}] command command
```

Use the **privilege** command without a **show**, **clear**, or **configure** parameter to set the privilege level for all the modifiers of the command. For example, to set the privilege level of all modifiers of the **access-list** command to a single privilege level of 10, enter the following command:

```
privilege level 10 command access-list
```

For commands that are available in multiple modes, use the **mode** parameter to specify the mode in which the privilege level applies. Do not use the **mode** parameter for commands that are not mode specific.

Next, to enable command authorization, use the following command:

```
pixfirewall(config)#aaa authorization command {LOCAL | tacacs-server-tag}
```

Consider the following example where privilege levels are set for the different command modifiers of the **access-list** command:

```
pixfirewall(config)#enable password Passw0rD level 10
pixfirewall(config)#privilege show level 8 command access-list
pixfirewall(config)#privilege configure level 10 command access-list
pixfirewall(config)#aaa authorization command LOCAL
```

The first **privilege** command entry sets the privilege level of **show access-list** to 8. The second **privilege** command entry sets the privilege level of the **configure** modifier to 10. The **aaa authorization command LOCAL** command is then used to enable command authorization. The user knows the highest privilege level to which the **access-list** command is assigned and also knows the password for that level. The user is therefore able to view and create ACLs by entering level 10.

To view the command assignments for each privilege level, use the following command:

```
pixfirewall#show running-config [all] privilege [all | command command |level level]
```

The system displays the current assignment of each command-line interface (CLI) command to a privilege level.

Use the **show privilege level** command with the *level* option to display the command assignments for a specific privilege level. Use the **show privilege command** *command* to display the privilege level assignment of a specific command. To view the user account that is currently logged in, enter the **show curpriv command**.

Lab 8.4.3a   Configure User Authentication and Command Authorization Using ASDM

In this lab exercise, you configure command authorization, local user authentication, and SSH.

 Lab 8.4.3b   Configure SSH, Command Authorization, and Local User Authentication Using CL

In this lab exercise, you configure and verify SSH operation. You then configure command authorization and local user authentication.

PIX Security Appliance Password Recovery

When configuring the command-authorization feature, do not save the configuration until it works as required. If an administrator gets locked out of the PIX Security Appliance, the administrator can usually recover access by simply reloading it. If the configuration has already

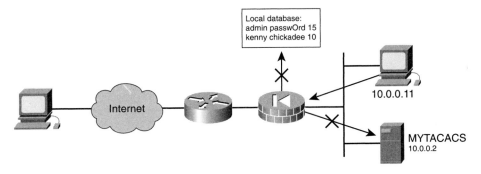

been saved, and authentication using the LOCAL database has been configured, but no usernames have been configured, a lockout problem is created. A lockout problem can also be encountered when configuring command authorization using a TACACS+ server if the TACACS+ server is unavailable, down, or misconfigured, as shown in Figure 8-18.

Figure 8-18   Lockout

If access to the PIX Security Appliance cannot be recovered by restarting the PIX, use a web browser to access http://www.cisco.com/ warp/customer/110/34.shtml.

This website provides a downloadable file with instructions for using it to remove the lines in the PIX Security Appliance configuration that enable authentication and cause the lockout

Note

If AAA has been configured on the PIX Security Appliance, and the AAA server is down, the PIX Security Appliance can be accessed by entering the Telnet password initially, and then **pix** as the username and the enable password for the password. If there is no enable password in the PIX configuration, enter **pix** for the username and press **Enter**. If the enable and Telnet passwords are set but not known, you must continue with the password-recovery process.

problem. If there are Telnet or console **aaa authentication** commands in PIX Security Appliance Software Versions 6.2 and later, the system also prompts to remove these.

The PIX Password Lockout Utility is based on the PIX Security Appliance software version that is running. Use one of the following files, depending on the PIX software in use:

- np63.bin (6.3 version)
- np62.bin (6.2 version)
- np61.bin (6.1 version)
- np60.bin (6.0 version)
- np53.bin (5.3 version)
- np52.bin (5.2 version)
- np51.bin (5.1 version)

A different type of lockout problem can be encountered when the **aaa authorization** command and *tacacs-server-tag* argument are used and the administrator is not logged in as the correct user. For every command that is entered, the PIX Security Appliance displays the following message:

```
Command Authorization failed
```

Note

Password recovery for PIX Security Appliance versions through 6.3 requires a TFTP server.

This occurs because the TACACS+ server does not have a user profile for the user account that was used for logging in. To prevent this problem, make sure that the TACACS+ server has all the users configured with the commands that they can execute. Also, make sure to be logged in as a user with the required profile on the TACACS+ server.

 Lab 8.4.4   Perform Password Recovery on the PIX Security Appliance

In this lab exercise, you learn to upgrade the PIX Security Appliance software image. You also learn to perform password-recovery procedures.

Adaptive Security Appliance Password Recovery

On the Adaptive Security Appliance, if the password is forgotten, you can boot the ASA into ROMMON by doing the following:

Step 1.   Press the **Esc** key on the terminal keyboard when prompted during startup.

Step 2.   Set the ASA to ignore the startup configuration by changing the configuration register using the **config-register** command. For example, if the configuration register is the default 0x1, change the value to 0x41 by entering the **config-register 0x41** command.

Step 3.   After reloading, the ASA loads a default configuration, and you can enter privileged EXEC mode using the default passwords.

Step 4. Load the startup configuration by copying it to the running configuration and reset the passwords.

Step 5. Set the ASA to boot as before by setting the configuration register to the original setting. For example, enter the **config-register 0x1** command in global configuration mode.

On the Adaptive Security Appliance, the **no** version of the **config-register** command prevents a user from entering ROMMON with the configuration intact. When a user enters ROMMON, the ASA prompts the user to erase all Flash file systems. The user cannot enter ROMMON without first performing this erasure. If a user chooses not to erase the Flash file system, the ASA reloads. Because password recovery depends on using ROMMON and maintaining the existing configuration, this erasure prevents the password from being recovered. However, disabling password recovery prevents unauthorized users from viewing the configuration or inserting different passwords. In this case, to recover the system to an operating state, load a new image and a backup configuration file, if available. The **service password-recovery** command, which enables password recovery, appears in the configuration file for informational purposes only—this command is on by default. When the command is entered at the CLI prompt, the setting is saved in nonvolatile random-access memory (NVRAM). The only way to change the setting is to enter the command at the CLI prompt. Loading a new configuration with a different version of the command does not change the setting. If password recovery is disabled when the ASA is configured to ignore the startup configuration at startup, in preparation for password recovery, the ASA changes the setting to boot the startup configuration as usual. If failover is used, and the standby unit is configured to ignore the startup configuration, the same change is made to the configuration register when the **no service password recovery** command replicates to the standby unit:

```
Ciscoasa(config)#no service password-recovery
WARNING: Executing "no service password-recovery" has disabled the password recovery
mechanism and disabled access to ROMMON. The only means of recovering from lost or for-
gotten passwords will be for a ROMMON to erase all file systems including configuration
files and images. You should make a backup of your configuration and have a mechanism to
restore images from the ROMMON command line.
```

File Management

Use the following command to display the directory contents:

```
pixfirewall(config)#dir [/all] [all-filesystems] [/recursive] [disk0: | disk1: | flash: |
system: ] [path]
```

The **dir** command without keywords or arguments displays the directory contents of the current directory.

The **pwd** command option displays the current working directory.

Example 8-2 demonstrates output from the **dir** command.

```
Example 8-2      Viewing Directory Contents
pixfirewall# dir
Directory of disk:/
1 -rw- 1519 10:03:50 Jul 14 2003 my_context.cfg
2 -rw- 1516 10:04:02 Jul 14 2003 my_context.cfg
3 -rw- 1516 10:01:34 Jul 14 2003 admin.cfg
60985344 bytes total (60973056 bytes free)
```

Use the following command to display the contents of a file:

```
pixfirewall# more [/ascii] | [/binary] [filesystem:] path
```

Example 8-3 demonstrates output from the **dir** command.

```
Example 8-3      Viewing File Contents
pixfirewall#more test.cfg
: Saved
: Written by enable_15 at 10:04:01 Apr 14 2005
xxx Version x.x(x)
nameif vlan300 outside security10
enable password 8Ty2YjIyt7RRXU24 encrypted
```

Use the **mkdir** command to create a new directory. If a directory with the same name already exists, the new directory is not created. To remove the existing directory, use the **rmdir** command. If the directory is not empty, the **rmdir** command fails. Use the **cd** command to change the current working directory to the one specified. If a directory is not specified, the directory is changed to the root directory. The syntax for the **mkdir**, **rmdir**, and **cd** commands is as follows:

```
pixfirewall#mkdir [/noconfirm] [dik0: | disk1: | flash:] path
pixfirewall#rmdir [/noconfirm] [dik0: | disk1: | flash:] path
pixfirewall#cd [dik0: | disk1: | flash:] path
```

To copy a file from one location to another, use the following command:

```
pixfirewall(config)#copy [/options] {url | local:[path] | running_config | startup-config}
{running-config | startup-config | url | local:[path | image | pdm]}
```

For example:

```
pixfirewall(config)#copy disk:my_context/my_context.cfg startup-config
pixfirewall(config)#copy disk:my_context/my_context.cfg running-config
```

When the PIX Security Appliance software is installed, the existing activation key is extracted from original image and stored in a file in PIX file system. On systems that support removable Flash media, when you log in to the security appliance during normal operation, you can copy the application software or Cisco Adaptive Security Device Manager (ASDM) software to the Flash file system from a TFTP, FTP, HTTP, or HTTPS server using the following command:

```
pixfirewall(config)#copy tftp://server[/path]/filename flash://filename
```

For example:

```
pixfirewall(config)#copy tftp://10.0.0.3/cisco/123file.bin flash://123file.bin
```

Image, configuration, and ASDM files can be installed in either internal or removable media, or both. Images stored on removable media are not booted by default, unless the **boot system** command exists in the startup configuration and points to that image.

For multiple context mode, the administrator must be in the system execution space. Make sure to have network access to the server:

- For single context mode, configure any interface, the IP address of the interface, and any static routes required to reach the server.

- For multiple context mode, first add the admin context and configure interfaces, IP addresses, and routing to provide network access.

In single context mode, or from the system configuration in multiple mode, the startup configuration, running configuration, or a configuration file by name on disk, such as the admin.cfg, can be copied.

To copy the configuration file from an FTP server, enter the following command:

```
pixfirewall(config)#copy ftp://[user[:password]@]server[/path]/filename[;type=xx]startup-
config
```

To copy the configuration file to an FTP server, enter the following command:

```
Hostname#(config)#copy {startup-config | running-config | disk0: [path/]filename}
ftp://[user[:password]@server[/path]/filename[;type=xx]
```

For example:

```
pixfirewall(config)#copy ftp://admin:letmin@10.0.0.3/configs/startup.cfg;type=an startup-
config
```

Image Upgrade and Activation Keys

The **show version** command enables the administrator to display the software version, operating time since the last reboot, processor type, Flash partition type, interface boards, serial number, or BIOS ID, activation key value, license type, such as R or UR, and time stamp for when the configuration was last modified, as demonstrated in Example 8-4. The serial number listed with the **show version** command is for the Flash partition BIOS. This number is different from the serial number on the chassis. When a software upgrade is obtained, the serial number that appears in the **show version** command will be needed, not the chassis number.

> **Example 8-4** Viewing Version Information
>
> ```
> pixfirewall#show version
> This machine has a Restricted (R) License.
> Serial Number:12345678
> Running Activation Key: 0xbd27f269 0xbc7ebd46 0x1c73e474 0xbb782818 0x071dd0a6
> Configuration has not been modified since last system restart.
> ```

The **copy tftp flash** command enables the administrator to change software images without accessing the TFTP monitor mode. The full syntax for this command is as follows:

```
pixfirewall(config)#copy tftp://server [/path]/filename flash:/filename
```

This command can be used to download a software image via TFTP with any PIX Security Appliance model running version 5.1 or later. The image that is downloaded is made available to the PIX on the next reload.

Be sure to configure the TFTP server to point to the image to be downloaded. For example, to download the pix611.bin file from the D: partition on a Windows system whose IP address is 10.0.0.3, access the Cisco TFTP Server **View > Options** menu and enter the filename path, such as D:\pix_images, where the image is located. Then, to copy the file to the PIX Security Appliance, use the following command:

```
pixfirewall#copy tftp://10.0.0.3/pix700.bin flash
```

Note

The TFTP server must be running when the **copy tftp** command is entered on the PIX Security Appliance.

The TFTP server receives the command and determines the actual file location from its root directory information. The server then downloads the TFTP image to the PIX.

Entering a New Activation Key

You can upgrade the license for the PIX Security Appliance using the following command:

```
Pixfirewall(config)#activation-key [activation-key-four-tuple | activation-key-five-tuple]
```

Before entering the activation key, ensure that the image in Flash and the running image are the same. You can do so by rebooting the PIX before entering the new activation key. The PIX also needs to be rebooted after the new activation key is entered for the change to take effect.

Enter the *activation-key-four-tuple* as a four-element hexadecimal string with one space between each element, or *activation-key-five-tuple* as a five-element hexadecimal string with one space between each element, as follows:

```
0xe02888da 0x4ba7bed6 0xf1c123ae 0xffd8624e
```

The leading **0x** specifier is optional. All values are assumed to be hexadecimal. The key is not stored in the configuration file. The key is tied to the serial number.

Use the **activation-key** command to enter an activation key. In this command, replace *activa-*

tion-key-four-tuple with the activation key obtained with the new license, as follows:

```
activation-key 0x12345678 0xabcdef01 0x2345678ab 0xcdef01234
```

After the activation key is entered, the system displays an indication that the activation key has been successfully changed.

Reload the PIX Security Appliance to activate the Flash activation key.

Upgrading the Image and the Activation Key

If the image is being upgraded to a newer version and the activation key is also being changed, reboot the system twice. After the key update is complete, the system is reloaded a second time so that the updated licensing scheme can take effect.

If an image is being downgraded, the PIX Security Appliance needs to be rebooted only one time, after installing the new image. In this situation, the old key is both verified and changed with the current image.

To view the current activation key, enter the **show activation-key** command. Table 8-1 shows error messages that might be returned in the output from this command, along with steps that you can take to resolve the errors.

Table 8-1   Troubleshooting the Activation Key Upgrade

Message	Problem and Resolution
The activation key you entered is the same as the running key.	Either the activation key has already been upgraded or you need to enter a different key.
The Flash image and the running image differ.	Reboot the PIX Firewall and reenter the activation key.
The activation key is not valid.	Either you made a mistake entering the activation key or you need to obtain a valid activation key.

Summary

Having completed this chapter, you should be familiar with virtual firewalls and how they allow the PIX Security Appliance to be separated into multiple, independent firewalls called security contexts. You should be able to discuss how security contexts can be managed and configured independently of one another.

You should also be familiar with methods of PIX Security Appliance failover, why it is necessary, and how to configure it. Failover options and their configurations were discussed. Also discussed in this chapter was the transfer of state information between failover peers. Hardware-based and stateful failover were discussed, and precautions about the type of interconnection between the peers were introduced.

This chapter also discussed the configuration of a PIX Security Appliance as a Layer 2, or transparent, firewall. You should be able to discuss the configuration and available features of a PIX Security Appliance that is in this mode.

Remote-access techniques for maintenance of PIX Security Appliances were introduced. This included the use of SSH and Telnet as access methods. The command-authorization system was discussed, along with how to assign users to levels and levels to command words.

Check Your Understanding

Complete all the review questions listed here to test your understanding of the topics and concepts in this chapter. Answers are listed in Appendix A, "Check Your Understanding Answer Key."

1. The system configuration does not include any network interfaces or network settings for itself. Instead, when the system needs to access network resources, such as downloading the contexts from the server, it uses one of the contexts that is designated as the admin context.

   a. True

   b. False

2. The security context mode has one of the following configurations:

   a. single or double mode

   b. single or multiple mode

   c. enabled or disabled mode

   d. static or dynamic mode

3. What are the two types of hardware failover? (Choose two.)

   a. Active/standby

   b. Primary/secondary

   c. Active/active

   d. Active/passive

4. A failover occurs when block memory exhaustion occurs for how many consecutive seconds:

   a. 5 seconds

   b. 10 seconds

   c. 15 seconds

   d. 20 seconds

5. What are the three types of failover links?

   a. Serial failover cable

   b. LAN-based failover cable

   c. Ethernet failover cable

   d. Stateful cable

6. A transparent firewall is a Layer 2 firewall that acts like a bump in the wire, or a stealth firewall, and is seen as a router hop to connected devices.

   a. True

   b. False

7. Which of the following is true of the transparent firewall mode?

   a. Transparent mode only supports two interfaces, typically an inside interface and an outside interface, and it can run both in single and multiple mode.

   b. Transparent mode only supports one interface, typically an inside interface, and it can run both in single and multiple mode.

   c. Transparent mode only supports two interfaces, typically an inside interface and an outside interface, and it can run only in the single mode.

   d. Transparent mode only supports one interfaces, typically an outside interface, and it can run only in the multiple mode.

8. The transparent PIX Security Appliance does not pass Cisco Discovery Protocol (CDP) packets.

   a. True

   b. False

9. The PIX Security Appliance supports up to how many privilege levels?

   a. 2

   b. 5

   c. 10

   d. 16

10. Password recovery for PIX Security Appliance versions through 6.3 requires a TFTP server.

    a. True

    b. False

Check Your Understanding Answer Key

Course 1

Chapter 1

1. C

   Network security goals are about protecting data. Protecting against denial-of-service attacks is one of the tools to help achieve the goals.

2. B

   Reconnaissance is the unauthorized discovery and mapping of systems, services, or vulnerabilities (see Figure 1-13). It is also known as information gathering and, in most cases, it precedes an actual access or denial-of-service (DoS) attack.

3. C

   A closed security model is most difficult to implement. All available security measures are implemented in this design. Administrators configure existing hardware and software for maximum-security capabilities in addition to deploying more costly hardware and software solutions such as firewalls, VPNs, IDSs, and identity servers. A PIX Appliance without access control lists or conduits will basically not allow anything in.

4. B

   The easiest hack involves no computer skill at all. If an intruder can trick a member of an organization into giving over valuable information, such as locations of files and servers and passwords, the process of hacking is made immeasurably easier.

5. A

   A Trojan horse differs only in that the entire application was written to look like something else, when in fact it is an attack tool. An example of a Trojan horse is a software application that runs a simple game on the user's workstation. While the user is occupied with the game, the Trojan horse mails a copy of itself to every user in the user's address book. The other users receive the game and then play it, thus spreading the Trojan horse.

6. C

   Access control is not a method of attack, as listed in the text.

7. B

   Confidentiality, authentication, and access have nothing to do with data. A company's data integrity is extremely important.

8. C

The security policy is developed with the security goals of the company in mind.

9. D

DoS attacks prevent authorized people from using a service by using up system resources.

10. A

A protocol analyzer is designed to analyze network traffic and examine packet contents.

Chapter 2

1. A and D

The steps of the Security Wheel are Secure, Monitor, Test, and Improve.

2. A

The CLI command **no cdp enable** turns off CDP.

3. B

Security procedures implement security policies. Procedures define configuration, login, audit, and maintenance processes. Security procedures should be written for end users, network administrators, and security administrators.

4. A

Telnet services would normally remain turned on to enable administrators access to the router via the network.

5. C and D

It is common practice and good network security procedure to change default names and passwords and to turn of any unnecessary services and applications.

6. C

Level 1 user EXEC and level 15 privileged EXEC is the right combination for the two default user levels on the Cisco IOS Software.

7. E

There are actually 16 privilege levels available. The levels run from level 0 to level 15.

8. D

The test component of the network security policy is used to test the effectiveness of the security safeguards in place, using various tools, such as port scanning, to identify the security posture of the network with respect to the security procedures that form the hub of the Security Wheel.

9. B

Type 5 uses an MD5 hash, which is much stronger. Cisco recommends that Type 5 encryption be used rather than Type 7 where possible. Type 7 encryption is used by the **enable password, username, and line password** commands.

10. A

Secure Shell (SSH) replaces Telnet to provide remote router administration with connections that support strong privacy and session integrity. This connection provides functionality that is similar to that of an outbound Telnet connection except that the connection is encrypted.

Chapter 3

1. B

All firewalls fall within three classes: appliance-based firewalls, server-based firewalls, and integrated firewalls.

2. C

The Cisco IOS Firewall features provide the following benefits: protection of internal networks from intrusion, monitoring of traffic through network perimeters, enabling of network commerce via the World Wide Web.

3. A

4. B

With PIX 501 Security Appliance Software Release 6.3, several product-licensing options are available. Each user license supports a maximum number of concurrent source IP addresses from the internal network to traverse through the PIX 501. Ten-user, 50-user, or unlimited-user licenses are available.

5. A

The PIX Security Appliance contains a command set based on the Cisco IOS Software and provides four administrative access modes: unprivileged mode, privileged mode, configuration mode, and monitor mode.

6. B

You can create configurations on a text editor and then cut and paste them into the configuration. The configuration can be pasted in one line at a time, or the entire configuration can be pasted at once. Always check the configuration after pasting large blocks of text to ensure that everything has been copied.

7. A

The first step in enabling NAT on a PIX Security Appliance is entering the **nat** command.

8. D

If the name is more than 16 characters long, the command fails.

9. A

The **show interface** command enables you to view network interface information. This is one of the first commands you should use when trying to establish connectivity.

10. B

The PIX Security Appliance supports up to eight additional physical interfaces for platform extensibility and security policy enforcement on publicly accessible services.

Chapter 4

1. B

TACACS+ uses TCP, RADIUS uses UDP.

2. B and C

TACACS+ and RADIUS are remote server protocols used by AAA.

3. B

RADIUS uses shared keys.

4. B

TACACS+ uses TCP, RADIUS uses UDP.

5. D and E

6. C

A network access server (NAS) operates as a client of RADIUS, as shown in Figure 4-2.

7. B

Authorization is the process that allows authenticated individuals access to resources.

8. A

TACAC+ features all but extensive accounting.

Chapter 5

1. A, D, and E

2. C

3. A

4. B

5. A, B, and D

6. B

7. B

Chapter 6

1. **D**

   After successful authentication, the user's authorization profile is retrieved, and the authentication proxy uses the information in this profile to create dynamic access control entries (ACEs) and add them to the inbound ACL of an input interface, and to the outbound ACL of an output interface if an output ACL exists at the interface.

2. **A**

   To use the authentication proxy with HTTPS, use the **ip http secure-server** command to enable the HTTP server on the router. Then use the **ip http authentication aaa** command to require the HTTP server to use AAA for authentication.

3. **C**

   Use the **show ip auth-proxy** command to display the authentication proxy entries, the running authentication proxy configuration, or the authentication proxy statistics.

4. **A, C, and D**

   Three types of authentication are available on the PIX Security Appliance: access authentication, cut-through proxy authentication, and tunnel access authentication.

5. **A**

   Configuring interactive user authentication is a three-step process. The three steps are as follows:

   Step 1. Specify a AAA server group. The administrator defines a group name and the authentication protocol:

   ```
   Pixfirewall (config)# radius-server key string
   ```

   Step 2. Designate an authentication server. The administrator defines the location of the AAA server and a key:

   ```
   Pixfirewall(config)# aaa-server server-tag [{if_name}] host ip_address
   ```

   Step 3. Enable user authentication. The administrator defines a rule to specify which security appliance access method to authenticate and which authentication server to reference:

   ```
   Pixfirewall(config)# aaa authentication [serial | enable | telnet |ssh | http]
   console server_tag [local]
   ```

6. **D**

   Use the **aaa new-model** global configuration command to enable the AAA access control system. Use the no form of this command to disable AAA. By default, **aaa new-model** is not enabled.

7. D

The **inactivity-timer** *min* command specifies the length of time in minutes that an authentication cache entry, along with its associated dynamic user ACL, is managed after a period of inactivity. Enter a value in the range 1 to 35,791. The default value is 60 minutes.

8. A

To set the authentication encryption key used for all RADIUS communications between the Cisco IOS Firewall router and the AAA server, use the **radius-server key** global configuration command.

9. C

Downloadable ACLs are supported with RADIUS only. They are not supported with TACACS+. Kerberos, LDAP, and PPP are protocols, not AAA servers.

Chapter 7

1. A, C, and D

The 802.1x framework defines three roles in the authentication process. The supplicant is the endpoint seeking network access. The supplicant may be an end-user device or a standalone device, such as an IP phone. The authenticator is the device to which the supplicant directly connects and through which the supplicant obtains network access permission. The authenticator acts as a gateway to the authentication server, which is responsible for actually authenticating the supplicant.

2. B

The authentication process consists of exchanges of Extensible Authentication Protocol (EAP) messages. This exchange occurs between the supplicant and the authentication server.

3. A

The authenticator is a network component that checks credentials and applies the access policy, usually implemented on a router, switch, or wireless access point. The supplicant is a software component on the user's workstation that answers the challenge from the authenticator.

4. C

Cisco has incorporated 802.1x and EAP into its Cisco Wireless Security Suite.

5. F

Cisco Secure ACS supports the following varieties of EAP:

- **EAP-MD5**—An EAP protocol that does not support mutual authentication

- **EAP-TLS**—EAP incorporating Transport Layer Security (TLS)

- **LEAP**—An EAP protocol used by Cisco Aironet wireless equipment. LEAP supports mutual authentication

- **PEAP**—Protected EAP, which is implemented with EAP – Generic Token Card (GTC) and EAP-MSCHAPv2 protocols

- **EAP-FAST**—EAP Flexible Authentication via Secured Tunnel (EAP-FAST), a faster means of encrypting EAP authentication, supports EAP-GTC authentication

6. C

EAP-TLS is an IETF standard that is based on the TLS protocol. EAP-TLS uses digital certificates for both user and server authentication.

7. A, B, and E

PEAP is an IETF draft RFC authored by Cisco Systems, Microsoft, and RSA Security.

8. A and B

The important policy decision regarding authentication in a Cisco Catalyst switch environment is which EAP authentication type to deploy. The two choices are EAP-MD5 and EAP-TLS.

Chapter 8

1. A

2. A

Context-Based Access Control (CBAC) intelligently filters TCP and UDP packets based on application layer protocol session information.

3. A, C, and D

When CBAC suspects an attack, the DoS feature can take the following actions:

- Generate alert messages

- Protect system resources that could impede performance

- Block packets from suspected attackers

4. A

DoS detection and prevention requires the creation of a CBAC inspection rule, which is applied to an interface. The inspection rule must include the protocols that will be monitored against DoS attacks.

5. A

Do not configure an ACL for traffic from the protected networks to the unprotected networks. All traffic from the protected networks is allowed to flow through the interface.

This helps to simplify firewall management by reducing the number of ACLs applied at the interfaces. This assumes a high level of trust for the users on the protected networks, and it assumes there are no malicious users on the protected networks who might launch attacks from the inside. Network access for users on the protected networks can be fine-tuned as necessary.

6. A

To turn on CBAC audit trail messages, which display on the console after each CBAC session closes, use the **ip inspect audit trail** command in global configuration mode.

7. B

Use the **ip inspect tcp synwait-time** global configuration command to define how long the software will wait for a TCP session to reach the established state before dropping the session.

8. B

Port-to-application mapping (PAM) enables administrators to customize TCP or UDP port numbers for network services or applications. PAM uses this information to support network environments that run services using ports that differ from the registered or well-known ports associated with an application.

9. D

Use the **no ip inspect** command to remove the entire CBAC configuration. This command also resets all global timeouts and thresholds to their defaults.

10. C

The timeout value in CBAC is configured in seconds.

Chapter 9

1. A

The Adaptive Security Algorithm (ASA) check applies to every packet of a communication. ACLs are only evaluated one time per connection. ACLs can work in both directions.

2. A and D

Higher to lower security; the ACL is used to restrict outbound traffic, and the source address argument of the **access-list** command is the actual address of the host or network.

Lower to higher security; the ACL is used to restrict inbound traffic, and the destination address argument of the **access-list** command is the translated global IP address.

3. A

PIX ACLs differ from ACLs on Cisco IOS routers in that the PIX does not use a wildcard mask like Cisco IOS routers. It uses a regular subnet mask in the ACL definition. As with Cisco IOS routers, the PIX ACL has an implicit deny all at the end of the ACL.

4. B

Use the **access-list id line** *line-num* command to insert an **access-list** command statement.

5. B

   - **Network**—Used to group client hosts, server hosts, or subnets.

   - **Protocol**—Used to group protocols. It can contain one of the keywords **icmp**, **ip**, **tcp**, or **udp**, or an integer in the range 1 to 254 representing an IP protocol number. Use the keyword **ip** to match any Internet protocol, including ICMP, TCP, and UDP.

   - **Service**—Used to group TCP or UDP port numbers assigned to a different service.

   - **ICMP-type**—Used to group ICMP message types that are permitted or denied access.

6. A

   MPF is configured via three basic commands:

   - **class-map**—This command is used to identify a traffic flow. A traffic flow is a set of traffic that is identifiable by its packet content. In Figure 9-18, voice traffic between Site B and Headquarters is an example of a traffic flow, as are remote-access VPNs that allow the system engineers and executives to access network resources at the headquarters.

   - **policy-map**—This command is used to associate one or more actions with a class of traffic. For example, in Figure 9-18, all voice traffic between Site B and Headquarters is provided low-latency queuing.

   - **service-policy**—This command is used to enable a set of policies on an interface. In the example in Figure 9-18, the voice priority queuing policy is applied to the outside interface.

7. A, B, and C

8. A

9. B

   SIP is an application layer control protocol used to set up and tear down multimedia sessions. These multimedia sessions include Internet telephony and similar applications. SIP uses RTP for media transport and RTCP for providing a quality of service (QoS) feedback loop. Using SIP, the PIX Security Appliance can support any SIP VoIP gateways and VoIP proxy servers.

10. A

    The PIX Security Appliance features full support for NAT of DNS messages originating from either inside or outside interfaces. This means that if a client on an inside network requests DNS resolution of an inside address from a DNS server on an outside interface, the DNS A record is translated correctly. It is no longer necessary to use the **alias** command to perform DNS doctoring.

Chapter 10

1. A

   In May 1999, the tool macof was released. It was written in approximately 100 lines of Perl code and was later ported to C language code and incorporated into the dsniff package. This tool floods a switch with packets containing randomly generated source and destination MAC and IP addresses.

2. A

   You can mitigate a CAM table overflow attack by configuring port security on the switch.

3. A

   A more administratively scalable solution is the implementation of dynamic port security at the switch.

4. B

   You can use this command to enter the maximum number of secure MAC addresses. If fewer secure MAC addresses than the maximum are configured, the remaining MAC addresses are dynamically learned.

5. A and C

   You can check the port security configuration in two ways:

   ```
   switch#show port-security interface interface_id
   ```

   This command displays port security settings for the switch or for the specified interface, including the maximum allowed number of secure MAC addresses for each interface, the number of secure MAC addresses on the interface, the number of security violations that have occurred, and the violation mode.

   ```
   switch#show port-security address
   ```

   This command displays port security settings for the switch or for the specified interface, including the maximum allowed number of secure MAC addresses for each interface, the number of secure MAC addresses on the interface, the number of security violations that have occurred, and the violation mode.

6. C

   Attackers can maliciously exploit GARP to spoof the identity of an IP address on a LAN segment. Typically, this is used to spoof the identity between two hosts or all traffic to and from a default gateway in a man-in-the-middle attack.

7. D

8. B

   DAI determines the validity of an ARP packet based on the valid MAC address-to-IP address bindings stored in a DHCP snooping database.

9. D

10. A

Course 2

Chapter 1

1. C

   Either technology can be implemented at a network level, host level, or both for maximum protection.

2. B

   The alarm action sends alarms to an internal or external log and then forwards the packet through.

   The reset action sends packets with a reset flag to both session participants if TCP forwards the packet.

   The drop action immediately drops the packet.

   The block action denies traffic from the source address of the attack.

3. A

   These categories are false alarms and true alarms.

4. A

   IDS signatures can be classified by how many packets it takes for the sensor to positively identify an alarm condition on the network. The two classifications are atomic signatures and compound signatures.

5. A

   Anomaly detection is also sometimes referred to as profile-based detection. With anomaly detection, the administrator must build profiles for each user group on the system. This profile incorporates typical user habits, the services normally used, and other relevant information.

Chapter 2

1. D

   Cisco IOS IPS can accurately identify, classify, and stop malicious or damaging traffic in real time and is a core component of the Cisco Self-Defending Network.

2. D

   When packets in a session match a signature, the Cisco IOS IPS can take any of the following actions, as appropriate: send an alarm to a syslog server or a centralized management interface, drop the packet, or reset the connection.

3. A

   The primary difference between Cisco IOS Software IDS and the new, enhanced Cisco IOS IPS is that an intrusion detection system monitors traffic and sends an alert when suspicious patterns are detected; whereas an intrusion prevention system can drop traffic, send an alarm, or reset the connection, enabling the router to mitigate and protect against threats in real time.

4. A

The performance impact of intrusion prevention depends on the number of signatures enabled, the level of traffic on the router, the router platform, and other individual features enabled on the router, such as encryption. Because the router is being used as a security device, no packet is allowed to bypass the security mechanisms. The IPS process in the router sits directly in the packet path and searches each packet for signature matches.

5. A

SDEE uses a pull mechanism, meaning that requests come from the network management application and the IPS/IPS router responds. SDEE uses HTTP and XML to provide a standardized interface.

6. B

To use SDEE, the HTTP server must be enabled with the **ip http server** command. If the HTTP server is not enabled, the router cannot respond to the SDEE clients because it cannot not see the requests.

7. B

To display IPS information such as configured sessions and signatures, use the **show ip ips** command in privileged EXEC mode.

8. C

When configured, Mail Guard allows only seven SMTP commands as specified in RFC 821 section 4.5.1: HELO, MAIL, RCPT, DATA, RSET, NOOP, and QUIT.

9. B

FragGuard and Virtual Reassembly perform full reassembly of all ICMP error messages and virtual reassembly of the remaining IP fragments that are routed through the Pix Security Appliance. They use syslog to log any fragment.

10. A

The **shun** feature of the PIX Security Appliance allows a PIX, when combined with a Cisco IDS sensor, to dynamically respond to an attacking host by preventing new connections and disallowing packets from any existing connection.

Chapter 3

1. B

2. A

3. A

4. A

In client-initiated VPNs, remote users use a VPN client or web browser to establish a secure tunnel across a public network to the enterprise.

In NAS-initiated VPNs, remote users dial in to an ISP NAS. The NAS establishes a secure tunnel to the enterprise private network that might support multiple sessions initiated by remote users.

5. B

There is no need for either a software or hardware client. WebVPN provides easy access to a broad range of enterprise applications, including web resources, web-enabled applications, NT/Active Directory (AD) file shares that are web enabled, e-mail, and other TCP-based applications from any computer connected to the Internet that can reach HTTP(S) Internet sites.

6. A

7. B

IPsec supports IP unicast traffic only.

8. A

IPsec is a framework of security protocols and algorithms used to secure data at the network layer

9. C

IPsec consists of two protocols. The first protocol is Encapsulating Security Payload (ESP). It encapsulates the data, but does not provide protection to the outer headers. ESP encrypts the payload for data confidentiality. The second protocol is Authentication Header (AH). The AH protocol provides protection to the entire datagram by embedding the header in the data. The AH verifies the integrity of the IP datagram.

10. A

Chapter 4

1. B

The main limitation of pre-shared secret authentication is the requirement to base the preshared secret on the IP address of the remote peer, not its IKE identity. This can impose significant problems in an environment with dynamic peer addresses such as dialup users, DHCP users, and so on.

2. A

Ensure that the ACLs on perimeter devices are compatible with IPsec. Ensure that perimeter routers and the IPsec peer router interfaces permit IPsec traffic. Use the **show access-lists** command for this step.

3. D

   See Table 4-1.

4. B

   Authentication Header (AH) is rarely used because authentication is now available with the **esp-sha-hmac** and **esp-md5-hmac** transforms. AH is also not compatible with NAT or PAT.

5. A

   ISAKMP uses UDP port 500. ESP is assigned IP protocol number 50, and AH is assigned IP protocol number 51.

6. C

   ISAKMP peers negotiate acceptable ISAKMP policies before agreeing upon the SA to be used for IPsec. When the ISAKMP negotiation begins in IKE Phase 1 main mode, ISAKMP looks for an ISAKMP policy that is the same on both peers. The peer that initiates the negotiation sends all its policies to the remote peer, and the remote peer tries to find a match with its policies.

7. A

8. B

   Cisco recommends that for every crypto access list specified for a static crypto map entry that is defined at the local peer a symmetrical, or mirror image, crypto access list be configured at the remote peer. This ensures that traffic that has IPsec protection applied locally can be processed correctly at the remote peer.

9. A

   You can apply only one crypto map set to a single interface.

10. D

   Use the **show crypto ipsec sa** EXEC command to view the settings used by current security associations.

Chapter 5

1. E

   The router does not store server certificates.

2. C

   To specify that certificates and CRLs should not be stored locally on the router, but should be retrieved when required, turn on query mode by using the **crypto ca certificate query** command in global configuration mode.

3. A

On certificates, there is a valid from and to date and time. When the certificate is validated by the router, the router determines whether its system clock falls within the validity range. If it does, the certificate is valid. If not, the certificate is deemed invalid or expired.

4. A

RSA keys are generated in pairs consisting of one public RSA key and one private RSA key.

5. A

6. C

To delete all RSA keys from the router, use the **crypto key zeroize rsa** command in global configuration mode.

7. C

8. B

Display the configured transform sets by using the **show crypto IPsec transform set** command.

9. A

The PIX Security Appliance generates an RSA public and private key pair to enable RSA encryption.

10. A

Chapter 6

1. E

The Cisco Easy VPN Remote feature provides for automatic management of the following details:

- Negotiating tunnel parameters, such as addresses, algorithms, and lifetime

- Establishing tunnels according to the parameters that were set

- Automatically creating the NAT or PAT and associated access lists that are needed, if any

- Authenticating users, that is, ensuring that users are who they say they are by way of usernames, group names, and passwords

- Managing security keys for encryption and decryption

- Authenticating, encrypting, and decrypting data through the tunnel

2. A

The Cisco Easy VPN consists of two components: the Cisco Easy VPN Server and the Cisco Easy VPN Remote features.

3. B

The Unity Protocol supports only Internet Security Association Key Management Protocol (ISAKMP) policies that use group 2 (1024-bit Diffie-Hellman) Internet Key Exchange (IKE) negotiation, so the Easy VPN Server being used with the Cisco Easy VPN Remote feature must be configured for a group 2 ISAKMP policy.

4. A

The first step when preparing the Easy VPN Server router for remote access is to establish a AAA section in the configuration file using the **aaa new-model** command in global configuration mode.

5. A

Enable RRI using the **reverse-route** command, as shown in Figure 6-21. This command has no arguments or keywords.

6. B

Dead peer detection (DPD) is a keepalive scheme that allows the router to query the liveliness of its IKE peer. There are two options for DPD: periodic and on-demand.

7. D

The Cisco Easy VPN Remote feature supports three modes of operation: client mode, network extension mode, network extension plus mode.

8. B

To verify or text the Easy VPN configuration, you use the **show crypto ipsec client ezvpn** command (for the configuration shown in Figure 6-45).

9. A

Specify which transform sets are allowed for the crypto map entry using the **crypto ipsec transform-set** command, as shown in Figure 6-58. When using this command, be sure to list multiple transform sets in order of priority, with the highest priority first. Note that this is the only configuration statement required in dynamic crypto map entries.

10. A

The NAT 0 **access-list** command defines which traffic is encrypted but not translated. In Figure 6-65, traffic sourced from network 10.0.0.0/24 and destined for a host on 10.0.11.0/24 network is encrypted. The remaining traffic is translated, using NAT, to the IP address of the outside interface and then transmitted in clear text.

Chapter 7

1. A and B

The SNMP community string is a shared secret between devices. Encapsulating traffic will make it more time-consuming for an attacker with the intent to sniff network traffic.

2. A

The Router MC can be defined as follows:

- A web-based application for the setup and maintenance of VPN connections using Cisco VPN routers.

- Centralizes the configuration of IKE and tunnel policies for multiple devices.

- Scalable to a large number of VPN routers.

- Router MC is a web-based application designed for large-scale management of virtual private network (VPN) and firewall configurations on Cisco routers.

3. A and B

Using SSH or an out-of-band management system helps avoid the use of clear-text management protocols such as Telnet or SNMPv1.

4. B

Building blocks in the Router MC refer to network groups and transform sets. Building blocks are reusable, named, global components that can be referenced by multiple policies. When referenced, a building block is incorporated as an integral component of the policy.

5. C and D

Security audit contains two modes:

- **Security audit**—Examines router configuration and displays the Report Card screen, which shows a list of possible security problems. The administrator can then pick and choose which vulnerability to lock down.

- **One-step lockdown**—Initiates the automatic lockdown using recommended settings.

6. A

The security features provided in SNMPv3 are as follows:

- **Message integrity**—Ensuring that a packet has not been tampered with in transit

- **Authentication**—Determining the message is from a valid source

- **Encryption**—Scrambling the contents of a packet prevent it from being seen by an unauthorized source

7. A

You can use the port security feature to restrict input to an interface by limiting and identifying MAC addresses of the workstations that are allowed to access the port. When you assign secure MAC addresses to a secure port, the port does not forward packets with source addresses outside the group of defined addresses. If you limit the number of secure MAC addresses to one and assign a single secure MAC address, the workstation attached to that port is ensured the full bandwidth of the port. However, if the security zone is large, this will become too time-consuming.

8. C

IP spoofing is a technique used to gain unauthorized access to computers, whereby the intruder sends messages to a computer with an IP address indicating that the message is coming from a trusted host. To engage in IP spoofing, a hacker must first use a variety of techniques to find an IP address of a trusted host and then modify the packet headers so that it appears that the packets are coming from that host. This is a Layer 3 and not Layer 2 vulnerability.

9. D

Mitigating VLAN hopping attacks requires several modifications to the VLAN configuration. One of the more important elements is to use dedicated VLAN IDs for all trunk ports.

10. D

In SNMPv1, community strings, or passwords, are sent in clear text and can easily be stolen by someone eavesdropping on the wire. These community strings are used to authenticate messages sent between the SNMP manager and the agent. SNMPv1 lacks any authentication capabilities, which results in vulnerability to a variety of security threats, including the following:

- Masquerading

- Modification of information

- Message sequence and timing modifications

- Disclosure

Chapter 8

1. A

2. B

Use the **show mode** command in privileged EXEC mode to show the security context mode for the running software image and for any image in Flash memory. The mode will be either single (in which case, multiple mode is disabled) or multiple (in which case, multiple is enabled).

3. A and C

There are two types of hardware failover: active/standby and active/active.

4. C

Block memory exhaustion occurs for 15 consecutive seconds or more on the active PIX Security Appliance.

5. A, B, and D

There are three types of failover links: serial failover cable, LAN-based failover cable, and stateful cable.

6. B

    A transparent firewall is a Layer 2 firewall that acts like a bump in the wire, or a stealth firewall, and is not seen as a router hop to connected devices.

7. A

    Transparent mode only supports two interfaces, typically an inside interface and an outside interface. Transparent mode can run both in single and multiple mode. The PIX Security Appliance bridges packets from one VLAN to the other instead of routing them. MAC lookups are performed instead of routing table lookups.

8. A

9. D

    The PIX Security Appliance supports up to 16 privilege levels, levels 0 through 15.

10. A

802.1x   An IEEE standard for port-based Network Admission Control, 802.1x is part of the IEEE 802 (802.1) group of protocols. It provides authentication to devices attached to a LAN port, establishing a point-to-point connection or preventing access from that port if authentication fails. It is used for certain closed wireless access points and is based on EAP, the Extensible Authentication Protocol.

access control   Limiting the flow of information from the resources of a system to only the authorized persons or systems in the network.

access control element (ACE)   Contain a number of values that are matched against the contents of an access control list.

access control lists (ACLs)   List kept by routers to control access to or from the router for a number of services. Can be used for security purposes by denying entry to a host accessing the network with a certain IP address, through a certain port, or through other upper-layer protocols.

Adaptive Security Algorithm (ASA)   A Cisco proprietary algorithm that provides stateful inspection firewall services by tracking the state of all authorized network communications and by preventing unauthorized network access.

Address Resolution Protocol (ARP)   The Address Resolution Protocol is the method for finding a host's MAC address when only its IP address is known. The sender broadcasts an ARP packet containing the Internet address of another host and waits for it to respond with its MAC address, which is then stored in a cache for later use.

anomaly detection   An anomaly-based intrusion detection system is a system for detecting computer intrusions and misuse by monitoring system activity and classifying it as either normal or anomalous. The classification is based on heuristics or rules, rather than patterns or signatures, and detects any type of misuse that falls outside normal system operation. This is contrast to signature-based systems, which can detect only those attacks for which a signature has previously been created. To determine what attack traffic is, the system must be taught to recognize normal system activity. This can be accomplished in several ways, most often with artificial intelligence types of techniques. Systems using neural networks have been used to great effect. Another method is to define what normal usage of the system comprises using a strict mathematical model and to flag any deviation from this as an attack.

asymmetric encryption   The term *asymmetric key cryptography* is a synonym for public key cryptography in most cases. It can use either the same algorithm or different but complementary algorithms to scramble and unscramble data. The required public key and a private key differ but are related.

attack guards   These are special techniques applied to the PIX Security Appliance that can prevent many problems that surround popular services such as e-mail and DNS.

Authentication Header (AH)   IPsec is a standard for securing IP communications by encrypting/authenticating all IP packets. IPsec provides security at the network layer. IPsec is a set of cryptographic protocols for (1) securing packet flows and (2) key exchange. Of the former, there are two: Encapsulating Security Payload (ESP) provides authentication, data confidentiality, and message integrity; Authentication Header (AH) provides authentication and message integrity but does not offer confidentiality. Originally, AH was only used for integrity, and ESP was used only for encryption; authentication functionality was added subsequently to ESP. Currently, only one key exchange protocol is defined: the Internet Key Exchange protocol.

authentication proxy   The process of having the access policy of the user downloaded from the authentication server and applied to the router interface. The policy determines what the user can access either inbound or outbound.

authentication, authorization, and accounting (AAA) architecture   In computer security, AAA stands for authentication, authorization, and accounting protocols:

Authentication   Authentication refers to the confirmation that a user who is requesting services is a valid user of the network services requested. Authentication is accomplished via the presentation of an identity and credentials. Examples of types of credentials are passwords, one-time tokens, digital certificates, and phone numbers (calling/called).

Authorization   Authorization refers to the granting of specific types of service (including "no service") to a user, based on authentication, what services the user is requesting, and the current system state. Authorization may be based on restrictions (for example, time-of-day restrictions, or physical location restrictions, or restrictions against multiple logins by the same user). Authorization determines the nature of the services granted to a user. Examples of types of service include IP address filtering, address assignment, route assignment, quality of service (QoS)/differential services, bandwidth control/traffic management, compulsory tunneling to a specific endpoint, and encryption.

Accounting   Accounting refers to the tracking of the consumption of network resources by users. This information can be used for management, planning, billing, or other purposes. Real-time accounting refers to accounting information delivered concurrently with the consumption of the resources. Batch accounting refers to accounting information saved until it is delivered later. Typical information gathered in accounting is the identity of the user, the nature of the services delivered, and when the services began/ended.

black hat   Black hat is another term for individuals who use their knowledge of computer systems to break into systems or networks that they are not authorized to use.

brute-force computation   This method uses a particular character set, such as A to Z, or A to Z plus 0 to 9, and computes the hash for every possible password made up of those characters. It always computes the password if that password is made up of the character set you have selected to test. The downside is that time is required for completion of this type of attack.

building blocks   Building blocks in the Router Management Center (MC) refer to network groups and transform sets. Building blocks are reusable, named, global components that you can reference by multiple policies. When referenced, a building block is incorporated as an integral component of the policy. If a change is made to the definition of a building block, this change is reflected in all policies that reference that building block. Building blocks aid in policy definition by eliminating the need to define that component each time a policy is defined.

certificate authority (CA)   In cryptography, a certificate authority or certification authority is an entity that issues digital certificates for use by other parties. It is an example of a trusted third party. CAs are characteristic of many public key infrastructure schemes.

certificate revocation lists (CRLs)   In the operation of some cryptosystems, usually public key infrastructures, a CRL is a list of certificates (more accurately, their serial numbers) that have been revoked, are no longer valid, and should not be relied upon by any system user.

Cisco Easy VPN   The Cisco Easy VPN consists of two components. The two components are the Cisco Easy VPN Server and the Cisco Easy VPN Remote feature. Both components work together to provide safe, reliable, and secure remote-access VPNs for users.

Cisco IOS Intrusion Prevention System (IPS)   Cisco IOS IPS can monitor and detect more than 700 of the most common attacks using signatures to detect patterns of misuse in network traffic. The IPS can automatically reset, drop, or alert an administrator about a suspicious packet. In addition, IPS provides the capability to configure, disable, and exclude signatures.

Cisco Unity Client Protocol   Allows most VPN parameters to be defined at a Cisco Easy VPN server and then "pushed" to Cisco Easy VPN remotes.

Context-Based Access Control (CBAC)   A protocol that provides internal users with secure access control for each application and for all traffic across network perimeters. CBAC enhances security by scrutinizing both source and destination addresses and by tracking each application's connection status.

cracker   An individual who attempts to gain unauthorized access to network resources with malicious intent.

Database Replication   Database Replication creates user accounts on a secondary Cisco Secure Access Control Server (ACS) by overwriting all existing user accounts on a secondary Cisco Secure ACS with the user accounts from the primary Cisco Secure ACS. Any user accounts unique to a secondary Cisco Secure ACS are lost in the replication.

DHCP snooping   DHCP snooping provides security against denial-of-service (DoS) attacks launched using the DHCP messages by filtering the DHCP packets and building and maintaining a DHCP snooping binding table. DHCP snooping uses both trusted and untrusted ports.

dictionary cracking   All the words in a dictionary file are computed and compared against the possible user passwords. This method is extremely fast and finds simple passwords.

Diffie-Hellman algorithm   A cryptographic protocol that allows two parties that have no prior knowledge of each other to jointly establish a shared secret key over an insecure communications channel. This key can then be used to encrypt subsequent communications using a symmetric key cipher.

Domain Name System (DNS)   Cisco IOS Software supports looking up host names with the Domain Name System. DNS provides the mapping between names, such as central.mydomain.com, to IP addresses, such as 14.2.9.250.

dynamic access control entries   Access list entries at the firewall interfaces that can be dynamically created/deleted, according to the information maintained in the state tables. These access list entries are applied to the interfaces to examine traffic flowing back into the internal network. These entries create temporary openings in the firewall to permit only traffic that is part of a permissible session.

Dynamic ARP Inspection (DAI)   Determines the validity of an Address Resolution Protocol (ARP) packet based on the valid MAC address-to-IP address bindings stored in a DHCP snooping database. In addition, DAI can validate ARP packets based on user-configurable ACLs. This allows for the inspection of ARP packets for hosts using statically configured IP addresses. DAI allows for the use of per-port and VLAN access control lists (VACLs) to limit ARP packets for specific IP addresses to specific MAC addresses.

Encapsulating Security Payload (ESP)   IPsec consists of two protocols. The first protocol is Encapsulating Security Payload (ESP). It encapsulates the data but does not provide protection to the outer headers. ESP encrypts the payload for data confidentiality.

Extensible Authentication Protocol (EAP)   Pronounced "eep," EAP is a universal authentication mechanism, frequently used in wireless networks and point-to-point connections. Although the EAP protocol is not limited to wireless LAN networks and can be used for wired LAN authentication, it is most often used in wireless LAN networks. Recently, the WPA and WPA2 standards have officially adopted five EAP types as their official authentication mechanisms.

external threats   External threats can arise from individuals or organizations working outside of a company. They do not have authorized access to the computer systems or network. They work their way into a network mainly from the Internet or dialup access servers.

failover protection   The process of the secondary unit taking over if the primary unit fails or is taken off line.

gratuitous ARP (GARP)   An unsolicited ARP reply, a GARP can be exploited maliciously by an attacker to spoof the identity of an IP address on a LAN segment. Typically, attackers use this method to spoof the identity between two hosts or all traffic to and from a default gateway in a man-in-the-middle attack.

hacker   Historically, a hacker is a computer programming expert. More recently, hacker is commonly used in a negative way to describe someone who attempts to gain unauthorized access to network resources with malicious intent.

Hashed Message Authentication Code (HMAC)   A keyed hash message authentication code, or HMAC, is a type of message authentication code (MAC) calculated using a cryptographic hash function in combination with a secret key. As with any MAC, it can be used to simultane-

ously verify both the data integrity and the authenticity of a message. Any iterative cryptographic hash function, such as MD5 or SHA-1, can be used in the calculation of an HMAC; the resulting MAC algorithm is termed HMAC-MD5 or HMAC-SHA-1 accordingly. The cryptographic strength of the HMAC depends upon the cryptographic strength of the underlying hash function and on the size and quality of the key.

host-based intrusion   Response is typically implemented as inline or passive technology depending on the vendor. The passive technology, which was the first-generation technology, is called host-based intrusion detection system (HIDS), which basically sends logs after the attack has occurred and the damage is done. The inline technology, called host-based intrusion prevention system (HIPS), actually stops the attack and prevents damage and propagation of worms and viruses.

Identity Based Networking Services (IBNS)   Expands network security by using 802.1x to automatically identify users requesting network access and route them to a VLAN domain with an appropriate degree of access privilege based on policy. IBNS also prevents unauthorized network access from rogue wireless access points.

internal threats   Internal threats occur when someone has authorized access to the network with either an account on a server or physical access to the network. According to the FBI, internal access and misuse account for 60 percent to 80 percent of reported incidents.

intrusion detection   The capability to detect attacks against a network.

intrusion prevention   Takes the capability of intrusion detection further by actually stopping attacks against the network.

jobs   A job is a deployment task in which administrators specify the devices to which VPN configurations should be deployed. The Router MC generates the command-line interface commands for the devices specified in the job, based on the defined VPN policies. These commands can be previewed before deployment takes place. Within the context of the job, administrators can specify whether to deploy the commands directly to the devices in the network or to a file.

man-in-the-middle attack   A man-in-the-middle attack requires that the hacker have access to network packets that come across a network. An example is someone who is working for an Internet service provider (ISP) and has access to all network packets transferred between the ISP network and any other network. Such attacks are often implemented using network packet sniffers and routing and transport protocols. The possible uses of such attacks are theft of information, hijacking of an ongoing session to gain access to private network resources, traffic analysis to derive information about a network and its users, denial-of-service (DoS), corruption of sent data, and introduction of new information into network sessions.

Message Digest (MD)   In cryptography, a cryptographic hash function is a hash function with certain additional security properties to make it suitable for use as a primitive in various information security applications, such as authentication and message integrity. A hash function takes a long string (or message) of any length as input and produces a fixed-length string as output, sometimes termed a message digest or a digital fingerprint.

Modular Policy Framework (MPF)   Modular policy provides greater granularity and more flexibility when configuring network policies. The MPF provides a consistent and flexible way to configure PIX Security Appliance features. One case where MPF can be used is to create a timeout configuration specific to a particular TCP application, as opposed to one that applies to all TCP applications.

Network Admission Control (NAC)   NAC is an industry initiative, sponsored by Cisco Systems that uses the network infrastructure to enforce security policy compliance on all devices seeking to access network computing resources, thereby limiting damage from viruses and worms.

network intrusion detection   Network intrusion detection is based on active or passive detection. Sensors are deployed at network entry points that protect critical network segments. The network segments have both internal and external corporate resources. Sensors capture and analyze the traffic as it traverses the network. Sensors are typically tuned for intrusion detection analysis. The underlying operating system is stripped of unnecessary network services, and essential services are secured. The sensors report to a central director server located inside the corporate firewall.

Network Time Protocol (NTP)   Cisco routers and other hosts use the Network Time Protocol to keep their time-of-day clocks accurate and in sync. If possible, configure all routers as part of an NTP hierarchy.

one-time passwords (OTPs)   A one-time password is one password in a set of passwords so constructed that it is extremely difficult to calculate the next password in the set given the previous passwords. Consider a computer system at an institution where a visitor needs to use the system for a given time period or login. An OTP system might consist of the user being presented with a one-time password on the screen, granting the visitor access for one day. When the given time period expires, no more passwords are available to the visitor, and thus the access to the system is removed.

phisher   A phisher uses e-mail or other means in an attempt to trick others into providing sensitive information, such as credit card numbers or passwords. Phishers masquerade as a trusted party who would have a legitimate need for the sensitive information.

phishing   Phishing is a type of social-engineering attack that involves using e-mail or other types of messages in an attempt to trick others into providing sensitive information, such as credit card numbers or passwords. Phishers masquerade as a trusted party who has a seemingly legitimate need for the sensitive information.

phreaker A phreaker is someone who manipulates the phone network to cause it to perform a function not normally allowed. A common goal of phreaking is breaking into the phone network, usually through a payphone, to make free long-distance calls.

port redirection Port redirection attacks are a type of trust exploitation attack that uses a compromised host to pass traffic through a firewall that would otherwise be dropped.

port security You can use the port security feature to restrict input to an interface by limiting and identifying MAC addresses of the stations allowed to access the port. When you assign secure MAC addresses to a secure port, the port does not forward packets with source addresses outside the group of defined addresses. If you limit the number of secure MAC addresses to one and assign a single secure MAC address, the workstation attached to that port is ensured the full bandwidth of the port.

private VLANs (PVLANs) Private VLANs provide Layer 2 isolation between ports within the same private VLAN. There are three types of private VLAN ports: A promiscuous port can communicate with all interfaces, including the community and isolated ports within a private VLAN. An isolated port has complete Layer 2 separation from other ports within the same private VLAN except for the promiscuous port. Private VLANs block all traffic to isolated ports except traffic from promiscuous ports. Traffic received from an isolated port is forwarded only to promiscuous ports. Community ports communicate among themselves and with their promiscuous ports. These interfaces are isolated at Layer 2 from all other interfaces in other communities or isolated ports within their private VLAN.

Remote Authentication Dial-In User Service (RADIUS) RADIUS is a AAA protocol for applications such as network access or IP mobility. It is intended to work in both local and roaming situations. RADIUS is an alternative to

TACACS+ and is important to network administrators. RADIUS is an access server AAA protocol developed by Livingston Enterprises, Inc. (now part of Lucent Technologies). It is a system of distributed security that secures remote access to networks and protects network services against unauthorized access.

Remote Database Management System (RDBMS) Enables an administrator to update the Cisco Secure user database with information from an Open DataBase Connectivity (ODBC)-compliant data source. The ODBC-compliant data source can be the RDBMS database of a third-party application. It can also be an intermediate file or database that a third-party system updates. Regardless of where the file or database resides, Cisco Secure Access Control Server (ACS) reads the file or database via the ODBC connection.

Reverse Route Injection (RRI) Reverse route injection ensures that a static route is created on the Easy VPN Server for the internal IP address of each VPN client.

Router Management Center (MC) Router MC is a VPN and Cisco IOS Firewall feature set configuration and deployment tool for Cisco IOS VPN routers. Router MC is a web-based application installed on top of Common Services.

Secure Hash Algorithm (SHA) The Secure Hash Algorithm family is a set of related cryptographic hash functions. The most commonly used function in the family, SHA-1, is used in a large variety of popular security applications and protocols, including Transport Layer Security (TLS), Secure Sockets Layer (SSL), Pretty Good Privacy (PGP), Secure Shell (SSH), Secure/Multipurpose Internet Mail Extensions (S/MIME), and IP Security (IPsec). SHA-1 is considered the successor to MD5, an earlier, widely used hash function. The SHA algorithms were designed by the National Security Agency (NSA) and published as a U.S. government standard.

Secure Shell (SSH) Replaces Telnet to provide remote router administration with connections that support strong privacy and session integrity. This connection provides functionality similar to that of an outbound Telnet connection except that the connection is encrypted. With authentication and encryption, SSH allows for secure communications over an insecure network.

Secure Sockets Layer (SSL) SSL provides endpoint authentication and communications privacy over the Internet using cryptography. In typical use, only the server is authenticated (that is, its identity is ensured) while the client remains unauthenticated; mutual authentication requires public key infrastructure (PKI) deployment to clients. The protocols allow client/server applications to communicate in a way designed to prevent eavesdropping, tampering, and message forgery.

security association (SA) After two peers agree upon a policy, the security parameters of the policy are identified by a security association established at each peer, and these security associations apply to all subsequent Internet Key Exchange (IKE) traffic during the negotiation.

security contexts You can partition a single security appliance into multiple virtual devices, known as security contexts. Each context is an independent device, with its own security policy, interfaces, and administrators. Multiple contexts are similar to having multiple standalone devices. Many features are supported in multiple context mode, including routing tables, firewall features, IPS, and management. Some features are not supported, including VPN and dynamic routing protocols.

Security Device Manager (SDM) SDM is a graphical user interface (GUI) utility that uses security configurations from Cisco Technical Assistance Center (TAC) and International Computer Security Association (ICSA) as a baseline for comparisons and default settings.

shunning The shun feature of the PIX Security Appliance allows a PIX, when combined with a Cisco IDS Sensor, to dynamically respond to an attacking host by preventing new connections and disallowing packets from any existing connection. A Cisco IDS device instructs the PIX to shun sources of traffic when those sources of traffic are determined to be malicious.

signature definition file (SDF) Integral to Cisco IOS IPS, the SDF is an Extensible Markup Language (XML) file with a definition of each signature along with relevant configurable actions. Cisco IOS IPS reads in the SDF, parses the XML, and populates its internal tables with the information necessary to detect each signature. The SDF contains the signature definition and configuration.

signature micro-engines (SMEs) Cisco IOS IPS uses signature micro-engines (SMEs) to load the SDF and scan signatures. Each engine categorizes a group of signatures, and each signature detects patterns of misuse in network traffic.

signature-based detection At a basic level, signature-based detection can be compared to virus-checking programs. IDS vendors produce and build signatures that the IDS system uses to compare against activity on the network or host. When a match is found, the IDS takes action. The actions taken can include logging the event or sending an alarm to a management console.

Simple Network Management Protocol (SNMP) The Simple Network Management Protocol is the standard Internet protocol for automated remote monitoring and administration. There are several different versions of SNMP with different security properties.

social engineering The easiest hack involves no computer skill at all. If an intruder can trick a member of an organization into giving over valuable information—such as locations of files, servers, and passwords—the process of hacking is made immeasurably easier.

spammer A spammer is someone who sends large numbers of unsolicited e-mail messages. Spammers often use viruses to take control of home computers to use these computers to send out their bulk messages.

stateful inspection and packet filtering   A method of filtering network traffic to allow only valid traffic and services. This method of filtering maintains complete session state information for each connection. Each time a TCP or UDP connection is established for inbound or outbound connections, the information is logged in a stateful session flow table.

structured threats   Structured threats come from hackers who are more highly motivated and technically competent. These people know system vulnerabilities and can understand and develop exploit code and scripts.

symmetrical encryption   Symmetrical encryption, also known as secret key encryption, is used for large volumes of data because asymmetrical encryption is much more CPU intensive. The three encryption algorithms available in Cisco IOS Software include Digital Encryption Standard (DES), Triple DES (3DES), and Advanced Encryption Standard (AES).

Terminal Access Controller Access Control System Plus (TACACS+)   TACACS is a remote authentication protocol used to communicate with an authentication server commonly used in UNIX networks. TACACS allows a remote-access server to communicate with an authentication server to determine whether the user has access to the network. TACACS+ is an improved version of TACACS. TACACS+ forwards username and password information to a centralized security server.

transparent firewall mode   Traditionally, a firewall is a routed hop and acts as a default gateway for hosts that connect to one of its screened subnets. A transparent firewall, on the other hand, is a Layer 2 firewall that acts like a "bump in the wire," or a "stealth firewall," and is not seen as a router hop to connected devices. The security appliance connects the same network on its inside and outside ports. Because the firewall is not a routed hop, you can easily introduce a transparent firewall into an existing network; IP re-addressing is unnecessary.

transparent tunneling   Transparent tunneling allows secure transmission between the VPN client and a secure gateway through a router serving as a firewall, which might also be performing Network Address Translation (NAT) or Port Address Translation (PAT). Transparent tunneling encapsulates ESP traffic within UDP packets and can allow for both Internet Security Association and Key Management Protocol (ISAKMP) and ESP to be encapsulated in TCP packets before they are sent through the NAT or PAT devices or firewalls. The most common application for transparent tunneling is behind a home router performing PAT.

trust exploitation   Although it is more of a technique than a hack itself, trust exploitation refers to an attack in which an individual takes advantage of a trust relationship within a network. The classic example is a perimeter network connection from a corporation. These network segments often house DNS, SMTP, and HTTP servers. Because all these servers reside on the same segment, the compromise of one system can lead to the compromise of other systems because these systems usually trust other systems attached to the same network.

unstructured threats   Unstructured threats consist of mostly inexperienced individuals using easily available hacking tools such as shell scripts and password crackers.

URL filtering   URL-filtering applications for a firewall are used to block specific URLs on the basis of a defined policy to effectively monitor and control network traffic.

virtual private network (VPN)   A VPN provides the same network connectivity for remote users over a public infrastructure as they would have over a private network.

white hat   Individuals who use their abilities to find vulnerabilities in systems or networks and then report these vulnerabilities to the owners of the system so that they can be fixed.